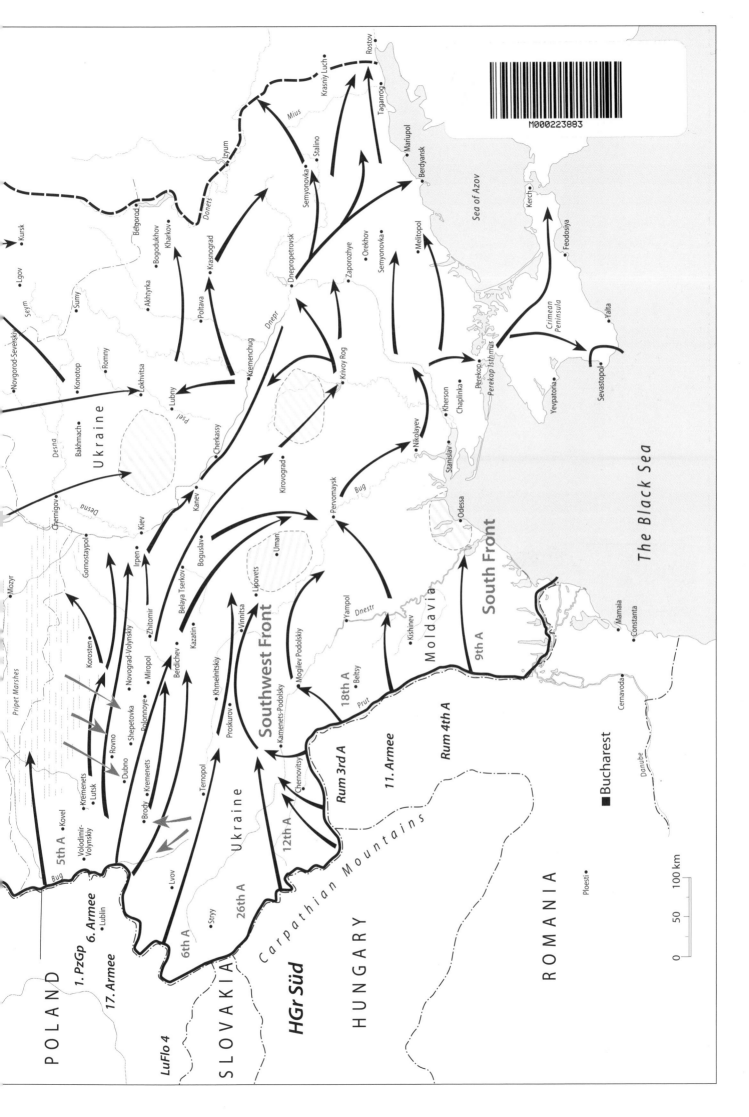

OPERATION BARBAROSSA

This edition of Operation Barbarossa: The Largest Military
Campaign in History – Hitler Against Stalin first published 2016.
First published in Swedish by Vaktel Förlag 2013.
Original Swedish edition: Operation Barbarossa: Världshistoriens
största fälttåg – Hitler mot Stalin © 2016 Christer Bergström.
English translation copyright © 2016 Christer Bergström.
Cover design: Katie Gabriel Allen
Insert layout: Fredrik Gustafson *fredrikgustafsondesign@gmail.com*
Maps: Samuel Svärd *info@samuelsvard.se*
Cover photos: Author's collection, Kuva-SA.
Printing: Printon Publishing House, Estonia.
ISBN 978-1-61200-401-3

Casemate UK
10 Hythe Bridge Street, Oxford,
OX1 2EW, United Kingdom
www.casematepublishers.co.uk

Casemate Publishers
1950 Lawrence Road, Havertown,
PA 19083, USA
www.casematepublishers.com

Vaktel förlag
Box 3027
S-630 03 Eskilstuna
Sweden
www.vaktelforlag.se
vaktelforlag@gmail.com

CHRISTER BERGSTRÖM

OPERATION BARBAROSSA

The Largest Military Campaign in History

Hitler Against Stalin

Vaktel Förlag Publishing • Casemate Publishers

Mikhail Katukov, the commander of Soviet 4th Tank Brigade/1st Guards Tank Brigade in 1941.

Swedish Waffen-SS volunteer Hans Lindén on the Eastern Front.

CONTENTS.

Offensive in the Center, June–September 1941.

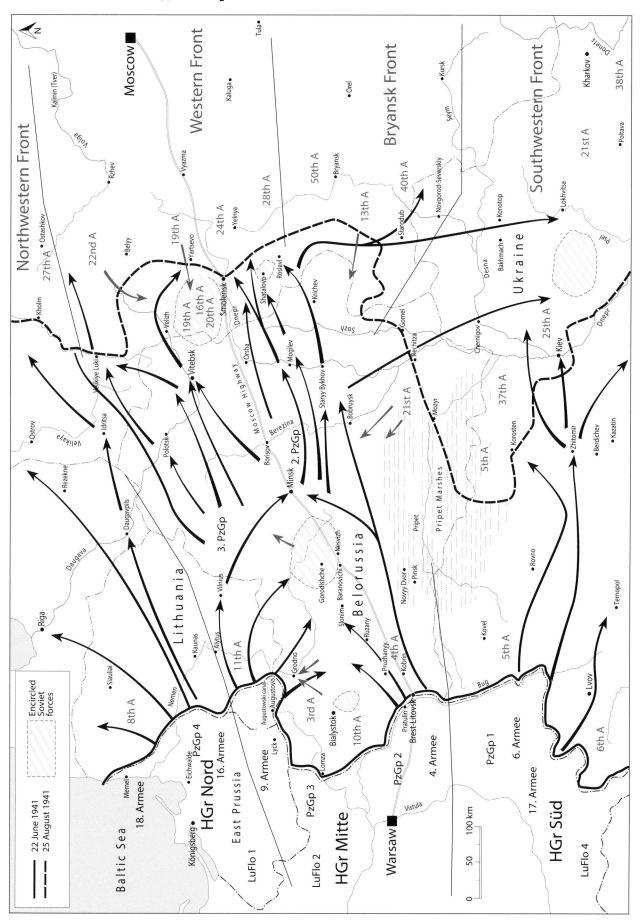

Offensive in the North, June–November 1941.

Offensive in the South, June–December 1941.

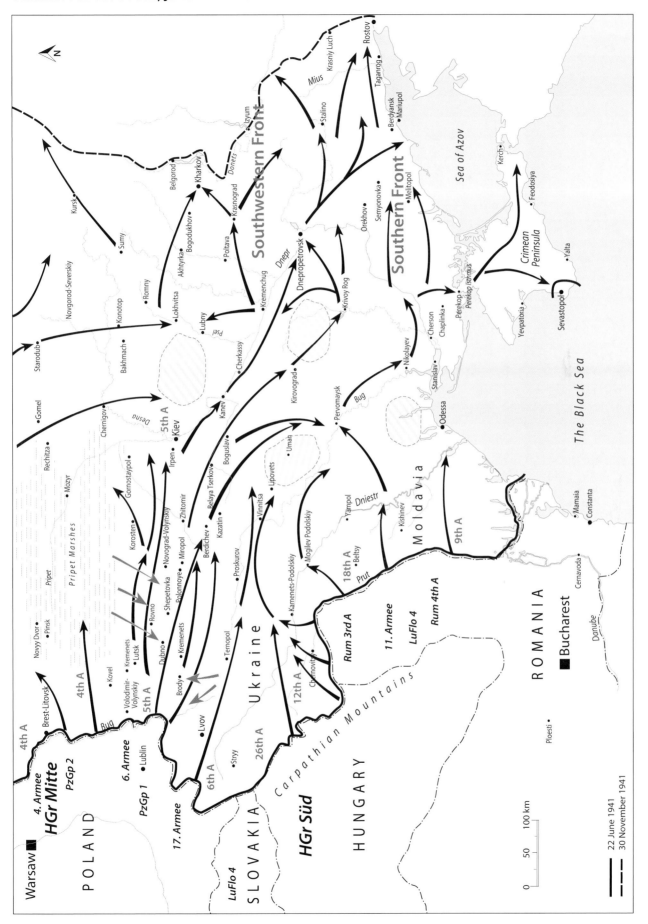

The Finnish front.

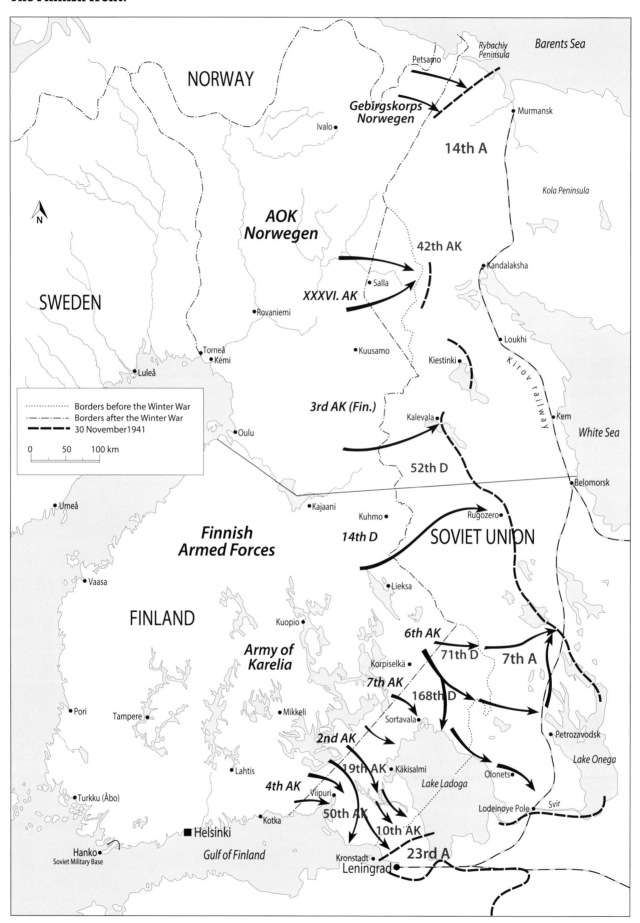

Operation Typhoon.

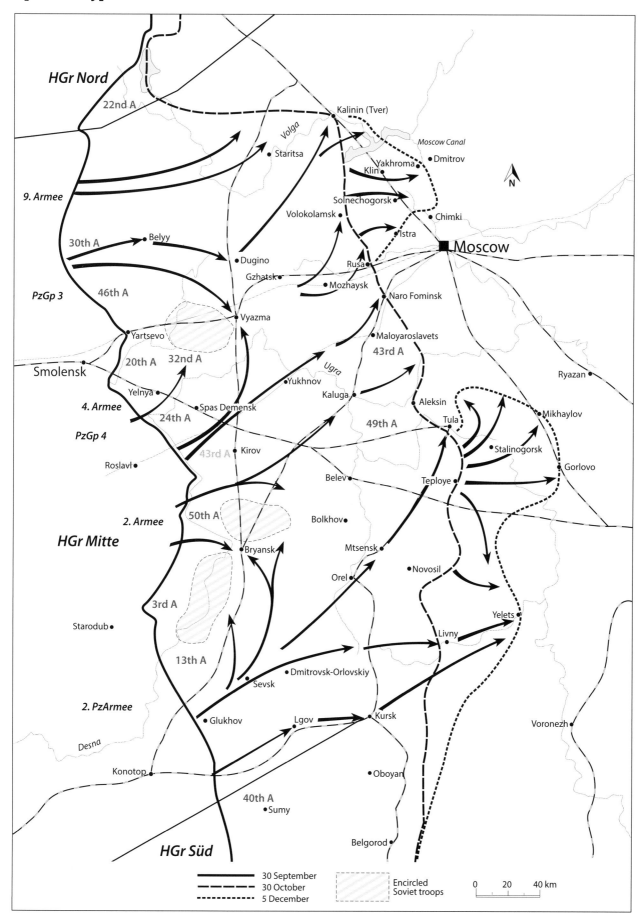

HGr Nord

22nd A

9. Armee

30th A • Belyy

PzGp 3

46th A

Smolensk

Yartsevo

20th A   32nd A

Yelnya

4. Armee

24th A

PzGp 4

Roslavl

43rd A • Kirov

2. Armee

50th A

HGr Mitte

3rd A

Starodub

13th A

2. PzArmee

Glukhov

Konotop

40th A
• Sumy

HGr Süd

Volga

• Staritsa

• Dugino

Gzhatsk •

Vyazma

• Yukhnov

Ugra

• Spas Demensk

Belev

• Bolkhov

• Bryansk

Mtsensk •

Orel •

• Dmitrovsk-Orlovskiy

• Sevsk

Lgov •

Desna

Kalinin (Tver)

Moscow Canal

Yakhroma   • Dmitrov

Klin

Solnechogorsk •

Volokolamsk •
• Istra   • Chimki

Rusa •   ■ Moscow

• Mozhaysk

Naro Fominsk

• Maloyaroslavets

43rd A

Kaluga •

49th A   Aleksin
Tula •

Teploye •

Novosil •

Livny •

Kursk •

• Oboyan

Belgorod •

Ryazan •

Mikhaylov •

• Stalinogorsk

Gorlovo •

Yelets •

Voronezh •

N

—————— 30 September
– – – – – – 30 October
· · · · · · · 5 December

Encircled
Soviet troops

0   20   40 km

13

The Soviet counter-offensive.

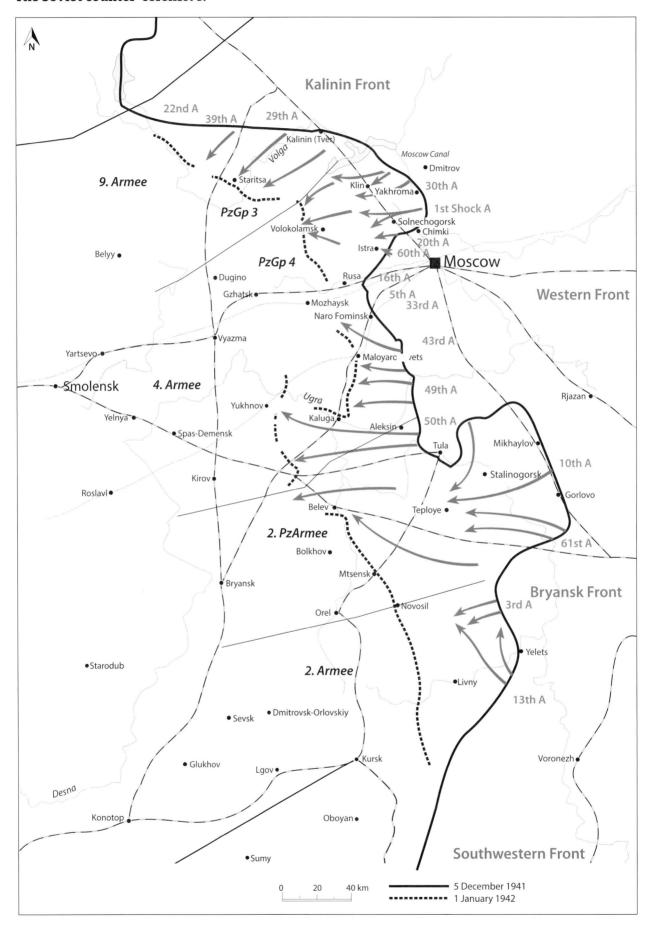

GLOSSARY AND GUIDE TO ABBREVIATIONS.

AAA Anti-aircraft artillery.

Abteilung (Armored, artillery or cavalry) battalion (German).

AD (Aviatsionnaya Diviziya) Aviation Division (Soviet).

AE (Aviatsionnaya Eskadrilya) Aviation Squadron (Soviet).

Aerial victory A confirmed shot down enemy aircraft.

AK (Armia Krajowa) Home Army, Polish resistance movement.

Albacore British single-engine Fairey carrier torpedo bomber biplane.

ANT (Andrey Nikolayevich Tupolev) Soviet aircraft designer.

Aufklärung Reconnaissance (German).

Aufklärungsgruppe Reconnaissance (aviation) group (German).

AufklObdL (Aufklärungsgruppe Oberbefehlshaber der Luftwaffe) Reconnaissance (aviation) group, commander of the Luftwaffe (German).

Ar (Arado) German aircraft designer.

Ar (Arkhangel'skiy) Soviet aircraft designer.

Ar-2 Soviet dive-bomber version of the SB twin-engine bomber.

Ar 95 German single-engine, three-place reconnaissance biplane.

Armee Field Army (German).

Armeekorps Army Corps (German).

Assault Ground-attack aviation.

Aviaeskadrilya or **Aviatsionnaya Eskadrilya** Aviation squadron (Soviet).

Aviadiviziya or **Aviatsionnaya Diviziya** Aviation division (Soviet).

Aviakorpus or **Aviatsionnyy Korpus** Aviation corps (Soviet).

Aviapolk or **Aviatsionnyy Polk** Aviation regiment (Soviet).

Aviatsiya Voyenno-Morskogo Flota Navy air force, VVS-VMF (Soviet).

Aviatsionnaya Shkola Pervonachal'nogo Obucheniya Primary flight training school (Soviet).

Aviazveno Svyazi Liaison flight (Soviet).

BAB (Bombardirovochnaya Aviatsionnaya Brigada) Bomber aviation brigade (Soviet); the equivalent in Soviet's navy aviation to the BAD of army aviation.

BAD (Bombardirovochnaya Aviatsionnaya Diviziya) Bomber aviation division (Soviet).

BAK (Bombardirovochnyy Aviatsionyy Korpus) Bomber aviation corps (Soviet).

BAP (Bombardirovochnyy Aviatsionyy Polk) Bomber aviation regiment (Soviet).

Bataillon Battalion (German).

BBAP (Blizhnebombardirovochnyy Aviatsionnyy Polk) Short-range bomber aviation regiment (Soviet).

Befehlshaber des Rückwärtigen Heeresgebietes Command of the rear area of a German army group.

Berück Abbreviation for Befehlshaber des Rückwärtigen Heeresgebietes Command of the rear area of a German army group.

Beriyev Soviet aircraft designer.

Bf (Bayerische Flugzeugwerke) German aircraft designer; original designation of Messerschmitt 109 and 110.

Bf 109 German single-engine, single-seat fighter.

Bf 110 German twin-engine, two-place heavy fighter and fighter-bomber.

Blenheim British-designed Bristol twin-engine bomber.

Blitzkrieg "Lightning War."

Bolshevik "Majority" (Russian) nickname of the Soviet Communist Party, formerly Social Democratic Party.

Brigadnyy Inzhener Brigade engineer; old Soviet military maintenance rank, approximately equivalent to general-mayor. Even if the general ranks were instituted in the Red Army in 1940, several commanders retained their old ranks.

Bristol British aircraft designer.

BT (Bystrokhodnyy tank) Fast tank (Soviet).

BT-5 Soviet light tank.

BT-7 Soviet light tank.

Blue Division (División Azul), Spanish infantry division which fought on the German side on the Eastern Front.

Chayka "Seagull," Soviet Polikarpov I-153 single-engine, single-seat biplane fighter.

Che-2 Soviet twin-engine Chetverikov amphibian reconnaissance aircraft.

Chetverikov Soviet aircraft designer.

ChF (Chernomorskiy Flot) Black Sea Fleet (Soviet).

Chief of Staff The leader of a supporting staff organization, not a military rank.

C-in-C (Commander in Chief) Senior commander, not a military rank.

Commissar or Politruk (politicheskiy rukovoditel) Political officer, responsible for the political education and control of the military (Soviet).

C.O. Commanding officer.

CSIR (Corpo di Spedizione Italiano in Russia) Expeditionary Corps in Russia (Italian).

Curtiss U.S. aircraft designer.

"Curtiss" An incorrect German designation of the Soviet Polikarpov I-153 single-engine, single-seat biplane fighter.

DB (Daimler-Benz) German engine designer.

DB (Dal'niy Bombardirovshchik) Long-range bomber (Soviet).

DB-3 Soviet twin-engine Ilyushin bomber.

DBA (Dal'ne-Bombardirovochnaya Aviatsiya) Long-range bomber aviation (Soviet).

DBAP (Dal'nebombardirovochnyy Aviatsionnyy Polk) Long-range bomber regiment (Soviet).

División Azul "Blue Division", Spanish infantry division which fought on the German side on the Eastern Front.

Diviziya Aviation wing (Soviet); composed of four to six regiments.

Do (Dornier) German aircraft designer.

Do 17 German twin-engine bomber and reconnaissance aircraft.

Do 215 German twin-engine bomber and reconnaissance aircraft.

Einsatzgruppe German extermination units charged with "political" mass executions of Jews and Communist functionaries in occupied area of Poland and the Soviet Union.

Einsatzkommando Element of an Einsatzgruppe.

Ergänzungsgruppe Replacement aviation group (German).

ErgGr (Ergänzungsgruppe) Replacement aviation group (German).

Escadrila Squadron (Rumanian).

Eskadrilya Squadron (Soviet).

F (Fernaufklärung) Long-distance (strategic) reconnaissance aviation (German).

FAB (Fugashnaya Aviatsionnaya Bomba) High-explosive aviation bomb (Soviet).

Fairey British aircraft designer.

Falco Italian Fiat CR.42 single-engine, single-seat biplane.

FARR (Fortele Aeriene Regale ale Romane) Royal Romanian Air Force.

Fernaufklärungsgruppe Long-distance (strategic) reconnaissance aviation group (German).

Fi (Fieseler) German aircraft designer.

Fi 156 Storch German single-engine liaison and reconnaissance aircraft.

Fiat CR.42 Falco Italian designed single-engine, single-seat biplane fighter.

Flak (Fliegerabwehrkanone) Antiaircraft artillery (German).

Fliegerdivision Aviation division (German).

Fliegerführer "Aviation command"; command of the aviation within a defined geographical area (German).

Fliegerkorps Aviation corps (German).

Flotiliya "Flotilla"; Soviet small regional fleet.

Focke Wulf German aircraft designer.

Front (In Soviet connection) Soviet equivalent to army group.

Frontovniki Nickname of Soviet front soldiers.

Fulmar British Fairey single-engine, single-seat carrier fighter.

Fw (Focke Wulf) German aircraft designer.

G or **Gv** (Gvardeyskiy) Guards (Soviet); see below.

Gauleiter "Branch leader," Party leader of a regional branch of the German Nazi Party.

Gebirgsjäger Troops specialized in fighting in mountainous areas (German).

Gebirgsjäger-Division Mountain division (German).

Gebirgskorps Norwegen Mountain Corps Norway (German).

General der Jagdflieger Fighter Aviation general; the German inspector of the Fighter Aviation.

Generalmajor der Polizei Major-General of the Police (German).

Generaloberstabsarzt German military medical rank equivalent to Generalleutnant.

Geschwader Aviation wing (German).

Geschwaderkommodore Aviation wing commander (German).

GKO (Gosudarstvennyy Komitet Oborony), State Committee for Defense (Soviet).

Gorbatyy "Hunchback," Soviet nickname for the Il-2 ground-attack aircraft.

GOSPLAN (Gosudarstvennyy planovyy komitet sovyeta ministrov) State Planning Commission of the Soviet Government.

Grossdeutschland "Great Germany" Name (in 1941) of a German infantry/mechanized regiment.

GRU (Glavnoye razvedyvatel'noye upravleniye) Main Intelligence Directorate of the General Staff of the Armed Forces of the Soviet Union.

Grupul Bombardament Bomber group (Romanian).

Gruppe Aviation group (German).

Gruppenkommandeur Aviation group commander (German).

Gruppo Aviation group (Italian).

Gruppo Autonomo Caccia Terrestre Independent fighter aviation group (Italian).

Grupul Vanatoare Fighter aviation group (Romanian).

Grünherz "Green Heart" (the name of JG 54).

Guards Honorary Soviet title to specially distinguished units.

Gv see "G."

H (Heeresaufklärung) Army (tactical) reconnaissance aviation (German).

Hawker British aircraft designer.

He (Heinkel) German aircraft designer.

He 60 German single-engine, two-place short-range reconnaissance float biplane.

He 59 German twin-engine reconnaissance and torpedo bomber biplane.

He 111 German twin-engine bomber.

He 112 German designed single-engine, single-seat fighter.

He 114 German single-engine, two-place reconnaissance floatplane.

He 115 German twin-engine, three-seat torpedo bomber.

Heer The Army of the Wehrmacht.

Heeresarzt (Heeresarzt beim Oberbefehlshaber des Heeres) "Army Medical [Department] at the Army High Command" (German).

Heeresaufklärungsgruppe Army (tactical) reconnaissance aviation group (German).

Heeresgruppe Army group (German).

Heeresgruppe Mitte Army Group Center (German).

Heeresgruppe Nord Army Group North (German).

Heeresgruppe Süd Army Group South (German).

Heereskommando Army detachment (German).

Heinkel German aircraft designer.

Henschel German aircraft designer.

Hero of the Soviet Union (Geroy Sovyetskogo Soyuza); title for the highest Soviet appointment for bravery in combat.

Hindenburg The name of KG 1 (adopted after the late World War I German Army commander in chief and later president Paul von Hindenburg, who helped to ensure Hitler's coming to power).

HMS (His Majesty's Ship) vessel of the British Royal Navy.

Holocaust (from the Greek holókaustos: hólos, "whole" and kaustós, "burnt"), the Nazi systematic genocide of millions of innocent civilians, including six million Jews.

Holzhammer "Wooden Club" (the name of KG 2).

Horst Wessel The name of ZG 26 (adopted after a Nazi street fighter "hero").

Hs (Henschel) German aircraft designer.

Hs 123 German single-engine, single-seat ground-attack biplane.

Hs 126 German single-engine, two-place Army cooperation and tactical reconnaissance aircraft.

Hurricane British Hawker single-engine, single-seat fighter.

I (Istrebitel) Fighter aviation (Soviet).

I-15 Soviet single-engine, single-seat, fixed-gear Polikarpov biplane fighter.

I-15bis Soviet single-engine, single-seat Polikarpov biplane fighter.

I-16 Soviet single-engine, single-seat Polikarpov fighter.

I-18 Erroneous German designation for Soviet MiG-1/MiG-3 fighter.

I-26 Alternate designation for Soviet Yak-1 single-engine, single-seat fighter.

I-61 An incorrect German name for MiG-1 and MiG-3 (see below).

I-152 Alternate designation for Polikarpov I-15bis.

I-153 Soviet single-engine, single-seat fighter and ground-attack Polikarpov biplane.

I-301 An incorrect German designation for Soviet single-engine, single-seat LaGG-3 fighter (see below).

IAD (Istrebitel'naya Aviatsionnaya Diviziya) Fighter aviation division (Soviet).

IAK (Istrebitel'nyy Aviatsionnyy Korpus) Fighter aviation corps (Soviet).

IAP (Istrebitel'nyy Aviatsionyy Polk) Fighter aviation regiment (Soviet).

I.A.R. (Industria Aeronautica Romana) Romanian Aeronautical Industry (Romanian aircraft designer).

I.A.R.37 Romanian single-engine, three-place light bomber, liaison and reconnaissance biplane.

I.A.R.39 Romanian single-engine, three-place light bomber, liaison and reconnaissance biplane.

I.A.R.80 Romanian single-engine, single-seat fighter.

Il (Ilyushin) Soviet aircraft designer.

Il-2 Soviet single-engine, single-seat (in 1941) ground-attack aircraft.

Ilyusha Soviet nickname for the Il-2 ground-attack aircraft.

Ilyushin Soviet aircraft designer.

Immelmann The name of StG 2 (adopted after World War I ace Max Immelmann).

Infanterie Infantry (German).

Ishak "Jackass," Soviet Polikarpov I-16 single-engine, single-seat fighter.

J (Jagd) Fighter aviation (German).

Jagdflieger (German) fighter pilots.

Jagdgeschwader Fighter aviation wing (German).

Jagdstaffel Fighter aviation squadron (German).

Jagdwaffe Fighter air arm (German).

JG (Jagdgeschwader) Fighter wing (German).

Ju (Junkers) German aircraft designer.

Ju 52 German three-engine transport aircraft.

Ju 86 German twin-engine bomber and reconnaissance aircraft.

Ju 87 German single-engine, two-place dive-bomber.

Ju 88 German twin-engine bomber/dive-bomber and reconnaissance aircraft.

Junkers German aircraft and engine designer.

KA (Krasnaya Armiya) Red Army.

KAE (Korpusnaya Aviatsionnaya Eskadrilya) Aviation squadron of the (ground army) corps (Soviet).

Kampfflieger "Combat aviators"; bomber aviators (German).

Kampfgeschwader "Combat Wing," German bomber aviation wing.

Kampfgruppe "Combat group", German ad hoc army force or German bomber aviation group.

Katyusha "Little Katya," Soviet rocket artillery.

KBF (Krasnoznamyonnyy Baltiyskiy Flot) Red Banner Baltic Fleet (Soviet).

Kette "Chain," German tactical air formation (three aircraft).

KG (Kampfgeschwader) Bomber wing (German).

KGzbV (Kampfgeschwader zu besonderen Verwendung) Special-purpose (transport) bomber wing (German).

KGr (Kampgfruppe) Bomber group (German).

KGrzbV (Kampfgruppe zu besonderen Verwendung) Special-purpose (transport) bomber group (German).

Knight's Cross One of the highest German military awards.

Kombrig Old Soviet military rank, equivalent to brigadnyy inzhener/general-mayor.

Kommandeur See Gruppenkommandeur.

Kommodore See Geschwaderkommodore.

Komsomol (Kommunisticheskiy soyuz molodyozhi) Communist Youth League (Soviet).

KOSOS (Konstruktorskiy Otdel Opytnovo Samolyoto-stroeniya) Experimental Aircraft Design Section (Soviet).

KOVO (Kievskiy Osobyy Voyennyy Okrug) Kiev Special Military District (Soviet).

Kradschützen-Bataillon Motor-cyclist infantry battalion (German).

KüFlGr (Küstenfliegergruppe) Coastal patrol aviation group (German).

KV (Kliment Voroshilov) Soviet heavy tank.

KV-1 (Kliment Voroshilov 1) Soviet heavy tank.

KV-2 (Kliment Voroshilov 1) Soviet heavy artillery heavy tank with a 152 mm howitzer.

LAF (Lietuvos Aktyvistų Frontas) Lithuanian Activist Front, Lithuanian anti-Soviet partisan movement.

LaGG (Lavochkin, Gorbunov, Gudkov) Soviet aircraft designers.

LaGG-3 Soviet single-engine, single-seat fighter.

Landser Nickname of German soldiers.

Legion Condor Condor Legion (also the name of KG 53).

LeLv (Lentolaivue) Aviation squadron (Finnish).

LeR (Lentoregiment) Aviation regiment (Finnish).

Letka Squadron (Slovakian).

LG (Lehrgeschwader) Training wing (German).

Locotenent Aviator Romanian Air Force rank equivalent to first lieutenant.

Locotenent Comandor Aviator Romanian Air Force rank equivalent to major.

Los Polish-designed twin-engine bomber.

Luftflotte Air fleet (German).

Luftwaffe Air Force (German).

Luftwaffenkommando "Air force command," command of the aviation within a defined geographical area (German).

M (Motor) Engine (Soviet).

Macchi Italian aircraft designer.

Magyar Királyi Honvéd Légierö Royal Hungarian Air Force.

"Martin bomber" Erroneous German designation for the Soviet SB twin-engine bomber.

MBR (Morskoy Blizhniy Razvedchik) Naval short-range reconnaissance aircraft (Soviet).

MBR-2 Soviet twin-engine Beriyev reconnaissance floatplane.

Mc.200 Saetta Italian single-engine, single-seat Macchi fighter.

Me (Messerschmitt) German aircraft designer.

Mechanized Corps Soviet tank corps.

Messerschmitt German aircraft designer.

MG (Maschinengewehr) Machine gun (German).

MiG (Mikoyan, Gurevich) Soviet aircraft designers.

MiG-1 Soviet single-engine, single-seat fighter.

MiG-3 Soviet single-engine, single-seat fighter.

Mikoyan and Gurevich Soviet aircraft designers.

MK (Maschinenkanone) Automatic cannon (German).

MTAP (Minno-Torpednyy Aviatsionyy Polk) Mine-torpedo aviation regiment (Soviet).

Nachtschlachtgruppe Night ground-attack aviation group (German).

Nahkampfführer "Close-support air command" within a defined area (German).

NBAP (Nochnoy Bombardirovochnyy Aviatsionnyy Polk) Night bomber aviation regiment (Soviet).

NCO (Non-commissioned officer) a military officer who has not earned a commission; all grades of corporal and sergeant.

Nebelwerfer (Smoke Mortar) German rocket artillery.

Neman Soviet aircraft designer.

NKGB (Narodnyy komissariat gosudarstvennoy bezopasnosti) People's Commissariat for State Security (Soviet).

NKVD (Narodnyy Kommissariat Vnutrennikh Del) People's Commissariat for Internal Affairs (Soviet).

Nordland (Northland) An SS infantry regiment.

OAG (Osobaya Aviatsionnaya Gruppa) Special aviation group (Soviet).

Oboronitel'nyy krug Soviet defensive air combat circle.

OIAE (Otdel'naya Istrebitel'naya Aviatsionnaya Eskadrilya) Independent fighter aviation squadron (Soviet).

OKH (Oberkommando des Heeres) Army High Command (German).

OKL (Oberkommando der Luftwaffe) Air Force High Command (German).

OKW (Oberkommando der Wehrmacht) Armed Forces High Command (German).

OMRAP (Otdel'niy Morskoy Razvedyvatel'nyy Aviatsionnyy Polk) Independent naval reconnaissance aviation regiment (Soviet).

ORAE (Otdel'naya Razvedyvatel'naya Aviatsionnaya Eskadrilya) Independent reconnaissance aviation squadron (Soviet).

Ordnungspolizei Order Police (German).

OshAE (Otdel'naya Shturmovaya Aviatsionnaya Eskadrilya) Independent ground-attack aviation squadron (Soviet).

OSNAZ (Osoboye Naznachenie) Special purpose (Soviet).

Osoaviakhim (Obshchestvo Sodeystviya Oborone, Aviatsionnomu i Khimicheskomu Stroitel'stvu) Society for the Support of Defense and of Aviation and Chemical Construction (Soviet).

Ostheer "Eastern Army," the German armed forces on the Eastern Front.

OUN (Orhanizatsiya Ukrayins'kykh Natsionalistiv) Organization of Ukrainian Nationalists, Anti-Soviet Ukrainian resistance movement.

OUN-B The faction of OUN led by Stepan Bandera.

OUN-M The faction of OUN led by Andriy Melnyk.

P-40 U.S. designed Curtiss single-engine, single-seat fighter.

Pak (Panzerabwehrkanone) Anti-tank gun (German).

Panzer Tank (German).

Panzer I German light tank.

Panzer II German light tank.

Panzer III German medium tank.

Panzer IV German medium tank.

Panzer 38(t) (Panzerkampfwagen 35tschechisch) German designation for a Czechoslovak-designed light tank used by Germany during World War II.

Panzergruppe Armored group; a grouping of German armored corps.

Panzerkampfwagen Tank (German).

Panzerkorps Armored Corps (German).

PBAP (Pikiruyushchiy Bombardirovochnyy Aviatsionnyy Polk) Dive-bomber aviation regiment (Soviet).

P (Petlaykov) Soviet aircraft designer.

Pe-2 Soviet twin-engine bomber.

Pik As "Ace of Spades" (the name of JG 53).

Po (Polikarpov) Soviet aircraft designer.

Polikarpov Soviet aircraft designer.

Politruk (politicheskiy rukovoditel) Political officer, responsible for the political education and control of the military (Soviet). See also Commissar.

Polizei Police (German).

Polk Regiment (Soviet).

Potez French aircraft designer.

Potez 63 French-designed twin-engine bomber.

PO Prisoner of war.

PQ Code name for U.S. and British Soviet-bound Arctic shipping convoys.

PVO (Protivo-Vozdushnaya Oborona) Home air defense (Soviet).

Pz (Panzer) Tank (German).

19

R (Razvedchik) Reconnaissance (Soviet).

R-5 Soviet single-engine Polikarpov light bomber and reconnaissance aircraft.

R-10 Soviet single-engine, two-place Neman reconnaissance aircraft.

RAG (Reservnaya Aviatsionnaya Gruppa) Reserve aviation group (of the Stavka) (Soviet).

Rata "Rat" (Spanish) German and Spanish nickname for Soviet Polikarpov I-16 single-engine, single-seat fighter.

Red Army The army of the Soviet Union.

Regia Aeronautica Royal Italian Air Force.

Reich "Empire" or "Realm" (German); the Third Reich, Hitler's designation for Nazi Germany.

Reichsführer (Realm Leader), the senior SS rank, held by the commander Heinrich Himmler.

Rifle Corps Infantry corps (Soviet).

Rifle Division Infantry division (Soviet).

RLM (Reichsluftfahrtministerium) Aviation Ministry (German).

Rotte German tactical air formation (two aircraft).

Rottenflieger Wingman (German).

Rottenführer Leader of a Rotte (German).

R (Reaktivnyy Snaryad) Aircraft-carried rocket projectile (Soviet).

Russki Russian.

R/T Radio-telephone.

R-Z An upgrade version of Soviet R-5 single-engine light bomber and reconnaissance aircraft.

S (Schlacht) Ground-attack/assault (German).

Saetta Italian single-engine, single-seat Mc.200 fighter.

SA (Smeshannaya Aviatsionnaya Diviziya) Composite aviation division (Soviet).

SA (Smeshannyy Aviatsionnyy Polk) Composite aviation regiment (Soviet).

SB (Skorostnoy Bombardirovshchik) High-speed bomber (Soviet); a particular Tupolev twin-engine Soviet bomber.

SBAP (Skorostnoy Bombardirovohchnyy Aviatsionnyy Polk) High-speed bomber aviation regiment (Soviet).

Savoia-Marchetti Italian aircraft designer.

SC (Splitterbombe, cylindrisch) Cylindrical splinter-bomb (German).

SchG (Schlachtgeschwader) Ground-attack wing (German).

Schlachtflieger Ground-attack airman (German).

Schlachtgeschwader "Assault Wing"; German ground-attack aviation wing.

Schützen-Brigade Rifle-brigade (German).

Schwarm "Swarm" or "flight"; German tactical air formation (four aircraft).

Schwarmführer Schwarm leader (German).

SD (Sicherheitsdienst) The German security service.

SD (Splitterbombe Dickwand) Fragmentation bomb, hard-covered (German).

SF (Severnyy Flot) Northern Fleet (Soviet).

ShAD (Shturmovaya Aviatsionnaya Diviziya) Ground-attack aviation division (Soviet).

ShAP (Shturmovoy Aviatsionnyy Polk) Ground-attack aviation regiment (Soviet).

ShKAS (Shpital'nyy-Komaritskiy Aviatsionnyy Skorostrelnyy) Rapid-firing aircraft machine gun; 7.62mm, by designers Komaritskiy and Shpital'nyy (Soviet).

Shturmovik Soviet ground-attack aircraft.

ShVAK (Shpital'nyy-Vladimirov Aviatsionnaya Krupno-kalibernaya) Large-caliber aircraft cannon; 20mm, by designers Vladimirov and Shpital'nyy (Soviet).

Sicherungsdivision Security division, army division responsible for security on the rear area (German).

SKG (Schnellkampfgeschwader) High-speed bomber wing (German).

SKR (Storozhevyye korabli) Patrol boat (Soviet).

SM (Savoia-Marchetti) Italian aircraft designer.

SM-79 Italian designed Savoia-Marchetti three-engine bomber and torpedo bomber.

SM-81 Italian designed Savoia-Marchetti three-engine multi-purpose bomber, transport, and utility aircraft.

Sonderkommando (Special Command), element of an Einsatzgruppe.

SP (Skorostnoy Pikiruyushchiy Bombardirovshchik) High-speed dive-bomber (Soviet).

Squadriglia Squadron (Italian).

SS (Schutzstaffel), Protection Section, Nazi political armed forces (German).

St (See Stuka).

Stab Staff (German).

Staffel Aviation squadron (German); usually composed of twelve aircraft.

Staffelkapitän Aviation squadron commander (German).

Stavka Headquarters of the Soviet Supreme High Command.

StG (Sturzkampfgeschwader) Dive-bomber wing (German).

Storch German Fi 156 single-engine liaison and reconnaissance aircraft.

Stuka (Sturzkampfflugzeug) Dive-bomber (German).

Stukageschwader German dive-bomber aviation wing.

Sturmgeschütz Assault gun (German).

Su (Sukhoy), Soviet aircraft designer.

Su-2 Soviet single-engine, two-place Sukhoy light bomber.

T (Tank) Tank (Soviet).

T-26 Soviet light tank.

T-34 Soviet medium tank.

T-35 Soviet heavy, multi-turreted tank.

T-40 Soviet amphibious light tank.

Taifun Code-name of the German offensive against Moscow in the fall of 1941; see "Typhoon."

Taran Air-ramming (Soviet).

T (Tyazhyolyy Bombardirovshchik) Heavy bomber (Soviet).

TB-3 Soviet four-engine Tupolev heavy bomber.

TB-7 Soviet four-engine Petlaykov heavy bomber.

TBA (Tyazhyolyy Bombardirovochnyy Aviatsionnyy Polk) Heavy bomber aviation regiment (Soviet).

Tomahawk U.S.-designed Curtiss P-40B and P-40C single-engine, single-seat fighter.

Totenkopf "Death's Head" (the name of KG 54).

Transportstaffel German transport aviation squadron.

Tu (Tupolev) Soviet aircraft designer.

Tupolev Soviet aircraft designer.

Typhoon See "Taifun."

U (Uchebnyy) Basic training (Soviet).

U-2 Soviet single-engine Polikarpov training and light bomber biplane.

USSR (Union of Soviet Socialist Republics) The Soviet Union.

UT (Uchebno-Trenirovochnyy) Basic training (aircraft) (Soviet).

UTI (Uchebno-Trenirovochnyy Istrebitel') Basic fighter trainer (Soviet).

Verbrechen der Wehrmacht "Crimes of the Wehrmacht" German exhibition of war crimes committed by the Wehrmacht.

Victory See "aerial victory."

Vitse-Admiral Vice admiral (Soviet).

VM (Voyenno-Morskoy Flot SSSR) Naval Forces of the USSR.

VO (Voyennyy Okrug) Military district (Soviet).

VVS (Voyenno-Vozdushnye Sily) Military air force (Soviet).

Waffen Weapons, arms (German).

Waffen-SS The (fighting) armed forces of the SS.

Wehrmacht Armed forces (German).

Wehrmachtführungsstab Armed forces staff (German).

Westa (Wetterkundungsstaffel) Weather reconnaissance aviation squadron (German).

Wetterkundungsstaffel Weather reconnaissance aviation squadron (German).

Wiking Viking (German).

WNr (Werknummer) Aircraft construction number (German).

Yad Vashem "Enduring memorial" (Hebrew); Israel's official memorial authority to the victims of the Holocaust of Jews in World War II.

Ya (Yakovlev) Soviet aircraft designer.

Yak-1 Soviet single-engine, single-seat fighter.

Yakovlev Soviet aircraft designer.

Yer (Yermolayev) Soviet aircraft designer.

Yer-2 Soviet twin-engine Yermolayev long-range bomber.

Yermolayev Soviet aircraft designer.

Z (Zerstörer) Heavy fighter (German).

ZAB (Zazhigatel'naya Aviatsionnaya Bomba) Incendiary aviation bomb (Soviet).

Zerstörer "Destroyer"; German heavy fighter or naval destroyer.

Zerstörerstaffel Heavy fighter aviation squadron (German).

Zerstörergeschwader Heavy fighter aviation wing (German).

ZG (Zerstörergeschwader) Heavy fighter aviation wing (German).

ZOVO (Zapadnyy Osobyy Voyennyy Okrug) Western Special Military District (Soviet).

Zveno 1. Soviet tactical air formation (three aircraft); 2. "Piggyback" – TB-3 heavy bomber carrying two I-16 fighter-bombers.

ZWZ (Związek Walki Zbrojnej) "Union for Armed Struggle"; Polish resistance movement.

RANK EQUIVALENCY.

Red Army.	German Wehrmacht.	German SS.	U.S. Army.
–	Reichsmarschall*	–	–
Marshal Sovetskogo Soyuza	Generalfeldmarschall	Reichsführer SS	General of the Army
General Armii	Generaloberst	SS-Oberst-Gruppenführer	General (4-Star)
General-Polkovnik	General	SS-Obergruppenführer	Lieutenant General
General-Leytenant	Generalleutnant	SS-Gruppenführer	Major General
General-Mayor	Generalmajor	SS-Brigadeführer	Brigadier General
Polkovnik	Oberst	SS-Oberführer	Colonel
Podpolkovnik	Oberstleutnant	SS-Standartenführer	Lieutenant Colonel
Mayor	Major	SS-Obersturmbannführer	Major
Kapitan	Hauptmann	SS-Sturmbannführer	Captain
Starshiy Leytenant	Oberleutnant	SS-Hauptsturmführer	First Lieutenant
Leytenant	Leutnant	SS-Untersturmführer	Second Lieutenant (2/Lt)
Mladshiy Leytenant	Stabsfeldwebel	SS-Sturmscharführer	Sergeant Major
Starshina	Oberfeldwebel	SS-Hauptscharführer	Master Sergeant
Starshiy Serzhant	Feldwebel	SS-Oberscharführer	Sergeant First Class
Serzhant	Unterfeldwebel	SS-Scharführer	Staff Sergeant
Mladshiy Serzhant	Unteroffizier	SS-Unterscharführer	Sergeant
–	Stabsgefreiter	–	–
–	Obergefreiter	SS-Rottenführer	Corporal
Yefreytor	Gefreiter	SS-Sturmmann	–
–	Oberschütze	SS-Oberschütze	Private First Class (PFC)
Krasnoarmeyets	Soldat/Schütze/Grenadier	SS-Schütze	Private

* Only Hermann Göring held this rank.

SOVIET POLITICAL RANKS AND THEIR EQUIVALENTS.

Rank of Political Instructor.	Equivalent regular Army Rank.
Mladshiy Politruk	Leytenant
Politruk	Starshiy Leytenant
Starshiy Politruk	Kapitan
Batal'yonniy Komissar	Mayor
Starshiy Batal'yonny Komissar	Podpolkovnik
Polkovoy Komissar	Polkovnik
Divizionny Komissar	General-Mayor
Korpusnoy Komissar	General-Leytenant
Armeyskiy Komissar Vtorogo Ranga	General-Polkovnik
Armeyskiy Komissar Pervogo Ranga	General Armii

TIME LINE.

1933: 30 January Hitler seizes power in Germany.

1936: 1 November The Berlin-Rome Axis between Germany and Italy is declared.

25 November Germany and Japan forms the Anti-Comintern Pact.

1937: 22 May Marshal Mikhail Tukhachevskiy, the commander of the Red Army, is arrested by Stalin: The Great Purge of the Red Army begins.

6 November Italy joins the Anti-Comintern Pact.

1939: 24 August The Molotov-Ribbentrop Pact is signed between Germany and the Soviet Union.

1 September Germany invades Poland.

3 September France, Great Britain and (successively) the Commonwealth declares war on Germany.

17 September The Soviet Union invades Poland.

28 September Poland surrenders and is partitioned between Germany and the Soviet Union.

30 November The Soviet Union invades Finland, the "Winter War" begins.

1940: 13 March Finland surrenders to the Soviet Union.

9 April Germany invades Norway and Denmark.

10 May Germany attacks in the West.

10 June Italy declares war on France and Great Britain.

25 June France surrenders to Germany.

29 June Hitler informs his service chiefs of his intention of invading the Soviet Union.

31 July Hitler orders the German High Command to prepare a plan for the invasion of the Soviet Union.

15–16 June The Soviet Union invades Lithuania, Latvia and Estonia, which are annexed in August 1940.

2 July The Soviet Union annexes Romanian Bessarabia and northern Bucovina.

July–October The Battle of Britain; Hitler fails in his attempt to bring Britain down on its knees.

12 September Finland agrees to allow German troops to be transited through its territory.

27 September Germany, Italy and Japan sign the Tripartite Pact.

7 October German troops are invited to Romania.

28 October Italy invades Greece, which results in an Italian tactical setback.

18 November Soviet spy Richard Sorge dispatches information to Moscow that Hitler has ordered preparations to be made for an invasion of the Soviet Union.

24 November Slovakia joins the Tripartite Pact.

18 December Hitler submits the formal order for the invasion of the Soviet Union, Directive No. 21, the plan is assigned with the code name "Barbarossa."

29 December A Soviet spy ring in Germany informs Moscow of Hitler's Directive No. 21.

1941: 1 March "Plan Oldenburg" (the "Green Folder"), a plan for the economic exploitation of the conquered territory in the East, is approved by Reichsmarschall Hermann Göring.

26 March Anti-German coup d'état in Yugoslavia.

5 April Yugoslavia enters a pact with the Soviet Union.

6 April Germany invades Yugoslavia and intervenes to support Italy in Greece.

10 April A Pro-German Croatian state is declared.

13 April A Non-aggression Pact is signed between Japan and the Soviet Union.

17 April Yugoslavia surrenders to Germany.

2 May The "Hungerplan" is presented to leading Wehrmacht commanders: "The war against Russia can only be carried out if the whole Wehrmacht is fed from Russia. The consequence of this will be that tens of millions of people will die from starvation."

13 June Soviet spy Richard Sorge informs Moscow that 150 German divisions will attack the Soviet Union at dawn on 22 June 1941.

15 June Croatia joins the Tripartite Pact.

22 June Germany and Romania invades the Soviet Union. Germany, Romania and Italy declares war against the Soviet Union.

25 June Finland declares war against the Soviet Union.

25 June Sweden agrees to allow German troops to be transited through its territory for deployment on the Eastern Front.

27 June Hungary declares war against the Soviet Union.

27 November Finland, Romania, Hungary, Croatia, Slovakia, Bulgaria and Denmark joins the Anti-Comintern Pact.

6 December Great Britain declares war against Finland, Romania and Hungary.

7 December Japan attacks Pearl Harbor and US and British territories in East Asia.

11 December Germany and Italy declares war against the USA.

1943: 31 January German 6th Army surrenders in Stalingrad.

1945: 16 April The Soviet army assaults Berlin.

30 April Hitler commits suicide in Berlin.

8 May Germany has surrendered unconditionally and the war in Europe is over.

PREFACE.

Although Operation Barbarossa, Hitler's invasion of the Soviet Union in 1941, remains the largest military campaign in history, it also is one of the least known military operations of World War II. Not that the campaign is not covered in books, articles and documentary films – on the contrary, it is one of the most covered – but the actual events have been seriously distorted in history writing.

In any war, the events described by each side during the war are colored both by the aims of conscious propaganda and by subconscious misconceptions and prejudices regarding the enemy. For instance, if one reads German newspapers during the time of the Battle of Britain, the impression is given of an entirely victorious Luftwaffe, and one wonders why Germany chose not to invade the British Isles. The distortion of both side's descriptions of events becomes even greater when the war is based on deep ideological differences, such as any civil war – or the conflict between Nazi Germany and the Soviet Union.

After the war, the Soviet Union prevailed, and thus also its history writing. Nazi Germany was crushed, but some of its conceptions of the war lingered on in the memoirs and accounts of its former generals and other servicemen. In the Cold War between the West and the East, which almost immediately succeeded World War II, the West – now regarding its former ally, the Soviet Union as its foremost enemy – allowed itself to be duped by the ideologically distorted accounts by former servicemen of Nazi Germany in its general concept of the war on the Eastern Front between 1941 and 1945. The fact that this was supplemented with a few translated official Soviet accounts only made the situation worse as far as a correct historical assessment is concerned.

With the fall of the Soviet Union and the subsequent opening of the former Soviet archives to all scholars, a re-evaluation of this part of history could take place. A small revolution in history writing took place when it was discovered that the former Soviet records were not only meticulously kept, but also in exemplary good order. But after all, this was what one could expect of a ruthless dictatorship where everyone and everything was subject to the strictest control and monitoring, with severe repercussions for anyone who was not able to account for every last detail of what he or she was responsible for. As a matter of fact, the German first-hand records are less useful – owing first of all to the fact that many of these were destroyed in Allied bombing raids or by the Germans themselves at the end of the war, but also due to the fact that the Soviet recorded events and facts more rigorously. (This is not to say that German records were entirely unreliable, which they weren't; but Soviet records were above average meticulous.)

Writers such as Christopher Lawrence, David Glantz, Nigel Askey, Niklas Zetterling, Artem Drabkin, Mikhail Bykov, Grigoriy Krivosheev, and Vlad Antipov have used Soviet and German records to create a new breed of balanced accounts of the war on the Eastern Front that would have been unthinkable prior to the 1990s. Christopher Lawrence's 1,652-page *Kursk: The Battle of Prokhorovka* (2015) is actually one of the most well-researched, detailed and balanced accounts of any single battle during World War II. This book gives a good example of what can be achieved if a writer seriously uses the access to first-hand accounts from both sides without any bias or preconception, and could be used by any department of history as an exemplary historical account.

However, human consciousness lingers behind science, and it is a fact that to this day, the formerly distorted accounts of the war on the Eastern Front dominate in literature. Even though the facts are readily available in archives and, in some cases, in publications, the image in most Western accounts of the war between Germany and its allies and the Soviet Union remains in general colored by old accounts by Germans and the former allies of Nazi Germany. The heated debate caused in Finland in recent times by certain revelations of facts that are not so flattering to the Finnish government during the war, shows that the subject still can be quite sensitive. (After all, among the warring states on the Eastern Front in World War II, Finland is the only one that remains today: Nazi Germany is gone, and so are the formerly Fascist regimes of Romania, Italy and Spain; today's independent states of Slovakia and Croatia have very little in common with the Slovakia and Croatia of 1941-1944, and today's Hungary is the result of a transformation via a Stalinist state fiercely opposed to Nazi Germany. Hence, it is hardly surprising that the strongest reactions against a re-evaluation of the perception of the enemy Soviet Union meets its strongest reaction in Finland, although this is not an all-pervasive attitude among the population.)

To mingle politics and one's political preferences into history writing always leads astray. But it should also be kept in mind that the human psyche makes us subconsciously apprehend things according to our former perceptions. It is only when we are aware of this fact that we can truly approach new facts with an open mind.

It has been the author's intention to make such an approach to the events during Operation Barbarossa. The account on the following pages is based on a substantial amount of first-hand records gathered during several decades of intense research work in several countries, among which Germany and Russia of course are the most important. This research work has led the author to discover evidence of a not insubstantial amount of misconceptions and pure errors concerning the Russo-German war, as well as large "white spots" in history writing.

The author has been occupied with the history of World War II for nearly five decades, and this has resulted in 27 books on the subject. More than half of these deal with the Eastern Front, opening with the author's ongoing book series *Black Cross/Red Star: Air War Over the Eastern Front* from the year 2000 and onward.

With the present book, it is the author's intention to give his contribution to set the records of the much misunderstood war on the Eastern Front in 1941 straight. The reader will find a fairly detailed account of Operation Barbarossa, presented equally from the view of both sides, built around a large number of eye-witness accounts – aimed at describing the events from the perspective of those who lived through it all – and several new facts which in many cases will present the history in a completely new light, compared with previous general preconceptions. It would be foreign to the author to claim personal honor for all these new findings; to a very large extent they are the result of a close cooperation with and contributions from many fellow scholars who generously and most kindly has shared their knowledge and access to records. The author is deeply indebted to and wishes to extend his warmest gratitude to the following persons:

Captain Christian Allerman, Alfons Altmeier, Ferdinando D'Amico, Alexey V. Andreev, Sergey V. Andreev, Vlad Antipov, Vladislav Arkhipov, Henrik Arnstad, Andrew Arthy, Michael Balss, Bernd Barbas, Vesvolod Bashkuev, Mirko Bayerl, Csaba Becze, Holger Benecke, Dénes Bernád, Lennart Berns, Christian Berring, Peter Björk, Jan Bobek, Andreas Brekken, Pawel Burchard, Don Caldwell, Toni Canfora, Brian Cauchi, Boris Ciglic, Larry deZeng, Andrey Dikov, Tadeusz Dobrowecki, Artem Drabkin, Chris Dunning, Eugene Dvurechenski, Olve Dybvig, Carl-Fredrik Geust, Octavian Ghita, Dr. Rainer Göpfert, Alexei Gretchikine, Jürgen Grislawski, Fredrik Gustafson, Håkan Gustavsson, Lars Gyllenhaal, Lutz Hannig, Bert Hartmann, Thomas Hasselberg, Bengt Högberg, Michael Holm, Ivanova Maya Ivanovna, Marko Jeras, Morten Jessen, Daniel Johansson, Thomas Jönsson, Ossi Juntunen, Seppo Juttula, Dmitriy Karlenko, Polkovnik Vsevolod Kanaev, Dmitriy Karlenko, Peter Kassak, Christian Kirsch, Aleksandr Anatolevich Kudriavtsev, Viktor Kulikov, Andrey Kuznetsov, Vitse-Admiral Yuriy Kvyatkovskiy, Pär Lagerqvist, Ola Laveson, Christopher Lawrence, Brigadier General Håkan Linde, Alexander Makienko, Raimo Malkamäki, Martin Månsson, Alexey Matvienko, George Mellinger, Rolf Mewitz, Andrey Mikhailov, Yekaterina Mikhailova, Gian Piero Milanetti, Eric Mombeek, Egor Nazarenko, Kamen Nevenkin, Jonathan Newton, Mathias C. Noch, Doug Norrie, Mikhail Fyodorovich Potapov, Bogdan Pavelyev, Donald Pearson, Roger Pedersen, Martin Pegg, Jim Perry, Gennadiy Petrov, Rodion Podorozhny, Valery Potapov, Dr. Jochen Prien, Rune Rautio, Ondrej Repka, Ivan I. Rodionov, Günther Rosipal, Yuriy Rybin, Pär Salomonson, Matti Salonen, Vitaly Samodurov, Carlo Sansilvestri, Alexandre Savine, Anneluise Schreier, Niclas Sennerteg, Yuriy V. Shakhov, Grzechu Slizewski, Hans E. Söder, James Sterrett, Harold E. Stockton, Samuel Svärd, Lieutenant Commander B. John Szirt, Peter Taghon, Kevin Troha, Dariusz Tyminski, Rustam Usmanov, Hannu Valtonen, Peter Vollmer, Dave Wadman, Manfred Wägenbaur, Walter Waiss, Bob Wartburg, Pierre Watteeuw, Carl-Johan Westring, Brigadier General Björn Widmark, Dave Williams, Nikita Yegorov, Mike Young, Admiral Vasilyevich Zelenin & Rolf Zydek.

World War II Soviet & Allied veterans:
Petr Vasilyevich Bazanov, Ion Lazarevich Degen, Mikhail Petrovich Devyatayev, John Francis Durham "Tim" Elkington, Nina Erdman, Mikhail Mikhailovich Filatov, Nikolay Ivanovich Gapeyonok, Vasiliy Matveyevich Garanin, Semyon Vasilyevich Grigorenko, Viktor Alekseyevich Grubich, Aleksey Filipinnovich Gubin, Aleksey Ivanovich Kalugin, Vitaliy Ivanovich Klimenko, Leonid Yakovlevich Klobukov, Aleksandr Vladimirovich Kostikov, Arkadiy Fyodorovich Kovachevich, Sergey Makarovich Kramarenko, Viktor Aleksandrovich Kumskov, Vasiliy Vasilyevich Kurayev, Ivan Davidovich Lazarev, Vasiliy Ivanovich Lutskiy, Ariya Simeon Lvovich, Malkus Boris Lyubovits, Dmitriy Aleksandrovich Makarov, Boris Dmitriyevich Melyokhin, Sergey Semenovich Merkulov, Stepan Anastasovich Mikoyan, Vsevolod Olimpev, Vladimir Vladimirovich Onishchenko, Sergey Andreyevich Otrochenkov, Aleksandr Aleksandrovich Pavlichenko, Georgiy Vasilyevich Pavlov, Nikolay Potapov, Vasiliy Yegorovich Rudenko, Viktorovich Rybalko, Georgiy Denisovich Safronov, Aron Savelyevich Shapiro, Petr Andreyevich Shvets, Sergey Sidorov, Vera Tikhomirova, Viktor Nikolayevich Yegorov, Ivan Petrovich Vasenin, Roman Yevseyevich & Gabass Zhurmatovich.

World War II German veterans:
Gerhard Baeker, Gerhard Barkhorn, Hansgeorg Bätcher, Arno Becker, Helmut Berendes, Hans-Ekkehard Bob, Johannes Braun, Johannes Broschwitz, Hugo Dahmer, Leutnant Hans Ellendt, Adolf Galland, Unteroffizier Arthur Gärtner, Rudolf Gloeckner, Gordon M. Gollob, Alfred Grislawski, Klaus Häberlen, Norbert Hannig, Hermann Heckes, Hajo Herrmann, Karl-Heinz Höfer, Franz Hohlmann, Hans Hormann, Udo Hünerfeld, Erhard Jähnert, Berthold K. Jochim, Otto Kaufmann, Fritz Klees, Benno Kohl, Hans Krohn, Wilhelm Kühl, Felix Lademann, Friedrich Lang, Heinz Lange, Erwin Leykauf, Friedrich Lühring, Friedrich Metz, Hans-Adolf Metz, Victor Mölders, Dagobert Paskowski, Gerhard Philipp, Günther Rall, Ernst-Wilhelm Reinert, Leutnant Edmund Rossmann, Günther Schack, Kurt Schade, Heinrich Scheibe, Friedrich Schmid Herbert Schmidt, Hans-Udo Schmitz-Wortmann, Walther Schröder, Walter Seifert, Johannes Steinhoff, Hannes Trautloft & Dieter Woratz.

To any helpers whose names we may have missed, please accept our apologies and our implied gratitude.

Last, not least, the author would like to extend his gratitude to his family, Maria, Bambi, Caroline, Albin, Benjamin and Kristoffer, for their great understanding during the work on this book.

Eskilstuna, Sweden, 15 April 2016
bergstrombooks.se

Preparing for the onslaught. A member of the ground crew is preparing a Junkers Ju 88 bomber of German bomber wing KG 51.

BRANDENBURGERS IN THE NIGHT.

Soviet border patrol at the western border of the USSR on 20 June 1941. (Photo: Viktor Temin.)

It was one of those wonderful, star bright Central European midsummer nights. Everything was still and quiet when a car came driving up the road that German engineers had constructed on the soft underground in the forest in southern East Prussia. Four men, dressed in Soviet army uniforms, sat in the car which approached the border with Soviet-occupied eastern Poland. Suddenly a large, felled tree blocked the road. Just as the car halted, two figures appeared in the darkness.

Everything was dead silent. The four men remained sitting in their car. A German officer's cap became visible. In the next second it was clear that the two figures were officers of the German army.

"Are you from Regiment Brandenburg?" one of them demanded to know, looking at the brownish greatcoats.

"Of course," came the reply.

The Brandenburgers were German special forces, trained for covert operations behind enemy lines, where they operated in enemy uniforms and with enemy equipment. They were to be the first German troops to cross into the Soviet Union in Operation Barbarossa, Hitler's attack against his former ally Joseph Stalin. All along the Soviet borders between the Baltic Sea and the Black Sea, dozens of Brandenburger teams prepared to slip through on the evening of 21 June 1941. Their tasks were to seize important river crossings and cut hundreds of telephone lines, rendering the Soviet troops leaderless when the German armies struck a couple of hours later. Behind them waited the largest army ever assembled for a single operation: 3.35 million German troops with 3,600 tanks, 600,000 transport motor vehicles, 625,000 horses and 3,400 Luftwaffe aircraft.

Just as during all of Germany's previous military campaigns, the first shots were fired by the Brandenburgers, or Lehr und Bau Kompanie z.b.V. 800 (or Special-Purpose Training and Construction Company No. 800), as was its official designation. Subordinated to the Wehrmacht and its Abwehr (Intelligence Section) under Admiral Wilhelm Canaris, Lehr-Regiment 800 was led by Oberstleutnant Paul Haehling von Lanzenauer. It employed all of its three battalions for Operation Barbarossa.

The strongest among these was the I. Battalion; commanded by Major Friedrich Heinz, it was employed in the northern operational zone of Heeresgruppe Süd, Army Group South, in southeastern Poland/northwestern Ukraine. It operated together with two battalions of Ukrainian insurgents – Nachtigall and Roland.

Heeresgruppe Süd was divided between southeastern Poland/northwestern Ukraine, where its main force stood, and Romania, where its 11. Armee was positioned. The Brandenburger's II. Battalion under Major Paul Jacobi was divided between two of the three German army groups that stood ready for the invasion of the Soviet Union: 6. Kompanie was in Romania, tasked to open the way for 11. Armee by seizing bridges across the Dnestr River. 7. and 8. Kompanie were assigned to the northern army group, Heeresgruppe Nord, in East Prussia, and aimed against Soviet Lithuania.

III. Battalion under Hauptmann Franz Jacobi consisted of two companies, 10. and 12., assigned to Heeresgruppe Mitte.

Leutnant Herbert Kriegsheim led the men of his small squad of four men through the barbed wire entanglement. This was one of eight squads of the 10. Kompanie, each tasked with capturing a vital bridge. The goal for Kriegsheim's group was a bridge across the Augustowski canal. Some five kilometers south of the Lithuanian border, the Augustowski canal runs west from the great river Neman. At Augustovo, 55 km northwest of Grodno, it turns south and eventually joins the Vistula River. Constructed in the 19th century, the waterway with its 102 kilometers, still is one of Europe's largest canals. On 22 June 1941, the crossings of this canal played a vital role for German 20th armored division (20. Panzer-Division) under Generalmajor Horst Stumpff. Subordinated to the 39th Armored Corps (XXXIX. Armeekorps) under General Rudolf Schmidt, this panzer division was tasked to surge ahead along the main road from Lyck (today's Elk), across the Augustowski canal and to the Lithuanian capital of Vilnius, via Alytus. General Schmidt's corps formed the northern force of Generaloberst Hermann Hoth's Panzergruppe 3, one of the four German armor groups that constituted the main breakthrough forces of Operation Barbarossa, Hitler's attempt to destroy the Soviet Union. It also constituted the northern flank of Generalfeldmarschall Fedor von Bock's Central army group (Heeresgruppe Mitte).

Just as Kriegesheim stopped to check the compass, a short but sharp cry froze the blood in his veins: "*Stoy!*" Two frontier guards of the NKVD, Stalin's feared secret service, emerged out of the thicket, pointing their rifles at the four intruders. Kriegsheim and his men began to raise their arms. In the moment when the two Soviets relaxed slightly at the sight of what they thought were harmless men in Soviet uniforms, the trained German élite soldier quickly pulled his pistol and put a bullet in each of the two NKVD men. Both fell to the ground, one hit in the face and one wounded in a leg. Before the latter had even time to shout, Kriegsheim had shot him in his head.

Immediately afterwards a whistle was heard at some distance in the darkness and a flare lit in the sky. The little group of Brandenburgers set off towards their goal when suddenly a machine gun opened fire. The commando soldiers immediately hit the ground, but it was too late: Two were wounded. In the next instant a group of soldiers rushed up with rifles aimed at the Brandenburgers. In panic, Kriegsheim yelled the codeword as he recognized them as German soldiers.
"You idiots!" he screamed at the suddenly completely terrified troops.

Leaving them behind, Kriegsheim and the other remaining of the Brandenburger, a Gefreiter Koch, disappeared into the pitch black forest.

After a while they reached the main road between Augustow and Grodno. There they spotted two Soviet soldiers. Koch, who spoke excellent Russian, approached them and asked where Lipsk was. Sensing no danger, one of the soldiers pointed into the right direction. Without anyone paying any special notice to them, the two disguised Germans continued along the road.

Large groups of Soviet soldiers in disarray passed by. The German attack has started! A terrible rumbling sound from the German artillery was filling the air. But the two Brandenburgers carried on, mingling with the Soviet sol-

diers. No one noticed their German weapons. They reached the road fork where a smaller dirt road crosses the main road from the south to the north. There they took a right and suddenly they came upon the bridge.

It was a steady wooden bridge, strong enough to carry heavy vehicles. The two Germans started looking for wires for explosives, and understandably the Soviets took them for pioneers preparing to blow up the bridge. Soon the flow of withdrawing Soviet troops diminished into individual soldiers who, looking scared, rushed past without bothering about the two Red Army-clad Brandenburgers. Finally, all movement died down and Kriegsheim and his comrade were the only ones left at the bridge.

They had just began to expect to see the first German troops advancing towards the bridge when a platoon of men in brown uniforms came rushing forward. Soviets! And half of the men were carrying a heavy cargo which the two Germans recognized as petrol cans. That could only mean one thing – they were the real pioneers who had been tasked to burn the bridge.

Kriegsheim and Koch jumped into a hollow and uncocked their submachine guns. But that drew the attention of the Soviets. Their officer deployed his men in combat formation and they approached carefully. Kriegsheim and Koch had to wait until the Soviets were within effective range, some 70 meters, before they opened fire. The first burst sent the Soviets plummeting to the ground, and soon their rifle bullets came whistling past the two Germans. Several hit the ground in front of them, spraying their helmets with dirt.

The duel had been going on for a couple of minutes when suddenly a clicking sound from his submachine gun told Kochs that he had emptied his last magazine. Then he blackened out – hit by one or more Soviet bullets.

"Kochs!" screamed Kriegsheim as he saw his comrade fall onto his face and drop his gun. At the same time, heavy machine gun fire was heard behind the Soviets, who stood up and ran towards the river bank, towards cover, towards Kriegsheim. Only too late did Kriegsheim notice the Soviet soldier behind him. He had a rifle with a fixed bayonet pointed at him. Before Kriegsheim could react the blade penetrated his neck and he too collapsed.

When he came to his senses, the area swarmed with German soldiers. Kriegsheim found himself lying on a stretcher. His head and neck were bandaged. Next to him was Kochs, dead. On all sides, across hundreds of kilometers, hundreds of thousands of German troops and tens of thousands of vehicles surged across the borders and into a completely unprepared Soviet Union. The Brandenburgers had done a fantastic preparatory work. Not only had they captured most of their assigned bridges intact, but they also had cut hundreds of telephone lines. Since the Red Army did not trust wireless radio messages and relied on regular telephone communications, the disruption of telephone lines deprived the Soviet commanders of any general overview. At Soviet headquarters, no one had any idea of the general situation.

Thus began Operation Barbarossa, the largest military campaign in history.

1: **HITLER AGAINST STALIN.**

"All along the line the incompetent scoundrel triumphs."

– Leon Trotsky, former commander of the Red Army, 12 June 1937.

It is hard to find any other major war in modern times that was fought between two states that both were in the hands of such autocratic leaders as the German-Soviet war of 1941–1945. The dominant personal influence exerted by the Nazi dictator Adolf Hitler over Germany is paralleled only by the power enjoyed by Joseph Stalin over the Soviet state.

Modern history writing has tended to point out the indeed striking similarities between these two dictators, but the states that they controlled were both quite opposed in nature, while they at the same time also showed several similarities. There also were great differences between Hitler and Stalin.

Adolf Hitler rose to power through a formally legitimate parliamentary process – the conservative and liberal parties in the German Reichstag voted unanimously to assign him with unlimited powers in order to "fight communism". Josef Stalin, on the other hand, owed his power to a socialist revolution in the name of the working class and oppressed peasants. His rise to power, however, was due to his own bureaucratic maneuvering – and outmaneuvering of his rivals – in a country which lay in shambles after a terrible civil war.

Both Hitler and Stalin set about consolidating their personal power through authoritarian and repressive means immediately after their seizure of power. While Hitler as the Führer, Leader, was able to transform Germany into a nationalist, authoritarian Nazi state, Stalin was able to bring about a similar change of the Soviet state due to his position as general secretary of the Communist (Bolshevik) Party, which gave him the power to decide which people would occupy responsible positions.

The greatest changes were undoubtedly brought about by Stalin. In a broad sense, Hitler merely developed the right-wing nationalist plans that had prevailed in Germany for two generations. Stalin, however, broke most of the ideological foundations of the Bolshevik Party: Where the Soviet government under his predecessor Lenin (who died in 1924) had set nations oppressed by the old Tsarist Russia free (Finland, Poland, the Baltic countries), Stalin set about to reverse this policy by re-conquering – or attempting to re-conquer – what had been released as a result of the October Revolution. (The great differences between Lenin's and Stalin's policy vis-à-vis the nations had been showed during the conflict between them both over Georgia in the early 1920s.) Where Lenin's slogan had been "all power to the workers' and soldiers' councils" (Soviets), and had regarded the extreme limitations of democratic freedoms that successively followed during the first year after the revolution as a temporary measure owing to the civil war, Stalin based his power on an increased repression.* Originally, the Bolshevik Party based itself on a Marxist class analysis, regarding the Russian revolution as merely the first stage of a global socialist revolution. Hence, the Bolsheviks addressed the working classes and oppressed masses of the colonies, urging them to rise and seize power, rather than engaging in diplomacy with the governments of these countries. Under Stalin, this was totally reversed. Stalin cancelled all support for the liberation movements in the colonies in order to achieve an alliance with the governments of the UK and France, and ultimately dissolved the tool for the intended world revolution, the Communist International, which had been formed on the initiative of the Bolsheviks in 1919.**

Finally, this policy led Stalin to the unfortunate pact with Hitler in August 1939.

By that time, both dictators had consolidated their absolute power. In order to do so, Stalin had been forced to turn not only against the ideology of the October Revolution, but against the Bolshevik Party itself.*** Between 1936

---

* In 1921, during the last year of the civil war, Soviet prison camps and other prisons had 21,724 inmates. In 1937, in peacetime, Stalin's prison camps and other prisons had 429,311 inmates. ("Victims of Stalinism and the Soviet Secret Police: The Comparability and Reliability of Archival Data – Not the Last Word" by Stephen G. Wheatcroft in Europe-Asia Studies, Vol. 51, 199, p. 338.)

** In an interview to Roy Howard, President of Scripps-Howard Newspapers, on 1 March 1936, Stalin described the idea of a world revolution as "a tragic misunderstanding". ("The Stalin-Howard Interview." Interview given by Joseph Stalin to Roy Howard, Representative of the Scripps-Howard Newspaper Chain, on March 1, 1936. International Publishers, 1936.)

*** The history of the Bolshevik opposition against Stalin's dictatorship is largely unknown and probably never will be written in full, owing to the fact that the Soviet authorities scrupulously destroyed both this opposition and nearly all traces and remembrances of it. In Pierre Broué's Trotsky biography, elements of this obviously quite widespread opposition is described on pages 662–673 (Swedish edition, 2011.)

Adolf Hitler had the aim of crushing Communism from his early days in politics in 1919. (Photo: Via Daniel Johansson.)

and 1939, more than one million members of the Bolshevik Party were purged.[1] Hundreds of thousands were executed, including the majority of the Central Committee which had led the revolution in 1917.[2] Concurrently with this, the Red Army was de facto beheaded by similarly large-scale purges – more on this later. All of this followed in the wake of a fearsome famine which had caused economic chaos and the death of millions of Soviet citizens, mainly – but not limited to – the Ukraine. The cause of this, which has been described as a genocide, was double: First, similar to the Great Famine in Ireland ninety years earlier, because the government exported grains that could have prevented the famine, and secondly due to what Stalin's main opponent, the revolutionary in exile Leon Trotsky, described as "the senseless bestialities that grew out of bureaucratic methods of collectivization."[3]

Hitler and Stalin indeed inspired each other. The Hitler Youth Organization (Hitler Jugend) was inspired by the Soviet Pioneer organization. Stalin's establishment of the cult of the leader clearly had Fascist roots.

The regimentation of the Nazi society also had striking similarities with the regimentation of Soviet society under Stalin. In the Soviet Union of the 1930s, the cultural explosion of the early years of the revolution lay crushed under a system of repressive control. But here also was a great difference between Hitler's Germany and Stalin's Soviet Union, the foundation of which was another basic dissimilarity between Hitler's rule and that of Stalin: While Hitler was quite open about his goals and intentions to change German society into a nationalist fascist state, the degree of popular support enjoyed by Stalin rested on an ignorance of his true aims: The socialist revolutions and its social gains enjoyed widespread popularity, and thus Stalin – who was fundamentally opposed to the continuation of a revolutionary policy in the way that the Bolshevik Party had foreseen when it carried out the October Revolution in 1917 – was forced to uphold false slogans that he in actual fact was opposed to.

This led to a need to strike down on any independent thinking, and to substitute this with formulas and slogans dictated by the leadership. Stalin's eternal critic, Leon Trotsky, wrote in 1937: "The Soviet school cripples a child no less gravely than the Catholic seminary, from which the Soviet school differs only in that it is less stable. Scholars, educators, writers, and artists who show the slightest signs of independence or talent have been terrorized, hounded, arrested, exiled, if not shot. All along the line the incompetent scoundrel triumphs."[4]

All of this is necessary to understand the double nature of the Red Army and the whole Soviet society when the war broke out. On one hand, the image of the social gains of the October Revolution created a Soviet-Russian citizen who was prepared to die for the cause of the socialist idea and the defense of the socialist Soviet Union. On the other hand, the massive repression left the Soviet soldier and citizen in the hands of "incompetent scoundrels", Stalinist cronies, and military and civilian leaders who were afraid of taking any own initiatives. Moreover, owing to the great famine created by the regime only eight years previously and the repressive policies against national minorities and

Leon Trotsky, the organizer of the October 1917 Revolution and leader of the Red Army, was a staunch critic of the Stalinist system, against which he attempted to organize a revolution. In 1929 he was deported from the Soviet Union, to be assassinated on the orders of Stalin in exile in Mexico in 1940.

(from 1939) subdued peoples (Poles, Balts), only Soviet Russians could be trusted to be motivated to defend the Soviet Union.

The German Armed Forces, the Wehrmacht, were the diametrical opposite in this regard. By 1941, it was a uniformly German nationalist force, consisting of generally highly motivated young men who had been effectively brainwashed in a totalitarian German nationalist and racist society. A sufficiently large amount of them were convinced that they were fighting a kind of final, "holy" war of decisive importance to generations of Germans for a thousand years to follow. In contrast to the Red Army, individual initiative was encouraged in the German Armed Forces, and the senior command was quite open to new methods and ideas – whereas their Soviet counterparts feared anything unorthodox.

In short, the double nature of Joseph Stalin's Soviet Union was clearly reflected in the Red Army and its methods, while means and methods formed an organic whole in Adolf Hitler's warfare in the East.

One final similarity between the two dictators is that both built their plans on unrealistic ideas: Hitler's plan to invade and colonize the Soviet Union was in fact doomed from the start. Stalin's attempt to permanently uphold a state with such a double nature as the non-revolutionary and conservative Soviet Union proved to be no less unrealistic.

2: LEBENSRAUM.

"Everything I undertake is aimed against Russia."

– Adolf Hitler, August 1939.[1]

When Germany invaded the Soviet Union in 1941, Adolf Hitler's and the Nazi movements' goal to invade the Soviet Union had been absolutely clear for at least fifteen years. The Nazi Party – or Deutsche Arbeiterpartei (DAP), as it was originally called – had been formed on the basis of two pillars: The peculiar German right-wing nationalism called *Völkisch* ("folkish") ideology, and a glowing hatred of Communism. In essence, both of these pointed in the direction of a confrontation with the Soviet Union with its communism and vast land masses.

To anyone in doubt of Hitler's goal, a cursory reading of the second part of his book *Mein Kampf*, which was published in 1926, is sufficient: In Chapter 14, Hitler openly declared his ultimate goal of invading, annihilating and colonizing the Soviet Union. He lamented that Germany was "limited to the absurd area of five hundred thousand square kilometers" and argued that it must become a world power through the aqcuisition of "an adequately large space." This was to be seized from the Soviet Union, which he compared with the Persian Empire in the time of Alexander the Great as "ripe for collapse." On the one hand, the Nazi leader argued that no justification was needed, but that "the right lies in this strength alone." On the other hand, he used the communist nature of the Soviet Union as a rationale for this conquest. He described "the international Jew," whom he claimed "completely dominated Russia," as "common blood-stained criminals" and "the scum of humanity" and wrote: "The fight against Jewish world Bolshevization requires a clear attitude toward Soviet Russia."

Once in power, the first violent action of the Nazi Party was directed not against the Jews, but against the socialists in general and the Communists in particular. Thousands of Communists were rounded up and sent to concentration camps. Simultaneously, the Nazi press launched a fierce campaign against communism and the Soviet Union. Horror stories related by the White emigrés from the Revolution and photos from the 1921 famine that followed in the wake of the Russian civil war were widely published. A special exhibition, ironically called "Das Sowjet-Paradies" (The Soviet Paradise) was created and toured throughout the country with the aim of "informing the German people about the dreadful conditions in the Soviet Union." All of this was done with the hidden object of preparing the population for war.

But Hitler was the born opportunist. His invasion of Poland in September 1939 was merely the first step of his planned expansion towards the East – the Soviet Union was next in turn, and besides, Germany needed the Polish territory as the springboard for the invasion of the USSR. Britain and France had been helpful towards Hitler as long as they regarded him as a reliable ally against communism, and one who could be controlled. When they belatedly – in early 1939 – realized that the Nazi dictator had no intention of being reigned in, they switched over to opposition to

Poster for the Nazi exhibition "Das Sowjet-Paradies" (The Soviet Paradise). Organized by Propaganda Minister Goebbels, the alleged purpose of the exhibition was to "inform the German people about the dreadful conditions in the Soviet Union." The true aim was to prepare the population for a war of aggression against the Soviet Union.

Hitler, although still refusing to heed to Stalin's overtures for an anti-Hitler alliance. This drove Stalin – who feared a "capitalist invasion" of the kind that had taken place during the Russian civil war – to seek to pacify Hitler. In April 1939, the Nazi government was courted by Soviet diplomats with proposals for an end to the ideological struggle and instead begin a "concerted policy."

Stalin intensified his flirting with the Nazis by replacing his Jewish foreign minister Maxim Litvinov with Vyacheslav Molotov, and ordered the latter to "purge the ministry of Jews."

When it began to be clear that Britain and France would not give Hitler a free hand against Poland as they had given him regarding the Rhineland, Austria and the Sudeten area of Czechoslovakia, the Führer cleverly seized the opportunity to heed to Stalin's proposals. For German war plans, an economic agreement with the Soviet Union could also mean that the country could overcome its desperate shortage in raw materiel needed for the war.

On 24 August 1939, the renowned Molotov-Ribbentrop Pact was signed in Moscow. Officially, it was a 10-year non-aggression pact, but its secret protocol to the pact divided the states of Northern and Eastern Europe into German and Soviet "spheres of influence." This gave Hitler the perfect opportunity to attack Poland (on 1 September 1939), leaving the Western allies more or less helpless.

Testifying to Stalin's eagerness to maintain the pact with Hitler, he instructed the Communist International to immediately suspend all anti-Nazi and anti-Fascist propaganda. This could be implemented owing to the fact that Stalin's secret police had purged the international with the same efficiency as it had purged the Bolshevik Party. Communist parties trained to adhere to any instruction from the Kremlin without asking questions began a campaign against the "capitalist states" (Britain and France), which would severely undermine France's ability to defend itself against the German attack in May 1940.

The German-Soviet relations were extended through the signing of a commercial agreement in February 1940. This helped Germany to surmount the British-French blockade; up until Hitler's invasion of the Soviet Union in June 1941, it allowed Germany to import large amounts of vital raw materials through the Soviet Union – including 200,000 tons of phosphates, 140,000 tons of manganese, 20,000 tons of chrome ore – as well as 900,000 tons of oil, 1,600,000 tons of grains and 200,000 tons of cotton, among other goods.[2]

But the invasion of the Soviet Union remained the centerpiece of Adolf Hitler's Nazi masterplan, and Stalin's concessions merely helped to lay the material foundation for that war. On 29 June 1940, less than a week after the surrender of France, the Nazi dictator Hitler informed his service chiefs of his intention to invade the Soviet Union. On 31 July 1940 he ordered the German High Command to prepare a plan for this invasion. The first result was the so-called Marcks Plan on 5 August 1940. According to this, the main centres of the Soviet economy in the Ukraine and Donets Basin and the armament industries of Moscow and Leningrad were to be occupied, and German armies were to advance to the line between the rivers lower Don

On 24 August 1939, the renowned Molotov-Ribbentrop Pact was signed in Moscow. Sitting at the desk is the Soviet foreign minister Vyacheslav Molotov.
Standing from left to right: Waffen-SS officer Richard Schulze-Kossens; Chief of the General Staff of the Red Army, Boris Shaposhnikov; German foreign minister Joachim von Ribbentrop; Joseph Stalin; and Vladimir Pavlov, First Secretary of the Soviet embassy in Germany. (Photo: Krigsarkivet Stockholm.)

–central Volga–north Dnepr. Generalmajor Erich Marcks, a member of the recently established Army Headquarters East in East Prussia, also pointed out that no offensive aims by the Soviet Union could be traced: "The Russians will not do us the favour of attacking. We must expect that the Russian Army will remain on the defensive against us." This was supplemented by another study by the OKW's Oberstleutnant Bernhard von Lossberg, presented on 15 September.

Lossberg's draft saw four strike forces: One which would strike from East Prussia through the Baltic States with the aim of capturing Leningrad. Another, the most powerful one with the bulk of the armored forces, would advance towards the east from eastern Poland, envelop and annihilate strong Red Army forces at Minsk and Smolensk, and finally capture Moscow. A third force in southeastern Poland and a fourth in Romania would link up in the Ukraine to encircle and annihilate the Soviet forces in that region. Next, the two southern forces would proceed to link up with the two northern forces.

The Chief of the General Staff, Generaloberst Franz Halder, instructed Generalmajor Friedrich Paulus to create a final draft based on the Marcks and the Lossberg studies. The result was a study nearly identical to Lossberg's work. On 5 December 1940 it was presented to Hitler, who emphasized that the most important objective must be the destruction of the Red Army through large-scale encirclement battles in the Baltic states, in Belarus and in the Ukraine. Having completed this, the next aim was to capture Leningrad, and for this the central army group would veer north to cooperate with the northern force. Paulus' study had been accepted in general, but with one important exception: "Moscow of no great importance," as a disgruntled Halder noted in his diary.[3] Although Halder chose not to confront Hitler on the matter at that time, he never relinquished his aim of seizing Moscow as one of the main objectives of the operation.

On 18 December 1940 Hitler submitted the formal order for the invasion, Directive No. 21, where the plan was assigned with the code name "Barbarossa" *. Hitler set the "general line Volga-Archangelsk" as the invasion's overall military objective.

The greater part of the German armed forces were to be divided into three major army groups in the east: Army groups North (Heeresgruppe Nord), Center (Mitte) and South (Süd). Heeresgruppe Nord was to be located in East Prussia and Heeresgruppe Mitte in northeastern Poland. The task assigned to these two army groups was to annihilate the Soviet armies in Belarus and the Baltic States through great encirclement battles, and then cooperate to capture Leningrad. In the end, it was thought that they would seize the capital Moscow.

Heeresgruppe Süd was split between southern Poland and eastern Romania. In between lay the still-neutral Hungary. Heeresgruppe Süd's task was to destroy the Soviet troops in Ukraine and capture the major industrial and mining areas in eastern Ukraine. This army group was to interact with the Romanian armed forces.

In the Far North, in northern Norway, a small German assault force was assembled with the goal of seizing the port of Murmansk – the Soviet Union's only port with direct access to the oceans that is ice-free year round.

On the question on Moscow, Führer Directive No. 21 read: "Only after the accomplishment [Erledigung] of this most important task, which must be followed by the occupation of Leningrad and Kronstadt, are the offensive operations aimed at the occupation of the important traffic and armament center of Moscow to be pursued." In an act of defiance, Halder self-willingly changed the Führer's word "accomplishment" in the above quoted sentence into "made safe" [Sicherstellung]. Thus, Operation Barbarossa would be launched without any defined directive as to the phase that would follow after the encirclement battles.

The political goal found its concrete form in the so-called Generalplan Ost (Master Plan East), which called for the colonization of all East European territories to the Ural Mountains, including the Caucasus. Led by the SS Chief Heinrich Himmler and the Nazi chief ideologist and ex-Russian Alfred Rosenberg, Generalplan Ost was a classic colonialist, racist and genocidal plan. At its core was ethnic cleansing and colonisation of these areas by Germans. No less than 45 million "racially undesirable" (Jews and Slavs) were to be subject to "annihilation or expulsion". Thus, a Lebensraum ("living space") would be created for Germany.

The plan for a colonization of the East occupied a central position in the late nineteenth century German

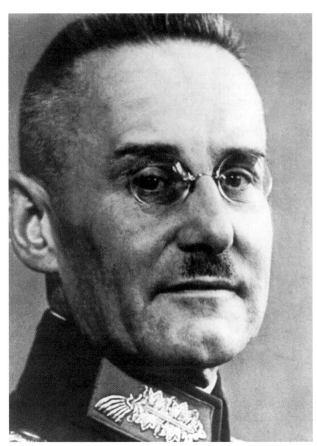

Generaloberst Franz Halder served as the Chief of the German General Staff from 1938, when he succeeded Ludwig Beck. He was relieved from his post by Hitler in September 1942. In July 1944 Halder was arrested by the Gestapo, suspected of involvement in the failed coup attempt against Hitler on 20 July 1944. Liberated by the US Army in April 1945, he worked for the US Army Historical Division, where he became Chief of the Historical Liaison Group. Halder passed away on 2 April 1972, at the age of 87. (Photo: Krigsarkivet Stockholm.)

nationalist movement, which was the breeding ground for the Nazi ideology. It was only logical that the Nazis inherited and developed the nationalists' ideas of Drang nach Osten ("yearning for the East") and Lebensraum. After all, the diabolic nature of Germany's Generalplan Ost was nothing but a consequence of this thinking. It led to the sinister Hungerplan. This was developed from Plan Oldenburg (also known as the "Green Folder") – drafted by Reichsmarschall Hermann Göring, the Luftwaffe commander and the Minister of Economics. Oldenburg was the plan for the economic exploitation of the conquered territory in the East. It included the total de-industrialisation of Eastern Europe: All stocks of raw materials and industrial enterprises between River Vistula and the Ural Mountains were to be either transported to Germany or destroyed, and the entire area would be turned into an agricultural appendage of Germany. By and by, Hitler also began to lean towards the pure economical aim with Operation Barbarossa.

Moreover, Göring demanded the seizure of the food supplies in the conquered Soviet territories. This led to the so-called Hungerplan, which was presented to leading Wehrmacht commanders on 2 May 1941: "The war against Russia can only be carried out if the whole Wehrmacht is

* "Barbarossa" was a pun on Emperor Frederick Barbarossa ("Red Beard"), a German crusader in the Middle Ages – a referral to Hitler's idea that the invasion would be a crusade against the "Red Menace" in the east. What Hitler however seemed to have forgotten was the fact that Barbarossa himself died during his crusade.

fed from Russia. The consequence of this will be that tens of millions of people will die from starvation." [4]

Although the genocidal nature of the Nazi planning for Eastern Europe derived from late nineteenth century German nationalism and colonialist ideas, it was further sharpened by a strong anti- Communism – or, in the Nazi vocabulary, the fear for the "Judeo-Bolshevik ideology." The Nazi Party was founded on a glowing hatred of Communism. As recent research has shown, it was not anti-semitic from the onset. This however changed with the influx of Russian White emigrés after the October Revolution in 1917. One of the most important among these was the Baltic-German Russian citizen Alfred Rosenberg. Anti-semitism had been one of the Tsarist Empire's most used weapons to divert dissent. In the early twentieth century, Russia was the scene of the most violent pogroms. This was not least due to a forgery by the Tsar's secret police called *The Protocols of the Elders of Zion*, purporting to describe a Jewish plan for assuming global power through means such as deliberate starvation.

The Russian White emigrés brought along *The Protocols of the Elders of Zion* to Germany and printed a German translation (the first foreign translation). In early 1919, Alfred Rosenberg became one of the first members of the Nazi Party (even before Hitler himself), and with the use of *The Protocols of the Elders of Zion* successfully managed to create a bridge between the Party's staunch anti-Communism and anti-Semitism simply by convincing the members that Communism was merely a tool invented by the Jews for world domination.

ORDNUNGSPOLIZEI UND SICHERHEITSPOLIZEI IM KRIEGSEINSATZ

The combination of racism and anti-Communism turned the German war in the East into a ruthless war of extermination. Not only were the Eastern territories to be plundered and subject to ethnic cleansing – Communism was to be totally eradicated, meaning the physical liquidation of Communists.

During a meeting on 30 March 1941with the commanders of the Wehrmacht's three armed services and the key Army commanders for the operation, Hitler informed them that the war against the Soviet Union was a war of "ideologies and racial differences," and thus could not be conducted "in a knightly fashion." He informed the senior military commanders of the intended "extermination of Bolshevik Commissars and of the Communist intelligentsia" without mercy because they were the "bearers of ideologies directly opposed to National Socialism." [5] Thus, the foundation for genocidal warfare was laid. He sought to justify this by claiming that the Soviet Union had not signed the Hague Conventions of 1899 and 1907, which was not true.

The official order was issued by the German High Command, Oberkommando der Wehrmacht under Generalfeldmarschall Wilhelm Keitel, on 6 June 1941. The instructions in this order began with the following line: "In this battle mercy or considerations of international law is false." It called for the execution of all captured Soviet political commissars and was dispatched to all senior commanders of the Wehrmacht, who were ordered to inform their subordinates verbally.[6]

This murderous order was supplemented by the employment of the so-called Einsatzgruppen, which would follow in the footsteps of the advancing armies. These were governmental paramilitary death squads assigned with the task of carrying out the most brutal of the Nazi state's goals. The Einsatzgruppen had been used in Poland in 1939, where they executed 65,000 people – intellectuals, Jews, Romani people, and the mentally ill.

Five Einsatzgruppen would take part in Operation Barbarossa: Einsatzgruppen A, B, and C attached to Army Groups North, Centre, and South respectively, Einsatzgruppe D specifically assigned to the 11th Army, and, from July 1941, Einsatzgruppe zu besonderen Verwendung (for Special Purposes) in eastern Poland. SS-Obergruppenführer Reinhard Heydrich, commander of the German Security Service, held the central command of the Einsatzgruppen. The task he assigned them with was to capture Soviet and Communist Party offices and documents, to execute Soviet officials, and to encourage pogroms against Jews. In this they would cooperate on a regular basis with the ordinary Police Force battalions that were dispatched to the occupied areas.

Operationally, each Einsatzgruppe, consisting of between 500 and 990 men, was subordinated to Army command, and the army was tasked to provide the Einsatzgruppen with logistical support.

This German propaganda poster for the "Day of the Police" on 16–17 February 1941 illustrates the close bonds between the German order Police and the Nazi Sicherheitsdienst (SD). The Order Police and the SD's Einsatzgruppen followed behind the advancing Army during Operation Barbarossa and carried out tremendous terrible atrocities against the civilian population.

3: THE WEHRMACHT VERSUS THE RED ARMY.

"All we have to do is to kick in the door and the whole
rotten structure will come crashing down!"

– Adolf Hitler, June 1941.

Under the command of Marshal Mikhail Tukhachevskiy, the Red Army reached a top-of-the-world level in the early thirties. Undoubtedly, Tukhachevskiy was one of the most brilliant military thinkers of the twentieth century. In a couple of years, he turned the Red Army into the most modern armed forces in the world. At a time when most military strategists were thinking along the lines of First World War, Tukhachevskiy and his close associate Vladimir Triandafillov (who was killed in an accident in 1931) developed the revolutionary "deep operation" (*Glubokaya Operatsiya*) defensive doctrine. This was a combination of the revolutionary ideas of British armored warfare theorist J. F. C. Fuller – who also had a major impact on German armored warfare theorists such as Heinz Guderian – and Leon Trotsky's development of protracted warfare. According to the Deep Operation doctrine, an attacking enemy's armor was to be led into "kill zones" consisted of fortifications and defense belts, where the enemy would be annihilated.* Simultaneously, own mobile formations would fall onto the deep rear of the enemy and destroy his ability to rebuild his defenses.

Unquestionably, *Glubokaya Operatsiya* was the most advanced military doctrine by the time it was launched, and would remain so for a considerable time. It was adopted in the Red Army's Field Regulations of 1929, was further developed in the 1935 Instructions on Deep Operations, and formed the basis for the Field Service Regulations of 1936. At the core of the Deep Operations doctrine lay the armored forces. In 1932 the Red Army's first mechanized corps (tank corps) were formed, several years before Germany set up its first armored divisions. Owing to Tukhachevskiy, the Soviet Union had the largest mechanized forces in the world in 1937.

With the Deep Operation, calling for a multi-echeloned offensive, conducted in waves, Tukhachevskiy also came to revolutionize tank design in a way that would be not only of great benefit to the Soviet Union in the war, but also would lay the foundation for modern tanks for nearly sixty years. Apart from the light tanks for infantry support that were at on hand in most modern armies, he saw the need

for heavy tanks to carry out the initial breakthrough and medium tanks for the exploitation of the penetration. Also in the position of Director of Armaments, Tukhachevskiy, and his close associate, Innokentiy Khalepskiy, chief of the Directorate of Mechanization and Motorization of the Red Army, drafted the requirement for a heavy breakthrough tank.

In 1927, Professor V. I. Zaslavskiy at the Leningrad Obukhov Factory had designed the first indigenous Soviet tank, the T-18 (MS-1). Because of the need to coordinate the tank operations, Zaslavskiy had a radio was installed in the tank in place of signal flags, which were standard in all other tanks across the world by that time. (As late as the Summer of 1943, not all U.S. tanks had two-way radios.) Three years later, the design bureau at the factory (now renamed the Bolshevik Factory**) received an order for a heavy tank. The result was the 45-ton T-35, which in 1933 was accepted for production. (Engineering was shifted to the Kharkov Locomotive Factory.) Through the multi-turret T-35, the Red Army had the only modern heavy tank in service in the mid-1930s. The only other heavy tank in service during the inter-war years, the vintage French Char C2*** from 1917 – of which only ten were brought into service – was outgunned and outrun by the T-35. The latter also led to the design of the heavy KV, which laid the foundation for all consecutive heavy tanks.

Tukhachevskiy also developed methods for close cooperation between ground and air forces, and thus the concept for the *Shturmovik* (assault) aviation was formed. This was included in the Field Service Regulations of 1936. Put into practice at Guadalajara in March 1937 during the Spanish Civil War, it resulted in a major Republican victory. Moreover, Tukhachevskiy was the driving force behind the Red Army's development of the world's first airborne troops: the display of 1,200 airdropped paratroopers during the Kiev maneuvers in 1935 both shocked and impressed the international observers, as did the use of tank formations and heavy bombers. By that time, the Soviet Union also had the largest and most modern bomber force in the world. Meanwhile, Soviet aviation

---

*   These fortified areas were later, quite misleading misleadingly, called the "Stalin Line" by the Germans.
**   After the murder of Leningrad's Party leader, Sergey Kirov, in 1934 again renamed, into the Kirov Works.
*** Occasionally, the French Char B1 from 1935 has been referred to as a heavy tank, but its weight (28 tonnes) hardly qualifies it
        as a heavy tank.

industry created some of the best fighter planes in the world – the I-15 and the I-16. A few years later, the quality of the Red Army had fallen far below Western standards, despite several war experiences between 1936 and 1939 that could have improved the tactics and qualities further. The dominant reason for this downfall was the Stalinist purging measures in the late thirties.

It began with the arrest of Marshal Tukhachevskiy and his closest associates in May 1937. Having undergone severe torture, Tukhachevskiy signed a confession and was executed the following month. The paper on which he signed his confession carries blood stains… Tukhachevskiy was accused of being part of a "Trotskyist Anti-Soviet Military Organization." Indeed, Tukhachevskiy had had close bonds with the first commander of the Red Army, Leon Trotsky (who was exiled from the Soviet Union in 1929).

The 1935 Soviet military display shocked the international observers. Modern armored maneuvers were displayed, as well as a mass airborne landing. In less than two hours, all-metal four-engine Tupolev TB-3 bombers such as the one in the photo delivered 1,975 soldiers, six trucks, ten artillery pieces, and one 3.2-ton T-37 tankette from the air. The TB-3 could carry a bomb load of 2,000 kg, twice the payload of the British standard bomber of the time, Handley Page Heyford, and had an operational range of 2,000 km. (Photo: Soviet Embassy, 1976.)

Trotsky had assigned Tukhachevskiy with the command of the 5th Army in 1920, with which he ousted Aleksandr Kolchak from Siberia. He also helped defeat General Anton Denikin in the Crimea in 1920.

The "Trotskyist" Tukhachevskiy was accused of cooperation with Nazi Germany – just as the distorted Soviet propaganda claimed that Trotsky was an agent of Germany (later, after the Hitler-Stalin Pact had been signed, to be changed into an agent of "British imperialism"). It has been proven that Stalin knew that this was a false accusation. In fact, he was so intimately involved that he sent a double agent to SS-Obergruppenführer Reinhard Heydrich, commander of the German Security Service, and convinced him to forge documents portraying Tukhachevskiy as a German spy.[1] Stalin used these documents, which lent greater credibility to the attack against Tukhachevskiy, to get rid of the commander of the Red Army. The actual reason why

Stalin attacked Tukhachevskiy is not known, but it would not be far-fetched to assume that he feared a commander of the Red Army who so clearly indulged independent revolutionary thinking – quite along the lines of Trotsky – in the Red Army: "Tukhachevsky saw the army as the cutting edge of the revolution, a legitimate and effective means of spreading the new gospel and its shield against all its enemies. [...] as Tukhachevskiy continually observed, the army is part of the Soviet system and should reflect its goals and its spirit."[2]

Everything and everyone who showed that tendency was ruthlessly rooted out by Stalin – hence the massive purges directed against the Bolshevik Party. With the killing of the popular commander of the Red Army, followed the logical need to strike against his subordinates, i.e. the entire Red Army. Of five Red Army Marshals, three were killed: Apart from Tukhachevskiy, the Soviet Far East Front commander Vasily Blyukher – who died, probably as a result of torture, on the same day as he signed the confession that was presented to him – and the Chief of the General Staff of the Red Army, Aleksandr Yegorov, who was executed. Only the two Stalin cronies Kliment Voroshilov and Semyon Budyonnyy survived. Thus, Stalin had spared two senior commanders who hated each other – Budyonnyy scorned Voroshilov for what he apprehended as his "military dilettantism" and they had both threatened each other with revolvers on several occasions – and thus were easy to control; that neither of them was particularly talented as a military commander obviously did not concern the dictator. Meekness towards Stalin rather than military competence became the rule among the senior commanders.

Grigoriy Kulik – Chief of the Main Artillery Directorate, Vice Commissar for the Defense, appointed a Hero of The Soviet Union and promoted to Marshal in 1940 – is a telling example. Kulik had gained Stalin's personal friendship by attacking Tukhachevskiy, claiming that the "deep operation" actually displayed "an ideological leaning" towards the "degenerate fascist ideology"! Attempting to distance himself from Tukhachevskiy as much as possible, Kulik even expressed an opposition to tanks in general. When the KV and T-34 tanks entered production, Kulik also meddled in a most unfortunate way. Owing to political preferences towards Leningrad, Kulik threatened the producers of the both more effective and cheaper F-34 anti-tank cannon in Gorkiy to the degree that they dared not produce the gun, as a result of which the new tanks were equipped with the inferior L-11 gun, which was produced at the Leningrad Kirov Plant. He also branded submachine guns as a "bourgeois fascist affectation," and prohibited their use in his units!

Kulik became famous for his personal motto, "Jail or Medal," which described his habit of either heaping awards on his subordinates or having them arrested – often on trumped-up charges.

All deputy defense commissars, all commanders of military districts, the commanders and chiefs of staffs of both the Air Force and the Navy, fourteen of sixteen army commanders, 60 of 67 corps commanders, 136 of 199 division commanders, 221 of 397 brigade commanders and

Grigoriy Kulik was one of the most faithful Stalinist cronies. On 8 May 1940, he was named a Marshal of the Soviet Union, along with Semyon Timoshenko and Boris Shaposhnikov. (Photo: Soviet Embassy, 1976.)

thousands of regimental commanders were imprisoned or executed.

The consequence was devastating in several aspects: Highly trained and skilled commanders were replaced by less skilled men, and a fear of undertaking any own initiatives spread among the survivors. Although thirty percent of the officers purged were later returned to service, the widespread slander against the officers undermined the soldiers' trust in their commanding officers and led to what can be described as a near collapse in discipline in the Red Army. Moreover, as Associate Professor of Strategic Studies at Johns Hopkins University, Mary R. Habeck, points out, most of the surviving officers were so intimidated by the purges that they "would spend the purge years trying to stay out of official notice, hide from responsibility for any decisions, and generally do nothing controversial or radical."[3]

In order to alleviate the sudden shortage in officers, the course of study at the officer schools was shortened by one-third, leading to the creation of a whole generation of inadequately trained military commanders at all levels. Still, by 1941, 75 percent of all officers in the Red Army had been in their position for less than one year.[4]

When Hitler invaded Poland on 1 September 1939, Stalin hurriedly instituted a universal military draft – which had never been done before in the Soviet Union. This led to an explosive expansion of the Red Army from 1.5 million men in 1939 to 5.7 million in June 1941. It goes without saying that the vast number of these received a totally insufficient military training. On top of that, the military training in Stalin's Soviet Union consisted mainly of "political education," and comparatively little true military training.

Moreover, the modern doctrine introduced by Tukhachevskiy was buried in the course of the purges. His theoretical writings were even withdrawn and destroyed. In 1939, the mechanized (tank) corps that had been created by Tukhachevskiy were ordered to be abolished. Instead, the tanks were dispersed among infantry units, just like during the First World War. True to Stalin's paranoid mind, he became convinced that Tukhachevskiy utilized the tank corps to create a "state within the state" in order to "wrest control of the military from the Communist Party."[5] Thus, the purges of the Red Army came to specifically target the mechanized units, and even the tank designers. Among the latter were Professor Zaslavskiy, the first Soviet tank designer, Konstantin Chelpan, the chief designer of the famous T-34 tank diesel engine V-2,* and the heads of the design bureaux of the Kharkov locomotive Works (where the T-34 tank was designed) and of the SKB-2 at the Kirov Works – they were all executed. Innokentiy Khalepskiy, the Directorate of Mechanization and Motorization of the Red Army (ABTU), was arrested in 1937 and died in prison. His replacement, Ivan Gryaznov, was executed in July 1938. By that time, nearly half the people in the ABTU had been purged. Only through "extraordinary" measures could 63 replacements be found.[6] One of those was Gryaznov's successor as the head of the ABTU, Dmitriy Pavlov, a Stalin crony who argued that only two main tank types were needed – a main "cavalry" (light) tank, a heavy "artillery tank" – plus an amphibious tank. He also lent Stalin support in insisting that tanks be shifted to infantry support roles.

A Marxist would say that the material circumstances forced the Stalinist leadership to back down and progressively return to the legacy of Tukhachevskiy, but often not before it was too late. The vast resources invested in the design of modern tanks made the leadership refrain from interfering against this – to the great benefit of the country as war broke out.

---

* The V-2 diesel engine was a technical marvel of its time. It was the first high-power diesel tank engine in the world, in many ways superior to carburetor ones: it was more economic, better stood overloads, and the diesel fuel lowered the risk of a fire. Another great advantage was its low specific weight of just 2,05 kg/hp. In various modifications, it became the standard Soviet tank engine during World War II. Its chief designer Chelpan, a veteran from the Civil War, where he had served under Trotsky, was arrested in December 1937, six months after the execution of Tukhachevskiy. He was formally accused of conspiracy and sabotage at the Kharkov locomotive Works. After a month of torture in the NKVD's Kharkov prison, he signed a confession of being a spy, whereafter he was sentenced to death and executed in the prison on 10 March 1938. The death of this brilliant engineer was covered up for many years, and only after several years was his wife told that he had died "from heart failure" in 1942. The actual cause of his death was revealed as late as 1988, in President Gorbachev's Glasnost and Perestroyka era. After Stalin's death in the 1950s, an examination of the case by the Military Collegium of the Supreme Court of the USSR found the accusations against Chelpan to be completely unsubstantiated and probably only trumped up.

The T-26 tankette, a Soviet version of the British-designed Vickers 6-ton light infantry tank from 1928, was the standard Soviet tank in 1941. (Photo: Soviet Embassy, 1976.)

Shocked by the amazing German victory achieved through the Blitzkrieg against France in June 1940, in panic the Soviet leadership ordered the re-establishment of the mechanized (tank) corps. Now the immediate creation of eight mechanized corps – each with an assigned strength of 36,000 men and slightly above 1,000 tanks was suddenly demanded. In February 1941, an order was submitted to form another twenty-one. The result was an organizational chaos. By the time the Germans attacked, only nine mechanized corps had been formed, and five of those were still not fully combat ready. Additionally, later on in the war, the Soviet leadership sought to re-implement Tukhachevskiy's Deep Operations doctrine – with the nearly complete annihilation of German Heeresgruppe Mitte in the summer of 1944 as a consequence.

In stark contrast to the Red Army of 1941, the German Armed Forces – the Wehrmacht with the Heer (Army), the Luftwaffe (Air Force) and Kriegsmarine (Navy) – stood at the height of its power in June 1941. Totally recreated in the thirties, it was rid of all conservatism that hampered the armies of the Allies, and based on the best traditions of the Prussian army and the experiences of the First World War, the Spanish Civil War and the Blitzkrieg campaigns of between 1939 and the spring of 1941 it had adopted the best military doctrine in the world. It had soldiers and commanders with greater battle experience than any other armed forces in Europe, and it had some of the best trained soldiers and airmen in the world.

While the Soviet commanders and soldiers feared individual initiative because that could get them arrested and possibly even executed, the German armed forces were based on the principle of *Auftragstaktik* (Mission Command), which encouraged own initiative in combat. This placed the German units at an immediate advantage to their Soviet counterparts, because it gave them the ability

to react with rapidity and flexibility in accordance with shifting situations on the battlefield.

Adolf Hitler was well aware of this, and he was further reinforced by his distorted racial view on the Russians as "subhumans." This led him to make an infamous statement to one of his field marshals, von Rundstedt: "All we have to do is to kick in the door and the whole rotten structure will come crashing down!" He would later regret these words…

In spite of the rapid build up of the numerical strength of the Red Army, the Germans and their allies enjoyed a numerical superiority in manpower on 22 June 1941. The largest invasion force in military history had been assembled against the Soviet Union. Between the Baltic Sea and the Black Sea the four Soviet western military districts had 2.3 million men, opposed to nearly 4.5 million Axis troops. The Wehrmacht had amassed 3.35 million troops.[7] To this the Romanian army contributed 600,000, and in the north, Finland had already mobilized its army and could muster 530,000 men.

As far as the technical equipment is concerned, Operation Barbarossa actually negates the image of the German Armed forces as "horse-carried" and not motorized. More than 600,000 transport motor vehicles were committed in support of Operation Barbarossa, plus 625,000 horses.[8]

The powerful KV-1 heavy tank was completely without equal among any other nation's tanks during the first years of World War II. (Photo: Soviet Embassy, 1976.)

39

Transport was a sadly neglected area in the Red Army, which had a severe shortage of trucks.

Quite interestingly, however, regarding the relation of strength between men and machine, the Red Army was – at least superficially – more modern than the Wehrmacht. The 2.3 million Soviet troops in the west were supported by 46,630 artillery pieces and mortars over 50mm* and 12,800 tanks, whereas the 3.35 million men of the German *Ostheer* (armed forces in the East) had 7,184 artillery pieces and 3,648 tanks and assault guns.[9] That gives an average of 49 Soviet and 466 German soldiers per artillery piece, and 180 Soviet and 917 German soldiers per tank. The total German force of tanks on 1 June 1941 was 5,264, of which 4,200 were operational.[10] That should be compared with the total strength of 23,058 tanks and 110,530 artillery pieces in the Soviet Union.

However, the relations were not as uneven as they might seem to be. Among the German armor employed against the Eastern Front, 2,406 were medium tanks – to which can also be added 272 assault guns (Sturmgeschütz III). Among the Soviet tanks, 21,122 were light tanks, inferior to the German medium tanks and assault guns, and only 1,373 medium and 563 heavy tanks.

Largely due to Stalin's purges of Soviet tank designers, the most common Soviet tank on the eve of the German attack was the T-26, a Soviet version of the British-designed Vickers 6-ton light infantry tank from 1928. More than 10,000 of this antiquated vehicle – barely qualified to be called a tank by 1941 standards – filled the ranks of the Red Army's brand new tank divisions in June 1941. Most of the T-26s at hand also were of the older models with just a 15mm vertical frontal armor and a 37mm gun. These could be easily destroyed not only by the 37mm Pak anti-tank guns with which the German infantry was abundantly equipped, but even with lighter weapons such as 20mm automatic guns.

7,500 of the Soviet tanks were of the better BT types. The BT – *Bystrokhodny Tank* (fast tank) – was based on the design of American tank designer Christie. It also was a light tank, but the world's fastest of its kind: Its maximum speed was between 72 and 100 km/h (depending on the models) on paved road (as compared with 31 km/h of the T-26). Another major feature of the BT tanks was that they had a sloped front armor. Thus, its 13mm front armor actually offered a better protection than that of the T-26. In June 1941 there were 580 BT-2s, equipped with the small 37mm gun, 1,688 BT-5s (with a larger turret and the same 45mm gun as the T-26 had), and 5,263 BT-7s. The latter, also armed with a 45mm gun, had a redesigned hull front and a sloped turret.

Still, the BT was quite vulnerable to any German anti-tank gun and definitely inferior to the German medium tanks. The most numerous among these was the 22-ton Panzerkampfwagen III (Panzer III). There were 965 of these in readiness for Operation Barbarossa. Equipped with a 50mm gun and with a 30 mm frontal armor sloped to 70–80°, it could penetrate the frontal armor of the Soviet light tanks at a range of more than 1,500 meters, a distance where the German tank was invulnerable by great margin to any of the Soviet light tanks.

Another 772 of the German medium tanks were captured Czech Panzer 38(t)*, which was older and approaching obsolescence. Originally, this tank was relatively weakly armored, and also had a mostly not sloped and riveted armor (in contrast to the majority of the German tanks, which had welded armor). However, by bolting on a 25mm shield, the front armor was increased to 50mm. The 37mm gun of the Panzer 38(t) was also capable of penetrating the front armor of any of the Soviet light tanks, while it was invulnerable to fire from even the 45mm guns at any distance below a couple of hundred meters. In order to facilitate supplies, all Panzer 38(t) were assigned to Panzergruppe 3 of Heeresgruppe Mitte in June 1941. Another tank of Czech origin, the light tank 35(t) – also with a 37mm gun but only 25mm front armor – was also assigned to Panzergruppe 3; in fact all 137 vehicles formed the tank strength of the 6. Panzer-Division.

The most modern German Panzer was the Panzer IV. A special feature of some Panzer IIIs and IVs was that they were converted into so-called *Tauchpanzer* ("diving tanks") or *U-Panzer*, submersible tanks that could travel on the bottom of body of water at the depths of 6 to 15 meters. A total of 168 Panzer IIIs and 42 Panzer IVs were modified into this type and assigned to the 3. and 18. Panzer divi-

This 1939 propaganda poster by Nikolay Dolgorukov gave a totally misleading image of the Red Army and the dictator Joseph Stalin. In actual fact, Stalin's purges had brought the Red Army to its knees. (Photo: Soviet Embassy, 1976.)

* (t) stands for tschechisch, Czech.

The Germans had many advantages over the Red Army. Among the most important was the combat experience of the German soldiers, who had been waging a war for nearly two years when Operation Barbarossa was launched. The photo shows a column of German tanks in Belgium in May 1940: A Panzer II driving behind a Panzer I. (Photo: Wittke-Scherl via Jessen.)

sions of Panzergruppe 2. Originally designed as an infantry support tank, the Panzer IVs of 1941 were armed with a short-barrelled 75mm KwK 37 L/24 gun. It was intended to destroy fortifications such as pillboxes, but even with armor piercing shells it could only penetrate 39 mm of armor at a distance of 500 meters. Its frontal armor, 30 mm sloped at 80°, was equal to that of the Panzer III.

On the eve of Operation Barbarossa, the Germans believed that they had the best tanks in the world. They were in for a nasty surprise. Already on the first day of the war, they had to rethink as they encountered the new Soviet KV and T-34 tanks. Named after defense minister Kliment Voroshilov, one of Stalin's favorites, the KV was a real monster, a heavy tank without any competition. The KV was the second Soviet heavy tank which followed after the T-35 had been designed in 1932 in response to the Deep Operations doctrine. Entering service in 1939, this 45-ton vehicle had an unsurpassed 90mm front armor. Although the 1941 versions of the KV-1 were mainly armed with the short-barrelled 76.2mm L/11 gun; this sufficed to penetrate the front armor of any German tank at a distance of 1,000 meters, while it was invulnerable to anything but the German 88mm Flak guns at any distance but point blank. In June 1941 the Red Army had 471 KV tanks. One-third of these were of the huge 52-ton KV-2 version, with a monstrous 12-ton turret sporting a 152mm howitzer.

However, even the KV was surpassed by the T-34 medium tank. Entering service in 1940, nearly all of its features were superior to the German tanks: It had a 45 mm welded front armor, sloped at 60° (corresponding to 90 mm vertical armor), and when armed with a 76.2mm F-34 anti-tank gun it was capable of knocking out any German tank frontally at a distance of 2,000 meters. Moreover, it had a diesel engine which extended its range and was less prone to catching fire when hit. It also was equipped with wide tracks that made it suitable for operations in soft terrain. The impression of the Germans in 1941 was that this was the finest tank in the world – an impression shared by the Soviet tank crews. In June 1941 the Red Army was able to field 821 T-34s. During the second half of 1941, another 1,886 T-34s were produced.

Nevertheless, the superiority of the T-34 should not be exaggerated. It had some serious flaws. First of all, owing to Marshal Kulik's political interference, by the time of the German attack nearly all T-34s were equipped with the short-barrelled 76.2mm L/11 gun instead of the superior F-34. Only after the German attack did the T-34s begin to be re-equipped with F-34s. The gearbox was quite heavy to handle and had poor reliability. Many T-34s also suffered from production flaws such as deficiencies with plate joins and welds.

Moreover, the T-34 was less agile than the German tanks in combat, for three main reasons. First of all, the T-34 had no vision cupola, which most German tanks were equipped with, restricting the vision to an area straight ahead, while a German tank commander had a 360° vision. Another deficiency which related to all Soviet tanks except the KV (with its crew of five) was that

One of the Wehrmacht's trump cards was the powerful and modern Luftwaffe. The photo shows one of the most modern aircraft of 1941, German bomber Junkers Ju 88. This aircraft could be used in a multitude of roles – as a level bomber, a dive-bomber, a reconnaissance plane and a night fighter. It had a top speed of 514 km/h, higher than many Soviet fighters of 1941. It superseded the TB-3 heavy bomber in both bomb load, 3,000 kg, and flight range, 2,430 km. (Photo: Klaus Häberlen.)

a Soviet tank crew consisted only of three men: driver, commander/gunner, and loader. A German tank crew, on the other hand, consisted of four men: apart from driver, gunner and loader it had a separate commander who was relieved from the task of aiming and firing the gun in order to observe the battlefield. Thirdly, while cooperation between individual German tanks was facilitated by the radio transmitters and receivers that each tank was equipped with, only Soviet command tanks had such a device.

The situation was quite similar regarding the equipment of the aviation forces. The Luftwaffe had been founded six years earlier on a basis of new ideas by a new generation of air force officers, free from the bonds of tradition which held many other air forces back. Its large force of dive-bombers, its modern fighter tactics, and its emphasis on tactical cooperation with the armored units on the ground placed Reichsmarschall Hermann Göring's Luftwaffe in a singular position of quality. To that should be added the combat experience which the men of the Luftwaffe had gathered from the Spanish Civil War and the campaigns from September 1939 through June 1941.

In 1941, no air force had a more modern equipment than the Luftwaffe. Its latest bomber type, the Ju 88, had a top speed of 500 km/h and thus was capable of out-running the main Soviet fighter aircraft in 1941, the Polikarpov I-16. At 3,000 meters' flight altitude – about where most air combats took place on the Eastern Front – the I-16 could

reach a top speed of between 425 km/h (Mark 17) and 490 km/h (Mark 24). The other Polikarpov fighters, the I-15bis and I-153 single-engine biplanes, was hopelessly outdated in 1941.

Just before Operation Barbarossa, the Soviet Air Force, the VVS, commenced a large-scale modernization of its fighter planes. Large numbers of new MiG-3 fighters arrived at the forward airfields in the West, and two other types, the LaGG-3 and Yak-1 were also beginning to arrive. But even among these three new inline monoplane fighters, only the Yak-1 could compete on equal terms with the Bf 109 F, while the MiG-3 and the LaGG-3 were both slower and less maneuvrable. The latest German fighter models, the Bf 109 F-2 and F-4, were superior to any Soviet fighter. At 3,000 meters, the Bf 109 F-2 could reach a speed of 531 km/h, while the F-4 reached 558 km/h.

Regarding bombers, the standard Soviet Army Air Force bomber, the Tupolev SB was a bit better than the also twin-engined German Dornier Do 17. Both were of the fast bomber (Russian: Skorostny Bombardirovshchik, SB) concept, but the most recent model of the Soviet aircraft, the SB-RK, was faster (480 km/h) and carried a heavier bomb load (1,500 kg against the German 1,000 kg). But the Junkers Ju 88 A-4, which was gradually replacing the older Do 17, was both faster than the SB and could carry a bomb load twice as large (3,000 kg). The main aircraft of the Soviet Long-Range Aviation (the DBA) was the twin-engine Ilyushin DB-3 with a maximum speed of

435 km/h and a bomb load of 2,500 kg. The main German bomber, twin-engine Heinkel He 111, was comparable in speed but had a better armament and a bomb load of 3,600 kg.

Moreover, the Germans had 376 single-engine Junkers Ju 87 dive-bombers ready to support the advance of its ground troops. The Soviet Air Force, the VVS, had nothing similar to this aircraft, which was able to bomb with utmost precision.

Another field where the Germans enjoyed a substantial superiority in the air was regarding reconnaissance. Among 3,400 aircraft employed against the Soviet Union, over 500 were reconnaissance planes. Aerial reconnaissance was largely neglected by the Soviets, who had to pay dearly for this in the war.

But the Soviets had advantages in some technical fields. The Polikarpov fighters (the biplanes I-15bis and I-153 and the monoplane I-16) could easily out-turn any German aircraft. Moreover, the Soviet 7.62mm ShKAS machine gun had a higher rate of fire than any other aircraft gun – 1,800 rounds per minute or, in the case of guns synchronized to the aircraft's propeller, 1,650 rounds per minute, at a muzzle velocity of 825 meters per second (850 for synchronized guns) – and in 1941 the Soviets were years before anyone else in arming combat aircraft with rocket projectiles, the RS-82 and RS-132.

The most important among the new Soviet aircraft which went into action in 1941 probably was the Il-2 Shturmovik assault plane. In exchange for a relatively small payload – 400 kilograms of bombs and eight rockets – it was fitted with a thick armor hull, unique among combat aircraft, which enabled the Il-2 to stay in the air in the target area, and sustain fire while locating its targets and performing several strikes. Other assault aircraft were hampered through the necessity to break off after only one quick strike – due to ground fire – which often also reduced the precision of the attack.

Also worth mentioning is the brand new twin-engine Soviet Petlyakov Pe-2 bomber, which was able to reach a speed of 540 km/h – thus being faster than any other bomber at the time. However, this was offset by the fact that it could only deliver a payload of 600 kg of bombs.

Figures on the German aircraft ready for Operation Barbarossa differ between various sources. However, the following figures are quite close to the actual figures: All in all, over 3,400 German aircraft stood ready for Operation Barbarossa on 21 June 1941. These included 993 fighters, 929 bombers, 376 dive-bombers, 138 ground-attack aircraft (Henschel 123 and Messerschmitt Bf 110), 287 long-range reconnaissance aircraft, 252 tactical reconnaissance aircraft, 292 transport planes and 168 of miscellaneous types. To this force should be added 550 Finnish and 621 Romanian aircraft, hence a total of over 4,500.

The Soviet aviation was not only generally inferior in terms of technical equipment – among its single-engine fighters, only those flown by unit commanders had radio transmitters, while this was standard in all German aircraft; it also was hampered by inadequately trained airmen (a result of the rapid expansion of the aviation) and inferior air combat tactics. The German fighter pilots used the Rotte tactic, developed in the Spanish Civil War, where they flew in pairs – the leader acting as the "sword" and the wingman as the "shield." The Soviet fighter pilots, however, were instructed to operate in the cumbersome three-plane V-formation, which in fighter combat always broke up, forcing each pilot to fight individually. Moreover, in 1941 most airmen of the Luftwaffe were quite experienced in combat. Some of the best German fighter pilots had amassed 40, 50 or more aerial victories. Hastily trained young Soviet airmen stood very little chance against these veterans.

In addition to that, the Luftwaffe had a homogenous structure. Indeed, the tactical reconnaissance aircraft (Heeresaufklärung) were subordinated to the Army, but

The MiG-3 was the first among the new generation of modern Soviet aircraft to reach the combat units in large numbers. On the eve of the German attack, there were 917 MiG-3s along the Soviet western borders. It was designed as a high-altitude fighter, with its top speed of at the time a nearly unsurpassed 640 km/h at 7,800 meters altitude. However, most air fighting on the Eastern Front took place at lower altitudes, where the MiG-3 was slightly slower but above all less maneuverable than the German Messerschmitt Bf 109 F. At 3,000 meters, the Bf 109 F-2 could reach a speed of 531 km/h, while the F-4 reached 558 km/h. Armament consisted of one 12.7 mm and two 7.62 mm machine guns. (Photo: Yuriy Rybin.)

apart from that and a few Navy aircraft, the Luftwaffe was an independent branch of Arms. The commander, Reichsmarschall Hermann Göring and his Headquarters (Oberkommando der Luftwaffe, OKL) could shift units between the various Luftflotten and Fliegerkorps in accordance with the shifting of the combat between various fronts.

The Soviet air force (VVS), however, was split between a myriad of commands. First of all, it was divided between the Army Air Force (VVS RKKA) and the Naval Air Force (VVS VMF). But within the VVS RKKA, the air units were divided between Front aviation (subordinated to the various Fronts, the designation of the Military Districts after 22 June 1941) and Army aviation (subordinated to individual ground armies). Frequently, a ground army commander would jealously guard his own aviation, and would not come to the assistance of a neighbouring army, even if this was under severe pressure. Then there was the independent Long-range (bomber) aviation, the DBA, and the regional Home Defense aviation, the PVO. All of this resulted in a lack of coordination which deprived the Soviets of the possibility of making the most rational use of their air forces.

The numerical strength of the Soviet aviation has often been exaggerated. Soviet archival sources show that on 1 June 1941, the RKKA mustered 5,841 fighters, 1,508 Long-range bombers, 3,726 Front and Army bombers, and 1,285

ground-attack (assault) aircraft – in total 12,360 combat aircraft. On 22 June, 5,863 were available to the Military districts in the West and 1,332 belonged to the DBA. Another 1,447 were assigned to the fleets in the North, the Baltic Sea and the Black Sea. When the Germans struck, only 2,600 Soviet aircraft were of modern types – 1,900 MiG-3, LaGG-3 and Yak-1 fighters (of which 980 were based in the western frontier Military districts), 458 Pe-2 bombers and 249 Il-2 Shturmoviks.

Quite ironically, the process of rapid modernization of the Soviet Air Force's equipment was a major factor in the Luftwaffe's enormous success during the opening attack. The Germans struck precisely in the moment when a large number of modern aircraft had arrived at the airfields in the western USSR, but before there had been time to train all pilots on these aircraft. An evaluation by the Air Force of the Western Military District (VVS ZOVO) on the eve of 22 June 1941 showed that while its fighter units mustered 201 MiG-3s and 37 MiG-1s, only four pilots were fully trained to handle these modern fighters. Thus, when the Luftwaffe attacked, the Soviet airfields – all of which had been closely pinpointed by German reconnaissance aircraft – were crowded with aircraft, often wingtip to wingtip, both newly arrived modern types and the old types.

The first task of the Luftwaffe on 22 June was to wipe out the Soviet air force on the ground and in the air, and then to support the advance of the ground troops.

Cavalry still played an important role in the Red Army during World War II.

4: TOWARDS THE ABYSS.

"You can't believe everything you read in intelligence reports!"

– Joseph Stalin, 14 June 1941.

The pact with Hitler of August 1939 did not relieve Stalin of fears that the Soviet Union would be invaded by hostile forces – either by the Western powers or by the Germans (both assumptions proved correct; documents have shown that the British and French planned an attack against the Soviet Union in the winter of 1939–1940). Hence, a series of aggressive maneuvers were commenced with the objective of improving the Soviet defensive capacity. One of these was the disastrous Winter War against Finland in 1939–1940. On 15–17 June 1940 – immediately after the fall of Paris – Soviet troops marched into Estonia, Latvia and Lithuania. The three Baltic countries were occupied without resistance and became integrated republics of the Soviet Union. Ten days later, the Soviet Union occupied Bukovina and Bessarabia, territories that Romania had seized from Soviet Russia in 1918.

Romania, governed by King Carol, who had banned all political parties and introduced severe anti-Semitic laws, occupied a key role in Hitler's plans – both through its oil resources and its geographical position for the attack on the Soviet Union – and, consequently, the Führer played a skillful but cynical game with this country. In the fall of 1940, he supported Bulgaria – another anti-Semitic right-wing dictatorship – in its seizure of southern Dobruja from Romania. All of this caused great social rift inside Romania. In September 1940 the king was toppled in a coup that brought his son Michael to the throne. But the real power was seized by the new dictator Marshal Ion Antonescu. Feeling threatened by the Soviet Union in the east, Bulgaria in the south, and Hungary to the north, Antonescu was driven into Hitler's arms in the hope that the support of the Nazi dictator would guarantee his country's borders. The Romanians gratefully accepted a German military mission. In the fall of 1940 large German army and air forces moved into Romania. All this was part of Hitler's plans to prepare for the attack on the Soviet Union.

Hitler was busy secretly forming an anti-Soviet front. On 27 September 1940, the German-Italian Military Pact (the Berlin-Rome Axis of 1936) was extended in that Japan joined. Even if Hitler failed to convince Japan to join the war against the Soviet Union, Hungary, Bulgaria, Romania, Slovakia, and Croatia soon additionally joined the Axis.

But above all, Hitler was interested in obtaining access to countries that bordered the Soviet Union, and thus three countries came into question – Finland, Hungary, and as already mentioned Romania. Hungary became a hard nut to crack. For 20 years Admiral Miklos Horthy had ruled this country with an iron fist. His main goal was to retake the territories which Hungary lost after the First World War, mainly to Romania. Admiral Horthy was able to take advantage of Hitler's various conquests to grab new territories for Hungary. Among other things, he was involved in the dividing of Czechoslovakia in 1938 and 1939. In April 1941, Hungary participated in Germany's war against Yugoslavia, which led to the seizure of the Yugoslav Backa region. Hungary also was successful in pushing Romania to cede – or return, as the Hungarians saw it – northern Transylvania. But when Hitler eventually invaded the Soviet Union, Hungary initially maintained a neutral position. This created a major flaw in Operation Barbarossa, whereby the southern German army group had to be dispersed between southern Poland and Romania, with the neutral Hungary in between.

Nevertheless, Romania was already secured, and Finland, who lost large territories due to the Soviet war of aggression in 1939–1940 (the Winter War), joined Hitler quite easily. On 12 September 1940, the Finnish government agreed that German troops could be transited through its territory. It is even possible that Finland directly participated in the planning for Operation Barbarossa, but if so any documents pertaining to this has been lost. Quite notably, Hitler's Directive No. 21 for Operation Barbarossa, which was signed on 18 December 1940, included the following paragraphs: "On the flanks of our operations we can count on the active support of Romania and Finland in the war against Soviet Russia. [...] Finland *will* cover the advance of the Northern Group of German forces moving from Norway (detachments of Group XXI) and will operate in conjunction with them. Finland will also be responsible for eliminating Hangö." (Author's italics.) Moreover, in his speech to the leaders of the Wehrmacht on 30 March 1941, Hitler said that "the Finns will fight bravely."[1] U.S. military historian Earl F. Ziemke concludes that "the presence of the Finnish General [Paavo] Talvela in Berlin in mid-December [1940] raises the possibility of Finnish participation in the

Finland suffered grievously in the Winter War. The civilian population was subject to 2,075 bomber attacks against 516 localities, claiming the lives of around 900 people, with another nearly 2,000 injured. This photo shows the aftermath of one of the aerial bombings. The war also led to Finland losing 11 per cent of its territory, with 30 per cent of its economic assets. 422,000 Karelians lost their homes and were evacuated from the territories annexed by the Soviets. Hardly surprisingly, this led to widespread bitterness. (Photo: Kuva-SA.)

formulation of Directive No. 21."[2] Oberst Erich Buschenhagen of the general staff of the Wehrmachtskommando Norwegen played a key role in the contacts with the Finnish senior military commanders. At the Nuremberg Tribunal hearings in 1946, he stated that already in December 1940, the Chief of the German General Staff, Generaloberst Halder informed the his Finnish colleague, General Erik Heinrichs, of the Barbarossa plan of attack on the Soviet Union during an OKH conference at Zossen.[3]

One of the great tragedies of the Soviet-German war is that the Soviet intelligence service by that time already knew almost everything about the plan, and the Red Army could have been ready to meet the attacker and inflict serious losses on him. But this opportunity was missed, and this was largely due to a single man; Joseph Stalin.

The Soviet intelligence service during World War II was fortunate to be assisted by ideological convictions when it recruited spies. The body mainly responsible for collecting international intelligence was the GRU (Main Intelligence Directorate of the General Staff of the Armed Forces of the Soviet Union), but the NKGB (People's Commissariat for State Security) also took part in these activities. Both had successfully recruited several Germans, some of them even in key high positions.

One of these, Willy Lehmann (code-named Breitenback), managed to infiltrated the Gestapo and even took part in the Röhm Putsch murders in order not to reveal himself. In 1939 Lehmann was employed in the Reich Main Security Office with the task of preventing the Soviets from spying on the German armaments industry, which made him one of the most important Soviet agents. Another important agent was Richard Sorge, a reporter from the *Frankfurter Zeitung* in Tokyo, where he enjoyed the confidence of the German military attaché and later ambassador Eugen Ott.

The largest spy ring was the so-called Schulze-Boysen/Harnack group in Berlin – known by the name it was assigned by the German counter-espionage, "Rote Kapelle". One of its most important members was the great-nephew of Admiral Alfred von Tirpitz, Harro Schulze-Boysen (codenamed Starshina), an Oberleutnant in the intelligence department of the RLM, the German Air Force Ministry in Berlin. Another leader of this group was Arvid Harnack (codenamed Korsikanets).

The information on the upcoming German invasion that these agents supplied the Soviet leadership with displays the appallingly low security surrounding the planning and preparation for the German offensive. It should have been sufficient for Stalin to realize the threat and take measures to meet the onslaught. But nothing of the kind took place, owing to one decisive factor – Stalin and the Soviet leadership stubbornly dismissed all of these reports. This was also due to the large-scale purges of the Soviet intelligence service, as David E. Murphy describes: "Hundreds of members of the NKVD's Foreign Intelligence Service were arrested, tortured during interrogation to extract confessions based on trumped-up charges, and then either shot or sent to the GULAG." [4] Similar to what was taking place all across Soviet society and in the Red Army, professional intelligence officers disappeared and were replaced by less talented people who were chosen with the only criterion of being obedient and uncritical towards the senior leadership. One of these was Filipp Golikov, who in July 1940 was appointed to lead the GRU, albeit having no intelligence experience at all. Golikov resembled a caricature of the subservient subordinate who worked hard to modify any report in the way that Stalin wished, and he knew well that the Soviet dictator did not want to hear anything about an impending German invasion. Hence Golikov routinely began to dismiss intelligence reports on the prepareations for Operation Barbarossa as "disinformation," which further reinforced Stalin's tendency to disregard any such information.

Already on 18 November 1940, i.e. while Generalmajor Friedrich Paulus was still working over the Marcks and Lossberg studies to come up with a final plan, Richard Sorge had obtained and dispatched information that Hitler had ordered preparations to be made for an invasion of the Soviet Union. [5]

Eleven days after Hitler's Directive No. 21, on 29 December 1940, Schulze-Boysen knew everything about it and informed the GRU, which forwarded it to Moscow. [6] But this obviously made no impression on Stalin, just as was the case with the supplemental information received from Schulze-Boysen on 4 January 1941, and again on 28 February – when he was informed that "the beginning of the attack is provisionally set for 20 May." [7] Although this supported a report from an agent in Switzerland, who on 21 February reported that the chief of the Swiss general staff had obtained information that the German offensive would begin in late May, Golikov branded it as "likely disinformation." [8]

In the USA, still neutral in the war at that time – although sympathetic towards the anti-Hitler coalition – the government also became aware of the impending German attack on the Soviet Union. Through American codebreakers who had intercepted communication between the Japanese Ambassador in Berlin and Tokyo, President Roosevelt learned about the German plans. On 20 March, this was forwarded to the Soviet Ambassador in the United States. Stalin's reaction was to declare it a "provocation."

From Romania and the agent "AVS" – the press officer at the German embassy in Bucharest, Kurt Völkisch – came the information on 26 March 1941 that the Romanian dictator Antonescu in January 1941 had been briefed on Germany's plan to attack the Soviet Union. But Stalin remained unshaken in his belief that all information on the impending invasion was false.

When German aerial reconnaissance over the Soviet Union increased, the NKVD commander Lavrentiy Beria issued an order on 29 March 1940 that "in case of violations of the Soviet-German border by German aircraft or balloons, do not open fire." [9]

In October 1940, Hitler had personally instructed Luftwaffe Oberstleutnant Theodor Rowehl to initiate a methodic aerial reconnaissance operation over the USSR. Rowehl was the commander of AufklObdL (Aufklärungsgruppe Oberbefehlshaber der Luftwaffe), an aerial long-reconnaissance unit directly under the command of the Luftwaffe C-in-C Reichsmarschall Hermann Göring. Its task now became to photograph military installations in the western area of the Soviet Union, with the emphasis on airfields. The task was to photograph all airfields in this whole region until 15 June 1941. Then, between 15 and 22 June 1941, all airfields should be photographed once again. But the Soviet response to this was absolute passivity – which frustrated many aircrews.

ORDERS FROM ABOVE.

"Look! A German reconnaissance plane!"
"A Junkers!"
"That is a German aircraft, comrade Mayor," Mironov exclaimed.
"What else," said the regimental commander. "And it isn't the first one. They carry out aerial reconnaissance and have surely taken aerial photographs." "Why is there no alarm?" I thought. "Why don't we pursue it?" And I said: "I would put a stop to this!"
"The aircraft already has reached above the Prut," answered Ivanov and sighed. "In order to catch it, we would need a faster aircraft than the I-16. However, to shoot it down is not allowed."
"Why not? Are we not entitled to do that when they fly over our territory? It can't be true!"
"The fascists carry out photo reconnaissance in broad daylight, and we are not even allowed to scare them?" Agitated, we watched our commander, as though he was personally responsible for this.
"Orders from above," Ivanov explained with an expression of resignation. "It's called diplomacy. . ."

From Aleksandr Pokryshkin's autobiography – an account of 55 IAP's encounter with a 3./ObdL Ju 86 P in the spring of 1941.

GÖRING'S FLYING EYE.

The history of the Aufklärungsgruppe Oberbefehlshaber der Luftwaffe goes back to 1926. In April of that year, Theodor Rowehl – who had been a reconnaissance pilot in World War One – started conducting target training flights for the German anti-aircraft artillery, taking off from the air bases Norderney, Kiel-Holtenau and Pillau. Thus he worked in close cooperation with the commander of the German Navy's Nordseestation, Wilhelm Canaris.

The Abwehrabteilung – the intelligence department of the Reichswehr – became interested in these flights. In 1930, the Abwehrabteilung asked Rowehl, who was still a civilian, to conduct secret aerial photo reconnaissance of the former German territories in the east and the west which Germany had lost under the Versailles treaty. Piloting a Ju W 34 which had been modified to reach extreme altitudes, Rowehr performed such flights regularly from 1930 to 1934.

Through close cooperation with Carl Zeiss of Firma Zeiss in Jena, Rowehr reported on the results of the reconnaissance flights and submitted his photographs to Amt Ausland Abwehr, Abteilung I, Section Luft, where the photographs were evaluated. In 1934, Rowehl was made commander of a small unofficial unit consisting of five camera equipped aircraft, the so-called Fliegerstaffel zbV.

From 1935, Rowehl and Canaris came together again when the latter was appointed chief of the Abwehr, but the following year, General Hermann Göring – who was building up his Luftwaffe – intervened to subordinate Rowehl's unit to Luftwaffenführungsstab Ic (Intelligence Department).

The photo reconnaissance missions over the Soviet Union began in 1934. At first, these were carried out only over the Gulf of Finland, Kronstadt and Leningrad, but soon they spread to the Pskov – Minsk region and finally they extended all the way down to Nikolayev on the Black Sea coast. These photo reconnaissance flights were performed at an altitude of between 8,000 and 10,000 meters altitude, and resulted in no German losses.

In 1937, Rowehl's unit was renamed into Hansaluftbild Abt. B. Using a variety of military and civilian aircraft they used the designation "route proving flights for the Lufthansa" as a cover for continued military air reconnaissance. In the late thirties, Rowehl's unit flew high-altitude missions over the Soviet Union and all of Europe. The unit earned much valuable experience in high-altitude flight, and one part of the unit was even actually transformed into the Luftwaffe's Test Unit for High Altitude Flight – the Versuchstelle für Höhenflugzeuge (VfH).

In January 1939, the unit was officially recognised as a Luftwaffe unit, given the designation Aufklärungsgruppe Oberbefehlshaber der Luftwaffe – i.e. a reconnaissance air unit directly subordinated to the Luftwaffe C-in-C, General Hermann Göring – with Theodor Rowehl, promoted to Oberstleutnant, as its commander. Two other strategic reconnaissance Staffeln – 2.(F)/122 under Major Wenz and 3.(F)/123 under Oberleutnant Schürmeyer – were incorporated into AufklObdL, which thus in late 1939 mustered four active Staffeln. The 1st Staffel flew Do 215 V aircraft, and all others were equipped with He 111s.

The crews of 1./ObdL initiated the operation by flying over Belarus from Seerappen-Königsberg. They used He 111s equipped with engines specially trimmed for high altitude flight. Later, the 2nd and 3rd Staffeln joined in. The former flew from Insterburg over the Baltic states and toward Lake Ilmen. The latter flew from Bucharest along the Black Sea coast and over the Ukraine. In addition, the VfH, based in Krakow and Budapest, flew both supplemental reconnaissance, and the most secret missions of them all – the parachuting of Abwehr agents into the USSR at night time. These units used Do 215s, Ju 88s, and Ju 86 P. The latter aircraft was fitted with an extended wing and a pressurized cabin, which enabled it to operate at altitudes close to 13,000 meters.

Up until 21 June 1941, Oberstleutnant Rowehl's crews conducted almost 500 long-range flights to pinpoint Soviet airfields, troop concentrations, and railheads – all tactical targets for Operation Barbarossa. Due to the high frequency of these flights, they could not be hidden from the Soviets. But Stalin himself ordered that no counter-action was to be taken. On 15 April 1941, a Ju 86 P crash-landed near Rovno in the Ukraine. Bad weather forced down another Ju 86 P near Vinnitsa. Even though these aircraft were found to be complete with cameras and exposed film, Stalin did not even protest.

On 22 June 1941 and the in the following days, the intelligence gathered by AufklObdL played a key role in the overwhelming initial German success in its war against the Soviet Union.

General Filipp Ivanovich Golikov led the GRU (Main Intelligence Directorate of the General Staff of the Armed Forces of the Soviet Union) between July 1940 and July 1941.

He had no previous experience in military intelligence. Prior to this, he had commanded the 6th Army, e.g. during the Soviet invasion of Poland in 1939. Golikov passed away on 29 July 1980, on the day before his 80th birthday. (Photo: Soviet Embassy, 1976.)

In fact, the deployment of the huge German army on the borders with the Soviet Union was carried out quite clumsily and absolutely openly; it was known to every single person in Warsaw, one of its main hubs. "From 10 to 20 April 1941," a report from a Soviet agent in Warsaw stated, "German troops moved eastward through Warsaw without stopping, both during the day and by night. Because of the uninterrupted flow of troops, all movement on the streets of Warsaw was halted. By rail, trains were moving in an easterly direction loaded mainly with heavy artillery, trucks, and aircraft parts. From the middle of April, military trucks and Red Cross vehicles appeared on the streets of Warsaw. [...] All motor vehicles belonging to private individuals and commercial firms, including German ones, [have] been mobilized for use by the army. Schools [have] been closed as of 1 April as their buildings [are] to be used as military hospitals. [...] River-crossing materials [are] being prepared along the river Bug." This report lay on Stalin's desk on 5 May 1941. On the very same day, the "master spy" Richard Sorge in Tokyo forwarded to the Soviets on a microfilm of a telegram from the German Foreign Minister Joachim von Ribbentrop to Ambassador Ott where it said that "Germany will begin a war against the Soviet Union in the middle of June 1941." Ten days later Sorge had the information that the attack would take place on 20–22 June, and this was immediately dispatched to Moscow.

The information on the large-scale build up of German troops on the border was confirmed by what the Soviet bor-der troops could see with their own eyes: troop transports, large quantities of pontoons, canvas and inflatable boats on the river sides, etc. Without any other reason than wishful thinking, Stalin refused to believe that Sorge had any credibility at all, nor did he think that the massing of German troops had any significant meaning; he chose to completely trust the Germans when they explained that they were stationed there to "remain out of reach for British bombers."

But the most able military commanders lost their patience. On 9 June, the commander of the Kiev Military District, General-Polkovnik Mikhail Kirponos, decided to order his troops to occupy the forward defense positions. This caused Stalin to panic, and he sent the new Chief of the General Staff, General Armii Grigoriy Zhukov, to rebuke Kirponos with a harsh message: "Such action could provoke the Germans into an armed confrontation fraught with all sorts of consequences. Revoke this order immediately and report who, specifically, gave such an unauthorized order!"

The NKGB also had highly valuable agents in the UK. One of them was Anthony Blunt, who had infiltrated the secret service MI5 and who recruited John Cairncross, one of only four people with full knowledge of Operation "Ultra", the British top secret decrypting of the German Enigma-coded messages. Thus Ultra information was delivered straight to the Soviet Union. This source also informed Stalin that Finland planned to join the war against the Soviet Union, which was confirmed by a similar report from an agent in Helsinki.

The British government also forwarded to the Soviets that they had secure information that Hitler was going to strike against the country, but although the Soviets could find confirmation of this in Ultra decrypts, which excluded that it could be a case of "disinformation," Stalin inexplicably chose to keep his eyes closed. "Stalin had, for whatever reason, succeeded in deluding himself that relations with Germany would proceed on the same comradely path as before," concludes historian Nikolay Tolstoy.[10]

When Sorge on 13 June returned with **even** more specific information – "150 divisions will begin an offensive at dawn on 22 June 1941"[11] – People's Commissar of Defense, Marshal Semyon Timoshenko, advised Stalin to place the border troops on alert. But Stalin refused, and instead accused Sorge of being "a little shit who has set himself up with some small factories and brothels in Japan!"[12] In desperation, Timoshenko turned to Zhukov, and on the following day the two of them turned to Stalin with the same proposal. The result was an outburst of rage. "You propose carrying out mobilization," Stalin exclaimed: "Alerting the troops and moving them to the Western borders? That means war! Do you understand that or not?" When Zhukov replied that, according to their intelligence reports, the mobilisation of the German divisions was complete, Stalin only said: "You can't believe everything you read in intelligence reports!"

The Soviet dictator maintained the same position when Schulze-Boysen at the RLM on 17 June reported that "all preparations for the armed attack on the Soviet Union have been completed and the blow can be expected at any time."[13] Stalin blurted out: "Starshina [Schulze-Boysen's codename] is not a 'source', but a disinformer!"[14] Two days later, Willy Lehmann forwarded to the Soviets that his Gestapo unit had received an order that Germany would initiate the attack on the Soviet Union at 0300 hrs on 22 June 1941.[15] Meanwhile, the German high-altitude reconnaissance flights were stepped up even more. On 19 June eleven such flights were recorded by the Soviets, and on 20 June thirty-six – as compared with a daily average of three since late March.

But the Stalin remained in his state of denial. On 21 June he sent Marshal Timoshenko to give General-Polkovni Fedor Kuznetsov, the commander of the Baltic Special Military District, a harsh dressing down. Like Kirponos eleven days previously, Kuznetsov had adhered to the warning signals of an impending attack, and attempted to prepare to meet the German attack before it was launched. On 20 June he ordered the evacuation of the families of the officers in Lithuania, and he ordered an extensive masking of artillery and troop positions and the dispersal and masking of combat aircraft. He also ordered the troops of his 8th and 11th armies, employed on the border between Soviet Lithuania and East Prussia, to begin laying mines. But on 21 June a raging Timoshenko arrived at Kuznetsov's headquarters, instructing him to remove all the masking of military equipment, forbidding any mining of strategic roads and even ordering the trains with the families of the soldiers back! A report from the 11th Army is quite telling: "Instead of accelerating the grouping of our forces into defensive positions, the High Quarters ordered us to carry out routine training, and on the evening of 21 June an order went out that all ammunition should be transferred to garrison stores."[16]

Meanwhile in Moscow, on the day before the attack, Beriya asked Stalin to "recall and punish our ambassador in Berlin, [Vladimir] Dekanozov, who keeps on bombarding me with 'disinformation' about alleged preparations of an attack on the USSR. He has reported that the 'attack' will begin tomorrow."[17]

At the western borders, loyal cronies in command of the troops echoed Stalin's sentiments. One of those was, most unfortunately for the Soviets, General Armii Dmitriy Pavlov – the commander of the Soviet Western Military District (ZOVO), which would receive the main German blow. As the Chief of the Directorate of Mechanization and Motorization of the Red Army in 1938, Pavlov had been a strong advocate of the idea of spreading out the tanks in support of the infantry. Being a favorite of Stalin, he was one of the first Soviet generals to be awarded the new second-highest rank of General Armii. When General-Leytenant Vasiliy Kuznetsov, the commander of the 3rd Army of the Soviet Western Military District, on 21 June

1941 reported that the Germans had removed the barbed wire entanglements from their side of the border and that the sound of many engines could be heard from the forests, the military district commander, Pavlov, retorted: "Our leaders in Moscow know the military and political situation better than we do," and refused to even ask for permission to put his units in a state of alert. Pavlov's Chief of Staff, General-Mayor Vladimir Klimovskikh, was appalled to hear this and protested. But this only annoyed Pavlov, who swept a map off the table and exclaimed, "War is not possible in the near future!" Then he left to see a patriotic musical in Minsk, 240 kilometers away from the border.[18]

At his headquarters at Kobrin, the commander of the 4th Army, General-Mayor Aleksandr Korobkov, was nevertheless also distressed at incoming reports of German troops moving close to the border. He called the Front headquarters and was put in touch with Klimovskikh. Korobkov told him of the serious situation and asked for permission to order his troops into combat positions. In agony, Klimovskikh could only reply that considering

General-Polkovnik Mikhail Kirponos commanded the Kiev Military District at the onset of Operation Barbarossa. Owing to the lack of senior officers due to the purges of the Red Army, Kirponos enjoyed a meteoric rise up the ranks. During the Winter War against Finland, he had led the 70th Rifle Division with good success. In April 1940 he was appointed to corps commander, and in June that same year he was elevated to command the Leningrad Military District. Kirponos commanded the Kiev Military District from February 1941. He died in combat on 20 September 1941, at the age of 49. (Photo: Archive of the National Military History Museum of Ukraine.)

Semyon Timoshenko earned his reputation from the turning of the fortunes in the Winter War against Finland, in which he assumed the position of senior commander in January 1940. For this he was appointed a Hero of the Soviet Union and the People's Commissar of Defense of the Soviet Union. Early in the war against Germany he took over the important position of commanding the Western Front, and Joseph Stalin personally replaced him as the People's Commissar of Defense. Timoshenko passed away on 31 March 1970, at the age of 75. (Photo: Soviet Embassy, 1976.)

Pavlov's opinion on the matter, he was unable to grant such a request. But he decided to send Polkovnik Nikolay Korneyev, the Western Front's Chief of Intelligence, to Minsk to inform Pavlov. Shortly before midnight, Korneyev entered Pavlov's box in the theater. Annoyed at getting disturbed, Pavlov's only reaction was to bark, "Nonsense! This can't be true!" [19]

Meanwhile in Moscow, Stalin held a meeting with members of the Politburo. A phone call from the Kiev Special Military District, telling of a German deserter who had said that the invasion would commence that night, had been received with skepticism by the dictator, who asked if this might be "a provocation." But then Klimovskikh called, frustrated with Pavlov's relaxed attitude, and stated what he knew. Marshal Timoshenko phoned Pavlov and asked, "What is going on? Is everything quiet?" Pavlov told him what he had learned, but the response he received from Timoshenko did not inspire him to take any immediate action: "Stay calm. Summon your staff in the morning. Something unpleasant might happen, but do not yield to any German provocations. Call me if something happens." But when even a report from the Baltic Special Military District reached the men gathered around Stalin, stating that the Germans had laid bridges across the Neman River and evacuated civilians from a zone of 20 kilometers from the border, the Soviet leadership finally began to realize that not everything was as calm as predicted.

Hesitatingly, Stalin agreed to transmit an order which spoke of the possibility of an imminent German attack. The troops were ordered to full combat readiness, but "not to respond to any provocative actions," and the aviation was instructed to disperse all aircraft to reserve airfields. But it was too late. The document was not sent to the troops until around 0230 in the morning.

At Kobrin, General-Mayor Korobkov had done what he could and sent for his staff officers in order to have at least the 4th Army headquarters prepared for the onslaught. Here, at two in the morning, he was informed that in the city of Brest the power and running water had been extinguished. Shortly afterwards, Kobrin too went dark and all telephone lines with Korobkov's troops and the military district headquarters went dead. The Brandenburgers had carried out their task.

By that time, the Luftwaffe aircraft had already taken off, laden with bombs, some of which was aimed for Korobkov's headquarters…

A formation of German Heinkel 111 bombers. (Photo: Hansgeorg Bätcher.)

Offensive in the Center, June–September 1941.

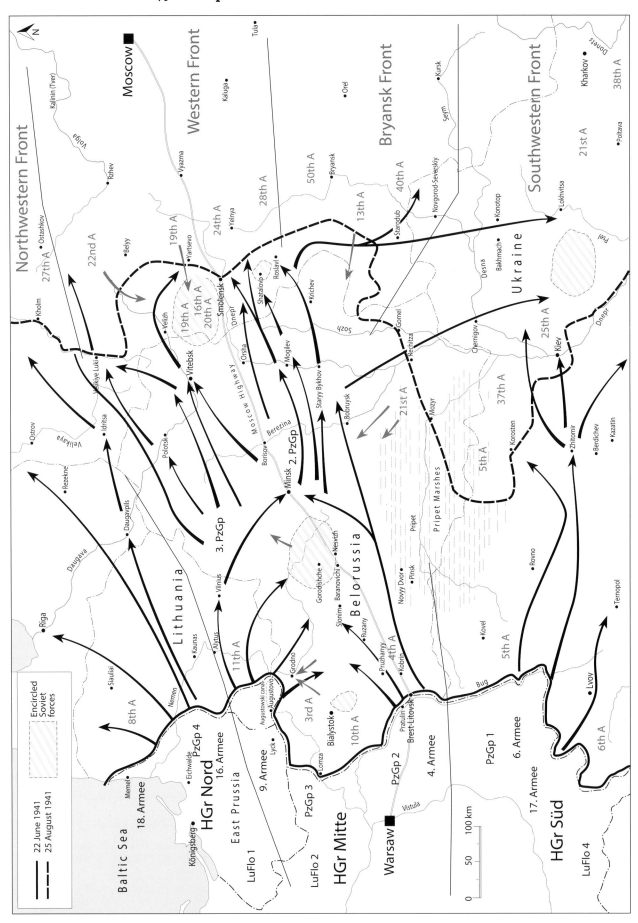

5: STRIKE AT DAWN.

"The entire area on our side was on fire. Everything, the towns, the villages, the settlements, everything was burning."

– Mladshiy Leytenant Fyodor Arkhipenko, 17 IAP, 22 June 1941.

At 0211 hours on Sunday 22 June 1941, the German air base at Eichwalde, just east of Labiau (Polessk), 30 kilometers northeast of Königsberg in East Prussia, was filled with a deafening sound when twenty-nine twin-engine Junkers Ju 88 bombers started their fourteen-hundred horse power Junkers Jumo engines. Then they began to lumber out, each carrying a payload of four thousand kilos of bombs, towards the runway. The engine sound rose as one after another raced across the field, heaved itself from the ground and disappeared in the darkness.

Major Walter Lehwess-Litzmann organized the third group of Luftwaffe Bomber Wing 1 (III. Gruppe/KG 1) "Hindenburg" into a combat formation and then the Junkers bombers headed towards the north. Beneath them, the airmen could distinguish the narrow strip of the Kursiche Nehrung and the small town of Rositten. "It struck me that at that place I had been admiring the sailplanes in the air during my last scout summer," said Lehwess-Litzmann. The Junkers bombers continued north over the Baltic Sea, passing Memel to the left. "It was a clear night and the horizon was bright from the midnight sun in the far north," recalled Hauptmann Gerhard Baeker, the unit's Technical Officer, who also took part in this mission. The twenty-nine Ju 88s were just one formation out of many dozen who took off from airfields all over East Prussia, Poland and Romania to carry out the first surprise onslaught against the Soviet Union. Red Army headquarters and billetings, Soviet cities and ports, and – above all – airfields were their targets. 870 medium bombers, Stukas, Zerstörer, assault planes and fighters were forming up in the air between the Baltic Sea in the North and the Black Sea in the south.

At 0300 hours Lehwess-Litzmann's Junkers bombers turned east out over the Baltic Sea, and headed for the coast south of Libau. By that time, the last train loaded with strategic minerals from the Soviet Union crossed the German-Soviet demarcation line in Poland.

The German airmen found the Soviet territories sleeping innocently, totally unprepared. Leutnant Max-Hellmuth Ostermann of Luftflotte 1's seventh squadron in the Luftwaffe's fighter wing 54 (7./JG 54), later wrote: "As we flew above the enemy's country, everything below seemed to be asleep. No anti-aircraft fire, no movement, and above all no enemy aircraft were present to confront us." [1]

Oberleutnant Georg Schirmböck, who flew a single-engine Messerschmitt Bf 109 fighter of fighter wing JG 77, based in Romania, with airfields of Soviet Black Sea Fleet Aviation's (VVS ChF) as its target, recalled that "Russia really was not prepared at all. Railway stations, villages, everywhere where there was light, the entire country was lit up. At railway stations we could see fully normal activity."

At 0305, the Luftwaffe's pathfinder force began to reach its targets. The largest military campaign in history could begin.

In an instant, incendiary bombs provided a beacon to thirty-one Soviet airfields along the 1,600-kilometer-border. At the airfield at Novyy Dvor, 90 kilometers northeast of Brest, Mladshiy Leytenant Sergey Dolgushin of Soviet 122nd Fighter Regiment (122 IAP) experienced a harrowing awakening. "At three o'clock, the alarm went off," he said. "We all ran towards our airplanes."

Around 100 kilometers farther to the southwest, the commander of the German 2nd Panzer Group (Panzergruppe 2), Generaloberst Heinz Guderian, observed the Soviet side from his command post tower northwest of Brest at 0310 hours. What he saw convinced him: "The Russians knew nothing of our intentions!"

Minutes later the main force of German aircraft struck their targets. The timing of the attack could not have been better chosen. The Luftwaffe struck just as the re-equipment program of the VVS stood at its height. An astonishing sight met the German airmen as they approached their targets. On most Soviet airfields hit by the Luftwaffe the planes stood parked in tight rows, wingtip to wingtip, with no camouflage measures being taken. Due to teething problems with the new aircraft types entering service, the front airfields – many of them only a few kilometers from the border – were packed with aircraft, both old types on their way "out," and the newly received more modern types. This was particularly the case in the relatively recently Soviet-occupied territories of Lithuania and eastern Poland, where the airfield construction program had simply not complied with the need to harbor such vast amounts of aircraft.

The Luftwaffe's primary mission was to neutralize the threat from the Soviet Air Force through massed attacks upon airfields.

The target for the Junkers bombers of Lehwess-Litzmann's III./KG 1 was the airfield at Libau (Liepaja) in Lithuania, where Soviet fighter regiment 148 IAP was based. The German airmen found its sixty-nine Polikarpov I-153 Chayka biplane fighters "parked in nice, tight rows," according to Gerhard Baeker, "offering us a good target in the bright night." Another pilot in III./KG 1, Hauptmann Manfred von Cossart, describes how the Ju 88s completely unopposed unloaded their bombs onto "long rows of completely uncamouflaged aircraft standing in close formation as though on parade along the edges of the Libau airfield."

Major Hannes Trautloft, commanding the fighter wing JG 54 "Grünherz," escorted other Ju 88s of Luftflotte 1 against Kaunas' airfield in Lithuania. Here, the 8th Composite Aviation Wing (8 SAD) of the Soviet Baltic Special Military District (PBVO) had established its headquarters, and the airfield was packed with 114 of the old and outgoing Polikarpov fighter types I-15bis, I-153 and I-16, plus 62 brand new MiG-3 monoplane fighters. Just as the bombers and Trautloft's Messerschmitts came in over the large, grass-covered airfield, the sun rose above the horizon and cast its bright rays on the deadly metallic birds. Trautloft watched as the fragmentation bombs exploded in devastating sequence among the double lines of neatly parked Soviet aircraft. Only two airborne I-153s appeared in front of the attacking aircraft, but they left as quickly as they came. Returning from this raid, the Luftwaffe aircrews reported 70 Soviet planes put out of commission.

At the airfield of Varena southwest of the old Lithuanian capital of Vilnius, Luftwaffe fighter squadron 8./

JG 53 shot up seven of the SB twin-engine bombers of fast bomber regiment 54 SBAP on the ground. 8./JG 53 was subordinate to Fliegerkorps VIII, commanded by General Wolfram Freiherr von Richthofen, one of the most able Luftwaffe commanders. In this first attack, Fliegerkorps VIII was mainly directed against 11 and 9 SAD of the Red Army's Western Special Military District (ZOVO) – two of three such composite air units that ZOVO had stationed in the vicinity of the Soviet-German demarcation line in Poland. 122 IAP, to which Sergey Dolgushin belonged, was part of 11 SAD. Sixty-five of 122 IAP's seventy-five I-16 Ishak (Rata) fighter planes were destroyed at Novyy Dvor.[2]

But 9 SAD, based in the Bialystok area in front of the attack forces of German Panzergruppe 3 northeast of Warsaw, took the heaviest beating from the aerial onslaught that morning. 9 SAD was a crack unit, commanded by the Hero of the Soviet Union General-Mayor Sergey Chernykh, a veteran from the Spanish Civil War, during which he had shot down three Franco-planes (including the first Bf 109 ever to be lost in air combat). According to an inspection shortly before the outbreak of the war, General-Mayor Chernykh's unit was one of the best in the entire VVS. The four fighter regiments under his command were equipped with 233 of the modern MiG-3 fighter and had only 156 obsolete Polikarpov fighters. The bomber regiment of the division, 13 SBAP, was equipped with 51 bombers, including 22 of the experimental twin-engine Ar-2 dive-bomber (a modified version of the SB 'high-speed bomber'). 9 SAD had the dubious luck of receiving the attention of both Fliegerkorps VIII and II – the two air corps of Generalfeldmarschall Albert Kesselring's Luftflotte 2, the air fleet

Bombs lying ready on a frontal airfield to be loaded onto Junkers Ju 88 bombers of the Luftwaffe.

When the Luftwaffe struck at dawn on 22 June 1941, many Soviet aircraft stood lined up, wingtip to wingtip, such as these I-16 Ishak fighters – also called Rata ("Rat") by the Germans.

assigned to support Heeresgruppe Mitte – and suffered heavier losses that any other VVS unit on this fateful Sunday morning. All of 9 SAD's airfields were targeted.

General Bruno Loerzer's Fliegerkorps II – tasked to support Guderian's Panzergruppe 2 on the right wing of Heeresgruppe Mitte – attacked 9 and 10 SAD. Thirty kilometers south of Novyy Dvor, Messerschmitt Bf 109 fighters from 2./JG 51 swooped down on the airfield at Pruzhanyy, destroying twenty I-16s of 33 IAP. 1./SKG 210, a squadron of Messerschmitt Bf 110 twin-engine assault aircraft, also attacked this target and General-Mayor Korobkov's 4th Army headquarters at Kobrin, destroying all the aircraft of 74th Assault Aviation Regiment (74 ShAP) at the adjacent airfield – fifteen old I-15bis biplanes, fifteen I-153 biplanes and eight of the brand new Ilyushin Il-2s – and destroying the Army headquarters.[3] General-Mayor Korobkov was only lucky to survive – altough he would be killed by a Soviet bullet only a few weeks afterwards.

Returning to attack Pruzhanyy a third time, nine Bf 109s from 2./JG 51 pressed home their strafing attacks for nearly 40 minutes and, according to Soviet sources, an additional twenty-one I-16s and five I-153s were put out of action. In total, 2./JG 51 reported the destruction of 43 Soviet aircraft on the ground on 22 June, 1941.[4]

To several German airmen, the first raid was like being on a shooting range. Leutnant Ernst-Wilhelm Ihrig of bomber squadron 3./KG 3 conducted six low-level runs with his Ju 88 against Pinsk Airdrome, 140 km east of Brest, and claimed sixty planes destroyed on the ground. In fact, Soviet 39th Fast Bomber Regiment (39 SBAP) lost 43 SB bombers and five Pe-2s on that airfield – the whole action nevertheless ending with Ihrig himself getting shot down by ground fire.

39 SBAP, 33 IAP and 74 ShAP were all part of the ZOVO's 10th Composite Aviation Wing (SAD), which lost 180 out of its 231 planes on 22 June 1941.

The situation looked much the same to the south of the Pripyat Marshes, where Generaloberst Alexander Löhr's Luftflotte 4 raided twenty-nine Soviet airfields over a wide area all down to the Black Sea coast. VVS-Kiev Special Mil-

itary District (KOVO) on the northern flank of this area took the full brunt of the attacks by Fliegerkorps V – the air corps of German air fleet Luftflotte 4 which was assigned with the task of providing the ground attack into northwestern Ukraine with air support. Hauptmann Hans von Hahn, flying a Bf 109 at the head of fighter group I./JG 3 wrote in his diary: "We could hardly believe our eyes. Row after row of reconnaissance planes, bombers and fighters stood lined up as if on parade." Dispatching 80 Ju 88s on the first mission of the day, bomber wing KG 51 was reported to have destroyed around 100 of KOVO's aircraft on the ground.

"That day I will remember for my entire life, I will remember it to the end of my life," said Fyodor Arkhipenko, Mladshiy Leytenant and Operations Duty Officer of 17 IAP at Lyublynets airfield near Kovel in northwestern Ukraine. He recalls: "Beginning at 0325 in the morning, around 50 German planes bombed our field, coming back four times. Only myself and the duty pilot, my squadron leader, Ibragimov, and the guards, the security forces, were there. Because it was Sunday, the rest had been allowed to go home on leave. The airfield was small, two by three kilometres. You can imagine the kinds of horrors that took place at the airfield. Then, by the afternoon, the pilots and ground crews started arriving. Many of them, their hair had turned white. And some of them had even begun to stutter from fear after experiencing that kind of bombing."

Starshiy Leytenant Aron Shapiro of 86 SBAP, based at Ternopol, around 150 kilometers further to the south, describes the bombings by KG 51 on this Sunday morning:

"Since the commanders of the Polk [regiment] had left for a staff meeting on Saturday, I was the senior highest ranking officer on the airfield. The alarm went off at 0400 [Russian time, i.e. 0300 Central European Time]. No one understood what was happening. At around [0330], three planes appeared. They looked very similar to our SBs. We watched silently as they approached at high speed at an altitude of 300 feet. Everyone believed that our commanders had ordered these planes to carry out a mock attack in order to test our combat vigilance.

THE RESULT OF THE GERMAN ONSLAUGHT FROM THE AIR ON 22 JUNE 1941.

1. Destroyed I-153 assault planes, U-2 training planes and (to the right) an SB bomber at Minsk's airfield.

2. Remnants of destroyed SB bombers. (Photo: Johannes Wiese.)

3. The tail of a DB-3 bomber and destroyed I-153s. (Photo: Arno Becker.)

4. Destroyed SB bombers. (Photo: Via Taghon.)

5. A destroyed I-153 Chayka. (Photo: Arno Becker.)

"As they buzzed above our heads, we suddenly saw that they didn't carry red stars but had black crosses under their wings! And then we heard bomb explosions. We didn't know what to do. The connection to headquarters was severed. In the control tower there was a radio transmitter. I managed to handle it, and from the very noisy conversations that I heard, I understood that war had broken out. Then we only heard German voices in the radio.

"Ten minutes after the first bombing, more alien aircraft appeared. By that time, we understood that they were German. We opened fire at them with everything that could shoot, but since we had no anti-aircraft artillery, we could only confront the Germans with light arms fire, including rifles. The aircraft gunners sat in the turrets of the bombers and fired vertically.

"One of the German bombers was hit and left a black trail of smoke. I think it was a Ju 88. The crew bailed out and landed on our airfield. Everyone rushed to where they came down and surrounded them. One officer who knew German served as interpreter. I particularly remember one of the Germans, a huge, red-haired young man. He acted most brazenly. 'Stalin kaputt, Heil Hitler,' he acclaimed, smiling scornfully. We had no intention of playing his game. A soldier gave him two punches, which made the German pilot more talkative. Finally we found out what was going on. It was war – the *Blitzkrieg* had started. He confidently declared that the Germans would be in Moscow by October: 'To all of you – *alles kaputt!*'"

Messerschmitt Bf 110 assault planes of the Luftwaffe's Fast Bomber Wing SKG 210 in action. This unit was credited with the destruction of no less than 344 Soviet aircraft on the ground on 22 June 1941.

During Operation Barbarossa, it operated in close support of Guderian's Panzergruppe 2, claiming another 479 Soviet aircraft destroyed on the ground and 92 shot down in the air, as well as the destruction of 2,136 vehicles and 165 tanks, while losing 57 Bf 110s to enemy action.

The Bf 110 was one of the most successful aircraft of World War II. Contrary to pre-war rumors, it performed very well in the role of a day fighter in 1939–1941. During Operation Barbarossa it served as Germany's most important night fighter in the Home Defense during most of the war. During Operation Barbarossa it as the Luftwaffe's most common assault plane. But its main success was attained as Germany's most important night fighter in the Home Defense during most of the war.

Further north, Hauptmann Baeker of III./KG 1 "Hindenburg" returned from his successful mission: "We landed undramatically, at 0351, before the sunrise."

By that time, it was as if a glowing snake had appeared on the ground below the returning German aircraft. At 0315 hours, while the bombs were raining over dozens of Soviet airfields, the German artillery opened up a massive fire along an 800-kilometer front ranging from the Baltic coast in the north and across the entire Soviet-German line of demarcation in Poland.

In the sky above the German soldiers, who were lined up in attack positions, a terrible sound passed by, as if a thousand freight trains had passed over their heads. Then the first salvoes exploded on the Soviet side. The night turned red and lit up in the east. "The sky was filled with bursting shells of every caliber," wrote German Gefreiter Hans Teuschler from his position near Brest. "It was an awful roaring, exploding, crackling and howling as if hell was actually about to come on earth." Next the German soldiers were hit by a powerful wind draft from the explosions. Thousands of shells continued to rain over the Soviet side. The shelling continued and continued. Meanwhile, at the Luftwaffe airfields, medium bombers were prepared for the task of isolating the battlefield through bombings of roads, rail lines and stations, bridges, etc. The artillery barrage was still continuing as the first of these planes passed to the east in the sky above.

Another of the German soldiers on the ground, Unteroffizier Hans Schmitz, even took his time to write a letter to his wife during the bombardment: "Our artillery has already been shooting for three quarters of an hour, and everything is on fire on the Russian side. So far the enemy has not returned any fire. It gives an overwhelming impression. Probably we will cross the border today. Ceaselessly we hear how it bangs and booms everywhere. Our aircraft are really busy."[5]

"As if hell was about to come on earth," said Hans Teuschler. On the other side of the border, it *was* hell that had broken out. "The dreadful bombardment lasted for about thirty minutes," said Roman Yevseyevich of Soviet 8th Army in Lithuania, and after it stopped the forest filled with the groans and screams from wounded men. Everything was covered with smoke. The survivors, dazzled and deafened by the explosions, wandered about between the shell craters and tried to help the wounded men who shouted for medics. But no one could conceive of carrying the wounded away, and we had no first-aid kits. The wood was littered with corpses..."[6] At 0400 hours, fourteen minutes before sunrise, the invasion army began to cross the border. "Silently, absolutely silently we crept up to the edge of River Bug," wrote Gerd Habedanck who followed 45. Infanterie-Division. "Sand had been strewn across the roads so that our hobnailed boots made no sound. Assault sections already grouped moved along the road edges in mute rows. Outlines of rubber dinghies were discernible as they shuttled along, raised up against the light of the northern sky. One boat after the other slid into the water. There were excited cries, splashing and the howling of assault boat engines. Not a shot from the other bank as blood red flames dance in the water. We jump on shore and press for-

A Soviet village in flames. (Photo: Arno Becker.)

ward. Verdant dykes between swampy ditches, barbed-wire fences, and the lower casemates. The body of a dead Soviet-Russian soldier, the carcasses of dead horses. Onward, onward! Trembling, individual groups of Soviet-Russians approach us with hands raised. Others are leaping between trees, fleeing with rifles in their hands."[7]

Stukas, assault planes, Messerschmitt Bf 109 and Messerschmitt Bf 110 fighter-bombers flew over the heads of the advancing German soldiers, striking defense positions, command posts, troop quarters, and fuel and ammunition dumps of the Red Army. The Soviet border troops were totally caught by surprise, and at in most places the entire front crumbled.

At Pratulin, 10 kilometers northwest of Brest, German pioneers in rubber assault boats had secured a bridgehead during the first thirty minutes of the assault. Next followed the tanks of 18. Panzer-Division. There were no bridges in the area, but Stabsfeldwebel Helmut Wierschin, platoon commander in Panzer-Regiment 18, drove his tank straight into the Bug river. While it disappeared under the water surface, other tanks followed. These were Tauchpanzer – modified Panzer IIIs and Panzer IVs – and after traversing the bottom of the river, they re-emerged on the other side. The rubber caps on the gun muzzles popped off, the wet turret hatches opened and the tank commanders became

visible. An arm thrust three times into the air: "*Panzer marsch!*" A formation of Soviet armored cars was detected. "Turret – One O'clock – armor piercing – 800 meters – group of armored scout cars – *Feuer!*" Bright flashes, explosions, smoke and fire, and the panzers clanked on – in all eight tanks from Major Manfred Graf Strachwitz's I. Abteilung of Panzer-Regiment 18.

In the southeastern part of German-occupied Poland, Oskar Scheja took part as 298. Infanterie-Division of Heeresgruppe Süd's 6. Armee stormed across the River Bug. "We moved quickly through the fields towards the enemy encampment and announced our arrival with a shower of bullets," he said. "We found no Russian artillery set up to counter our assault and few defensive positions. Large numbers of Russian soldiers fled their encampment still in their underwear. Many were gunned down as they ran, still more quickly surrendered. The artillery strike proved very effective as we captured [the border town Ustilug, 60 km southwest of Kovel] without much of a fight."[8]

"Our troop command was totally demoralized," said Starshiy Leytenant Ivan Kovalyov of Soviet 30th Rifle Division. "No one knew exactly what was going on at the borders. The drumfire of the enemy artillery, and the sabotage by German special forces in Red Army uniforms caused tremendous and irreparable damage."[9]

58

Ivan Chernov, a young Soviet Leytenant was among 1,600 newly trained officers on board a train en route to Lutsk in the Ukraine that morning when suddenly bombs began to explode around the train, which halted with shrieking brakes. Everyone on board fell over. Having moments before been fast asleep, the men jumped from the train, still in their underwear and leapt away as the first railway waggons caught fire. Hearing but not seeing any aircraft, Chernov ran barefoot into a small wood patch, from where a terrible screaming could be heard. There he saw a girl weeping with her arms wrapped around a Leytenant who had been killed by shrapnel. After about fifteen minutes, the German aircraft left the scene, leaving an indescribable chaos behind. Over two hundred of the officer recruits had been killed, many more were wounded, and scores of shell shocked soldiers ran around. "We did not know what to do, no officers in charge could be seen. Total chaos reigned," said Chernov. After a while, a Mayor from the corps staff in Rovno appeared. But he did not know what had taken place either. All he knew was that Rovno had also been bombed.[10]

It actually took the Soviet High Command several hours to realize the full extent of the disaster. The whole scene on the Russian side was characterized by total confusion. "From beleaguered command posts, field telephone-centres and bomb-ravaged aerodromes, messages poured into Moscow: 'We are under fire. What are we meant to do?' Back came the reply: 'You must be feeling unwell. And why isn't your message in code?'"[11]

This reply from the High Command perfectly reflects the Stalinist mentality of appeasement at this time: "Do not give in to provocation! Do not open fire!" According to Soviet Marshal Aleksandr Vasilevskiy, the Red Army had received strict orders to avoid "any action that the Nazi leaders could use to exarcerbate the situation or make a military provocation". The Soviet leaders desperately clung to the hope that the German attack was an act of " self-motivated German generals" attempting to provoke a war against the will of Stalin's ally Hitler!

In Minsk, the commander of the Western Military District, General Armii Dmitriy Pavlov, received a message from General-Leytenant Vasiliy Kuznetsov, the commander of the 3rd Army, informing him that German troops had broken through in the border area between Sopotskin and Augustovo, that aircraft were bombing Grodno, and the 3rd Army headquarter's communications with its troops were cut.[12] Pavlov was completely taken aback. "I don't understand what's going on," he was heard mumbling.[13] Shortly afterward, Marshal Timoshenko phoned Pavlov to check the situation again. Pavlov reported what he had heard, but Timoshenko's only reply was that "Stalin will not permit artillery fire to be returned against the Germans."[14]

Over the next 30 minutes, the Western Military District's headquarters was overwhelmed with reports of German air raids. The picture of the whole Western Military District crumbling began to take shape. The headquarters of its 3rd and 4th armies reported that communications with most of their troops were severed. But what was of

German soldiers carrying a rubber assault boat. (Photo: Dagobert Paskowski.)

greatest concern to Pavlov and his staff was the complete silence from the General-Mayor Konstantin Golubev's 10th Army headquarters in Biyalystok. "I will fly to Biyalystok," Pavlov said in panic, and ordered his deputy, General-Leytenant Ivan Boldin, to take over at the military district headquarters. But Boldin protested: "I consider such a decision incorrect," he retorted. "The commander can't abandon the leadership of his armies!" After the war, Boldin wrote: "But he persisted. Nervously, he went back and forth, leaving the office and then coming back again and again." [15]

A Soviet T-26 tankette is hit by German fire.

Then Timoshenko phoned – the third time in two hours that he contacted the Western Military District. He forbade Pavlov from leaving the headquarters. Instead, the Vice Commissar for the Defense, Marshal Grigoriy Kulik was instructed to fly from Moscow to the 10th Army's headquarters to establish the situation. Kulik was the infamous Stalin crony who had voiced an opposition against tanks in general and branded submachine guns as a "bourgeois fascist affectation." * It would take him two days to reach Biyalystok – which by then was enveloped by the Germans, and as we shall see further on, he was of no help whatsoever.

During one of the moments when Pavlov was gone, Timoshenko phoned again.

Boldin took the call. "Our troops are forced to retreat, cities are burning, people are dying!" Boldin shouted into the receiver. But Timoshenko was cold. "No action is to be taken against the Germans without our consent," he said. "Inform Pavlov that comrade Stalin will not allow the artillery to open fire." Boldin was told that Stalin believed that all aggressive action by the Germans might be provocations on the part of a couple of German generals.
By the time the Western Military District finally was brought into action, the Luftwaffe had destroyed a large part of its artillery as well as most of the fuel and ammunition dumps in the vicinity of the front line.

To the north, elements of Soviet 11th Army, supposed to defend the Lithuanian capital of Vilnius, received orders

* See Chapter 3.

not to engage the Germans as late as around six in the morning.[16] In this sector, Mladshiy Leytenant Nikolay Gapeyonok, an SB-pilot in fast bomber regiment 202 SBAP, had an experience quite symptomatic of the general confusion during these hours, at an airfield 25 kilometers north of Kingisepp on the first day of the war. Gapeyonok told the author: "No one had expected war. It broke out on a Sunday. On the previous day, Saturday, most of the Regiment's airmen had left for athletic games. I was one of the few who remained on duty at the airfield. Suddenly we could hear sirens, but we expected it was training. Since the radio operator was gone, we couldn't receive any radio calls. It was not until 1100 hours, as the airmen returned to the airfield, that we learned that it was war. Fortunately, our airfield was not bombed."

"As a result of our tactical surprise, enemy resistance directly on the border was weak and disorganized, and we succeeded everywhere in seizing the bridges across the border rivers and in piercing the defense positions", Halder happily noted in his diary.[17]

However, contrary to a popular belief, the Luftwaffe was far from alone in the skies over the Eastern Front on 22 June 1941. In fact, after the initial German onslaught there were at least as many Soviet as German planes in the air, although dispersed in many small groups. It is estimated that 6,000 VVS sorties were made on this day. In the center, the strongest German air fleet – Luftflotte 2 – conducted 2,272 sorties throughout the day,[18] while the battered VVS ZOVO brought 1,900 aircraft into the air, to which the sorties undertaken by the DBA in this area should be added.

Despite the surprise attack and patchy communications, Soviet pilots scrambled individually or in small formations to fight back. Bitter dogfights raged in the skies all along the front during these early morning hours. The first recorded air fight took place when I-153s from Mayor Boris Surin's fighter group 123 IAP of 10 SAD scrambled from Kobrin and intercepted I./StG 77's Ju 87s, which, escorted by IV./JG 51's Bf 109s attacked the fortress at Brest. While Oberleutnant Karl Schmidt's Ju 87 B-1 of 2./StG 77 was shot down by an I-153, Oberleutnants Karl Führing and Franz Hahn claimed the first German aerial victories in the Russo–German war, between 0340 and 0347 hours. Hahn alone contributed three.[19]

The Stabsstaffel of KG 2 experienced both the skills lacked by the Soviet fliers, and their rage. Hans Kowwwnatzki, Feldwebel and radio operator in a Do 17 Z, recalled: "At around 0415 hours, approximately 24 kilometers southeast of Lomza, near Zambov, we came under attack from enemy fighters."[20] This was an Eskadrilya of MiG-3s and I-16s led by Mladshiy Leytenant Dmitriy Kokorev from 124 IAP/9 SAD, which made a series of gunnery runs straight into the German bomber gunners' coordinated defensive fire, as Kownatzki describes: "During the air combat, we managed to shoot down three enemy fighters, while I received two light bullet wounds." Three Soviet fighters were actually lost, while 124 IAP's pilots claimed to have shot down one Do 17 – which in reality managed to limp back with battle damage. But Mladshiy Leytenant Kokorev's determination was stronger. "Shortly afterward we got shot down ourselves," said Feldwebel Kownatzki.

But in reality, Kokorev – with empty guns – pushed his MiG-3 close to the Do 17, and used the propeller to cut the bomber's stabilizer. The powerful impact knocked Kokorev unconscious while, in Kownatzki's words, the Do 17 was thrust into a spin: "Oberleutnant [Hans-Georg] Peters and I were flung out of the aircraft and came down to earth in our parachutes. We landed in a wheat field. There we were found by a Polish civilian who told us that our two comrades Oberfeldwebel Stockmann and Unteroffizier [Hans] Schuhmacher went down with the aircraft and burned."

Meanwhile, the slipstream brought Kokorev back to consciousness, and he managed to resume control of his damaged MiG-3 and force-landed near Zambov. For this feat, Kokorev was awarded with the Order of the Red Banner. He carried out another hundred sorties and achieved a total victory score of five before being shot down and killed in October 1941.

This was the first successful taran – air-to-air ramming – of the war. With Kokorev as an example, the taran would become a not-uncommon and most heroic way of destroying enemy aircraft by Soviet pilots. Around 600 German planes were reportedly destroyed by taran between 1941 and 1945.

In 127 IAP/11 SAD alone, three pilots were reported to have made air-to-air rammings on 22 June 1941 – Leytenant Petr Kuzmin, a Bf 109; Starshiy Politruk Andrey Danilov, who claimed two Bf 110s shot down and a third rammed with his I-153 during a single dogfight near Lida; and Leytenant Aleksandr Pachin, who reportedly rammed a Ju 87. Altogether, 11 SAD's 122 IAP and 127 IAP claimed seventeen Bf 109s, eleven Bf 110s, and seven Ju 88s destroyed on 22 June, 1941.[21]

The German aircraft losses during the first day of the attack against the Soviet Union were surprisingly high. Seen in this photo is a shot down and belly-landed Dornier Do 17 Z bomber. (Photo: Erwin Leykauf.)

Soviet fighter pilots would keep fighting tenaciously throughout the day, disregarding their losses, and this is the dominant assessment by most of their German counterparts. Just as the Soviets were stunned by the fierce and massive German attack, many Luftwaffe airmen describe how they were completely taken aback by the incredible stamina displayed by Soviet fliers throughout the first day, and beyond.

On their approach flight to attack 14 SAD at Mlynov Airdrome, northwest of Dubno in northwestern Ukraine, at about 0425 hours, six crews of Luftwaffe bomber group III./KG 55 experienced the determination with which

A dead Red Army soldier, one of the first victims of the German attack.

A shot down Soviet SB bomber. The Soviet bomber force made incessant attempts to halt the German attack on 22 June 1941, suffering terrible losses at the hands of Messerschmitt Bf 109 fighters in the process. (Photo: Karlheinz Höfer via Günther Rosipal.)

many Soviet airmen fought. Led by Leytenant Ivan Ivanov, a group of 46 IAP I-16 Ishaks had scrambled and cross-cut the twin-engine Heinkel 111 bombers before these had managed to drop their bombs. Two of the He 111s were shot down (the Soviets actually only claimed one!) and the remainder jettisoned their bombs and started escaping toward the west. While his compatriots returned and landed, Ivanov decided to continue pursuing the fleeing enemy. He caught up again, but spent the rest of his ammunition without any decisive effect. In that moment, Ivanov simply crashed his small Ishak fighter right into the He 111 piloted by Unteroffizier Horst Wohlfeil of bomber squadron 7./KG 55. Both planes went down, and none of the airmen involved survived. Ivan Ivanov posthumously received the Soviet Union's highest recognition, the appointment to a Hero of the Soviet Union.

Among other taran victims this day was the commander of JG 27, Major Wolfgang Schellmann. A total of at least nineteen tarans were recorded on 22 June 1941. When analysed, some of these turn out to be optimistic exaggerations of close-hits, or even attempts to cover up a simple shootdown. This testifies to both the Soviet determination to fight back and the awe felt by those who were attacked by the German military machine on this Sunday morning. Losses on the Soviet side were indeed horrendous, both on the ground and in the air combats.

Soviet bombers were also in action to strike back. 40 SBAP, with 52 serviceable SBs, took off from Ventspils in northwestern Latvia. The unit commander, Mayor Mogi-

lyov, led his formation along the coastline until it reached the northernmost German city of Memel. There the regiment divided into Eskadrilya formations, carrying out surprising dawn attacks against Memel, Königsberg and Tilsit. All SBs managed to return to base without getting intercepted by any German fighters.

At 0538, German fighter group II./JG 53 in East Prussia was scrambled against approaching Soviet bombers. In the ensuing clash, eight SBs fell in flames while the Soviet gunners succeeded in knocking down one of the Bf 109s. It was piloted by Hauptmann Heinz Bretnütz, whose 37 victories made him one of the top aces of the Luftwaffe at that time. Bretnütz made a belly landing in enemy territory and was lucky to be hidden by friendly local people. But this could not save his life. Recovered by advancing German troops on 26 June, Bretnütz died of his wounds the following day.

It was not until 0715 hours – four hours after the German onslaught – that it dawned on Stalin that the Soviet Union was actually subject to a massive German invasion. He now issued "Directive No. 2," authorizing an active defense. But by that time, the German armies, spearheaded by large tank concentrations, were flooding into the Soviet-held territories of Lithuania and Poland. ZOVO's unwise grouping of its three armies (the 3rd, 10th and 4th) in a forward line just along the demarcation line in Poland, facilitated the German plan to destroy them. Generaloberst Hermann Hoth's Panzergruppe 3 immediately cut a wedge in the

AIRCRAFT LOSSES ON 22 JUNE 1941.

The aircraft losses on the Eastern Front on 22 June 1941 were the highest ever in the history of air war for a single day. Soviet records actually confirm most of the German claims. The Air Force of the Baltic Special Military District saw eleven of its airfields bombed, and lost 56 aircraft. VVS ZOVO had twenty-six airfields bombed, and lost 738 of its 1,789 aircraft. Twenty-three airfields in western Ukraine were bombed, and although VVS KOVO managed to escape total annihilation, it still lost 192 aircraft – including 95 on the ground. In addition, 109 training aircraft in the same area were destroyed in the German air attacks on 22 June 1941.[1]

VVS OVO had six airfields bombed and lost 23 aircraft.[2] To these losses should be added those by the DBA and the Navy Air Force. It is interesting to note that whereas Soviet sources list 336 Soviet planes shot down in the air – including 204 in the operational area of VVS ZOVO alone – on 22 June 1941, the Germans claimed 322 aerial victories, to which of course should be added a number of victories by Romanian pilots and anti-aircraft batteries.

The hardest blow was inflicted on General-Mayor Sergey Chernykh's 9 SAD: Of 409 planes, no fewer than 347 were destroyed, including the majority of the 57 MiG-3s and 52 I-16s of 129 IAP alone. General-Mayor Chernykh, Hero of the Soviet Union, was arrested by the NKVD and executed.

But the losses sustained by the Luftwaffe were also absolutely shocking in some cases. The operations against VVS KOVO on 22 June 1941 came at a heavy price for Fliegerkorps V of Luftflotte 4: KG 51 lost fifteen Ju 88s, KG 54 three Ju 88s (with another three belly-landed), and KG 55 ten He 111s. Klaus Häberlen, who flew as an Oberleutnant with III./KG 51 by that time, confessed that "we felt really depressed that night, and this feeling could be relieved only through some bottles of wine."[3] That amounted to over ten per cent of the bombers in Fliegerkorps V. The fighter wing of the air corps, JG 3, was even more battered, with 15 of its 98 Messerschmitt Bf 109s – five of those total losses – being put out of action.

Other Luftwaffe units escaped with only negligible losses – like III./KG 27, which claimed the destruction of over 40 Soviet aircraft on the ground without sustaining any own losses.

Total Luftwaffe losses in the East on 22 June 1941 amounted to 78 aircraft destroyed (24 fighters, 23 Ju 88s, 11 He 111s, 7 Bf 110s, 2 Ju 87s, 1 Do 17, 10 miscellaneous types).[4] Added to these losses were those sustained by the Romanian Air Force – four Blenheims, two PZL P.37s, two Savoia-Marchetti 79Bs, one Potez 633, one I.A.R. 37, and one I.A.R. 39 – bringing total Axis aircraft losses on 22 June 1941 to almost 90.

The day's most successful Soviet fighter pilot in terms of shot down enemy aircraft, was Leytenant Ivan Kalabushkin of 10 SAD's 123 IAP; he claimed two Ju 88s at dawn, a He 111 before midday, and two Bf 109s in the evening. During the last combat of the day he was wounded in both his legs when a cannon shell exploded in the cockpit. He nevertheless was able to bring his I-153 back to base, where he had to be lifted out of the cockpit by mechanics and taken to hospital.

1 TsAMO, f. 229, op. 181, d. 47, l. 21; Skripko, *Po tselyam blizhnim I dalyim*, p. 130.
2 Kornyukhin, *Sovetskie Istrebitel v Velikoy Otechestvennoy Voyne*, p. 264.
3 Interview with Klaus Häberlen.
4 Bundesarchiv/Militärarchiv RL 2 III/754.

seam between ZOVO's northernmost army, the 3rd, and the Baltic Special Military District.

At Augustovo, tank commander Gefreiter Otto Carius rode one of 20. Panzer-Division's 121 Czech-made Panzer 38(t) tanks across the bridge that had been captured by Brandenburgers early in the morning. The tanks raced along the highway towards the northeast and managed to capture the airfield at Alytus – where smoking remnants of I-15bis biplanes of Soviet 240 IAP were found – without encountering much resistance.

This created opportunities for General Erich von Manstein's LVI. Panzerkorps on Heeresgruppe Nord's southern flank. On this day alone, von Manstein's forward elements advanced 80 kilometers, seized the vital Airogola road viaduct across River Dubysa, and established a bridgehead on the eastern side of the river. At Alytus, von Manstein's 8. Panzer-Division met with 20. Panzer-Division. On Heeresgruppe Mitte's southern flank, Guderian's Panzergruppe 2 captured Kobrin and Pruzhany.

Only at the fortress of Brest and to the south of the Pripyat Marshes were the defenders barely able to hold their positions. In Heeresgruppe Süd's northern sector, in what previously was southern Poland, NKVD border troops and three under-strength divisions of Soviet 5th Army fought hard against the initial onslaught by ten divisions, including two Panzer divisions, of Generaloberst Ewald von Kleist's Panzergruppe 1.[22] The attacking German troops found that all bridges across the rivers in the border area had been blown up by the retreating Soviets, and they also became entangled in bitter fighting with a most resolute enemy. A German soldier said:

"Until we attacked, we had heard the singing of the Soviet broder troops, and we could not imagine that people who sing so beautifully were able to defend theuir country with such bitter stamina. Their fire was terrible! We left many dead behind on the bridge, and still were not able to capture it. Finally, our battalion commander ordered us to wade across the San river to the left and to the right of the bridge. But we had barely entered the water before Soviet border troops subjected us to an intense fire. We sustained significant losses. Nowhere, neither in Poland, nor in France, had my battalion sustained such heavy losses as during those minutes when we attempted to cross the San. As the battalion commander realized that his attempt was about to fail, he ordered the mortars to open fire. Only under the cover of this fire were we able to force the river, but on the other side we were not able to advance as fast as had been anticipated. The Russians had established several fire positions along the river bank, and they fought literally to the last bullet. We had to bring forward pioneers. They crawled forward and blew up one stronghold after another with explosive charges. But often the Russians continued to offer resistance even after their bunkers had been destroyed. … When we launched our attack, our battalion had 900 men. We lost 150 killed and over 100 were wounded."[23]

Sporadic and uncoordinated counter-attacks were made. At Vladimir-Volinskiy on the main road to Kiev in the east, a battalion of Soviet 41st Tank Division was hurled straight against German Panzer III tanks and anti-tank guns. Thirty of the fifty light-skinned T-26 tankettes were rapidly picked off by the German guns.[24]

But to the north, the entire border defense had collapsed and the invasion army kept streaming over bridges across rivers Dubysa, Neman and Bug in the border area. The confused directives sent from the Soviet High Command during the early morning hours had prevented the destruction of most of these bridges. As the Soviet High Command finally reacted, the VVS was instructed to launch every available bomber against these arteries of the invasion armies.

Initially, the SB fliers of the Front and Army aviation carried the main burden of counterstriking from the air. They had to stand alone against the German fighters, because of the chaotic situation which gave no room for organizing any fighter escort. In addition to this, due to indecisiveness on behalf of the higher headquarters, the DBA remained inactive, with all its bombers in the rear for many hours.

18 SBs of 39 BAP/10 SAD managed to take off around 0700 and attacked the German tanks and motorized units of Heeresgruppe Mitte that crossed River Bug. At least one bridge was hit, but all 18 bombers were downed on the return flight.

The unescorted Soviet bomber missions during the first days of the war furnished the overall catastrophe with additional multiple losses. Nevertheless, the bomber crews kept flying, literally "to the last man," against the aggressor. This was not only a matter of obeying orders; these airmen were convinced that they represented the Motherland's last resort. From the air they could clearly see the full extent of the crisis. The courage and discipline displayed by the Soviet bomber crews during these first days of the war are almost unrivalled.

But it was only in the afternoon, more than ten hours after the German attack had started, that the forces of the Soviet Long-Range aviation, in the rear began to react. Again, the inability of the High Command stood in stark contrast to the desire among the lower ranks to strike back immediately. The Long-range aviation, the DBA, had been saved from attacks by its more remote airfields. But it took three and a half hours – until 0644 hours – before the order intake through the hierarchy of Stalinist bureaucracy allowed the DBA units to be placed in alert status. And typical to the Stalinist rule of behavior, the political leadership opened by displaying distrust in the airmen. Instead of immediately dispatching the bomber crews to support the hard-pressed troops in the border regions, political commissars summoned the fliers to meetings where they were lectured on the necessity to defend and die for Stalin and the Motherland. Only at around twenty to two in the afternoon could the orders from VVS KA's commander, General-Leytenant Pavel Zhigarev, for Bomber Corps 3 BAK to take off and attack the German troops at Suvalki be implemented.[25]

Due to both the vast destruction of the forward fighter bases, and the chaos wrought upon Soviet command and control through the German onslaught, there was no fighter escort available. The seventy twin-engine DB-3F bombers that were dispatched by 96 DBAP of 3 BAK on the

The German Messerschmitt Bf 109 F-4 fighter was without compare the best fighter plane in service by the time Germany invaded the Soviet Union. (Photo: Via Günther Rosipal.)

unit's first combat mission stood no chance of intercepting German fighters; twenty-two of these bomber crews failed to return to base, and many more returned with their aircraft badly shot up.[26]

Meanwhile, the devastating air base raids continued while other Luftwaffe planes pounced on Soviet command posts, troop billetings and communication centers, which contributed to the collapse of the entire command and control system on the Soviet side. At 1330 hours the Germans reported "wild flight on the Brest-Litovsk road" and "Russian command organization in complete confusion" in Heeresgruppe Mitte's combat zone.[27]

Throughout the afternoon of 22 June 1941, unescorted formations of Soviet bombers flew in desperate attempts to strike at the invasion forces. Over and over again they were shot down in large numbers. On several occasions, whole formations were completely wiped out by the Messerschmitt fighters. The highly trained German fighter pilots in their Bf 109s reaped an unprecedented harvest of aerial victories. Never before had the German fighter pilots been presented with such a large number of relatively "easy targets." JG 53 was the most successful Luftwaffe fighter unit, with seventy-four claims on 22 June, against only two own combat losses. Hauptmann Wolf-Dietrich Wilcke's III./JG 53 alone contributed with thirty-six Soviet aircraft shot down, and another twenty-eight destroyed on the ground.[28] JG 51 was credited with twelve fighters and fifty-seven bombers shot down, plus 129 reportedly destroyed on the ground. JG 54, operating from East Prussia, reported forty-five aerial victories, plus thirty-five aircraft destroyed on the ground, against only one own Bf 109 damaged due to hostile activity.[29] Regarding aircraft destroyed on the

ground, SKG 210 superceded all other units by reporting no less than 344 Soviet planes wrecked on the ground during attacks against fourteen airfields on 22 June, against seven own Bf 110s destroyed or damaged due to hostile activity. On this first day of the war with the USSR, the German report stated that 1,489 Soviet aircraft were destroyed on the ground. These figures appear incredible. They were even doubted by the Luftwaffe's commander in chief, Reichsmarschall Hermann Göring, who had them secretly checked: "For days on end, officers from his command staff picked their way about the airfields overrun by the German advance, counting the burnt-out wrecks of Russian planes. The result was even more astonishing: their tally exceeded 2,000."[30]

On the evening of 22 June, the Headquarters of the German Armed Forces described the overall picture of the first day of the offensive: "The enemy was surprised by the German attack. His forces were not in tactical disposition for defense. The troops in the border zone were widely scattered in their quarters. The frontier itself was for the most part weakly guarded. As a result of this tactical surprise, enemy resistance directly on the border was weak and disorganized, and we succeeded everywhere in seizing the bridges across the border rivers and in piercing the defense positions (field fortifications) near the frontier. Our divisions on the entire offensive front have forced back the enemy on an average of 10 to 12 km. This has opened the path for the offensive."[31]

The greatest results had been achieved by the two army groups north of the Pripyat marshes. In particular Hoth's Panzergruppe 3 of Heeresgruppe Mitte achieved "a remarkable success," pushing through the forest

SOVIET REACTION TO THE GERMAN ONSLAUGHT.

Young Soviet women volunteer to fight against the invaders.

The reactions to the German onslaught differed widely between the Soviet leadership and the population. The official mobilization began only on the second day. But already on the first day, recruitment offices in towns and cities all across the Soviet Union were flooded by huge numbers of volunteers. As if taken from a scene in a Soviet propaganda film, places of work and universities marched as entire groups to enlist for military service. This was something that the government had not anticipated – such was the degree of mistrust in its own population – so there was no structure, no planning to handle this storm of Soviet patriotism. Semyon Silberstein, a 17-year old Komsomol member remembers that the news of the outbreak of war was received with great cheering among the Komsomol members of his group. "We felt that at last we will be able to beat those terrible fascists", he said.

Robert Borok, a Red Army artillery soldier, remembers that he was very excited when he learned that war had broken out and immediately wanted to go to the front. "We were all united by the sentiment of defending our beloved motherland from the enemy," said Yevgeniya Gurulyeva-Smirnova, an 18-year-old aviatrix who volunteered to become a bomber pilot.

The mobilization brought in 5.3 million men to the Red Army, but there was not enough equipment for all of them. Many were sent to the front without firearms. In order to take in all the volunteers, militia units were set up parallel to new regular military units. These so-called istrebitelnyy (fighter) and Narodnoe Opolcheniye (people's militia) battalions were hastily formed and badly equipped. "They gave us hunting rifles, one for every five men, and five sabres. That was it!" said Vladimir Dolmatov, who by the age of seventeen volunteered for such a unit. "No uniforms – everyone wore whatever they came in with, and went to fight." With little or no military training, these militias were sent straight to the front, where they were mercilessly butchered by the Germans. But testifying to the stalwart desire to fight the invaders, Dolmatov, as one of a handful of survivors from his first People's Militia battalion immediately volunteered for front service again.

ADVANCE INTO THE SOVIET UNION.

1. *Wehrmacht troops mounted on Panzer IIIs during the attack against the Soviet Union.*

2. *German troops advancing past a deserted Soviet railway station.*

3. *Panzer III tanks on the advance.*

1.	
2.	
3.	

A destroyed Soviet BA-10 armored car.

and lake country to the Neman river and capturing the important Neman river crossings at Alytus and Merkine: "There is no organized enemy resistance in front of it. Full operational freedom of movement appears to have been achieved in this sector," was reported in the forenoon of 22 June.[32] Before midday, 7. Panzer-Division of Panzergruppe 3 managed to secure a bridgehead across River Neman at Alytus in southern Lithuania. Under interrogation, a captured Soviet pioneer officer revealed that he had been ordered to blow up the bridges at Alytus at 1900 hrs on 22 June. However, fearing repercussions if he on his own initiative destroyed the bridges earlier, he failed to act when the German advance group approached the site earlier than the appointed time.[33] But then elements of Soviet 5th Tank Division of the Baltic Special Military

District appeared, launching for the first time a handful of T-34 tanks against the Germans – with devastating effect. Eleven German tanks (including four Panzer IVs) were destroyed and many more knocked out (although later on they were able to be salvaged and repaired).[34] The Germans were lucky that only weak elements of the Soviet tank division managed to reach Alytus. While their tanks withdrew out of range of the Soviet guns, the Luftwaffe was called in. The aircraft struck down on the Soviet force just as 20. Panzer-Division – which just had seized the airfield at Alytus – appeared from the southwest. The Soviets withdrew, leaving 73 tanks behind. 16 of these were T-34s and the remainder light tanks.[35]

Generaloberst Franz Halder, the Chief of the German General Staff, noted that Guderian's Panzergruppe 2 had

THE MYTH OF STALIN'S COLLAPSE.

In his famous speech to the 20th Congress of the Communist Party of the Soviet Union in February 1956, First Secretary Nikita Khrushchev said: "After the first severe disaster and defeat at the front Stalin thought that this was the end. In one of his speeches in those days he said: 'All that Lenin created we have lost forever!' After this Stalin, for a long time ceased to do anything whatever."

This has transferred into one of the most long-lasting misunderstandings surrounding Operation Barbarossa. However, according to research made by Steven Main of the University of Edinburgh into Stalin's appointments diaries this was nothing but disinformation on behalf of Khrushchev. Interestingly, the story was not repeated in Khrushchev's post-war autobiography, a large part of which deals with World War II and Stalin.

Main shows that Stalin's official working day on 22 June 1941 began at 0545 and ended at 1645: "Stalin held meetings with a variety of senior Soviet government and military figures, including Molotov (People's Commissar for Foreign Affairs), Timoshenko (People's Commissar for Defence), Zhukov (Chief of Staff of the Red Army), Kuznetsov (Commander of both North Caucasus and Baltic Military Districts), and Shaposhnikov (Deputy People's Commissar for Defence). All in all, on the very first day of the attack, Stalin held meetings with over 15 individual members of the Soviet government and military apparatus".

On 23 June, when the Soviet dictator was supposed to have suffered from his "collapse," he worked for 22 hours and 35 minutes. Following such an exhausting day, Stalin's shortest working day was 24 June, lasting a little over five hours. This might be the nucleus of Khrushchev's allegations. However, for 25/26 June, Stalin held 24 hours of meetings. On 27 June, according to Main, "his recorded working days ran to a little over ten hours and, possibly as a result of this physically and mentally punishing schedule. his working day for 28 June again lasted a little over 5 hours".

Thus, far from slipping into a state of paralyzation, Stalin worked for 168 hours during the entire week of 22–28 June.

Source: "Stalin in June 1941: A Comment on Cynthia Roberts" by Steven J. Main in *Europe-Asia Studies*, Volume 48, No.5 (July 1996).

"gained operational freedom of movement" and "will start rolling on the Brest – Minsk highway", although its southern wing (3. and 4. Panzer divisions) had been held up for a time in difficult wooded terrain. To the south, Kleist's Panzergruppe 1 had encountered the heaviest resistance, but was able to get moving around noon.

But the report also also noted that "after the first shock, the enemy has turned to fight." Concerning Heeresgruppe Nord, Halder wrote that Generaloberst Erich Hoepner's Panzergruppe 4 "has battled its way to the Dubysa River and captured two crossings intact. Here the enemy will be able to throw fresh forces against us from his rear area in the next few days."

The image was more dismal from the Soviet perspective. Late in the afternoon on 22 June, Mladshiy Leytenant Fyodor Arkhipenko, a fighter pilot of of 17 IAP, made a reconnaissance flight along the border, from Brest to the region of Lvov. He recalled: "The entire area on our side was on fire. Everything, the towns, the villages, the settlements, everything was burning."

Offensive in the Center, June–September 1941.

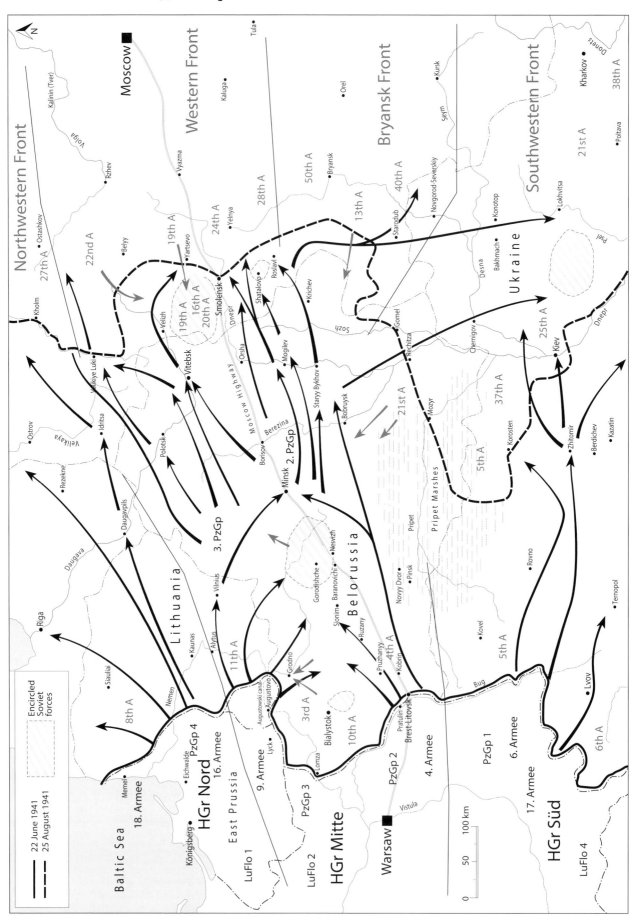

6: THE FIRST BATTLES OF ANNIHILATION.

"Shorn of communications, running low on ammunition and out of fuel, fighting against enemy encirclements."

– Soviet Marshal Grigoriy Kulik on the state of the 10th Army, 24 June 1941.

In spite of the devastating blows inflicted on the Red Army units during the first hours of the German attack, Stalin issued Directive No. 3 in the evening on 22 June. Signed by Marshal Timoshenko, this demanded a general counter-offensive to push back the Germans "without any regards for borders." This was nothing less than a death sentence for the Western Military District (ZOVO). Simultaneously, the military districts were brought to a state of war, renamed "fronts," the Soviet equivalent of the German army groups. The Leningrad Military District became the Northern Front; the Baltic Special Military District became the Northwestern Front; ZOVO became the Western Front; KOVO became the Southwestern Front; and OVO (Odessa Military District), the Southern Front. The Soviet leadership also established a new High Command, the so-called Stavka.

The confused commander of ZOVO/Western Front, General Armii Pavlov, decided to launch the five mechanized corps under his command in a counter-attack. But the headquarters of ZOVO's 3rd, 4th and 10th armies remained cut off from communications with most of their troops, and thus were unable to forward the instructions. Initially, Pavlov only managed to contact the 13th and 14th Mechanized corps. The former, however, had only half its assigned tank strength, consisting of 540 obsolete tankettes, mainly T-26s, and it had been so badly mauled by German air attacks in the Kobrin area that it simply could not be organized for any attack.* The 13th Mechanized Corps attacked Guderian's Panzergruppe 2 late on 22 June, but was severely hampered by many faults, several owing to pure mismanagement – mechanical failures, shortage of fuel and a lack of armor-piercing ammunition.[1] The 25th Tank Division of this mechanized corps reported, "Motorized enemy units operate only on the roads, boldly drive into the rear and position themselves in the settlements... Thus, the enemy is tied to the roads, the speed of his advance depends on the quality of the roads. The enemy's motorized units operate with a total impudence; when [our forces] withdraw, he looks for the weakest flanks, when his attacks are unsuccessful he immediately switches to an artillery barrage, and when KV tanks appear he concentrates all means against them..."[2]

In an attempt to restore communications with the 10th Army at Biyalystok, which was not even able to contact ZOVO headquarters in Minsk, Pavlov's deputy, General-Leytenant Ivan Boldin, decided to do what Pavlov was prohibited from – to fly to Biyalystok in the afternoon of 22 June. This would give him quite an illustrative picture of the situation.

En route the SB bomber in which he traveled was damaged by Bf 109 fighters and had to force-land 35 kilometers from Biyalystok. Reaching the highway, where he intended to take a truck to Biyalytsok, he found the road to be filled with confused people not knowing where to go. "Everything is on fire!" said a man with a look of exhaustion in his face.[3] Boldin hitch-hiked with a truck, but after only a few minutes he heard the sound of aircraft engines. "Three bombers appeared," he explained. "They dived until they were only two hundred meters above the ground and then they began to rake the road with machine gun fire. People ran – but where to? Where is shelter to be found against these impudent Hitlerites, who even hunt individual people on the road! Our truck was hit by their machine guns. The driver was killed, and I was barely able to escape by jumping from the cabin of the running vehicle. Except for my adjutant and an orderly, no one on board the truck

Civilian refugees and Red Army soldiers lie side by side at a road, victims of a Luftwaffe attack.

* In consequence, Stalin had its commander, General-Mayor Stepan Ilich Oborin, arrested and executed.

A Soviet T-34 medium tank in an ambush position. (Photo: Ivan Nartsissov.)

survived. I approached a body. It was still warm, but the head was completely shattered by bullets. Next to the wreck of our truck lay a ZIS-101 limousine. Everyone inside, women, children and the driver, had been killed." [4]

Boldin continued on foot. He met an engineer who came from Biyalystok and said that the city was completely destroyed. Over and over again, Boldin had to take cover from strafing German aircraft. The road was lined with traces of death and destruction. When he arrived at Biyalystok he found that the engineer had not exaggerated. He continued his narrative: "Ahead there is a railway crossing. A freight train crammed with people slowly passes by. But the steam from the engine obviously draws the attention of the enemy. Suddenly Fascist aircraft appear. Explosions are heard, followed by the heart-breaking screams from women and children. Hundreds are killed or maimed before our eyes. In the midst of the turmoil, two medical nurses in white dressing gowns show up. The military commander of the station comes running towards me. His head is bandaged and his shirt is covered with blood. I order him to immediately clear the destroyed cars from the tracks, remove the bodies of the dead and evacuate the wounded. He looks at me with begging eyes: 'Comrade General, that is not possible. There are no people to carry out your orders.'" [5]

The headquarters building of the 10th Army lay in ruins. It was not until late in the evening that Boldin managed to locate the command post, comprised of two tents and a car, on the outskirts of Biyalystok. He found the Army commander, General-Mayor Konstantin Gol-

ubev, who told him that all telephone lines were cut and that hardly any radio communication worked. His voice agitated, Golubev reported the situation: "At dawn, three enemy army corps, supported by a large number of tanks and bombers, attacked the 5th Rifle Corps on my left flank. We already sustained heavy losses during the initial hours. The 113th Rifle Division was particularly badly hit. In order to prevent the enemy from advancing further, I have ordered the 13th mechanized Corps to River Kurets, but there are only few tanks in the divisions." Then he vented his feeling of hopelessness: "And, by the way, what can be expected from our old T-26s? They are good only for shooting sparrows!" Continuing his report, Golubev said, "In the center, straight towards Biyalystok, the enemy's 42nd [XLII.] Army Corps is attacking my 1st Rifle Corps. I have ordered my 6th Mechanized Corps to establish positions at River Tsarev."

Then he let fly again, "But how can we fight with any success when almost all our aircraft and anti-aircraft artillery are destroyed, only very little ammunition is available, and we are running out of fuel!" When Boldin asked how this could be, Golubev sighed and explained, " Right from the start of the attack, enemy aircraft bombed our fuel depots. They are still burning. Fuel tanks were also destroyed on the railway…"

In that moment, General-Mayor Igor Nikitin, the commander of the 6th Cavalry Corps, appeared. With a most distressed look he reported, "The 6th [Cavalry] Division is annihilated. As the enemy attacked, it was south of Lomza. In the beginning everything went well. 'Konniki' [the divisional commander General-Major Mikhail Petrovich Konstantinov] fought well. They literally covered the ground with enemy corpses and did not fall back a single step. But then the enemy brought in a group of aircraft." Nikitin made a gesture of hopelessness with his hands: "How is cavalry supposed to fight against aircraft! There was no protection, and the Fascists mowed down the entire division!" Then he looked at Boldin and said in a low voice, "Poor people. They were good lads, all of them. They died like eagles, one after another. . ."

At that moment, an orderly reported that communication with Pavlov's headquarters had been established, and that Pavlov was on the line. "Here are my orders," Pavlov said, "organize a counter-attack in the direction of Biyalystok - south of Grodno with the 6th Mechanized Corps, the 36th Cavalry Division and elements of the 11th Mechanized Corps. Your task is to eliminate the enemy force on the left bank of River Neman. You will answer personally for the carrying out of this order!" Boldin objected, asking how Golubev would be able to carry out the order when his units had sustained heavy losses and were barely able to defend themselves against the enemy. Pavlov was silent for several minutes, and then he just said, "That is all. Follow my orders," and then he hung up.

"I reflected on how divorced from reality Pavlov was," Boldin wrote after the war. "We had only weak forces for

Fallen Red Army troops next to a BT-7 tank which has been abandoned, possibly due to a lack of petrol. (Photo: Arno Becker.)

a counter-attack. All units that Pavlov demanded should attack were already involved in severe fighting and had taken heavy losses. To detach them would mean a weakening of the defense. Moreover, we had lost communication with the 11th Mechanized Corps and had no idea where it was and in what state, but what could we do? Orders are orders!"[6]

Before the counter-attack by this the so-called "Boldin Group" had even been launched early on 23 June, a German air attack hit the 10th Army's command post, killing General-Major Ivan Mikhailin, the Assistant Commander in Chief for Fortified Areas in the Western Special Military District. Meanwhile, another Luftwaffe formation caught the 36th Cavalry Division in open ground and inflicted a terrible bloodbath on the horsemen, rendering the division completely unable to take part in the counter-attack.

Then the "Boldin Group" struck German VIII. Armeekorps at Grodno on the right flank of Generaloberst Hoth's Panzergruppe 3. "At the onset of our tank attack, the enemy suffered heavy losses in tanks and withdrew his armor behind his infantry," the subsequent report of the 11th Mechanized Corps read, "but then they brought in their aviation…"[7] Almost without any interference from Soviet fighters, Fliegerkorps VIII's close-support aircraft were able to break the backbone of the counter-attack. General Wolfram von Richthofen, commanding Fliegerkorps VIII, in fact despatched almost all aircraft types – bombers, Stukas, Zerstörer, assault planes and strafing fighters – against the counter-attacking forces.

Feldwebel Hermann Neuhoff, who flew a Messerschmitt 109 with JG 53, recalled: "We found the main roads in the area heavily congested with Russian vehicles of all kinds, but no fighter opposition and very little Flak. We made one gunnery run after another and caused a terrible destruction on the ground. Everything was on fire when we returned to base."[8]

On 24 June, desperate General-Major Ivan Khatskilevich, the 6th Mechanized Corps' commander, called the 10th Army headquarters. "Comrade General, we are running out of fuel and ammunition," he reported with an agitated voice. "Our tankmen are fighting courageously, but without ammunition and fuel our tanks are helpless! If you can provide us with what we need we shall beat the Nazis!" Boldin replied, shouting at the top of his voice to make himself heard while the air was filled with the droning of dozens of German aircraft engines, "Can you hear me, comrade Khatskilevich? Wait! I shall take vigorous measures to supply you with what you need!" With all communications with the headquarters in Minsk severed, he despatched two aircraft – in the hope that at least one of them would arrive – to deliver the message to Pavlov of an urgent need of air-dropped supplies of fuel and ammunition. But neither of them reached their destination; they were both shot down.

To make things worse, Marshal Grigoriy Kulik landed at the headquarters of the 10th Army. Boldin briefed him on the difficult situation. Kulik listened, and then he just made a helpless gesture. "Yes," he said with nothing but uncertainty in his voice.[9] A report from the 10th Army described Kulik's very strange appearance: "The behaviour of Marshal Kulik was incomprehensible. He ordered everyone to remove their rank insignias, throw away all documents and then change into peasant garb, which he himself did also. He carried no documents. He suggested that we throw away our weapons, and he asked me personally to get rid of my awards and documents. However, except for his adjutant, a Mayor whose name I have forgotten, no one threw away their documents or weapons. He explained this by saying that if the enemy caught us, they would take us for peasants and let us go. Kulik left in a horse-drawn cart along the very road where German tanks had just passed. At a river he waited while some men constructed a raft for him."[10]

Later on 24 June, General-Major Khatskilevich arrived at the 10th Army headquarters to inform Golubev and Boldin that he had decided to use the very last shells to destroy the remaining tanks rather than giving them up to the enemy. Then he departed for the battlefield, never to return again. His charred body was found in the wreck of a destroyed tank near Grodno. The 6th Mechanized Corps scattered, with the surviving troops withdrawing to the east in small groups, and the equipment abandoned or destroyed en masse. "Our troops had to retreat and spread out in small groups and hid in the forests," Boldin wrote.[11] Apparently, his opponent, Generaloberst Heinz Guderian, ran into one of these scattered groups. "On 24 June at 0825 hrs. I left my headquarters and drove towards Slonim [100 km southeast of Grodno]," he wrote. "The 17. Panzer-Division had meanwhile arrived at this town. Between [Ruzany] and Slonim I ran into Russian infantry which was laying down fire on the main road. A battery of the 17. Panzer-Division and dismounted motor-cyclists were returning enemy fire without any particular success. I joined in this action and by firing the machine gun in my armored command vehicle succeeded in dislodging the enemy from his position; I was then able to drive on. At 1130 hrs, I arrived at the headquarters of the 17. Panzer-Division."[12]

The charred body of a Soviet tank man who attempted to abandon his burning BT-2 tankette too early during a tank battle in Belarus in the summer of 1941. (Photo: Arno Becker.)

The aerial onslaught against the Western Front's counter-attacking forces continued until nightfall on 24 June, long after the Soviets had consumed their last assets of fuel and ammunition. The German airmen reported 105 tanks destroyed. In effect, Pavlov's counter-attack was completely routed. The 11th Mechanized Corps alone lost 275 of its 305 tanks, and of 60,000 men, only 600 survived. The 6th Cavalry Corps sustained more than 50 percent casualties, mostly due to air attacks.[13]

Alexander Cohrs, a German soldier, described the scene as it looked when he arrived a couple of days later: "Around 150 tanks were spread out in the terrain, some of them of the heaviest kind, as well as hundreds of trucks and other materiel. Between them lay large numbers of dead Russians, probably more than a thousand. We saw terrible scenes; soldiers who had been flattened by tank tracks.

Once I stepped on something soft. To my dismay I discovered that it was a flattened head. We saw many who had been unable to abandon their tanks and had been burned alive inside – they had shrunk into tiny figures. The sun scorched this forested, hilly area. On the right hand side a cavalry attack had probably been made. The ground was filled with dead Russians and horses."[14]

Right from the outset, the German invasion army conducted the war of annihilation that Hitler had spoken of. "I saw many lying about, having been shot with their hands raised and without any arms or belts," German soldier Unteroffizier Robert Rupp wrote in his diary. "I saw at least one hundred in that position. It was said that even a parliamentarian who came with a white flag had been shot. Wounded men had also been shot."[15]

Only comparatively few Wehrmacht commanders are known to have raised their voices against such atrocities. One of them was General Joachim Lemelsen, the commander of LXVII. Armeekorps of Panzergruppe 2. On 24 June, he issued the following instructions to his troops: "I have observed that senseless shootings of both POWs and civilians have taken place. A Russian soldier who has been taken prisoner while wearing a uniform and after he put up a brave fight, has the right to decent treatment."[16] But obviously this had little effect. Five days later, Lemelsen complained at "scenes of countless bodies of soldiers lying on the roads, having clearly been killed by a shot through the head at point blank range, without their weapons and with their hands raised."[17] Still, not even Lemelsen had any objections to the execution of political commissars. In the same report, he emphasized that the fight was against "the oppression of a Jewish and criminal group"; he said that "the instructions of the Führer calls for ruthless action against Bolshevism (political commissars)" and demanded that "people who have been clearly identified as such should be taken aside and shot," albeit "only by order of an officer."[18]

Generalfeldmarschall Günther Kluge, the commander of 4. Armee, personally ordered the execution of women in uniform.[19] At the outbreak of the war, very few Soviet women served in the first-line forces – their participation in fighting was not encouraged by the conservative leadership – but many women had gone through paramilitary civil defense training. On the day the war broke out, however, tens of thousands of young Soviet women volunteered to fight, and some of them managed to make it to the frontline.

The Soviet command became absolutely stunned by the ferocious onslaught. On 24 June, Pavlov seemed to have slipped into an astounding passivity, making no attempts to close the gaps that had been torn in his frontlines. However, the reaction of the majority of the *Frontovniki* – as the Soviet soldiers were called – was quite different. Indeed, they felt that they had been let down by their own leadership, which had not prepared them for this assault. "The people said that they have betrayed us," said Red Army radio operator Boris Lyubovits. "They said: 'All our life we have been working, giving our last money for defense loans, and now we have been deceived and betrayed by

German machine gun crew advances to obtain a firing position against a Soviet point of resistance. (Photo: Via Daniel Johansson.)

those above.'"[20] But quite contrary to what the Germans had expected, they offered a determined resistance to the attackers everywhere, and this completely stunned the *Landser*, the German soldiers. "We had never seen soldiers fighting with such determination," said one of them. "Although we passed by and surrounded them, groups of two or three Russians refused to give up their positions. They preferred death to any retreat. The only possibility of taking any prisoners was if they were wounded and unconscious."[21] On 23 June the Chief of the German High Command, Generaloberst Halder, lamented over "the absence of any large gathering of prisoners."[22]

Although lacking any escort fighters, the Soviet bomber fliers continued their persistent attempts to hit the invading enemy, at a terrible cost for themselves. On Heeresgruppe Mitte's right flank, General-Mayor Fyodor Polynin's bomber wing 13 BAD attacked Panzergruppe 2 in the area of Grudopole, Pilovidy, and Ivantsevichi, halfway between Brest and Minsk. These Soviet bombers, and scattered remnants of VVS Western Front's SB units, continued to fly against Guderian's armored forces throughout 24 June. In doing so, they ran the gauntlet of JG 51's fighter pilots. For ten hours, these hurled themselves against numerous unescorted bomber formations, each consisting of between 12 and 20 aircraft. Oberleutnant Karl-Heinz Schnell claimed seven victories on 24 June 1941 – including four SBs in just two minutes. Leutnant Ottmar Maurer claimed another six, including three in a single minute. On one mission against the highway east of Brest, Soviet bomber regiment 212 DBAP lost 28

DB-3s.[23] One of the pilots, Leytenant Yevgeniy Borisenko recalled:

"The bombers caught fire all along the line and fell as burning torches, leaving black trails of smoke behind. All around them hung the parachutes of the airmen, which the Germans attacked and killed them with their machine guns. My plane was above the target. I dropped the bombs and started turning the crate when suddenly a gang of German fighters turned their attention towards me. My gunner Nechayev defended us bravely, and even managed to shoot down one of the German fighters. But suddenly his machine gun went quiet. Now the Fascists could open fire at me without any hindrance. The navigator Fetisov was wounded, and then the right engine was ablaze. In a hailstorm of enemy bullets, Fetisov fell dead to the floor."

All in all, the Germans claimed to have destroyed 557 Soviet aircraft on 24 June. As Russian historian Viktor Kulikov proves, the Soviet losses were actually higher than the German estimations. While the Germans reported the destruction of around 3,100 Soviet aircraft during the first three days of the war, Soviet records list 3,922 aircraft losses during the same period.[24]

However, one fighter wing that had escaped destruction because it was based in the rear was 43 IAD, assigned with the task of defending Minsk against air attacks. On 24 June the pilots of Soviet fighter wing fought hard against repeated waves of German bombers and dive-bombers which came in to attack Minsk. On this day, Kesselring had decided to destroy the Belorussian capital. "Our mission read: Destroy the northern exits from Minsk in order to block the supply traffic, and as a secondary objective target the enemy columns on the roads northwest of Minsk," wrote Hauptmann Helmut Mahlke, the commander of Stuka group III./StG 1.

As his formation of twenty-six Ju 87s approached the target, they were met by a breathtaking sight: "Far ahead… a vast sea of flames: Minsk! Other Luftwaffe units have apparently been successful in their attacks." [25]

Right above the burning city, six I-16s of 43 IAD's 163 IAP fell upon twenty-six Ju 87s of StG 1 and StG 2. Led by Starshiy Leytenant Zakhar Plotnikov, a veteran from the Spanish Civil War, the I-16 pilots shot down seven dive-bombers (according to German loss records) without any own losses.[26] In all, 163 IAP/43 IAD claimed twenty-one aerial victories in this area on 24 June. Total Luftwaffe combat losses on the Eastern Front on 24 June were 70 aircraft, of which 40 were totally destroyed.[27] But as Mahlke so laconically put it from the perspective of the attacker, other Luftwaffe units had been successful in their attacks: large parts of the city lay in ruins, and the number of victims probably counted in the thousands. "The city is bombed throughout the whole day," reads an account from one of Minsk's citizens. "The entire center of the city was destroyed – all that remained was a pair of large buildings. Everything else in the center is in ruins. When the bombing began in the morning, I was in at work in the Pedagogical Institute. We sought shelter in the basement, and the sight that met us when we came out was terrible! Burning houses, ashes, ruins, and everywhere in the streets – dead bodies. The people tried to flee out of the city during the bombing, but the streets were crammed. And those who in getting out were mown down by German aircraft that came swooping down at low level." [28]

Having dropped their bombs – which exploded "as gigantic mushrooms right where they were supposed to," according to Mahlke – the dive-bombers swept down over the masses of people and vehicles that jammed the highway to Minsk. "And then – onwards! At low level against

Dead Soviet soldiers in a roadside ditch. Considering the fact that they carry no belts, it is probable that these men were shot after being captured.

the road," wrote Mahlke.[29] On the ground, a Russian on the highway to Minsk recalled, "people were fleeing eastward in panic, on foot, to look for a place to hide from the onrushing enemy. The highway was jammed with demolished trucks, smashed cannon, and discarded machine guns. Now and again, aircraft with Nazi emblem swooped over this pile of assorted weapons. They flew so low that we could see the mocking, contemptuous faces of the German thugs. They made one foray after another, 'playfully' firing their machine guns into groups of terror-stricken people on the road, mostly women holding children by the hand or in their arms." [30]

On Heeresgruppe Mitte's southern flank, Panzergruppe 2 surged ahead on the Brest-Minsk highway to occupy Baranovichi and Slonim on 24 June, while Panzergruppe 3 on the northern flank seized the Lithuanian capital Vilnius. Thus the Soviet troops in the so-called Suvalki border pocket northwest of Biyalystok were sealed off. They immediately initiated desperate but fruitless attempts to break out. Leutnant Georg Kreuter of German 18. Panzer-Division wrote, "Everything is upside down at the command post. A Russian column had attacked our advance road from the west. These men probably tried to get out of the encirclement. Some of their trucks were able to be set ablaze by a tank that by chance was under repair at the command post. They are a strange people. Even some German communists were among them. Most of them were civilians, even women and children."[31] It should be pointed out that Kreuter received his impression from the dead Soviets that he saw after the combat, in which he did not take part himself…

In the occupied towns and villages, a complete rule of terror began. A Soviet woman interviewed after the war recalled, "The Germans would settle into houses in the villages and take what they needed to live, and they did whatever they wanted to here. They took our hope. They came in quickly and asked for eggs and milk, yelling, screaming, running after girls, taking everything. They were even killing pigs. They destroyed everything and ate eggs, milk, running under the houses and yelling, 'where are those eggs and milk?' They were already taken!" [32]

The occupiers also immediately set about to root out any Communist presence. Friedrich Falevich, a Jewish youngster, recalled: "Right from the start the Germans started arresting and killing Communists, Komsomol members and activists. On the first day they killed 26 people. The Germans didn't act on their own. There were traitors, who thought the Soviet regime had mistreated them. All this mud got stirred up. They were former prisoners in jails or camps, or those who had been exiled and had been hiding their attitude towards the Soviets regime. These people served the Germans and worked in the police. They helped the Germans to make the lists and showed them the right houses where Communists or Jews lived. This was the first time I heard the word '*zhyd*' [a derogative Russian word for Jews]. During the German occupation it became a normal part of our everyday life. We stayed at home as if it was a cage expecting to be arrested or killed. Everybody in Slutsk knew we were the family of a communist and that we were Jews. However, people helped us

↑ The commander of the Soviet Western Front, General Armii Dmitry Pavlov (left), with (from left to right) General-Leytenant Maksim Purkayev, (the Chief of Staff of the Southwestern Front), General Armii Kirill Meretskov, and Marshal Semyon Timoshenko. This photo was taken before the war. Both Pavlov and Meretskov were arrested in July 1941. While Pavlov was executed, Meretskov survived, albeit suffering terrible torture by the NKVD. According to Nikita Khrushchev, the torture was so severe that Meretskov could hardly speak.

← German infantry with an armored troop carrier enter a village where Soviet troops offer a stiff resistance. (Photo: Via Daniel Johansson.)

even in this critical situation. Some policemen knew and respected my father. They helped us to survive; otherwise we would have been killed."[33]

The large-scale atrocities committed by the Germans led to frequent cases of Soviet civilians or soldiers taking a bloody revenge on German soldiers that fell into their hands. This in turn led to further German killings of civilians. When a regiment of 9. Armee's 5. Infanterie-Division discovered the bodies of five murdered German POWs on 28 June, the execution of 50 Jews was ordered.[34] On 25 June, the Soviets desperately launched new counter-attacks at Grodno. Following the failure to break through the German fighter shield on the previous day, the bombers units of VVS Northwestern Front and the Long-Range Aviation DBA now instead were tasked with wiping out Fliegerkorps VIII's fighters on the ground. But the continuing lack of escort fighters caused these efforts also to end in failure. To be able to intervene more rapidly, the German fighter units were brought forward. Early on 25 June, Messerschmitt Bf 109s of fighter wings JG 27 and JG 53 were shifted to the large air base on the outskirts of Vilnius. As they moved in to that airfield, the Germans found 56 Soviet aircraft wrecks, the sad remnants of 57 SAD.

The vicinity of the air base at Vilnius became the scene of another carnage in the air. Throughout 25 June, formation after formation of Soviet bombers tried to break through and attack the airfields. Each time, they were pounced on by fighters from JG 27 and JG 53. One of the German fighter pilots involved in this melee, Leutnant Gustav Langanke, succeeded in shooting down seven bombers.[35] At dusk, the burned-out wrecks of 53 DB-3s and SBs – and one Bf 109 – lay scattered around Vilnius.

The counter-attacking Red Army forces meanwhile became subject to intense air attacks – Fliegerkorps VIII directed over five hundred sorties against the Soviet coun-

ter-attack on 25 June, reportedly destroying 30 tanks and fifty lorries.

Farther south, Soviet bomber units continued to be dispatched against Panzergruppe 2's spearheads. This led to terrible new bomber losses at the hands of German fighter wing JG 51, which was led by the top ace Oberstleutnant Werner Mölders. From 24 June onwards, the German fighter units on the Eastern Front maintained continuous fighter patrols, their Bf 109s operating in independent four-plane Schwarm or two-plane Rotte formations over the tank spearheads. Using this tactic, Mölders and his pilots claimed to have downed 70 Soviet aircraft, all SBs, on 25 June – this time against only four own aircraft shot down.[36] Werner Mölders himself blew two SB bombers out of the sky in a single minute, thus increasing his total victory score in World War II to 75 (89 if those in the Spanish Civil War are included).

The claimed score for the Luftwaffe on 25 June, 1941, was 351 Soviet aircraft destroyed, while twenty-five German aircraft were destroyed in combat and twenty-two received battle damage on the Eastern Front.[37] At the end of the day, bomber and Stuka units returned from their missions, reporting that it was increasingly difficult to find "sufficient" amounts of undamaged Soviet aircraft to attack on the ground. Flying over Soviet-controlled areas, airfield after airfield was seen littered with scores of aircraft wrecks, with very few remaining serviceable. Hence it was decided to shift the main mission of the bombers, the Stukas, and the Zerstörer from air-base raids to tactical support at the front.

On 26 June, the bombers of Luftflotte 2 were brought in to attack roads and railways in the Soviet rear area, where trains and large columns of fresh Soviet troops were seen to be moving *towards* the front. While the Western Front seemed to be approaching total annihi-

THE MINSK GHETTO.

When the Germans occupied Minsk, large parts of the city had been turned into a heap of rubble through Luftwaffe bombings, and of its 250,000 inhabitants, 60 percent had either fled or been killed. Among the remaining 100,000, half were Jews. The Germans herded them into the ghetto, where they would soon meet a grim fate.

The Minsk ghetto was the largest Jewish ghetto in the German-occupied parts of the Soviet Union. It had over 100,000 Jewish inhabitants – including 50–60,000 original Minsk inhabitants, at least 30,000 Jews resettled from the vicinity, and 7,000 German Jews who were deported there in November and December 1941. Crammed in a two square kilometer-area, the population had to survive on a daily ration of 200 grammes of bread per person.

Subject to hard forced labor, daily intimidations and regular shootings from the guards from the SS and Lithuanian and Belarussian auxiliary policemen, the ghetto population rapidly diminished. On 7–8 November the Germans and their allies "celebrated" the 24th anniversary of the October Revolution by executing between five and eighteen thousand of the ghetto's inhabitants. On 20 November another 20,000 were killed. Further massacres followed on 21 January 1942, with over 12,000 Jews killed, and on 2 March 1942 with 8,000 killed. During the spring of 1942, a large number of the ghetto's children were gassed. Another mass killing took place on 28 July, claiming 25,000 victims.

In August 1942, only 9,000 survivors remained. The last inhabitants were killed when the Germans annihilated the ghetto on 21 October 1943.

However, the Minsk ghetto also was characterized by its strong resistance movement. One of its most important leaders was Hersh Smolar, a dedicated Communist and writer. Jewish forced workers in German factories in Minsk regularly managed to smuggle both arms and ammunitions from these factories and to the Belarus partisans. In fact, about 10,000 Jews managed to escape the ghetto and formed independent partisan groups in the forests in the surrounding area.[1]

The Minsk ghetto. (Photo: Fold3.)

1 Epstein, *The Minsk Ghetto 1941–1943: Jewish Resistance and Soviet Internationalism*, p. 41.

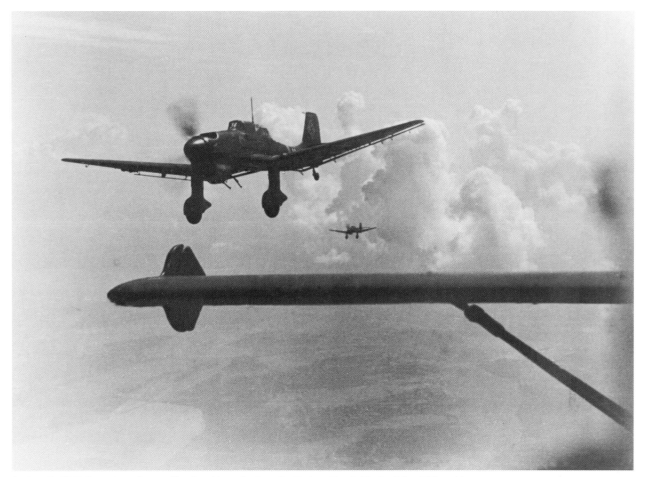

Junkers Ju 87 Stukas return from a dive-bombing attack on the Eastern Front. (Photo: Erhard Jähnert.)

lation, new Red Army forces were streaming westwards. In desperation, the Soviet High Command sent its entire reserve, five armies (the 13th, 19th, 20th, 21st and 22nd) to save the Western Front. Commanded by Marshal Semyon Budyonnyy, the new Front of Reserve armies was under instruction to form a rear defense line from Vitebsk on the Dvina River to Kremenchug on the Dnepr River. But constant air raids kept taking a heavy tribute of these units, especially where there was congestion of troops and vehicles at river crossings.

The Germans also brought forward fresh troops. Generaloberst Maximilian von Weichs' German 2. Armee, which had been in Heeresgruppe Mitte's reserve, was now ordered forward to assist in the battle. Panzergruppen 2 and 3 swung around to capture the city of Minsk, the Belarus capital, which took place on 28 June.

Minsk was a tremendously important communications hub, with highways and railway links to Brest in the southwest, a hard-surface highway to Vilnius in the northwest, rail connection with Gomel in the southeast, and the famous hard-surface highway running from Minsk, through Smolensk, to Moscow. Also possessing a large, well-equipped airfield, Minsk was of utmost importance to the continued German campaign in the central combat zone of the Eastern Front, and would remain so until the Red Army recaptured the city three years later.

With Panzergruppen 2 and 3 linking up at Minsk, the 3rd, 4th and 10th Soviet armies – with a combined strength of nearly half a million men positioned to defend Minsk to the west of the city – became sealed off and left mainly leaderless. On 26 June, Marshal Kliment Voroshilov, the People's Commissar for Defense, arrived at the headquarters of the Western Front in Mogilev. There he found the C.O., General Armii Pavlov, completely broken down. "I am done with!" Pavlov exclaimed. He pointed out that the collapse of his Front had been almost inevitable, considering the belated information from Moscow and the peacetime dispersal of his troops. Still, Pavlov knew that he would take the full blame.

Sure enough Voroshilov fired multiple accusations at Pavlov, and then went to search for Marshal Kulikov. The latter had just made it back to his own lines and had changed from his peasant clothes that he had taken in the 10th Army's headquarters. The two marshals – both of whom had saved their lives by denouncing military colleagues during the Great Purge – agreed that Pavlov was "done with."

Indeed, Stalin had refused to allow the Front commanders to withdraw to avoid being outflanked. However, once sealed off, the Soviet forces never received any "hold out to the last man order". Instead, the doctrine of the Red Army was to immediately attempt a break-out when surrounded. This proved to be a sinister combination.

Masses of Soviet vehicles were destroyed by Luftwaffe attacks, particularly at river crossings such as this. (Photo: Arno Becker.)

The fact that the Soviets failed to defend Minsk in dogged street-to-street fighting of the same type as later occurred in Stalingrad was one of the main Soviet mistakes during Operation Barbarossa. In fact, the Soviet doctrine ordained a maneuver warfare in the open and not close combat in cities. Had Minsk been held as the same kind of "breakwater" as the Germans later on used in fortified towns such as Demyansk and Rzhev, Heeresgruppe Mitte's Blitzkrieg could have been thwarted after just the first few days.

A new army, the 16th, arrived from Orel and went into action straight from the railway cars on 26 June. But the same mistake as at Minsk was repeated: Instead of fortifying the next major city to the east, Smolensk, this army was positioned in the open fields between the two cities.

The 3rd, 4th and 10th Soviet armies immediately began to attempt a breakout. As a matter of fact, the three Soviet armies were not entirely surrounded. While Panzergruppen 2 and 3 raced on eastward on both flanks of Heeresgruppe Mitte, the two German infantry armies had not yet arrived to seal the pincers around the Soviet armies.

Günther von Kluge had been appointed to Generalfeldmarschall for his most skillful command of German 4. Armee during the offensive in the West in 1940. It was forces under his command that had completed the encirclement of the British army at Dunkirk in May 1940. Now

he led the 4. Armee in another highly successful battle of envelopment, where he had been temporarily appointed to command both the Panzergruppe commanders Hoth and Guderian. Albeit drawing upon him the rage of the latter, von Kluge ordered 29. Infanterie-Division of Panzergruppe 2 to be released to establish a blocking position. Thus Soviet 10th Army was finally isolated from the two other enveloped armies. With the telephone lines still blocked as a result of the Brandenburger operations on the eve of the attack, the various enveloped Soviet units had no contact with each other, with the result that the breakout efforts were completely uncoordinated.

But the *Frontovniki* refused to give in. Contrary to the widespread image of a Soviet mass surrender, many of the multitude of isolated units fought on stubbornly until running out of ammunition. At the Brest fortress on the border in the west, a small garrison held out against an enemy widely superior in troops and artillery, inflicting over one thousand casualties on German 45. Infanterie-Division.

"The enemy is fighting with the utmost stamina and courage," Heeresgruppe Mitte reported to the German Army High Command on 28 June.[38] German 4. Armee described the Soviet soldiers as "exceptionally tough and stalwart."[39] "White" émigres who had fled Russia after the October Revolution were used to try to convince the encircled Red Army troops to surrender and join the anti-

THE BATTLE OF THE BREST FORTRESS.

1. A German soldier during the Battle of the Brest fortress. For nine days, German 45. Infanterie-Division was tied down by the Soviet garrison at Brest. (Photo: Via Daniel Johansson.)

2. "I am dying but I will not surrender. Farewell, Motherland. 20 July 1941." Inscription on a wall inside the Brest fortress by one of the last Soviet defenders. (Photo: Author.)

3. The head of the nursing staff of the surgical department at the Brest Fortress Hospital, Praskovya Leontyevna Tkachyov, with soldiers' wives and children, surrounded by German soldiers at the Brest Fortress.

4. The last known defender of the Brest fortress was 41-year old Mayor Pyotr Gavrilov, commander of the 44th Infantry Regiment. On 23 July – having fought for over a month – he attacked a group of German soldiers inside the fortress, wounding several with his pistol and hand grenades. Gavrilov was subsequently badly injured himself and captured by the Germans. He survived the captivity and was appointed a Hero of the Soviet Union in 1957. Gavrilov passed away in Krasnodar on 26 January 1979 and received a hero's burial in Brest. In the film "Fortress of War" from 2010, Alexander Korshunov plays the role of Pyotr Gavrilov.

1.	
2.	
3.	4.

Bolshevik side, but this was "categorically refused," according to a German Army report.[40] Another German account reads: "What has become of the Russian of 1914-17, who ran away or approached us with his hands in the air when the firestorm reached its peak? Now he remains in his bunker and forces us to burn him out, he prefers to be scorched in his tank, and his airmen continue firing at us even when their own aircraft is set ablaze. What has become of the Russian? Ideology has changed him!"[41]

A massive breakout of the Soviet encircled forces probably would have succeeded, had it not been for the Luftwaffe and the air superiority it had gained through the strikes on the Soviet airfields on the first day. This German dominance in the air was a factor not anticipated by the Soviets. Carried out mainly along major highways, the breakout efforts were immediately targeted by hundreds of aircraft of Luftflotte 2, who exacted a terrible toll on Red Army soldiers and equipment, forcing the survivors to scatter into the surrounding terrain.

Well informed of the ground situation through their aerial reconnaissance, the close-suppport units of both Fliegerkorps II and Fliegerkorps VIII were dispatched against the scattered Soviet ground units in the enveloped area. "Flying on a broad front in flights of three planes or in formations of five to six, the bombers did their own scouting and immediately attacked every enemy target seen."[42] The slow-flying Hs 123 biplanes of 10.(S)/LG 2 were particularly successful during these missions.

This caused unit cohesion and command and control on the Soviet side to completely break down, even at army level, often with the result that even battalions and companies scattered. This in turn made it completely impossible for Soviet army and Front headquarters to get a grip on the situation. On top of that, the supply system of the Western Front collapsed altogether, so that most troops were left with only the amounts of ammunition that each man could carry.

Soviet aircraft sent to locate their own troops failed to find them, as they hid in the forests in daytime to avoid Luftwaffe attacks. When the Soviet Chief of Staff, General Armii Georgiy Zhukov called General Armii Pavlov and demanded to know whether it could be true, as the German radio reported, that two Soviet armies had been surrounded east of Biyalystok, Pavlov could only answer vaguely that "there is some truth in that".[43]

The Red Army's instruction to open fire with any arms available at any enemy aircraft sighted also brought severe losses to the Luftwaffe units which were engaged in close support missions, and only being in close proximity to their own airfields saved the Germans from suffering even higher losses in terms of aircraft totally destroyed. Nevertheless, after one week of action in the East, seventeen of SKG 210's Bf 110s had been shot down. Between 27 and 29 June the Luftwaffe lost 61 aircraft in combat on the Eastern Front, with another 42 damaged.[44] The loss rate rose from

0.5 percent on 26 June to 1.9 percent on the 29th. Consequently, the number of sorties conducted by Luftflotte 2 dropped from 1,072 on 26 June to 862 on 27 June, 458 on 28 June and just 260 on 29 June.

But owing to these air missions, Heeresgruppe Mitte's two infantry armies could move in to mop up the scattered Soviet troops, who were now often without ammunition, disorientated and demoralized. Farther to the west, the Germans were able to seize most of the Brest fortress after a Junkers 88 bomber had dropped a gigantic 2500-kg bomb on the citadel. Inside the ruined fortress, the walls were filled with inscriptions such as "We will die but never leave the fortress." Still, some individual Soviet soldiers continued to offer resistance in isolated parts of the fortress for several weeks. When those parts were finally cleared, the Germans found a final inscription on a wall: "I am dying but I will not surrender. Farewell, Motherland. 20 July 1941."

Meanwhile the panzer forces continued their drive forward. It was an unusually hot and dry summer, the sun blazing from an often cloudless sky. The long vehicle columns threw up enormous dust clouds that often wreaked havoc on motor vehicles, clogging dust filters. Fire, smoke and the stench of decomposing corpses mingled with the dust. The soldiers on both sides suffered from the heat, sweating profusely in their uniforms and jackboots. Dehydration among the troops was a constant problem. No rain fell during the first eight days of the war. The situation was incomparably worst on the Soviet side, where supplies more often than not failed to arrive owing to German air attacks against the rear areas. With German forces on all sides, tormented by hunger and thirst, with officers and men often in a state of bewilderment due to a lack of situation reports, and with ammunition and fuel running low, thousands of Soviet troops were approaching the bitter end in dry pine tree, spruce and birch forests during those days. Meanwhile, although they were subject to a constant harassment from groups of enveloped Soviet troops that lay in ambush, inflicting bloody losses on both sides, the Germans at least felt assured of a victorious end to the war within short period of time. "Signs of victory were everywhere along the road," said Hans-Martin Wild, then a Gefreiter in 4. Panzer-Division of Panzergruppe 2. "Vast quantities of light Russian T-26s were shot up or bogged down or abandoned in panic along the roadside. Extremely modern artillery, anti-aircraft weaponry, prime movers, and antitank guns loomed over us – tipped over or pushed into the ditch by our tanks. We frequently saw the results of German aerial attacks. Humans, animals, and equipment were mown down, jumbled together. Dead horses stretched their legs into the air, their stomachs swollen from decomposition. The sweet smell of carrion lingered over the roadway. The trunks of trees – cut down, shredded by bombs – jutted out of the limbs of collapsed crowns. Onward…onward…the march continued without interruption. By night we reached Bereza Kartuska. The town was burning. The amount of destroyed Russian war materiel was immense. The area was saturated with rubble far and wide."[45]

← *A German soldier about to hurl a hand grenade in close combat. The resistance encountered by the Germans was far above what had been expected.*

The commander of Panzergruppe 2, Generaloberst Heinz Guderian (with binoculars), studying the map with the German fighter ace Werner Mölders, who commanded fighter wing JG 51. (Photo: Johannes Broschwitz via Wägenbaur.)

The next goal for the German panzers was to cross the main waterway of Berezina, which ran from the north to the south across Heeresgruppe Mitte's entire assigned advance route. At Minsk, General Walther Nehring, commander of 18. Panzer-Division in Panzergruppe 2's XLVII. Panzerkorps, was ordered to continue "at full speed" along the Moscow highroad to take the important bridge across River Berezina at Borisov, 60 km northeast of Minsk.

An advance force consisting of a few tanks, some armored reconnaissance vehicles and motor cycles were put together under the command of Major Willi Teege and set off on the road. At noon they reached the outskirts of Borisov, only to be subjected to an intense fire. With the regular Red Army forces in the area in disarray, the local armor school had reacted quickly, employing its trainers and cadets to man defensive positions. The first assault was beaten back with heavy German losses. A company of light T-26 tanks from the 2nd Rifle Corps was alerted and set off towards the bridge from the eastern side of the river. But before these were able to reach the site, more elements from the German panzer division appeared. One by one the Soviet defense positions were flushed out. Just as some of the last remaining Soviet troops prepared to blow up the bridge, a group of German soldiers led by Unteroffizier Otto Bukatschek attacked. Although wounded in the shoulder, Bukatschek ran across and managed to kill the remaining Soviets. Thus the advance on the important Minsk-Moscow highway could be secured. For this feat, Bukatschek

became the first soldier in the division to be awarded with the Knight's Cross.

Shortly afterward, the T-26 company arrived. Finding the bridge in enemy hands, it immediately attacked. General Nehring himself was an hair's breadth from being killed as one of the Soviet tanks rammed his car. But a German Flak Abteilung had just reached the site, with orders to set up an air defense of the important bridge, and its 88 mm guns quickly annihilated the Soviet light tanks.

Meanwhile, further south along the river, German 3. Panzer-Division captured Bobruysk – where it found the airfield littered with the wrecks of destroyed Soviet aircraft – and managed to capture the Berezina bridge.

On the same day, 29 June, General-Leytenant Andrey Yeremenko replaced the Front commander Pavlov, who on the following day, together with members of his staff was summoned to Moscow, where they were eventually shot. Among those was Pavlov's Chief of Staff, General-Mayor Vladimir Klimovskikh; the fact that he had tried to persuade Pavlov to place the troops in alert position on 21 June would not save him.*

Yeremenko issued "Directive No. 14," according to which the enemy must be prevented from reaching River Dnepr. The remainder of VVS Western Front, and the Long-Range Aviation's 3 BAK, was instructed to employ all available aircraft to prevent crossings of the Berezina.

Coming in over and over again in relatively small formations at about 2,000 meters height throughout 30

* See Chapter 4.

84

German troops pass by the result of a Luftwaffe attack, a whole column of destroyed tanks and other vehicles of Soviet 6th Mechanized Corps. Closest to the camera is a T-34 which was probably abandoned because of a lack of fuel.

June, the Soviet bombers were met by a savage fire barrier from the Luftwaffe's Anti-Aircraft regiment 10, which inevitably tore the attack formations apart. Then JG 51's Bf 109s engaged the Soviet planes. The Germans recorded twenty-four separate air combats over fourteen hours. The fiercest combat was fought between 1400 and 1500 hours in the afternoon, when JG 51 was dispatched against 42 DBAD and 52 DBAD, claiming 13 DB-3s shot down. Two hours later, III./JG 51 met 3 TBAP's TB-3s and claimed five of the four-engine giants shot down.[46] The actual number of Soviet aircraft shot down by JG 51 on 30 June is unclear. The figure of 113 JG 51 claims is frequently mentioned, but the RLM statistics actually list 146 claims filed by JG 51 on that day. Afterward, it was found that with the SB shot down by 10. Staffel's Leutnant Bernd Gallowitsch, JG 51 – the most successful Jagdgeschwader at that time – surpassed the one-thousand victory mark. JG 51 lost five own aircraft in combat on 30 June.

After this disastrous air battle, VVS Western Front could muster no more than 374 bombers and 124 fighter aircraft out of an initial force of 1,789 ten days earlier. On the ground, the Western Front meanwhile was down to a at merely mere 145 tanks in the front line.[47]

In the forests between Biyalystok and Minsk, large numbers of Soviet troops were still fighting desperately to try to break out of the envelopment, while they were mercilessly butchered by German artillery and air attacks. On 30 June, Heeresgruppe Mitte reported: "Partly rugged but uncoordinated resistance … enormously bloody Russian

losses, only a few surrender."[48] In the air above, the few remaining Soviet aircraft were flown by bitterly determined pilots until they were shot down.

On 1 July, a flight of six I-16 Ishak fighters from Soviet fighter regiment 161 IAP had just landed at an airstrip inside the surrounded area, when a formation of Heinkel 111 bombers appeared and attacked the parked aircraft. Leytenant Nikolay Terekhin took off in the midst of the exploding bombs. His chubby little Polikarpov fighter climbed rapidly. Terekhin aimed at a bomber on the right side of a flight formation and without hesitating started cutting its tail fin with his propeller. With the rudder cut to pieces, the German aircraft flipped over to the left and hit the flight leader's aircraft. This bomber in turn veered to the left and collided with the last aircraft of the Kette. It was a fantastic scene. In the next minute, all four planes – the three Luftwaffe bombers and the I-16 – went down. Six or seven parachutes opened in the sky, but the combat was not over. On their way to the ground, the German airmen and Terekhin started firing at each other with their small flight pistols.

Meantime, a group of Messerschmitt 109s appeared and started attacking the I-16s that had followed Terekhin aloft. One or two I-16s went down in flames as the remaining German bombers withdrew to the west. Leutnant Heinz Bär, one of the most daring pilots in JG 51, blasted away an I-16 for his 28th victory. A bit farther away the He 111s came under attack by another flight of I-16s. But Terekhin was fully occupied with his strange air duel with the parachuting Luftwaffe fliers.

Exhaustion is painted in the faces of these Wehrmacht soldiers during the arduous march towards the east during the rapid advance through Belarus in June 1941.

As they landed in Soviet-controlled territory, the parachuting German bomber fliers were disarmed and tied up with a rope by members of a local collective farm. As if taken from a scene from a Western movie, Terekhin appeared at the headquarters of Soviet fighter division 43 IAD with his pistol in one hand and the rope with the tied-up Luftwaffe airmen in the other, presenting his prisoners to the C.O., General-Mayor Georgiy Zakharov.

But no amount of bravery could save the enveloped 3rd, 4th and 10th Soviet armies from annihilation. On 1 July, the Germans had taken around 100,000 prisoners; on 5 July that number had increased to 300,000, and on 11 July, the number of prisoners had increased to over 400,000. Actual losses sustained by the Western Front through 9 July were 341,000 killed or missing and 77,000 evacuated as wounded or sick – out of an original strength of 627,000, in other words, two of every three men had become a casualty in just two and a half weeks.[49] The number of killed is impossible to calculate, but it was without doubt in the tens of thousands.* Also, during the following weeks a large number of Red Army stragglers managed to reach their own lines after a long time hiding in the large forests and swamps behind enemy lines. The discrepancy between the actual figure of maybe a quarter of a million Red Army soldiers captured and 400,000 POWs registered by the Germans is explained through the fact that the Germans as a rule rounded up a large number of civilians – suspected of being Red Army soldiers who

had changed into civilian dress – and sent them to POW camps. Thus, for instance the following order was issued by XII. Armeekorps on 5 July 1941: "Any man with a short haircut between the ages of 17 and 30 is suspected of being a soldier. It is demanded that all such elements are picked up from the streets and forests and brought to the closest POW camp."[50]

Additionally, there never were any mass surrenders. The soldiers were seized in small groups or individually, often wounded or with no ammunition left. "Most soldiers were captured in small batches in a multitude of separate instances across a vast landscape," wrote historian Roger R. Reese: "Those men were not captured all at once in the manner of the German mass surrender of 90,000 men at Stalingrad in February 1943 and a quarter million at Tunis, the British surrender of 70,000 men to the Japanese at Singapore in February 1942, or the American surrenders at Bataan and Corregidor in April–May 1942."[51] A Soviet officer described how he ended up in captivity: "I was captured in a state of shock by the Germans. Our whole unit was cut off and slowly being decimated by the German artillery … and then all hell broke loose. When I recovered I was under a German guard … a POW."[52]

In addition to the huge numbers of prisoners, the Germans also captured no less than 2,585 Soviet tanks. Several thousand others lay as burned out hulks along Heeresgruppe Mitte's advance routes. Of the 6,784 tanks in the Western Front on 21 June, less than 200 remained on 1 July. In his hunt for scapegoats, Stalin had the commander of the 4th Army, General-Mayor Aleksandr Korobkov – who in vain had attempted to order his troop into battle positions on 21 June (see Chapter 4) – and the Chief of the Western Front's Artillery, General-Leytenant Nikolay Klich, arrested and shot.

The decisive role played by the Luftwaffe in this huge German victory is often obscured in modern accounts of Operation Barbarossa. However, in an order at that time, Heeresgruppe Mitte's commander, Generalfeldmarschall Fedor von Bock, emphasized that "the success of this battle of annihilation was possible *only* through the support of Luftflotte 2."[53]

Not only had the Luftwaffe provided the ground forces with air support of immense value – it had also obliterated a deadly threat from 1,789 aircraft of VVS Western Front and 1,332 bombers of the Long-Range Aviation. In huge air combats, 1,669 Soviet aircraft were shot down between 22 June and 30 June 1941.[54] The VVS had put up stiff opposition, claiming to have shot down 662 German aircraft between 22 and 30 June – 613 in air combat and 49 through ground fire.[55] The Luftwaffe's actual losses on the Eastern Front during this period were 699 aircraft destroyed or damaged, of which 480 (276 destroyed and 208 damaged) were due to enemy action.[56]

The stage was now set for Heeresgruppe Mitte's continued offensive. But one question remained unanswered – where to? Moscow or Leningrad?

* The Wehrmacht sustained over 22,000 killed on the Eastern Front through 10 July 1941. (Bundesarchiv-Militärarchiv, RW 6/543.)

1. *A female private soldier among other Soviet prisoners of war.*

2. *After the battle. Two captured Red Army soldiers are watched suspiciously by the German troops.*

3. *A Jewish Red Army soldier in German captivity. The prisoners of war of Jewish origin often suffered a fate even worse than that of ordinary Soviet POWs.*

4. *The Soviet prisoners of war were herded together in enormous concentrations, without any sanitary or medical installations, and lacking food and water.*

5. *Next to a destroyed T-26 tank, two Soviet men in civilian clothes are seized as prisoners of war by German troops.*

	1.	
2.		
3.	4.	
	5.	

87

This Red Army soldier has just been captured. An uncertain fate awaits him. (Photo: SA-Kuva.)

THE FATE OF SOVIET PRISONERS OF WAR.

After being captured, Soviet prisoners of war were forced to march hundreds of kilometres with little or no rations or water during this incredibly hot and dry summer. No transportation was made available. Any POW who collapsed or who even showed exhaustion was shot on the spot. "I will never forget the endless columns of prisoners of war under the blazing sun on Russia's dusty roads," recalled one of the Soviet POWs, Yakov Diyorditsa. "Many among us were wounded, but the guards shot anyone who could not march on with the rest of us. Now and then a shot was heard. Without belts or army caps, many barefoot, unshaved, the back of our uniform shirts covered with gray-white spots, dirty, hungry and tormented by thirst we dragged on towards the Unknown." [1]

Whips, rifle butts and sticks were used to drive on increasingly exhausted body of prisoners of war. Red Army medic Yevgeniy Livelisha described the absolutely inhumane treatment of the prisoners by their German guards: "Peaceful civilians came to meet us, and tried to supply us with water and bread. However, the Germans would not allow us to approach the citizens, nor would they let them approach us. One of the prisoners stepped five or six meters out of the column and without any warning was killed by a German soldier." [2] Nikolay Obrynba, another Red Army medic captured in 1941, said: "I watched with horror how healthy people were reduced to a state of complete helplessness and death."

Following long death marches, the POWs were placed in so-called *Russenlager* – "POW camps" that were nothing but large fields, surrounded by barbed wire, without any housing, no sanitary installations, and no medical care. There they were slowly starved, with rations amounting to only one-fourth of what normally is required for a male person to survive. "The prisoners of war sometimes go six to eight days without food, and, in the animal apathy caused by hunger, have but a single craving: to get something to eat," was noted in a report submitted to Alfred Rosenberg – the revengeful former "White emigré" who had joined the Nazi Party in 1919 and now was Minister for the Occupied Eastern Territories. [3]

↑ *Soviet prisoners of war herded like animals by German soldiers with sticks.*

→ *German attitudes to the Soviet people were shaped by racist propaganda such as this book, Der Untermensch ("The Subhuman"), nurturing hatred and contempt against what was labeled as "Jewish-Bolshevik subhumans." They were described as "terrible animals" with "a lust to destroy."*

1 Kempowski, *Das Echolot*, p. 276.
2 "Soviet Prisoners of War: Forgotten Nazi Victims of World War II" by Jonathan North, in *World War II Magazine*, January/February 2006.
3 *The German Army and the Genocide*, p. 142.

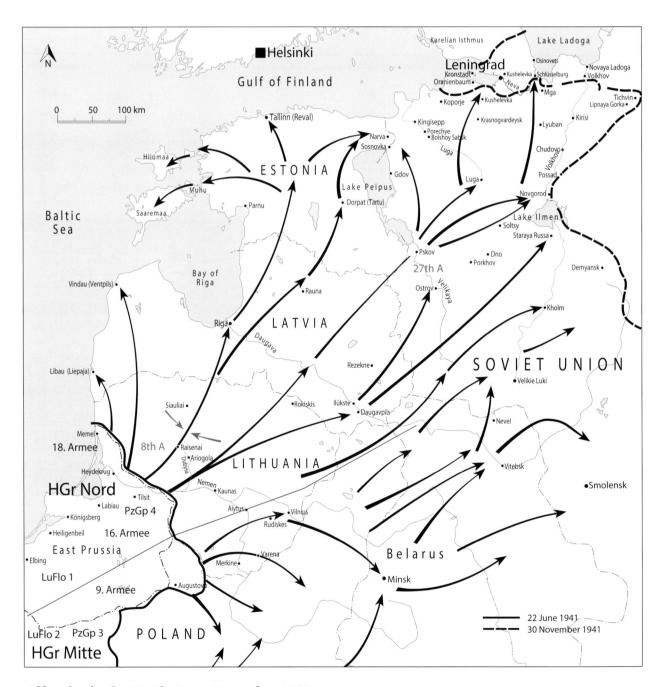

Offensive in the North, June–November 1941.

7: TANK BATTLES IN THE NORTH.

"The Russian is a colossus and strong!"

– Adolf Hitler, 13 July 1941.

In the Baltic states, Soviet Northwestern Front by contrast was able to avoid getting its forces surrounded like the dismal fate which met the Western Front. As we have seen previously, its commander, 42-year old General-Polkovnik Fedor Kuznetsov, was one of the few senior military commanders who had attempted to mobilize his forces to meet the German onslaught before it came – and had been reprimanded for it. But at least he was psychologically prepared when the attack came, and on 22 June he immediately ordered the 3rd and 12th Mechanized corps from the 11th and 8th armies to move forward and counter-attack the German forces that had crossed the border into Lithuania. The 3rd Mechanized Corps, with 2nd and 5th Tank divisions located in the Kaunas area, had been overlooked by the German intelligence prior to 22 June, and thus came as a most unpleasant surprise to Generalfeldmarschall Wilhelm Ritter von Leeb, the commander of Heeresgruppe Nord, and his generals. The 12th Mechanized Corps, located north of Siauliai, some 100 km farther to the northwest, consisted of the 23rd and 28th Tank divisions and the 202nd Motorized Division. Altogether, these two mechanized corps mustered 60,000 troops and 1,400 tanks, including 110 of the modern T-34 medium tanks and KV heavy tanks, against which the German tanks were more or less helpless.

Generaloberst Erich Hoepner's Panzergruppe 4, von Leeb's main strike force, surged forward into the area between these two powerful Soviet concentrations of armor. Without encountering much resistance, 8. Panzer-Division, the only panzer division in General Erich von Manstein's LVI. Panzerkorps on Hoepner's southern flank, advanced 80 kilometers on the first day of the attack, and captured an bridge across River Dubysa near Ariogala intact.[1]

With surprising rapidity, the 12th Mechanized Corps started its march towards the south and the 3rd began to traverse towards the west. The opposing forces were still widely apart. But while Northwestern Front's six Rifle divisions – with an average of only 8,700 men per division – withdrew rather than taking up a hopeless fight with numerically superior German panzer forces, Kuznetsov's armored strike forces were detected by German aerial reconnaissance. Generaloberst Alfred Keller's Luftflotte 1, assigned to provide Heeresgruppe Nord with air support, was immediately alerted, and soon scores of planes with black crosses came raining down on the Soviet columns. Lacking fighter cover, the Soviets sustained some severe losses during these attacks late on 22 June. Soviet 23rd Tank Division of the 12th Mechanized Corps sustained particularly severe losses. Ju 88s from Luftflotte 1 that attacked in low-level flight left 40 tanks or lorries destroyed.[2]

Moreover, the two divisions of the 3rd Mechanized Corps were widely dispersed, and as we have seen in the previous chapter, the 5th Tank Division also had to be hurriedly turned southwards in an effort to destroy the bridgehead across River Neman established at Alytus (45 km south of Kaunas) by 7. Panzer-Division of Heeresgruppe Mitte. This not only tore both the corps and the division apart, but also cost the 5th Tank Division a loss of 73 tanks.[3] The Neman bridgehead remained in German hands and was used as a springboard for next day's attack towards the Lithuanian capital of Vilnius.

Only about one third of the 600 tanks in the 12th Mechanized Corps managed to reach the battlefield, and these clashed in piecemeal fashion with three infantry divisions of 18. Armee on von Leeb's left flank late on 23 June and during the following night.[4] German 1. Panzer-Division also became embroiled in fighting with some of the

A Soviet BT-7 light tank in the midst of a blazing tank battle.

German soldiers in combat with a Soviet BA-10 (Broneavtomobil 10, i.e. armored car 10). The BA-10 entered service in 1938 and was armed with a 45mm gun. It only had a 10 mm thin armor.

12th Mechanized Corps's armor. In this soon to become legendary tank clash, the Germans encountered the KV and T-34 tanks for the first time."In a fantastic exchange of fire," a German tank soldier said, "the Russian tanks continued their advance while our anti-tank shells simply bounced off them."

With clear and warm weather, both sides sent their air forces into action to support the ground forces in this expanding tank battle. While the Soviets for a short while held the upper hand on the ground, the situation was the absolute opposite in the air. German fighter pilot Oberleutnant Hans-Ekkehard Bob of JG 54 recalls: "Russian bombers kept coming throughout the day, each time in formations of around twelve bombers. To us fighters, these bombers were an easy harvest, and we flew relentless interception missions in Staffel strength."[5] The German fighter pilots were greatly aided by the fact that most of these bomber formations came in without any fighter escort – a result both of the blows against the Soviet airfields and of the severed telephone lines on the Soviet side.

Meanwhile Luftflotte 1 were in constant action against the Soviet attack formations on the ground, often bailing out German ground units from difficult situations caused by Soviet armored attacks. As we have seen, the German aircraft succeeded in putting a large number of Soviet tanks – mainly light tanks of the type T-26 – out of action, but the most important result of this air action was that it cut the Soviet supply lines. Thus, most of these Soviet armor formations went into action with only one day's supply of ammunition and fuel.[6] A large share of the Soviet tank losses were caused when the crews had to abandon the vehicles when they ran out of fuel and ammunition.

Luftflotte 1 had only one air corps, Fliegerkorps I under General Helmuth Förster, and this was hampered by a lack of close-support aircraft, so the Ju 88 twin-engine bombers had to be employed in hazardous low-level attacks. During these first days of the battle between Luftflotte 1 and Northwestern Front's armor, these Junkers 88 crews met only few Soviet fighter planes, but losses due to ground fire were not insignificant. The Red Army troops were ordered to open fire with all arms – including rifles – at any enemy aircraft within range. The bomber units of Luftflotte 1 – three Geschwader with a total of 270 aircraft – recorded 18 Ju 88s shot down on 23 June alone.[7] The fact that the Luftwaffe on 23 June lost 76 aircraft in combat, of which 40 were totally destroyed, showed that the Soviets were far from beaten.

In spite of all its difficulties, Soviet 12th Mechanized Corps succeeded in slowing down the German advance, allowing the infantry units of the 8th Army to evacuate Lithuania and the Kurland Peninsula in western Latvia. On 24 June, von Leeb's northern flank remained stalled, although Soviet 23rd Tank division was ordered to pull back to secure its supply lines.

While all of this took place, a civil war was raging in the rear of Northwestern Front's front troops. On 22 June, the Lithuanian Activist Movement (LAF) started an armed rebellion against the Soviet forces and attacked small retreating forces and supply columns.

The LAF had been formed in November 1940 by Kazys Škirpa, former Lithuanian representative in the League of Nations. It consisted of representatives of most of the main non-communist political parties, with the Nationalist Unionists and the Christian Democrats being the most dominant. Secretly cooperating with the Germans, its aim was to end the Soviet annexation of Lithuania. The LAF's underground Provisional Government of Lithuania under Škirpa was announced on 22 April 1941, and the planned armed uprising came closer. Partisan cells grew stronger all over Lithuania, particularly in the capital of Vilnius and in Kaunas. The NKVD struck back by deporting some 17,000 "anti-Soviet elements" between 14 and 19 June. Five of those arrested and deported were ministers of the underground Provisional Government – including the Minister of Defense Vytautas Bulvičius, who was supposed to hold a key role in the uprising.

The LAF and the Provisional Government was not only nationalist, but also vehemently anti-Semitic. The LAF clearly declared: "The Lithuanian Activist Front, by

THE KAUNAS FORT OF DEATH.

Having killed large numbers of Jews and Communists in pure lynchings in the streets, the Lithuanian partisans began to organize the repression. Thousands of Jewish men, women and children were locked into a fort at Kaunas, where they were held under appalling conditions. An eyewitness described the conditions: "When somebody moved or were caught talking, the partisans would open automatic fire into the crowd. Not everyone was lucky enough to be killed outright. ... Many of the wounded were twisting around in agony and asking the bandits to kill them, but the bastards would laugh and say, 'You were told to keep quiet,' but would not shoot, and instead let them die in pain."[1] There was an artesian well within the fort, but the thousands of people who were held there were forbidden by the partisans who guarded them on the walls above to drink: anyone who approached it was shot.[2] A woman who survived, said: "For several days we had no food and no water. The nights were the worst. Partisans would come in and beat up the women. They picked up the most beautiful ones and took them out by force and raped them."[3]
End fact box

1 Rhodes, *Masters of Death*, p. 44.
2 Ibid.
3 Ibid., p. 45.

restoring the new Lithuania, is determined to carry out an immediate and fundamental purging of the Lithuanian nation and its land of Jews."[8] Jews had been subject to harsh anti-semitic laws in Lithuania prior to the Soviet annexation in 1940, and anti-Semitic street violence was part of everyday-life. This ended when the Soviet Union took control. The anti-Semitic laws were abolished and Jews found easier ways to positions within the new authorities. Hardly suprisingly, many Jews – the country's largest ethnic minority – preferred the Soviet rule.

Throughout 22 and 23 June, heavy fighting raged, mainly in the cities of Vilnius and Kaunas – in the seam between Heeresrguppen Nord and Mitte – between LAF partisans and Soviet forces.* The Lithuanian insurrection was strengthened by the influx of thousands of Lithuanian deserters from the Red Army's 29th Lithuanian Territorial Corps. Several Jews also volunteered to fight on the Soviet side. The struggle was ruthless. In Vilnius and Kaunas, the NKVD murdered all the political prisoners – 260 in Kaunas alone – lest they were liberated by the LAF to reinforce its strength. By the evening of the 23rd, both cities were mainly in the hands of the Lithuanian partisans, who immediately initiated reprisals against the Communists and the Jewish population. When the Germans entered the cities, the bloodbath was in full swing. Generalmajor der Polizei Franz Stahlecker, the commander of Einsatzgruppe A, reported on the events in Kaunas: "In the first pogrom during the nights of 23–26 June, the Lithuanian

The burned corpse of a Soviet tank man lies on the hull of his gigantic KV-2 tank. The 57-ton KV-2 was the heavy artillery version of the Soviet KV heavy tank. It was equipped with a 152 mm M1938 howitzer and aimed at fighting enemy pill boxes. However, the powerful recoil of the gun often caused the small turret ring to jam, rendering it unable to defend itself against attacking enemy forces. This tank has been set ablaze by incendiary bombs dropped by the Luftwaffe. (Photo: Hannes Trautloft.)

* The whole situation was utterly complicated through the fact that the ZWZ, the Polish armed resistance movement (the precursor of the Home Army, AK) – fighting to bring back Vilnius under the Polish rule that it had been between 1920–1939 – was also active in Vilnius.

THE LITHUANIAN PROVISIONAL GOVERNMENT AND THE HOLOCAUST.

The LAF's Provisional Government was officially established on 23 June in Kaunas and Vilnius. Kazys Škirpa returned to Lithuania, where he was appointed Prime Minister. He set up a police force and issued several laws. The daily paper *Iaisvę* (Towards Freedom) was issued. However, the Provisional Government's main influence was to instigate further pogroms. According to historian Timothy Snyder, Prime Minister Škirpa used radio broadcasts to incite mobs to murder.[1] But the Germans would only tolerate the Provisional Government to the extent that it could be used for their purposes. They were not the least interested in a truly independent Lithuania.

On 5 August 1941 the Provisional Government dissolved itself and the German Reichskommissariat Ostland – Alfred Rosenberg's administration for the Baltic countries, led by Hinrich Lohse – took over. Its main task was to prepare the "Germanization" of the area by the settlement of ethnic Germans, which also was supposed to require an ethnic cleansing. This soon resulted in plans for the complete annihilation of the Jews in the Baltic countries, a task which was nearly completely fulfilled. The Lithuanian partisans reportedly killed 18,490 Jews, but the Nazi Einsatzgruppe A took over with far greater efficiency, liquidating another 114,856 in the country through December 1941. In total, at least 190,000 Jews were killed in Lithuania between 1941 and 1944, representing around 95 per cent of its Jewish population.

1 Snyder, *Bloodlands: Europe Between Hitler and Stalin*, p. 192.

partisans did away with more than 1,500 Jews ... and burned down a Jewish residential quarter consisting of about 60 houses. During the following nights, approximately 2,300 Jews were rendered harmless in a similar way. In other parts of Lithuania, similar actions followed the example of Kaunas."

This suited the German SS leader Himmler well, and he issued the following order to the Einsatzgruppen: "The attempts of self-cleansing on the part of anti-Communist or anti-Semitic elements in the areas to be occupied are not to be hindered."[9] When Generalfeldmarschall von Leeb reported to Hitler's Headquarters about the Lithuanian pogroms, Oberst Rudolf Schmundt, Hitler's adjutant, told him not to intervene.[10] The 7. Panzer-Division of Panzergruppe 3, operating south of Heeresgruppe Nord, entered Vilnius on 24 June, and on 25 June German infantry marched into Kaunas peacefully, in parade order.[11] They received an enthusiastic welcome from large segments of the Lithuanian gentile population.

However, while the Red Army folded back in southern Lithuania, the tank forces continued to hold back all but the southernmost flank of Heeresgruppe Nord. A final Soviet offensive move in the Battle of Lithuania was made with the 2nd Tank Division against German 6. Panzer-Division's bridgehead across River Dubysa near Raisenai on 24 June. Although only the Soviet 2nd Motorized Rifle Regiment managed to reach the designated area, the few KV tanks that it was equipped with sufficed to cause a severe crisis to the German division. Following an artillery barrage, these

KVs rumbled forward to attack. The motorcycle battalion Kradschützen-Bataillon 6 was completely mashed up, with its commander Major Schlieckmann being among those killed. Oberst Erhard Raus, commanding the German division's 6. Schützen-Brigade, described the impact made by the heavy tanks:

"Even the concentrated fire of the artillery and all other heavy weapons did not deter the steel pachyderms. Though enveloped in fire and smoke, they immediately lumbered to attack, crushing everything in their paths. Untroubled by the shower of heavy howitzer shells and debris raining down upon them, they attacked a roadblock, shrugged off the flanking fire of our anti-tank guns in the woods, turned and overran those positions, and then broke into the artillery area."[12]

100 tanks, including thirty Panzer IVs, of 6. Panzer-Division arrived to ward off the counter-attack, striking from three sides. But their shells only bounced off the KVs, and soon one German tank after another was knocked out. Those remaining had to beat a hasty retreat "to escape destruction," as Raus put it.[13] "The danger of a general panic became imminent," Raus continued. "Nearer and nearer rolled the giant tanks, echeloned in width and depth. One of them encountered a marshy pool in which a [German] Panzer 35(t) had become mired. Without hesitating, the black monster rolled over the helpless panzer. The same fate befell a German 150mm howitzer, which had not been able to escape in time."

Only when German air support and 88mm anti-aircraft guns from a Luftwaffe unit arrived, could the Soviet tanks be destroyed. Owing mainly to the German air superiority, these attacks however soon petered out. Throughout 24 June, Soviet 28th Tank Division was unable to move at all due to a total lack of fuel, chiefly caused by air attacks. When the battle was over, this division left behind 198 tanks. Nevertheless, through the counter-attacks on 23 and 24 June, the Soviet tank units saved the bulk of the men and women of the Northwestern Front's 8th and 11th armies, who managed to conduct a swift retreat and avoid being enveloped by Heeresgruppe Nord.

The fact that the Soviet counter-attack was beaten back did not immediately save the situation for German 6. Panzer-Division. One of the KV tanks had broken through and alone advanced deep into the German rear area, where it on 24 June took up position on the only road along which the German division received its supplies. A column of twelve supply trucks which arrived from Raisenai were shot up to the last vehicle and left burning on the road, as a warning sign to others.

Oberst Raus dispatched a battery with 50mm anti-tank guns to neutralize the KV. The gun crews labored through a forest to sneak up on it without being noticed, and got into position at a distance of 600 meters. One shell slammed against the KV, followed by another and another. But nothing happened – the KV remained unscathed and motionless. Only when at least eight shells had bounced off its thick armor did the turret begin to rotate. The Soviet tank commander took careful aim and fired. One anti-tank gun was torn apart. Then the KV's gun banged again, another anti-tank gun with its crew was obliterated. Methodically, the Soviet tank commander knocked out all of the German guns. The supply road remained blocked.

In the afternoon, an 88mm anti-aircraft gun could be removed from the battle at the bridgehead and employed against the KV. The Soviet tank commander saw the 88mm piece being moved closer and closer, but waited for the right moment to strike. The whole tank crew waited, knowing that the "88" could only fire when it had stopped.

Suddenly the "88" stopped and its crew began the preparations to take up a firing position. We don't know exactly what went through the mind of the Soviet tank commander at that moment. Maybe he smiled in triumph, maybe he cursed the Fascist invaders? But the tank turret rotated and its powerful 76mm gun banged. In a bright flash, the "88" was overthrown. Then the area was raked with machine gun fire from the tank.

At the isolated bridgehead, the mood among the troops of 6. Panzer-Division began to drop. During the following night, twelve volunteers from the pioneer group attempted to destroy the tank with a powerful explosive charge. Under the cover of darkness, they silently crept forward to the tank and placed the device. Then they withdrew into the forest and lit the fuse. The stillness of the night was broken by a violent explosion and a flickering light between the dark trees. A violent clattering from the tank's machine guns told them that the KV still was very much active.

On the morning of 25 June, the Germans tried to get the Luftwaffe to employ dive-bombers against the tank, but the request was turned down.

Finally, hunger drove the Germans to come up with a new idea as to how to neutralize the mortal threat embodied in a single Soviet "super tank." This time, a combined operation was launched. Since the forest was quite sparse, the small German tanks of the type Panzer 38(t) were able to advance to a position near the tank. Utilizing bushes,

The Luftwaffe's 88mm anti-aircraft guns employed in ground combat would be the most important German asset with which to fight the heavily armored modern Soviet tanks of the types T-34 and KV. (Photo: Krigsarkivet Stockholm.)

The charred body of a Soviet tankman is all that remains of the crew of this burned T-26 tank. (Photo: Karl-Heinz Höfer via Rosipal.)

trees and small hills to seek cover, they began to take the KV under fire. Of course, their comparatively small 37mm guns were totally insufficient to inflict any harm on the heavy tank, but their repeated hits shook the Soviet tank crew and drew their attention. The KV started to shoot back at the annoying panzers. In the meantime, unnoticed by the Soviet tankmen, a new 88 mm anti-aircraft gun was brought into position behind the steel colossus.

The anti-aircraft crew fired seven shells, each a full hit. The tank shook violently and apparently the traverse mechanism for the turret became blocked. Then the German engineers rushed forward and quickly dropped hand grenades into a shell hole in the turret. A muffled bang was heard from the interior of the tank and the hatch lid flew open. Then everything became quiet.

Carefully peeking down into the open hatch a German engineer was met with the gruesome sight of the shredded remnants of the Soviet tank men's bodies. Deeply impressed by their courage, the Germans buried them with all honors. An inspection of the KV showed that among all the shells that had been fired at it only two of the last seven – fired by the 88mm gun from close distance – had managed to penetrate the armor.

A similar achievement was pulled off by a solitary Soviet 5th Tank Division BT-7 tank crew commanded by Starshiy Serzhant Grigoriy Naydin, who on 25 June ambushed a German vehicle column near Rūdiškės, southwest of Vilnius, knocking out fifteen armored vehicles and ten artillery pieces.

But none of these accomplishments could turn the tide. On the southern flank of Panzergruppe 4, General Erich von Manstein's LVI. Panzerkorps exploited the gap that had been created between the Northwestern Front's 8th and 11th Armies as the former pulled back north, into Latvia, while the latter withdrew to the east, past Vilnius and into the northern part of Belarus. This was a mistake that would cost Kuznetsov dearly. However, the powerful attack by von Manstein's Panzerkorps, with Heeresgruppe Nord's 16. Armee on its southern flank, also made it nearly impossible for the 11th Army to move north from its initial position in southwestern Lithuania.

The evacuation of the 8th and 11th armies was indeed an impressive feat. "They marched very quickly, even when retreating in extremely large numbers," commented Erhard Raus. "When they decided to withdraw, they did so in one jump and then immediately began an active defense again. When our panzer divisions, which had torn through their lines, chased them off the roads, the Russians disappeared into the terrain with remarkable skill. In retreating, retiring from sight, and rapidly reassembling, the Russians were masters. Large forces covered long distances over terrain devoid of roads or even paths. For example, south of Leningrad, the 6. Panzer-Division would take prisoners from the same regiment of the 125th Rifle Division that had first opposed us when we crossed the border at Tauroggen, having withdrawn 800 kilometers to fight again." [14]

That the three armies which constituted the Northwestern Front on 22 June 1941 – the 8th, 11th and 27th – were among very few Soviet armies that escaped destruction during Operation Barbarossa is an often overlooked fact. Had Heeresgruppe Nord managed to achieve a swift and major breakthrough all along its front, both the 8th and the 11th could have been enveloped and annihilated, and this might well have led to the fall of Leningrad.

On 25 June, von Manstein's most advanced troops reached Ilūkste, 10 km northwest of the city of Daugavpils on River Daugava. Kuznetsov was now instructed to halt the Germans at this large waterway. However, a task force from the Brandenburger Regiment with four captured Soviet trucks and fifty soldiers in Soviet uniforms were sent towards the main bridge in Daugavpils on 26 June, while von Manstein's armor attacked the city from the west. The Brandenburgers found the bridge bustling with Soviet transport in full swing, but at the checkpoint at the approach to the bridge, the men on the last "Trojan horse" truck were revealed as Germans. A firefight broke out, but the Brandenburgers managed to hold the bridge until the German panzers arrived. By then thirty-five of the Brandenburgers had been killed, but the vital bridge was in German hands.

This was a heavy blow against Kuznetsov's strategy. On 28 June, the 21st Mechanized Corps launched a counter-attack which turned the situation, in von Manstein's own words, "quite critical". Once again the Luftwaffe decided the outcome. As noted earlier, an important flaw of Luftflotte 1 was its lack of close-support aircraft, which forced Generaloberst Keller to deploy his medium bombers in low-level attacks for which they were not suited. This produced unnecessarily high losses to ground fire. An operation against a concentration of Soviet tanks south and southwest of Riga on 28 June cost KG 1 a loss of six Ju 88s.[15] III./KG 1's Hauptmann Gerhard Baeker recalls: "The mission was carried out in bad weather, with a cloud ceiling of only 50 to 100 meters. During the attack, my aircraft was hit in a liquid cooler hose and left a white trail. I made a forced landing at Siaulai."[16]

With his ground forces in disarray, Kuznetsov brought in the aviation to destroy the bridge. But VVS Northwestern Front was in no condition to intervene. Between 22 June and 30 June, it had lost 425 aircraft during combat missions, plus 465 on the ground. Another 187 had sustained serious battle damage. Out of 403 SB bombers at hand on 22 June, 205 had been shot down, 148 lost on the ground, and 33 damaged by 30 June. Fighter losses included 110 I-153s, 81 I-16s, and 17 MiG-3s in the air.[17]

Other air commands had to be called in, and on 30 June, the Air Force of the Red Banner Baltic Fleet (VVS KBF) employed all available bombers in an attempt to knock out the Daugava bridges at Daugavpils and neutralize the German fighters at Daugava's aerodrome. Both efforts failed as the naval SBs and DB-3s, without escort flew straight into swarms of Bf 109s. Major Hannes Trautloft, the commander of German fighter wing JG 54, described the situation in his diary: "A wild air combat unfolds. Everywhere you can see Russian bombers go down like comets. The sky is filled with burning planes. We take a terrible toll on them. I attack a single Russian, apparently separated from his formation by anti-aircraft fire. A long burst sets him on fire and one crew member bails out. The burning aircraft hits the ground in a wood, ten kilometers to the north of our airfield, but I'm already after the next. I fire once, twice, and flames envelop his left engine and his undercarriage opens. He goes into a steep dive and approaches a small lake. The bomber hits the surface, bounces across the water like a skimmed stone, is flung over the shore, and finally it crashes in the woods in a huge cascade of fire. To the left I can see another plane being shot down, in front of me yet another. It is a horrific picture. Suddenly an Me 109 falls on its back and plunges to the earth at high speed. Apparently the pilot had been mortally wounded in the air. As we return to base, almost every aircraft is waving victory signs with its wings."[18]

Out of 78 bombers dispatched, 37 were shot down (the Germans claimed 65) while only two Bf 109s were lost. Soviet bombs hit and destroyed a few pontoon bridges, but the main river crossings remained intact. One extraordinary feat nevertheless was credited to Mladshiy Leytenant Petr Igashov, a pilot in the naval mine-torpedo regiment 1 MTAP. His DB-3 was attacked by four Messerschmitt Bf 109s coming in from two directions. After two attacks the bomber was severely damaged and three Bf 109s closed in to deal the coup de grace. In that moment one of the fighters received the full brunt of the nose and aft gunners' combined fire. The Messerschmitt burst violently into flames and immediately went down. In spite of heavy battle damage to his airplane, Igashov decided to carry on. Seconds later, four other Bf 109s made another attack. The bomber pilot realized that he had no chance of escaping and made a swift decision. Guiding his crippled twin-engine plane against the approaching enemy formation, he managed to hit the closest Bf 109 with the wing of his DB-3. Then the bomber rolled on its back and crashed right into a concentration of vehicles on the main road below, performing what was known as a "fire taran" according to Soviet terminology.

Two other Soviet bomber pilots reportedly carried out fire tarans during the raids against the Daugava crossings on 30 June 1941 – Leytenants Aleksey Glukhov and Pyotr Ponomaryov, both of whom flew SBs with bomber regiment 73 BAP.

On 1 July, VVS Northwestern Front's commander, General-Mayor Aleksey Ionov, was removed from his post – and shortly afterward arrested. His successor, General Timofey Kutsevalov, took charge of a depleted force that was brushed aside in more than one way. VVS Northwestern Front actually ceased to be a force to reckon with. General-Mayor Aleksandr Novikov's VVS Northern Front was ordered by the Stavka to take over the mission of providing the Northwestern Front with air support. VVS Northern Front had escaped the destruction that had been wrought upon other Soviet air commands. But on the other hand it was widely stretched out, from the Leningrad sector and along the whole of the Soviet-Finnish border to Murmansk in the Far North. Finland's entrance into the war on the German side on 25 June compelled General-Mayor Novikov to deploy two whole aviation wings, 5 SAD and 39 IAD, to the Karelian Isthmus.

To compensate this loss, the Northern Front's composite air division 2 SAD was shifted forward to airfields around Ostrov, east of River Velikaya south of Lake Peipus on 1 July. This unit consisted of three regiments with a mixed composition of SB and Pe-2 bombers; a fighter regiment with MiG-3s, and 65 ShAP with new Il-2 Shturmoviks. Another composite aviation wing – 4 SAD with three SB bomber regiments and a fighter regiment – meanwhile stood ready in northern Estonia. Moreover, the two fighter wings 3 IAD and 39 IAD were held in readiness in the Leningrad area.

These wounded Red Army troopers were ambushed by Lithuanian partisans. The more unlucky ones were shot dead. (Photo: Krigsarkivet Stockholm.)

But when Panzergruppe 4 opened its attack early on 2 July, no aircraft could intervene on either side. Heavy downpours during the previous night had turned all airfields into quagmire. When the skies cleared in the west toward the evening, as many aircraft as possible took off on both sides. JG 54 clashed violently with 2 SAD's bombers and claimed 28 shot down without any own losses.[19] One of the shot down Soviet planes was the SB piloted by Starshiy Leytenant Pavel Markutsa of 44 SBAP/2 SAD. While on a reconnaissance mission west of the Daugava River, Markutsa's lone bomber was pounced on by five Bf 109s. The rear

Maintenance of a Messerschmitt Bf 109 F-4 of JG 54 "Grünherz." (Photo: Hannes Trautloft.)

gunner claimed to have shot down one of the enemy fighters but was immediately afterward thrown out of his cabin by a large explosion caused by a full salvo of 15mm shells hitting the fuselage and wings. With the Tupolev bomber on fire, the pilot decided to force-land behind enemy lines. Leaving his dead navigator in the cockpit of the crashed and burning bomber, Markutsa managed to make contact with a large group of Red Army soldiers of 749th Rifle Regiment, which had been left behind enemy lines during the retreat. Following five days of repeated skirmishes with enemy troops in the area, the Soviet bomber pilot and 312 of 749th Rifle Regiments soldiers managed to break through to the Soviet lines. Two weeks later, Markutsa was appointed a Hero of the Soviet Union. Immediately back in action again, he would not survive the year.

While The German fighters effectively shielded off the Soviet attempts to bomb the advancing panzer columns, the bomber units were focused on the prevention of Soviet retrograde movements.[20]

After the crippling bomber losses on 2 July, General-Mayor Novikov held back his bombers on the following day; they were rested while fighters were tasked with covering the Northwestern Front's supply routes against the devastating German bomber attacks. 39 IAD – with three fighter regiments – was shifted southwestward from the Leningrad area. These fighter pilots, and those of VVS Northwestern Front farther southeast, were instructed to focus on the bombers and reconnaissance aircraft and avoid combat with fighters. This was fulfilled quite successfully. While JG 54's airmen flew all day long on 3 July without sighting a single Soviet aircraft, Fliegerkorps I's bombers were intercepted by Soviet fighters at Pskov, Ostrov, and Opochka, and lost five Ju 88s.[21]

With the Northwestern Front in full retreat, General-Polkovnik Kuznetsov, the commander of the Front, was removed from command on 3 July. Succeeded by the former commander of the 8th Army, General-Leytenant Pyotr Sobennikov, Kuznetsov was demoted to command only a single army, the newly formed 21st of the Western Front. He, who in vain had attempted to place his troops in position to successfully meet the German attack before it started, was only lucky not to share the fate of his colleague in the Western Front, Pavlov, and get executed. This was probably only due to his successful withdrawal of the 8th and 11th armies from the German trap.

Meanwhile, the Stavka ordered four reserve corps – including one mechanized from the Northern Front – against Heeresgruppe Nord. However, the blows dealt by Fliegerkorps I's bombers contributed decisively to slowing down the march of fresh Red Army troops to meet Panzergruppe 4. As a result, the panzer spearhead could advance rapidly in a northeasterly direction, encountering only weak opposition. 16. Armee's infantry followed behind, turning toward the east in order to secure the flanks. The skies above the forward panzer columns were dominated by Major Trautloft's Messerschmitt fighters. Lacking air reconnaissance, the Soviets were belatedly informed of the fact that German 1. Panzer-Division had managed to seize the bridge across River Velikaya near Tizhina, at Ostrov – having accomplished an astounding march of 200 kilometers in 36 hours. However, when Sobennikov's and Novikov's headquarters were informed of this, strong counter-measures were taken. In the afternoon of 4 July,

THE MYTH OF THE STALIN LINE.

During its 200 kilometer-advance to River Velikaya on 2–4 July, German 1. Panzer-Division actually breached what has gone down into history writing as the "Stalin Line." This designation, never used by the Soviets, but deriving from German propaganda, is however most unfortunate. It was not a defense line like the French Maginot Line or the German West Wall. The so-called "Stalin Line" was a series of fortifications, forming Tukhachevskiy's "kill zones" – corridors into which an attacking enemy's armor was to be led and annihilated. Thus it was deliberately perforated. But by the time the Germans attacked, the artillery, anti-tank guns and machine guns had been removed from these fortifications and moved to a new defensive line along the new 1939 border. This new defensive line, actually called the "Molotov Line," is far less known – probably owing to the fact that it was rapidly penetrated by the Germans on 22–23 June 1941.

41 SAD was dispatched against the bridge. The first SB formation ran straight into 5./JG 53, which shot down three bombers. Next followed seven SBs from 10 SBAP, led by Kapitan Leonid Mikhailov. In a fierce clash with II./JG 53, six bombers were lost, while the bomber gunners claimed to have shot down four Bf 109s.[22] II./JG 53 actually had three Bf 109s shot down. Leonid Mikhailov reportedly directed his burning SB straight into a German vehicle column below.[23]

In order to thwart any further Soviet air attacks, Luftflotte 1 struck with force against Soviet airfields on 5 July, claiming 40 aircraft destroyed on the ground at Dno-Grivochki alone and 25 at Tuleblya.[24] In consequence, Northwestern Front's counter-attack against the Velikaya bridgehead initially received only weak support from the air. Still, their heavy tanks completely annihilated a whole task force from 1. Panzer-Division.[25] Again the Luftwaffe was called in, and dive-bombing attacks by KG 1, KG 76, and KG 77 broke up the Soviet counter-offensive. The Ju 88s flew both close-support missions at Ostrov, and preventative raids against retrograde movements at Pskov in the north. 140 Soviet tanks were reported as destroyed, and virtually all Soviet supply lines to the Ostrov sector were cut off.

The Soviets worked throughout the night to repair what had been damaged in the previous day's airbase attacks, and on 6 July, General-Mayor Novikov dispatched all flyable aircraft against the Velikaya bridges at Ostrov. But by that time, Trautloft's fighters were on full alert, and some had even been shifted forward to Ostrov, close to the front line. According to German sources, 73 Soviet bombers were dispatched, few of which would return. Major Trautloft himself became witness from the ground to how a formation of five Soviet bombers were totally annihilated by Bf 109s. In total, Trautloft's fighter pilots claimed 62 victories on 6 July – almost all against bombers. Included among the Soviet losses was 202 SBAP's commander, Polkovnik Nikolay Yefimov. The few Soviet fighters that were tasked with escorting the bombers failed utterly, but in a sense that applies to the Bf 109s too. Albeit at a dreadful price, the Soviet bombers nevertheless succeeded in dealing heavy blows against Panzergruppe 4's troop and vehicle columns. On 7 July, Novikov's last remaining bombers were sent out against the same target, again spreading havoc among the congested concentrations of German troops and vehicles at the Velikaya bridges, and again suffering tremendously at the hands of the Messerschmitts. This time JG 54 claimed 42 planes shot down – including the 750th victory of the Geschwader.*

In total, the VVS carried out 1,200 sorties, dropping 500 tons of bombs against the German armored columns in the Ostrov sector between 1 July and 10 July. The encounters with Major Trautloft's fighters almost completely obliterated the VVS bomber units in the northern combat zone. Between 4 July and 9 July, 2 SAD and 41 SAD alone sustained 60 aircraft losses.[26] Indeed, these bomber units were at the end of the rope, but they had completed their task. All the bridges at Velikaya were destroyed. On 10 July, the German Army Headquarters reported "heavy losses in arms and other equipment through enemy air attacks against 1.Panzer-Division."[27] Generalmajor Franz Landgraf meanwhile reported that his 6. Panzer-Division sustained particularly heavy personnel losses through these air attacks.[28]

* One of the Soviet pilots who was shot down by JG 54 on this day, Ivan Shiyan of SB-equipped 35 SBAP, was captured by the Germans and later sided with the Germans, flying Messerschmitt fighters in the Luftwaffe. After the war he was sentenced to 25 years in prison by a Soviet court. (Zvyagintsev, *Tribunal dlya "Stalinskikh sokol"*, p. 199.)

Heeresgruppe Nord finally reached the stage where it could begin the advance towards Leningrad, one of the main goals for Operation Barbarossa. This however required that the flanks were covered. On the southern flank, the infantry of 16. Armee had difficulties in keeping pace with the motorized columns of Panzergruppe 4. On 4 July, when 1. Panzer-Division seized the railway bridge across Velikaya at Ostrov, 16. Armee still lagged 150 kilometers behind. Heeresgruppe Nord had been the weakest among the three German army groups already when Operation Barbarossa was launched, and its lines grew even thinner as it fanned out across 350 kilometers, from the Bay of Riga to the area north of Velikiye Luki. Thus, Generalfeldmarschall von Leeb was compelled to split up both Panzergruppe 4 and 18. Armee. Two of 18. Armee's three army corps were assigned to cover Panzergruppe 4 and support its southern flank, while XXVI. Armeekorps was swung northwards against Soviet 8th Army in Estonia. Simultaneously, from Velikaya, Panzergruppe 4 diverted General von Manstein's LVI. Panzerkorps

A German 20mm Flak 38 anti-aircraft gun mounted to protect the Velikaya bridge at Pskov against Soviet air attacks. (Photo: Hans-Ekkehard Bob.)

towards the east in the direction of Lake Ilmen, while the attack against Leningrad could only be made by General Reinhard's XLI. Panzerkorps.

Meanwhile, on 10 July, the Stavka reorganized the command structure of the Soviet armed forces. Three new supreme commands were created: the Northwestern Direction, comprising the Northern and Northwestern fronts; the Western Direction, comprising the Western Front; and the Southwestern Direction, comprising the Southwestern and Southern fronts.

Command of the Northwestern Direction was assigned to Marshal Voroshilov, and General-Mayor Novikov took overall command of the army air forces in the North-

western Direction. These two men were of quite opposite character. Quite unimaginative, Voroshilov ordered stiff resistance at all places. At this stage, the Northern Front had only thirteen divisions to defend Leningrad and the whole Karelian region as far north as Murmansk. But Leningrad's civilian population was mobilized in a way that could only be done in a country like the Soviet Union. Tens of thousands of men volunteered for worker's militias and set off to the front. Meanwhile, many more men and women labored night and day to create new defense lines. The most forward of these was constructed at River Luga, 100 kilometers south of Leningrad. Here the Luga Operational Group was organized with three Rifle divisions and a half-formed Mountain Troop brigade.[29]

General-Mayor Novikov was one of the most competent Soviet senior commanders. Drawing lessons from the bitter defeats in the air produced by the use of unescorted bombers operating in daylight, he decided to shift the bomber missions to night time, a far less hazardous business due to the lack of effective German night fighters. In daylight, all bomber missions were to be provided with fighter escort. Novikov placed an increasing reliance on his fighter units, demanding a more aggressive stance against enemy aircraft. The VVS fighter units were also called on to carry out incessant, swift, low-level harassment attacks against the German ground troops. On 11 and 12 July, Soviet airmen claimed to have put fifteen German tanks and ninety armored vehicles out of commission and destroyed two bridges in the area southeast of Lake Peipus. Even though Fliegerkorps I claimed that it had shot down 487 Soviet planes in the air and destroyed 1,211 on the ground between 22 June and 13 July, resistance in the air was clearly mounting. On 13 July, Heeresgruppe Nord reported 354 Soviet aircraft in action over the front.[30] All of this compelled the Germans to return repeatedly to fresh air-base raids.

While escorting Ju 88s against a Soviet airfield in the Novgorod region near Lake Ilmen on 13 July, Oberleutnant Gerhard Ludwig of I./JG 54 was rammed by Leytenant Aristotel Kavtaradze of 38 IAP, and both pilots were killed. Soviet air rammings became a particular preoccupation of the airmen of Luftflotte 1 during this period of the war. In fact, almost half of the sixty tarans – air-to-air rammings – performed by Soviet airmen during the month of July 1941, were made in the northern combat zone. Several so-called fire tarans, i.e. the deliberate crashing of an aircraft against a ground target, were also reported. Two days previously, Starshiy Leytenant Fedor Turkin of 38 IAP had crashed his I-153 biplane straight into a vehicle column of von Manstein's LVI. Panzerkorps.[31]

After the fall of the Velikaya line, the Soviets withdrew rapidly to the Luga line in the northeast, while offering a determined resistance against von Manstein's forces in the south. General-Mayor Novikov concentrated a force of 235 aircraft, including units from VVS Northwestern Front, 2 SAD of the Northern Front, and 1 BAK of the DBA, against LVI. Panzerkorps. On 14 July, as von Manstein's panzers seized the town of Soltsy, 30 km west of Lake Ilmen, Novikov dispatched all available aircraft in continuous attacks against German troops, tanks, and artillery batteries in the Soltsy region. The Germans described this as some of the heaviest Soviet air attacks encountered so far. This was the prelude to the counter-offensive organized by General-Leytenant Sobennikov, the Northwestern Front's new commander. Soviet 11th Army blundered straight into von Manstein's forces with overwhelming effect. Having escaped annihilation through a quick withdrawal in June, while Northwestern Front's armor held up Heeresgruppe Nord, this army was now able not only to take up positions on Northwestern Front's otherwise quite endangered southern flank, but also to mount a counter-offensive against von Manstein's exhausted troops.

When the 11th Army struck with its 70th Rifle Division on 15 July, it was with such force that von Manstein's infantry was pushed back 40 kilometers, leaving 8. Panzer-Division enveloped by the Soviets. Next, Soviet 21st Tank Division with 128 T-26 tankettes and a small number of heavy KVs attacked the 8. Panzer. In the ensuing tank battle, 39 German tanks were knocked out (of which 12 were total losses) at a cost of 54 Soviet tanks, nearly all of them T-26s. The 8. Panzer-Division was able to hold out only due to supplies brought in from the air by three-engine Junkers Ju 52 transport planes. The battle around Soltsy raged for four days, during which the air force of the Northwestern Front carried out fifteen hundred close-support sorties. These could be carried out without much interference from the fighters of Luftflotte 1, who were handicapped by the long distance from their airfields west of the Velikaya.

A detachment from JG 54 which had been brought forward to an airstrip at Porkhov, 60 km southwest of Soltsy, was driven off by a Soviet tank raid against the airfield on 16 July.[32] Meanwhile, a single Soviet Pe-2 bomber crew carried out a lightning strike against the German main airbase

A Soviet sniper. (Photo: Krigsarkivet Stockholm.)

A destroyed Panzer III. (Photo: Krigsarkivet Stockholm.)

in the area, at Pskov, 130 km from Soltsy. Major Hannes Trautloft, commanding the German fighters in Luftflotte 1, received an urgent report: "The air base has been attacked by a Russian Pe-2 bomber coming in at low level. We have several badly wounded men. Urgently request a Ju 52 transport plane for immediate evacuation of the wounded."[33]

While this took place, XXVI. Armeekorps of 18. Armee became bogged down in heavy fighting with Soviet 8th Army in Estonia. Here the Germans received invaluable support from the Estonian nationalist partisans, the so-called "Forest Brothers," who were substantially reinforced when elements of the Soviet-Estonian 22nd Rifle Corps revolted on 9-10 July and joined forces with the "Forest Brothers". The Estonian nationalists attacked the Soviet positions in Dorpat (Tartu) on the western side of Lake Peipus, 110 km northwest of the Velikaya bridges at Pskov. In bitter fighting, the "Forest Brothers" managed to take control of the southern part of Dorpat, and were able to welcome the troops of German XXVI. Armeekorps when these arrived on 12 July.*

When Sobennikov had been appointed to replace Kuznetsov as the commander of the Northwestern Front a few days earlier, General-Leytenant Fedor Ivanov was called in from the Southwestern Front to lead the 8th Army. Ivanov, who had organized armored counter-attacks against Heeresgruppe Süd, now quickly organized a quite successful defense in central Estonia against the German advance from the south. He dispatched 16th Rifle Division against Dorpat, and with the support of the aviation of the Red Banner Baltic Fleet these troops managed to hold northern Dorpat and thus block the German attack. The battle for Dorpat raged for several days.

Reporting on the situation to Hitler on 13 July, the Commander-in-Chief of the German Army, Generalfeldmarschall Walther von Brauchitsch, and the Chief of the General Staff, Generaloberst Franz Halder, had to admit that although the Soviet lines were held by weak forces

---

* According to a German narrative, Dorpat was captured through a daring raid by a Wehrmacht force, but both Soviet and Estonian reports prove that this is wrong. (Baltic Defence Review No. 9 Volume 1/2003.)

or troops of dubious quality, the Soviets "surely have no thought of giving ground."[34] Apparently reconsidering his previous contemptuous opinion on the Russians as "sub-humans," Hitler blurted out that "the Russian is a colossus and strong" and ordered "terror raids against Moscow."[35] Halder found it "absolutely intolerable" that a whole army corps could be held back at Dorpat by just "three [sic] enemy divisions," as he wrote in his diary.[36] (One can only guess what Halder's reaction would have been, had he known that it in fact was just a single Soviet division that blocked XXVI. Armeekorps in eastern Estonia.) When still no progress had been made three days later, Halder ordered von Leeb to move 93. Infanterie-Divison from the army group's reserve and employ it against Dorpat "with all available means and to report on compliance."[37]

Soviet signal troops in the frontline. (Photo: Semen Friedland via Mikhail Filatov.)

In Heeresgruppe Nord's center, on the road to Leningrad, Panzergruppe 4 meanwhile was also halted after it had managed to establish two bridgeheads across River Luga at Porechye and Bolshoy Sabsk, 120 km southwest of Leningrad, on 14 July. This was accomplished through a daring dash by a combat group from 6. Panzer-Division under Oberst Erhard Raus through an area just east of Lake Peipus. Marshal Voroshilov had not expected the Germans to advance in this sector – he was focused on the main forces of Panzergruppe 4, which 60 kilometres farther to the east was moving towards Leningrad straight from the south, along the highway from Pskov. Neither did he have any forces available to plug in the gap just to the east of Lake Peipus, having concentrated his troops to block the highway.

This German advance was conducted with the utmost skill. By ordering a "quasi-peacetime march," Oberst Raus managed to give the Soviet aerial reconnaissance the impression that his force was a Red Army unit on the move. The western Luga was forced before noon on 14 July. A tank detachment carried on in the direction of Leningrad on the other side of the river to make a surprise raid on the airfield at Yastrebina, just 105 km southwest of Leningrad, "driving through the hangars and over the planes standing about on the ground."[38]

All that Voroshilov had to plug in the gap into which 6. Panzer-Division poured, was the 2nd People's Volunteer Rifle Division, and this had just been formed and was in Leningrad when 6. Panzer-Division crossed the Luga. Mustering 7,200 men with often no military training, and supplemented with a handful of KV tanks fresh from the factory in Leningrad and manned by cadets from Leningrad's tank school, the fresh division was loaded onto trains in Leningrad. In the meantime, the only means with which the Soviets could counter the German breakthrough towards Leningrad was its aviation, and Novikov acted quickly. All airfields in the Leningrad area were instantly alerted. "Hardly an hour had passed before our completely worn-out troops, who had only just arrived in their assigned defensive sectors, were roughly jolted out of sleep," wrote Oberst Raus. "Out of a clear sky the villages, farms, roads and adjacent fringes of forest were subjected to a veritable downpour of bombs. A particularly large share was meted out to the villages of Muravina and Porechye, situated on both sides of the bridges [at the Luga bridgehead]. Waves of enemy aircraft continued to attack in succession until the day drew to a close."[39]

In fact, a swift German flanking move northwest of Voroshilov's forces at Luga and straight towards Leningrad was averted by the Soviet aviation alone. Just as in the case with von Manstein's force at Soltsy, the VVS dominated in the air over the Luga bridgehead because the distance from the German fighter airfields west of Velikaya was so large. Oberst Raus's force was held down by these air attacks until the first elements of the 2nd People's Volunteer Rifle Division arrived in the morning of 15 July. But all the untrained civilians in uniform could do was to sacrifice their lives in futile and terribly badly conducted counter-attacks, thus forcing the Germans to revert to the defensive. The Leningrad volunteers were mowed down in large numbers by German artillery, mortars and machine gun fire. 1,398 of them were returned to Leningrad for treatment of their injuries; the number of killed has never been established. But the combination of their death-defying counter-attack and the continued attacks by Soviet aircraft had the effect of halting 6. Panzer-Division. Shortly afterward, the Soviet 60th Separate Armored Train "Karl Liebknecht" arrived, adding significant weight to the Soviet defenses.

With Soviet aviation constituting a great hindrance to Panzergruppe 4 both at Luga and at Soltsy, it was decided that Fliegerkorps I would dispatch all available aircraft in a massive operation against the Soviet airfields on 17 July. About forty twin-engine Messerschmitt Bf 110 long-range fighters of Stab and I./ZG 26 were rapidly brought in from Fliegerkorps VIII, thus reducing the aerial support for Panzergruppe 3 of Heeresgruppe Mitte just as this was subject to increasingly powerful Soviet counter-attacks. But the Soviets struck first. The '110s had barely landed at the airfield at Pskov before the same Pe-2 that had struck the airbase on the previous day launched another lightning strike. "Again," wrote Major Trautloft of JG 54, "the

Members of the 2nd People's Volunteer Rifle Division return to Leningrad after bitter fighting with German 6. Panzer-Division.

LATVIAN PARTISANS.

Just like in Lithuania, although on a smaller scale, Latvian partisans began to attack Soviet officials and retreating Red Army units shortly after the German attack on 22 June. Latvia had also suffered from the NKVD deportations of 14 June 1941, when 15,000 citizens were forcefully transported to Siberia.

A large number of soldiers from the Red Army's 24th Latvian Rifle Corps changed side and joined the partisans. These achieved a major feat on 1 July, when they seized control of the capital, Riga, ahead of the German troops.[1] When a German motorcycle scout entered Riga a few hours later, as the first German soldier, the people covered him with flowers and wreaths.[2] On 2 July the town of Sigulda, northeast of Riga, was taken by the Latvian partisans, who held it for two days until the Germans arrived.

Also similar to the situation in Lithuania, the Latvian partisans immediately initiated pogroms against the Jews. Many of these were instigated by the Germans, but Latvian officers also made radio broadcasts where they called for the people to get rid of Soviet functionaries, Communists and Jews. On 2 July, Latvian partisans with red and white armbands began to search Riga for Jews, and arrested all they could find. In the process, a large number of Jews were beaten to death, others were shot on the spot. Most of the perpetrators belonged to the so-called "Arjas Commando," formed by the Latvian partisan Viktors Arājs on 1 July, and placed under the direct command of Generalmajor der Polizei Walter Stahlecker, the commander of Einsatzgruppe A. On 4 July, the "Arajs Commando" burned all the synagogues in Riga, whereby many people were burned alive.

On 20 July, on the instruction of the Germans, Latvian Lieutenant Colonel Voldemārs Veiss formed a Latvian Auxiliary Police Force, which would also take part in the mass killings. The "Arjas Commando," integrated into this force, alone would murder approximately 26,000 people in both Latvia and Belarus. On 30 November and 8 December, the Latvian Auxiliary Police Force and the bodyguards of German SS-Obergruppenführer Friedrich Jeckeln executed 25,000 Jews in the Rumbula forest near Riga; 24,000 of those were Jews from Riga, and over one thousand were Jews recently deported from Germany. In total, Latvian collaborators and the Germans would kill 95 percent of Latvia's 100,000 Jews.

Supervised by a German soldier, a group of Latvian partisans have apprehended a Jewish man.

1 Mangulis, *Latvia in the Wars of the 20th Century*, p. 95.
2 Ibid.

Through a daring dash in the flank of the Soviets, Kampfgruppe Koll of 6. Panzer-Division managed to cross River Luga on 14 July 1941. Seen in this photo is the commander, Oberst Richard Koll – who also commanded Panzer-Regiment 11 of that division – in the turret of his command Panzer III, cigarette-holder in his mouth. Koll was awarded the Knight's Cross for this feat on 15 July 1941. He survived the war and passed away on 13 May 1963, at the age of 66. (Photo: Helmut Ritgen.)

same Russian aircraft appeared. With incredible impudence this Russian dropped his bombs on the airbase at Pskov. We have losses in personnel and aircraft. Three aircraft were totally burned out."[40]

Testifying to the determination with which the Soviets fought to defend Leningrad, Politruk Ivan Chebotaryov of 38 IAP followed the example set by Starshiy Fedor Turkin six days previously and crashed his I-153 into a German ground position at Soltsy on 17 July.[41]

It was only with the arrival of I. Armeekorps from 18. Armee on 19 July that von Manstein's Panzerkorps could be relieved from its critical situation. By then, the battle had cost 8. Panzer-Division 70 destroyed or damaged tanks.[42] The men of the previously surrounded 8. Panzer-Division were found to be so shaken that the whole unit had to be temporarily pulled out of combat and sent into the army group's reserve – even though that meant that von Manstein was deprived of all his armor.[43] Von Leeb had no choice; he could only establish that his army group had been halted all along the line.

The Blitzkrieg in the northern combat zone had come to an end. Resistance was sharpening, both on the ground and in the air. The VVS was becoming increasingly active and aggressive, even though the Luftwaffe maintained its qualitative superiority. The new concentration on Soviet fighters rapidly provided the invaders with mounting difficulties. This became a main preoccupation of the German ground troops, who became subject to continuous strafing and bombing from fast-flying fighter-bombers dropping out of the clouds. This would become an important benchmark of the entire war on the Eastern Front. This dominant ground-support air doctrine, in fact, emerged spontaneously from the shortcomings of the Soviet light and medium bombers during the initial weeks of the war.

One spectacular feature of the war in the northern combat zone during the first four weeks of hostilities was that Heeresgruppe Nord had succeeded in one important operational goal – to race across the Baltic states – without achieving its main strategic goal, the annihilation of the Soviet Northwestern Front. Down to about 350 aircraft in mid-July, Luftflotte 1 was unable to meet the increasing demands of supporting an army group in three directions. During the remainder of July 1941 and well into August, this weakness of Luftflotte 1 ground down Heeresgruppe Nord to slow and exhausting fights on the two flanks, mainly involving its two infantry armies.

One aspect of Soviet 11th Army's devastating strike against von Manstein's panzer corps that has not been observed in many accounts is the influence that it had on operations along the road to Moscow. In fact, it directly led Hitler – who was informed in detail of the sorrowful situation for Heeresgruppe Nord on 26 July – to order Fliegerkorps VIII to immediately shift from Luftflotte 2 to the Soltsy-Lake Ilmen sector on 29 July.[44] Thus deprived of half its aerial support, Heeresgruppe Mitte's capacity to continue immediately towards Moscow was thwarted.

Offensive in the South, June–December 1941.

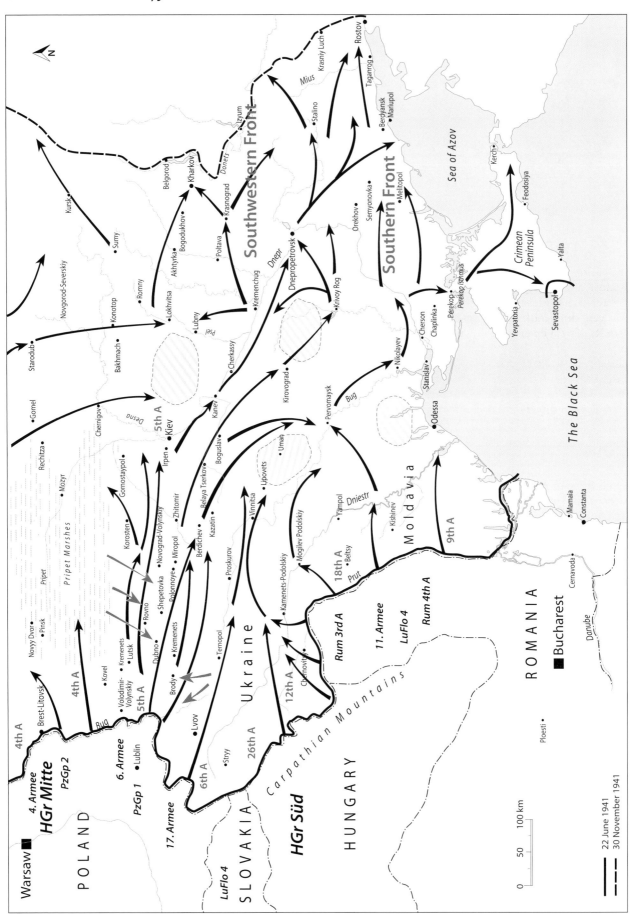

8: THE ADVANCE TOWARDS KIEV.

"These massive air attacks were absolutely terrible. People went mad from fear. One had the feeling that every bomb was directed against yourself,. High in the sky we saw this whole armada floating; we were afraid. Then they came down to attack us, with all of them howling, and dropped a hailstorm of bombs."

– Soviet tankman Ariya Lvovich.

To the south of the Pripyat Marshes, along the 1,200 kilometer front assigned to Generalfeldmarschall Gerd von Rundstedt's Heeresgruppe Süd, with air cover provided by Generaloberst Alexander Löhr's Luftflotte 4, the situation was very different from that to the north of the Marshes. Von Rundstedt opened his offensive by launching the German 6. and 17. armies, together with Generaloberst Ewald von Kleist's Panzergruppe 1 on the left flank, between the Pripyat Marshes and the Hungarian-Slovakian border. These forces were intended to strike in an eastern and a southeastern direction, while the Romanian 3rd and 4th armies and the German 11. Armee were held back along the Soviet-Romanian border. The purpose of this operation was to encircle and destroy most of the Red Army troops west of the Dnepr River.

The northern group of Heeresgruppe Süd was the strongest, but it also faced the largest concentrations of Red Army forces along the entire Eastern Front. Stalin had placed the main emphasis on General-Polkovnik Mikhail Kirponos' Southwestern Front. Kirponos was one among many senior Soviet commanders who, as a result of the purge of the Red Army, had been promoted beyond his ability. Arguably, he was an able divisonal commander.

In early March 1940, during the Winter War, he had decided the fate of the Finnish defense by dispatching his 70th Rifle Division around Vyborg on the ice of the Gulf of Finland, for which he was appointed a Hero of the Soviet Union. As we have seen, he had also attempted to place his forces in combat readiness before the Germans struck – although he was sharply rebuked for this by the Red Army's Chief of Staff, General Armii Georgiy Zhukov. However, he lacked both the education and the experience to command an entire army group; he was promoted from divisional to corps commander and then to army group commander in only three months.

In the evening of the first day of the war, Zhukov also was sent to "advise" Kirponos. This may be seen as a reflection of the great importance that Stalin placed on the defense of the Ukraine, but without doubt Zhukov also had the mission of controlling the "self-minded" Kirponos.

At the outbreak of the war, 5,956 tanks, nearly half the 13,000 tanks in the Military districts in the western parts of the USSR, were available to Kirponos alone – against which Panzergruppe 1 deployed 908 tanks and assault guns. But the Soviet numerical superiority was not as great as it appears to be. Among the Soviet tanks, only one thousand were equipped with cannon able to deal with enemy armor (the remainder were light tanks of the types T-26, T-40 or BT), while among the German tanks 211 were of the light Panzer I type with only machine-guns while nearly 700 were armed with cannons.[1] Nevertheless, Kirponos had 278 out of the total number of 471 KVs available to the Red Army, and 514 of 821 T-34s. Thus, nearly 800 of his tanks were widely superior to anything that von Kleist could put forward. However, this superiority could not be used because of the dispersal of the mechanized units in the depths of the rear: Whereas von Kleist's armor was concentrated, Kirponos could only launch his dispersed tanks piecemeal, and they would also be destroyed piecemeal.

Moreover, von Rundstedt was the undoubtedly finest among the three German army group commanders in Operation Barbarossa, and it is hard to find a senior commander in World War II who can be described as superior to von Rundstedt. Sixty-five years of age, he was one of the war's most experienced staff officers and senior commanders. He had served with Imperial Germany's General Staff already in 1907, and was Chief of Staff of several units in World War One. During the war against Poland, he held a key position as the commander of the southern army group, and during the Western Offensive in May 1940, it was his army group that made the decisive breakthrough in the Ardennes and sealed off the British army at Dunkirk. He had worked closely with Generaloberst Ewald von Kleist, who commanded Heeresgruppe Süd's only armored group, Panzergruppe 1, since the beginning of the war: von Kleist had led the armor of von Rundstedt's army group in all previous campaigns.

Von Rundstedt's attack on 22 June was directed towards the main road leading from southeastern Poland straight towards Kiev, the capital of the Ukrainian Soviet republic, in the east. Here the Germans enjoyed a considerable numerical superiority, initially encountering only elements of Soviet 5th Army and NKVD border troops. However, as we have seen, Heeresgruppe Süd became bogged down in heavy border fighting during most of 22

The crew of a Ju 88 of KG 51 study the result of a Soviet anti-aircraft hit. (Photo: Klaus Häberlen.)

June. Only after very heavy and bloody battles was Panzergruppe 1 able to start advancing into a 30-kilometer wide gap during the afternoon on the offensive's first day. A key element to the breakthrough was the support offered by the bombers of Fliegerkorps V –as described by Polkovnik Ivan Fedyuninskiy, the commander of Soviet 15th Rifle Corps: "German aircraft attacked the railways and the supply lines. We suffered from a severe shortage of radio equipment, and most soldiers did not know how to handle this equipment. Orders and instructions were delayed or did not reach the troops at all. This enabled the enemy to break through our defense lines rapidly, and then they could attack our staff headquarters. Although the Germans were in control of the air, our columns undertook no measures to avoid detection from the air. Frequently, congestion of troops, artillery, vehicles and field kitchens occurred on narrow roads. Such clusters inevitably became rich targets for the enemy air force."

In fact, the battle in Heeresgruppe Süd's sector was not decided on 22 June, as it was further north, but in fierce battles during the following days, and much owing to a most unfortunate order from Moscow. In the evening of 22 June, the Soviet High Command ordered the Southwestern Front to "carry out concentric strikes in the direction of Lublin, utilizing at least five mechanized corps and the aviation of the Front, in order to encircle and destroy the enemy and by the end of 24 June to occupy the region of Lublin [130 kilometers inside German-occupied Poland]." Nothing could more clearly illustrate the incompetence of the Soviet High Command. Not only had Southwestern

Front's forces been dispersed to the depth, but the Front also had lost contact with several of its subordinate units.

General-Leytenant Maksim Purkayev, the Chief of Staff of the Southwestern Front, and his deputy, General-Mayor Ivan Bagramyan, were completely stunned as they received the wire that ordered the Southwestern Front to launch a counter-attack against the concentrated German forces. "We were both of the same opinion," the latter wrote after the war: "An attack under the present conditions would be disastrous." Purkayev explained the situation: "Ten enemy infantry and tank divisions are attacking in the Sokal-Lyubachuv [Lubaczów] sector alone." This was actually an understatement of the force deployed by Panzergruppe 1 in this 75-kilometer wide sector northwest of Lvov. "What are we able to launch against them?" Purkayev continued: "We know that here we only have two regiments each of the 45th, 62nd, 87th and 124th Rifle divisions. Their third regiments are still on the march towards the front. In this sector we will by tomorrow be able to have, if we are fortunate, the 135th Rifle division and two divisions of the 22nd Mechanized Corps also – although its best division, the 41st Tank Division, will hardly make it to the front in time. . . . Also, we must not forget that our units that are marching towards the border are subject to massive strikes by the enemy's air force." Purkayev turned to the Front commander, Kirponos, and said: "We have no choice but to inform the People's Commissar of the true situation and ask him to change the order."

This caused an outburst from the commissar of the Southwestern Front's Military Council, Nikolai Vashugin.

"Do you know, Maksim Alekseyevich," he said, turning to Purkayev, "you are our officer with the greatest war experience, and had I not known you as an experienced Bolshevik, I would have thought that you had panicked. . ." This was a clear threat. Kirponos could not afford another stand-off with the High Command. With a stern face he said: "Orders are orders . . . We have to concentrate the mechanized corps as rapidly as possible. Special attention has to be paid to the task of providing our ground forces with air cover. Potapov [Soviet 5th Army's commander, General Polkovnik Mikahil Potapov] must be instructed to cooperate with the 6th Army, and with strong support by our Front Air Force they must prevent the enemy from advancing deeper into our territory." Vashugin yelled: "That is right!" Purkayev said nothing. He just nodded his head. Shortly afterwards, General Armii Georgiy Zhukov and Nikita Khrushchev, the head of the Communist Party in Ukraine, arrived, and demanded the attack to be launched as soon as possible. This sealed the fate of the Southwestern Front.

One cause of optimism for the Soviets was their still substantial air assets. While the VVS in the central combat zone was more or less paralyzed on 23 June by the crippling blows dealt by the Luftwaffe on the first day of the war, the Soviet Air Force in the southern combat zone managed to maintain a high level of activity. VVS Southwestern Front had lost 192 aircraft on 22 June, but it had since mustered 1,913 aircraft when the German invasion began, it still was a force to be reckoned with. It was led by General-Leytenant Yevgeniy Ptukhin, a Hero of the Soviet Union and veteran of the wars in Spain and against Finland. On the first day of the war, Ptukhin instructed his bomber and ground-attack units to concentrate all efforts against the attacking enemy columns and the airfields of the enemy. Two of the Long-Range Aviation's bombers corps took part in this also.

VVS Southwestern Front was opposed by Fliegerkorps V of Luftflotte 4, which had also sustained some heavy losses on the first day of the war, when 10 per cent of its 226 bombers and 15 per cent of its 98 fighters were put out of commission. However, the better quality of the German aircraft and the greater experience among their aircrew would prove to be decisive.

Early on 23 June, a large formation of DB-3s from bomber corps 4 BAK caught a German tank column in open field. Vasiliy Kurayev, who served as a radio operator with bomber regiment 8 DBAP, recalled: "Our whole wing took off. There were nine formations of nine aircraft each. Without encountering any opposition, we detected a large German tank column in the vicinity of Shepetovka. We were instructed to attack individually. One by one, our 81 DB-3s made individual passes and bombed the column from an altitude of only 800 meters. The result was absolutely devastating. Our bombs destroyed a large number of vehicles. Fire, explosions and thick smoke soon covered the entire column. As we left, nothing could be seen but burning and overturned tanks and other vehicles. All of us made it to the base, where we received an enthusiastic welcoming. We felt that we would defeat the enemy!"[2]

But this proved to be an exception. The fighter wing assigned to provide von Kleist's Panzergruppe with air cover, JG 3, was commanded by Major Günther Lützow, one of the best wing commanders of the Luftwaffe. On this day, Lützow dispatched all his fighters in standing patrols in formations of two or three over the whole battlefield. As soon as Soviet bombers arrived, any such small fighter formation would attack and call for reinforcements. During

This Soviet SB bomber crashed and burned during an attempted belly-landing after it was shot down by German fighters. (Photo: Hans-Ekkehard Bob.)

A light T-26 tank and Soviet infantry join the raging tank battle.

the next Soviet bomber mission that same day, twenty-seven DB-3s of 8 DBAP were intercepted by a large number of JG 3's Messerschmitt Bf 109s and lost nine bombers. JG 3 claimed eleven shot down.[3] Vasiliy Kurayev recalled: "I did not participate in this mission because my own aircraft was unserviceable due to technical malfunction. But I was there to witness the scenes as our aircraft returned. We had the wives of the airmen at our base. As our bombers began to return, damaged and with wounded crewmembers on board, the women became greatly disturbed and began to gather at the landing strip. After a while, when it began to become clear that only 18 out of 27 bombers would return, and that we had lost around thirty airmen, a total chaos broke out as the women began to weep and wail. This of course had a strong impact on our nerves, and the main task of our commander was to remove all the women from the airfield. When they had left, the feelings of the men came out. Now we understood that this would be a terrible war and that it would cost bitter losses."[4] All in all, Lützow and his men were credited with the destruction of 34 Soviet bombers and four fighters on 23 June, with only three of their own aircraft getting downed in force-landings. Meanwhile, Luftflotte 4's bombers were deployed against Soviet airfields as well as against the large armor columns that were detected marching towards the front. If the Luftwaffe played a vital role in the operations of Heeresgruppe Mitte, it was of absolutely decisive importance to Heeresgruppe Süd – not only during the initial days, but throughout the whole campaign. Fifteen Soviet airfields were attacked by

Luftflotte 4 on 23 June alone, with substantial success. At Stanislav, 20 fighters of 64 SAD were reported destroyed, and at airfields such as Stryy (home of 63 SAD), Tarnopol (16 SAD) and Chernovits (64 SAD), many more aircraft were destroyed on the gorund ground.[5] A force of just two hundred German bombers performed a total of 1,600 sorties against seventy-seven Soviet air bases between 22 and 25 June, claiming the destruction of 774 aircraft on the ground. In addition to that, Lützow's Messerschmitt fighters reportedly shot down 89 Soviet planes.[6] The Luftwaffe's own losses were also high – 55 German planes were lost in the same period.[7] But these air actions resulted in the near collapse of VVS Southern Front, which was unable to perform more than 523 combat sorties during those four days.[8] Quite remarkably, at the same time Fliegerkorps V also managed to wreak havoc among the columns of Soviet tanks en route to attack the German ground troops. In the absence of ground-attack aircraft in Fliegerkorps V, the medium-bomber units – KG 51, KG 54 and KG 55 – carried out continuous low-level attacks against the counter-attacking Soviet forces that blocked the way of Panzergruppe 1 on the road to Kiev. Although costly to the air units, these missions were of paramount importance to the outcome of the battle.

Early on 23 June, 27th Rifle Corps of Soviet 5th Army launched a counter-attack against the northern flank of Panzergruppe 1 in the Volodimir-Volynskiy area. German bomber wing KG 54 intervened with 74 bombers which destroyed twenty T-26 tanks and damaged another four-

Destroyed T-26 tanks from the 19th Tank Division of Soviet 22nd Mechanized Corps, near Lutsk in June 1941. In a large tank battle on 24 June 1941, the 19th Tank Division lost 118 of its 163 tanks. During this battle, the divisional commander, General-Mayor Kuzma Semenchenko, was wounded, and the corps commander, General-Mayor Semyon Kondrusev, was killed. Despite his wounds, Semenchenko continued to fight. In July, he organized a successful break-out from a German encirclement, and was appointed a Hero of the Soviet Union on 22 July 1941.

teen.[9] Soviet tankman Ariya Lvovich recalled: "These massive air attacks were absolutely terrible. People went mad from fear. One had the feeling that every bomb was directed against yourself. High in the sky we saw this whole armada floating; we were afraid. Then they came down to attack us, with all of them howling, and dropped a hailstorm of bombs. I remember Nekrasov, how he almost went crazy. When the air attack was over, he was gone. Finally we found him crouched in a trench which he refused to leave. There was wild horror in his eyes."[10] Following this onslaught, three German divisions attacked, tore the remainder of the Soviet units apart and forced them to undertake a hasty retreat.

Further to the north, when 6. Armee, Heeresgruppe Süd's northernmost army, was attacked by Soviet 15th Rifle Corps, the Soviet artillery was effectively wiped out by the Luftwaffe. Deprived of this support, the soft-skinned T-26 tanks of 41st Tank Division, which had arrived to bolster the Soviet attack, were mercilessly butchered. By the evening, all but ten of the 64 committed Soviet tanks had been destroyed.[11]

Unteroffizier Gustav Schrodek of 11. Panzer-Division participated in the German counter-attack against the 41st Tank Division: "A divisional reconnaissance plane – a Fieseler Storch – flew over the regiment and threw out a message in the proximity of the regimental commander Oberstleutnant Riebel's car. Afterwards, the entire regiment

received orders: 'Clear for combat!' … The gunners on all vehicles re-sighted their guns in such a manner as to take the enemy tanks under fire. Then it's time, and shell after shell flies towards the Russians. Most of the first shells were hits, some even direct hits. Others tear away whole sections of armor from the enemy tanks. One can see damaged enemy tanks everywhere, with their crews dismounting the best they can. … When the enemy withdrew in the afternoon of 23 June and our first taste of combat in the Russian campaign was over, 46 enemy tanks remain destroyed on the battlefield.[12]

Next day, 24 June, German 6. Armee repelled the attack by 22nd Mechanized Corps, during which the 19th Tank Division was almost completely obliterated.* Notwithstanding these setbacks, the Military Soviet (the military counsel, i.e. a political organ) of the Southwestern Front – where Nikita Khrushchev was the political commissar – ordered an attack against von Kleist's Panzergruppe in the vicinity of Brody, 60 kilometers into northwestern Ukraine, where 9. and 16. Panzer divisions and SS-Division "Wiking" were advancing. Six mechanized corps were mobilized for this operation, and might well have wiped out these three divisions, had it not been for incessant Luftwaffe attacks against their marching columns. Hence, when they reached contact with the enemy's ground forces, they had been reduced to a fraction of their original strength, and were unable to attack other than in piecemeal fashion.

* On 22 June, 19th Tank Division mustered 163 tanks. After losses sustained during the march to the front, 45 were left. On 26 June, the division's tank strength had been reduced to just four. (Isayev, *Ot Dubno do Rostova*, p.147.)

The very first attack on 24 June was launched by no more than the remnants of a single tank division, and by then the Germans were prepared, warned by their aerial reconnaissance.

"Our 12th Tank Division attacked, but failed to achieve any success," wrote General-Leytenant Dmitriy Ryabyshev, commanding the 8th Mechanized Corps. "The enemy's artillery fire was too dense. But the decisive cause was the sudden appearance of enemy aircraft. These came in large groups, 50 to 60 aircraft, and bombed our troops at will. Nowhere could any of our own fighters be seen…"[13]

The effect of these German air attacks can be read in the war diary of the 8th Mechanized Corps on 25 June: "40-50% of the equipment lost to technical failure and enemy air attacks."[14] The original strength of this corps had been around 900 tanks. When 19th Mechanized Corps went into action, it had only 35 tanks (all of which were light tanks), and the 9th Mechanized Corps attacked with 66. "This was our first large miscalculation: while we prepared the counter-offensive, we failed to consider the enemy's superiority in the air," commented Ryabyshev.[15]

On top of this, the headquarters of the Soviet mechanized corps knew very little of the general situation, as was noted by the 43rd Tank Division: "During the march, up to 26 June 1941, there was no information from higher headquarters about situation at the front."

The 9th Mechanized Corps, which was tasked to strike against the German left flank, was sent more or less to its own annihilation. "I watched with bitterness as our old T-26s, BT-5s and few BT-7s marched towards the front, understanding that they would not last long", wrote the corps commander, General-Major Konstantin Rokossovskiy. "They went into combat piecemeal and straight from the march, without any consideration given to their condition."[16]

This was a consequence of the permanent presence of German bombers over the battlefield – any delay in the attack only resulted in mounting Soviet losses. Their only chance to avoid the devastating blows from the air was to get close to the German ground forces, i.e. to attack.

One of the tankmen in the 9th Mechanized Corps described the battle as they blundered straight into German 13. Panzer and 299. Infanterie divisions: "Instead of taking time to prepare us for the combat, our brave commanders decided to carry out a cavalry-like shock on the enemy. 'Hooray! For the Motherland! For Stalin!' we yelled. The engines roared and we set off for the attack. It was a terrible carnage. The Germans laid down an artillery barrage. Around seventy T-26 light tanks took part in the attack, and afterwards only twenty remained."[17]

The operations of Fliegerkorps V against the Soviet aviation also started to have a considerable effect. On 24 June, much of the remnants of 14 SAD were wiped out in

An abandoned KV-2 tank. The KV-2 was virtually invulnerable to direct fire, but suffered from severe technical problems. The gearbox often broke, and of 22 KV-2s lost by 41st Tank Division of 5th Army, only five were due to enemy action. Production of the KV-2 version ceased in October 1941. Out of 1,596 KVs produced in 1940-1941, most were KV-1s, and 334 were KV-2s. (Photo: Hannes Trautloft.)

German air attacks against their airfields at Lutsk. Meanwhile, nine Ju 88s of KG 51 attacked 17 SAD on the airfield at Proskurov. Two of the attackers were shot down, but 55 Soviet aircraft were destroyed or damaged on the ground.[18] Late in the afternoon of 24 June, Soviet 5th Army's commander, General Polkovnik Mikahil Potapov, reported: "14 SAD is under my command. This morning it consisted of 41 aircraft. According to the Front order, we should receive cover from 62 BAD and 18 BAD, but I have no idea where they are. I have lost all contact with them."[19] The failure of VVS Southwestern Front led to the immediate removal of the commander, General-Leytenant Ptukhin. In spite of the accomplishments of his aviation on the first day, he was arrested, accused of sabotage, sentenced to death and executed.

By now, von Rundstedt had torn up a 50-kilometre wide wedge between Soviet 5th Army in the north and 6th Army in the south, which further complicated the Southwestern Front's counter-actions.

It took until 26 June before the significantly weakened 8th Mechanized corps could assemble to join the counter-attack. By that time, Fliegerkorps V's bombers units had completely shifted their focus from air-base raids to direct support of the German ground troops.[20] "The Russians tried to break through everywhere and thereby temporarily created quite critical situations", said Unteroffizier Schrodek of 11. Panzer-Division: "Our own aviation eliminated the activity of the Russian aircraft, which is as usual pleasantly noted." Then 88mm Flak guns were employed against the Soviet tanks. By the evening of 26 June the situation was, in Schrodek's word, "again quite secure".[21] That evening, the 15th Mechanized Corps had lost 473 out of its originally 733 tanks, and in one German air attack, the commander, General-Mayor Ignat Karpezo, had been wounded.[22]

The renewed Soviet counter-attack was supported by the last planes of VVS Southwestern Front. With fighter group I.(J)/LG 2 temporarily brought in from Fliegerkorps IV to support JG 3 in its task of clearing the skies above 6. Armee and Panzergruppe 1, the Soviet airmen met a more powerful fighter opposition than before. In this last major battle between VVS Southwestern Front and Fliegerkorps V's Bf 109s on 26 June, the Germans claimed 24 SBs shot down. With one of them – possibly downed by I./JG 3's Oberleutnant Max Buchholz in the Brody area – 86 SBAP lost its commander, Podpolkovnik Sorokin.[23] After that day, a few dozen aircraft was all that remained of the 251 SBs that had been possessed by VVS KOVO four days previously.

While all roads in the Soviet rear area were subject to massive air attacks, the Germans were able to bring forward seven divisions from the reserve to the battlefield, and this settled the outcome. Kirponos wanted to disengage his forces on 27 June, but this was denied by Zhukov – with the consequence that masses of Soviet tanks that had stopped when their fuel ran out were lost.

On 27 June, German 11. Panzer-Division managed to tear up a gap in the Soviet defenses at Dubno and raced almost unopposed towards the east. Further to the south, on the same day, StuG III assault guns of Sturmgeschütz-

Abteilung 243, assigned to 1. Gebirgsjäger-Division of 17. Armee, made a daring raid straight into a formation of Soviet tanks that had gathered in the Yanovovo forest northwest of Lvov. The Soviets were caught totally by surprise, and in half an hour their position was totally annihilated. One of the assault gun commanders, Oberwachtmeister Ernst Alex, was credited with the destruction of ten tanks. With this battle, the Germans managed to break through towards the city of Lvov. Next day, 1. Gebirgsjäger-Division stood only nine kilometers from Lvov, where a total chaos reigned as Soviet officials fled the city. On 11. Panzer-Division's front, General-Leytenant Ryabyshev's 8th Mechanized Corps made a futile attempt to counter-attack, with the sole result that it became surrounded itself. To Nikolai Vashugin, the commissar of the Southwestern Front's Military Council who had pushed Kirponos for counter-attacks on the 22nd, the full disaster and his own complicity was absolutely clear. On 28 June he shot himself.[24]

On 29 June, Ryabyshev held a conference with his staff officers, surrounded by "burning vehicles that had been destroyed by the German aviation," and it was decided to attempt a breakout during the following night. No sooner had the Soviet set off in darkness, with twenty KV-1s and T-34s of the 12th Tank Division in the lead, than the Germans opened a hellish fire with artillery and anti-tank guns. The night was completely lit up by explosions and the flames of numerous blazing Soviet tanks. Commanding one KV-1 each, Ryabyshev and General-Mayor Timofey Mishanin, 12th Tank Division's C.O., rode in the lead. Suddenly Ryabyshev saw his colleague's tank burst into flames. It had sustained a direct hit from a Panzer IV positioned on the road, barely 60 meters away. Glimpsing Mishanin bail out of the KV-1 as the only survivor of the crew, and running into the darkness, Ryabyshev ordered fire against the Panzer IV, which was promptly destroyed.

Testifying to the ruggedness of the KV-1, Ryabyshev made it back to their own lines with sixteen hits in his tank. However, Mishanin was never seen again, and of around 900 tanks and 172 armored cars in the 8th Mechanized Corps, only 207 tanks and 21 armored cars remained.[25]

Next day, 30 June, the Germans and their Ukrainian collaborators marched into Lvov. It was only now that the Stavka realized that there was no option but to pull back what remained of the Southwestern Front. It withdrew toward the line Korosten – Novograd-Volynskiy – Shepetovka – Proskurov.

The whole Battle for Ukraine in fact was settled during the week-long air and tank battle around Brody. The Southwestern Front sacrificed the bulk of its tanks, sustained around 200,000 troop casualties (one quarter of its original strength) and lost over fifteen hundred of its 1,900 aircraft.[26] The German ground losses were comparatively small, but it was Fliegerkorps V that had won the battle, and its losses were quite severe. Around one-third of the bombers in Fliegerkorps V had been lost or put out of commission by 30 June. Major Lützow's fighter wing JG 3 was even harder hit, with around half of its Messerschmitt 109s lost or put out of commission. Such losses inevitably had an impact on the moral, and after ten days it was already noted that the mood among many airmen in Fliegerkorps V had plummeted.[27]

However, the heavy demands placed on these airmen could not be eased up. Fliegerkorps V would continue to play a key role in the continued operations by Panzergruppe 1 and German 6. and 17. Armee in northwestern Ukraine. A renewed Soviet counter-attack on 1 July against Panzergruppe 1, aimed at covering the withdrawal of the Southwestern Front toward Kiev, was completely routed by Fliegerkorps V. On this day the bombers of Fliegerkorps V reported the destruction of 220 motor vehicles of all kinds, including 40 tanks, west of Lvov.

Soviet Leytenant Grigoriy Melnik of the 170th Artillery Regiment described the scenes that met him when he travelled on the road from Kiev to Zhitomir, en route to the front: "The road Kiev-Zhitomir was blocked by masses of our own fleeing troops. I have never seen such chaos. The sight of the mass of fleeing troops was terribly depressing."[28] Another Red Army officer, Feodosiy Avdeyevskiy, recalled, "The German aircraft mercilessly destroyed our retreating troops as well as the troops that were marching towards the frontline, so that everything fell to pieces. There was no longer any possibility of halting our fleeing units, not to mention the impossibility of bringing them to order. […] The fleeing masses gathered at every water source to still their thirst. This was observed by the German airmen, who lay in wait for this to happen. We all wondered where our own aviation was. Along the roadsides were several wrecks of our own shot down aircraft, but no German ones. […] On house tops and in high buildings there were alien sharpshooters who fired at us."[29]

In many places, activists of Stepan Bandera's Ukrainian nationalist organization (OUN-B) took over as soon as the Red Army departed, and similar to the situation in Lithuania, the Wehrmacht could march into localities already controlled by the partisans. Oberst Otto Korfes, regimental commander in 295. Infanterie-Division of 17. Armee noted in his diary a ghastly sight that met his troops on 2 July: "We saw trenches 5 m deep and 20 m wide. They were filled with men, women and children, mostly Jews. Every trench contained some 60–80 persons. We could hear their moans and shrieks as grenades exploded among them. On both sides of the trenches stood some 12 men

German soldiers study an abandoned Soviet T-35 heavy tank. Entering service in the early 1930s, the T-35 was the only five-turreted heavy operational tank in the world. Its main armament consisted of a 76.2mm gun, coupled with two 45mm guns and five to six 7.62mm machine guns. It had a crew of no less than eleven. When the Soviet Union was attacked by Germany on 22 June 1941, only 48 T-35s remained in service with the Red Army, all with the 67th and 68th Tank regiments of the 34th Tank Division/8th Mechanized Corps. Participating in the tank battle at Rava-Russkaya in June 1941, seven T-35s were lost in combat. However, all other T-35s were lost due to technical malfunction. (Photo: Benno Kohl.)

dressed in civilian clothes. They were hurling grenades into the trenches. Later, officers of the Gestapo told us that those were Banderists."[30]

The Germans also acted with greater brutality in the Ukraine than in any other sector of the Eastern Front, at least during the initial phase of Operation Barbarossa. To a large degree, this was as a result of the impact of the scores of murdered political prisoners that the NKVD left behind here. Prior to Operation Barbarossa, the Ukrainian nationalist organization OUN-B had as many as 27,000 members of the underground movement in Soviet western Ukraine. During the course of the conflict between the OUN and the Soviet authorities, many Ukrainians were arrested, but the greatest wave of arrests came on 22 June 1941, when Germany invaded. On 24 June, Lavrentiy Beriya, the head of the NKVD, ordered the execution of these prisoners, since they could not be evacuated fast enough. Over the course of the next few days, 8,789 prisoners were killed in the Ukrainian SSR, including 2,800 in Lvov.[31]

A Soviet female soldier lies dead among vehicles destroyed in a Luftwaffe air attack against a Red Army column on a road. (Photo: Krigsarkivet Stockholm.)

The prisons of Lvov were the scene of a terrible carnage in late June 1941, when the NKVD executed 2,800 political prisoners lest they joined the anti-Soviet resistance. This photo was taken at a place where the victims of the NKVD were gathered together.

BLOODBATH IN LVOV.

The city of Lvov (Lviv) had been the scene of bloody ethnic conflicts ever since the Polish-Ukrainian war in 1918, when Polish troops murdered up to 150 Jews in a three-day pogrom. During the Polish war against the Soviet Union in 1919-1920, Poland annexed this Ukrainian city with its predominantly Ukrainian population. Polish policies discriminating against the city's large Ukrainian minority led to terrorism and counter-terrorism between the right-wing Ukrainian nationalist organization OUN and Polish police and military forces.

Many Ukrainian nationalists, including the leader of the OUN, Stepan Bandera, were placed in the Bereza Kartuska concentration camp. During the German-Soviet invasion of Poland in September 1939, Lvov was returned to the (Soviet) Ukraine, while Bandera began cooperating with the Germans. Shortly afterward the OUN split into OUN-M and Bandera's more radical OUN-B, which was decidedly anti-Semite. Leading OUN-B member Yaroslav Stetsko publicly branded Jews as "parasites".[1] In their strategy document "The Struggle and Activities of the OUN in Wartime", Bandera, Stetsko and other OUN-B leaders called for "terror for enemy aliens" and declared that "Muscovites, Poles and Jews" were to be "destroyed".[2] The Germans supported OUN-B with 2.5 million marks to be used for subversive activities inside the USSR, and Bandera formed two Ukrainian battalions – "Nachtigall" and "Roland – in the Brandenburger commandos.

OUN-B presence in Lvov was quite strong, and this would characterize the city during the first weeks of Operation Barbarossa. But Lvov was also the headquarters of the section of the Polish underground guerilla movement, ZWZ, which operated in Soviet-controlled former parts of Poland. Of 8,789 political prisoners killed by the NKVD in the Ukrainian SSR, 2,800 were in in Lvov alone.[3] This of course caused a great rage among many of the city's inhabitants, and, among many Christian Ukrainians, sympathy for the Germans. A Jewish eye-witness recalled the German entrance into the city on 30 June: "Thousands of jubilant Ukrainian nationalists took to the streets to greet them while disquieted Jews remained shuttered in their homes." Blue and yellow Ukrainian flags and swastika flags were on display "side-by-side on every available pole, on every street in the City of Lvov."[4]

While OUN-B declared independence, the Ukrainian nationalists initiated a terrible pogrom to retaliate for the NKVD killings, and this was applauded by the new invaders. "During the first hours after the departure of the Bolsheviks, the Ukrainian population took praiseworthy action against the Jews... About 7,000 Jews were seized and shot", was noted in a German report.[5] "Shot" here is a euphemism for a lynching, beating to death and mutilating that went on in the streets of the city for several days. Lvov citizen Nomi Levenkron testified: "Women were raped in the middle of the streets. The murderers dragged Jewish women out of their apartments and cut off their breasts."[6] One of the Lvov Jews to get arrested was the later famous Nazi hunter Simon Wiesenthal; he was lucky to avoid getting killed, but was sent to a concentration camp.

The perpetrators of the atrocities against prisoners in Lvov's jails however escaped. Immediately after the first German air attack against the city on 22 June, the party leaders had left with their families.[7]

Within a short space of time, German Einsatzkommando 5 of Einsatzgruppe C arrived for a more systematical killing. It executed approximately 2,000 Jews plus a number of Polish intellectuals, including the famous Polish author Tadeusz Boy-Zelenski before it carried on to Dubno, Zhitomir, Kiev, Cherkassy and Uman. In total, the 700 men of Einsatzgruppe C executed 150,000 people during January 1942.

A third Ukrainian pogrom in Lvov took place at the end of July, the so-called "Petlura days" (named after the Ukrainian nationalist leader during the Russian Civil War), when more than 2,000 Jews were killed by Ukrainian nationalists. This was in the aftermath of the frustration felt when the Germans on 5 July had Bandera arrested – Hitler would not tolerate any Ukrainian independence.

1   Rossolinski, Grzegorz, *Stepan Bandera: the Life and Afterlife of a Ukrainian Nationalist: Fascism, Genocide and Cult*, p. 174.
2   Ibid., p. 181.
3   Ibid., p. 193.
4   Weiss, *The Lemberg Mosaic*, p. 167.
5   Ibid., p. 173.
6   Goldenberg and Shapiro, *Different Horrors/Same Hell: Gender and the Holocaust,* p. 104.
7   TsAMO, f. 9. Op. 39. d. 98. ll. 250–253.

Many people in western Ukraine, including much of the population in Lvov, greeted the German Army as liberators.

German troops who marched into Lutsk on 25 June discovered that the NKVD had murdered thousands of political prisoners in this place just two days previously.* In retaliation, the SD began killing Jews of the town. It began on 30 June, when 300 Jews and 20 "looters" were executed. Red Army troops retributed got_in due course, as Leytenant Nikolay Dupak said, "We shot those whom we captured on the spot for their crimes. War is a brutal thing."[32] Shot down and captured German airmen were particularly hated, and they often suffered a grim fate at the hands of enraged Soviet soldiers or civilians. When German troops captured the village of Oziyutichi, 40 km west of Lutsk on 28 June, they found the mutilated body of a Luftwaffe flier who had been shot down on 26 June 1941. The German troops accused the local Jews and killed about 100 of them, some near the pilot's grave.

A massacre of German soldiers taken prisoner was reported to have taken place on 1 July 1941. Gefreiter Kurt Schäer, who managed to escape alive, later testified: "When retreating from Klewan to Broniki we were taken prisoner by superior Russian forces, who had turned our flank. We were driven into the street from all sides. I noticed that my comrades took off their belts. I wanted to take mine off too, but it caught in the rear buckle. A Russian immediately approached me and tore it off. We then had to take off our coats, shirts, boots and socks. The Russians ordered us to do that by gestures. As far as I know, none of them spoke German. They were mainly young people. Those who did not immediately take off their shirts were roughly mistreated. I saw, for example, how one man was struck in the ribs with a rifle butt. Others were stabbed. It is true that I did not see that myself, but I later saw the bleeding wounds. I saw how a Russian hit a wounded soldier, lying an the ground, over the head with the butt of his rifle. One

was always seeing a Russian close to a wounded soldier. The latter were screaming. We were now herded into the field, and then the hands of twenty men were tied behind their backs. Why this happened, I don't know. They were then shot down with rifles, pistols and submachine guns. At the same time other Russians standing near us began to shoot at us, who were standing away from the 20 whose hands had been tied behind their backs. While the first ones were falling, I made a jump between two Russians in the direction of the corn field 3 meters away and fled through it. A number of other comrades also ran away. Shots were fired after us. I did not meet any more Russains on the way. After 6 kilometers we found men of the motorcycle rifle battalion."[33]

The next day, 2 July, over one thousand Jews were brought to the citadel in Lutsk, where they were killed by the Germans – both SD men and soldiers from 17. Armee.[34] Over the following weeks, more than 20,000 Jews would be killed at this place.

The Southwestern Fronts sank deeper into the crisis. Kirponos and Zhukov turned to the aviation to save the situation. General-Leytenant Fyodor Astakhov – who succeeded General-Leytenant Ptukhin as VVS Southwestern Front's commander – was ordered to throw in all aircraft against the German spearheads. But with what? VVS Southwestern Front was in a sorrowful state, with only 340 serviceable aircraft remaining on 30 June. But the situation would not allow any rest. On 1 July, the skies almost entirely belonged to the Luftwaffe, and when the Soviets returned with a large number of aircraft formations on the following day, Major Lützow's Bf 109 pilots were in place and slammed down on the red-starred planes. Astakhov's remaining SB bombers flew to attack the advancing enemy columns or, in cooperation with I-153 fighter-bombers, to provide the retreating army with close support at the front. The fighter planes were directed to cover the retreating army from air attacks. But there was one obstacle: The Messerschmitt fighters of Fliegerkorps V. Throughout 2 July, the skies over the battlefield was were the scene of fantastic aerial fighting, with scores of Soviet aircraft falling in flames towards the ground. When it all was over, JG 3 had shot down 40 planes for only a single own loss. In the meantime, the German ground forces continued to slice through the gap between Soviet 5th and 6th armies and took Tarnopol, 90 kilometers southeast of Lvov, thus posing an additional threat to the rear area of the 26th Army.

On that day also, came alarming news for the Soviets from the south: German 11. Armee began its attack from northern Romania, across River Pruth, and towards Mogilev Podolskiy on the Dnestr River. Simultaneously, the Romanian 3rd Army started advancing toward Chernovtsy, and the Hungarian Army crossed the Soviet border. Hungary had joined the war on the German side on 27 June, following an attack by three unidentified twin-engine bombers on the city of Kassa on the previous day. One of the bombs that did not explode turned out to be

* The figures vary between 2,800 and 4,000.

Soviet civilians on the road to an uncertain destiny pass an abandoned Red Army BT-7A, an artillery support tank with a 76.2 mm howitzer.

With VVS Southwestern Front in shambles, one composite aviation wing from the Moscow Military District and two bomber corps from the Long-Range Aviation were hurriedly brought in. On 6 July these faced Major Lützow's fighters in new large air battle that became a repeat of what had happened four days previously. The results were precisely the same: JG 3 shot down 41 Soviet planes for the loss of a single Bf 109. Owing to this excellent cover in the air, Panzergruppe 1 reached Miropol, 30 kilometers east of the previous day's point of departure. Here the Germans blasted into a series of fortifications. Although greatly outnumbered and outgunned, the Soviet defenders refused to give in. The Germans had to flush out one bunker at a time. By the end of the day, the defense line had been penetrated. The Soviet dictator Stalin found another scapegoat in VVS Southwestern Front's Chief of Staff, General-Major Nikolay Laskin, who became next in line to be arrested.

But the Soviet airmen would ironically be aided by the rapid pace of the German advance. Slicing through the gap between Soviet 5th and 6th armies, 11. Panzer-Division took Berdichev on 7 July, after a 60-kilometer advance in only three days. This increased the distance from JG 3's main base at Lutsk to the frontlines to 250 kilometers, which reduced the time the Messerschmitt fighters could spend over the front area. Thus, on 7 July Soviet fighters were able to shoot down four KG 55 He 111s, while KG 51 lost four Ju 88s to hostile action on 7 July and three on the following day.[36]

In order to render fighter escort more effective over the frontlines, the Germans brought forward a small detachment from I./JG 3 to an airstrip at Polonnoye on 8 July. The bulk of Panzergruppe 1's reconnaissance planes also gathered here. But Soviet aerial reconnaissance discovered this new concentration, and VVS fighters came roaming in over the field just as a Ju 52 arrived to bring in technical personnel from JG 3. The transport plane was shot down and several men were killed or injured on the ground in the following strafing runs. In the afternoon, a formation of 4 BAK bombers arrived and knocked out several of Panzergruppe 1's reconnaissance planes and caused twenty casualties among the ground personnel. That I./JG 3's Bf 109s scrambled and pursued the withdrawing bombers, shooting down three DB-3s for the loss of two Bf 109s, was a poor consolation to the Germans.

Owing to the support from unchallenged VVS formations, a weak Red Army task force managed to push German 298. Infanterie-Division from the main road between Novograd Volynskiy and Zhitomir, blocking the German advance to the latter city. But this relief was only temporary. The remnants of Soviet 4th, 15th and 22nd Mechanized Corps were sent to the breakthrough area, but their divisions had shrunk to the size of battalions.[37] "We have nothing to defend Zhitomir with," reported a dejected General-Leytenant Purkayev, the Chief of Staff in the Southwestern Front, "All we have there are some weak battalions of railway troops."[38]

Since the fall of Berdichev, the connection between Southwestern Front's 5th and 6th armies was broken,

a FAB-100 of Soviet designation.* The élite of Hungary's army, the "Carpathian Group" with some 40,000 men, was assigned to German 17. Armee and would take part in all of its operations in Operation Barbarossa.

Heavy rains restricted air activity for some days – without doubt a blessing for the battered Soviet air and ground units. Although the downpours turned the roads into deep mud, Panzergruppe 1 took Shepetovka on 4 July. Even though that meant that the Germans had reached half-way between the border and Kiev, the disastrous situation in the Smolensk area farther north caused the Stavka to transfer the 5th Cavalry Corps, eleven artillery regiments and eight anti-tank regiments from the Southwestern to the Western Front.

When the skies cleared again on 5 July, the German bombers fell upon the retreating Soviet columns with rage as if trying to compensate for the previous day's inactivity. While also claiming the destruction of 18 trains and more than 500 trucks, Panzergruppe 1 smashed the Soviet attempts to form a frontline at Polonnoye, 30 kilometers east of Shepetovka. During a single raid with ten bombers against Soviet vehicle and cavalry columns east of Proskurov on 6 July, over 200 vehicles were claimed destroyed.[35]

---

* It is still disputed today, who carried out this particular bombing. It is possible that the attack was merely a tragic mistake, the result of navigational error by three Soviet aircrews. After the war the Soviets maintained that it was a plot, and they even mentioned the aircraft that carried out the attack – three P.37 Los bombers of the Romanian Grupul 4 Bombardament. (Glass et al, Samoloty bombowe wrzesnia 1939, p. 52.)

A Soviet I-153 Chayka assault plane takes off. As the German forces approached Kiev, the Soviet airmen fought with desperation to support the poor remnants of the Southwestern Front's ground troops. But this also cost the Soviet fliers themselves dearly.

with the latter being pushed to the south. On 10 July the Southwestern Front was in full retreat towards the Dnepr between Berdichev-Zhitomir and Kiev. German air attacks against the retreating columns in combination with Panzergruppe 1's rapid advance threatened to envelop a large part of Southwestern Front on the western side of the Dnepr. All that stood in front of German 13. and 14. Panzer divisions which approached Kiev, was a single Soviet tank regiment and the 213th Rifle Division. "All our hopes rested with our aviation," wrote the deputy chief of staff in the Southwestern Front, General-Major Ivan Bagramyan.[39]

But even in this desperate situation, VVS Southwestern Front had to hand over 46 SAD to VVS Western Front to help out in the battle of Smolensk. The new supreme commander of the army air forces in the Southwestern Direction, General-Major Falaleyev, even brought old four-engine TB-3 heavy bombers into action in this area. During a late afternoon mission in the Irpen – Zhitomir area on 10 July, the II./JG 3 Rotte composed of Oberleutnant Franz Beyer and Unteroffizier Werner Lucas came across twelve of these "dinosaurs" from 14 TBAP. The Soviet bombers flew without any fighter escort, and the two German pilots claimed five of them shot down. In fact, Soviet sources show that seven TB-3s were downed, though the bomber gunners claimed one Bf 109 destroyed.[40] In other air combats that day, fighter pilot Hauptmann Walter Oesau of III./JG 3 alone blasted five Soviet planes out of the sky.

That day, 13. Panzer-Division reached Zhitomir, 120 km west of Kiev. The next day, almost without encountering any opposition, its tanks penetrated Kiev's inner defense perimeters.[41] Once again Kirponos, the commander of the Southwestern Front, demanded an intensification of the air operations in order to halt the German advance towards Kiev, to which his air force commander, General-Leytenant Astakhov, helplessly replied, "We try that all the time, but we have too few aircraft remaining!" The arrival on 11 July of assault aviation regiment 74 ShAP, equipped with 20 Il-2 Shturmoviks, looked promising, but this was far from sufficient. The average life expectancy of the pilots in that unit would be no more than sixteen days during its operations against the German forces outside of Kiev.[42]

Less promising for the Soviets was the appointment of Marshal Semyon Budyonnyy to command the new Red Army Southwestern Direction – as supreme commander of the Southwestern and Southern fronts – on 10 July. This was a most unfortunate decision, from the Soviet point of view. Budyonnyy was renowned for his conservative standpoints in military matters. He was suspicious of new methods and quite ignorant of modern warfare. He had been a cavalry commander during the Civil War, but never managed to understand the use of tanks, which he actually despised!* Such a man was to lead the Red Army against Generalfeldmarschall von Rundstedt, one of the world's most brilliant military commanders…

* During the Great Purge trial against Marshal Tukhachevskiy, Budyonnyy had been called as a witness and happily accused Tukhachevskiy of deliberately "destroying" the Red Army through the focus on creating an armored force.

THE STRATEGIC BOMBER OFFENSIVE AGAINST ROMANIA IN 1941.

In the far south, the Soviets actually took the initiative by attacking the Romanian Black Sea port of Constanta on the war's very first day. Six SBs and three DB-3s of VVS ChF's 63 BAB performed this first raid. From then on, 63 BAB's 2 MTAP, equipped with DB-3Fs, and 40 SBAP, equipped with SBs and an Eskadrilya with Pe-2s, made regular attacks against Constanta. On 23 June, forty-nine DB-3Fs of 2 MTAP and twenty-four SBs of 40 SBAP were dispatched. The 53.3 tons of bombs they dropped fell scattered in the intense anti-aircraft fire, which – together with intercepting fighters – cost a loss of sixteen bombers. Locotenent Aviator Horia Agarici of FARR's Escadrila 53, equipped with Hurricane fighters, became the Romanian hero of the day when he managed to down three DB-3s in this fight.

Following these first sporadic attacks, VVS commander General-Leytenant Pavel Zhigarev organised a regular strategic bomber offensive with the intention of destroying the Romanian oil fields. For this purpose, the DBA, the Front aviation and VVS ChF united forces. Early on 24 June eighteen SBs and eighteen DB-3s were employed against Constanta. They dropped 178 bombs over the airfield and oil fields without causing much damage, and then were intercepted by III./JG 52 and Romanian fighters and lost ten bombers. Nevertheless, another formation with thirty-two SBs and DB-3s which arrived shortly afterward, and knocked out several of III./JG 52's Bf 109s on the ground at Mamaia.

63 BAB's operation against Constanta early on 26 June was different. That time the purpose was to divert the attention of the defenders from a fleet force, numbering two flotilla leaders, a cruiser and two destroyers, which subjected Constanta to shelling. But the Soviet raid backfired. The bombers were intercepted by Bf 109s from III./JG 52 during the approach flight and lost nine bombers, all SBs from 40 BAP/VVS ChF. In addition, the flotilla leader *Moskva* was sunk by a mine, and coastal artillery damaged the flotilla leader *Kharkov*.

Next, the Soviets focused on attacking Romanian oil producing facilities. During the afternoon of 13 July, six Soviet bombers raided the Romanian Astra, Romana, and Orion oil refineries on the southern outskirts of Ploesti. The attack destroyed seventeen lubricating oil storage tanks and twelve loaded railway tanker wagons, with a total of 9,000 tons of oil set ablaze. The Unirea oil refinery would remain on fire for three days. Nevertheless, only two of the attackers against Romania on 13 July made it back to base; the other four were shot down by Romanian fighters. From mid-July, the Soviet bombers resorted mainly to nocturnal raids against objectives in Romania.

In the face of mounting fighter interception, the Soviet aviation introduced a new tactic – the Zveno method. Zveno was a TB-3 heavy bomber carrying two I-16 Ishak fighters, each loaded with two 250-kilogram FAB bombs. The I-16s were released at high altitude between ten and thirty miles from the target and then were supposed to carry out a high-speed diving attack. Since they were much smaller and faster than conventional bombers, the I-16s could strike with surprise and evade enemy AAA fire and fighters. Having effected the attack, the I-16s returned home on their own.

The original idea of the Zveno tactic came from designer Vladimir Vakhmistrov. At first it was intended that the two fighters carried by a TB-3 would be launched to ward off attacks – a flying aircraft carrier in effect. This proved impracticable but gave birth to the concept of a "piggyback" dive-bomber. Six I-16s were modified for dive-bombing and redesignated I-16SPB. A special unit was set up with these aircraft, the 2 Eskadrilya of 32 IAP/VVS ChF. Together with three TB-3s converted for the new role, the planes were based at Yevpatoria in the Crimea early in the war, and training commenced immediately.

The first Zveno raid was carried out on 26 July, 1941. Two TB-3s released four I-16SPBs led by Kapitan Arseniy Shubikov about thirty miles from the Romanian coast. Two of the fighter-bombers attacked oil plants near Constanta, while the other two raided the floating docks in the harbor. A couple of III./JG 52 Bf 109s scrambled from Mamaia and pursued the escaping I-16SPBs sixty miles over the sea. As they finally caught up with the Ishaks, Kapitan Shubikov made a 180-degree turn and carried out a frontal counter-attack. Aware of the vulnerability of the liquid-cooled Bf 109 – as opposed to the I-16's air-cooled radial engine – the Germans broke off in a split-S. When they recovered from the dive close above the waves, the little Ishaks were gone. The only Soviet loss on that mission was one fighter-bomber which ran out of fuel and crash-landed on the shore near Odessa. The German fighter pilots nevertheless found and reportedly shot down two MBR-2s. In return, Feldwebel Tepan was shot down by a Soviet aircraft over the sea off Constanta. Afterward, Rossmann and other III./JG 52 pilots flew over the area to search for Tepan, but found no trace of him.

Interview with Edmund Rossmann.

119

THE STRATEGIC BOMBER OFFENSIVE AGAINST ROMANIA IN 1941.

Cont.

III./JG 52 was released from its duty of providing the Romanian oil fields with air cover on 31 July, and began its transfer to to Biyala Tserkov. The Soviets immediately took advantage of the weakened fighter defense in Romania, and on 1 August, six Pe-2s of 40 BAP/VVS ChF undertook a swift attack against the harbor and rail Marshaling yards of Constanta. The ship Amarilis was sunk and the Durostor was damaged, six train cars were damaged, six people on the ground were killed, and four were injured. On 2 August the next Zveno mission was launched by three TB-3s with six I-16SPBs. This time enemy fighters – probably Romanian – bounced the TB-3s before they had released the I-16SPBs. The fighter-bombers were jettisoned, and the heavy bombers turned away from a hopeless encounter. The intercepting fighters concentrated on the I-16s. Later, four I-16 pilots landed at Odessa Airdrome. Two of their comrades were missing.

On 3 August, 63 BAB and 2 Eskadrilya/32 IAP dispatched the third Zveno mission from Odessa Airdrome. An escort of two MBR-2 flying boats was furnished the two TB-3s. Released ten miles from the target, the fighter-bombers spread out and struck an oil refinery, an oil storage depot, harbor installations in Constanta, and a hydroplane base on the Black Sea coast. All Soviet planes returned home. Thirty-two Soviet medium bombers that flew against the same target on that day fared worse. By that time, the whole I.(J)/LG 2 had been shifted to the defense of Romania instead of III./JG 52, and its pilots claimed six bombers shot down against one own loss.

But the Soviet bomber units – in particular those of VVS ChF's 62 IAB and 63 BAB, which were stationed in Nikolayev and the Crimea – would not be deterred by these losses. On 10 August, three waves of bombers were dispatched to interrupt traffic across the important Danube bridge at Cernavoda, which connected the port of Constanta with the interior. The first two attack formations – five DB-3s from 2 MTAP, followed by six Pe-2s from 40 BAP – failed to inflict any decisive damage on the target. But the last wave's six I-16SPB Zvenos from 32 IAP/VVS ChF damaged nearby oil pipelines. On this day, I.(J)/LG 2, was unable to inflict any losses on the attackers.

The next Zveno attack followed on 13 August. Three TB-3 Zvenos took off from Yevpatoria in the Crimea at 0330 hours. Two hours and ten minutes later, six I-16SPBs were released ten miles off the coast. They dived down on the bridge, catching the defenders totally by surprise, and placed five FAB-

250 bombs directly on the span. This caused considerable disturbance to the road and railway traffic across this bridge and destroyed the nearby oil pipelines. During the return flight, the six I-16SPBs strafed a Romanian infantry column. Finally they landed at Odessa Airdrome at 0705 hours. Later that day they returned to Yevpatoria, where the I-16 Zveno commander, Kapitan Arseniy Shubikov, became the first in VVS ChF to be awarded the Lenin Order. Again I.(J)/LG 2 was forced to admit a failure against the Zveno planes, none of which was shot down.

32 IAP/VVS ChF and 63 BAB carried out another successful Zveno mission on 17 August, scoring bomb hits on three ships in the Romanian port of Constanta. Two I-16SPBs were claimed shot down by I.(J)/LG 2. In fact, what caused the Soviets to discontinue the Zveno raids against Romania was not the fighter opposition; it was the deteriorating situation at the front lines which finally compelled the Soviets to shift the Zvenos to tactical support missions.

Although VVS ChF's regular bombers units also had to be employed to provide tactical support – mainly around Odessa, which became isolated on 13 August – these continued to carry out small raids against Romania on an almost daily basis. On 9 October the oil pipeline at Cernavoda was heavily damaged by Soviet bombs.

Undefeated by enemy aircraft, this last string of small-scale attacks eventually also ended due to the need to focus on tactical operations. On 14 October, Vitse-Admiral Oktyabrskiy dispatched his entire Black Sea Fleet to conduct a rapid evacuation of Odessa. In order to divert the enemy's attention, a final Soviet air raid against Constanta was flown on 15 October. In all, Constanta was subject to a total of thirty-four day raids and twenty-five night raids, mostly of a nuisance character.

An I-16SPB fighter-bomber mounted under the wing of a TB-3 heavy bomber.

9: THE ADVANCE TOWARDS MOSCOW.

"It looked like a scene from Dante's inferno."

– Gefreiter Hans Gärtner, German soldier.

While the German infantry armies destroyed the large elements of Soviet Western Front which had been surrounded between Biyalystok and Minsk in the rear, the Panzergruppen of Heeresgruppe Mitte raced on toward the east. On the northern flank, Panzergruppe 3, supported by Fliegerkorps VIII, approached the city of Vitebsk, to the north of the highway to Moscow. On the southern flank, following the failed Soviet attempt to block the Berezina river crossings through concentrated air attacks, Panzergruppe 2 seemed unstoppable. Here, Fliegerkorps II established a special close-support air command, Nahkampfführer – comprised of assault wing SKG 210 and fighter wing JG 51 – in order to render command and control of close support air operations more effective. With his headquarters placed in a train not far from the frontline, Generalfeldmarschall Kesselring directed the medium bombers of his Luftflotte 2 day and night against the communication lines in the Soviet rear area; roads, railways and railway junctions were the main targets.

The Germans assumed that Soviet Western Front was more or less obliterated. "Practically, the Russians have already lost the war," Hitler said on 4 July, asserting that they would be unable to replace their huge losses in tanks and aircraft.[1] But in this, the Führer was gravely mistaken. Indeed, the The Western Front's 3rd and 10th armies were indeed completely annihilated and only poor remnants of the 4th Army had managed to break out of the envelopment. The Front had lost two-thirds of its troop strength and was down at 389 aircraft – 103 fighters and 286 bombers – and less than 200 tanks on 1 July. But the Stavka took

German motor cyclist troops advance past burning and destroyed Soviet tanks. (Photo: Via Daniel Johansson.)

A Heinkel 111 bomber of Stab/KG 53. This unit operated from the airfield at Minsk against Soviet troop columns, trains and other targets in the Red Army's rear area during the Battle of Smolensk. This particular aircraft, piloted by Feldwebel Robert Mayer and with the commander of the Stabsstaffel, Oberleutnant Jürgen von Horn, was recorded as missing on operation on 30 January 1942. (Photo: Via Eric Mombeek.)

resolute steps to rebuild the battered forces. Within a couple of hours on 2 July a more or less new Western Front was created, from top down: Following the arrest of the Western Front's C.O., General Armii Pavlov, VVS Western Front's commander, General Andrey Tayurskiy, was sacked and replaced by Polkovnik Nikolay Naumenko. Pavlov's successor, General-Leytenant Andrey Yeremenko, also was replaced by Marshal Timoshenko (demoting Yeremenko to deputy commander). Eight days later, when the central command Western Direction was created, Timoshenko took command of that too.

Moreover, as we have seen, on 26 June a new army, the 16th, had been assigned to the Western Front west of Smolensk. Of even greater importance was the formation on 25 June of the new Reserve Front, with five armies from the Stavka reserve – the 13th, 19th, 20th, 21st and 22nd. On 2 July, the Reserve Front was integrated into the Western Front, which thus was beefed up to a strength of over half a million men and more than 2,000 tanks.[2] Additionally, the Western Front was supplied with 900 new aircraft through July.

General-Leytenant Fyodor Remezov's Soviet 20th Army was assigned with the defense of both sides of the Minsk-Moscow highway on a 85-km wide front west of Orsha, about half-way between Minsk and Smolensk. Remezov received two mechanized corps, the 5th and 7th. Mustering 75 % of the Western Front's armor – over 1,500 tanks – its first task was to wipe out the bridgehead across

River Berezina that the Germans had established at Borisov on the highway from Minsk towards Smolensk. But before Remezov's hastily employed army was ready to strike, the 1st Moscow Motorized Rifle Division under Polkovnik Yakov Kreitzer arrived to carry out the first attack.

Under the impact of this, Joseph Stalin found the strength to hold his first radio broadcast speech to the nation on 3 July. With a low voice, revealing just how shocked he was by the massive German onslaught, he began by addressing "comrades, citizens, brothers and sisters, men of our army and navy . . . my friends." His whole speech was monotonous, admitting that "the enemy continues to push forward," and ended – in a hardly convincing tone with an "onward, to our victory."[3] However, the forces gathered to counter-attack the Germans were only

The dead Soviet driver never got out of his hit T-26 light tank. (Photo: Franz Hohlmann.)

Pilots of a Soviet assault regiment lined up in front of one of the unit's Il-2 Shturmovik. The Il-2 was undoubtedly the world's finest assault plane by 1941. Although fitted with a thick armor hull it had a top speed of 450 km/h. It could carry 400 kg of bombs and eight RS-82 rocket projectiles. (Photo: Viktor Kumskov.)

sent to their own destruction. The 1st Moscow Motorized Rifle Division had 229 tanks, but only 24 were T-34s or KVs.[4] The Germans had also intercepted an uncoded radio message transmitted *about* the Soviet plans, and this was confirmed by Luftwaffe aerial reconnaissance.

On 4 July, when Kreitzer attacked, XLVII. Panzerkorps, defending the Borisov bridgehead, was ready, supported by Luftwaffe 88mm Flak guns and the aircraft of Fliegerkorps VIII. "1st Moscow Motorized Rifle Division suffered heavy losses", wrote Yeremenko, "One regiment defending north of Borisov suffered heavy losses from air attacks." The counter-attack was blunted. In the afternoon, the sky suddenly blackened and a thunderstorm with torrential rain covered the battlefield, littered with corpses and the hulks of burned out tanks and other vehicles. In the heavy rain, fuel and ammunition in the destroyed vehicles continued to burn, with the fire smoke adding to the darkness from the clouds. "It looked like a scene from Dante's inferno," commented Gefreiter Hans Gärtner, one of the *Landser* (German soldiers).

Meanwhile, the new Soviet 21st Army began to take up positions on the Western Front's southern flank. This army was commanded by General-Polkovnik Fedor Kuznetsov, the former commander of the Northwestern Front. He had executed a successful withdrawal of the Northwestern Front's armies in June, and now prepared to block the German advance south of the Minsk–Smolensk highway. Here, the advance column of German 4. Panzer-Division reached

River Dnepr at Staryy Bykhov. Oberleutnant Hans-Detloff von Cossel, commander of the division's 6th Company, was ordered to seize the Dnepr bridge through a lightning strike with six tanks. As the panzers raced towards the bridge, they came under fire from anti-tank guns which knocked out one of the tanks. But the remaining five continued at full speed while artillery shells crashed all around them. "Faster! Faster!" Von Cossel urged on his crews. The first tank reached the wooden bridge and crossed, and within a couple of minutes all five were across, while Soviet artillery fire increased in intensity. The tanks went into cover along the slope of the river bank, but suddenly three mighty explosions caused the bridge to collapse. Trapped on the western side of the river, the five German tanks were knocked out by Soviet guns, one after another. Two of the tank crews attempted to surrender to a group of Soviet soldiers, but they were promptly killed. For 36 hours, von Cossel and six other survivors hid in an abandoned Soviet bunker that soon was covered with earth from exploding shells. This saved them from being detected, but when they attempted to sneak through to the river at night, they were discovered by Soviet posts who opened fire and killed two of them. The remaining five managed to escape and made it across the river in a small rowboat. When they reached their own lines, they found that letters had already been sent to their families, informing them that their sons were missing in action. Two months later, von Cossel was awarded with the Knight's Cross.

123

Troops of SS-Infanterie-Regiment 11 "Das Reich" in bitter fighting on the road to Moscow. The typical mottled camouflage of the SS, here seen on the helmets of the soldiers, was invented by the unit's commander, SS-Obersturmbannführer Dr.Ing. Wim Brandt. He was killed in a Soviet air attack on 13 July 1941.

It was a ruthless war where little mercy was shown. On 4 July, German army surgeon Hermann Türk wrote in his diary, "One of our drivers has captured a Russian aviation officer, the commander of an airfield. He remains composed. Only when he is brought out to be shot does he break down.[5]" The Germans also took a fearsome revenge on the civilian population for their own losses and frustrations, such as a case at Borisov which was included in historian Wendy Jo Gertjejanssen's doctoral studies on sexual violence on the Eastern Front during World War II: "75 women and girls attempting to flee at the approach of the German troops fell into their hands. The Germans first raped and then savagely murdered 36 of their number. By order of a German named Hummer, the soldiers marched L. I. Melchukova, a 16-year-old girl, into the forest, where they raped her. A little later some other women who had also been dragged into the forest saw some boards near the trees and the dying Melchukova nailed to the boards. The Germans had cut off her breasts in the presence of these women, among whom were V. I. Alperenko and V. N. Bereznikova."[6]

Ion Degen, a Soviet soldier of Jewish origin, recalled, "We constantly attacked small groups of Germans. Often it was close-quarter fighting, man against man. On one such occasion I rammed the butt of my rifle against a German soldier's helmet with such force that he passed out. When he regained consciousness, the gigantic German was very haughty and acted as if we were his prisoners and not the other way around. I started to interrogate him, but the German was silent, until he suddenly screamed, 'Verfluchte Jude!' – 'You damned Jew!' – whereupon I immediately shot him."[7]

However, in the midst of the gruesome killing, acts of respect for the enemy could also be shown. On 17 July, Oberleutnant Henfeld of 4. Panzer-Division wrote in his diary: "In the evening we buried an unknown Russian soldier. He was alone with his anti-tank gun, but he kept firing at our column of tanks and infantry until he was killed. All were amazed at his courage. We gave him a funeral with all mil-

itary honor. Speaking before the grave the colonel said that if everyone was fighting for Hitler with the same determination as this Russian had fought, then we could capture the whole world. We fired three rifle volleys to honor that brave man." Before they buried the soldier, the German battalion commander brought some local residents to the place. They showed one of them a sheet of paper with the dead man's address. "Write a letter in your mother tongue," the German officer said. "Let his mother know what a hero her son was and how he died."

The German trump card still was their supremacy in the air. Thus, Soviet aerial reinforcements were also brought in, even though this meant scraping the barrel to the bottom. Equipped with thirty-eight of the new Pe-2 bombers, 410 BAP was assigned to the Western Front on 5 July. Shortly afterward, 46 SAD arrived from the Southwestern Front. Podpolkovnik Nikolay Malyshev's Il-2-equipped 430 ShAP was rushed to the front to join forces with the battered 4 ShAP. On 5 July these two Shturmovik regiments were employed in a combined operation against the German bridgehead at Bobruysk. While 4 ShAP attacked the Luftwaffe airfield at Bobruysk – an attack which won the unit commander, Mayor Semyon Getman, the title of Hero of the Soviet Union – 430 ShAP struck down on the bridge itself. In spite of heavy fire from light AAA – Podpolkovnik Malyshev's Il-2 received more than 200 hits – all of the Il-2s returned to base afterwards. The destruction they caused sufficed to delay the German offensive on this sensitive sector for a decisive twenty-four hours, enough to allow 20th Army with its fifteen hundred tanks to march up into attack positions. That 4 ShAP's formation was intercepted by Messerschmitt Bf 109s from JG 51 on their return flight, costing the loss of two pilots, including the commander of the 3rd squadron, Kapitan Nikolay Satalkin, was of comparatively little importance.

Bomber regiment 53 DBAP of the Long-Range Aviation was also dispatched in daytime attacks against Bobruysk bridge in the afternoon of 5 July; they were intercepted by I./JG 51 which shot down four of the bombers, two of them by the ace Leutnant Heinz Bär.[8] The pilot of one of the DB-3s, Leytenant Nikolay Bolygin, crashed his burning plane straight onto the bridge.[9]

But at the same pace as new Soviet aircraft arrived, others were lost. On the same day, Luftflotte 2 claimed to have destroyed 57 Soviet aircraft on the ground.[10] Throughout 5 July, the bombers, Stukas and assault aircraft of Luftflotte 2 were employed in rolling attacks against Soviet troops. In bitter air fighting, the top ace Oberstleutnant Werner Mölders shot down four planes in a single combat. His JG 51 bagged a total of 29 victories that day, against only two Bf 109s shot down.

On 6 July, General-Polkovnik Kuznetsov's 21st Army launched a counter-offensive against Guderian south of the Minsk–Smolensk highway. The attack struck 10. Infanterie and 3. Panzer divisions heavily, with the latter losing 22 tanks.[11] Hermann Türk wrote in his diary, "Our tanks suffer heavy losses. One of the companies is left with just one vehicle operational. The Soviets allowed our tanks to approach to a short distance away and then opened fire. Some of their heavy tanks had been built into the houses, and these allowed our tanks to approach to within 75 meters."

The most serious counter-attack on 6 July was made by the 5th and 7th Mechanized corps of Soviet 20th Army, which struck against the seam between German Panzer-gruppen 2 and 3. "We encounter red tanks everywhere," wrote Leutnant Georg Kreuter of German 18. Panzer-Division. "They appear to be badly led. We knock out several of them and many trucks. But who is encircling whom here? That's the question! Only now and then does a courier manage to get through. Russian tanks attack! Some of them are of the heaviest types. Our anti-tank guns, even those of 5 cm caliber, are having a quite difficult time with them. My own tank is hit and burns out. Our Nebelwerfer have heavy losses. Their positions are revealed through the enormous smoke clouds that their rocket bursts create."

The German ground forces desperately called for rein-forced air support. Guderian noted that "the air became

clear" wherever Mölders' fighters appeared, but they were unable to be everywhere.[12] An irritated General von Rich-thofen, the commander of Fliegerkorps VIII, burst out, "The Army will not realize that we can't disperse our air-craft all over the front, but that we have to concentrate them to the most important sectors."[13] The Soviet attacks against Panzergruppe 2 and its seam with Panzergruppe 3 were initially successful, not least owing to the fact that the elements StG 77 previously assigned to Fliegerkorps II had been shifted to Luftflotte 4 in the south. 7. Panzer-Division on the southern flank of Panzergruppe 3 was driven back 30 kilometers, while Panzergruppe 2's 18. Panzer-Division sustained heavy losses, and 17. Panzer-Division found itself sealed off. By 9 July, 18. Panzer-Division had only 83 opera-tional tanks, or 39 per cent of its original force, left, and the divisional diary noted "high casualties among officers" and "fighting strength greatly reduced."[14]

Again it was the Luftwaffe that saved the situation. Fliegerkorps VIII brought in III./StG 1 to aid StG 2 to sup-port the troops at Bobruysk. With the weather clear, hot and dry again, von Richthofen's Stukas carried out "roll-ing attacks" that managed to bail out 17. Panzer-Division on 8 July. Soviet 17th Tank Division – of 5th Mechanized Corps – noted the German armor's tactic of avoiding any clashes with Soviet tank formations of equal size, while at the same time displaying an excellent interaction between ground and air units.[15] With Luftflotte 2 hammering the Western Front with nearly twelve hundred sorties on 8 and 9 July, the 5th and 7th Mechanized corps became com-pletely routed. German 17. Panzer-Division contributed by picking off over 100 Soviet tanks, mainly T-26 tankettes, on 9 July alone.[16]

Meanwhile, both Western Front's flanks began to carve in. To the north, Panzergruppe 3 continued towards Vitebsk, 60 km WNW of Orsha. In the south, Guderian's Panzergruppe 2 outflanked Soviet 13th Army at Mogilev, 60 km south of Orsha. En route to the Western Front head-quarters near Mogilev on 8 July, the vehicle which carried the 13th Army's commander, General Petr Filatov, was strafed by a German aircraft. Filatov was badly wounded and died six days later.

Optimism again soared on the German side. On 8 July, Hitler instructed Heeresgruppe Mitte to "force the last resistance group north of the Pripet Marshes out of the overextended Russian front" and "open the road to Moscow." The Führer outlined his strategic plans, "After destroying the Russian armies in a battle at Smolensk, we shall block the railroads across the Volga, occupy the coun-try as far as that river and, after that, proceed to destroy the remaining Russian industry centers by armored expe-ditions and air operations." He also informed his senior commanders of his "firm decision to level Moscow and Leningrad, and make them uninhabitable" through

Oberstleutnant Werner Mölders was the top ace of the war in 1941, and became the first pilot to reach 100 victories. In July 1941 he received the highest German military award, the Diamonds to the Knight's Cross with Oak leaves and Swords, and was appointed In-spector of the Luftwaffe's fighter arm. Mölders was killed in a flying accident on 22 November 1941, at 28 years old. (Photo: Johannes Broschwitz via Wägenbaur.)

attacks by the Luftwaffe.[17] On 9 July, Hoth's Panzergruppe assaulted Vitebsk, 40 kilometers northeast of Soviet 20th Army's northern flank. Farther south, Guderian's first attempt to cross River Dnepr at Staryy Bykhov, south of Mogilev, through a lightning strike by Oberleutnant Hans-Detloff von Cossel's small group of tanks from 4. Panzer-Division on 4 July had failed. But with the support of 872 Luftwaffe sorties on 10 July, the Panzer division managed to establish itself on the eastern side of the river and severed the road from Gomel to Mogilev in the northwest. The next day Luftflotte 2 conducted a total of 1,048 sorties – the highest number in over two weeks. On 12 July Guderian's panzers captured Gorki on the eastern side of the Dnepr, about 50 km southeast of Orsha. This move blocked the retreat of Soviet 13th Army's 20th Mechanized Corps and 61st Rifle Corps, which had been left to defend Mogilev.

The Soviets responded with an intensified aerial effort, directed mainly against Panzergruppe 2. 28 SAD, 9 IAP and 135 BBAP were employed against the Dnepr crossings at Bobruysk, destroying several bridges, thus delaying the advance by Panzergruppe 2.[18] On 13 July, at the the German salient at Gorki, 10. Panzer-Division complained loudly, "[Soviet] dive-bomber attacks against Gorki. No defense available!" During one of these air attacks the headquarters of SS-Infanterie-Regiment 11 "Das Reich" was completely wiped out.*

In another effort to halt the Germans, the Soviets brought in a new "secret weapon", the 132 mm BM-13 rocket, later to become known as the "Katyusha". At 1515 hours on 14 July, Kapitan Ivan Flyorov's 1st Special Rocket Artillery Battery, equipped with seven BM-13 rocket launchers, fired a volley of 112 rockets at Orsha. According to a popular myth, these first rockets fired in anger were not directed against the Germans, but destroyed the railway station in a town still in Soviet hands, thus preventing it from being used by the Germans. Indeed, Orsha fell into German hands only two days later. But as confirmed by German sources, the airfield west of Orsha was occupied on 14 July and was in fact used by a forward detachment of air reconnaissance unit Heeresaufklärungsgruppe 32 and SKG 210. Four aircraft of the former unit were actually destroyed on the ground at the Orsha airfield on 14 July.[19]

Here it should be pointed out that – contrary to a common notion – the Soviets were not the first to introduce the rocket weapon in World War II. In fact the Germans were the first to bring rocket weapons into use – their 15 cm Nebelwerfer 41 multiple rocket launchers were in service, with quite some success, from the first day of Operation Barbarossa.

While large columns of defeated Red Army contingents were streaming eastward, retreating from annihilation, other Soviet motorized columns were on their way to join the counter-offensive. The tactical units under command of Luftflotte 2 were launched in "rolling attacks" against both these streams. Ulf Balke, the chronicler of KG 2, noted that each mission was intercepted by Soviet fighters at this time. JG 51 claimed twenty-seven victories on 13 July, before a violent summer thunderstorm grounded

Utilizing an abandoned KV-1 tank as cover, these two German soldiers take part in the advance into the city of Smolensk. (Photo: Via Daniel Johansson.)

all air activity in the late afternoon. In clear skies again on the 14th, another fifteen Soviet aircraft were claimed shot down, but eight of JG 51's own aircraft were shot down on these two days, and the Staffelkapitän of 7./JG 51, Oberleutnant Hermann Staiger, was seriously injured. A remarkable feat took place on 15 July, an extremely hot and dry summer day, when Oberstleutnant Werner Mölders became the first fighter pilot ever to surpass the 100-victory mark. In his enthusiasm at this achievement, Hitler instituted yet another new top military award, the Knight's Cross with Oak Leaves, Swords, and Diamonds. Mölders became the first holder of this extravagant distinction. Afraid of losing such a gem for the Nazi propaganda machine, Hitler removed Mölders from frontline service and appointed him the first Inspector of the Fighter Arm. Ironically, this young favorite of Adolf Hitler would turn away from the Nazi regime in disgust within three months.

In the forests and fields in the huge area between Vitebsk and Minsk, 200 km further to the south, semi-encircled Soviet troops meanwhile fought a desperate defensive battle against the pursuing infantry of German 9. Armee, while simultaneously trying to escape across River Berezina. In these confused battles, Stalin's son, Yakov Dzhugashvili, serving as a Leytenant in the 7th Mechanized Corps, was captured by the Germans.

---

* Among those mortally wounded in this raid was the regimental commander, SS-Obersturmbannführer Dr. Ing. Wim Brandt, the man who had invented the famous mottled camouflage of the SS.

A scene from the battle of Smolensk. The fierceness of the battle is read in faces of these German soldiers, who are standing before a barricade where the Soviet defenders fought to the last man. (Photo: Via Daniel Johansson.)

forest and the bridge lay a rye field, but striking so surprisingly the Red Army soldiers managed to oust the German infantry from their positions. Shortly afterwards, however, German tanks arrived and caused a terrible bloodshed among the Soviet ranks. Across the whole field, men were shredded by exploding shells. In that moment, Ostapchuk's platoon commander, Aleksandr Dubinin, grabbed two anti-tank mines and ran towards the German tanks, hurled himself under one of them and blew it up together with himself. That caused the other German tanks to hesitate a bit, which gave the remaining Frontovniki a chance to escape back into the forest.

Hiding in among the trees, the Soviets established that of the whole battalion, only 32 men remained. They kept hiding in the forest until nightfall, and under the cover of the darkness they approached an unoccupied sector of the river. They found a mass of logs floating on the water, and by jumping from log to log, managed to cross to the eastern side.

At a small village, they encountered another group from their division. They learned that the division was more or less destroyed and that the commander had ordered all survivors to make it to Vitebsk in small groups. Should the Germans be there (which they actually were), the order was to march towards Smolensk.

Ostapchuk set off in a group of ten men. They darted from one small wood to another. On one occasion a little girl from a nearby hamlet came running towards them, yelling, "Hide, comrades! There are German tanks here!" But as they cautiously came closer, it turned out to be Soviet tanks. A tank commander who sat in the turret hatch studying a map informed the group of soldiers that Vitebsk was already a battle zone. "It's better that you follow our tracks to Orsha, and from there go to Smolensk."

A tank captain with three soldiers armed with submachine guns suddenly approached the group. "Halt, you deserters! I will have you shot!" the captain blurted out and started to yell obscenities at them. The mladshiy leytenant who led Ostapchuk's group replied angrily, "Comrade Captain, have you finished? I will tell you, we have been in hard combat, and where were you, if I may ask? We were near Minsk for two weeks, waiting for you, so where were you?" At this the captain softened, "All right, all right, you can go..."

Ostapchuk remembers that the people of Belarus were most kind to the Red Army soldiers. In every village the people shared all they had with them. One farmer gave him a pair of shoes, which was a great relief to Ostapchuk's sore feet. Ultimately reaching Orsha, the soldiers were divided between various other units. Ostapchuk was given a loaded rifle, and in a warehouse that had been bombed to ruins, he got a new soldier's blouse and boots. Having seen no further combat, Ostapchuk's new unit was sent off to Smolensk.

In Smolensk, he experienced heavy fighting with the Germans. He was drawn into the maelstrom of Soviet soldiers and civilians retreating towards the Dnepr Bridge. But this was blown up by Stukas, and thousands of soldiers swam across the river. Ostapchuk saw before his own eyes how many drowned in the strong current. He himself saved

Former Red Army private Grigoriy Ostapchuk was 91 when he was interviewed in 2011. He is one of very few Frontovniki (Soviet soldiers) who survived this battle. His unit held positions at daytime, well camouflaged against German air attacks, and at night time they retreated as fast as possible, often running for hours. The soldiers said to themselves that once across River Berezina, the great water barrier about half-way between Minsk in the southwest and Vitebsk in the northeast, they would be safe. But they had little information on the front situation. As the river came within sight, they discovered that the bridge was already held by the Germans.

Fortunately, the troops were in a small forest and had not yet been detected by the Germans. In the afternoon, the Soviets made an attempt to storm the bridge. Between the *a little girl from drowning by pulling her across to the other shore.*

Ostapchuk was again put into a newly reformed regiment. Shortly afterward, his frontline service would come to an end. Ostapchuk remembers that he and his comrades were in a forest when suddenly all hell seemed to break loose as they came under heavy fire. The next thing he can remember is a harsh "Hände hoch!" – Hands up!

Cold and hungry, the Frontovniki were rounded up and herded towards Orsha by German soldiers with dogs. He was brought to a prison camp which was nothing but a huge field, surrounded by barbed wire. The Soviet prisoners received nothing to eat at all, and everyone in the camp was only talking about food. Together with three other prisoners he attempted to escape one night. One of them was caught in the barbed wire, but the others got away. They reached a village where friendly inhabitants fed them and gave them civilian clothes. But this would not help. He was discovered by German field police, arrested and severely beaten, and then brought back to the same prison camp.

A while later the prisoners were transported to a prison camp near Fürth in Germany, where Ostapchuk would spend the rest of the war. The conditions in the camp were extremely harsh. There was daily hard labour, and the prisoners were fed with only boiled cabbage and 250 grams of bread per day. "Many of us died there," remembered Ostapchuk, "and I was only lucky to survive again." He described all the Germans that he met as "very cruel," with the exception of a few old people. After liberation in 1945, Ostapchuk was first interrogated and then again placed in the Red Army. Only in May 1946 – more than five years after he had left home – was he able to return to his home village in Bashkir. There he learned that his father had been killed in the war, and his brother had been injured in Leningrad.[20]

Attempting to halt the German advance against Smolensk from the northwest, Kapitan Flyorov's 1st Special Rocket Artillery Battery was rushed to Rudnya, 60 km northwest of the city, where it fired three powerful volleys against German 5. Infanterie-Division on 16 July. But this would not save Smolensk, which was entered from the south by LXVII. Armeekorps of Panzergruppe 2 on the same day. "Almost nothing remains of Smolensk from the first bombs by the Germans and the large fires set by the retreating Red Army. … These attacks have left the city as not much more than a skeleton. The city is a heap of rubble. … Left standing are Hotel Smolensk, the State Bank, and the cathedral turned museum." Thus Miguel Arena, correspondent from the Spanish news agency ABC, described the scene that met him when he arrived shortly afterward in this city, which before the war had a population of around 160,000.[21]

On 16 July, Luftflotte 2 carried out 615 sorties, reporting the destruction of 514 trucks, 14 tanks, two anti-aircraft guns and nine artillery pieces. On 17 July, Panzergruppe 2 reached Yelnya, 70 kilometers southeast of Smolensk. With

Wherever the German army advanced, the roads were littered with destroyed Soviet war equipment.

this, Soviet 16th and 20th armies became outflanked in the area west of Smolensk. These immediately began a large-scale operation to evacuate towards the east, but were seriously hampered by German air attacks.

Filled with enthusiasm at the latest victories, Hitler awarded the commanders of Panzergruppen 2 and 3, Guderian and Hoth, with the Oak Leaves. The Luftwaffe's contribution to these German accomplishments – in the face of a fierce Soviet resistance, including repeated counter-attacks – simply cannot be over-emphasized. In consequence, Hitler also awarded General von Richthofen, Fliegerkorps VIII's C.O., and Oberstleutnant Oskar Dinort and Major Walter Storp – the commanders of StG 2 and SKG 210 respectively – with the Oak Leaves.

At this point the terrible losses placed the Soviet Western Front in a qualitative as well as numerical inferiority. Generalfeldmarschall Fedor von Bock's Heeresgruppe Mitte enjoyed a superiority of five to one in tanks and almost two to one in artillery, and Luftflotte 2 could muster twice as many serviceable aircraft as its Soviet opponents in this sector.

On 19 July, Hitler issued his Directive No. 33, in which he instructed Heeresgruppe Mitte to continue the advance towards Moscow with only the infantry armies. The Führer believed that the road to Moscow lay open, with only limited opposition against a fast advance to seize the Soviet capital.[22] Three days later, under the impression created by the successes achieved by Heeresgruppe Mitte, and Heeresgruppe Nord's failure to push forward towards Leningrad, he issued an amended Directive (No. 33a), which would split Heeresgruppe Mitte into three directions: The infantry armies would march on towards Moscow, Panzergruppe 3 was to turn north to assist the onslaught against Leningrad, and Panzergruppe 2 would veer south to participate in the conquest of the Ukraine. Obviously, Hitler greatly exaggerated Heeresgruppe Mitte's striking capacity – a position that he would soon retreat from.

BLACK CROSS OVER MOSCOW — RED STARS OVER BERLIN.

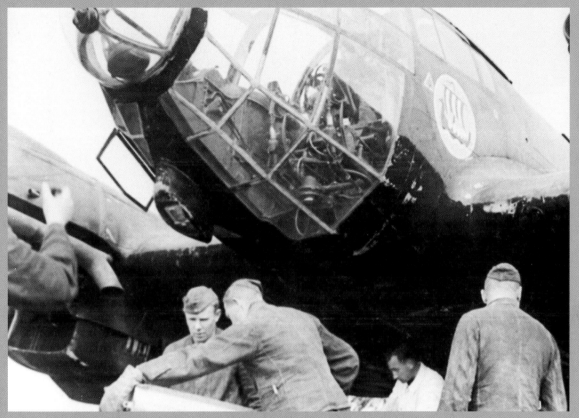

A German Heinkel He 111 bomber of KGr 100 "Wiking" is loaded with bombs for a mission against Moscow. With a crew of five and a top speed of 440 km/h, the He 111 could carry a bomb load of 3,600 kg. Defensive armament consisted of one 20 mm automatic cannon, one 13 mm gun and up to seven 7.92 mm machine guns. Soviet fighter pilots regarded it as sturdy and heavily defended. (Photo: Hansgeorg Bätcher.)

On 8 July 1941, Adolf Hitler ordered Reichsmarschall Göring to level Moscow and Leningrad to the ground – "in order to ensure that there will be no inhabitants left that we will have to supply during the winter." The final order for the implementation of these terror raids came with the Führer's Directive No. 33 of 19 July 1941. New bomber units – KG 4, KG 28, and KGr 100 – that arrived from Western Europe would strengthen the attack force.

General-Major Mikhail Gromadin, the commander of Moscow's Air Defense District (Moskovskaya Zona PVO), however had powerful resources at his disposal. First of all, there was an anti-aircraft artillery mustering 1,044 cannon and 336 machine guns. Then there were 585 fighters – of which more than half were of the modern types MiG-3, Yak-1, and LaGG-3 – divided among twenty-nine fighter regiments in fighter corps 6 IAK, commanded by Polkovnik Ivan Klimov. By that time, the Soviet night fighter force was at a rudimentary stage and still had no guidance from radar on the ground. However, within an 80-kilometer wide "light belt" that began 120 kilometers west

of Moscow, hundreds of searchlights had been deployed to illuminate the incoming enemy aircraft. It was in this sector that the fighter pilots would try to locate the Luftwaffe bombers.

The first air raid against the Soviet capital was launched during the evening on 21 July. A total of 195 bombers were dispatched. The main target was the Kremlin, and the operation was ironically dubbed Operation "Klara Zetkin," after the famous German Communist. Polkovnik Klimov sent 170 fighters into the air to meet the raiders. Heavy air fighting took place in the Searchlight Concentration Zone in the Solnechnogorsk – Golitsyno area northwest of Moscow. The first Soviet shoot down was recorded by Starshiy Leytenant Ivan Chulkov of the MiG-3-equipped 41 IAP, who claimed a Heinkel 111 at 0210 hours. A Dornier 17 piloted by Leutnant Kurt Kuhn of 9./KG 3 was brought down by the famous test pilot Kapitan Mark Gallay.

Closer to Moscow, the German bombers were met by anti-aircraft fire which grew in intensity as they approached the capital. Oberfeldwebel Broich, a Do 17 pilot in 3./KG 2 wrote about this first night over Moscow, "A searchlight caught us, and immediately afterward no less than thirty searchlights focused on us. The first anti-aircraft shells exploded close by. We jettisoned our bombs, and then commenced our battle with the flak. . ."[1] In total, Moscow's anti-aircraft units reported the expenditure of 29,000 cannon shells and 130,000 machine gun bullets during this raid. Oberleutnant Hansgeorg Bätcher of Luftwaffe bomber group KGr 100 recalled, "The night missions against Moscow were the most difficult that I ever carried out on the Eastern Front. The anti-aircraft fire was extremely intense, and the gunners fired with a frightening accuracy."[2]

At the cost of seven aircraft shot down, 104 tons of high explosives and 46,000 incendiaries were dropped by the attackers during this first raid. These caused heavy losses among the civilian population. But the real aim of the mission – to burn the Kremlin to ashes – failed completely. Erskine Caldwell of American radio station CBS reported directly from Moscow: "I have seen the Moscow air defence in action, and it is one of the marvels of the age. I am unable to compare it with the air defence of London and Berlin; but, judging from reports, if the Moscow defence is not superior it certainly must be every bit as effective in beating back air attacks as any air defence anywhere."[3]

The very next night, 115 bombers were launched. While the I-16 pilots of 27 IAP claimed three Ju 88s shot down, Mladshiy Leytenant Anatoliy Lukyanov of 34 IAP managed to bring down his second bomber in Searchlight Concentration Zone 5.[4] The Germans admitted to the loss of five bombers, and still no great damage was caused in Moscow. Discontent with the reports from aerial reconnaissance, Hitler ordered a new attack on the third consecutive night, this time with 125 aircraft. All in all, these first 435 bomber sorties against Moscow resulted in no more than 336 people killed in the Soviet capital.

On each occasion they were faced with an effective air defense. The most successful Soviet fighter pilot during the brief "Air Battle of Moscow" was Kapitan Konstantin Titenkov, who scored one bomber on each of the first four raids, for which he was both awarded with the Order of Lenin and appointed a Hero of the Soviet Union.[5] Due both to the strong Soviet defense and the difficulty of keeping such a large portion of the declining German bomber force away from the growing difficulties at the front, the number of aircraft participating in each raid decreased from 100 on the third night to 50, 30, and finally no more than 15 on successive missions. Within a short time the trumpeted Luftwaffe offensive against Moscow had been reduced to mere nuisance raids.

Already after the first five raids, the Luftwaffe's failure was obvious to Erskine Caldwell, who scornfully reported, "In five nights of raiding they have accomplished little more than the entire Swiss Navy accomplished in the World War."[6]

In Hansgeorg Bätcher's opinion, the bomber offensive against Moscow was a great mistake, leading to no German gains at all but only producing exhaustion and demoralization among bomber crews who were badly needed for military goals. The attacks did not even influence the moral of the Muscovites, who quickly learned to adapt everyday life to the raids. Similar to the Londoners, they waited out the raids in the subway – Moscow's luxury built underground communications system. Anatoliy Dreitser, one of the Muscovites, recalls, "Down below people lie in four rows, mostly women and children. They lie in careful order. Each family has its area. They spread out newspapers, then blankets and pillows. Children play, adults amuse themselves in various ways. They drink tea, even with jam. They visit each other. They talk quietly. They play dominoes. There are several pairs of chess players, surrounded by 'fans.' Many read books, knit, darn stockings, repair linens." (Thurston and Bernd Bonwetsch, *The People's War: Responses to World War II in the Soviet Union*, p. 114).

The first nocturnal taran during the air battle of Moscow was carried out by Leytenant Petr Yermeyev of 27 IAP on the night between 27 and 28 July. Another night time air-to-air ramming was performed by Mladshiy Leytenant Viktor Talalikhin of 177 IAP on the night of 6/7 August. While the whole German crew was killed in the crash, Talalikhin survived by bailing out. When the Luftwaffe returned to Moscow on the night of 10/11 August, they were confronted with Pe-2s acting as night fighters. These aircraft had been equipped with powerful searchlights to locate the enemy bombers in the dark. The original intention was to use the Pe-2s as "flying searchlights" to assist the single-engine night fighters, but once the German aircraft were sighted, the eager Pe-2 pilots pressed home their own attacks with vigor. The success was immediate. Four German bombers were reported downed by the Petlyakov night fighters on their first night out. Following this raid, the Germans decided to cancel the bomber offensive against Moscow. Between 22 July and 22 August, the air offensive against Moscow claimed the lives of 736 of the city's inhabitants, and 3,513 were injured.

More air raids would follow against the Soviet capital – a total of eighty-seven took place between 12 July 1941 and 5 April 1942 – but the systematic air offensive had ended. Of seventy-six air raids during 1941, fifty-nine were carried out with no more than between three and ten planes. According to Soviet sources, air raids against Moscow through 1 October 1941, cost the Luftwaffe 173 aircraft (110

A row of Soviet Ilyushin DB-3F bombers ready for a new bombing operation. The DB-3F was comparable to the German He 111 in that it was quite sturdy. However, it was slower (the maximum speed was 410 km/h), and had a maximum bomb load of 2,700 kg, one ton lower than that of the He 111. But its main weakness was the light defensive armament – only three machine guns. (Photo: Vasiliy Kurayev.)

shot down by fighters and 60 by AAA, with another three destroyed in collisions with the steel wires of the barrage balloons). In any case, it was a humiliating blow to the prestige of the Luftwaffe, particularly as it occurred just at the time when Soviet bombs were starting to fall on the Reich's capital itself.

On 7 August 1941, the Berliners had begun to hope that they had the worst British air raids behind them. Between August 1940 and mid-June 1941, there had been 46 RAF attacks against the city, sometimes with over 100 participating aircraft. But since then, only two weak raids had been made by the British – with eleven planes on the night of 3 June and with nine planes on the night of 26 July. But the calm was to be broken not by the British, but by the Soviets.

At nine in the evening of 7 August, 15 Ilyushin DB-3 bombers of the Red Banner Baltic Fleet's mine-torpedo regiment 1 MTAP took off from the airfield at Kagul on the island of Saaremaa (Ösel) off the Estonian coast. The twin-engine machines divided into three groups, commanded by the regimental commander Polkovnik Yevgeniy Preobrazhenskiy, Kapitan Vasiliy Grechishnikov, and Kapitan Andrey Yefremov, and set course for the German capital. Navigating nearly one thousand kilometres to their target, five aircraft arrived over Berlin shortly after midnight. These dropped thirty 100-kg high-explosive bombs over the city area, and other aircraft bombed the approaches and outskirts of Berlin. Six people were killed and seventeen injured in Berlin (Bundesarchiv-Militärarchiv, RL II/267. Geheim-Akten über Lagebericht (Lw) vom 25.7. 1941 bis 9.8. 1941. Lagebericht Nr. 699). The German capital's AAA defenses were taken completely by surprise, and all Soviet aircraft were able to return safely to base.

It was the commander of the Soviet Navy Air Force (VVS VMF), General-Leytenant Semyon Zhavaronokov, who in July 1941 took the initiative to launch a nightly bomber offensive against Berlin. It was clear that owing to a lack of resources and poor navigational means, an air offensive against such a distant target as Berlin could only affect morale – but what the Soviets needed by that time was some kind of victory to maintain the fighting spirit.

With German forces already standing east of Smolensk and at the gates of Kiev, the shortest distance to Berlin was from the Estonian island of Saaremaa, and thus the role fell to the Red Banner Baltic Fleet's aviation and its bomber brigade 8 BAB. The best crews of 8 BAB's 1 MTAP and 57 BAP, equipped with twenty DB-3s, were earmarked for the Berlin raids. On 4 August, a first group of these bombers was flown over to Kagul Airdrome on the island of Saaremaa. The following night, five DB-3s were dispatched on a reconnaissance mission over Berlin. Ten of the veteran bomber crews also bombed the Latvian port of Ventspils on the night of 5/6 August. Two nights later, the first attack on Berlin followed, with great success.

The second Berlin raid was carried out on the night of 8/9 August. This time all twelve DB-3s participating in the mission reached Berlin and dropped seventy-two 100-kg FAB-100 high-explosive bombs and 2,500 propaganda leaflets. One aircraft, piloted by Starshiy Leytenant Ivan Finyagin, was shot down by Berlin's anti-aircraft guns.

These first Berlin raids aroused great enthusiasm, and Stalin instructed the Long-Range Aviation to deploy forces to strengthen the Berlin raids. 22 BAP and 200 BAP sent two groups of DB-3s to the airdrome at Aste on Saaremaa, while bomber wing 81 BAD moved forward to Pushkin Airdrome near Leningrad. 81 BAD, formed only on 15 July 1941, had not yet seen combat. It was comprised of the most modern bombers in the DBA's inventory – 432 TBAP and 433 TBAP, equipped with the four-engine TB-7 bombers, and 420 and 421 DBAP, equipped with twin-engine Yermolayev Yer-2s. The wing was commanded by Kombrig Mikhail Vodopyanov, one of the first Heroes of the Soviet Union, and mustered a large number of highly experienced pilots and navigators. It was regarded as the best the DBA could afford. Still, the unit and its aircraft were untested in combat. It would turn out that the diesel engines in the TB-7s were unsuitable for such long-range missions.

On the evening of 10 August, Kombrig Vodopyanov led 81 BAD's first operation, aimed at Berlin. It was a disaster right from the onset. One TB-7 and one Yer-2 crashed on take-off, and another Yer-2 which was called back also crashed. So only seven TB-7s and three Yer-2s departed for Berlin. Of these, three TB-7s failed to reach Berlin,

two of which crashed during their return flights. Among the aircraft that reportedly bombed Berlin, two TB-7s and two Yer-2s were lost. Vodopyanov's own TB-7 first was attacked in error by a Soviet naval fighter over the Baltic Sea, then German ground fire put one of its engines out of action before it reached Berlin, and during the return flight more anti-aircraft fire pierced one fuel tank. Finally it force-landed in German-occupied southern Estonia. After a two-day walk, the crew managed to reach the Soviet lines, only to learn that Vodopyanov had been removed of his command and replaced by Polkovnik Aleksandr Golovanov. 81 BAD's total losses overnight amounted to seven aircraft destroyed (five TB-7s and two Yer-2), and two Yer-2s damaged. The Soviet analysis showed that the diesel engines of the TB-7s had proved to be completely unreliable. "I could tear out those damned diesels with my teeth!" Vodopyanov was reported to have burst out in front of Stalin.

Soviet bombers returned to Berlin during the night of 11/12 August – this time DB-3s from both the Navy and the Long-Range Aviation. Eight reached Berlin, dropping six FAB-250s, twenty-six FAB-100s, forty-eight FAB-50s, and more than 100,000 propaganda leaflets. Five other bombers failed to reach Berlin – four of them attacked Libau, while one unloaded its bombs over Kolberg. All aircraft returned safely to base. In recognition of their feats, Polkovnik Preobrazhenskiy, who commanded 1 MTAP, and four of his pilots were appointed Heroes of the Soviet Union the next day.

On the night of 15/16 August the next Berlin mission took place, involving seventeen bombers from both commands. Fifteen reached Berlin, and the other two dropped their bombs over Stettin and Neubrandenburg. Again all aircraft were able to return to base – where two DB-3s of 1 MTAP crashed.

However, the increasingly critical situation in Estonia by this time called for 1 MTAP to be deployed against German forces in this area. In consequence, the Berlin raid on the night of 18/19 August was undertaken only by DBA crews. Five DB-3s dropped their bombs over the German capital while a sixth attacked Schweinemünde.

To compensate for the reduced attack force, Stalin ordered the use of heavy bombs, 1,000-kg FAB-1000s and 500-kg FAB-500. This put a great strain on the pilots, since the runways used were too short for a DB-3's take-off with such a heavy cargo. Because only external racks could be used, a take-off with these bombs was under all circumstances very dangerous. Despite the fact that two DB-3s crashed on the runway at Aste during take-off on 19 August, nine other DB-3s were employed on the night of 20/21 August, loaded with heavy bombs. Another two crashed on take-off, and of the seven remaining aircraft only three managed to locate Berlin. Following this, 22 BAP and 200 BAP were withdrawn from further participation in the Berlin raids. Another setback followed on 21 August, when ZG 26 Bf 110s attacked 81 BAD's base at Pushkin, causing severe damage to the airfield's ground installations (TsAMO, f. 302, op. 6169, d. 1, l. 56).

On the night of 31 August /1 September, 1 MTAP went into action against Berlin again, dispatching six DB-3s from Kagul. But only two of them were reported to have reached Berlin, where they dropped two FAB-500s and twelve ZAB-50 incendiary bombs, plus thousands of propaganda leaflets. Three other crews claimed to have attacked Memel, Libau, and Danzig, while the sixth failed to return to base. However, in the adverse weather all Soviet aircraft made navigational errors; in fact, no bombs hit Berlin that night (Girbig, *Im Anflug auf die Reichshauptstadt*, p. 238).

Simultaneously, Polkovnik Aleksandr Golovanov led three TB-7s on a mission against the East Prussian city of Königsberg.

Two nights later, 1 MTAP sent only two DB-3s against Berlin. One managed to drop its bombs over the city centre, while the second failed to reach Berlin and instead reportedly attacked Libau. On the night of 4/5 September, four DB-3s were sent out again. This time they were subject to both anti-aircraft fire and night fighter interception. The latter prevented one of the bombers reaching Berlin, and another DB-3 was shot down.

That would prove to be the last Soviet air raid against Berlin in 1941. The Germans were now preparing to invade Saarema, and on 6 September, six of 1 MTAP's DB-3s were destroyed in an attack by II./ZG 26 against Kagul's airfield (M. Morozov, *Torpedonostsy Ilyushina v nebe Baltiki* in *Istoriya Aviatsii*, No. 3/2002). On the next day, the three DB-3s that remained serviceable in 1 MTAP flew over the ground personnel from Kagul to Bezzabotnoye near Leningrad. On 8 September, the German operation to occupy Saarema was started. With the loss of the island's airfields, the twin-engine Ilyushin bombers could no longer reach Berlin. The unfortunate experience of the TB-7s and Yer-2s also compelled the Soviets to discontinue the use of these aircraft against such a distant target as Berlin. Nevertheless, 81 BAD would continue to fly against Germany through the autumn of 1941, although in small numbers and against closer targets, like Königsberg or Danzig.

In total, the bomber units that operated from Saaremaa conducted nine missions against Berlin, with a total of 54 sorties. The total losses for these units amounted to 20 aircraft. In addition to the five naval fliers who had previously been appointed Heroes of the Soviet Union for their participation in the Berlin raids, this honorary rank was on 16

September bestowed upon five of the Long-Range Aviation pilots for their participation in the Berlin raids. However small in size, the fact of Red stars over Berlin was greatly capitalized on by the Soviet propaganda, and it unquestionably had a strong impact on the morale of Soviet populace. It also piqued the British into resuming their Berlin raids: On the night of 13 August, 70 aircraft were dispatched in the largest RAF raid against the German capital since April. On the night of 7/8 September, the British carried out the largest Berlin raid so far, with nearly 200 bombers, resulting in 250 civilians killed or injured and nearly 3,000 rendered homeless.

A Soviet bomb aimer.

1 Quoted in Balke, *Der Luftkrieg in Europa 1939–1941*, p. 334.
2 Interview with Hansgeorg Bätcher.
3 Caldwell, *Moscow Under Fire: A Wartime Diary*, p. 36.
4 TsAMO, f. 146 GIAP.
5 TsAMO, f. 6 IAK.
6 Caldwell, p. 39.

10: THE BLITZKRIEG IS HALTED.

"Had I known the figures for the Russian tank strength
I would not – I believe – ever have started this war."

– Adolf Hitler, 3 August 1941.

Generalfeldmarschall von Bock, the commander of Heeresgruppe Mitte, exploded with rage when he was informed of Hitler's Directive No. 33a. He knew very well that his forces were becoming worn down, and aerial reconnaissance had shown that massive Soviet reinforcements were arriving.

Without exaggeration, it might be stated that the Soviet Union was saved by its impressive capacity of generating new forces in those few days. In fact, for the second time in a fortnight, the nearly obliterated Western Front was recreated. On 14 July a new Reserve Front with six new armies (the 24th, 28th, 29th, 30th, 31st and 32nd) was formed under the command of NKVD General-Leytenant Ivan Bogdanov, and ordered into position behind the Western Front. This also was placed under the Western Direction, which was commanded by Timoshenko – at the same time as he maintained his command over the Western Front.

A terrible mistake by German intelligence before the war was its failure to realize the ability of a society like the Soviet Union to generate new forces. Under Tukhachevskiy's command, the Red Army emphasized the combination of a peacetime cadre army and massive wartime mobilizations. A plan was made for mobilization in "waves," allowing the army to be fully replaced every four to eight months of heavy combat.[1] This idea was neglected after the execution of Tukhachevskiy, but the plans were in place, preparations had been made, and when the German onslaught came, they could easily be put into practice, at least on a quantitative level. Indeed, the newly mobilized forces were marked by Stalinist neglect and incompetence, suffering from a terribly inadequate training and often a desperate shortage of equipment – leading to immense losses in combat – but the mobilization in "waves" which began on the fourth day of the German attack saved the Red Army from being simply wiped out.

Between the Western and the Southwestern fronts, the Stavka placed the 13th and 21st armies under a new command, the Central Front, which also was subordinated to the Western Direction. With the appointment of General-Polkovnik Fedor Kuznetsov to command the Central Front, Kuznetsov was rehabilitated – after first being demoted from commanding the Northwestern Front to lead the 21st Army. The new Front was provided with an air force consisting of the rebuilt 11 SAD (under General-

Leytenant Grigoriy Kravchenko) and the newly arrived 28 SAD, plus five independent regiments.

On 20 July the Stavka instructed Timoshenko to launch a major counter-offensive, the largest to date, with the objective of relieving the semi-enveloped 16th and 20th armies at Smolensk and the 13th at Mogilev. For this purpose, the 28th, 29th and 30th armies of the Stavka reserve were assigned to the Western Front.

At that stage, the relentless heavy fighting was wearing down the German strength at a frightening pace, particularly with regard to tanks and aircraft. 7. Panzer-Division had by this time recorded 77 tanks as total losses and had another 120 in repair. 10. Panzer-Division, meanwhile, had lost over one third of its vehicles.[2] The situation was even worse in 4. Panzer-Division, which on 17 July reported only 40 tanks remaining out of the 169 that it had begun the campaign with.[3] 18. Panzer-Division had started the campaign with 218 tanks – two thirds of which were Panzer IIIs or Panzer IVs – and received 30 new Panzer IIIs and Panzer

Next to a destroyed tank, two Red Army soldiers enjoy a smoke during a pause in the fighting. (Photo: Soviet Embassy, 1976.)

German infantry in bitter fighting over a Soviet village. (Photo: Via Daniel Johansson.)

IVs on 22 July, but further losses brought down the number of operational tanks to a mere twelve on 24 July.[4]

In the air war, Luftwaffe losses to all causes (including non-combat related) on the Eastern Front during the first month of war with the USSR amounted to 1,284 aircraft destroyed or damaged – nearly half the original force. On 22 July fighter group III./JG 53 reported a "frightening lack of aircraft; the Gruppe has only six serviceable aircraft!"[5]

But the situation was no less desperate on the Soviet side, where large forces were sealed off at Smolensk. A narrow corridor to the east still remained, and here terrible scenes took place as scores Luftwaffe planes attacked tightly packed masses of escaping Red Army soldiers. Nina Erdman, a Red Army nurse, said, "It was terrifying – weapons lying around, no one knew where to go, panic! How awful! And we were not traveling light, we had wounded with us. We drove out into a field: in which direction to move? Everything around us was burning. The commanders were running about, they didn't know where to go."[6]

Timoshenko's counter-offensive was opened in a rush on 23 July when the 28th Army attacked in the Roslavl area, some 100 kilometers southeast of Smolensk, striking towards the northwest. The critical situation at the front allowed virtually no time for preparations. The 28th Army had just recently been formed, and consisted mainly of either inadequately trained recruits or conscripts with no military training at all. It suffered from shortages in everything, including ammunition, and with the exception of its commander, General-Leytenant Vladimir Kachalov (who had previously commanded the Arkhangelsk Military District), nearly all the officers lacked even the most basic understanding of troop command in battle.

In the air, 411 BAP – which had arrived with ten Petlyakov Pe-2 bombers at the front only the day before – conducted its first mission to support the 28th Army's offensive early on 23 July. Five Pe-2s were tasked with attacking Shatalovo Airdrome between Smolensk and Roslavl. Intercepted by Bf 109s, all were shot down.[7] Later that day, the remaining five Petlyakovs of the 411th went for Shatalovo again, this time escorted by four LaGG-3s from 239 IAP. Three Petlyakovs were lost in a short engagement where JG 51's Oberleutnant Karl-Gottfried Nordmann and Leutnants Heinz Bär and Herbert Huppertz destroyed one each.

In spite of all difficulties, Timoshenko widened his counter-offensive to the north on 24 July, when the Reserve Front's 24th and the Western Front's 30th armies attacked on a 140-kilometer wide front between Yartsevo (45 km northeast of Smolensk) and Belyy in the north. The 153 aircraft of General-Mayor Boris Pogrebov's new Reserve Front Air Force and 120 bombers of the Long-Range Aviation's 3 BAK were launched in wave after wave against the forces of Panzergruppe 3 that were pushing southwards in an effort to close the gap east of Smolensk.[8] These forces complained loudly on 25 July of, "Attacks by bombers which cost time and resulted in particular in personnel and material losses."[9] General von Richthofen immediately sent the bulk of his Messerschmitt 109s to the area, and in large-scale air battles on 26 and 27 July, these reportedly shot down 83 Soviet planes and swept the Soviet air force from the skies. The fact that only six own fighters were shot down in the process is quite telling.

The air battle east of Smolensk on these two days captures the whole air situation in a nutshell. Inadequately trained fliers that had seen their training schemes consid-

erably reduced in order to make up for the losses at the front took off and had immense losses inflicted on them as swarms of Messerschmitt 109s pounced on them from above. But with their fighting spirit unbroken, they took off the next day and the next day again, until all had been shot down. The average life expectancy in such air units at this stage was no more than a couple of weeks, and this even if they were equipped with the most modern aircraft straight from the factories. 410 BAP began operations with 38 Pe-2 bombers on 5 July; in the course of 235 sorties during the next three weeks, 33 of these were lost. Although the Air Force of the Western Front mustered a total of around 1,300 aircraft in July – 900 new aircraft arrived to bolster the strength of 389 on 1 July – only 188 remained on 29 July.[10]

On 27 July the German ring around Smolensk was sealed to the east of the city. At this point, 185,000 Soviet POWs had been taken in the Smolensk area. With almost all of their ammunition used up and now deprived of the possibility of receiving new supplies, the 16th and 20th armies rapidly crumbled. During mopping-up operations over the following week, the number of prisoners of war captured by the Germans at Smolensk rose to 310,000.

Another great battle of annihilation had been won where the Luftwaffe had played a decisive role. As a measurement of the Luftwaffe's contribution, assault wing SKG 210 – one of the most important among Luftflotte 2's close-support units – claimed to have put 823 Soviet aircraft, 2,136 motor vehicles, 194 artillery pieces, 52 trains, and 60 locomotives out of commission on the ground between 22 June and 26 July.

The intensity of the air war during the Battle of Smolensk is clearly displayed by the number of sorties carried out by the belligerent air forces in this sector between 10

A Soviet anti-tank gun crew under enemy fire.

been assigned to the *Ostheer* – the Eastern Front Army – by the end of July.[14]

Individual units had been severely mauled, such as 18. Panzer-Division, which sustained 3,353 casualties between 22 June and 27 July – amounting to 19.5 per cent of the overall strength on 22 June and an appalling 38.3 per cent of all officers on 22 June 1941! The unit's 18. Schützen-Brigade, originally composed of two regiments, was reorganized into a regiment of two battalions of no more than 600 men. The motorcycle battalion had lost 352 men, the equivalent of three companies, including most of its group and platoon leaders.[15]

In spite of the defeat at Smolensk, Timoshenko's armies continued to attack Heeresgruppe Mitte. On 26 July, the Chief of the German General Staff Halder wrote in his diary, "Overall picture: Enemy defense is becoming more aggressive: more tanks, more planes."[16] On 27 July, the day that German 20. Panzer-Division closed the ring around Smolensk, Helmuth Dittri, a soldier in the division, wrote in his diary, "From early dawn the enemy [artillery] rake our lines with his accurate, well-directed fire... The Russians have been shooting for 48 hours now, the only lull having been 3 hours during the night... Several German bombers wheeled above our heads and as long as they were about the Russians warily abstained from firing. But as soon as they disappeared... we landed in a cross-fire so terrific that we did not know if we were dead or alive. A few more tanks went the way of all flesh – or metal, rather, to be exact. They're bringing in an endless line of wounded. The motor-cyclist [battalion] fared very badly. Their casualties were tremendous."[17]

Meanwhile, 70 kilometers farther to the south, Lemelsen's XLVII. Panzerkorps reported "strong enemy air superiority, many low-level attacks and bomber raids, many casualties," and called for reinforced air support.[18] With only nine serviceable aircraft, IV./JG 51, the only German fighter group in the area, was unable to ward off these Soviet air attacks. Even more so since the unit's air base, Shatalovo, came under attack from Red Army forces that had broken through on 27 July. The Luftwaffe units at that place had to fly their missions to defend themselves instead of carrying out the ordered missions to support the attempts to break through at Yelnya, 60 km further to the northeast.[19] Another fighter group, III./JG 51, was hastily shifted to Shatalovo on 28 July, and managed to relieve the pressure from the air on Lemelsen's troops by shooting down nine Soviet planes, four of them by Leutnant Joachim Hacker.

In fact, by this time it was only in the battle in the air that the Germans still had the initiative, and a permanent maximal air effort was a prerequisite for Heeresgruppe Mitte's ability to withstand the mounting pressure from Timoshenko's attack forces. On 28 July Luftflotte 2 carried out 696 sorties, while the battered Soviet air units managed to perform only 327.

Although Timoshenko's counter-offensive failed to relieve the enveloped armies at Smolensk and led to terrible Soviet losses, it succeeded in halting the German advance towards Moscow – at least for the time being. In the Veli-

and 31 July – 12,653 German and 5,200 Soviet. In total, the Germans claimed to have destroyed 4,908 Soviet aircraft on the Eastern Front in July 1941 – 2,656 fighters, 1,806 bombers, and 446 miscellaneous aircraft.[11] The claims of a total of 7,564 destroyed Soviet aircraft since the war began on 22 June are in fact quite in line with actual Soviet losses.

The Luftwaffe's own combat losses were fairly heavy as compared to its initial strength, but very low in relation to the damage it inflicted on its enemy – a total of 760 aircraft had been lost in combat by the end of July, amounting to 20 per cent of the initial strength.[12] The German panzer units meanwhile had sustained losses on the same level – 850 out of 3,400 tanks had been lost by 31 July.[13] Personnel losses meanwhile were less than 10 per cent – by 31 July the force of some 3.3 million men had sustained 318,333 casualties killed, missing and wounded. But whereas material losses could be replaced, only 47,000 personnel replacements had

German troops seek cover as they come under Soviet artillery fire. (Photo: Via Daniel Johansson.)

The driver of a T-34 tank receives food from a Soviet woman, not far from the battlefield.

kiye Luki sector in the north, Soviet 22nd Army – soon to be reinforced by the 29th Army – launched a series of counter-attacks with heavy air support that managed to halt Panzergruppe 3 and 9. Armee. Mayor Ivan Polbin, commanding 150 SBAP of Soviet 22nd Army, wrote, "Our people are doing a great work! We beat the Germans both day and night. For them, our regiment is a terrible, merciless force. We often receive expressions of gratitude from our ground troops, to whom we provide support from the air."[20], In fact Panzergruppe 3 and 9. Armee would remain stalled not only during the remainder of July, but also throughout August.

In the German headquarters, quite serious strife began to emerge. In the Air commanders' view, it was increasingly obvious that the never slackening Soviet resistance – in combination with the Luftwaffe's growing role as a fire brigade – was beginning to have a negative effect on the German ground troops. The observations previously made by General von Richthofen that the ground forces expected air cover at every point and all the time were supported by Luftwaffe Oberst Hermann Plocher, who said that the army at this point "had become outrageously spoiled by the con-

tinuous employment of Luftwaffe units in direct support on the battlefield."[21] While von Richthofen accused the ground troops of a tendency to retreat prematurely whenever confronted with any serious Red Army resistance if Luftwaffe aircraft were not present, the ground forces frequently complained that the liaison with the close-support units of the Luftwaffe did not work quickly enough.

Hitler began to realize that he had been overly optimistic when he submitted directives 33 and 33a. He was particularly concerned with the threatened southern flank of Heeresgruppe Mitte.* On 27 July he revised his previous instructions for Guderian's Panzergruppe 2 and ordered it turn southwestwards to deal with the Central Front's 21st Army at Gomel, 250 km southwest of Smolensk. Thus Guderian's spearhead was to be used defensively. "The appearance of new, powerful enemy forces in front of and on the flank of Heeresgruppe Mitte in the last few days have convinced the Führer that the idea of large-scale operations as outlined in Directive 33 must stand back in favour of the destruction of enemy forces," was noted in a memorandum of Hitler's instructions on 28 July.[22] He also gave up on the plan to shift Panzergruppe 3 to Heeresgruppe Nord. Instead he subordinated it to 9. Armee, commanded by Generaloberst Adolf Strauss.

This caused outrage in Heeresgruppe Mitte's headquarters. On 28 July, von Bock summoned all the senior commanders of his army group to a conference on the new situation. "Because the Russian is so tough his tactical methods are unpredictable," he said. The frustrations caused by a de facto halted offensive were vented. "The nerves of those burdened with great responsibility are starting to waver," von Bock worriedly noted.[23] Von Kluge complained about the long and vulnerable flank of his 4. Armee. Guderian accused von Kluge – who was still his superior – of having frittered away the possibility of breaking through in the east by tying down some of the forces of his Panzergruppe 2 against the enveloped enemy forces at Smolensk. In Guderian's words, the relations between him and von Kluge became "strained to an undesirable degree."[24] Concern was also voiced about the state of Panzergruppe 2, whose tank strength had dropped from 953 on 22 June to only 286.[25]

* Possibly under the looming threat of these Soviet counter-offensives, Germans and collaborating Belorussian auxiliary policemen executed more than 3,000 Soviet POWs and 700 Jews in a large-scale massacre in Nesvizh, 45 km northeast of Baranovichi, on 27 July. (Smilovitsky, *Holocaust in Belorussia, 1941–1944*, p. 189.)

T-26 tankmen receive the last instructions before they launch an attack against the Germans. (Photo: Soviet Embassy, 1976.)

Above all, everyone was against Hitler's new directives. "I expected to be told to push on towards Moscow or at least Bryansk," wrote Guderian. "To my surprise I learned that Hitler had ordered that my 2nd Panzer Group was to go for Gomel in collaboration with the Second Army. This meant that my Panzer Group would be swung round and would be advancing in a south-westerly direction, ie towards Germany."[26] In clear defiance of the Führer's orders, von Bock instructed Guderian to open a new offensive towards the east, directed against Roslavl, around 100 kilometers southeast of Smolensk. The formal goal was to annihilate Soviet 28th Army, which was attacking in this area, but as von Bock admitted in a phone call with Halder, Roslavl was necessary as a jump-off base for the continued eastward advance.[27]

Both Generaloberst Halder, the Chief of the General Staff, and Generalfeldmarschall von Brauchitsch, the Commander-in-Chief of the German Army, were actually also opposed to Hitler's new directive and tried to convince the Führer to concentrate all forces on the offensive towards Moscow.

On 29 July, Guderian made a doomed but passionate attempt to make Hitler change his mind – to no avail; instead, that day the Führer ordered von Richthofen's entire Fliegerkorps VIII to move to Heeresgruppe Nord's southern flank, without even notifying the Army High Command. The next day, Hitler issued Directive No. 34 with a completely new tone. "The appearance of strong enemy forces," he wrote, made it necessary for Heeresgruppe Mitte "to go over to the defensive." The new orders suddenly called for

shifting the next main objective of Operation Barbarossa to the seizure of Leningrad, and returned to his idea of having Panzergruppe 3 shifted northwards to support Heeresgruppe Nord. All of this was a complete volte-face of what Hitler had maintained throughout most of July.

In German and many other Western post-war accounts, the discussion between Hitler and Generaloberst Alfred Jodl (the Chief of the OKW Operations Staff) on one hand and the commander of Heeresgruppe Mitte, Halder and von Brauchitsch on the other is said to have paralysed the activities of Heeresgruppe Mitte during most of August 1941, and it is implied that this is the reason why the offensive against Moscow was discontinued. However, Heeresgruppe Mitte's orders and actions refute this conclusion. The advance against Moscow had been explicitly ordered by Hitler on 8 July, then again on 19 July, and a third time on 22 July. Without any doubt, it was the Red Army that thwarted this, although the German commanders blamed each other and Hitler for their failure.

On 1 August Guderian launched his attack towards Roslavl in the east. His 4. Panzer-Division advanced around 50 kilometers in one day and thus sealed off Soviet 28th Army. Two days later Hitler flew to the headquarters of Heeresgruppe Mitte to enforce his decision to cancel the costly attempts to break through towards Moscow. By that time, von Bock's headquarters had turned into a nest of conspiracy against Hitler. Several officers in the headquarters planned to kidnap Hitler when he arrived at. Only a strong presence of SS bodyguards prevented this from happening. During the conference on 3 August, Hitler and his generals clashed, with the former declaring that Leningrad and the Ukraine were the main goals, while von Bock, Guderian and also Halder wanted to make an attempt to break through to Moscow – which Guderian was actually in the process of attempting.

According to the image created by German generals after the war, Hitler was always wrong in his conflicts with his generals. This simplified picture disregards the fact that the Blitzkrieg in the West in 1940 was Hitler's idea, which he carried out in defiance of his generals, who believed it to be impossible.* Now the generals were overly optimistic while Hitler – again – proved to be more realistic.

On 26 July, Hitler had received a gloomy report on Heeresgruppe Nord's situation; it had become stalled south of Leningrad, with both of its flanks threatened by enemy armies, and greatly intensified Soviet air activity was posing a mounting problem.

To leave the army group in that situation would definitely cool down the Finnish eagerness for aggressive action in cooperation with the Germans. In fact, Finland's own offensive against Eastern Karelia had become bogged down by that time. A reinforcing of Heeresgruppe Nord brought the prospect of a breakthrough to Leningrad, which was probably required to encourage the Finns to resume their own offensive. Moreover, in order to secure the Baltic Sea and the vital shipping of Swedish iron ore to Germany, it was vital to at least lock the mighty Red Banner Baltic Fleet into the Gulf of Finland, and this required that Estonia's northern coast was occupied.

To put more forces against the Ukraine also was to target some of the Soviet Union's most important industrial areas and mining regions, and its largest agricultural area. The capture of those assets would not only put an end to the Red Army's proven ability to generate new forces, but in fact was one of the most important aims of Operation Barbarossa.

If the Crimea could also be taken, the Soviet bomber offensive against the Romanian oil fields would be brought to an end, since it departed from there. In any case, it was necessary to deal with the mounting threat against Heeresgruppe Mitte's southern flank, in the shape of the new Soviet Central Front. To turn Guderian's Panzergruppe 2 to the south also gave the Germans a chance of annihilating the Soviet Southwestern Front through a gigantic encirclement – an aim that eventually was fulfilled, providing Germany with the largest tactical victory in military history.

Upon his return to his headquarters in East Prussia, the Wolf's Lair, Hitler collapsed. Dr. Morell, the Führer's doctor, wrote in his diary that he found Hitler pale, "very irritable," with trembling hands, and complaining of a loud buzzing sound in his ears. He was throwing up and his blood pressure was dangerously high, 170 mm.

Meanwhile, in the aftermath of the annihilation of Soviet 16th and 20th armies at Smolensk, Stalin and his generals also had a heated argument. At a conference with Stalin on 29 July, the Chief of the Soviet General Staff, General Armii Zhukov, proposed an attack against the Yelnya Salient and that Kiev be evacuated in order to save the Southwestern Front. "Attack Yelnya? Such a stupidity!"

the Soviet dictator blurted out, and he also opposed the idea of evacuating Kiev. Zhukov was so upset that he asked to be relieved of his post, which Stalin accepted. Zhukov was replaced by Marshal Boris Shaposhnikov, who thus was reinstated in this position. Shaposhnikov was a quite a talented military commander. He had been appointed Chief of the General Staff for the first time in 1937, but had resigned in 1940 because of the failures of the Red Army during the Winter War against Finland – although his original plan had been ignored by the military commander of the invasion of Finland, Stalin's favorite, Marshal Voroshilov (which led to the terrible losses sustained by the Soviets in that war). Zhukov was ordered by Stalin to replace NKVD General-Leytenant Bogdanov as the commander of the Reserve Front, so that he could organize the Yelnya attack that he wished.

Another failed Soviet counter-attack. The only result is a row of fallen Red Army troopers and destroyed tanks. (Photo: Arno Becker.)

In the meantime, the main fighting on the road to Moscow was utterly contradictory. On the northern flank, the Soviet forces continued to pounce on Hoth's Panzergruppe 3, while Guderian's Panzergruppe 2 was attacking Soviet 28th Army at Roslavl. After Fliegerkorps VIII had been sent northwards, General Bruno Loerzer's Fliegerkorps II was the only air corps remaining in Luftflotte 2. However, owing to the weakness of the Soviet aviation in this sector, it was actually sufficient to interfere decisively in both of these sectors. Fliegerkorps II had already previously been deprived of its only Stukageschwader, StG 77, which had been shifted to Luftflotte 4, but the assault wing SKG 210 continued to wreak havoc on the Soviet forces. Between 29 July and 4 August, Fliegerkorps II claimed to have destroyed 1,500 trucks, 100 tanks, 41 artillery pieces, and 24 anti-aircraft batteries.

From Roslavl, Soviet 28th Army's commander, General-Leytenant Vladimir Kachalov, sent a desperate call for help on 4 August, "Requesting air support, particularly fighters!"[28] Kachalov personally fought to the bitter end,

---

* Those who hold the simplified view that Hitler was always wrong in the clashes with his generals should consider the fact that von Rundstedt, arguably the most competent among the German field marshals in Operation Barbarossa, supported Hitler in his view that Leningrad should have top priority.

Troops of German 29. Infanterie-Division (mot.) of Panzergruppe 2 in combat against counter-attacking Soviet tanks. The anti-tank gun is a 50mm PaK 38, one of the most modern guns of its kind at the time. The PaK 38, which entered service shortly before Operation Barbarossa, was one of few guns capable of penetrating the sloped armor of the T-34 tank. When firing Panzergranate PzGr 40 Hk (Hartkern, hard core) shells with a hard tungsten core, it was even possible to penetrate the armor of the heavy KV tank.

side by side with his troops. Leading a brave attempt to break out on 4 August, he was killed.* When the battle died down at this place a couple of days later, the 28th Army had been annihilated. The Germans netted 38,000 POWs.

Fliegerkorps II had been reinforced with three new bomber groups – III./KG 26, I./KG 28, and KGr 100 – in addition to the five that it already had (of KG 3 and KG 53). A heavy pressure was put on these bomber fliers, who at night time were engaged in the air offensive against Moscow, and during the day flew pre-emptive missions against bridges and railway junctions in the Soviet rear area. In these, 126 trains and 15 bridges were destroyed, affecting the Soviet deliveries of supplies to the front quite severely. This was a major cause to the withering of Timoshenko's counter-offensive.[29] By the time the Battle of Roslavl was over, the whole Soviet counter-offensive had shrunk down to attacks against the wedge driven into the Soviet lines by German troops at Yelnya, 70 kilometers southeast of Smolensk.

The fighters of Fliegerkorps II meanwhile were rushed from one sector to another in a fire brigade fashion. A Soviet attempt to reinforce Central Front's weak air force on 2 August 1941 backfired. En route to be employed in first-line service, a squadron of Il-2 Shturmoviks from 174 ShAP ran into four Messerschmitt Bf 109s led by the commander of fighter group IV./JG 51, Oberleutnant Karl-Gottfried Nordmann. In only slightly more than ten minutes,

German soldiers cautiously approach a destroyed BT-2 light tank.

nine Shturmoviks were shot down – four by Oberfeldwebel Heinrich Hoffmann (actually his first victories), three by Oberleutnant Nordmann, and two by Leutnant Hans Boos.[30]

After the victory at Roslavl, Guderian intended to pull back the bulk of his armor to recuperate for what was intended to be the final strike against Moscow, which he imagined could be made on 15 August – in defiance of a sickly and weakened Führer's demands. But in the meantime, southwest of Mogilev, cavalry forces from Soviet 21st Army were approaching Bobruysk on River Berezina. This compelled the Army High Command on 6 August to request that Guderian detach at least two Panzer divisions to support the 2. Armee in the Rogachev-Bobruysk sector.

And at Yartsevo and Yelnya, northeast and southeast of Smolensk, Timoshenko and Zhukov launched renewed attacks against German 9. Armee and Panzergruppe 3. While VVS Western Front encountered only light opposition in the air over Yartsevo, VVS Reserve Front was drawn into heavy air fighting as it attacked the German troops in the salient created by the Germans at Yelnya. There were practically no German fighters available in the former sector, but most of JG 51 operated over Yelnya. Here VVS units were depleted at the same pace as new units arrived. 57 BAP, which joined the air force of the Reserve Front's 24th Army on 7 August, was badly mauled by IV./JG 51 over Yelnya on 8-9 August. In the afternoon on 8 August, 57 BAP conducted its first combat mission with twenty-seven SBs flying against German armored forces at Yelnya. Messerschmitt Bf 109s from JG 51 intercepted just before the bombers had reached their target. The escorting MiG-3s of 10 IAP failed to prevent the German pilots from attacking the SBs. The Bf 109s concentrated their attack against 57 BAP's 2nd squadron, commanded by Starshiy Leytenant I. T. Krasnochubenko. Starshiy Leytenant G. A. Osipov, who piloted an aircraft with the 1st squadron, recalled how he looked back and in horror saw how all nine planes of the 2nd squadron were on fire simultaneously – while still flying in formation! But they managed to make it to the target and drop their bombs, after which the nine SBs descended to the left and to the right and parachutes filled the sky.[31] Next, the Messerschmitts turned their attention to the 1st squadron and blew two of its SBs out of the sky before one of the Bf 109s was shot down. The German pilots returned to base and reported eleven victories – this time exactly matching the Soviet losses.

On 9 August, the turn of 57 BAP's 3rd squadron had come, which lost five planes to IV./JG 51 when eight SBs were sent out without fighter cover. In this combat, Leutnant Heinz Bär scored his 55th victory. In return, Serzhant Listratov, the gunner in one of the SBs, managed

---

* Kachalov was buried in the village of Stodolishche, but owing to the chaotic situation, the report on this could not reach Moscow. Stalin did not hesitate to brand General-Leytenant Kachalov a "traitor" and had him sentenced to death in absentia. Only after Stalin's death in 1953 was the Soviet Supreme Court able to withdraw the disgracing sentence.

to shoot down a Bf 109. The German pilot, 33-victory ace Leutnant Herbert Huppertz, survived the crash without injuries. On 10 August, 57 BAP was down at a strength of only 14 SBs and was shifted to night operations – a fact which was noted by German radio interception.[32]

Meanwhile, 10 IAP – which had been posted to VVS 24th Army with 32 MiG-3s in late July – reported a strength of no more than ten planes.[33] The radio message on this was also intercepted by the Germans, who appeared to have a fairly good view on their opponent's strength in this sector.[34]

But while all these battles took place in Fliegerkorps II's area of operations, the sector farther north saw a reversal of the situation, owing much to the departure of Fliegerkorps VIII for the Leningrad offensive. In the area east and northeast of Smolensk, VVS Western Front and 3 BAK took control of the air, even though one of 3 BAK's units, 42 DBAD, was shifted south to help the hard-pressed Southwestern Front at Kiev.[35] On 11 August, the war diary of the German High Command reported the situation in the area on Heeresgruppe Mitte's northern flank, "The enemy enjoys air superiority in the whole army sector."[36]

The regiments of Soviet 43 SAD (numbered 43 IAD until 6 August 1941) and 47 SAD were divided into elements consisting of one or two eskadrilyas, which made it possible to increase the number of flights. Luftwaffe Oberst Hermann Plocher later wrote: "Especially troublesome were the continuous attacks upon the German front lines by Soviet ground-attack planes. Although these attacks were generally of relatively slight effect, they nevertheless influenced the morale of the ground forces. … The struggle against these ground-attack aircraft was very difficult because they approached from afar and at low level, flying singly, in two-plane formations, and in weak squadron strength; dropped their bombs on the front lines; and immediately turned back toward their own territory. Scrambling German fighters usually arrived too late to block the attack, and their pursuit of the Soviet ground-attack aircraft, which were retiring at low altitudes, was too costly for the unarmored German fighters because of the strong Soviet ground fire."[37]

This relentless pressure in the air and on the ground cost the Soviets heavily but also prevented the progress of Panzergruppe 3 northwards, which would have tremendous repercussions for Hitler's offensive against Leningrad. It also compelled the Germans to bring back III./JG 53 from Fliegerkorps VIII to the sector north of Smolensk. But this unit was quite worn out. On 17 August, when General-Polkovnik Ivan Konev's Soviet 19th Army, supported by a tank brigade and new aircraft of 43 SAD, attacked 9. Armee at Yartsevo, III./JG 53 was down at six operational aircraft. Two of these were lost – without any own successes – on that same day. The disastrous shortage in deliveries of replacements and spare parts rendered the whole of III./JG 53 practically unserviceable.

The subsequent ground battle is quite illustrative of the situation when German ground troops had no support from the Luftwaffe. 9. Armee 161. Infanterie-Division's forward positions were overrun. On 18 August, the last operational aircraft of III./JG 53 was lost.[38] On top of

Soviet soldiers are being rounded up by the Germans.

this, a contagious stomach disease affected most men of the Gruppe. On the whole, the mood among III./JG 53's men was on the decline during this period.[39] This also was the case with 161. Infanterie-Division, which lost 75% of its combat strength and much equipment in just a couple of days' fighting. After a week, it had to be pulled out of the front line. The Germans had to dispatch 7. Panzer-Division, 5. Infanterie- Division, and two anti-tank units to prevent the Soviet breakthrough. But in spite of these counter measures, Panzergruppe 3 still had to retreat on 20 August.

The tenacity with which the Soviets fought to block the advance towards Moscow is displayed by an event over the battlefield at Yartsevo on 21 August. A formation of Il-2s of 190 ShAP suddenly and quite unexpectedly came under attack from Bf 109s. The Soviets had not seen any German fighters in this sector for several days, but these came from I./JG 51, which had just arrived in this sector. The German unit commander, the ace Hauptmann Hermann-Friedrich Joppien, managed to blow one of the escorting MiG-3s of 129 IAP out of the sky – this was his 65th victory. But in the next moment, MiG-3 pilot Starshiy Leytenant Pyotr Kovats sacrificed his life by ramming one of the Bf 109s, and this compelled Joppien to return to base.[40]

On 22 August the battle reached a new peak, with 7. Panzer-Division losing 30 tanks in its efforts to block the Soviet attacks at Yartsevo.[41] Heeresgruppe Mitte reported heavy Soviet air activity with the focus on the Yelnya Bulge and the Yartsevo area.[42] JG 51 made a major effort to support their heavily pressed ground troops and claimed twelve Soviet aircraft shot down against a single loss. Hauptmann Joppien was again in the thick of the fighting, bagging two DB-3 bombers.[43]

In the south, Guderian's Panzergruppe was meanwhile rushed back and forth in tactically successful mopping-up operations which nevertheless cost the Germans much valuable time. Following the victory at Roslavl, Guderian's armor was sent southwestward, where it routed Soviet 13th and 21st armies in a massive battle between Krichev and

Soviet soldiers with a PTRD-41 anti-tank rifle. The PTRD-41 (ProtivoTank-ovoye Ruzhyo Degtyaryova, i.e. Degtyaryov Anti-Tank Rifle of model 1941) was the main individual, close combat anti-tank weapon in the Red Army in 1941. This single-shot weapon fired a 114mm round with a muzzle velocity of 1,012 m/s. At a distance of 100 meters this was sufficient to penetrate the 30mm side armor of a Panzer III or Panzer IV. (Photo: Krigs-arkivet Stockholm.)

Gomel, netting 78,000 prisoners of war. That the war booty meanwhile was limited to 144 tanks and 700 artillery pieces is indicative of the declining Soviet strength in armor and artillery.

As a result of Heeresgruppe Süd's failure to capture Kiev in the south, and the rugged Soviet defense on the highway to Moscow, Hitler ordered Panzergruppe 2 on 21 August to continue southwards from Gomel, 250 kilometers south of Yelnya, to help break the deadlock at Kiev. Thus, the fighter wing of Fliegerkorps II, JG 51, became spread out over an area measuring 250 kilometers from the north to the south. With only around 70 operational Messerschmitt planes available, it was inevitable that the skies belonged to the Soviets most of the time.

The Soviets took advantage of this to step up their aerial activity over Yelnya. Intercepting 190 ShAP's Il-2 Shturmoviks and 57 BAP's SB bombers in this sector on 25 August, Hermann-Friedrich Joppien, victor in seventy aerial combats, was shot down and killed.[44] "The Red Air Force has not been defeated", the War Diary of JG 51 dryly remarked.

By bringing in aircraft from other parts of the USSR, replacements from aviation industry, and eleven hundred obsolescent planes from flight-training schools, the VVS was able to increase the number of first-line combat aircraft to 3,700 at the end of August. Even if this was far below the impressive resources available at the front at the outbreak of the war, it meant that the VVS had once again managed to gain at least a numerical superiority in the air. With massive support from the air, Soviet 24th and 43rd armies launched a new attack against the Yelnya Wedge on 30 August. That I./JG 51 claimed thirteen Soviet planes shot down on the two first days of the offensive brought no real relief to the German ground troops.

Many accounts speak of von Bock's decision to withdraw from the Yelnya Wedge on 2 September, but the *Landser* at Yelnya were of a different opinion, as Franz Frisch, an artillery soldier of 4. Armee said: "Officially it was called a 'planned withdrawal,' and a 'correction of the front lines,' but to me it was so much bullshit. The Russians were kicking us badly... We on the front line were running like rab-

bits in front of the fox. ... I well remember the retreat from the Yelnya line. We had almost exhausted our supplies of artillery ammunition, and did not provide the proper counter-battery support to the infantry. As such our battery received a constant amount of Soviet artillery fire and casualties. ... Nobody knew where the battery commander was, and I guess he did not know where his guns were – happily or unhappily, he participated in the retreat like any little soldier – without organization, without communication, and without command. This was perhaps the most vicious battle I remember of the entire war, including even [Monte] Cassino."[45]

Following the victory at Yelnya, the first units of the Red Army received the honorary "Guards" designation, with the 100th, 127th, 153rd and 161st Rifle divisions being renumbered into the 1st, 2nd, 3rd and 4th Guards Rifle divisions, respectively. It has sometimes been asserted that the Guards units were particular "crack" units, but in fact it was only a sign of recognition of a special feat and had nothing to do with the composition of the unit as such.

But it had cost the Red Army dearly to halt the Germans: the Western Front alone registered 218,000 casualties in August and September 1941, including 41,000 killed and 49,000 missing.[46] 903 Soviet aircraft were lost in the Smolensk – Yelnya sector between 10 July and 10 September 1941. Losses inflicted upon their enemy were lower but nevertheless quite heavy. By 7 September, Heeresgruppe Mitte had sustained a total of 160,000 casualties since the invasion of the USSR began.[47]

As an effect of the tenacious Soviet resistance, Heeresgruppe Mitte had been reduced from the main force of Operation Barbarossa to a mere supplement to the two other army groups. Another consequence of this rugged Soviet resistance was heavy German aviation losses. By 31 August, the accumulated losses sustained by the Luftwaffe to all causes on the Eastern Front had reached 1,320 combat planes destroyed and 820 damaged. In addition, 170 Army reconnaissance aircraft were destroyed, and another 124 were severely damaged. Ninety-seven transport, liaison, and other non-combatant aircraft were also lost. The

After the battle. The faces of these German troops are clearly marked with fatigue and bewilderment. The failure to break through to Moscow in the summer of 1941 had a negative impact on the German morale.

overwhelming majority of these losses were due to hostile action.

After the disheartening defeats in June and July, optimism soared in Moscow. Since this coincided with the end of the Luftwaffe bombings of Moscow, the inhabitants of the Soviet capital began to hope that the worst crisis was over. In their triumph, they noted the humiliating inability of the vaunted Luftwaffe to maintain the air offensive against their city. They were aware that German ground forces stood fewer than 200 miles away, but at the same time they felt reassured by the obvious fact that the Blitzkrieg along the road to the east had stopped. Many started to hope for an imminent turning point in the war. However, this would prove to be a futile hope, and the Soviet armies west of Moscow were in for another devastating blow.

For now, the focus of the war was shifted from the central combat zone to the two flanks – to Kiev in the south and Leningrad in the north.

The health of the Nazi dictator, which had deteriorated following his visit to von Bock's headquarters on 3–4 August, continued to be bad. He tried to participate in a war conference on 9 August, but then the buzzing in his ears had started again. On 18 August, he had another clash with von Bock, who again demanded an immediate resumption of the attack towards Moscow. Meanwhile, the Commander-in-Chief of the German Army, von Brauchitsch, submitted a written proposal for the continued operations on the Eastern Front which supported von Bock's viewpoint. Obviously lacking the strength to dictate a reply, Hitler received Propaganda Minister Joseph Goebbels that same day. Goebbels found the Führer "strained and sickly."

Added to thwarted hopes on the Eastern Front and exhausting clashes with his senior commanders was the news of Churchill's and Roosevelt's signing of the Atlantic Charter on 14 August, which Hitler, not without reason, interpreted as a potential alliance against Germany. According to Goebbels, Hitler "astonishingly expressed serious doubts about the war in the East and even suggested that a peace initiative from Stalin should be accepted."[48]

Strengthened by Goebbel's visit, Hitler dictated a harsh letter to von Brauchitsch on 21 August. It began with the following words: "The army's proposals of 18 August for continuing the operations in the East does not accord with my intentions," followed by clear orders that Guderian's Panzergruppe 2 was to turn south to support Heeresgruppe Süd. When he received this, von Brauchitsch suffered a mild heart attack.

During the conference on 3 August Hitler even showed signs of regrets for having launched the attack against the Soviet Union. "Had I known that the figures for the Russian tank strength which you gave in your book were true ones, I would not – I believe – ever have started this war", he told Guderian.[49] (In 1937, Heinz Guderian estimated the Soviet tank pool at over 10,000.)

Characteristically, Hitler put the blame on the Jews. He now demanded that all German Jews should carry the David's star, and that preparations should be made to deport them to the East. At his meeting with Goebbels on 18 August he also emphasized that what he had said in a speech before the war now would come true: "If the international Jewry should succeed in plunging the nations once more into a world war, then the result will not be the bolshevization of the earth, and thus the victory of Jewry, but the annihilation of the Jewish race in Europe!"

144

SOVIET PARTISANS.

No partisan force wrought such havoc on the occupier as the Soviet partisans in World War II. During Operation Bagration, the Red Army's greatest offensive which practically wiped out Heeresgruppe Mitte in the summer of 1944, partisans undoubtedly played a crucial role. However in 1941, things looked very different. The first partisan year was marked by immense problems and a relative weakness. The history of the Soviet partisans is to a large degree clouded by extremely biased German reports and a glorification by Soviet official historiography. That is particularly true when it comes to 1941. Germans exaggerated partisan activity in order to justify their mass killings of civilians, particularly Jews, and Soviet propaganda did the same for the sake of upholding morale.

In his famous radio broadcast speech on 3 July 1941, Joseph Stalin urged the population to form guerilla units in the areas occupied by the enemy. However, in reality Stalin and the Soviet leadership feared individual initiative beyond their own control more than anything else, and during the first fifteen months of the war "actual Soviet policy discounted and even discouraged popular initiative and participation."[1] The national directives for partisan activity, issued on 18 July 1941, stated that partisan members were to include only "participants in the Civil War and those comrades who have already showed their worth in the destruction battalion [NKVD sabotage units], the people's militia, and also workers from the NKVD."

Many modern analysts conclude that the main task assigned by the Soviet leadership to the partisans was not so much to fight the occupants but to carry out the political tasks assigned to them, i.e. to reinstate and uphold the authority of the Soviet government in the occupied territories.[2] It is fairly clear that in 1941, the Soviet partisans mainly focused on scorched earth activity and terror against what was broadly defined as collaborators. As Kenneth Slepyan writes, these were "often labeled by the prewar epithets of 'spies,' 'kulaks,' 'sons of kulaks,' and 'enemies of the people'" – i.e. the old victims of Stalin's rule.[3] A partisan wrote in his diary in January 1942, "We shot a traitor. Morale 'good.' In the evening I went to do the same to his wife. We are so sorry that she leaves three children behind. But war is war!"[4] Of course, a large number of the victims of partisan killings were local anti-Semites and anti-Communists who had participated in the mass murders of Jews, but others could be absolutely innocent. For instance, cases of partisans executing families of suspected Red Army deserters are documented in the Russian State Archive of Social-Political History in Moscow, RGASPI.[5]

The commander demonstrates a Browning Hi Power semi-automatic pistol to a group of Soviet partisans in 1941.

SOVIET PARTISANS.

Cont.

Since the presence of partisans led to ruthless German collective punishment, they were feared even by sympathetic civilians. One partisan commander in the Vitebsk region complained that the local population pleaded, "You can take our milk, you can take our bread, only please leave."[5] But the terror used by the partisans also made them many enemies among otherwise neutral civilians. To that should be added that the forests in Belarus – which saw the heaviest partisan activity – were infested with a myriad of armed groups: Regular partisans, cut-off Soviet troops who lived on looting, pure bandit gangs, "black partisans" organized by the Germans in order to turn the population against the actual partisans, and some independent armed resistance groups. The largest among the latter were Jewish self-defense groups.

The most famous among the Jewish partisan groups was the one organized by the four Belskiy brothers who managed to flee from the ghetto in Novogrudok near Grodno in Belarus in August 1941. Together with 13 other Jews from the ghetto they formed a partisan group which gradually expanded through more escapes via a tunnel from the ghetto. The main aim of these independent Jewish partisans was self-defense, including the organization of escape routes for Jews to be saved from the Holocaust, and the creation of defended living areas deep inside forests and swamps.

Owing to German army reports, it seems as though the degree to which the partisans inflicted any serious harm on the German occupiers was mainly confined to local incidents in 1941. In general, the partisans were continually on the run from German security units – far better equipped and supplied with aerial reconnaissance and, not infrequently, even Luftwaffe aerial bombings of partisan strongholds and whole villages. Out of 11,733 partisans organized by the NKVD in Leningrad between 22 June 1941 and 7 February 1942, nearly two thirds – 7,582 partisans – had been killed or listed as missing by the latter date.[7] It is hardly surprising therefore, that only one case of rail sabotage was recorded in Heeresgruppe Nord's rear area in December 1941.[8]

This German train was destroyed by partisans in 1941. In general, however, such incidents remained rare during the first year of the war, when partisan activity against German military targets were not that effective. (Photo: Hannes Trautloft.)

A Soviet civilian tortured to death, accused of supporting the partisans.

1   Slepyan, *Stalin's Guerillas*, p. 24.
2   Grenkevich and Glantz, *The Soviet Partisan Movement, 1941-1944: A Critical Historiographical Analysis*, p. 157.
3   Slepyan, p. 83.
4   Armstrong, *Soviet Partisans in World War II*, p. 751.
5   RGASPI, f. 69, op. 1, d. 196, l. 21.
6   Slepyan, p. 80.
7   Boyarskiy, *Partizany i armiya: Istoriya uteryannyykh vozmozhnostey*, p. 80.
8   Cooper, *The phantom war: The German struggle against Soviet partisans, 1941–1944*, p. viii.

11: ANNIHILATION IN THE UKRAINE.

"The German isolation of the Kiev pocket was exemplary, with the bombers of Fliegerkorps V operating from the Kirovograd area in the south and those of the Fliegerkorps II from north of Gomel and Orsha in the north."

– Oberst Hermann Plocher, Chief of Staff in Fliegerkorps V.

While Heeresgruppe Mitte was held up on the road to Moscow, Heeresgruppe Süd fought a battle of annihilation in the Ukraine. By mid-July 1941, Panzergruppe 1 and 17. Armee had created a 375-kilometer wedge in the Soviet lines, extending all the way to the gates of Kiev, and had destroyed most of Soviet Southwestern Front's armor and aviation. Meanwhile, German 11. Armee were advancing from the Soviet-Romanian border in the south. The situation opened the possibility of encircling and destroying Soviet 6th and 12th armies in the area between these two German forces.

Generalfeldmarschall von Rundstedt, the commander of Heeresgruppe Süd, proposed that Panzergruppe 1 and 17. Armee would leave the sector west of Kiev to be held by 6. Armee, and veer southwards, towards the Biylaya Tserkov sector, 50 kilometers south of Kiev, and thence towards the southwest, in order to link up with 11. Armee, which was pushing towards the northeast. Hitler worried that this would pose too great a threat to the northern force's right flank, and instead told von Rundstedt to limit his goal to an advance towards Vinnitsa, 100 kilometers farther to the west. But von Rundstedt protested strongly against this: Vinnitsa was located only 75 kilometers north of the point where German 11. Armee stood on that day, and to drive his forces to that point would only lead to a quite meaningless

linking up with 11. Armee, without any hope of enveloping any Soviet forces. He managed to convince the Führer, and on 10 July his northern force turned south.

Marshal Semyon Budyonnyy, the commander of the new Soviet Southwestern Direction, imagined that his forces had managed to halt the Germans at the gates of Kiev – an opinion that can still be found in Soviet and Russian literature on the war – but in fact a far greater threat against the 6th and 12th armies in the south loomed. Instead of taking action to avoid encirclement, Budyonnyy ordered the 6th and 12th armies to remain in place, southwest of the German wedge in the north, and the 26th Army to take up positions along the western bank of River Dnepr. His intention was to smash the new German advance through a two-pronged strike. Again he demanded that the Southwestern Front's aviation_ deliver the first "devastating" strikes against the enemy.[1]

It was a classic example of one skilfull commander completely outmaneuvering his less able opponent. The 6th and 12th armies had no more than around 400 tanks between them, and after a series of bloody air battles with JG 3, VVS Southwestern Front was down at a strength of only 249 serviceable aircraft.

Nevertheless, on 12 July Budyonnyy launched all available tanks against Panzergruppe 1 at Berdichev.

Soviet T-26 tanks attack with infantry support.

During the ensuing battle on 12 July, an SS-Unterscharführer and commander of a StuG III assault gun in the SS-Division "Leibstandarte Adolf Hitler" (LSAH or just plainly Leibstandarte), Michael Wittmann would distinguish himself particularly. Positioned on a hill, SS-Rottenführer Klinck, Wittmann's gunner, spotted eighteen Soviet tanks approaching in two groups. Wittmann ordered his driver Koldenhöff to reposition the vehicle on the left side of the hill and took aim at the enemy tanks. The first shot with the StuG III's 75mm gun was a hit. The Soviet tank stopped and emitted smoke. With considerable skill, Koldenhöff maneuvered the turret-less assault gun into a new position. Another shot and a second tank was hit, bursting into flames.

But now Wittmann's own vehicle also came under fire, and although this was badly aimed, he decided to withdraw into a small forest. There Wittmann left the vehicle and car-

SS-Reichsführer Heinrich Himmler during a visit in the Ukraine in August 1941. (Photo: Via Daniel Johansson.)

ried out a quick recce on foot. Only too late did he spot a third tank. In the next second a terrible explosion hurled him onto the ground. Having established that he was not wounded, Wittmann found himself staring at the smoldering wreck of a Soviet tank. Klinck, his faithful gunner, had seen the enemy first and destroyed it with a well-aimed armor-piercing projectile. Back in his own vehicle, Wittmann directed the driver against another Soviet tank. The loader Petersen slammed a new armor-piercing round into the gun, and – Feuer! – the next Soviet tank was engulfed in flames. Koldenhöff increased speed again, turned the StuG III and on Wittmann's order Klinck fired the gun. Soviet tank number five exploded.

By now, two Soviet tanks had spotted the solitary German assault gun and subjected it to a hailstorm of fire. Koldenhöff drove back and forth, constantly zigzagging, tormenting the Maybach engine, and avoided all the shells, that instead blew up high, black fountains of dirt all around them. On Wittmann's command he suddenly stopped. The gun was aimed straight at a Soviet tank, and off went a round. It bounced off! Another round hit, but without any visible damage. At this stage, the Soviet tank they had just hit was alone. The others had simply vanished. Wittmann watched it cautiously, and as its turret began to rotate, he sent a third round against it, with terrible impact. A large flame shot vertically out of its hatches. Wittmann saw dark figures silhouetted against the fire – the tank crew – desperately fighting to bail out. With their uniforms burning, they fell onto the ground.

That evening Wittmann received the Iron Cross Second Class from the hands of the unit commander, SS-Obergruppenführer Josef "Sepp" Dietrich. SS Leibstandarte was infamous for its ruthless methods in the war. It had killed civilian Jews in Poland, and during the Western Offensive in May 1940 it had carried out the notorious so-called "Wormhout massacre," where 80 captured British soldiers were executed. Nevertheless, when Wittmann was asked by Dietrich if he had any particular wishes, he replied: "Yes, Obergruppenführer, that the three wounded Russians from that last tank are to be given the best medical treatment!"

During the course of the war, Wittmann would develop into the fourth-ranking German tank ace, credited with 138 tank destructions, before he was killed in action in 1944.

On 14 July, Halder noted in his diary, "The battle around Berdichev, which at times was very bitter and turned into wholesale slaughter of the senselessly attacking enemy, is now also abating." Had Budyonnyy pulled back 6th and 12th armies, with altogether 300,000 men and around 400 tanks, to a defensive position along the Dnepr, the next disaster for the Red Army could have been avoided. But instead the 6th Army was worn down in hopeless counter-attacks.

Panzergruppe 1 continued its advance along the western side of the Dnepr, smashing up Soviet 26th Army as this made repeated attempts to counter-attack. Meanwhile 11. Armee in the south made its way across the Dnestr at Yampol and continued to the northeast, effectively sup-

ported by Stukas of StG 77. The German double envelopment operation was aimed at Uman.

Generaloberst Alexander Löhr, Luftflotte 4's C.O., focused his air units on severing the Soviet rear communication lines leading to and from the Uman area.[2] The effects of this are apparent from the message sent by Marshal Budyonnyy to the Stavka on 25 July, when Panzergruppe 1 stood 60 kilometers northeast of Uman: "All efforts to withdraw the 6th and 12th armies to the east and to the northeast are fruitless." Too late had Budyonnyy ordered a withdrawal.

However, most of VVS Southern Front was flown back to the area around the Dnepr bend with the primary task of preventing the Germans from crossing that river. Some of VVS Southern Front's units were also transferred to the defense of Kiev. Thus Budyonnyy more or less abandoned the two armies in the Uman area.

On 29 July, Panzergruppe 1 achieved a breakthrough and advanced nearly 150 kilometers in one day, covering the entire area east of Uman and reached a point 20 kilometers southeast of the city. In doing so, the tanks ran straight into Soviet retreat columns, wreaking havoc. The next day, Kirovograd, 120 kilometers ESE of Uman, was captured. Inside the sealed off area, unit cohesion of the Soviet forces rapidly disintegrated, as a Soviet soldier described: "On 30 July we arrived at Uman. The airfield and the railway station was on fire. Workers, Jews and Party and Komsomol activists have left the town; the local authorities were the first to be evacuated… Everyone takes whatever they want from the shops. Our guys are absolutely indifferent to the situation – they are only searching for any alcohol… In general, full anarchy and a total breakdown of all public order dominates the picture. Most of the people are morally dead."[3]

On 3 August, Panzergruppe 1 managed to connect with 11th Armee southeast of Uman. Thus the two Soviet armies were completely encircled and became subject to concentrated attacks. No attempts to relieve the enveloped troops were made before 7 August, when the weakened Soviet

The Nazi propaganda against the Communists and Jews was closely connected with the propaganda of the "White" side in the Russian Civil War, such as this propaganda poster. The image – a caricature of an "evil Jewish Bolshevik" – was made by the "Whites" in 1918, and the Nazi propaganda added a photo of victims of an NKVD execution of political prisoners in 1941. The text reads "Vinnitsa," and its purpose is to put the blame for the killings on the Jews. Vinnitsa soon became the scene of repeated massacres of Jews, committed by the SD Einsatzgruppen.

26th Army – in the Boguslav sector, half-way between Kiev in the north and Uman in the south – attacked from Kanev on River Dnepr in the northeast. The attack succeeded in tearing up the German flank and on 8 August Boguslav, 35 kilometers southwest of Kanev and 70 kilometers northeast of the encircled troops, was reached. Halder found the attack to be "very impressive in its daring an embarrassing for our troops."[4]

But again, the Luftwaffe tipped the scales. Despite adverse weather conditions of rain showers and a cloud ceiling of less than 100 meters, every available aircraft in Fliegerkorps V was dispatched in "rolling attacks" against 26th Army. They reportedly destroyed 148 motor vehicles and 48 tanks in the Boguslav-Kanev area between 7 and 9 August, bringing the offensive to a halt.[5]

Meanwhile, the units of Fliegerkorps IV carried our systematic attacks to help annihilate the encircled Soviet 6th and 12th armies in the so-called Uman Pocket. "Rolling aerial attacks" against troops attempting to escape the encirclement provided vital preconditions for the destruction of the entrapped forces. On 10 August alone, the bombers of Luftflotte 4 reported the destruction of 300 Soviet trucks and 54 tanks. The Battle of Uman came to a gruesome end in which 79,220 soldiers of Soviet 6th and 12th Army perished.[6] (That the Germans registered 103,054 prisoners as a result of this battle[7] indicates that a large number of civilians were also rounded up and sent into an uncertain confinement.) Among the prisoners were Leytenant-General Ivan N. Muzychenko and General-Mayor Pavel Ponedelin, the commanders of the 6th and 12th armies respectively, as well as General-Mayor Nikolay Kirillov, the commander of the 13th Rifle Corps.*

This battle had displayed, for the first time in history, the ability of a superior air force to completely "envelop an army from the air." The intensive aerial bombardment had brought virtually all major Soviet troop movements to the west of the Dnepr River to a halt.

Izo Adamskiy was one of one thousand Komsomol members in Dnepropetrovsk who volunteered for military service when the war broke out. Quite interestingly, 30 per cent of these were Jews. After only eight days of military training, Adamskiy was placed in a "battalion of students" called 1st Communist Regiment, and was dispatched to the front. Each soldier was armed with a rifle with a knife instead of a bayonet, plus a Molotov cocktail. Thus equipped the young volunteers experienced their first combat on 13 July, when they managed to repel a German patrol.

Two days later the battalion was reinforced by tank soldiers who had lost their tanks. The majority of these troops were utterly demoralised and thought of nothing but escaping. But the young volunteers refused to give in. During the envelopment battle at Uman, the German infantry made repeated attempts to attack, but the 1st Communist Regiment held their positions with bitter determination. Each time they allowed the Germans to come within a distance of 200 metres, and then opened fire with all arms. After each repelled attack, the German artillery would bombard them, and then aircraft attacked with bombs and machine guns.

On a couple of occasions, the young Communists even repelled the German infantry in bloody bayonet fighting. Adamskiy remembers how he felt nauseated when he discovered that he had killed a man for the first time, but he soon grew used to it.

However, after a while the enemy broke through on the flanks. Adamskiy recalls how the Red Army forces melted away as soldiers were killed or captured in large numbers. At night the Germans called to the youngsters: "Communists, surrender!" and their aircraft dropped propaganda leaflets saying that "All Jewish commissars will be exe-

Endless marching characterized the first weeks of Operation Barbarossa for the German troops.

cuted." From prisoners that had been taken, the Germans knew very well who they were fighting against. According to Adamskiy, all recognised members of the 1st Communist Regiment that were captured were immediately executed by the Germans.

On 1 August, a terrible artillery fire set in. It lasted for two days and totally destroyed the Soviet positions. On 2 August, Adamskiy took part in a final, failed, counter-attack. They advanced across ploughed up terrain completely strewn with dead and mutilated bodies, and when they later pulled back, the whole regiment was nearly completely annihilated. The Sinyokh River was red with blood.

By 5 August, the 18 remaining young Communists – three of whom were wounded – decided to attempt a break-out. They had no rifle ammunition, only bayonets and Walther pistols captured from dead Germans with which to fight. But the youngsters promised to fight to the end and to never surrender. During the night they managed to slip through to the north.

Marching northwards for several days and nights the little group finally came upon a German position near Lipovets, 85 kilometers northwest of Uman. Believing that this was the front line and that Soviet troops were on the other side, the young Communists decided to attack. Surprising the enemy, they managed to kill all fifteen of them in close combat, some of them by strangling. But the sound

* Ponedelin and Kirillov were immediately arrested by Soviet authorities after their release from German captivity in 1945. Both were sentenced to death and executed in 1950. Muzychenko, however, was saved from any repression punishment.

Romanian R-2 tanks entering Kishinev on 16 July 1941. In the background the cathedral of the city can be seen. The 1st Romanian Armored Division, Romania's only armored division in 1941, was equipped with 255 light tanks, including 105 R-2s, 75 Renault R-35s and 75 Renault FT-17s of 1918 design. The R-2 was the Romanian designation of the Czech Škoda LT VZ 35, which in German service was called Panzer 35(t).

One of the main targets of the Romanian Army was the capture of Kishinev, the capital of Bessarabia – the province which had been seized by Romania from Russia in 1919, and taken back by the Soviet Union in 1940. The attack begun on 2 July, watched by the Romanian dictator Ion Antonescu. But the Soviets counter-attacked, inflicting severe losses on Romanian 35th Infantry Division, where 2,200 soldiers ended up in Soviets captivity. A humiliated Antonescu had to ask for German assistance. Only on 16 July were the Axis forces able to enter Kishinev. In total, the Bessarabian campaign cost 22,765 Romanian and 17,893 Soviet troops casualties.

of the fighting alerted other Germans and the Soviets had to run. Adamskiy was wounded in the neck and foot by shrapnel from a hand grenade and fell to the ground, but two of his comrades grabbed him and pulled him to safety.

On approaching Lipovets they came upon a railway track where a train was approaching. The train slowed down and the engine-driver shouted at them: "Children! Where are you going? There are Germans at the station!" The man urged them to board one of the box cars. They found that it was loaded with boxes of cookies from a confectionery factory. In the chaotic situation, a large area between Vinnitsa and Rover Dnepr was practically a no man's land, and through this area the train journeyed, reaching Dnepropetrovsk in Soviet-controlled territory. In fact, every single one of the 18 youngsters that had broken out from the envelopment remained alive.[8]

In the path of the advancing German troops in the Ukraine followed security forces from the Wehrmacht, the SS and the German police. These were subordinated to General Karl von Roques, the commander of Rückwärtigen Heeresgebietes ("Berück") 103 – the Rear Area of Heeresgruppe Süd. The two Einsatzgruppen C and D cooperated in the task of "securing the area," which first of all meant the liquidation of Soviet political functionaries.

But there was some confusion as to who was in charge, as at the same time SS-Reichsführer Heinrich Himmler had appointed SS-Obergruppenführer Friedrich Jeckeln as Higher SS and Police Commander in Southern Russia. Jeckeln commanded two of the four Kommandos of Einsatzgruppe C.

From the beginning of the war, Jews were occasionally blamed for maltreatment of German POWs or accused of cooperating with the Communists and killed in large numbers. However, just as in Lithuania and Latvia, local Anti-Semites initiated the mass killings of the Jews in this area. We have already dealt with the pogroms in Lvov, Lutsk and Tarnopol in late June and early July. These were actually preceded by Romanian pogroms in the town of Iasi on 29 June. Following rumors that Jews in Iasi had signaled to Soviet planes that bombed the city, over ten thousand Jews were killed by the Romanian police. Actually, von Roques was initially opposed to German soldiers taking part in such pogroms, although it frequently occurred.[9] Such pogroms continued, such as at Kremenets, northwest of Lutsk, where a German reporter noted on 20 July that Ukrainian nationalists beat 130 Jews to death.

On 17 July, Reinhard Heydrich, the commander of the German Security Police, issued the first instructions that not only Jews who belonged to the Communist Party were to be killed, but all Jews among both POWs and other prisoners. Two days later, Reichsmarschall Göring assigned Heydrich the task of preparing a "total solution" to the "Jewish question."

One of the first organized German massacres took place in the small village of Annopol near Khmelnitskiy, where policemen gunned down twenty-five Jews on 20 July. Eight days later all Jewish men from Annopol and the neighboring village Kilikiyev were forced to dig three pits in a field, and then more than two hundred were shot.

At the same time, the motorized 1. SS-Infanterie-Brigade – newly formed from concentration camp guards – arrived in the Ukraine with the task of fighting Red Army stragglers in the Zhitomir corridor. Between 25 July and 9 August it reported the capture of some 7,000 Soviet troops, but in the meantime it also killed 1,658 Jews.[10]

A new killing method was applied on 1 August, when about 720 Jews from the village of Olyka were killed in a so-called gas van. This was a truck with an air-tight compartment for victims, into which exhaust fumes were transmitted while the engine was running.

But the real, planned massacres with the express purpose of extermination of Jews began only after Hitler's meeting with Goebbels on 18 August. Previously, mainly Jewish men had been killed by the Germans, but on 22 August, on orders issued by the commander of Sonderkommando 4a/ Einsatzgruppe C, SS-Standartenführer

REINHARD HEYDRICH'S NARROW ESCAPE.

Reinhard Heydrich, the notorious commander of the German Security Police, also had personal ambitions to show off in first-line service. Trained as a fighter pilot, he had flown combat missions with II./JG 77 over Norway and JG 1 over the Netherlands in 1940. It might be assumed that he chose those sectors because he wished to avoid serious combat. However, when Operation Barbarossa began and the papers became filled with reports of fantastic victory scores by German fighter pilots, Heydrich turned to the material inspector of the Luftwaffe, Ernst Udet, and asked him to arrange for him to be accepted in a Luftwaffe fighter unit. Heydrich's own prejudices against what he apprehended as "useless subhumans" probably weighed in to his decision to engage in the thick of fighting.

Udet agreed, and even assigned Heydrich with a "private" Bf 109 fighter. When he arrived at the Eastern Front for "political issues" – he was appointed the central commander of the Einsatzgruppen – he took advantage of the situation to fly combat missions with his "old" II./JG 77, in action over the Moldavian front sector.

On 22 July, three days after Reichsmarschall Göring – incidentally also the Luftwaffe commander – had instructed Heydrich to prepare a "total solution" to the "Jewish question," the SS-Obergruppenführer flew his first combat mission on the Eastern Front. Ironically, the Nazi who dismissed the Russians as belonging to an "inferior race," would come to face one of the best Soviet fighter aces of the entire war.

At around two in the afternoon, Heydrich and Leutnant Joachim Deicke flew a patrol mission over the front line when they were informed via radio that Soviet planes were bombing the Dnestr bridges at Yampol. The two Germans immediately turned their fighters in that direction and increased speed. It didn't take long before they spotted the enemy – nine single-engine light bombers of flight bomber group 210 BBAP, escorted by two I-16 Ishaks.

The pair of Soviet fighters turned to meet them and succeeded in locking the Messerschmitts into a combat which allowed the bombers to escape. Eager to score his first victory, Heydrich attacked one of the Ishaks. But he had no idea that the Soviets could be so clever as to maintain a top cover. High above, two modern MiG-3 fighters lay in position, and these now came hurtling down towards the Germans. The leading MiG-3 was piloted by 55 IAP's Starshiy Leytenant Aleksandr Pokrysjkin, who by this time had chalked up four victories. Without doubt, he was one of the most talented fighter pilots of the Soviet Air Force. When the war ended

he had an official score of 59 kills, which rendered him in second place in the list of the most successful Allied fighter pilots during the war. (The first place was also held by a Russian, Ivan Kozhedub, with 62 victories.)

Without realizing who the enemy pilot was, Pokryshkin closed in on Heydrich's Bf 109. Afterwards, Pokryshkin commented on the German pilots' behavior: "He must have been possessed by hunting fever, for he flew totally carelessly."[1] Pokryshkin fired a short burst, which was sufficient. The Messerschmitt went down, trailing smoke.

SS-Obergruppenführer Reinhard Heydrich, one of the cruelest among the Nazi leaders, feared by many even in the Nazi hierarchy itself, was lucky to manage a belly-landing in no-man's land. He had to be bailed out by a commando group who snatched him in front of Red Army troops. Following this unpleasant experience, Heydrich made a swift return to safety in his headquarters.[2]

SS-Obergruppenführer Reinhard Heydrich survived getting shot down by the Soviet ace Aleksandr Pokryshkin, but died on 7 June 1942 of wounds sustained in an attack by British agents in Prague eleven days previously. (Photo via Martin Månsson.)

Soviet fighter ace Aleksandr Pokryshkin was credited with 59 aerial victories during World War II, making him the second most successful Soviet ace. He passed away on 13 November 1985, at the age of 72.

1 Pokryschkin, *Himmel des Krieges*, p. 71.
2 Prien, *Geschichte des Jagdgeschwaders 77*, p. 710.

Paul Blobel, Ukrainian nationalists shot dozens of Jewish children to death at Biyala Tserkov. This was witnessed by a couple of German military chaplains, who immediately wrote a in protest to General von Reichenau, the commander of 6. Armee. Oberstleutnant Helmuth Groscurth, operations officer in 295. Infanterie-Division, also tried in vain to prevent these killings. In a report to von Reichenau, he noted that the troops were greatly upset by this, and that they were "waiting for the officers to intervene."[11]

During a meeting between the OKH and the Reich Ministry for the Occupied Eastern Territories on 25 August, Jeckeln was said to have announced "the liquidation" of the thousands of Jews that had been assembled in Kamenets-Podolskiy.[12] On the request of the Hungarian government, over 10,000 Hungarian Jews had been deported to this Ukrainian city. On 26 August Jeckeln flew to Kamenets-Podolskiy to lead the action. In the course of three days, 23,600 Jews were murdered, according to the report submitted by Jeckeln himself on 11 September 1941.[13]

The "action" at Kamenets-Podolskiy was thus a milestone in the Holocaust: It was the first massacre of Jews by Nazi forces with a five-digit number of victims. Together with the massacre at Biyala Tserkov, it laid the path for the continued indiscriminate murder of Jews regardless of age or sex, and thus the Holocaust.

After the defeat at Uman, Marshal Semyon Budyonnyy decided to abandon most of western Ukraine. Only the important Black Sea port of Odessa was to be held. The remnants of his 26th Army, which had been counter-attacking the Germans at Boguslav, some 100 km south of Kiev, were pulled back across the Dnepr. By 30 July, the armored strength of the entire Southwestern Front was down at just 380 tanks – out of an original strength of 5,956 on 21 June.[14]

Generalfeldmarschall von Rundstedt meanwhile aimed at encircling the 26th Army west of the Dnepr. By virtually closing down all Soviet troop movements, Luftflotte 4's bombers had been a key factor in the success at Uman. Now Generaloberst Löhr, the Luftflotte's C.O., intended to repeat this by directing his air units against 26th Army's main retreat route, the large Dnepr bridges at Kanev. This called for pinpoint attacks, for which the Ju 87 Stukas were most suited. StG 77 was called on to carry out unbroken dive-bombing raids against the bridges. Meanwhile, the Soviets concentrated strong fighter forces to defend these bridges, and fierce air combats developed.

It began on 13 August, when I-16-equipped 88 IAP recorded two Ju 87s shot down but lost Mladshiy Leytenants Yakov Kozlov and Ivan Novikov in combat with the escorting Bf 109s.[15] 88 IAP was in hot water over Kanev the next day again. This time it tangled with I./JG 3. Hauptmann Hans von Hahn of I./JG 3 recalled, "All previous air combat had been a children's game compared to what we encountered above the Dnepr bridge at Kanev. We met six Ratas.... Before you had even started thinking of attacking them, the Russian pilots quickly turned around and met us head-on, shooting and laughing cold-bloodedly." Hauptmann Hahn, Leutnant Detlev Rohwer, and Oberfeldwebel Detlev Lüth claimed one I-16 each in this melee. In return,

A Waffen SS trooper gives the signal to attack.
(Photo: Via Daniel Johansson.)

35-victory ace and Knight's Cross holder Oberleutnant Robert Oljenik, and Leutnant Heinz Ressel, credited with five victories, were shot down by the I-16s.[16] Both were lucky to survive, contrary to the two 88 IAP pilots who were shot down in the same combat. These too belonged to their unit's best pilots: Mladshiy Leytenant Vasiliy Demyonok had been credited with eight, and Mladshiy Leytenant Vasiliy Lipatov with three victories. A comparison with 88 IAP's records show that Oljenik and Ressel were shot down by Starshiy Leytenant Vasiliy Moskalchuk and Leutnant Vasiliy Maksimenko.[17]

All German attempts to destroy the bridges failed, and the 26th Army was able to be pulled back across the Dnepr. The Luftwaffe's failure to accomplish its task was obvious when the large railway bridge at Kanev was blown up on 16 August – by the Soviets! Next, Generaloberst Löhr ventured to prevent the scattered remnants of Soviet Southern Front from retreating across the lower Dnepr. Thus, on 17 August Fliegerkorps V opened a series of intensive air raids against the traffic center of Dnepropetrovsk. The main targets for these raids were the railroad station, thoroughfares, and bridges. But the past two months had worn down Luftflotte 4's bomber units considerably, so this attempt failed also. Instead their mission was shortly shifted to support Heeresgruppe Süd's attempts to establish various bridge-heads on the Dnepr's eastern (left) bank. Panzergruppe 1 managed to establish the first bridgehead at Zaporozhye, in the Dnepr bend, on 19 August.

Northwest of Kiev, Soviet 5th Army meanwhile with-drew across the Dnepr. Pursuing these forces, German 11. Panzer-Division on 23 August managed to capture a wooden bridge across the Dnepr at Gornostaypol, 50 km north of Kiev, before the Soviets had time to destroy it. That same evening, the Germans had gained a foothold on the eastern side of the Dnepr at this point too.

23 August in fact marked a turning point in the Battle of Kiev. Following Hitler's new directive to move the focus of the war toward Leningrad in the north and Kiev in the south, Generaloberst Guderian's Panzergruppe 2 of Heeres-gruppe Mitte delivered a heavy blow from the Starodub area towards the south, with Generaloberst Maximilian von Weichs' 2nd Army attacking further to the west, from the Gomel area, 200 kilometers north of Kiev. The aim was to cooperate with Heeresgruppe Süd in a gigantic envelop-ment maneuver at Kiev. Fliegerkorps II of Luftflotte 2, with JG 51 and I./SKG 210, provided air support for Guderian's drive to the south. The tank columns of Panzergruppe 2 paved their way through weak Red Army forces in the seam

TRAGEDY AT ZAPOROZHYE.

On 18 August 1941, elements of German Panzergruppe 1 seized the outskirts of Zaporozhye in the Dnepr Bend. With almost no Soviet troops in the area, and the threat of a general German breakthrough towards the industrial area in the Donets Basin, the Soviets took the drastic measure of blowing up not only the large triple-arched Dneper railway bridge at Zaporozhye, but also the huge Dneper Hydroelectric Dam (DniproHES). The latter was the largest single construction project in the USSR and one of the largest power plants in the world. The 60-meter high dam had been built between 1927 and 1932, and with a reser-voir containing 33.3 cubic kilometers of water, it generated some 650 MW.

At 1600 hours on 18 August 1941, the 157th Regiment of the NKVD Special Protection Troops blew a 120 meter wide hole in the dam, using 20 tons of explosives.[1] A wave several dozen meters high swept the Dnepr flood plain with the impact of a tsunami. The number of people affected by the avalanche of water is impossible to calculate, since many residents in the towns and villages that were flooded had been evacu-ated, while on the other hand thousands of refugees arriving from the west were in the area. Moreover, two Soviet armies – the 9th and the 18th – with a total of 150–170,000 men were assigned to hold positions along the Dnepr in this sector.

Coverage of this event was suppressed in the Soviet Union – which accused the Germans of the destruc-tion of the dam at the Nuremberg trials after the war – and no official study has ever been made. Not even today's Ukrainian authorities have put up any official monument or plaque in Zaporozhye to honor its victims. Thus, the number of victims of this flood is nearly impossible to calculate. Estimations range from 20,000 up to 100,000.[2] Still to this day, most accounts of the war in the Ukraine in 1941 omit this huge humanitarian disaster, owing to the fact that it is virtually unknown – even to many citizens of today's Zaporozhye.

The blowing up of this dam certainly did great harm to the German war economy, which otherwise could have made good use of it – the Germans were unable to repair it during the two years that the city was under their control. However, in 1941 it did not prevent the Germans from seizing Kherson, at the Dnepr's mouth, on 20 August. And the feared advance of Panzergruppe 1 towards the Donets Basin did not come about until late September, because the envelopment of Southwestern Front at Kiev in the north was given first priority.

Due to the suppression of details surrounding the blowing up of the dam, it has not been possible to establish who gave the orders.[3] It has been asserted that Marshal Budyonnyy issued them, but according to historian Vladyslav Moroko, Joseph Stalin gave the order.[4]

1 Moroko, *Dviproges: Chyornyy serpen 1941 roku*, p. 7.
2 Ibid.
3 TsAMO, f. .228, op.754, d. 60.
4 Moroko, p. 17.

between Soviet 13th and 40th armies. Any attempt to resist was met by rapid aerial attacks from Messerschmitt Bf 110 assault planes from SKG 210. Meanwhile, medium bombers were dispatched against the railway junction at Chernigov, on the Desna River, 160 kilometers south of Gomel. On 24 August, Guderian's armored troops seized the Desna Bridge at Novgorod-Severskiy intact.

Soviet reaction to this new double threat was swift. To the south, General-Polkovnik Kirponos, the commander of the Southwestern Front, ordered his aviation assets to attack the German Dnepr bridgeheads. These forces were met by strong concentrations of German fighters and anti-aircraft fire, which together were credited with the destruction of thirty-three attacking aircraft on 24 August alone. But late on that day, the pilot of one of the new Il-2 Shturmoviks, Leytenant Sergey Kolybin of 74 ShAP, managed to place two incendiary bombs on the wooden bridge at Gornostaypol. Kolybin's plane was hit by AAA fire and crashed into a concentration of vehicles.[18] The surviving *Landser* helplessly witnessed the costly bridge falling prey to the flames.[19] Fliegerkorps V's Oberst Hermann Plocher was not wrong that the loss of this bridge "adversely affected further river-crossing operations and considerably delayed the attack by the Sixth Army."[20]

When Panzergruppe 1 established a new bridgehead across the Dnepr at Dnepropetrovsk on 25 August, the Germans were immediately confronted with heavy air attacks from the DBA and VVS Southern Front, including Il-2 Shturmoviks entering service with 210 ShAP.[21] During the first two days, the aircraft of 210 ShAP were reported to have put several tanks and eighteen vehicles out of commission at the Dnepropetrovsk bridgehead. Thirteen airmen from 210 ShAP were decorated for these missions, which were carried out in defiance of the intercepting Bf 109s of II./JG 3. The diary of the German High Command noted, "In spite of own fighter cover, there are heavy and uninterrupted low-level attacks against the bridge and bridgehead at Dnepropetrovsk. These attacks were intensified during the evening hours."[22]

During these air combats the Soviet fliers were opposed by pilots of several different nationalities who were fighting on the German side. Apart from the Romanians in the South, there were already Hungarian and Slovakian airmen flying alongside the Luftwaffe in the Ukrainian skies. On 27 August the Italian fighter group 22 Gruppo Caccia, equipped with fifty-one Macchi MC.200 Saetta single-engine fighters, commenced operations. On this day the Italian aviators covered the Dnepropetrovsk bridgehead and in their first air combat they claimed six SBs and two I-16s, plus two each as probables, for no own losses.*

While the Southwestern Front managed to hold out along the Dnepr, the new Soviet Bryansk Front under command of General-Leytenant Andrey Yeremenko was employed against Panzergruppe 2 and 2. Armee in the north. The Bryansk Front had recently been formed on the battered remnants of the Central Front (which was disbanded) and the 13th Army, but received a powerful reinforcement in the shape of the new 50th Army. Equipped with the best Soviet material, including Katyusha rockets

and T-34 tanks, the Bryansk Front intended to annihilate Guderian's presumptuous Panzergruppe through a threefold attack from the east, south and west. An air force consisting of 464 combat aircraft was assigned to Yeremenko's new front. The foundation of VVS Bryansk Front, commanded by General-Mayor Fyodor Polynin, is quite telling with respect to the Soviet reinforcement capacity. In August 1941 the new Stavka Reserve, including strong aviation units, was built up. Within a short time, six reserve aviation groups (RAGs), equipped with the most modern aircraft, were commissioned. The first RAG was allocated to the Bryansk Front, and all Il-2 Shturmovik regiments from the Reserve Front were transferred to the VVS Bryansk Front. Other units arrived from the Transcaucasus Military District, from the Moscow PVO, from the Naval Air Force, and by means of the absorption of the Central Front into the Bryansk Front. These forces were supplemented with aircraft brought in from flight schools.

Yeremenko launched his offensive on 29 August and immediately brought the German advance from the north to a halt. VVS Bryansk Front launched all available aircraft

Panzer III tanks of 9. Panzer-Division co-operate with troops of 17. Armee's 1. Gebirgs-Division (1st Mountain Division) during the Battle of Uman. The soldiers in the photo are manning an MG 34 machine gun. The MG 34 was considerably superior to the Maxim Gun in Soviet use. The German weapon's rate of fire was 800-900 rounds per minute, as compared with the Maxim's 500–600. With a weight of 12.1 kg, the MG 34 was more than half as heavy as the Maxim, and changing the barrel was done in a matter of seconds. (Photo: Krigsarkivet Stockholm.)

* 22 Gruppo, with 51 MC. 200s, and the reconnaissance unit 61 Gruppo O.A. – with 33 Ca.311s and S.M.82s – formed the aviation of the Italian Expeditionary Corps, CSIR (Corpo di spedizione Italiano in Russia; Italian Expeditionary Corps in Russia), which joined German Heeresgruppe Süd.

Panzer I tanks crossing River Dnepr on a makeshift raft.
Panzergruppe 1 established its first bridgehead across the mighty
Dnepr River at Zaporozhye on 19 August 1941.
(Photo: Hans-Udo Schmitz-Wortmann.)

to support the ground battle and managed to overwhelm the Luftwaffe. On the first day of the counter-offensive, crews in four-engine TB-3 bombers of 42 BAD made two sorties each; the SB, Pe-2 and Il-2 crews, three or four sorties each; and the fighter pilots, six or seven sorties each. VVS Bryansk Front carried out a total of 1,500 sorties on 30 and 31 August.

While heavily pounced on from the air, 17. Panzer-Division of Panzergruppe 2 was attacked on 30 August by Soviet 108th Tank Division, with 90 tanks, including a number of heavy KVs. "We were young, we were carefree and above all: we hated the invaders," said Nikolay Filatin, a Soviet KV tank commander. "We all felt joy and yelled enthusiastically when a German tank was hit. We were so excited that we didn't feel the fumes and the jolting as our big tank drove across the field. There! Another target! Stop! Fire! Another team of 'Fritzes' are scorched. A German infantry position! We crush it beneath our big tracks. War is relentless. Bang! Bang! Two hits on our tank. For a couple of seconds we are all shaken. But no harm done. Onwards! I remember the battle as in a dream."

Taking heavy losses, 17. Panzer-Division withdrew several kilometers. On 31 August, 108th Tank Division repelled an attempt to regain the ground lost by 17th Panzer Division, which cost the Germans a loss of 11 tanks.[23]

"The morning picture is dominated by a decidedly uncomfortable development in Guderian's Group," wrote Franz Halder in his diary on 31 August. He was very critical of Guderian's maneuvers: "Carrying out his drive as a flank movement", he wrote, "he squarely invited heavy attacks into his eastern flank; then his advance, striking far to the east and leading him away from 2nd Armee, produced a gap which was exploited by the enemy for attacks from

the west also. These two developments have reduced his power to strike south to a point where his movements are paralyzed. Now he is blaming everyone in sight for his predicament and hurls accusations and recriminations in all directions."[24]

In the bitter air fighting in the skies above the battlefield, IV./ JG 51's Leutnant Heinz Bär surpassed his own personal one-day record by downing six enemy planes on August 30. Bär had achieved an amazing victory total since the opening of the war with the USSR, increasing his kill tally from seventeen to seventy in only two months. But after scoring his seventy-ninth and eightieth victories against two Pe-2s on 31 August, his Messerschmitt Bf 109 was badly damaged, leaving the ace with no choice but to force land behind enemy lines north-east of Novgorod-Severskiy. Despite having both feet sprained in the violent crash, he leapt out from the Messerschmitt as fast as he could, hid in some bushes, and managed to evade capture by Soviet soldiers arriving at the wreck. In a state of terror, confusion, and pain, Bär remained in hiding during the rest of the day and the following night. The next morning he pulled himself together and decided to try to make it back to the German lines. Turning his leather jacket inside out, stuffing it with hay, and throwing away his flight boots, he attempted to pass himself off as a Russian peasant. He could have thrown away the Knight's Cross and the Oak Leaves he had been awarded two weeks earlier, but his vanity prevented him from doing that; he just put them in his pocket, together with his watch and his small flight pistol. Then Bär started walking with two sprained ankles. He actually made it back to the German lines. By that time he was so injured that he would remain in hospital for two months.

On 1 September, "heavy Red air activity" was reported to the German Army High Command: "Unequivocal Russian air superiority in the sector of the 2nd. Armee."[25]

These setbacks put Guderian under severe pressure from his superiors. Halder and the army group commander von Bock were already quite upset with him, and now Hitler also became enraged over the Panzer general's failure. Guderian defended himself vehemently, blaming

The encirclement battle at Uman resulted in another very large batch of Soviet prisoners of war. (Photo: Krigsarkivet Stockholm.)

An Italian fighter pilot climbs into his Macchi MC.200 Saetta single-engine fighter for a combat mission on the Eastern Front. The MC.200 Saetta was quite outdated in 1941, with a top speed of only 504 km/h at 4,500 meters altitude, whereas the German Messerschmitt Bf 109 F-4 could reach 582 km/h. Armament consisted of two 12.7 mm machine guns. (Photo: Collection D'Amico – Valentini.)

von Bock for dispersing 2. Armee on the western flank of Panzergruppe 2. This caused von Bock to ask the Army High Command to relieve Guderian from his post.[26] This request was nevertheless turned down.

The situation for Guderian and his men was finally saved through the intervention of Reichsmarschall Göring, the Luftwaffe commander. Two close-support groups – II./StG 1 and II./SKG 210 – were brought back from the Leningrad sector, and joined I./SKG 210 and III./StG 1 in their attacks on the troops of the Bryansk Front. Guderian described the Stuka attacks as the turning point of the battle: "The enemy here had up to now resisted stubbornly, even against our tanks. But after the dive-bombers had gone in, his main resistance seemed to be broken."[27] On 6 September the forward elements of Panzergruppe 2 reached River Seym north of Konotop – half-way between Kiev and Kursk further in the east. The next day KG 28 was ordered to attack the rear area of the Bryansk Front troops that initiated a new counter-attack against German 2nd Army's bridgehead across the Desna at Chernigov.[28] On 8 September, KG 28 was tasked with attacking both the Soviet-held bridge north of Chernigov with the heaviest bombs, and the Soviet artillery concentration north of Chernigov.[29] These attacks created further problems for the Bryansk Front, as they disrupted the flow of Soviet reinforcements. The effectiveness of these Luftwaffe operations can be measured through the fact that bomber wing KG 3 was credited with the destruction of 349 trains, 488 trucks, 30 tanks and 450 Soviet aircraft on the ground – to which

should he added twenty-one Soviet aircraft claimed shot down in the air – during the first eleven weeks of Operation Barbarossa

The Bryansk Front's counter-offensive against Guderian's Panzergruppe 2 was completely smashed, and on 8 September the Soviet forces withdrew in disarray. A joyful Halder wrote in his diary on 9 September: "Second Army has made the crossing of the Desna, smashed several enemy units and started moving in a south-eastern direction. Armd. Gp. 2 has taken Romny and is clamoring for its opposite number, Kleist. Curiously, there are no attacks against its east flank. Perhaps this has something to do with the extensive railroad demolitions by our air effort."[30] That there were no more Soviet attacks against Guderian's eastern flank after all was not so "curious," considering that this sector was covered by Soviet 40th Army, which was down at only 5,000 soldiers and ten tanks.[31] In fact, the road to the great cities of Bryansk, Orel and Kursk lay wide open for Panzergruppe 2, had it veered towards the east.

In panic, Stalin ordered the 157 political prisoners in Orel's prison to be executed on 11 September. Among the victims of this mass execution – later to become known as the "Medvedev massacre" (named after the forest where the killings were made) – were internationally famous Old Bolsheviks such as Christian Rakovsky and Olga Kameneva, Trotsky's sister. They had been imprisoned for several years, but with the gradual collapse of the defense in the Ukraine, Stalin feared that they might be freed through

Soviet troops with a Maxim Gun, the Red Army's standard machine gun in 1941. Invented by Sir Hiram Stevens Maxim in 1884, it was the first portable, fully automatic and recoil-operated machine gun. It was purchased in large numbers by the Russian Imperial Army in 1910, and remained in large service in the Soviet Union through World War II. The Maxim Gun was fed by a 250-round canvas belt.

Antonina Vasilyevna Lebedeva, called "Tonya," was one of the most famous Soviet female combat pilots during the war. She learned to fly at the Dzerzhinskiy Air Club in Moscow before the war. On 17 July 1943, Lebedeva was shot down and killed.

an uprising against him of the same kind as the one that had toppled the Tsar as a result of defeats in World War I. Two days later, Stalin in his desperation turned to the British Prime Minister Churchill and pleaded for 25–30 British army divisions to be shipped to the Soviet Union for participation in the war on the Eastern Front.*

On 12 September, 17. Armee and Panzergruppe 1 began their offensive northward from the Dnepr bridgehead at Kremenchug. Budyonnyy had proposed the evacuation of the Southwestern Front from Kiev, in order to save it from being encircled. Now that events seemed to prove him right, a raging Stalin had him sacked and replaced with Marshal Semyon Timoshenko, who just like Stalin demanded that the city should be held at all cost.** Next, Stalin personally ordered VVS Southwestern Front to commit 90 percent of its aviation against Panzergruppe 2's eastern flank in the Konotop-Romny sector, 200 km to the east of Kiev.[32] The missions carried out in this area on 12 September claimed one of the first Soviet female-pilot casualties of the war, Starshiy Leytenant Yekaterina Zelyenko. She was one of the first women to enter service in the VVS as a combat pilot. Having had her baptism of fire in the Winter War against Finland, Zelyenko was appointed deputy commander of a Sukhoy Su-2 light bomber squadron of 135 BAP in 1941.

On this 12 September, the Su-2s of 135 BAP were in full action against the German armored breakthrough at Romny. During the return flight from the day's second mission, Starshiy Leytenant Zelyenko flew in a formation of three Su-2s led by Kapitan Antonina Lebedeva when they came under attack from four Bf 109s from JG 51. During the initial fighter attack, one '109 was claimed shot down by Zelyenko's gunner – apparently unsubstantiated. The Messerschmitts continued to attack the bombers. Kapitan Lebedeva's aircraft was shot down, and a full burst

killed Zelyenko's rear gunner and set her aircraft ablaze. According to the Soviet account, Zelyenko directed her crippled Su-2 right into the closest Bf 109, getting herself killed in the process. UnteroffizierAnton Hafner of II./JG 51 returned from that engagement with claims for two "R-3s" – his eighth and ninth victories. No German losses were reported in that combat.***

From the Kremenchug bridgehead in the south, the German forces fanned out with Panzergruppe 1 racing northward and 17. Armee pushing towards the northeast. Any attempt by battered remnants of Soviet 38th Army to resist was effectively crushed by Luftwaffe attacks. Due to the excellent support from the air, Panzergruppe 1's forward elements were able to seize a bridge across the Sula River at Lubny, 100 km north of the previous day's point of departure. 40 kilometers farther up the Sula, Panzergruppe 2 meanwhile captured an important crossing near Lokhvitsa.[33]

German fighters actually established an almost 100 % screen in the air over Panzergruppe 1. On 13 September JG 3 claimed to have shot down 26 Soviet aircraft, while Panzergruppe 1's XXXXVIII. Armeekorps, advancing from Kremenchug to Lubny, only eight recorded air attacks, involving a total of 23 airplanes.[34] Next day, a task force broke out from the Sula bridgehead at Lokhvitsa in the north, and after a seven-hour march established contact with Panzergruppe 1 at Lubny. The door closed behind virtually the whole Southwestern Front at Kiev. Four Soviet armies – the 5th, 21st, 26th, and 37th – with over 450,000 men were caught in the trap. Oberst Hermann Plocher, the Chief of Staff in Fliegerkorps V, wrote: "The German isolation of the Kiev pocket was exemplary, with the bombers of the Fliegerkorps V (Luftflotte 4) operating from the Kirovograd area in the south and those of the Fliegerkorps II (Luftflotte 2) from north of Gomel and Orsha in the

---

* For a while, Churchill nurtured a similar idea, but it never was materialised was never put into action.

** As we have seen in a previous chapter, the debate over Kiev also cost General Armii Georgiy Zhukov his post as Chief of the General Staff. He was appointed to command the Reserve Front in August 1941, but was sent to Leningrad in September, with Marshal Budyonnyy replacing him in the Reserve Front on 13 September.

*** On 5 May 1990 Mikhail Gorbachev awarded Yekaterina Zelyenko the title of Hero of the Soviet Union posthumously.

north."[35] By September 14, Fliegerkorps V had destroyed or damaged 727 trucks in this sector.[36] Hauptmann Rudolf Kiel's I./KG 55 Greif was alone credited with the destruction of 58 railway cars, 675 trucks, and 22 tanks during the envelopment battle of Kiev.

But the intense activity in the days leading up to the closing of the Kiev pocket had consumed far more fuel than the brittle German logistical system was able to bring forward. After all, the railways in the rear area had been completely wrecked by the previous month's successful German envelopment from the air, and the roads were crammed with thousands of destroyed Soviet vehicles. The fuel shortage reached a critical point on 16 and 17 September, when Fliegerkorps V was compelled to ground most its bombers and instead send less fuel-consuming Ju 87s into action. StG 77's airmen found the pocket littered with dense masses of vehicles and equipment of all kind, and inflicted enormous losses on the more or less defenseless Soviet troops on the ground. On one day alone, at least 920 vehicles were destroyed in air attacks, and the losses in Soviet personnel were "extraordinarily heavy".[37] Interrogations with Soviet prisoners afterward revealed that these devastating Stuka attacks caused morale to crumble among the trapped Red Army troops.

On 18 September, German 6. Armee renewed its offensive against Kiev from the west. StG 77's airmen made four to six sorties each day to support the attack, and bombed bunkers and artillery positions in the approaches to the Kiev citadel, which broke all resistance. On 19 September the fortress was in German hands.

Hoping that the German lines at Lokhvitsa were still not completely sealed, the Red Army senior commanders in the Kiev area attempted to escape the envelopment, but they proved to be wrong. During the night of 19-20 September, they hid in a small wood about 11 km southwest of Lokhvitsa. Troops of German 3. Panzer-Division received information of this tempting bait, surrounded the forest

An image from the Battle of Kiev, where vast amounts of Soviet war material was destroyed or abandoned due to air attacks. (Photo: Krigsarkivet Stockholm.)

and then went in. The Soviet force of 800 men fought literally to the last man.

On 20 September, General-Polkovnik Mikhail Kirponos, the commander of the Southwestern Front, led the fighting until he was injured. He was carried deeper into the wood, only to get killed by a mortar shell. General-Mayor Vasiliy Tupikov, his Chief of Staff, and General-Mayor Dmitriy Pisaryovskiy, the Chief of Staff of the 5th Army, also fell during the fighting. The 5th Army's commander, General Polkovnik Mikahil Potapov, was wounded and fell into German captivity, as did the artillery commander in the 5th Army, General-Mayor Vladimir Sotenskiy, and a number of members of the Ukrainian Soviet Council.

Timoshenko ordered a general breakout, and Soviet 26th Army made a desperate attempt on 21 September. The Messerschmitt Bf 110 assault planes of SKG 210 were brought into action against this maneuver, with devastating results. General-Leytenant Fyodor Kostenko, commanding 26th Army, radioed an urgent appeal to the Stavka: "All efforts to cross the river are futile. No ammunition left. Help required from the air force!" But no such support was received. The skies over the Kiev sector entirely belonged to the Luftwaffe. Even though the fuel shortage would not permit Fliegerkorps V to carry out more than an average of 140 sorties per day during the last days of the Battle of Kiev, this was fully sufficient to deal crippling blows against the tight concentrations of Soviet troops and equipment inside the narrow Kiev pocket. Between 12 and 21 September, Fliegerkorps V claimed 42 aircraft, 23 tanks, and 2,171 motor vehicles destroyed on the ground. The fact that no more than 65 Soviet planes were claimed shot down in the air during this ten-day period is quite indicative of the low Soviet air activity.

On 26 September, the greatest encirclement battle in history was over. The Soviet 5th, 26th, and 27th armies had ceased to exist. According to German reports, 665,000 prisoners were taken in the Kiev pocket.[38] In reality, the Southwestern and Central fronts lost 621,183 troops either killed or missing, 28,419 artillery pieces and 411 tanks during the Battle of Kiev from 7 July to 26 September 1941.[39] VVS Southwestern Front recorded 1,561 aircraft losses between 22 June and 26 September.[40] Its C.O., General-Leytenant Fyodor Astakhov, went missing in the encirclement battle. In reality, he managed to evade capture and reached Soviet lines in November 1941 – having made it three hundred miles through enemy-held territory. His colleague General-Mayor Petr Shelukhin, commanding VVS Southern Front, was made the scapegoat for the failure to prevent the disastrous German punitive bombings in the Ukraine, and was replaced on 24 September by Polkovnik Konstantin Vershinin. Stalin's favourite, Marshal Timoshenko – who had forbidden the evacuation of the Southwestern Front in time – nevertheless maintained his position as the commander of the Southwestern Direction.

To Kiev's population, who had been classified as "superfluous eaters" according to the Nazi "Hunger Plan," a hell began that lasted over two years. When the city was liberated by the Red Army in November 1943, the population

These Red Army female soldiers were singled out by their German captors. It seems obvious that they are aware of the fate that awaits them. The Germans called them Flintenweiber ("gun broads"), and frequently orders were issued to liquidate them when caught – although the OKH issued instructions that female soldiers were to be treated as prisoners of war.

had gone down from 900,000 to just 180,000. Over 100,000 had been sent to Germany as slave workers.

The mass killings of the inhabitants of Kiev began only days after the German occupation. On 24 September 1941 a bomb exploded at the German headquarters. Over the following days, this was followed by more explosions in various buildings occupied by the Germans. According to their prejudices, the Germans blamed the Jews. On 28 September, signs with the following message were put up all over the city:

"All *Zhidi* [a pejorative Russian word for Jews] living in the city of Kiev and its vicinity are to report on Monday 29 September1941, at 0800 in the morning at the corner of the Melnikov and Dokterivsky streets (near the cemetery). Bring your documents, money, valuables, warm clothes, linen, etc. Any *Zhid* who disobeys this instruction and who is found elsewhere will be shot."

The Germans rounded up 665,000 Soviets as prisoners of war during the Battle of Kiev – an unsurpassed number in the history of modern warfare.

Arriving at the assigned spot, tens of thousands of Jews were brought to Babiy Yar, a deep ravine in the northwestern part of Kiev. There they were ordered to undress. Then they were forced to run a gauntlet and finally mown down by machine guns.

According to the Einsatzgruppe Operational Situation Report No. 101, a total of 33,771 Jews were killed at Babiy Yar on 29 and 30 September. The killings continued for months. The Nazis next rounded up Roma people and killed them at the ravine. Next, a steady stream of more

Jews and Roma people, Communists, POWs and civilians accused of disobedience were brought to Babiy Yar, where they were gunned down by Germans and Ukrainian nationalists.

Before the return of the Red Army in 1943, the German authorities ordered a large number of POWs to exhume the bodies and scatter the ashes over the fields in the vicinity. Thus, the exact number of victims at Babiy Yar will never be known. Estimations range from 100,000 to 150,000.

12: LENINGRAD HOLDS OUT.

"When we arrived with spades, picks and shovels, the constant sound
of the artillery cannonade was still distant. Then we became accustomed
to the whine of shells, to nearby explosions. We went on digging until
the Fascist tanks approached our sector."

– Ada Vilm, citizen of Leningrad 1941.

While the great battle of Smolensk raged in the Central combat zone, Heeresgruppe Nord's strategic offensive had come to a standstill. Generalfeldmarschall von Leeb's limited forces of Heeresgruppe Nord had simply reached the end of their strength.

Along River Luga, halfway between Pskov south of Lake Peipus and Leningrad, the Northern Front had held back Generaloberst Erich Hoepner's Panzergruppe 4 on the road to Leningrad in the north since mid-July 1941, a state of affairs that continued for four weeks. This was a remarkable accomplishment by the so-called Luga Operational Group, which mustered no more than three Rifle divisions and a half-formed Mountain Troop brigade, supported by two armored trains.

However, with 6. Panzer-Division remaining in a small bridgehead at the western Luga, leaving just a 30-kilometer wide strip for the 8th Army in Estonia to be supplied, Marshal Voroshilov, the Soviet overall commander in the region, decided to slowly pull back from Estonia. This was conducted with utmost skill by the army's commander, General-Leytenant Fedor Ivanov, who accomplished a fighting withdrawal, tying up substantial elements of German 18. Armee for as long as possible. The withdrawal commenced from a line across Estonia from Dorpat (Tartu) at Lake Peipus in the east to Parnu on the Gulf of Riga's coast in the west. To support this movement, Soviet air and sea units became much more active in the region. VVS KBF, the Air Force of the Red Banner Baltic Fleet was responsible for most of the air support in the Estonian sector. The bomber and torpedo-bomber crews of its bomber brigade 8 BAB were assigned to drop anti-shipping mines and bomb German airfields and ports at night time, and to attack German supply shipping in the Gulf of Riga in daytime. On 13 July, eighteen DB-3s and five Ar-2s (the dive-bomber version of the SB bomber) from 8 BAB's mine-torpedo regiment 1 MTAP attacked a large German seaborne convoy in the Gulf of Riga. This was Erprobungsverband Ostsee (Test Unit Baltic Sea), with forty-two small naval vessels en route from Libau to Riga. But this air operation met with little success. Although forty-two Soviet sorties were made, only one assault boat was sunk.[1] Also, an attack by the two Soviet destroyers *Serditnyy* and *Steregushchiy* against a German supply con-

voy in the Gulf of Riga on 19 July was warded off by Ju 88s of bomber group KGr 806, which hit *Serditnyy* so decisively that it later had to be sunk by its own crew. However, in the air over Estonia itself, VVS KBF was more successful. In mid-July the German High Command noted that Soviet fighters made air reconnaissance difficult in Estonian airspace.[2]

The Soviet air activity in general was of great concern to the Germans, who shifted II./ZG 26 from Fliegerkorps VIII to join the wing's I. Gruppe in Fliegerkorps I. But when KG 76 launched a bomber raid against Leningrad with the escort of Bf 110s from ZG 76 on 20 July, it met hard resistance from fighters of the 7th Air Corps (7 IAK) of Leningrad's Air Defense. Three German and two Soviet aircraft were shot down, and the bombs dropped fell widely scattered.[3]

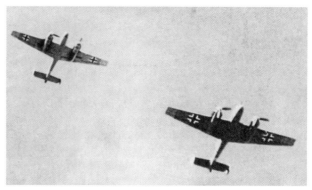

Two German Messerschmitt Bf 110s in the air. German heavy fighter wing ZG 26, operating this aircraft, claimed to have destroyed about 1,000 Soviet aircraft in the air and on the ground, plus 300 vehicles and 250 tanks during Operation Barbarossa. (Photo: Adolf Galland.)

On 22 July, nine SBs attacked the German airfield at Dorpat, killing or injuring several men on the ground and putting six German aircraft out of commission. After that, II./JG 53 could field only six serviceable aircraft, and had to be brought back to Germany to recuperate – leaving Luftflotte 1 without this fighter group for three weeks. Soviet 8th Army would hold German 18. Armee's advance down to a snail's pace for over a month, thus constituting a potential threat to Heeresgruppe Nord's flank. Greatly concerned,

The commander of Luftflotte 1, Generaloberst Alfred Keller (center), and the commander of JG 54, Major Hannes Trautloft (right), in front of a Messerschmitt Bf 109 F-4 of JG 54 at an airfield near Sarudinye. Both had a parallel career – Keller led Luftflotte 1 between August 1940 and June 1943, when he retired from active service, and Trautloft led JG 54 between August 1940 and July 1943, when he was appointed Inspector of the Day Fighters. Both were awarded with the Knight's Cross. Keller passed away on 11 February 1974, at the age of 85. Trautloft, credited with 53 aerial victories in World War II and five in the Spanish Civil War, passed away on 11 January 1995, at the age of 82. (Photo: Hannes Trautloft.)

Hitler flew to meet the commanders of Heeresgruppe Nord and Luftflotte 1, von Leeb and Keller. He was discontent with the failure to annihilate any larger Soviet forces in the northern combat zone, and issued a new directive for the general conduct of Operation Barbarossa. The new main target was to be the seizure of Leningrad. To create the necessary preconditions for this offensive, 18. Armee needed to finish its occupation of Estonia in the rear as quickly as possible.

On 26 July, Hitler received a dismal situation report about Heeresgruppe Nord: "Hoepner, Manstein and Reinhardt concur that the area between Lake Ilmen and Lake Peipus is unsuited to operations of armored units. The situation with Reinhardt's corps is very uncomfortable. Reinhardt vehemently demands to be given the go-ahead signal. But this is out of the question as long as the offensive from the direction of Luga has not become effective. Greatly intensified enemy air activity is reported also in that area."[4] Four days later, Hitler issued a new Führer Directive, No. 34, which changed the goal from the seizure of Leningrad to the envelopment of the city. He also ordered Fliegerkorps

VIII to be shifted from Luftflotte 2 to cover the endangered southern flank of Heeresgruppe Nord, where von Manstein's panzer corps had just received a heavy beating.

Thus, the Ju 88 bombers of Fliegerkorps I could wholly focus operations against the rail lines which brought supplies to Estonia.[5] This rapidly created a disastrous supply situation for the 8th Army. But there was not much help to be expected from the aviation of the Red Banner Baltic Fleet, which itself came under heavy pressure. On 25 July Tallinn's aerodrome was subjected to a devastating strike by ZG 26's Messerschmitt Bf 110s.

This support from the air allowed the Germans to achieve a strategic breakthrough on 8th Army's western flank. Driving boldly towards the east, German 61st Infanterie-Division reached the northwestern shore of Lake Peipus on 25 July, thus sealing off Soviet 11th Rifle Corps, which had held out at Dorpat for two weeks. Efforts to supply the 8th Army from the sea also were fraught with mounting difficulties. On the night of 25/26 July, the Soviet destroyer *Smelyy* was sunk by a 1000-kg mine dropped by German aircraft.[6]

With an acute shortage in ammunition and fuel, and one of the divisions of the 11th Rifle Corps down at a strength of three thousand men and twenty-two guns or mortars, Ivanov, 8th Army's commander, had no choice but to order a quick withdrawal to Tallinn on the northern coast. In spite of Ivanov's previous accomplishments in holding 18. Armee back, Marshal Voroshilov had him relieved from command, accusing him of "passivity and retreat from battle." Ivanov, a veteran of the Civil War and a highly esteemed commander, was arrested by the NKVD. Following long interrogations, he "confessed" that he had "spread anti-Soviet propaganda" and displayed "cowardice." He was demoted to private and spent the remainder of the war in prison.*

But his successor, General-Mayor Ilya Lyubovtsev, could not do much about the situation either. By 31 July, the enveloped 11th Rifle Corps had been annihilated. The Germans took 8,794 prisoners, and only three thousand exhausted and utterly demoralized soldiers managed to break out. The amount of the equipment captured by the Germans is quite revealing of the weakness of the enveloped corps – just 68 artillery pieces, five anti-tank guns, five tanks, and three armored cars.[7]

On 2 August, ZG 26 struck Tallinn's aerodrome again, claiming about 40 Soviet aircraft destroyed on the ground. Three days later the Germans occupied Rakvere, thus cutting off 8th Army's connection with Leningrad. On 6 August, while ZG 26 managed to completely annihilate all 16 aircraft at a VVS KBF seaplane station on a lake northeast of Narva, Lyubovtsev also was discharged. He was replaced by General-Leytenant Petr Pshennikov, formerly 23rd Army's commander. Another devastating blow

Soviet troops in combat against German tanks. The 45 mm 53-K anti-tank gun model 1937 seen in the photo was the Red Army's standard anti-tank gun in 1941. It had a rapid rate of fire – 15 to 20 rounds per minute – but had an insufficient armor penetration capacity, which made it useful only against German light tanks. Panzer III and Panzer IV tanks could be destroyed only at close range.

against the last remaining supply line by sea was dealt when Ju 88 bombers from bomber group KGr 806 attacked and sank the destroyer *Karl Marx* in Loksa Bay near Tallinn on 8 August.

With the threat from the 8th Army thus neutralized, the German High Command saw time as ripe for the final offensive against Leningrad. The arrival of Fliegerkorps VIII brought Luftflotte 1 its first Stuka units with altogether 130 serviceable Ju 87s. Two entire air corps, the first and the eighth, could now be dispatched in a massive air offensive against the Soviet defense positions of the Luga line, southwest of Leningrad. Day in and day out German aircraft pounced on the Soviet positions. This could be carried out without much interference from the Soviet air force. Of the 560 aircraft available to VVS Northern Front, 142 were deployed in Karelia farther north, where the situation had become more critical since the Finns opened their offensive on 31 July. Most of VVS KBF meanwhile was tied up supporting the 8th Army in northern Estonia.

One of the defenders at the Luga front, Aleksandr Pavlishkov, recalled, "From dawn to dusk we were subject to relentless air attacks. It was obvious to us that the enemy was in total control of the air. The enemy aircraft attacked us, left to refuel and then came back to attack us again. Quite surprisingly, their attacks were not particularly efficient. We sustained only few casualties. I grew so used to it that one day I even slept for five hours while we were under air attack. Finally they dived down over us without dropping any bombs or firing their machine guns. They came down so low that we could see the faces of the pilots. The noise from their engines was terrible, but we all remained lying flat at the bottom of the trenches,

German pioneers attack Soviet fortified positions with flame throwers. The Flammenwerfer 35, seen in use in the photo, weighed 35.8 kg and could fire for 10 seconds, at a distance of up to 30 meters. The flame thrower pioneers earned a special hatred among the enemy and were a favorite target for snipers. The Soviets were aware of this and produced made their flame throwers to be that were less conspicuous, looking like normal infantry rifles. (Photo: Via Daniel Johansson.)

* In 1946 Ivanov was quite unexpectedly released and had his general's rank restored.

waiting for one and a half hours for their bombs and machine gun fire."

On 8 August Panzergruppe 4 launched its attack on the Luga front. Initially, heavy rain hampered most air activity on both sides, and for several days both sides were locked in fierce fighting at Luga, with the Germans unable to achieve a decisive breakthrough. With clearing skies on 10 August, the air forces on both sides launched all available aircraft in close-support missions in the Luga sector. Fliegerkorps I and VIII conducted 1,126 sorties on 10 August, claiming the destruction of ten tanks, more than two hundred vehicles, and fifteen artillery batteries.[8] Meanwhile, General-Mayor Aleksandr Novikov, the supreme VVS commander in the Northwestern Direction, had reinforced the Soviet air asset at Luga by bringing in 2 SAD from the area south of Lake Ilmen, and 7 IAP from 5 SAD on the Karelian Isthmus.[9] On 10 August his air units flew 908 sorties, exerting a heavy pressure on the attacking German tank forces. The Il-2 pilots of 288 ShAP claimed particularly large successes in low-level attacks against concentrations of enemy motorized troops, without losing a single own aircraft. "Heavy enemy low-level air attacks against Panzergruppe 4," noted the German High Command's war diary.[10]

The fact that both sides lost eleven aircraft each during the air fighting in the northern combat zone on 10 August indicates quite an improvement on the Soviet side.[11] (On the other hand, both sides claimed to have "won" the day's air battle – the Germans claiming fifty-four enemy aircraft shot down,[12] and the Soviets reporting twenty-three.[13]) In one incident, ZG 26's Oberleutnant Alfred Möll and his radio operator were lost when their Bf 110 was rammed by the MiG-3 flown by Kapitan Ivan Gorbachyov of 71 IAP/ VVS KBF.[14]

The Soviet ground troops offered a frantic resistance at Luga, but owing to the dive-bombings by KG 77's Ju 88s against Soviet fortifications, artillery positions and tanks, the Germans managed to push forward, albeit at an agonizingly slow pace. "Every single trench and bunker had to be taken individually," noted Oberst Raus of 6. Panzer-Division.[15]

On the southern flank, the situation was utterly contradictory. North of Lake Ilmen, German 16. Armee was approaching the city of Novgorod, which General-Leytenant Sobennikov, Northwestern Front's commander, was ordered to hold at any cost. Situated on River Volkhov, which runs between lakes Ilmen and Ladoga, Novgorod was an important cornerstone of the Soviet defense. By bringing up the 34th Army from the Stavka reserve to join the 11th, 27th and 48th armies, the Northwestern Front had gathered a powerful force of nearly 400,000 men. But instead of concentrating this number to hold Novgorod, Sobennikov split up his forces: Novgorod was held by only the newly formed 48th Army with 70,000 men, and the remainder of Sobennikov's forces were concentrated south of Lake Ilmen to carry out a counter-offensive in the area where von Manstein's panzer corps had been blunted the previous month.

The objective was to break through at the point where the Germans were weakest – only X. Armeekorps of 16.

Armee stood in the sector south of Lake Ilmen – and advance to Pskov at Lake Peipus, thus cutting off the whole of Heeresgruppe Nord. Through sheer weight of numbers, the Soviets managed to overpower X. Armeekorps and reached the rail line between Dno and Staraya Russa on 14 August. Initially, it seemed as though Sobennikov would repeat the feat of the previous month, when he had blasted von Manstein's corps and neutralized 8. Panzer-Division. But this time, von Manstein would be able to exact a terrible revenge on his opponent.

Sobennikov underestimated not only the German ability to redeploy their forces quickly, but also the effect of the German air superiority. The situation was completely different now than it had been a month before, with around one hundred Messerschmitt 109 fighters based at Soltsy. VVS Northwestern Front and forces from the DBA were dispatched to support the counter-offensive by attacking the German supply lines. On 14 August, when the counter-offensive was launched, Il-2s from 288 ShAP dropped out of the skies and fell upon a single German column near Soltsy, wreaking havoc. As they left the scene, fire and black smoke covered the vehicle column. More than fifty vehicles were claimed destroyed or damaged. But on their return flight, the Il-2s were jumped from above by a pair of Bf 109s which shot down two of the assault planes. That same afternoon, Bf 109s of III./JG 27 intercepted a formation of DB-3s and claimed five shot down, four by Oberleutnant Erbo Graf Kageneck.

Red Army soldiers in bitter fighting south of Leningrad.

While the bombers of Fliegerkorps I and VIII were dispatched against Sobennikov's attack forces, 16. Armee continued to focus on the seizure of Novgorod north of Lake Ilmen. Assigned to support this assault, the Stukas of Fliegerkorps VIII carried out large-scale softening up attacks on 15 August. In spite of strong resistance from both Soviet fighters and anti-aircraft fire, the Stukas conducted their attacks until late in the afternoon, destroying

A column of German Panzer 38(t), version C, on the advance towards Leningrad.

most of Novgorod's fortress. Hauptmann Ernst-Siegfried Steen, III./StG 2's commander, contributed greatly to by destroying the large railway bridge over the Volkhov River at Novgorod – the main Soviet supply line in this sector – through a direct bomb hit. Then the infantry charged, and early on 16 August Novgorod was in German hands.

On that same day, bombers of KG 1 managed to cut all traffic on the rail line to the Luga front. With their enemy deprived of supplies, Panzergruppe 4 finally managed to smash their way forward. "The enemy broke through our front," said Aleksandr Pavlishkov. "We withdrew on foot into a forest since the Germans as a rule came on motor cycles or other motorized vehicles. They were terribly afraid of the woods. At first, we were overwhelmed by a collective fear, panic. But while running I came back to my senses and decided to stop and to halt the others. This succeeded. We continued backwards. We had no bread, we drank water in wheel tracks on the roads, and stilled our hunger with berries and mushrooms."

Contrary to the quite clumsy way in which Voroshilov and Sobennikov led their forces, the Germans operated methodically. The breakthrough at Luga enabled von Leeb to release von Manstein's LVI. Panzerkorps and send it back to the Lake Ilmen sector. This regrouping was conducted both rapidly and with such disguise that it was never detected by the Soviets. Von Manstein's strike against Sobennikov's flank at Staraya Russa on 19 August came as a total surprise to the Soviets. The result was a carnage, and shortly afterwards, X. Armeekorps surged into the Soviet positions from the north.

The 22nd Territorial Rifle Corps – built on the foundations of the former Estonian army – was almost completely obliterated and shortly afterward was disbanded.* The

34th Army, originally 55,000-men strong, sustained nearly 33,000 casualties and lost 74 out of 83 tanks and 628 out of 748 artillery pieces. The Germans took 12,000 prisoners and captured 141 tanks and 246 artillery pieces.

Sobennikov and General-Major Kuzma Kachanov, the commander of the 34th Army, had to pay dearly for this failure. While Sobennikov was deprived of his rank and awards and sentenced to five years of forced labor, Kachanov was executed. Stalin's faithful crony, Marshal Voroshilov, nevertheless got away without any repercussions.

However, quite a different turn of events would also come to cost Voroshilov his post. A particular feat of Leningrad's defense was the participation of its population. Aleksandr Pavlishkov was one of thousands of Leningraders who served in Workers' Militia units. One million inhabitants worked day and night to establish a wide defense perimeter. Ada Vilm, a scientific secretary of the Hermitage, took part in this work. "When we arrived with spades, picks and shovels," she said, "the constant sound of the artillery cannonade was still distant. Then we became accustomed to the whine of shells, to nearby explosions. We went on digging until the Fascist tanks approached our sector." [16]

All this mobilization of civil society evoked memories of the days of the October Revolution in 1917, and on 20 August a local Military Soviet for the Defense of Leningrad was formed. This outraged Stalin, who feared that this might "form the nucleus of a breakaway administration which could menace his own internal authority", and was a major reason why he shortly afterward abolished the Nortwestern Direction, placing it directly under control of the High Command, and replaced Voroshilov with Zhukov.

But this massive mobilization of Leningrad's citizens, in combination with aerial and armored operations against Hoepner's Panzergruppe 4, saved Leningrad during these crucial days. General-Major Novikov now threw in everything he had – including 126 naval aircraft, the bulk of VVS KBF – to the Luga-Leningrad front, even though this meant that the 8th Army in Estonia was left with virtually no air support. The war diary of a Luftwaffe unit reads, "Our squadron is involved in daily air combat with numerically superior enemy formations southwest of Leningrad. These engagements frequently last for an hour at a time. The maneuverability of the Russian fighters makes it hard to shoot them down." [17]

On the German side, Hoepner brought back 8. Panzer-Division – which was rested since it had been pulled out of combat after the debacle at Soltsy five weeks previously – to take the lead in the drive on Leningrad. But as this division's tank column approached Krasnogvardeysk on the road from Luga to Leningrad on the morning of 19 August, elements of Soviet 1st Tank Division had laid an ambush. Commanded by Leytenant Zinoviy Kolobanov, five well-hidden KV-1s had taken up position in a grove at the edge of a swamp through which the road to Krasnogvardeysk passed. When the vehicles of 8. Panzer-Division's armored reconnaissance battalion approached, Kolobanov ordered his men to hold their fire until the Germans were at point-blank range. Then he fired the first

* Out of 7,800 Estonians in this corps when the war began, 6,800 remained with the Red Army. (Õispuu, *Estonians in Russian Armed Forces in 1940–1945*, Part 3, p. 15.)

165

The crew of a Soviet KV-1 tank. (Photo: Soviet Embassy, 1976.)

shot, hitting and immediately knocking out the leading German vehicle. The Germans wrongly assumed that the vehicle had hit an anti-tank mine, and the entire column stopped. This gave Kolobanov the opportunity to knock out a second vehicle in the lead and then the last one in the column. In panic, the remaining German vehicles moved off the road, but got stuck in the moist terrain. There the armored cars, half-tracks and other vehicles were picked off one by one by the KV-1s.[18] III. Abteilung of Panzer-Regiment 10 rushed to the site, but its' Panzer 38(t) and Panzer IV tanks stood no chance against the KV-1s. Kolobanov broke off the action when he had fired the last of his ninety-eight rounds. Afterward, 135 hits were counted on his own tank No. 864, none of which had penetrated the armor. Through this single action, Heeresgruppe Nord's advance towards Leningrad again came to a standstill.[19] This feat earned Kolobanov the Order of Lenin.* He was credited with the destruction of 22 German tanks in this engagement, with another 20 by the other tank crews in his platoon. Without doubt, in their excitement the Soviets had counted every armored vehicle as a tank, but "there was little doubt that General Erich Brandenberger's 8. Panzer-Division had gotten another bloody nose," as historian Robert Forczyk points out.[20]

On 20 August, 6. and 8. Panzer divisions changed over to the defensive, and four days later the entire Heeresgruppe Nord was instructed to revert to the defensive again, and was not able to resume its offensive until two weeks later. Instead, the Germans requested the Finns start their advance against Leningrad from the north.

---

* Kolobanov had previously been appointed a Hero of The Soviet Union for bravery against the enemy during the Winter War. But for "fraternizing with the enemy" on the day when the armistice was signed, he was demoted and deprived of the honorary title.

THE AIR-SEA BATTLE AT TALLINN.

On 20 August German 18. Armee crossed the old Estonian – Russian border at Narva and thus completed the isolation of the Soviet garrison in Tallinn. The Soviet Red Banner Baltic Fleet organized a large naval operation to evacuate the enveloped Tallinn garrison. Under the cover of darkness, the troops successfully embarked the transport ships on the night of 27/28 August, but a storm in the Gulf of Finland prevented the fleet from leaving the port immediately. That settled its fate. The ships could set out to sea only at noon on 28 August.

Meanwhile, eight Junkers 88s from Hauptmann Dietrich Peltz's German bomber group II./KG 77 had been dispatched on a mission against the locks of the Stalin Canal, which linked the Baltic Sea with the White Sea. Under Peltz's command, this bomber group had become specialized in pinpoint attacks against small targets such as the Stalin Canal's locks, and on several occasions the unit had succeeded in blocking the canal for sustained periods. But this time, thick clouds prevented any bombing. In addition to that, intercepting Soviet fighters had shot down one of the Ju 88s. It was late in the afternoon on 28 August when the seven II./KG 77 crews on their return flight spotted the mass of Soviet ships. They immediately formed up to perform their dive attacks while the radio operators reported the sighting. Soon Ju 88s from KGr 806 also arrived to attack. Petr Makeyev, who made the journey on board the Estonian passenger steamer *Vironia*, recalled:

"One of the bombs detonated close to us in the water, damaging the steering gear and the main steam pipe. The vessel went off course and turned starboard. The steam rushed out from the boilers with an infernal noise, drowning all other sounds. People jumped overboard and soon a mine exploded, and the *Vironia* went down."

In addition to *Vironia*, the transport ships *Skrunda*, *Lake Lucerne* and *Atis Kronvalds*, and ice breaker *Krisjanis Valdemars* were sunk. But the indirect effect of the bombing led to an even greater result. Attempting to avoid the attacking aircraft, the Soviet ships veered toward the "Juminda" minefield. In the hours of darkness, a huge tragedy took place in the middle of this minefield. No less than twenty-one Soviet warships – including five destroyers – struck mines and went down, together with twelve transport ships and one tanker.

The next morning, 29 August, the remaining Soviet ships were again attacked by the Luftwaffe. Now II./KG 77 and KGr 806 were supplemented by KG 1, and nine I./KG 4 He 111s – the latter commanded by Hauptmann Klaus Nöske. While the Ju 88s conducted dive-bombings, Hauptmann Nöske had instructed his He 111 crews to attack at low level. This proved to be highly successful, since the anti-aircraft gunners on board the ships were apparently giving all their attention to the diving Ju 88s above. By attacking individually, Nöske's men succeeded in scoring bomb hits on six ships, three of which sank. However, as they pulled up after their attacks, the slow He 111s became exposed to the alerted anti-aircraft artillery, and all of the participating Heinkels were hit, although none of them was shot down.[1] The transport ships *Vtoraya Pyatiletka* and *Kalpaks*, and the training ship *Leningradsovet* sank. Four ships were damaged by the bombs – the freight ship *Ivan Papanin*, *Saule* and *Kazakhstan*, and repair ship *Serp i Molot*.

It is estimated that the air-sea battle at Tallinn on 28-29 August 1941 cost around 15,000 lives – 8,600 of the Soviet fleet, 4,771 civilians and 1,740 Red Army soldiers.[2] This was an even higher number than the Battle of the Leyte Gulf in 1944 – considered to be one the largest naval battles in history. The German price for this accomplishment was confined to two aircraft that were shot down.

The Junkers Ju 88 was one of the best aircraft in service in 1941.

1 Bundesarchiv-Militärarchiv, RL 10/487.
2 Zubkov, *Tallinskiy Krasnoznamyonnogo flota*, pp. 320–324.

The Finnish front.

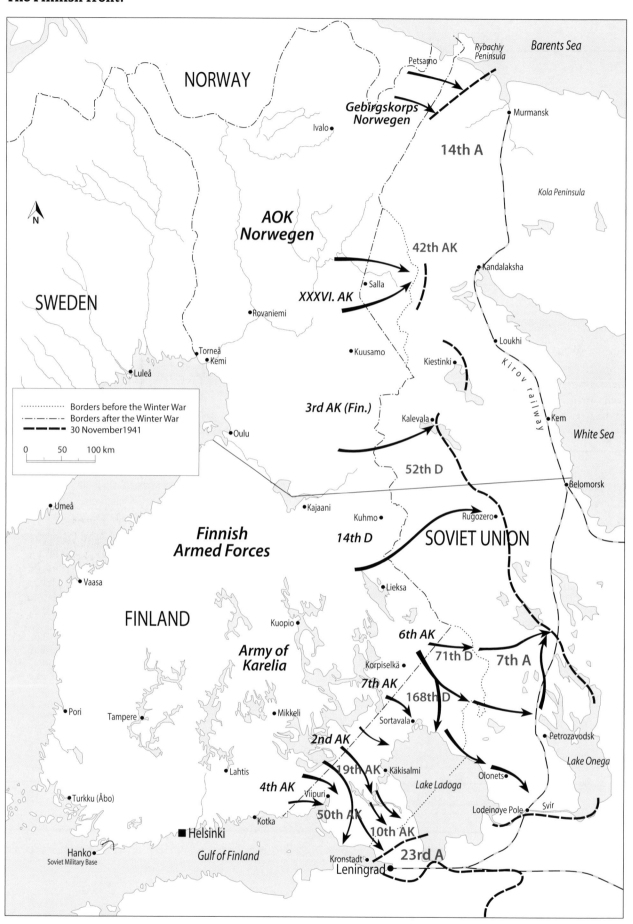

13: THE FINNISH FRONT.

"Orders are issued to Finland, with the request to launch the offensive on 10 July."

– Generaloberst Franz Halder, 6 July 1941.

As we have seen previously, Finland – badly hurt by Soviet aggression in the winter of 1939-1940 – quite willingly agreed to join Hitler's war against the USSR, although for political reasons it was to be under the pretext of a "defensive war." As early as 12 September 1940, the Finnish government signed a secret treaty with Germany, allowing the Wehrmacht to establish strongholds in northern Finland. A series of meetings between the Finnish and German general staffs commenced, where – as we have seen previously (chapter 4) – it is entirely possible that the Finns took an active part in the planning for Operation Barbarossa.

It is not entirely clear when the Finnish government was informed of Hitler's plans – according to official documents this took place in May 1941, but circumstances indicate that the actual date was much earlier. In early 1941, the Finnish government under the liberal Johan (Jukka) Wilhelm Rangell made an agreement with SS-Reichsführer Heinrich Himmler according to which the Finnish authorities would cooperate to form a Finnish volunteer SS battalion.* In connection with this agreement, Foreign Minister Rolf Witting informed the German Foreign Ministry that Finland "might be able to join the Three-Power Pact" (Germany, Italy and Japan).[1]

On 25–28 May 1941, a Finnish military delegation under General Heinrichs met with the Chief of the OKW, Generalfeldmarschall Wilhelm Keitel, and his chiefs of the OKW Operations Staff and of the General Staff, Generalobersts Alfred Jodl and Franz Halder, to discuss the upcoming war against the Soviet Union. Heinrichs declared that Finland was "interested in" Karelia, while the Germans explained that they were forming a combat group in northern Norway with the aim of passing through Finland to attack the Soviet port of Murmansk and the Kirov railway. Finnish President Risto Ryti and Rangell's government were informed about the plan for Operation Barbarossa.[2]

During a follow-up meeting on 3 June, the final plans were agreed upon. Generaloberst Nikolaus von Falkenhorst, the German C-in-C in occupied Norway, would control the German troops and Finnish III Army Corps in northern and central Finland, with the main aim of occu-

Finnish Lieutenant-Colonel Lars Woldermar Klärich (left) discussing the attack with a German staff officer. Klärich was the commander of Finnish Field Artillery Regiment 4. (Photo: SA Kuva.)

pying Murmansk – the only Soviet port that remained ice-free throughout the year – and the Kirov railway which connected Murmansk with the Soviet interior. In southern Finland, the main Finnish forces would be commanded by the Finnish C-in-C, Marshal Carl Gustaf Mannerheim, who would direct the onslaught from southern Finland in accordance with German instructions. It was also decided that Finland would start a general mobilization on 15 June.

---

* A total of 1,408 Finnish men – of which about 80 percent had served with the "White" forces during the Civil War in 1918 – joined the so-called SS Freiwilligen-Battalion Nordost, with Finnish officers and NCOs. Having completed training in Germany, the Battalion was sent into combat at the Mius River in January 1942, where it was offically attached to the 5. SS Wiking Division.

The Finnish C-in-C, Marshal Carl Gustaf Mannerheim, salutes German 163. Infanterie-Division, the so-called "Engelbrecht Division" after it had arrived via train through neutral Sweden. To the right of Mannerheim stands the divisional commander, General Erwin Engelbrecht. (Photo: SA Kuva.)

Moreover, it was agreed that Finland would occupy the Åland islands (which were demilitarized according to an international agreement) and retake the maritime base at Hanko in the western Gulf of Finland, which had been handed over to the Soviets after the Winter War. In fact, the whole Finnish strategy was subordinated to the Germans, as historian Earl F. Ziemke points out, "The Finnish main force would be assembled in such a manner that, depending on the wishes of the OKH, an attack could be launched either east or west of Lake Ladoga on five days' notice."[3] One concession given to the Finns was that the Finnish main operation was to begin only two or three days after the German attack because the Finns wished "to create the impression among their own people and people's representatives of being drawn in by the course of events."[4]

Thus, it was decided that the initial attack would be undertaken by Generaloberst Eduard Dietl's German Mountain Corps Norway, Gebirgskorps Norwegen – with 2. and 3. Mountain Divisions numbering 27,500 men – with the limited goal of establishing positions in the Finnish Petsamo area in the Far North. After that, the offensive would continue towards Murmansk, 100 kilometers to the east. The operations plan, dubbed Operation Platin Fox, called for a two-pronged attack. Dietl's mountain corps, assisted by a Finnish reinforced battalion of 1,200 men (Separate Detachment P/Ivalo Border Guard Battalion), would to strike east from Petsamo, attacking along the Barents Sea

coast. German XXXVI. Armeekorps with 40,600 men and Finnish III Corps with 28,000 men would strike further south in the Salla-Kestenga/Luokhi region. Air support was to be assigned by Generaloberst Hans-Jürgen Stumpff's German Luftflotte 5, which comprised 240 aircraft – of which nevertheless about half remained for the defense of Norway.

On 7 June 1941, large quantities of German military equipment and troops began to disembark in Finnish ports and were deployed to Laponia. Two days later, the Finnish mobilization commenced. On 12 June, the Finnish government ordered the British observers to leave the Petsamo area.

The attack against the Soviet Union from Finnish territory actually got off to quite a slow start, although it began early. On the night between 21 and 22 June, Finnish naval vessels took part in the German mining of the Gulf of Finland.[5] Meanwhile, Finnish commando troops located a Soviet airfield for the Germans, and, aided by the Finnish Army scouts, the German Brandenburgers started seizing bridges inside Soviet territory over which the main German invasion force in this area would march.[6] Early on 22 June, Finnish troops landed on the demilitarized Åland Islands and arrested the Soviet consulate.

While the Luftwaffe struck with tremendous impact on the "main Eastern Front," most aircraft of Luftflotte 5 were grounded due to bad weather during the first days of the war. Only a handful of aircraft flew operations near

Murmansk on 22 June, while Dietl's troops seized the Petsamo area with little fuss.

During the night of 22–23 June, two German Heinkel 115 seaplanes flew from Oulujärvi in Finland, bringing a fifteen-man strong Finnish Army long-distance scouting patrol to the Stalin Canal. When the He 115s returned after accomplishing the mission, four Brewster B-239 fighter aircraft of the Finnish Air Force's fighter group 4./LLv 24 flew into Soviet airspace to escort the Heinkels back to base. According to Finnish historian Carl-Fredrik Geust, it was a "top secret mission which was not recorded in LLv 24's War Diary."[7] From 23 June, German long-range reconnaissance aircraft flew regular reconnaissance missions from the air base at Luonetjärvi in Finland.[8] On 23 June, the Stalin Canal – which connected the White Sea with the Baltic Sea – was attacked by Junkers 88 bombers from KGr 806 which were able to use the Finnish airdrome at Utti.

Meanwhile, the Germans began negotiations with the Swedish government for the transit of the 163. Infantry Division, the "Engelbrecht Division," through neutral Sweden. After three days, the government in Stockholm accepted the German demands, leading to another German division being rapidly deployed to support the Finnish offensive.

There is no doubt that the Soviet intelligence was well informed of the Finnish war plans. On 24 June, the OKH had decided to instruct the Finns to undertake an operation east of Lake Ladoga with at least six divisions with the weight of the attack on the left and the objective set at a distance.[9] The next day, Halder noted in his diary that Finnish Major General Harald Öhquist arrived in the OKH headquarters "for orientation on our ideas concerning the conduct of the Finnish offensive east of Lake Ladoga, and is informed of the instruction."[10]

The Soviets decided to launch a pre-emptive strike against the Finns from the air. On 25 June, the bombers of the Northern Front and VVS SF went into action against airfields across a huge area between the Gulf of Finland and the Barents Sea, attempting to wipe out the forces available to both Luftflotte 5 and the Finnish Air Force.

Nikolay Gapeyonok was one of the Soviet bomber pilots who participated in the fateful operation on 25 June. By that time he served as a Mladshiy Leytenant and pilot with bomber regiment 202 SBAP, based near Leningrad as

A fresh graveyard for troops of German 6. SS Mountain Division Nord in northern Finland. The first contact of the SS troops with Soviet 1st Tank Division at Salla on 4 July 1941 resulted in a humiliating German defeat. (Photo: SA Kuva.)

a part of VVS Northern Front. On his first combat mission on 25 June, Gapeyonok flew as the number three with two other SBs, piloted by Starshiy Leytenant Rudenskiy and Leytenant Kuznetsov, men with experience from the Spanish Civil War and the Winter War. Gapeyonok suddenly found himself alone: "An anti-aircraft shell directly hit the bomb hatch of the leading SB, seriously wounding Starshiy Leytenant Rudenskiy, who barely managed to reach friendly territory. He was hospitalized and never returned to the regiment again. Kuznetsov's aircraft was also seriously damaged and one of the engines was put out of order. Nevertheless, the pilot managed to make an emergency landing in friendly territory."

Having lost orientation over enemy territory, Gapeyonok finally returned to base on the last drops of fuel. During the landing approach, both engines of his SB stopped: "I received a stormy welcoming. The fire engine came rushing, it was overtaken by the ambulance car, and people came running to meet me, including the C.O., Polkovnik Nikolay Yefimov. I climbed out of the cockpit, soaked with sweat as after a Russian sauna, anxious because I had lost two of my commanders. I reported to the C.O. that the Mladshiy Leytenant had returned. I couldn't think of anything clever to say."[11]

On only the first day of the air offensive, twenty-three bombers were lost.[12] Still, due to an order from the staff of the Northern Front, the Soviet air-base offensive would continue for another five consecutive days. But owing to German and Finnish preparations, the Soviets failed to destroy any Luftwaffe airplanes during these rather limited raids, while the Finns counted no more than two slightly damaged aircraft. The only main result was Finland's de facto declaration of war against the USSR on 25 June 1941.

The commander of a Soviet T-26 tank company instructs his men in the Karelian front. (Photo: Yevgenniy Khaldey.)

The German-Finnish ground forces enjoyed a quite convincing numerical superiority. The Finnish army, far better equipped than it had been during the Winter War, mustered 530,000 men in June 1941. The German army in Norway constituted 150,000 men, of which nearly half were immediately pitted against the Soviet Union. For their defense, the Soviets had the Leningrad Military District/ Northern Front, with slightly more than 400,000 troops grouped into three armies: the 23rd on the Karelian Isthmus in the south; the 14th along the 600-kilometer border zone from the shore of the Barents Sea in the Far North down to Kostumksha, and the 7th holding a 400-kilometer area in the center.

In the air the Soviets initially enjoyed a numerical superiority, with 1,136 planes of the Leningrad Military District/Northern Front, 116 of the Northern Fleet (VVS SF) and 624 of the Baltic Fleet (VVS KBF) against 550 Finnish and about 200 German aircraft. But this soon changed, when the Soviets were compelled to relocate the bulk of these forces against German Heeresgruppe Nord.

On 28 June the Finns presented a plan of attack which, according to Ziemke, "fulfilled the German request." This finds support in what Halder wrote in his diary, "Plan of attack entirely in line with our ideas. Troops are keen to attack."[13]

A Soviet Maxim machine gun crew in action against the Germans in the Far North.

On 29 June, Dietl's German offensive in the Far North began. The operation was immediately hampered by the difficult terrain and the inadequate roads in this desolate Arctic region. The Soviets immediately replied by launching eighteen SB bombers against the port of Liinahamari on 29 June, whereby one freight ship was sunk and severe damage was inflicted on the wharf area in the small harbour. This worsened the German supply situation, and greatly aided Soviet 23rd Fortification Region to repel all German attempts to seize the Rybachyy Peninsula, some 80 kilometers northwest of Murmansk. Pinpoint attacks by Ju 87 Stukas of IV.(St)/LG 1 – the only dive-bomber group available to Luftflotte 5 – posed a great threat to the Soviet

defenders during the initial stage, but this ended when the second main drive in the Far North commenced at Salla 300 kilometers to the south on 1 July.

The Finnish 6th Division opened the onslaught, with 6. SS Mountain Division Nord following suit. The aim was to advance to the Kandalakshka Bay in the northwestern tip of the White Sea, thus cutting off the Kirov railway and isolating the Kola Peninsula. But the SS troops were immediately embroiled in stiff fighting with Soviet 122nd Rifle Division. IV.(St)/LG 1 had to be brought in, but this was not entirely a blessing. SS-Brigadeführer Karl Demelhuber, commanding SS Mountain Division Nord, wrote: "Stukas of IV.(St.)/LG 1 were to suppress Soviet artillery positions before the assault. This opening barrage had some effect on the defenders, but more importantly set much of the forest on fire, which severely degraded visibility for the Stukas and artillery observers."[14]

On 4 July, the mere encounter with 1st Tank Division at Salla caused panic among the SS troops, who abandoned their positions and fled in disorder. In fact, the Soviet tank division had not even made a counter-attack, and no reports of heavy fighting are to be found in the unit's war diary. Between 30 June and 7 July, 1st Tank Division recorded only 28 troops killed in action, 30 missing and 58 injured.[15] More Stukas and German 169. Infanterie-Division had to be brought in. On 6 July, five attacks involving a total of 74 Stuka sorties were made against Soviet 1st Division, followed by three attacks with 43 sorties on the following day.[16] Thirty-three BT-7 tanks and three Soviet armored cars were destroyed, enabling the Germans to capture Salla.[17] Further to the north, the arduous march of the German Mountain Corps across the tundra towards Murmansk was further complicated by the fact that the Soviets dominated in the air. The air forces of the 14th Army and the Northern Fleet (SF) had concentrated 263 aircraft, i.e. a two-to-one numerical superiority against the Germans, to the defense of Murmansk. Over and over again the Soviet aviation in the area attacked the German rear area. On 2 July, one regiment of VVS SF alone, 72 SAP, carried out 45 ground-attack sorties and dropped 400 bombs in just three hours.[18] In response, II./KG 30 set out on 3 July to bomb the Soviet airfield at Varlamovo. 72 SAP took off to meet the formation, and Starshiy Leytenant Vasiliy Volovikov shot down the Ju 88 flown by the Gruppenkommandeur of II./KG 30, Hauptmann Eberhard Roeger, who was posted as missing.

On 5 July the Germans had managed to push forward 50 kilometers and reached River Litsa, 50 kilometers west of Murmansk. They just managed to establish a bridgehead on the eastern side of the river when they were beset by a counter-attack.

The Soviets dominated not only the skies, but also the sea, where their Northern Fleet mustered 8 destroyers, 15 submarines, 7 patrol boats, 2 torpedo boats, and 2 minesweepers. On 6-7 July the Northern Fleet landed around one thousand troops at Litsa Bay, in the rear of the Germans. Meanwhile Soviet 52nd Rifle Division counterattacked at the Litsa River. Also, on 7 July, nine Soviet SB bombers attacked Kirkenes Airdrome, causing 42 casualties among the ground personnel and knocking out several

German aircraft on the ground. Lacking air support, the Germans were pushed back across the river.

This Soviet success caused great concern on the German side. Dietl desperately pleaded for greater air support. Hitler became preoccupied that a larger naval landing might even be undertaken at Petsamo and demanded the shifting of elements of the Mountain Corps to that area – thus weakening the strength at the front. The German Navy decided to station a flotilla of five destroyers at Kirkenes. On 7 July the OKW ordered elements of XXXVI. Army Corps in the Salla sector north to support Dietl, and Mannerheim was asked to commence his offensive in the south. "Orders are issued to Finland, with the request to launch the offensive on 10 July," Halder wrote in his diary.[19] This was coordinated with German Heeresgruppe Nord's breakthrough at River Velikaya (see chapter 7), and the plan was that the German and Finnish forces would meet at River Svir, between lakes Ladoga and Onega.

The Finns struck on schedule, 10 July. Their Karelian Army under Lieutenant General Erik Heinrichs enjoyed a substantial numerical superiority, mustering six infantry corps with sixteen divisions. The first attack was directed against Ladoga Karelia, i.e. the territory between lakes Ladoga and Onega. Here the Finns concentrated the VI Corps (5th and 11th Divisions), the VII Corps (7th and 9th divisions) and Group O (Cavalry Brigade, 1st Jäger Brigade and 2nd Jäger Brigade) against Soviet 7th Army with just two Rifle divisions, the 71st and 168th, and one composite aviation division, 55 SAD, with around 30 bombers and 30 fighters.[20]

The weak Soviet forces fell back, and on 14 July the Finns cut the Sortavala-Petrozavodsk railroad, reaching the shores of Lake Ladoga the next day. Thus the Soviet routes around the lake were severed. Four days later the Finns crossed the 1939 border and continued into Soviet East Karelia, prompting the defenders to bring in rein-

Inspection of a shot down Junkers Ju 87 Stuka of IV.(St)/LG 1 in the Karelian wilderness. (Photo: SA Kuva.)

173

A DEMOCRATIC COUNTRY ALONGSIDE THE NAZIS.

The fact that Finland as a democratic country joined the war on Nazi Germany's side may be regarded as an absurdity, but had its counterpart in the composition of the country's government – a six-party coalition between Conservatives, Liberals, the Extreme Right and Social Democrats.

The Commander-in-Chief, Marshal Gustaf Mannerheim, had been the commander of the "Whites" during the bloody civil war between the "Whites" and "Reds" in 1918, and when Finland's armed forces launched its offensive on 10 July 1941, Mannerheim issued a quite controversial Order of the Day: He called the war against the Soviet Union a "holy war," praised the fight "alongside the mighty German army" and promised the conquest of Soviet East Karelia: "In 1918 during the War of Liberation I stated to the Finnish and Viena Karelians, that I would not set my sword to the scabbard before Finland and East Karelia were free."

Finnish Marshal Gustaf Mannerheim and some of his most important generals. Standing to the left in the photo is General Vilho Nenonen, the commander of the Finnish artillery, which mustered over 1,000 guns when the war against the Soviet Union broke out in June 1941. To the far right is Major General Paavo Talvela, the commander of VI Army Corps, and obliquely to the right of him is Lieutenant General Erik Heinrichs, who commanded the Karelian Army. All of these senior officers had led troops on the White side in the Finnish Civil War of 1918. They all wear the Mannerheim Cross, which was awarded to 191 servicemen during World War II. Mannerheim himself and Heinrichs however were the only two persons to be awarded the Mannerheim Cross of the First Class. (Photo: SA Kuva.)

This caused concern among many Finnish soldiers and civilians, and subsequently within the government also. The Social Democrat ministers agreed that Finland should retake the territories lost as a result of the Winter War 1939-1940, but voiced some discontent when the Finnish troops crossed the borders of 1939. However, even the Social Democrat leader Väinö Tanner called for the "crushing" of the left-wing Vapaa Sana Group, which had six members of parliament. In August 1941 all six MPs were imprisoned, not to be released until Finland had sought peace with the USSR in 1944.

Eager to get rid of the enmity with Finland, Stalin sent U.S. President Roosevelt a letter on 4 August, asking him to assist in peace negotiations with Helsinki. On 18 August, the Finnish Embassador in Washington, Hjalmar Procopé, was informed that the Soviet Union wished to end hostilities and that it was prepared to "discuss the Moscow Peace Treaty" after the Winter War – i.e. to return the Finnish territories that had been seized. But the Finns did not even bother to reply. Three months later, on 12 November, the Finns rejected a U.S. proposal for peace with the Soviet Union. The aggressive policy vis-a-vis Soviet East Karelia led the British government to declare war on Finland on 6 December 1941. Canada, Australia and New Zealand duly followed suit the next day, while the USA – fully occupied with Japan's simultaneous attack against Pearl Harbor – remained neutral vis-a-vis Germany's ally Finland.

A similar dichotomy is also reflected in the treatment of Finland's Jews. Over 200 Jews fought in the Finnish Army during the Winter War, and many also fought under Mannerheim's command in the Continuation War from 1941. Three of them were even awarded the swastika-embellished Iron Cross by the Germans (but refused to accept them). However, one reason why Finnish Jews continued to serve while fighting on the same side as the Nazis was that they feared that otherwise they might end up in German concentrations camps. Marshal Mannerheim had said that "as long as Jews serve in my army I will not allow their deportation."

In fact, recent research has showed that Finland extradited a quite large number of Jews to Germany. In *Luovutetut; Suomen ihmisluovutukset Gestapolle* ("Finland's handing over of people to the Gestapo") – awarded the Tieto-Finlandia Prize for the best non-fiction book – Finnish historian Elina Sana (Suominen) presents figures that Finland deported 2,829 Soviet POWs – among them 500 Jews or "politicals" (i.e. commissars) – to Nazi Germany, in return for POWs of Finnish origin in German custody. Although these figures have been questioned, the names of sixty-four Jews that were handed over to the Germans by Finland have been identified.[1]

The Finnish government also allowed a German Einsatzkommando, Einsatzkommando Finnland, to operate on its territory. The Finnish State Police (Valpo) cooperated closely with the Einsatzkommando in Salla, handing over 521 political commissars or Jewish POWs, who were probably all executed in Finland.[2] Thus, Finland took an active part in pursuing Hitler's infamous Commissar Order.

Finland also had concentration camps of its own. When East Karelia was occupied, an ethnic cleansing of Russians was undertaken. These were expulsed from their homes and put into what were actually designed as concentration camps. Most of the non-Finnish population in East Karelia were evacuated by the Soviet authorities, but some 24,000 Russians were placed into these camps, where, according to Finnish sources, 4,500 died – of which about one-third reportedly were children. Russian sources however show other figures – 14,000 deaths.[3]

Around 47,000 Soviet men and women ended up in Finnish POW camps in 1941. There they met a grim fate in terrible camp conditions with poor supply of food, shelter, clothing, and health care, added to inhumane treatment. For instance, the Finnish High Command gave the camp commanders the right to flog POWs as punishment for offences, and indeed thousands of POWs were publicly flogged. POWs who had managed to escape and were caught again could be executed.[4] In a ten-month period, more than 16,000 Soviets perished in these Finnish POW camps. Around one thousand of these were shot.[5] "These prisoner-of-war deaths were usually reported as 'shot while attempting to escape,'" noted Finnish historian Oula Silvennoinen. "This formulation, however, was also clearly used to mask illegal executions of prisoners, often committed out of a variety of causes including fear, hatred, incompetence, alcoholism or simple sadism."[6] Revealingly, the death rate was nearly eight times higher among prisoners of Russian origin than among those from the Baltic Soviet republics.

↑ A Soviet prisoner of war is led to the rear by Finnish soldiers. (Photo: SA Kuva.)

← Inmates of a Finnish concentration camp for Russian civilians in the parts of the Soviet Union that Finland occupied in 1941. The sign reads: "Any access to the camp or contact across the fence is prohibited under the threat of shooting." (Photo: Galina Sanko/Central Archive of Republic of Karelia.)

1   Arnstad, *Skyldig till skuld*, p. 43.
2   *"Limits of Intentionality"* by Oula Silvennoinen in Kinnunen and Kivimäki, *Finland in World War II*, p. 374.
3   Morozov, *Kareliya v godyy Velikoy Otechestvennoynyy (1941 – 1945)*, p. 10.
4   *"Limits of Intentionality"* by Oula Silvennoinen in Kinnunen and Kivimäki, *Finland in World War II*, p. 364.
5   Westerlund, *Prisoners of War and Internees: A Book of Articles by the National Archives / Sotavangit ja internoidut: Kansallisarkiston artikkelikirja*, p. 9.
6   *"Limits of Intentionality"* by Oula Silvennoinen in Kinnunen and Kivimäki, *Finland in World War II*, p. 378.

Soviet fighter ace Kapitan Boris Safonov (facing the camera) and British fighter pilots at Vayenga aerodrome in October 1941. Safonov achieved 24 victories in 34 aerial combats before he went missing on a combat sortie over the sea on 30 May 1942. (Photo: Tim Elkington.)

British Hurricanes in action on the Eastern Front, Vayenga airfield, near Murmansk, September 1941. (Photo: Krigsarkivet Stockholm.)

forcements: The 198th Rifle Division arrived from the 23rd Army on the Karelian Isthmus. 65 ShAP, equipped with a mixture of I-15bis biplanes and new Il-2 Shturmoviks, arrived on 19 July, and a couple of days later the new 197 IAP with nineteen I-153 fighters began operations in this sector.[21] The most powerful reinforcement arrived in the shape of 135 tanks – including four KV-1s – from 1st Tank Division. Going into action on the eastern shore of Lake Ladoga on 23 July, it managed to halt the Finnish advance. On 24 July the Soviet Ladoga Flotilla landed a Marine brigade on the northeastern shore of Lake Ladoga, in the rear of Finnish VII Corps. The Finns had to reposition their forces, and in a three-day battle managed to wipe out the Soviet bridgeheads, but their offensive had been strategically halted.

Meanwhile, the situation further north had deteriorated further for the Finns and the Germans. On 14 and 16 July Soviet Northern Fleet landed more troops at Litsa Bay, in the rear of the German Mountain Corps. With Soviet destroyers and patrol ships shelling the German troops and their supply lines, the Stukas of IV.(St)/LG 1 had to move back from the central sector of the Finnish border. On 20 July, Oberleutnant Johannes Pfeiffer of 12.(St)/LG 1 managed to sink the destroyer *Stremitelnyy* and the patrol ship SKR-20/*Shtil* in Kola Bay. For this, Pfeiffer was awarded with the Knight's Cross. But soon afterward, IV.(St)/LG 1 had to be shifted even further south, where the combined German-Finnish drive was desperately trying to reach Luokhi on the Kirov railway. Rushed from one critical sector to another like a fire

brigade throughout the month of July, IV.(St)/LG 1 bled white. No Stukagruppe was more battered than this unit in the summer of 1941. By 31 July, it had lost 25 of its original 36 Ju 87s.[22] And in fact, none of the German-Finnish targets were reached; the offensive bogged down all along the line, with Murmansk and the Kirov railway remaining in Soviet hands.

Thrilled by Hitler's increasing troubles on the Eastern Front, British Prime Minister Winston Churchill decided provide Stalin with material support. U.S. President Franklin D. Roosevelt would follow in due course. On 25 July 1941, the London government earmarked 200 Curtiss P-40 Tomahawk single-engine fighters to be delivered to the Soviet Union. But before the shipping could commence, Churchill decided to actively intervene in the war in the Far North, personally ordering a Fleet Air Arm strike against the northern ports of Kirkenes in Norway and Liinahamari in Finland. The Royal Navy dispatched aircraft carriers *HMS Furious* and *HMS Victorious* to the north, and on 30 July the double-strike was launched.

The force to attack Kirkenes took off from *Furious* – nine Fairey Albacores of Fleet Air Arm's 817 Squadron, nine Fairey Swordfish torpedo planes of 812 Squadron, escorted by six Fairey Fulmar fighters of 801 Squadron. But the port was virtually empty, and one Albacore and two Fulmars were lost to Flak. The operation from *Victorious* against Liinahamari ended in complete disaster. The twenty Albacore torpedo bombers from 827 and 828 Squadrons and nine Fulmars from 809 Squadron were intercepted by four Messerschmitt Bf 110s and nine Bf 109s, later reinforced by further '109s. The German fliers

completely broke up the attack formations and claimed seventeen British planes shot down, for the loss of only one Bf 110. British Fleet Air Arm statistics show that the Liinahamari task force lost eleven Albacores and two Fulmars. Nine Albacores limped back to the carrier, and only one of them had escaped battle damage. 827 Squadron lost six Albacores, with fourteen airmen made POWs, and five killed. 828 Squadron lost five out of eight Albacores, with eight made POWs, and seven killed. However, the psychological impact of this British intervention was significant – not least as it posed the Finnish government with the possibility of facing a British invasion.

While the whole offensive along the Finnish border was bogged down, the main forces of the Finnish Karelian Army attacked in the south, on the Karelian Isthmus. This territory had been the immediate cause of the Winter War in 1939: the Soviets had demanded the border be relocated from a 30 to a 60 km distance from Leningrad. The Finnish defeat in the Winter War however led to the border being moved over 100 kilometers.

Coordinated with the planned German attack at the Luga front, southwest of Leningrad, the Finnish attack against the Karelian Isthmus was launched on 31 July 1941. By that time the defenders – Soviet Northern Front's 23rd Army – had been substantially weakened in this sector. With 10th Mechanized Corps sent to defend Lenin-

↑ *Swedish volunteer troops withdraw under fire from the Soviet defenders at Hangö. The Hangö Peninsula, located at the mouth of the Gulf of Finland, is Finland's southernmost tip. As part of the 1940 Moscow Peace Treaty which ended the Winter War, Hangö was leased to the Soviet Union as a naval base for 30 years. It was bombed by the Luftwaffe on 22 June 1941, and placed under siege by the Finnish Army from 25 June. On 17 August 1941, the new Swedish Volunteer Battalion, Svenska Frivilligbataljonen (SFB) – with 500 men commanded by Lieutenant-Colonel Hans Berggren – arrived at the Hangö front. Owing to the deteriorating situation on the other side of the Gulf, in Estonia, the Soviets began to secretly evacuate their garrison on 26 October 1941, and this operation was completed by 2 December. Two days later a patrol led by Swedish Captain Anders Grafström entered Hangö to find that it was deserted. The siege of Hangö cost the Finns 272 killed in action and 529 wounded, while the Swedish casualties amounted to 178 men, including 25 killed, 75 wounded and 78 missing. Some of the latter had been captured by the Soviets. (Photo: SA Kuva.)*

grad from the south and the 198th Division transferred to Ladoga Karelia, all that remained to fight two Finnish Army corps with seven divisions were four Rifle divisions. However, two full air divisions – 5 SAD and 39 IAD – were available for air support, and just as the Finns had been in 1939–1940, the Soviets were greatly aided by the difficult terrain. Fighting a delaying action in the deep forests, the Red Army withdrew step by step, forcing the Finns to pursue them only slowly and with great caution. Over and over again the Finnish troops were subject to local counter-attacks and took some heavy losses. The 198th

Finnish troops, with a captured Soviet T-26 tank, advance deep into Karelia. (Photo: SA Kuva.)

Rifle Division was brought back from the other side of Lake Ladoga, and a new division arrived to reinforce the defense on the eastern flank of the Isthmus. On 14 August, when the Finns reached Kamennogorsk, 25 kilometers south of the new border and some 30 kilometers northeast of Viborg, these forces counter-attacked 40 kilometers farther to the northeast and managed to push the Finns back two kilometers.

In the Far North the Germans had meanwhile more or less given up the prospect of capturing Murmansk and instead resorted to bombing the vital port city. But even this was not without a cost. Each mission against Murmansk was confronted with heavy AAA fire and a Soviet fighter force that proved to be quite effective. The latter was not least due to one fighter pilot, Kapitan Boris Safonov of 72 SAP/VVS SF – undoubtedly one of the best fighter pilots of the entire war. Although he flew an outdated and slow I-16, Safonov managed to attain an impressive string of victories. Sergey Kurzenkov, who served with 72 SAP as a Starshiy Leytenant in 1941, dedicated a chapter to Safonov in his war memoirs: "The first months of the year were a very hard time for the fliers of the Northern Fleet. The enemy was numerically superior. Without any regard to losses, [the Germans] attempted to break through to Murmansk. Safonov and his comrades flew five, six, and even ten sorties daily. They hardly got any

sleep. Using their parachutes as pillows, they slept during short intervals, literally under the wings of their planes, while the ground crews were busy refueling and reloading the guns. This took no more than fifteen to twenty minutes. And then they sat in their cockpits again and were in the air, attacking the enemy."[23] The operation against Murmansk on 9 August cost the Luftwaffe a loss of seven aircraft while only two Soviet fighters were shot down.[24] Safonov contributed by shooting down four Ju 88s (exactly matching the German losses).

When the Germans sent three destroyers into Kola Bay on 10 August, attempting to block the entrance to Murmansk, bombers from the Air Force of Soviet Northern Front attacked, damaged the destroyer *Richard Beitzen* and compelled the whole force to withdraw.

Intercepting yet another of KG 30's raids against Kola Bay on 23 August, Kapitan Safonov shot down one more Ju 88 while Leytenant Leonid Zhdanov of the same unit shot down the German fighter ace Leutnant Hans Mahlkuch of 14./JG 77. Mahlkuch, credited with 16 aerial victories, was posted as missing.

When the Germans on 20 August demanded that the Finns attack Leningrad, the situation along the entire Finnish-Soviet front was completely different from what had been anticipated in Helsinki when the war plans were made. The Karelian Army remained locked in bitter fighting

MURMANSK SAVED BY THE SOVIET AIR FORCE.

Murmansk continued to be of vital importance to the Soviet Union throughout the war: As the only port with access to the oceans that was ice-free throughout the year, it became a lifeline for Lend Lease-deliveries from the West. The first of the regular convoys to northern Soviet Union, the so-called PQ convoys, sailed to Arkhangelsk in the White Sea. Following "Devon" in August, five PQ convoys arrived at Arkhangelsk between 12 October and 13 December 1941. But owing to ice in the White Sea, PQ-6 had to be directed to Murmansk, where it arrived on 20 December 1941. By that time, the PQ convoys had delivered 800 aircraft, 750 tanks, 2,300 vehicles and more than 100,000 tons of general cargo to the Soviet Union. Among the eleven subsequent convoys, during May 1942, all but one sailed to Murmansk.

In spite of repeated attempts, the Luftwaffe failed to destroy the port installations in Murmansk. This was much owing to the VVS in the area, which in addition also dealt the death blow to Dietl's efforts to reach Murmansk with his Mountain Corps.

On 28 September 1941, the airmen of 72 SAP/VVS SF carried out one of the most successful aerial missions ever conducted in the Far North. Between 1705 and 1830 hours, all available aircraft of that unit - twenty-six fighters and nine bombers - were dispatched against the bridge spanning the Petsamojoki River near Petsamo and other targets nearby.[1] Close hits by two 250-kilogram bombs near the vital river crossing resulted in a landslide, and three million cubic meters of earth destroyed the 30-meter span. This created a flood that drowned whole birch forests and swept away all crossings along the entire river. The whole invasion force heading for Murmansk on the eastern side of the river was isolated for ten days. This single air raid, in fact, dealt a decisive death blow to German hopes of capturing the vital port of Murmansk. German war correspondent Paul Karl Schmidt (Paul Carell) wrote, "Military history has never seen another case like this, that so spectacularly and dramatically cut off the supply lines of an entire front with two divisions."[2]

1 *Boyevoy put' Sovetskogo Voyenno-Morskogo Flota*, 4th edition, p. 186.
2 Carell, *Unternehmen Barbarossa*, p. 377.

in the forests and among rivers and small lakes 100 kilometers north of Leningrad and was sustaining bloody losses. The prospect of a successful Finnish offensive through the difficult terrain towards Leningrad looked bleak. Moreover, in the south, German Panzergruppe 4 stood just 50 kilometers south of the city. Pointing at the fact that the Finns lacked the extra heavy artillery and bombers needed for an assault on the large city, the Finns turned down the request. The Finnish Social Democrats were also growing increasingly concerned over the new occupation policy on the other side of the pre-1939 border.

Nevertheless, Mannerheim concentrated all available forces for a powerful attack in the northwestern part of the Karelian Isthmus on 22 August. Five days later he ordered the forces in Ladoga Karelia – which had now been reinforced by German 163. "Engelbrecht" Division – to resume their offensive with the aim of reaching River Svir, where they were supposed to meet German Heeresgruppe Nord. Thus, Leningrad would be effectively cordoned off and was expected to be starved into submission.

Under heavy pressure from the Karelian Army in the north and a considerably reinforced German Heeresgruppe Nord in the south, the Soviets decided to pull back. Viborg was recaptured by the Finns on 29 August. However, a repeated German demand for a Finnish drive towards Leningrad on 31 August coincided with the arrival of the first British convoy, "Dervish", to the Soviet White Sea port of Arkhangelsk. The timing could not have been worse for the Germans, and the request was once again declined.

With "Dervish" – the first of many British and American convoys with Lend-Lease material to the Soviets – arrived 60 fighter planes from United Kingdom. These included twenty-one Curtiss P-40 Tomahawks and thirty-nine Hawker Hurricane IIBs. The Tomahawks arrived

PHOTOS FROM THE FINNISH FRONT IN 1941.

	1.	5.
2.	3.	6.
4.		7.

1. Soviet marines holding the Litsa line against the Germans.

2. Gallows humor among Finnish soldiers during the extended positional warfare in Karelia. (Photo: SA Kuva.)

3. Finnish armored forces enter the burning Soviet city of Petrozavodsk. (Photo: M. Manninen.)

4. Destroyer Razumnyy of the Soviet Northern Fleet. This ship's main offensive armament consisted of four 130mm guns, six torpedo tubes and 25 depth charges.

5. An Italian-manufactured Fiat G-50 fighter from the Finnish fighter squadron Lentolaivue LLv 26. With a maximum speed of 470 km/h and an armament of two 12.7mm machine guns, the G.50 was roughly equal to the Soviet I-16. The swastika was the national insignia of the Finnish Air Force. It was adopted from Swedish count (and later Nazi activist) Eric von Rosen, who in 1918 donated a military plane to the "Whites" in the Finnish Civil War. (Photo: SA Kuva.)

6. Finnish artillery. The Finnish Army was far better equipped in 1941, as compared to the situation during the Winter War. (Photo: SA Kuva.)

7. Wounded Finnish soldiers are evacuated in an ambulance train. The Finnish army losses in 1941 were very heavy – 25,000 killed and 50,000 wounded, 14 per cent of the strength of the entire armed forces. (Photo: SA Kuva.)

Between the fall of 1941 and the summer of 1944, the Soviet-Finnish front was locked into a positional warfare. Finnish soldiers at the frontline. (Photo: SA Kuva.)

together with the American test pilot Lieutenant Hubert Zemke, and were sent southward to Moscow's defense. The Hurricanes arrived with pilots from RAF 151 Wing's 81 and 134 squadrons, who were to operate alongside with the Soviets in the Murmansk area for two months, and then hand over their machines to the Soviets.

Although Finland had officially turned down the request for an attack aimed at Leningrad, their Karelian Army was ordered to cross the 1939 border when this was reached on 2 September, and advance to a position at Beloostrov, just 15 kilometers from Leningrad's northern outskirts. The battle of Beloostrov began on 3 September and raged on for several weeks; in spite of Russian claims to the contrary, the town remained in Finnish hands until 1944.

Meanwhile a new Finnish offensive was opened to the east of Lake Ladoga with the aim of reaching River Svir and cutting off the Stalin Canal and the Kirov railway, thus contributing to Hitler's new plan to strangle Leningrad; both of these transport routes were of utmost importance to the supply of Leningrad.

The attack into Soviet East Karelia on 4 September was initiated by the heaviest artillery barrage ever laid by Finnish forces. With Soviet 7th Army weakened through the transfer of 1st Tank Division to the endangered Leningrad sector, the Finns were able to achieve a major breakthrough.

On 5 September the town of Olonets was reached.* On 7 September the leading Finnish forces reached River Svir, which connects lakes Ladoga and Onega. Thus the Stalin Canal was severed. The next day, the Kirov railway was also cut when the Finns occupied the northern end of the railroad bridge over the Svir. Thus they had completed their part of the plan to strangle Leningrad.

The battle along the Soviet-Finnish border in 1941 finally ended in a stalemate. It had cost both sides dearly. The Soviets recorded 32,470 killed, 66,660 missing in action and 90,936 wounded or sick soldiers during the battle on the Finnish front in 1941. The Finnish and German losses amounted to nearly 100,000 men – 75,000 Finnish (including 25,000 killed) and 21,500 German.[25]

The air war over Karelia in 1941 resulted in a loss of 221 Soviet aircraft, including 107 in air combat.[26] Most of these were due to Luftflotte 5, which recorded 89 own planes destroyed or severely damaged due to enemy action in the air (including at least 44 to Soviet fighters, 21 through anti-aircraft fire, and 23 to unspecified causes).[27] The Finnish Air Force recorded 54 combat losses in 1941.[28]

Following these bloody battles, a positional warfare which would last for nearly two years commenced along the Soviet-Finnish front.

* Annexed by Finland, this town was renamed first into Aunus, and in 1943 into Aunuksenlinna.

14: THE FINAL ATTEMPT AGAINST LENINGRAD.

"I have visited many divisions and everywhere I saw a strong determination and confidence, a desire to fight, and a firm decision not to give up one more meter of our ground to the enemy."

– Soviet reporter Pavel Luknitskiy, 18 September 1941.

Following bloody battles in August 1941, the Soviets had managed to evacuate their 8th Army from Estonia to a bridgehead on the southern shore of the Gulf of Finland at Oranienbaum – between Leningrad and Narva – while the Leningrad Front constructed by the splitting of the Northern Front into the Leningrad and Karelian fronts on 23 August) held back the Germans south of Leningrad and along River Volkhov in the east.

The main battle at Lake Ilmen, where River Volkhov flows out to the north, ended in a stalemate and the bulk of Heeresgruppe Nord and Luftflotte 1 were concentrated for the final attack against Lenin's City. As we have seen in the previous chapter, the attack against Leningrad was de facto initiated by the Finns – although they had told the Germans that they would not do so. The Finnish attacks against Beloostrov, just 15 kilometers north of Leningrad, on 3 September and against River Svir on the following day preceded Heeresgruppe Nord's final attack against Leningrad. This was initiated through "softening up" attacks from the air. On 6 September, Luftflotte 1 – mustering both Fliegerkorps I and the reinforcement from Luftflotte 2, Fliegerkorps VIII – conducted 1,004 sorties. Of these, 186

were brought to bear upon a sector of only 25 square kilometers.

Most of these air attacks could be conducted without being intercepted by Soviet fighters. By concentrating two whole Fliegerkorps in the Leningrad sector, the Germans managed to reach a numerical superiority in the air. When the offensive against Leningrad opened, Luftflotte 1 mustered 481 aircraft – 203 bombers, 60 Stukas, 166 fighters, 39 Zerstörer, and 13 long-range reconnaissance aircraft – to which the Army reconnaissance aircraft should be added. To counter them, the air forces of the Leningrad Front and the Red Banner Baltic Fleet had 420 planes – 288 fighters, 122 bombers and 10 Shturmoviks.[1]

Heeresgruppe Nord attacked on 8 September, with Panzergruppe 4 in the center, flanked by the 18. Armee to the left and XXXIX. Armeekorps of the 16. Armee to the right. Under the pressure from Fliegerkorps VIII's Stukas and XXXIX. Armeekorps, Soviet 54th Army was pushed out of Schlüsselburg on the southern shore of Lake Ladoga. Thus Leningrad was isolated from the Soviet hinterland. The focus of the battle was now shifted directly toward the city of Leningrad itself.

In the afternoon of 8 September, Luftflotte 1 began to bomb the city in order to soften up the defenses before the next German ground attack. The bombers continued to arrive throughout the night. From 1855 hours onward, 27 Ju 88s dropped 6,327 incendiary bombs, which caused 183 individual fires, of which the largest were in the Badayevo warehouses, in which Leningrad's entire-sugar reserve of 2,500 tons was set ablaze. A second air attack followed at 2235 hours. These were the first of several hundred raids against Leningrad. Even if the bomber forces available were considerably smaller than those engaged against London the previous year, the Germans made a great effort to destroy Lenin's city from the air. Karl Gundelach, who flew a He 111 in KG 4 during the war, wrote, "Frequently, the crews are launched twice a night against Leningrad."[2]

On 9 and 10 September, over 900 bomber sorties were flown. But 7 IAK of Leningrad's Air Defense had been bolstered by five new fighter regiments, and the fighting in the air became harder than before. On 10 September, the LaGG-3 pilots of 5 IAP/VVS KBF carried out five to seven combat sorties each, and claimed five victories against four

German troops with an MG 34 machine gun advance during street fighting. (Photo: Via Daniel Johansson.)

A Panzer IV of German 12. Panzer-Division enters Schlüsselburg. This strategically important town on the southern shore of Lake Ladoga, east of the Neva River, was captured by the Germans on 8 September 1941. XXXIX. Armeekorps, to which 12. Panzer-Division belonged, was shifted from Panzergruppe 3. to 16. Armee in late August 1941, and took part in the battle south of Lake Ilmen on 26 August 1941. By that time, 12. Panzer-Division had been severely depleted. Of 32 Panzer IV's at hand in June 1941, only nine remained on 26 August, and of 109 Panzer 38(t), there were only 42 left. However, the divisional commander, Generalmajor Josef Harpe, was awarded with the Knight's Cross on 13 August. Later, 12. Panzer-Division took part in the offensive towards Tikhvin, for which Harpe received the Oak Leaves on 31 December 1941. Following this battle, the badly depleted division was pulled out of combat to rest and refit. (Photo: Via Daniel Johansson.)

own aircraft destroyed or severely damaged.[3] Five I-16 pilots of 195 IAP engaged fifty bombers escorted by Bf 109s and claimed five shot down, including two by Leytenant Ivan Pidtykan, without own losses.[4] In one of the fiercest aerial

A Soviet 7.62mm Degtyaryov anti-aircraft machine gun position near Leningrad. (Photo: Via Artem Drabkin.)

clashes on the 10th, four I-16 pilots from 191 IAP attacked a large formation of Ju 87 Stukas and Messerschmitt Bf 109s near Ropsha, claiming six victories without loss. Counted among the downed Stuka airmen was Gefreiter Erich Peter, a newcomer in 3./StG 2, who had achieved considerable success during his first month of first-line service. Peter survived but was seriously injured. At least two more StG 2 Ju 87s are believed to have been shot down in this scrap. During another air combat on 10 September, Starshiy Leytenant Aleksey Storozhakov of 154 IAP was shot down and killed by a Messerschmitt. Storozhakov had been credited with eight individual and three collective kills, including one air-to-air ramming.

While these fierce air combats raged on 10 September, General Armii Georgiy Zhukov flew in to the besieged Leningrad to organize the city's defense. The transport plane that flew him across Lake Ladoga only barely escaped getting shot down by a group of Bf 109s.

The main attack against Leningrad the city commenced on 11 September, with German troops advancing into the breaches created by Luftflotte 1 bombers. Krasnoye Selo, just 15 km from the shore of the Gulf of Finland, west of Leningrad, fell to the attackers. In the Kremlin, Stalin panicked. "We might have to give up 'Peter' [Leningrad]," he yelled.

A group of Germans tanks during a pause in the fighting. To the left a Panzer I, and in front of it a Panzer II. (Photo: SA Kuva.)

But the Soviet soldiers and airmen fought on with furious determination. Throughout 12 September, the German ground troops lamented incessant Soviet air attacks against their artillery positions and marching columns.[5] Most of these were quick strikes by fighter-bombers, which had often left the scene by the time German fighters appeared. Also on 12 September, Soviet naval fighter ace Kapitan Petr Brinko shot down a Junkers 88.

Brinko was a veteran of the combats against the Japanese at Lake Khasan and Khalkhin Gol in 1938 and 1939, and had participated in the Winter War against Finland. During the first months of the 1941 war with Germany and Finland, he had operated over Hanko and Tallinn, reaping large successes. For this he was appointed a Hero of the Soviet Union on 17 July. The Ju 88 that he shot down on 12 September was his 15th aerial victory, making him the top scoring Soviet fighter ace to date. But he would not

live to see his 26th birthday on 17 September; on 14 September, when Soviet ground troops were about to launch a counter-attack, the German observation balloon at Krasnogvardeysk, from which artillery was being directed, had to be eliminated. Brinko volunteered to carry out the mission. Flying straight into intense German anti-aircraft fire, Brinko hit the balloon's basket with a salvo of RS rocket projectiles. In the next moment, Brinko's I-16 received a direct anti-aircraft hit and crashed into a power line, killing the pilot.

With support from all available aircraft, plus the mighty guns of the KBF's heavy vessels off the coast, the Soviets drove the Germans away from Sosnovka and Finskoye Koyrovo southwest of Leningrad. The Germans replied with a furious aerial onslaught that eclipsed even the opening attack one week earlier. Luftflotte 1's bomber units alone made 606 flights on 15 September. "Bombs are

185

STUKAS VERSUS SOVIET BATTLESHIPS.

Cruiser Kirov of the Soviet Red Banner Baltic Fleet provided a valuable fire support to the defense of Leningrad through her nine 18 cm and six 10 cm guns. With ten anti-aircraft guns of between 45 and 12.7 mm and a 50 mm deck armor she was able to withstand all attempts by the Luftwaffe to sink her. Kirov was launched on 30 November 1936. In 1961 she was reclassified as training cruiser, and was scuttled in 1974. Today, two of the cruiser's gun turrets can be seen as a monument in St Petersburg. (Photo: Krigsarkivet Stockholm.)

The large warships of the Soviet Red Banner Baltic Fleet posed a great problem to the German ground forces due to their heavy guns. Thus the Luftwaffe was tasked with neutralizing this threat, and General-oberst von Richthofen ordered Stukageschwader 2 "Immelmann" to destroy the ships.

On 16 September, StG 2 was sent out over the Gulf of Finland to hunt for the Soviet ships. As he led thirty Ju 87s, Hauptmann Ernst-Siegfried Steen – III./StG 2's Gruppenkommandeur – spotted the battleship *Marat* off Leningrad. He immediately radioed an attack order and commenced diving. Before the anti-aircraft guns could open fire, a 500-kilogram bomb struck the ship. The *Marat* steamed into the naval fortress island of Kronstadt to be repaired. Meantime, two Yak-1s and four LaGG-3s of 5 IAP/VVS KBF intercepted the Luftwaffe formation, and claimed to have shot down four Ju 87s and a Bf 109, while one of the LaGG-3s force-landed with battle damage.[1] The Germans registered only one loss – a Ju 87 which received a direct AAA hit.[2]

On 21 September, another Stuka attack hit the destroyer *Steregushchiy* in Kronstadt, but the large armored vessels escaped damage. To neutralize this threat once and for all, StG 2 received a batch of 1,000-kilogram armor-piercing bombs.

Loaded with these bombs, StG 2 took off for Kronstadt at 0845 hours on 23 September. Intense anti-aircraft fire, "virtually blackening the entire sky," according to Oberleutnant Hans-Ulrich Rudel of III./StG 2, met the dive-bombers and their escorts as they approached at an altitude of 5,000 meters. While attacking the cruiser *Kirov*, Hauptmann Steen's Ju 87 received a direct hit and crashed into the water just beside the ship. Nevertheless, the remaining Stuka pilots defied all opposition and pressed home their attack. Oberleutnant Lothar Lau, the StG 2 technical officer, dived straight down against the *Marat* and managed to place his bomb directly on the deck, causing a huge fire. Another bomb caused the ammunition of the 30.5cm forward turrets to explode, with the result that the entire forecastle was blown off the great ship.

Next, Oberleutnant Hans-Ulrich Rudel scored a direct hit, causing an enormous explosion that put the 23,600-ton battleship out of action for several months. And Leutnant Egbert Jaekel scored a direct hit on the flotilla leader *Minsk*, causing it to sink. Apart from this, the destroyer *Steregushchiy* and submarine M-74 were sunk, while other bomb hits damaged the battleship *Oktyabrskaya Revolutsiya* and the destroyers *Silnyy* and *Grozyashchiy*.

As they turned away from the anti-aircraft zone after the raid, the German planes were intercepted by large formations of Soviet fighters. In the ensuing dogfight, the Soviet pilots claimed ten enemy aircraft shot down, while 13 OIAE/VVS KBF alone lost two pilots killed and one wounded.[3] Soviet anti-aircraft batteries claimed another five German planes destroyed. German loss statistics note that six Luftflotte 1 aircraft were shot down on 23 September 1941 – two Ju 87s, two Ju 88s, one Bf 109, and one Bf 110.[4] On the other hand, JG 54 reported 17 victories this day.

StG 2 continued to appear daily over Kronstadt from 25 to 28 September. Hauptmann Ernst Kupfer, of I./StG 2, displayed an almost fanatical determination to destroy the Soviet naval vessels during these final raids. After Kupfer scored a bomb strike on a cruiser on 28 September, his Ju 87 was attacked and severely damaged by Soviet fighters. He barely managed to escape and brought his airplane down in a crash landing at the German forward airfield at Krasnogvardeysk. But this did not deter Kupfer. A few hours later, he was airborne again, heading for Kronstadt with another bomb-loaded Ju 87. This time, his aircraft was hit by anti-aircraft fire and he had to perform a second forced landing. On his third mission against the same target that day, Kupfer's Stuka received a direct hit in the engine. The dive-bomber went down and crashed in a forest, seriously injuring both the pilot and the radio operator. Two months later, Ernst Kupfer was awarded the Knight's Cross. Following eight surgical operations, the stubborn Stuka pilot returned to front-line service and flew an incredible total of 600 dive-bomber missions before he was finally killed in a flying accident.

A German aerial reconnaissance plane took this photo of Marat in Kronstadt's harbor. It can clearly be seen that the entire forecastle has been blown off as a result of a hit with a 1,000-kg bomb. However, the shallow water in the basin saved the ship, and it could continue to use its twelve 30.5 cm and sixteen 11.9 cm guns against the German troops that lay siege to Leningrad. 26,900-ton Marat was an old battleship, actually a dreadnought, and had been launched before World War I as Petropavlovsk. In 1921 the Soviet government renamed it after Jean Paul Marat, one of the legendary leaders of the French Revolution. In May 1943 she was again renamed Petropavlovsk.

1 TsVMA, f. 3 GIAP.

2 Bundesarchiv/Militärarchiv RL 2 III/754-756.

3 Achkasov and Vayner, *Krasnoznanennyy Baltiyskiy flot v Velikoy Otechestvennoy voyne*.

4 Bundesarchiv/Militärarchiv RL 2 III/754-756.

Red Army troops counter-attack. (Photo: Dmitriy Baltermants.)

up one more meter of our ground to the enemy. People are ready for heroic deeds, and these are made simply, naturally and easily, with a complete selflessness and a will to victory. No one shows any doubt in our final victory; this helps people to hold out and even to be occasionally cheerful in their personal life."[7]

On the other side of the front line, a Gefreiter Kramer of 121. Infanterie-Division wrote in his diary on 19 September, "We stand before a great victory. Petersburg is expected to fall within the next few days, but the fighting is terrible. The enemy is fighting to the last drop of blood. I shall never forget the three Russians who, subjected to our intense fire, fought to their last gasp in their entrenchments."

That day was one of the worst so far for Leningrad's citizens. Between 0814 and 2300 hours, the Luftwaffe raided the city six times. Soviet fighter planes and anti-aircraft artillery claimed seventeen German bombers shot down, whereas the Germans recorded six aircraft losses.[8] On the ground, 442 people were killed or injured when a hospital was hit by two bombs.

Meanwhile, the increasing demands from the Stukas and Ju 88s for fighter escort to counter the stiffening Soviet fighter resistance over Leningrad left the VVS in control of the skies over the battlefield itself. On 22 September Major Trautloft visited the army front lines. Suddenly a soldier next to the JG 54 commander cried, "*Achtung!* Low-flying enemy aircraft at ten o'clock! Take cover!" Trautloft and the artillery officers dived for the ground as two sections of I-16 fighters came roaring in at treetop level, spraying the German trenches with machine-gun bullets. Unhurt but covered with mud, the shocked German fighter commander spontaneously exclaimed, "Where the hell are our fighters?"

The experience of weathering the plight of the ordinary *Landser* on the Eastern Front had caused Trautloft himself to express one of the most common questions in the German language on the Eastern Front during World War II.

While heavy losses caused the German ground attacks against Leningrad to slacken, the focus of the battle was shifted eastwards. In the sector east of Schlüsselburg on Lake Ladoga's southern shore, a bitter fight began to push back General Rudolf Schmidt's XXXIX. Armeekorps from the wedge at Schlüsselburg, which the Germans had driven in between Leningrad and the Soviet hinterland in the east. Soviet 54th Army attacked the German eastern flank, and the "Neva Operational Group" attacked from within the beleaguered area. Provided with quite effective air support, these Soviet counter-attacks forced 8. Panzer-Division of XXXIX. Armeekorps to retreat on 24 September. This was only achieved by using the last Soviet resources.

raining from the sky," Major Trautloft, the commander of fighter wing JG 54, wrote in his diary. "One squadron after another arrives and drops its bombs. Fighters zigzag between the bombers. All aircraft types are present: Ju 88, He 111, Do 17, Ju 87, Hs 123, Me 109, and farther above, the Hs 126 reconnaissance planes. We have to watch out so that we don't collide with each other."[6] Air reconnaissance spotted three large supply ships bound for Leningrad on Lake Ladoga. Each vessel carried a thousand tons of wheat. StG 2 appeared before the grain had been unloaded and sank two of the ships.

However, with an incredible stamina the Soviets held their positions, thwarting one German attack after another. On 18 September, Soviet reporter Pavel Luknitskiy scribbled down in his personal diary, "I have visited many divisions and everywhere I saw a strong determination and confidence, a desire to fight, and a firm decision not to give

Leytenant Vasiliy Golubev and Mladshiy Leytenant Dmitriy Tatarenko – the only pilots remaining of the group of six from naval fighter squadron 13 OIAE/VVS KBF that had been stationed on Komendantskiy Airfield in Leningrad eight days earlier – contributed by carrying out eight sorties each on 24 September. Led by Starshiy Leytenant Aleksandr Avdeyev, a formation of I-153 biplanes from 153 IAP fell upon a German motorized column on the eastern outskirts of Leningrad and shot up more than ten vehicles.

Countering these air attacks, Luftwaffe fighter group III./JG 27 suffered a heavy loss on 25 September: "Ratas and ground-attack aircraft were attacking," wrote Hans Ring and Werner Girbig in the chronicle of JG 27. "The Gruppe is airborne to meet the enemy. When the Messerschmitts landed following this combat, Oberfeldwebel [Franz] Blazytko is missing. Later, it was found out that this outstanding airman and victor in twenty-nine aerial combats had fallen into Russian captivity."[9] The Soviet fighter pilot Vasiliy Golubev describes what most likely was Franz Blazytko's last fight. On 25 September, Leytenant Mikhail Klimenko led two Il-2 Shturmoviks – the only aircraft remaining of 57 PShAP/VVS KBF) on a ground-attack mission in the Ivanovo area. Fighter protection was provided by the "last two" Ishaks of 13 OIAE/VVS KBF, which were piloted by Golubev and Tatarenko. The Shturmoviks flew at treetop level, with the I-16s positioned roughly a thousand feet above them as top cover. Suddenly four Bf 109s fell upon them.

The German fighters split into two-plane Rotte formations, one attacking the fighter cover and the other going after Klimenko's Ilyushins. Mladshiy Leytenant Tatarenko was presented with an easy target as the latter Bf 109s came diving just beneath him. The first burst from his guns was a direct hit. The leading Bf 109 never pulled out of its final dive and hit the ground.

Having seen their leader shot down, the three remaining Messerschmitts left the Shturmoviks and turned against the I-16s. A sudden AAA barrage saved Tatarenko and Golubev. Meanwhile, the Shturmoviks were able to reach the target area and started attacking. This was enough to persuade the German fighter pilots to disengage and leave the scene. The anti-aircraft guns, however, were not altogether a blessing to the Soviets. Leytenant Klimenko's Shturmovik received a near-miss and later belly-landed in friendly territory.[10]

With Heeresgruppe Nord's offensive grounded to a halt, Hitler decided to return Fliegerkorps VIII to Luftflotte 2. And not only that, Fliegerkorps I's III./KG 4 and KG 76, and the whole of Panzergruppe 4 also left the Leningrad front and transferred to the central combat zone, where they were designated to participate in the upcoming offensive against Moscow. General Erich von Manstein – one of the most able German Army commanders, who had led LVI. Panzerkorps through the Baltic states – was posted to the south to assume command of the 11. Armee, which had just lost its C.O.

In this situation, the counter-attacks against German XXXIX. Armeekorps south of Lake Ladoga were close to re-establishing Leningrad's overland connection with the Soviet hinterland – which would have meant a great setback for the German strategy, which was now to isolate and starve the defiant Leningrad. By this time Heeresgruppe Nord's total losses since the invasion of the USSR amounted to 60,000 men.[11]

Again, the Luftwaffe was called in to help the Army out. Historian Werner Haupt wrote: "In view of this dire situation at the end of September, the OKH ordered 20,000 men to be flown immediately to [Heeresgruppe Nord].

A well-hidden Soviet position with a Maxim machine gun. (Photo: Soviet Embassy, 1976.)

This was taken care of by the [paratroopers of the 7th Fliegerdivision]. The 250th ID – this was the Spanish "Blue Division" – which had been seconded to Heeresgruppe Mitte, was immediately stopped and turned back to the north. The 72nd ID loaded up in France with the objective of 'Leningrad'."[12]

The air transport units KGzbV 1, KGrzbV 106 and LLG 1 were instructed to take charge of this operation. I./KGzbV 1 was even brought in from Greece for this purpose.

The airlift to Lyuban was accomplished successfully – and with only limited losses among the participating transport units. Major Edgar Stentzler's Luftlande-Sturmregiment became the first German paratrooper unit to be brought into action on the Eastern Front, and it succeeded in pushing back the Soviet bridgehead at Petroshkino. The German paratroopers managed to stabilize the situation south of Lake Ladoga. The XXXIX. Armeekorps (from 2 October a Panzerkorps) was able to hold the wedge, which condemned Leningrad to starvation.

A parallel operation by Heeresgruppe Nord met with success, albeit after severe difficulties. Following the seizure of Estonia, the Germans prepared the invasion of the islands of Hiiumaa (Dagö), Saaremaa (Ösel), and Muhu (Moon) between the Gulf of Riga and the Baltic Sea. On 8 September, the operation was launched through a landing on the small islands east of Hiiumaa (Dagö). However, it would take six weeks of bitter fighting – until 21 October – before the islands were secured for the Germans.

189

Operation Typhoon.

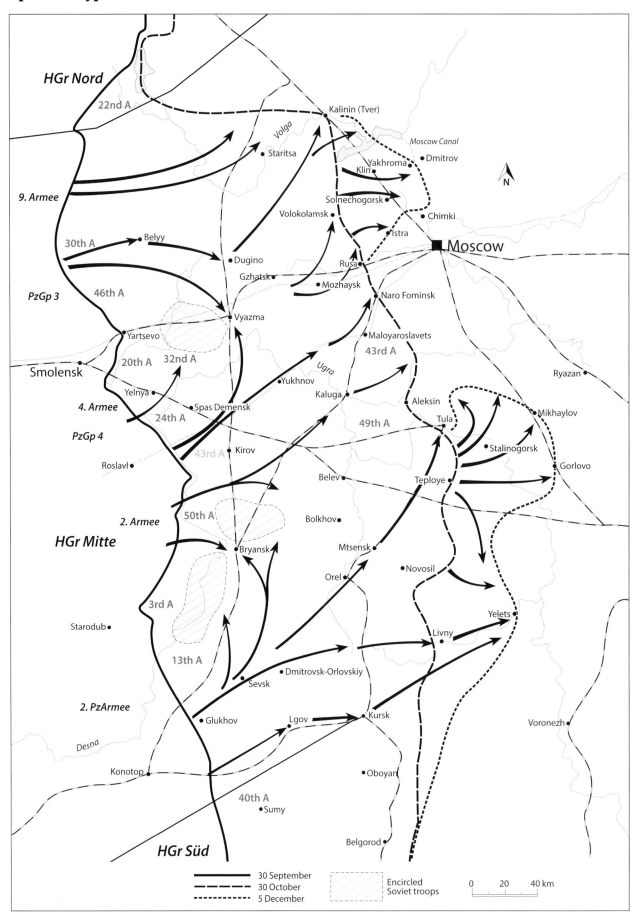

15: TYPHOON AGAINST MOSCOW.

"In the event of enemy forces arriving at the gates of Moscow,
the NKVD – Comrade Beriya and Comrade Shcherbakov – are ordered
to blow up business premises, warehouses and institutions which cannot
be evacuated, and all subway electrical equipment."

– Soviet State Defense Committee, 15 October 1941.

In late September 1941, the situation looked grim for the Soviet Union. Most of the Red Army's forces in the western parts of the USSR had vanished from the Earth. Official Soviet records indicate that in the period 22 June-30 September 1941, the Red Army sustained 2,774,765 casualties, plus materiel losses of tens of thousands of tanks, artillery pieces and mortars. The exact number of Soviet aircraft lost is unclear, but the Germans claimed the destruction of 15,311 for the same period.[1] At this point the final offensive against Moscow was launched.

Soviet troops with a mortar in combat against German forces.

Heeresgruppe Mitte was considerably strengthened and received the bulk of tank units on the Eastern Front. Luftflotte 2 – back at nominal full strength with the return of Fliegerkorps VIII from the Leningrad sector and reinforced by units from Luftflotte 4 and bombers from Luftflotte 1 – was tasked with providing the operation with air support. The operation was given the illustrative code name Typhoon (Taifun).

Operation Typhoon was planned to take place in two stages. During the opening stage, Panzergruppen 3 and 4, covered by the infantry of the 4th and 9th armies, were placed on the highway to Moscow to attack to the north and south of Smolensk, aiming at the city of Vyazma, in order to surround Soviet Western and Reserve fronts. At the same time, Generaloberst Guderian's Panzergruppe 2 was to strike from the Konotop-Romny sector, in the south, and advance in a northeasterly direction. The aim of this operation was to envelop the Bryansk Front, which had been severely crippled by Guderian's troops in the Battle of Kiev. Following the planned annihilation of the three Soviet fronts, the second stage of Operation Typhoon was to be aimed at the direct capture of Moscow. The ancient city was not only the Soviet capital, it was also the most important Soviet communications hub. The Germans assumed that the seizure of Moscow would deal a death blow to Soviet morale and ability to organize resistance and one from which the USSR would not be able to recover.

On paper, the troop strength of both sides was more or less equal: The three Soviet fronts had 1,250,000 men against Heeresgruppe Mitte's 1,183,000.[2] However, while the Germans concentrated their forces, the Soviet units were widely dispersed deep into the rear area, creating a German numerical superiority at the front. Not only was Panzergruppe 4 shifted from Heeresgruppe Nord to the center of Heeresgruppe Mitte for Operation Typhoon, two completely fresh Panzer divisions, the 2nd and 5th, were also released from Germany to bolster the strength of Panzergruppe 3 and 4 respectively. Out of slightly more than 2,000 German tanks and assault guns on the Eastern Front on 30 September 1941, 1,800 were assigned to Heeresgruppe Mitte.

Against these, just 939 tanks remained in the three Soviet fronts.[3] Few of the Soviet tanks were still of modern types: out of Western Front's 477 tanks, 21 were KVs and 51 T-34s, while two-thirds were light T-26 tanks.[4] Altogether, the three Fronts were able to muster no more than a total of 133 T-34s.

Only in the air were the two sides of about the same strength – with around 550 serviceable aircraft each – and that would also characterize the fighting during the first days.[5]

The Bryansk Front, formed only a few weeks previously, was commanded by General-Leytenant Andrey Yeremenko. The Reserve Front had been commanded by Marshal Semyon Budyonnyy since 12 September, when he had succeeded Zhukov in this position after being removed from the post of commanding the Southwestern Direction. From 12 September the Western Front was commanded by General-Polkovnik Ivan Konev, when Marshal Timoshenko had been sent to replace Marshall Budyonnyy.

As a consequence of the prolonged battles in the previous months, Operation Typhoon was opened just when the autumn set in – with its implications to movements on the roads. In the third week of September, the first frost set in, and when it thawed, the dirt roads turned into deep mud. Hence, the Germans rushed the commencement of Typhoon. When Guderian's Panzergruppe 2 opened its attack from the Konotop-Romny sector in the south on 30 September, the whole force was not yet in its departure position. Thick morning fog hardly permitted any air activity. But the roads in the area were still dry and the vanguard force, Kampfgruppe Eberbach under Oberst Heinrich Eberbach – consisting of elements of 4th Panzer Division – made a rapid advance against only weak resistance. On the evening of 30 September, Eberbach's troops had pushed 25 kilometers deep into Soviet defenses. The next day the weather cleared and Luftflotte 2 could be dispatched. With the support of Stukas, Sevsk was captured and the Kampfgruppe surged forward to Dmitrovsk-Orlovskiy, another 60 kilometers to the northeast. Thus the communications between Bryansk Front's 13th Army and "Operational Group Yermakov" were severed.

The following three nights, German bombers attacked Moscow, where they again encountered a heavy AAA barrage.[6] These air attacks contributed to increased worries in the Soviet capital, and were of great concern to Stalin.

On 2 October, the crisis multiplied as Soviet Western and Reserve fronts were attacked by Heeresgruppe Mitte's other forces east of Smolensk. With clear skies, Luftflotte 2 conducted a total of 1,387 sorties throughout the day, directed against troop concentrations, artillery positions and marching columns.[7] With Soviet artillery silenced through these German air operations, Panzergruppe 3, to the north of Smolensk, was able to advance rapidly towards the southeast and cut the connection between Western Front's 19th and 30th armies straightaway on the first day.

A German halftrack drives past a soldier's grave.
(Photo: Hannes Trautloft.)

Red Army soldiers in close-quarter fighting with submachine guns and hand grenades. The submachine gun is of the model PPSh-41, which reached the front line troops in the Fall of 1941.
(Photo: Dmitriy Baltermants.)

These T-34 tanks were abandoned, possibly due to a lack of fuel, and fell into German hands. (Photo: Hannes Trautloft.)

Generaloberst Erich Hoepner's Panzergruppe 4, grouped on the western side of River Desna southeast of Smolensk, was the strongest among the German forces in Operation Typhoon: It had eleven divisions, including five Panzer – with altogether 765 operational tanks, including over 300 Panzer IIIs and 75 Panzer IVs. They were opposed only by the Reserve Front's 43rd Army, with four rifle divisions, with on average less than 2,000 men and one anti-tank gun per kilometer of front. The German tanks were able to ford the shallow Desna river, and made a rapid advance towards the northeast. The aim was to link up with Panzergruppe 3 in the Vyazma area, 150 kilometers to the northeast.

Further to the south, Panzergruppe 2 split its forces in two directions – towards Bryansk in the north, with the aim of enveloping the Bryansk Front in conjunction with German 2. Armee; and, with Kampfgruppe Eberbach in the lead, towards Orel in the northeast.

With the cohesion of the various armies breaking down, the Soviets realized that much depended on their aviation. Western Front's Air Force was backed up by five Long-Range Aviation wings and several aviation regiments from the Moscow Military District, detached from the 6 IAK/PVO and GKO reserve air groups. The Stavka's 6 RAG – with two fighter regiments, one Shturmovik regiment, and a light bomber regiment with single-engine biplanes – arrived to reinforce the Bryansk Front's depleted aviation.

In daylight, the Soviets dispatched formations of three to six aircraft in incessant low-level attacks against the panzer spearheads. After only the first day of the offensive, the German fighter bases had been left too far behind the most advanced panzer spearheads. This was one of the Blitzkrieg's dilemmas: In order to sever the Soviet supply lines, the armored columns raced far ahead of the infantry, leaving large numbers of Red Army units behind in a far from cleansed area. At noon on 2 October, forty Pe-3 twin-engined fighters of 95 IAP and sixty fighters of 27 and 120 IAP were dispatched against Kampfgruppe Eberbach. The twin-engine Petlyakov bombers struck first, followed by rocket-firing I-153s. In thirty minutes the Soviet airmen claimed the destruction of thirty trucks and forty-three tanks. Even if this is a wild exaggeration, it clearly was a Soviet success; more so since no German fighters appeared on the scene. Soviet fighters also engaged the Luftwaffe heavily in the air. Luftflotte 2 lost 18 aircraft in combat on 2 October, while its fighters succeeded in claiming no more than eight victories.[8] In response to the mounting Soviet air activity, Fliegerkorps II's bombers were called upon to carry out a number of attacks against the airfields at Orel on 2 October and Kursk the next day. III./JG 3 also was moved forward to Glukhov in Panzergruppe 2's rear, and on 3 October managed to catch 74 ShAP's Il-2 Shturmoviks as these were beating up German 10th Motorized Division south of Sevsk – claiming four Shturmoviks in the process. But this did not help Kampfgruppe Eberbach in the lead, which during 3 October increased the distance to Glukhov to 200 kilometers. There were no German fighters available to intercept the three 215 ShAP Shturmoviks and six 129 IAP MiG-3s which reportedly

A column of Soviet refugees is caught up with a German Army column. (Photo: Hannes Trautloft.)

put twelve motor vehicles and at least two artillery batteries out of commission in a single attack. Panzergruppe 2 had reason to complain: "Own fighter escort lacking due to too large distance."[9]

However, the most effective air strikes were still dealt by the Luftwaffe. On 3 October, Luftflotte 2 conducted 984 combat sorties and reported the destruction of 679 enemy vehicles and the serious disruption of Soviet troop movements.[10] This enabled a small detachment from Kampfgruppe Eberbach to carry out a surprise lightning attack against the city of Orel on the same day. "Our tanks moved as fast as their engines would allow," said Feldwebel Hermann Bix, a tank commander who took part in this bold operation. "We raced across open terrain in a long line. Who dares, wins! The city of Orel was open in front of us. We fired to the left and right, kicked up a ruckus as if we were an entire tank regiment and charged into Orel in a race with the devil. We received heavy fire from anti-aircraft weaponry off to the left, but we disappeared between the rows of houses in the blink of an eye. Perplexed soldiers gazed at us. We stormed past them. Over there, yes, over there… a streetcar was still running! Then everything went ass over teakettles. Trucks flipped over. Anti-aircraft guns were overrun before they could get into position. We

moved along the main street of Orel and advanced as far as the railway station, exploiting the confusion of the Russians. Everyone was fleeing in the direction of Tula. Orel was ours!"[11]

Yeremenko and the rest of his Bryansk Front headquarters only narrowly managed to escape from the city. With all telephone lines to the headquarters severed through the fall of Orel, the Bryansk Front became leaderless in this critical situation.

Meanwhile, north of Panzergruppe 2, Hoepner's Panzergruppe 4 made a breathtaking advance against only weak troops of the Reserve Front, whose command left much to be desired. The Front commander, Marshal Semyon Budyonnyy, not only failed to get a grip on the situation, he also made the mistake of visiting the 43rd Army's headquarters, where he became temporarily trapped through the rapid German advance, and was unable to lead his forces during the first crucial days. On 3 October, 10. Panzer-Division in the vanguard of Hoepner's forces reached Ustrozheno, 40 kilometers from its point of departure on the previous day.

The Soviet aviation continued to be a serious opponent. On 3 October, one of the major aces of JG 51, Oberfeldwebel Heinrich Hoffmann, was lost. Hoffmann took off for his

194

last mission at 0830 hours[12] and claimed his 63rd and last victory against an "I-18" south of Yelnya, after which he was shot down – reportedly in combat with an Il-2. It is possible that he fell prey to 233 IAP's Starshiy Leytenant Sergeyev, who claimed a Bf 109 (his first victory) in the same area at that time.[13] In total, 233 IAP was credited with seven aerial victories – three Ju 88s, three Ju 87s, and one Bf 109 – on 3 October.[14] On 4 October, Generaloberst Heinz Guderian himself narrowly escaped death in a strafing attack by Pe-3s.

Meanwhile, the first Soviet counter-attacks on the ground got going. LIII. Armeekorps of German 2. Armee, operating on the northern flank of Guderian's force in a pincer movement aimed at surrounding the Bryansk Front, was subjected to an attack by Soviet 108th Tank Division, which pushed 167. Infanterie-Division three kilometers back before Luftflotte 2 was brought in.[15] A total of 152 dive-bomber and 259 medium bomber sorties were flown against this counter-attack, and this saved the situation for 167. Infanterie-Division. These raids were followed up by strikes by 202 Stukas and 188 medium bombers against long supply columns in the Bryansk-Spas-Demensk area. The Luftwaffe airmen claimed the destruction of 22 tanks (including four of the very heavy KV type), 450 motor vehicles, and 3 fuel depots, and they completely routed the Soviet counter-offensive.

Early on 4 October, 48 Stukas and 32 medium bombers were dispatched against rail lines and troop movements in the Sumy-Lgov-Kursk area, where they cut the communications between the Bryansk and Southwestern fronts.[16] The importance of the role played by the Luftwaffe for Operation Typhoon is demonstrated by two cases on 4 October. The first involved Soviet 4th Tank Brigade of 1st Guards Rifle Corps, which dispatched its brand new T-34 tanks in a counter-attack against the 4. Panzer-Division of Guderian's 2. Panzerarmee (the new designation of Panzergruppe 2) at Mtsensk.*

Polkovnik Mikhail Katukov, the commander of the tank brigade, described the battle: "In the gray, rainy morning a column of German tanks crept along the road to Mtsensk. Armored troop carriers towing anti-tank guns were in the lead. Behind them followed tanks, and behind them were armored troop carriers with infantry. Starshiy Leytenant A. Burda, commanding the T-34 company in ambush position, waited until the column had passed. Then his tanks opened fire. Several enemy vehicles exploded and others turned back, exposing their vulnerable rear to our guns. Pieces of destroyed vehicles flew through the air. The Nazis panicked.

"At this moment, Leytenant Lavrinenko's group of four T-34 intervened and also opened fire against the Hitlerites, and Leytenant A. M. Kukarkin began to shoot along the column of Hitlerites. Standing on Kukarkin's tank, the assistant politruk Bagurskiy fired at the fleeing Fascists, first with a rifle, then with his pistol. He caught sight of a fat officer who, breathing heavily, tried to escape from a tank.

The remnants of a fallen Red Army soldier on the road to Moscow. (Photo: Dmitriy Baltermants.)

* Panzergruppen 1 and 2 were designated Panzer armies in October 1941, while Panzergruppen 3 and 4, subordinated to 9. and 4. armies respectively, retained their old designations until January 1942.

Bagurskiy jumped off the tank and shot down the Fascist. He then searched the corpse and found important documents that revealed the enemy's plans to us.

"Almost the entire enemy column was wiped out. However, some of the Hitlerites tried to escape into a little valley. But there they came across Petr Molchanov's tank, which stood in an ambush position. Again heavy losses were inflicted on the enemy. As usual in similar situations, the Hitlerites requested assistance from their aviation. But when nine Junkers arrived, Burda had moved his company to the forest near the village of Kofanov. Having dropped their bombs over the canopy without inflicting any harm, the German planes left. Meanwhile, Lavrinenko's group of tanks had penetrated the enemy's rear area, and hardly surprising, six newly arrived enemy aircraft mistook them for their own. Our men laid a cloth on the grass to indicate 'friendly forces,' and the trick succeeded. The German pilots waggled their wings and departed. The outcome of this combat raised the mood among all the men in the unit." [17]

Thus, with the absence of any effective intervention from the Luftwaffe, T-34s and KVs were able to inflict considerable losses on their enemy. Farther to the north on that same day, Soviet 128th Tank Brigade attacked 6. Panzer-Division. This German division was part of Panzergruppe 3's LVI Panzerkorps, whose task it was to advance southeastwards to envelop the Western Front in the area west of Vyazma. The other division of the Panzer corps, 7. Panzer-Division, was unable to participate owing to fuel shortage, so the 6th was left alone.

Seven of 128th Tank Brigade's tanks were heavy KVs. Political Instructor Ivan Soldatov, commissar of the brigade's 1st Company, led two of these that in a space of twenty minutes knocked out five German tanks.[18] In fact fifteen of 6. Panzer-Division's tanks were put out of action.[19] But then the Luftwaffe arrived. While a screen of anti-tank guns and arriving infantry managed to halt the 128th Tank Brigade, the air attacks prevented the Soviets from bringing in reinforcements. In just two days, the 128th Tank Brigade lost 60 per cent of its strength, mainly

After the collapse of the Western, Reserve, and Bryansk fronts in October 1941, hundreds of thousands of Soviet prisoners of war were forced to march long distances to POW camps.

The Panzer III of Knight's Cross holder Oberleutnant Hans-Detloff von Cossel (standing next to the tank) of 4. Panzer-Division during Operation Typhoon.

due to air attacks. In total, Luftflotte 4 carried out 958 sorties on 4 October, while the Soviet aviation only managed to perform 328.

Meanwhile Luftwaffe transport planes flew in 55 cubic meters of fuel to 7. Panzer-Division, thus enabling this division to join the offensive on 5 October.

As the Soviet lines of communication broke down following the rapid advance of the panzer units deep into the Soviet rear area and the devastating blows by the Luftwaffe, the Red Army came to rely completely on air reconnaissance. But the full dimension of the impending disaster was not discovered by the Soviets until it was too late.

On 5 October, a Pe-2 reconnaissance crew discovered a 15-kilometer-long German tank column – the 10. Panzer-Division of Hoepner's Panzergruppe 4 – which was approaching Yukhnov from the southwest. The aim was to meet the 6. and 7. Panzer divisions of Panzergruppe 3 east of Vyazma.

But the new Chief of the Soviet General Staff, Marshal Boris Shaposhnikov, doubted the report. Although two further reconnaissance missions by fighter pilots from 120 IAP, who swept over the column at low altitude, confirmed this report, it was dismissed as "false" by the Soviet High Command. Polkovnik Nikolay Sbytov – the commander of Moscow Military District's Air Force – who had forwarded the report, was interrogated by the NKVD and accused of being a "panic-monger."[20] Only when 10. Panzer-Division seized Yukhnov – in actuality in the forenoon of 5 October, but it took several hours for this news to get through to the Soviet High Command – was Sbytov saved from being court martialled and possibly even shot.

Suddenly it dawned on the Stavka that the pincers were closing behind the bulk of the Red Army forces charged with defending Moscow. All VVS units were launched

to confront Panzergruppe 4. On 6 October, all available aircraft, ranging from Il-2 Shturmoviks to biplane trainers converted to light bombers, took off in the fog and attacked the German troops in the Yukhnov sector. The Soviet airmen managed to destroy a bridge over the Ugra River, but were met with strong enemy fighter opposition. The German fighters and ground-attack units had begun to employ a "leapfrogging" method to provide the rapidly advancing panzer spearheads with air cover. Aircraft detachments from these Luftwaffe units were shifted to forward airstrips in not sufficiently "cleared" areas close to the most forward troops in daytime. There they were supplied from the air by Ju 52s, and in the evenings the aircraft were flown back to the main bases. Although this took a severe toll on the rate of serviceability in these units, it gave the panzer troops an improved air support. Major Günther Lützow, who commanded both JG 3 and JG 51, was able to increase his personal victory tally to 76 by attaining four kills on 5 October.[21]

Hauptmann Gordon Gollob's II./JG 3 was particularly successful against the new Pe-2s, claiming four of 173 BAP's Petlyakovs on 6 October, of which two fell before the guns of Hauptmann Gollob's Bf 109 – his fifty-second and fifty-third victories. 215 ShAP's Leytenant Aleksandr Novikov reportedly sacrificed his life by crashing his Il-2 against German ground troops after it had been shot down in flames.[22]

Meanwhile, to the south, TB-3s from the DBA and PS-84s (license-built DC-3s) of MAGON GVF – a Special Purpose group of the civil air fleet – were employed to fly en masse to meet the German advance from Orel. Between 4 and 6 October, they flew 5,500 troops and 13 tons of ammunition to the Mtsensk sector, northeast of Orel. These forces formed the nucleus of the 1st Guards Rifle Corps.

197

On 6 October, the 4th Tank Brigade of 1st Guards Rifle Corps again dispatched its T-34s against the 4. Panzer-Division of Guderian's 2. Panzerarmee at Mtsensk. Brigade commander Katukov described the battle in a report: "Leytenant Kukarkin's T-34 closed the distance to 600-800 m and opened fire. With the first three shots, the gunner Serzhant Ivan Lyubushkin destroyed three Fascist tanks and hit another vehicle with a fourth shell.

"Almost all of the German tanks opened fired at the T-34. One of the shells hit its target and pierced the side hull. Our tank was covered with smoke. But Lyubushkin still fired. Another shot, and another tank was destroyed. Kukarkin ordered to the driver Fyodorov to reverse – the German tank shells were not dangerous for the T-34 at long ranges. As we discovered afterwards, the driver was wounded by shell fragments, but overcame the pain and drove the vehicle backward to the forest. When the tank stopped, Lyubushkin opened fire once again. The Fascist tankists began to leave the scene in a cowardly fashion."

Aleksandr Kukarkin and his gunner Lyubushkin were credited with the destruction of nine German tanks, for which Serzhant Lyubushkin became the first man of the brigade to be appointed a Hero of the Soviet Union. Actual German losses in this engagement were ten tanks and five artillery pieces.[23] The Soviet losses were confined to two destroyed and four damaged T-34s.[24] Shortly afterwards, the 4th Tank Brigade was adopted as the 1st Guards Tank Brigade.

Afterwards, Guderian visited the battlefield and could see with his own eyes the result of the T-34's superiority. "The tanks which were knocked out on both sides were still there," he wrote. "The Russians had inflicted a lot more damage than they had suffered themselves." Later he reported: "On 6 October, our headquarters was moved up to Sevsk, the 4. Panzer-Division was attacked by Russian tanks and had some difficult hours. This was the first time that the T-34's great superiority was clearly discovered. The division sustained heavy casualties and our planned fast advance to Tula had to be temporarily abandoned. The description of the quality and especially the new tactical use of the Russian tanks was very worrying. Our defensive weapons, when available, were only effective against the T-34 when the situation was unusually advantageous. The short gun of the Panzer IV was only effective when attacking the T-34 from the rear and at short range, and even then the shell had to hit the engine plates to knock it out. This required great skill from the crew to both maneuver into the right position and then fire with pinpoint accuracy. The Russians launched frontal attacks with infantry as they sent in tanks in mass formation on our flanks. They learned."

This Soviet attack also received strong aerial support. The Germans reported "heavy fighter activity" at Mtsensk.[25] Meanwhile four Il-2 pilots of 74 ShAP took part in the attack against the 4. Panzer-Division column on the road from Orel to Mtsensk, claiming to have destroyed fifteen armored vehicles and three fuel trucks in low-level bombing passes. Employed in conjunction with a well-defined tactic – going down "to the deck" when attacked by fighters to protect the vulnerable radiator in the belly

The body of an unknown man lies next to a shot down and overturned German Junkers 87 Stuka. (Photo: Pavel Troshkin)

– the Il-2 gave the Soviet ground-attack pilots a completely different chance in air combat. Unteroffizier Walter Tödt of I./JG 52 describes the Il-2's ability to withstand even heavy cannon fire: "During a return flight from the front area, Leutnant [Karl] Rung and I came across a lone Il-2. We attacked and the Ivan dived in the direction of Moscow. He was too low to permit us to attack him from below, where we could have hit his Achilles heel, the radiator. We fired from both sides, aiming at the tailfin, which blew apart. But the Il-2 kept flying! Suddenly, light anti-aircraft fire was thrown up against us, and we had to disengage at tree-top level. These birds were a most difficult target. When you attacked them from behind, the shells simply

A German halftrack moves through a completely flooded area on the road towards Moscow. (Photo: Arno Becker.)

bounced off their springy plywood fuselage. And the pilot was seated in an armored tub!"[26]

But although this combined air and armor assault shocked Guderian, the effect was nullified by the general collapse of the Soviet defense positions elsewhere. While this took place in the south, Guderian's XLVII. Armeekorps, which had veered towards the north to meet German 2. Armee, took Bryansk.

During the night between 6 and 7 October, Kapitan Ivan Flyorov's 1st Special Rocket Artillery Battery, which had brought the Katyusha rocket batteries into action for the first time in July, was ambushed and annihilated by German 5. Panzer-Division near Ugra, southwest of Vyazma – with Flyorov getting killed.*

The following day, Luftflotte 2 employed 692 aircraft, claiming the destruction of 20 tanks, 34 artillery pieces, several bunkers, and 650 vehicles of various kinds.[27] One of the Soviet casualties was General-Mayor Mikhail Petrov, the commander of the 50th Army, who had been assigned to lead the Bryansk Front in Yeremenko's absence. He was badly injured and died three days later.

On this day, 7 October, XLVII. Armeekorps and 2. Armee met at Bryansk, and 10. Panzer-Division linked up with Panzergruppe 3 in the vicinity of Vyazma.** Thus the main forces of both the Western and the Bryansk fronts – altogether half a million troops, the bulk of the defense forces in front of Moscow – were caught in two huge traps. General-Polkovnik Ivan Konev, the Western Front's C.O., was of the opinion that "incessant withering bombing" of the Soviet troops was a major reason for the failure to withdraw the bulk of the Western Front before the German trap slammed shut in their rear.[28]

In Moscow, the Soviet leadership despaired. Marshal Voroshilov – who had been discharged from his command position in Leningrad and succeeded by Zhukov – was fighting to rehabilitate himself in the eyes of Stalin. He flew to Konev's headquarters in Mozhaysk, where he accused Konev of being a traitor. General-Polkovnik Nikolay Bulganin, a senior member of the Military Council of the Western Front who was also present, gladly supported Voroshilov in an attempt to save his own skin.

Meanwhile, Stalin called Zhukov in Leningrad and begged him to fly to Moscow. On his arrival early on 7 October, Zhukov heard Stalin instruct Lavrentiy Beriya, the head of the NKVD, to utilize his secret service abroad to try and find out whether there was a possibility of reaching a separate peace with Hitler.[29] Stalin asked Zhukov if he considered Konev to be a traitor, and ordered Zhukov to replace him in command of the Western Front. Zhukov accepted, but said that he would need Konev's skills for military purposes. Thus one of the most able Red Army commanders was saved.

Early on 8 October, Zhukov frankly reported the disastrous situation to Stalin: "The main danger now is that the roads to Moscow are left virtually without any defense!"

However, the weather also began to deteriorate. The first snow fell, and early on the 7th, the ground was covered with a white coating. A few hours later, a thaw set in, turning the dirt roads and front line airstrips into muddy quagmires.

But the Germans felt assured that the war was practically won. "We have finally and without exaggeration won this war," Generaloberst Alfred Jodl, the Chief of the OKW Operations Staff, said on 8 October. "The Russian armies have been annihilated. All that remains in Russia is policing work." a jubilant Hitler declared on the following day. Headlines in Germany's large papers on 9 October read, "The Great Hour has struck: The campaign in the East Decided!"

Eager to reach his 100th victory before the whole campaign was over, Major Günther Lützow put in a flurry of activity during those days. On 8 October, he attained his 81th through 85th victories against Soviet bombers. On 9 October, a thick fog set in, bringing down the number of Luftflotte 2 sorties to just 139 – compared with 690 on the seventh.[30] Yet Lützow was in the air again, bagging another four kills. On 10 October, Luftflotte 2 managed to carry out 537 sorties, and reported the destruction of 450 vehicles and 150 artillery pieces.[31] During the air fighting, Lützow claimed two Pe-2s for his 90th and 91st victories. II./JG 3's Hauptmann Gordon Gollob increased his tally to 58 by bringing down two Yak-1s, one of them possibly flown by Kapitan Konstantin Titenkov, a six-victory ace in 11 IAP, who got shot down and killed in his Yak-1 on that day.

Fighting spirits did indeed begin to wane on the Soviet side in the Moscow area. But there still were those who offered a frantic resistance. On 11 October snow squalls and

---

* Inhabitants from the nearby village of Bogatyr rescued the wounded survivors. However, the Germans found out about this and entered the village and killed all the injured soldiers and those who had helped them.

** From 5 October, Panzergruppe 3 was commanded by General Georg-Hans Reinhardt, the previous commander of one of the armored corps in Panzergruppe 4, after Hoth had been assigned to lead 17. Armee in the Ukraine.

Three of the most successful German fighter pilots on the Eastern Front in 1941. From the left: Oberst Werner Mölders, Major Günther Lützow, and Hauptmann Karl-Gottfried Nordmann. In July 1941, Mölders became the first pilot to reach 100 victories in World War II. Next followed the commander of JG 3, Lützow, who shot down his 100th aircraft in World War II on 24 October 1941. Nordmann commanded IV./JG 51 and had achieved 70 victories by the end of 1941. Mölders was killed in a flying accident on 22 November 1941. Lützow was posted as missing on 18 April 1945, but Nordmann survived the war and passed away on 22 July 1982, at the age of 66.
(Photo: Johannes Broschwitz via Wägenbaur.)

icy roads hampered movement on both sides. That day, a couple of BT-7 light tanks and four T-34 tanks commanded by Starshiy Leytenant Dmitriy Lavrinenko of 4th Tank Brigade once again ambushed German 4. Panzer-Division as this advanced from Orel towards Mtsensk. The driver of Lavrinenko's tank, Starshiy Serzhant Ponomarenko, described the opening of the action: "Suddenly we saw the German tanks. I stopped and we fired. In the next moment we received a hit which nevertheless failed to penetrate our armor. But next to us we could see two of our light BT tanks in flames. But a German tank also was burning. We saw one more enemy tank. It tried to escape. Another shot. A flame. Three German tanks were now burning. The crews bailed out and crawled away."

The war diary of 4. Panzer-Division noted, "The Russian tanks are led with great skill; they often pull back in order to appear again in a flank attack. Their heavy tanks inflict severe losses upon us during the course of the afternoon. As our tanks slowly move over the hill on both sides of the road, they become subject to fire from heavy tanks. One of our tanks is destroyed. … We bring an anti-aircraft gun into position on the road. … Other enemy tanks open fire and our anti-tank gun receives a direct hit. The battery commander is wounded and most of the gun crew is killed or injured. … After the third gunshot, the second anti-aircraft gun, in position to the right of the road on

the hill, also is hit and destroyed. Our own tanks withdraw from the hill. … The Russian shells explode on our side of the ridge, and we have some wounded, including Oberleutnant Esser, the adjutant of I. Abteilung/Panzer-Regiment 35."

Ponomarenko continued his account. "In 300 meters I saw one more tank, I reported my observation to Lavrinenko, and he took careful aim. The second shell destroyed this one too, his fourth in this combat." 4. Panzer-Division's war diary wrote, "After a fierce tank duel, another two of our tanks are hit and lost." By constantly moving back and forth, the four T-34s gave the impression that they were many more. "The enemy dispatches more tanks, so that we finally are up against 25 heavy tanks," was noted in 4. Panzer-Division's War Diary. "More of our tanks are hit, while our tanks are unable to do any harm to the enemy at this distance. The enemy intensifies his fire, and thus forces us to withdraw further."

Finally, the Germans managed to repel the attack in close combat, but by that time the Soviet ambush had cost them a loss of 10 tanks (including 6 irrevocably lost), two 88mm guns, two artillery pieces and over 30 personnel casualties.[32]

For the first time in the war, the Red Army forces in this sector were placed under very competent command also. General Armii Georgiy Zhukov had taken over the

Western Front on 10 October. This was reinforced by the influx of the disbanded Reserve Front – whose incompetent commander, Budyonnyy, was sent "into the cold." One week later, the northern armies of the Western Front (the 22nd, 29th, 30th and 31st) were siphoned off to the new Kalinin Front, which was placed under General-Polkovnik Ivan Konev.

Reinforced by four bomber regiments from the Central Asian Military District on 10 October, the Moscow Military District initiated an offensive against Luftflotte 2's air bases. This began on 11 October, when Il-2 pilots from 214 ShAP and 288 ShAP defied the snow flurry to attack the airfield at Dugino just as the inspector of the Fighter Air Arm, Oberst Werner Mölders, arrived for an inspection. III./JG 27 scrambled, and Oberleutnant Erbo Graf Kageneck blew three Il-2s out of the sky. In fact, five Il-2s were lost, and with one of them 214 ShAP's commander, Mayor Shchelkunov, was killed.[33]

During these operations, the Soviets had the advantage of raiding air bases where they themselves had been stationed only a few weeks earlier. Hence the attacking air crews had a good picture of the targets they were sent against. An NCO from the ground crew of I./JG 52, stationed at Dugino, wrote: "12 October ... Several Russian bombers attacked us again today. They set fire to a fuel depot, and this in an outrageously brazen manner which clearly showed that they were well acquainted with our airfield."[34] But the whole airbase offensive was characterized by poor bomb-aiming – the direct and indirect results of the punishment the VVS units had taken at the hands of German fighters. No aircraft were destroyed on the ground at Dugino, where I. and II./JG 52 reported forty Bf 109s serviceable on 12 October.[35] Eight days of repeated Soviet airbase raids actually resulted in no more than a single German aircraft destroyed on the ground – a Bf 109 of 9.(H)/LG 2 at Orel on 11 October.[36]

Luftflotte 2 meanwhile continued to pounce on the surrounded Soviet troops with nearly 900 sorties on 12 and 13 October. On the twelfth, Bryansk Front's C.O., General-Leytenant Andrey Yeremenko, was severely wounded by bomb splinters and was flown out of the encirclement.[37] By 13 October, the Western Front in the northern pocket had been almost completely annihilated by Luftwaffe attacks.[38] That day, too, Kaluga, 160 km southwest of Moscow, fell to German 4. Armee.

The annihilation of the two southern pockets of the Moscow front on 17 and 20 October was the climax of Operation Typhoon. The German armies reported that 673,000 prisoners had been taken. Total losses sustained by the armies of the Soviet Western, Reserve, and Bryansk fronts between 30 September and 5 November, were 514,338 soldiers killed or missing – indicating that a fairly large amount of those rounded up by the Germans as POWs were in fact civilians.

Once again the dreadful scenes of suffering Soviet prisoners herded along the roads, with almost nothing to eat, were displayed – this time in cold weather with rain, sleet and snow on icy or muddy roads. Erwin Hackler, a soldier in German 4. Armee, describes the view that met him on one of those dismal roads: "Along the roadsides lay one horse carcass after another, slit open and swollen. They had all been shoved aside to allow our vehicles to pass. It was gruesome to watch as a column of Russian prisoners passed. They were covered with mud, wore thick blankets and had rags wrapped around their feet. They could not have been walking for so long, since the front was only ten kilometres distant. But apparently they suffered from a terrible hunger. They jumped from the column onto the horse carcasses, from which they tore large pieces of meat."[39]

In the uniform of a dead *Frontovniki* inside the "pocket" at Vyazma, a German soldier found a diary where the unfortunate man bitterly had written his final lines: "Why must we suffer like this? The Fascists show no mercy, we are running out of ammunition, we no longer have any possibility of taking care of all the wounded, and our generals are deserting us. When will all of this come to an end?" This sentiment in fact also reflected the feelings among very many people in Moscow by that time.

In the Kremlin, Stalin and the leadership were busy making preparations to leave the capital. On 15 October, the State Defense Committee issued a secret document, according to which "the Presidium of the Supreme Soviet and the top levels of Government" were to be evacuated, and "in the event of enemy forces arriving at the gates of Moscow, the NKVD – Comrade Beriya and Comrade Shcherbakov – are ordered to blow up business premises, warehouses and institutions which cannot be evacuated, and all subway electrical equipment." Stalin told Anastas Mikoyan, a member of the Soviet Politburo, that he intended to leave the capital. Government documents and signals equipment were loaded onto Stalin's train, which was waiting at one of Moscow's railway stations. That night, a car was waiting outside the Kremlin. "We were driven away. Moscow was completely dark," said Nikolay Ponomaryov, Stalin's telegraphist. "The weather was wet.

The population in Moscow was mobilized to dig anti-tank ditches or, as seen in the photo, erect barricades on the streets of the Soviet capital itself. (Photo: Krigsarkivet Stockholm.)

201

I saw we were heading for the railway station. I saw the armored train and Stalin's guards walking to and fro on the platform. It became clear to me that I would have to wait for Stalin and go into evacuation with him."

The next day, 16 October, has gone down in official Soviet and Russian history as the day of the great panic in Moscow. Indeed, in certain layers of the society full-scale panic broke out, but it would be more correct to talk of the day of the Moscow rebellion – which was what contributed to stopping the panic. It began early in the morning when the Muscovites woke up to find a very strange kind of snowflakes falling down over their city: black snowflakes. It turned out to be ashes from all official documents that were burned in great heaps outside government offices. Then as the workers arrived at their factories, they were met by closed gates. Soon they began to notice more and more cars and trucks carrying the bosses with their families and valuables, heading for the highways leading out of the city.

Large crowds of factory workers and women began to gather. Screams were heard: "The rats are leaving the ship!" The first stones were hurled against the cars that passed by at high speed, splashing down the people. Fury rose. "Some workers of Factory No. 219 attacked cars with evacuees from Moscow who were traveling on the Highway," the commander of the NKVD's directorate for Moscow, Mikhail Zhuravlyov, wrote in a report: "They seized the evacuees' belongings. Six cars were thrown into a ravine."[40] Zhuravlyov's lengthy report on the events in Moscow during those days contains numerous similar accounts of an outright rebellion.

The NKVD naturally branded these actions by vast numbers of Muscovites as "anarchy" and "counter-revolutionary activity." Of course there were cases where individuals shouted anti-Semitic or anti-Communist slogans, and a significant number of panicked ordinary citizens also flocked at the railway station or began to flee out of the city. But the action taken by thousands of workers of both

Red Army soldiers west of Moscow in October 1941. The gun is a DP-27 light machine gun, a 7.62mm calibre Pulemyot Degtyaryova Pekhotnyy ("Degtyaryov's infantry machine gun").

sexes was carried out in a rage over the "rats" that were "abandoning the ship." Even in his NKVD report, Zhuravlyov admitted that "the workers were furious." Journalist Nikolay Verzhbitskiy wrote in his diary, "Everyone is boiling with indignation. They make their voices heard. They shout out loud that they have been betrayed, that 'the captains are the first to leave the ship,' and that the leaders had escaped with all their valuables. People are saying things out loud that would have brought them before a military tribunal three days ago."[41]

The masses flooded the streets and blocked them to the escapees. The NKVD attempted to quell the unrest with its usual methods. On 16 October, they shot down over 200 people in Moscow, the highest figure in a single day since 1938. But workers armed with hammers and spades assaulted the NKVD officials and police officers, as well as their bosses and local Party leaders.[42] This went on for four days.

Stalin must have realized that had he left Moscow, he might well have nothing to return to – either it would be in the hands of the Germans or in the hands of rebellious workers. He had just clamped down on independent action in Leningrad (see chapter 12), and now he took the decision to stay and fight. And the first fight was not against the Germans, but against the people who had taken matters into their own hands in Moscow.

Probably fearing that the rebellious masses would find leaders in previously arrested military and political leaders, the convicts in the NKVD prison Lublyanka in Moscow were sent by train to Kuybyshev on the second day of the rebellion. On 18 October, Beriya ordered the execution of twenty-eight of these – including three former Air Force commanders: Aleksandr Loktionov, Yakov Smushkevich, and Pavel Rychagov. Within the next few days, all of those and many more – in total 300 former military and political leaders – were shot by the NKVD.

On 19 October, the State Committee of Defense declared a state of siege in Moscow. Army troops were

A destroyed German Panzer III tank.

called in – a measurement of the leadership's fright, bearing in mind that this was at a stage when the German army was approaching the gates of Moscow – to take control of the streets. Tens of thousands of citizens were arrested, 40,000 were sent to prison and nearly 900 sentenced to death. On 20 October a decree dictated by Stalin was issued, warning the population that anyone breaking civil order would be arrested and brought before a military court; "provocateurs, spies and anyone propagating disorder" would be "shot on spot."[43]

Maneuvering with both repression and concessions, Stalin managed to quell the uprising. Politburo Member Anastas Mikoyan went to address the rebellious workers at the Stalin Moscow Vehicle Plant: "Comrades, why are you so outraged? Who told you the government left Moscow? Stalin is in Moscow, Molotov as well – all the people who have to be here, are here!" Aleksandr Shcherbakov, the Moscow Party Chief, also set convincing the citizens that the leadership had not given in. "We shall fight, resolutely, desperately, to the last drop of blood," he thundered. "Comrade Muscovites! Let each of you, whatever your past, whatever your work, be a soldier in the army defending Moscow from the Fascist aggressors!"

More than 600,000 people were mobilized to create a defense belt with anti-tank ditches, trenches, firing positions and barricades. Contrary to what had been the situation in Leningrad and many other cities, this was not allowed to be based on volunteers, but the people were simply conscripted into this work. But there was no need to force people. The energy of the uprising was skilfully channelled into activity for the defense against "the Fascist killers." Nearly everyone worked under fear of the approaching German army. In scenes as taken from a propaganda film, people helped each other, sharing food and shelter. Those who had come from villages in the region to work on the defense belt were given accommodation by the Muscovites. 75 per cent of those taking part in this work were women, of all ages from youngsters at school to old ladies.[44]

This great upsurge in patriotic defense activity among the masses took hold on the exhausted and demoralized soldiers who had survived the carnage at Vyazma and Bryansk. Inspired by the population in Moscow, their fighting spirits revived. A new determination to fight to the last, one more time, was born out of the rebellion in Moscow during those days.

On 7 November, Stalin used the twenty-fourth anniversary of the October Revolution to rally the people under his flag. In spite of the fact that the thunder from the guns at the front could be heard, the traditional military parade was held on the Red Square in Moscow. This time many a Red Army soldier took part in the march with his heart

Polkovnik Mikhail Katukov, the commander of Soviet 4th Tank Brigade of the 1st Guards Rifle Corps, during a field conference with his staff officers. Katukov was a veteran of the Civil War, where he had served with the new Red Army. His greatest feat during World War II was when he led the 1st Tank Army during Operation Bagration in the summer of 1944 and the Battle of Berlin in 1945. Mikhail Katukov passed away on 8 June 1976, at the age of 75.

pounding with pride and determination to fight until the last drop of blood. Stalin's speech was heard in loud speakers all over Moscow:

"Comrades, men of the Red Army and Red Navy, commanders and political instructors, men and women guerrillas! The whole world is looking to you as the force capable of destroying the plundering hordes of German invaders! The enslaved peoples of Europe who have fallen under the yoke of the German invaders look to you as their liberators. A great liberating mission has fallen to your lot. Be worthy of this mission! The war you are waging is a war of liberation, a just war. Let the manly images of our great ancestors – Alexander Nevsky, Dimitry Donskoy, Kuzma Minin, Dimitry Pozharsky, Alexander Suvorov and Mikhail Kutuzov – inspire you in this war! May the victorious banner of the great Lenin be your lodestar! For the complete destruction of the German invaders! Death to the German invaders! Long live our glorious Motherland, her liberty and her independence! Under the banner of Lenin, forward to victory!"

It was a masterful speech, and it hit home. "That day, the anniversary of our great October Revolution, I felt that it was true: We were going to beat the enemy," said Natalya Medvedev, a Moscow citizen. Gabass Zhurmatov, a Khazakian recruit, was sent straight to the front with a throbbing heart after taking part in the parade. Taking up positions on a hill in the Mozhaysk sector, his small artillery group suddenly found themselves surrounded by German troops. Having consulted his comrades, Zhurmatov radioed the command post to vector in artillery fire from another position. "Have you gone mad!" the battalion commander exclaimed back, "that is exactly your own position!" Zhurmatov retorted, "What importance do our lives have! Annihilate the enemy!" But the commander refused to kill his own men in such a way, and shortly afterward the advanced artillery group was relieved by counter-attacking T-34 tanks. Speaking about this after the war, Zhurmatov said, "This was the most terrible moment of the entire war; I shall never forget the feeling of sitting there and waiting to get killed. During those minutes, my friend Astapov's hair turned grey, and I practically lost the ability to speak for some time. Afterwards, the battalion commander asked me how I was doing. All I could say was, 'It's normal.'" [45]

On the German side, optimism soared for quite obvious reasons. "The last elite troops of the Bolsheviks have been destroyed," Feldwebel Karl Fuchs of 7. Panzer-Division wrote in his diary. "I will never forget my impression of this destruction. From now on, their opposition will not be comparable to previous encounters. All we have to do now is roll on, for the opposition will be minor." [46]

Self-assuredly, the OKL began to partly dismantle the Luftwaffe forces that had been used for Typhoon, diverting them to sectors where they were assumed to be of better use. During the following weeks, more than thirteen Gruppen departed from the Moscow front. JG 3, plus

Stab and III./JG 27, and III./JG 53 sent to Germany, from where they departed for further operations in the Mediterranean area. (II./JG 3 was first shifted to Luftflotte 4, where it bolstered Luftflotte 4 in the difficult effort to seize the Crimean Peninsula.) The elements of StG 77 that had participated with Fliegerkorps II in Typhoon were also shifted to Luftflotte 4. III./StG 1 and I./StG 2 were sent to rest. III./KG 4 and I./JG 51 were returned to Luftflotte 1, which still had some "unfinished business." I./ZG 26 was sent to Germany to reinforce the night fighter force by transforming into II./NJG 1 – leaving II./ZG 26 and II./SKG 210 as the only Bf 110-equipped close-support units in the East. Stab and I./KG 2, and KGr 100 were shifted to the West, where they were assigned to operations against British shipping. The German certainty of an imminent final victory is displayed by the fact that the whole aviation in front of Moscow was actually promised that they would be leaving. Fliegerkorps VIII was told that it would spend the New Year in Germany,[47] and the headquarters of both Luftflotte 2 and its other air corps, Fliegerkorps II, received orders to shift to the Mediterranean area. The OKL even printed a map of the how "Luftgau Moskau" (Air District Moscow) was to be geographically organized after the seizure of the Soviet capital.

The German army steadily closed in on Moscow. The dirt roads had been completely destroyed by hundreds of tanks and other heavy vehicles that had passed in both directions, and when the snow thawed, long strips of road became almost impassable streams of soft, deep mud. "Rain, rain, rain. We stand up to knees in mud on the village streets," Walter Stoll, a *Landser* in 4. Armee's 34. Infanterie-Division wrote in his diary.[48] While supply columns got stuck on the roads leading to the front, advance tank units found themselves almost completely cut off from their supply columns.

Here the Luftwaffe's large fleet of Junkers 52 transport planes came to play an invaluable role. Through air-dropped supplies, the offensive could continue unabated, albeit at a slower pace. The southern end of the outer defense belt around Moscow – the line Volokolamsk-

A Soviet workers' militia mobilized in Moscow.

Mozhaysk-Maloyaroslavets-Kaluga – had been cracked when Kaluga fell on 12 October. On the 19th, Mozhaysk, 90 kilometers west of Moscow, was captured. 45 kilometers to the southeast, the motorized 3. Infanterie-Division surged through the defense line, took Naro Fominsk on 22 October and established a bridgehead on the other side of the Nara, the last river before Moscow. "It's going well!" the men said to each other. One of the unit's regiments obliterated a weak Soviet counter-attack and took 1,700 prisoners. The POWs were found to be quite demoralized, and many could be heard shouting *Voyna kaput* – "To hell with the war!"[49]

"Weak enemy resistance," Walter Stoll noted in his diary on 22 October.[50] 34. Infanterie-Division, to which he belonged, had more casualties to diseases caused by the cold and damp weather than to enemy action in the third week of October.[51]

But just as the Germans seemed to be within reach of victory, the Soviet resistance stiffened considerably. Pushing towards Volokolamsk, 90 km WNW of Moscow, 2. Panzer-Division was drawn into what was described by the tankmen as the most fierce fighting they had so far experienced. Their opponents belonged to Soviet 316th Rifle Division, which had just recently been formed with fresh recruits. These had arrived at the front only on 12 October, and went into combat straight from the rail cars on Volokolamsk's railway station. Supported by two artillery regiments, the 316th managed to inflict bloody casualties on 2. Panzer-Division.[52] "Our own losses were also considerable," wrote General-Mayor Konstantin Rokossovskiy, the commander of 16th Army, to which the 316th Division belonged. "Gunners, infantrymen, sappers and signalmen displayed heroism on a mass scale, and thus warded off the enemy's attacks. Often the gunners continued firing even though their equipment was damaged. The infantrymen met the tanks with explosives and Molotov cocktails. The infantry units covering the artillery were killed together with the artillery soldiers, but they never abandoned their positions."[53]

Massive Luftwaffe attacks – eighteen hundred bomber sorties were flown on 22-25 October – assisted the panzer force to flush out the tenacious defenders from one position after another. On 27 October all of Volokolamsk was in German hands, after several days of fighting. But there 2. Panzer-Division shifted to defense positions.

"Continuous raining. Bad road conditions makes it possible to traverse only on the highways," the War Diary of the German High Command noted on 26 October. But the troops were pushed to continue attacking, even though the fighting became fiercer each day. On the northern flank of Heeresgruppe Mitte, Panzergruppe 3 managed to establish a bridgehead north of River Volga at Kalinin (Tver), 150 km northwest of Moscow, on 28 October. But it would come no further. On 29 October, Oberfeldwebel Kurt Warmbold, a member of the ground crew of I./JG 52 Kalinin's airbase, wrote in his diary: "This is the darkest day during our entire Eastern Campaign. The Russians have covered our airfield with systematic artillery shelling since early this morning. … The Gruppe Weiss lost seventeen aircraft in today's heavy shelling."[54]

The situation grew so desperate for the Germans that even Luftwaffe ground crews had to be dispatched in the ground fighting. One of them, Martin Remer of StG 2, recalled: "A large number of dead soldiers, Germans and Russians lay next to each other on both sides of the road, just as they had fallen. Russian women searched among the dead for their beloved husbands, who had recently been mobilized for the defense fight from the factories in Kalinin. Several were in civilian clothes or half uniformed. … There was no time to bury the dead."[55]

In his astonishment, Oberst Günther Blumentritt, Chief of Staff of 4. Armee, wrote: "The defeated Russians seemed quite unaware that as a military force they had almost ceased to exist!"

Wounded German soldiers in the mud on the Eastern Front.

On Heeresgruppe Mitte's southern flank, XXIV. Panzerkorps of Guderian's 2. Panzerarmee attacked towards the north along the highway from Orel to Moscow. The first tactical goal was Tula, a key road and rail junction 170 km south of Moscow. "It must be taken at all cost!" demanded Guderian. By that time, there was not much left of Red Army forces to defend Tula. The only Soviet army in the area was the 50th, which had been nearly annihilated in the envelopment battle at Bryansk. The poor remnants of three of its divisions, each with between 500 to 1,000 men, with very little equipment, was all in terms of regular Red Army troops that stood between XXIV. Panzerkorps, with its two panzer and one infantry divisions, and Tula.

On 29 October German infantry regiment "Grossdeutschland" and 3. Panzer-Division conducted a dazzling 20-kilometer advance and stormed Tula. But the citizens of Tula were determined not to surrender their city to the Germans. A worker's regiment from the city's factories engaged the Germans as they entered the southern workers' suburbs. German war correspondent Paul Karl Schmidt (Paul Carell) describes the fighting that erupted: "Tula lies in front of them, covered in the October evening's fog. Explosion clouds hang in the sky above the city. They fight with pistols and hand grenades, one leap after the other, man against man, through the enemy-occupied ravine. The Russians catch the hand grenades in the air and throw them back."[56]

This family of Soviet collective farmers were killed by the Germans.

Ivan Kravchenko, a 36-year old Mayor who had been appointed a Hero of the Soviet Union in 1940, took charge of the defense of Tula. The battle continued to rage, day in and day out, with the worker's regiment clinging on to their positions, while reinforcements poured in on both sides. In spite of all German efforts, Tula remained in Soviet hands, with XXIV. Panzerkorps bleeding to no avail.

By now, the Soviets had managed to halt Heeresgruppe Mitte along the entire frontline, which extended from Kalinin and 200 kilometers straight south, at a distance of 75-80 km from Moscow, and thence to Tula. The Germans attributed the atrocious state of the roads as the main reason for their sudden lack of success, and expected everything to change once these froze. On 30 October Hoepner, the commander of Panzergruppe 4, wrote in his diary, "The roads have become quagmires – everything has stopped. Our tanks are unable to move. No fuel gets through. Dear God, give us fourteen days of frost and we shall surround Moscow."

Soviet and Russian historiography has often underestimated the effect the mud season had on the German advance, while Western accounts tend to explain the German halt in late October as only due to the weather. Indeed, revitalized fighting spirits on the Soviet side in the second half of October was the direct cause of the bogging down of Heeresgruppe Mitte; had these troops remained in their demoralized state and offered only limited resistance, the Germans would have been able to enter Moscow – in spite of any road conditions. Nevertheless, it must be kept in mind that the German forces that were warded off at the gates of Moscow in late October 1941, suffered from great shortages in fuel and ammunition, owing to the extreme problems of bringing supplies forwards on the bottomless

roads. Had the entire Heeresgruppe Mitte been able to attack with all its might, the Soviet persistence would not have sufficed.

Imagining that the war would soon be over, Hitler and the Nazi leaders took further steps towards the Final Solution of what they regarded as "the Jewish problem." On 15 October the deportation of Berlin's Jews to ghettos in the East began. Ten days later, Hitler uttered that "it would be a good thing if we preceded the horror and eradicated Judaism." [57] After a visit to the ghetto in Vilnius, Propaganda Minister Joseph Goebbels dictated: "The Jews are like the lice of civilized mankind. They have got to be exterminated somehow." [58] At around the same time, Adolf Eichmann approved a proposal from Gauleiter Hinrich Lohse, appointed by Alfred Rosenberg to administer the Baltic countries, to kill Jews in Riga by mobile gas trucks. [59]

While waiting for the weather conditions to permit the resumption of the attack against Moscow, a large-scale operation against the Jewish population in Heeresgruppe Mitte's rear area was also initiated. Caught in their racial prejudices, the Germans believed that thus they would get rid of a potentially growing partisan threat against their strung out supply lines. Between 20 October and 20 December 1941, between 60,000 and 80,000 Jews were killed in Heeresgruppe Mitte's hinterland.

Even Wehrmacht units under the command of the army group's Befehlshaber des Rückwärtigen Heeresgebietes took part in these atrocities. These were so-called "security divisions" (*Sicherungsdivision*), not first-line units, and were composed of older men with only limited military training. The 707. Infanterie-Division particularly stood out among these units. On 30 October, it went into action against the Jews in Nesvizh, northeast of Baranovichi. Four thousand were killed and the surviving nine hundred herded into a closed ghetto.* Three days later, 707. Infanterie-Division assembled over one thousand Jews in the central square of Lyakhovichi, a small town near Brest, and then brought them to a sand pit near the village of Lotva, where they were all executed. The remaining Jews of the town were forced into a ghetto surrounded by barbed wire. In Slonim, west of Baranovichi, 9,000 Jews were killed by members of the same unit, in cooperation with the SD and police forces.[60]

Shmuel Ryvkin experienced one of those massacres, at Klimovichi, southeast of Mogilev: "6 November 1941 was the most horrible day. Young people were sent to work at the distillery. Under the Germans' guidance, policemen began to chase old people and children out of their homes, ordering them to take valuables and warm clothes. The sound of wailing hung over the city. Groups of Jews were taken to the garages near the hospital. Some Russians looked at this with sympathy and others, with curiosity, readily helping the police. In the outskirts of the city, behind the Kalinitsa River, near the old airport facing the village of Dolgaya Dubrava, a tank for fuel had been dug in the ground. Not long before the war, it was taken out and a huge pit remained. It was turned into a common grave. The line to the execution stretched from the garages across the bridge and up the road to the pit itself – 900 people. All around there was an open field – there was nowhere to run to. The execution went on all day long. Then those who worked in the morning were brought in. The SS men themselves did not fire – on their order, the policemen did this. Children were killed with shovels – blood was flowing on the ground."[61]

But there were also cases of individual acts of courage by German soldiers to save people from execution. A couple of such cases occurred in Klimovichi on 6 November. Alla Levina, a 15-year-old Jewish girl at the time, was warned by several German officers, who said to her: "You are young,

you have a long life ahead of you, why don't you run away? You will be shot!" On 6 November, a young German soldier took Alla, two of her sisters, Lyuba and Basya, and two girlfriends aside, gave each of them a loaf of bread, and said: "Don't go home, your relatives are no longer there. If you want to live, go wherever your feet take you. We did not see you and don't know you." This saved their lives. A young girl, Faina Manevich, was even saved at the edge of an execution pit by an elderly *Landser* who led her away by hiding her between his rifle and his arm.[62]

Future holder of the Knight's Cross with Oak Leaves and Swords, Oberleutnant Friedrich Lang of Stuka unit StG 2, told the author of a rare incident at his billeting during one such day: "We were billeted into some small wooden house in a village around 3 kilometers from the airfield. We, the officers of the 1st squadron, took possession of such a house, which was made up of an anteroom, a large room with a baking stove, a smaller room and a chamber. The grandmother of the house slept in the stove room together with her four to eight kids.

During one of the last days of our stay at this house, we returned from the airfield earlier than usual because of heavy snowfall. The woman came to meet us and seemed more excited than ever. From the flow of words that came from her lips we could understand that her dear husband, who definitely was no communist, had returned home. He had been left in the Vyazma pocket, and had made it through the woods until he arrived at his village. We had barely made the woman understand that we understood her, before she flung the door open. A man dashed into the house, threw himself on his knees and attempted to kiss my tunic. To us, his flow of words appeared as nothing but an incomprehensible sound effect. We responded to the shining faces of the family and I patted the man on his shoulder and said something, which he didn't understand anyway. The performance was over and he dashed out of the room, in the same way as he had arrived, beaming with joy, followed by his family. We never saw him again."[63]

---

* As we have seen previously (page 138), Nesvizh had been the scene of a massacre on Soviet POWs and Jews in July. But Nesvizh also saw what probably was the first among the ghetto uprisings during World War II. Following the killings in October 1941, an underground resistance movement was created under the slogan, "We shall not go like sheep to slaughter." When Germans and collaborating Belorussians stormed the ghetto in July 1942, the resistance fought back. Following this, about 25 Jews managed to escape and joined the partisans. (See Cholawski, *Soldiers from the Ghetto: The First Uprising Against the Nazis*.)

THE STARVING OF LENINGRAD.

While the Red Army was practically obliterated at the gates of Moscow in October 1941, Heeresgruppe Nord initiated an operation aimed at strengthening the isolation of Leningrad. The German and Finnish tactic was to starve the city to death. One important step in this direction was taken when the Germans managed to drive a narrow wedge to the southern shore of Lake Ladoga at Schlüsselburg east of the city. Thus Leningrad's overland connection with the inland was severed. From then on, hunger became an increasing problem for the 3.4 million people in the besieged city. With the exception of the small amounts that could be flown in, the main supply line to Leningrad was henceforth the sea lane across Lake Ladoga.

The next stage in the war against Leningrad was an offensive across the Volkhov River, which connects Lake Ladoga with Lake Ilmen. The goal of this operation was the city of Tikhvin, 70 kilometers east of the Volkhov. Located on the only road that connected Lake Ladoga with the Soviet hinterland, and with a railway leading to the lake, Tikhvin was a question of life or death for Leningrad.

The Soviet forces in the region were under severe pressure from both the Germans in the south and the Finnish Army in the north. By mid-September, they had barely succeeded in halting the Germans at River Volkhov, east of Leningrad, and the Finnish Karelian Army at River Svir, only 140 kilometers north of Tikhvin,.

On 16 October German XXXIX. Panzerkorps and I. Armeekorps attacked. Major Hannes Trautloft, the commander of JG 54, watched the onslaught from the air: "The Army's attack was preceded by a violent artillery barrage. From the air I see lots of black and brown shell craters; it looks as if the snowy landscape has got freckles. The enemy soldiers rise, clearly silhouetted against the snow, and start falling back. Our bombs fall among them."[1]

Here the Spanish so-called "Blue Division" *(División Azul)* saw its first action. Integrated into the Wehrmacht as the 250. Infanterie-Division, this – and a fighter squadron assigned to JG 51 – was the Spanish dictator Francisco Franco's contribution to Hitler's "Crusade against Communism." Commanded by General Agustín Muñoz Grandes, it was said to consist of volunteers, but in reality a large number were not particularly motivated conscripts. The Spaniards drew their first blood on 17 October, when the 269th Regiment of Colonel José Martinez

Esparza crossed the Volkhov – only to be driven back by a local Soviet counter-attack. The first fighting cost the "Blue Division" tremendous losses – 139 killed and 434 wounded.[2]

Later, a battalion of Spaniards were subject to another local Soviet counter-attack at the villages of Posselok and Possad on the east bank of Volkhov. "Defend Possad as if it were Spain," General Muñoz Grandes demanded. "Share the glory and the danger!" But the Spanish lines broke. Survivors who fled in panic described the village of Posselok as "A living hell. . . Bodies with the young faces of university students were stacked like cordwood at the command post."

But with 70 per cent of the Soviet troops south of Lake Ladoga concentrated against the German wedge at Schlüsselburg, the two German corps were able to slice forward through relatively weak Red Army troops, mainly from the newly formed 4th Army.

The weather was dominated by rain, snow and sleet, and with the Germans marching on small, winding roads through the marshy area, and with the Luftwaffe in control of the skies, the Soviets were unable to get a clear picture of the threat against Tikhvin.

The Soviets only became aware of the seriousness of the situation on 27 October, when the Germans had covered half the distance to Tikhvin and netted 12,500 POWs. The immediate reply was to transport the 60th Tank Division by train to Tikhvin. Arriving on 29 October with 6,000 men and 179 tankettes, it was dispatched to attack the Germans.[3] But the Soviets followed the post-Tukhachevskiy textbook, dispersing the tanks among the infantry formations. Many became bogged down in the marshlands, and when on 6 November fourteen T-26s attacked the Panzer 38(t) tanks of 8. Panzer-Division, only two escaped destruction.

With 8. and 12. Panzer divisions in the forefront, the Germans captured Lipnaya Gorka, a small village just 10 kilometers from Tikhvin, in heavy snowfall on 7 November. The following day they reached the rail line between Tikhvin and Volkhovstroye on Lake Ladoga's southern shore, which was blown up. Under the cover of darkness, the tanks of 12. Panzer-Division rumbled into the southern outskirts of Tikhvin. Total confusion broke out among the inexperienced Soviet troops. Many fled, others were captured. General-

Georg-Hans Reinhardt, commanding German XXXIX. Panzerkorps, greets soldiers of the Spanish "Blue Division" (División Azul) in early October 1941. Shortly after this photo was taken, Reinhardt was appointed to command Panzergruppe 3 (later 3. Panzerarmee). His Panzerarmee was wiped out by the Soviets during Operation Bagration in the summer of 1944, but Reinhardt went on to become C.O. of the nearly annihilated Heeresgruppe Mitte until he was relieved from his post in January 1945. After the war, Reinhardt was sentenced to prison for murder and ill-treatment of prisoners of war and Soviet civilians. He was released in 1952 and passed away on 22 November 1963, at the age of 76. (Photo: Hannes Trautloft.)

Cont.

Soviet engineer troops are cutting barbed wire in no-man's land ahead of a counter-attack.

Leytenant Vsevolod Yakovlev, the 4th Army's commander, barely managed to escape.

The Germans vented their frustration on the unhappy civilians that remained in the city of Volkhov. Many were killed outright, others expulsed from their homes in the bitter cold, and raping took place, here as everywhere on the Eastern Front. In her doctoral studies, historian Wendy Jo Gertjejanssen recorded a particularly cruel case: "In the town of Tikhvin, in the Leningrad region, a 15-year old girl named G. Koledetskaya who had been wounded by shell splinters was taken to a hospital (a former monastery) where there were wounded German soldiers. Despite her injuries the girl was raped by a group of German soldiers and died as a result of the assault." [4]

The result of the fall of Tikhvin was, if possible, even more disastrous for the people in Leningrad. They had been dealt a heavy blow on 4 November, when German aircraft had sunk the patrol ship *Konstruktor* on Lake Ladoga, with 200 casualties as a result – mainly women and children who were being evacuated from the starvation in Leningrad. [5] On the following day, the Luftwaffe played a grim psychological game on the suffering population, dropping leaflets over Leningrad that promised

Cont.

to "celebrate" the anniversary of the Russian Revolution, 7 November, with terror bombings against this "the cradle of the Revolution."[6] General-Major Aleksandr Novikov, commanding the Northwestern Direction's Soviet air forces, decided to forestall these raids with strikes against the German bomber bases. When aerial reconnaissance reported a concentration of forty Ju 88s, thirty-one Bf 109s, and four transport planes at Siverskaya Airdrome on 6 November, he instructed his units to attack.[7]

Major Hannes Trautloft recalled that the first raid was totally unexpected.[8] Ten I-153 biplanes dropped out of the sky with rattling machine guns. Five minutes later seven Pe-2s and six MiG-3s came in from the southwest. While the Germans were focused on this attack, four Il-2 Shturmoviks of 174 ShAP, led by Kapitan Sergey Polyakov, a veteran from the Spanish Civil War and the Winter War, surprisingly buzzed in from the north. Five Messerschmitt Bf 109s scrambled in the midst of the raid and claimed two Soviet airplanes shot down – one of them, Mladshiy Leytenant Anatoliy Panfilov's Il-2 recorded as Oberleutnant Hans-Ekkehard Bob's 38th personal victory, III./JG 54's No. 400, and JG 54's fifteen hundredth. Panfilov bailed out over German-held territory and was killed in an exchange of fire with Wehrmacht soldiers rather than giving himself up.

Polyakov and his men however achieved a remarkable feat, claiming the destruction of eleven German aircraft on the ground. In fact, seven Ju 88s were lost, and a large part of the fuel depot was burned down. A follow-up raid by seven Pe-2s of 125 BAP in the afternoon rendered Siverskaya's runway unserviceable.[9]

But this would not prevent the Luftwaffe from carrying out their threat during the following night. Among thousands of incendiary bombs, huge one-ton sea mines were dropped over the city, with terrible effect. One of the mines penetrated the thick roofs of the Peter and Paul Fortress, killing thirteen people. At the Finland railway station, whole waggons filled with wounded soldiers and women and children who were about to be evacuated were hurled into the air. Another mine hit the railroad bridge near Kushelevka, blocking the traffic between Leningrad and Lake Ladoga. The bombs continued to fall throughout the night, and the only German loss was the Ju 88 piloted by Leutnant Harry Kollrarczig of KG 77.

Harrison E. Salisbury wrote, "In the morning the freight station was strewn with the corpses of women and children. There were enormous bomb holes everywhere. The rail cars were twisted masses of metal. Two trainloads of heavily wounded had been in the station. Now there was nothing but formless wreckage, piled high with bodies." Suddenly a crowd of women appeared, bringing with them one of the young KG 77 airmen. "They brought him up to the mountain of bodies which lay where the trains of the heavily wounded had been obliterated. 'Do you see what you did, you murderer?' they shouted. 'Do you see?'"[10] The fate of Leutnant Kollrarczig and his crew of three is unknown – they are all listed as missing.

Then came the news of the fall of Tikhvin. Now the trains that brought supplies to Leningrad had to be unloaded at Zaborye, a small station 35 kilometers southeast of Tikhvin. From Zaborye, trucks had to traverse 320 kilometers through thick forests, bogs and swamps in a wide arc around the German wedge to Tikhvin, in order to reach the port Novaya Ladoga, where ships and barges destined for Leningrad could be loaded. Often there was nothing but ancient forest trade tracks, which became almost impassable as the snow grew thicker. To traverse the route would take a GAZ truck a whole day or more. Thousands of people from the surrounding areas were mobilized to improve the road with picks and shovels and handsaws to cut down trees.

Meanwhile, the Red Army forces in the Volkhov area were regrouped and began to exert pressure on the German Tikhin wedge. But in Leningrad conditions worsened day by day. Rations had already in October been 400 grams of bread (equivalent to 500 calories) per day to workers and 200 grams to other civilians. On 13 November, the deteriorated supply situation compelled a reduction to 300 grams to workers and 150 grams for everyone else. That day the temperature also plummeted to minus 20 degrees Celsius.

The hunger gave way to famine, and the hospitals began to receive an increasing number of cases with dystrophy – a degeneration of tissue due to malnourishment. Then the dying began. People collapsed on the sidewalks and never rose again. In this situation the diminishing food stocks enforced another reduction in rations on 20 November – to 250 grams of bread per day for factory workers and 125 (just two slices) for everyone else.

Cont.

Victims of German bombardment and malnutrition in Leningrad's pediatric institute.

The winter turned out to be the coldest in decades, and this increased the mortality among a whole population weakened by malnourishment. However, it also gave the chance of establishing a road across the icy crust of Lake Ladoga. On the night of 22 November, the first sixty trucks, carrying 33 tons of flour, made it across what soon become known as the Road of Life.

On the last day of November, it was established that 11,085 Leningraders had died of starvation. In their desperation, the Soviets attempted to bring some KV tanks fresh from the Kirov works in Leningrad across the ice. Owing to the extreme cold, the ice had become so thick that it could actually support the 45-ton steel monsters.

Fighting with a desperation stronger than ever before, the Red Army intensified the efforts to take back Tikhvin. General Armii Kirill Meretskov, who had replaced Yakovlev as the 4th Army's commander on 9 November, was also fighting for his life; he had been arrested in July 1941, accused of "anti-Soviet activity," and still carried scars from two months of torture in the Lubyanka Prison. Released in September, he knew that his future hung on the efforts to retake this crucial town.

On 6 December the battle was fought in up to two meters of snow and a temperature of minus 38 degrees Celsius. On 8 December the Soviet troops managed to fight their way into the city. The next day it was in Soviet hands again. By the end of the year, the Germans had been pushed back to River Volkhov. Shortly afterward, a new Volkhov Front was formed from the left wing of the Leningrad Front, with Meretskov as its commander.

Dmitry Pavlov, in charge of Leningrad's food supply, wrote, "Without exaggeration, the defeat of the German Fascist forces at Tikhvin and the recapture of the northern railway line up to the Mga station saved thousands of people from starvation."

However, the suffering had only just begun. Even with Tikhvin back in Soviet control, the food supplies that could be brought in would still not suffice to provide the whole population with adequate nutrition. People in Leningrad were becoming increasingly weak, and in December alone, 52,881 people died of starvation. During the next two months, nearly 200,000 succumbed to the famine. Leningrad would remain under blockade for 900 days, during which an estimated one million people starved to death.

1 Hannes Trautloft, Diary, 16 October 1941.

2 "La División Azul" by Ramón Salas in *Espacio, Tiempo y Forma, Serie V, H.° Contemporánea*, No. 2/1989.

3 Isayev, *Kotlyy 41-go: Istoriya VOV, kotoruyu myy ne znali*, p. 351.

4 Gertjejanssen, *Victims, Heroes, Survivors: Sexual Violence on the Eastern Front during World War II*, p. 300.

5 TsVMA, f. 161, op. 6, d. 683, l. 44.

6 Novikov, *V nebe Leningrada*, p. 215.

7 Ibid., pp. 217-218.

8 Hannes Trautloft, Diary. 6 November 1941.

9 Archiv JG 54. Staffel-Chronik der III. Jagdgeschwader 54, 9. Staffel.

10 Salisbury, *The 900 Days*, p. 385.

16: THE RACE FOR THE "SOVIET RUHR AREA".

"It is a country which flows with milk and honey."

– Adolf Hitler, 23 July 1941.

Following the nearly complete annihilation of the Southern and Southwestern fronts in the gigantic envelopment battles at Uman and Kiev in August and September 1941, the whole of the Ukraine east of the Dnepr – the home of huge heavy industrial areas at Kharkov and the Donbasss – as well as the gigantic "natural aircraft carrier" of the Crimean Peninsula seemed to lay wide open for Generalfeldmarschall Gerd von Rundstedt's Heeresgruppe Süd.

As we have seen, the seizure of the Soviet Union's large industrial assets was one of the most important goals for Operation Barbarossa. Göring's Oldenburg Plan called for the transportation of all industrial enterprises between River Vistula and the Ural Mountains to Germany, and two days before the launching of the invasion in June 1941, Hitler told his closest associates that "the target is to capture all these areas, which are of particular economic interest to us."[1] The greatest concentration of Soviet industries was in the Donets-Kharkov area, the "Eastern Ruhr."

But the Soviets did not sit idle and hope that the invasion of their industrial heartland could be warded off by the Red Army. No plans for an evacuation existed before the war, but already on 4 July 1941, the State Planning Commission of the GOSPLAN – the organ for the planning of the economy – began working on a plan to evacuate the industry to the east. This was a challenge of astronomic proportions. Since the October Revolution, Soviet industry had grown by a fantastic 857 per cent, nearly five times the world average.[2] Steel and pig iron production increased from 3.5 and 3.0 million tons respectively in 1910 to 17.7 and 14.5 million tons respectively in 1937, surpassing the United Kingdom by a large margin and almost reaching Germany's levels.[3] Most of this was located in the western areas of the country which would be under German occupation by November 1941: 68 per cent of the production of pig iron, 58 per cent of that of steel, and 60 per cent of the total aluminum output.[4] Moreover, not just industries were to be evacuated west, but also their workers. Nonetheless a Council for Evacuation had already been appointed, and intense work began with hundreds of local committees using the five-year plan structure with 3,000 agents controlling the movement.

The first evacuations were soon made in June and July, but after the collapse at Uman in August, the large-scale, organized evacuation of all industries in the western parts of the country commenced. Between 7 and 15 August, nearly 30,000 rail cars were used in a huge operation to evacuate the industries in the Dnepr area. Nikolay Voznesenskiy, the director of the Soviet State Planning Commission, wrote: "Millions of people, hundreds of plants, and tens of thousands of machine tools as well as rolling mills, die presses, drop hammers, turbines, and motors were on the move."[5] Up to the end of September, 700 factories were evacuated, and the operation sped up in October 1941.

Hitler's Directive No. 33a had specifically ordered von Rundstedt to occupy the Kharkov industrial area and thrust forward across the Don River to Caucasia. When the

Generalfeldmarschall Gerd von Rundstedt was one of the most able senior military commanders during World War II. He was 65 years old when he commanded Heeresgruppe Süd during Operation Barbarossa.

Production of T-34 tanks. This superior Soviet tank was designed at Kharkov Locomotive Works, Factory No. 183, which in 1941 was the only T-34 producer in the Soviet Union. (Photo: Via Artem Drabkin.)

matter of Moscow or the Ukraine became the subject of a heated debate between him and von Brauchitsch, Halder and Heeresgruppe Mitte's senior commanders, he said that the South was more important, because "it is a country which flows with milk and honey."[6] Hardly surprisingly, von Rundstedt – undoubtedly the most able German senior commander in Operation Barbarossa – supported the Führer.

In a way, the Battle for the Ukraine can be regarded as a struggle between Nikolay Voznesenskiy and Generalfeldmarschall von Rundstedt. Simultaneously on 13 September, the former ordered the dismantling of the industries in Kharkov to begin, and the latter ordered 17. Armee's commander, General Carl-Heinrich von Stülpnagel, to begin the advance from the Dnepr bridgehead at Kremenchug towards Kharkov, 200 kilometers farther to the northeast. With its 900,000 inhabitants, Kharkov was the third largest industrial center of the Soviet Union. The most important enterprise was the huge industrial complex called Factory No. 183, the Soviet Union's most powerful tank producer. Employing 14,000 workers, it had not only produced eight thousand BT tanks; it was this factory that had designed the T-34 tank, and until 1941 it was the only plant where this superior tank was produced. By the time the dismantling of the plant began, Factory No. 183 had produced 1,675 T-34 tanks, including more than half the total number of T-34s that were manufactured in the second half-year of 1941.

While the GOSPLAN worked to dismantle and relocate the industries and their workers, the Red Army fought hard to hold back the advancing German armies to give the GOSPLAN time to carry out its huge operation. However, since 17. Armee's attack coincided with the drive to the north by Panzergruppe 1, aimed at encircling the bulk of the Southwestern Front, most of Soviet 38th Army – assigned to the Kremenchug sector – had been pushed northwards. Only three Rifle divisions, the 199th, 300th, and 304th, were left between Kharkov and von Stülpnagel's 17. Armee. The latter had also been considerably strengthened, and now consisted of five army corps – compared with three on 22 June.

The German attack was initiated with the worst possible timing for the Soviets – just as Marshal Budyonnyy was relieved from his post as the commander of the Southwestern Direction and Marshal Timoshenko took over. Timoshenko rushed to Kiev, with his full focus on the lumbering catastrophe there, and that also was where the commanders of both the Southwestern Front and its aviation were.

The three Soviet divisions immediately launched an absolutely futile counter-attack, faced by both a tremendous German superiority on the ground and massive air attacks by Stukas from StG 77. It was no wonder that the Germans completely smashed the Soviet forces north of Kremenchug. 38th Army reported, "Impossible to move in open terrain due to aerial attacks."[7]

On 15 September, 17. Armee had already advanced 45 kilometers and was half-way to Poltava, 120 kilometers southwest of Kharkov. The next day the Germans were slowed down mainly by torrential rains that transformed the roads into almost impassable mud streams. "The utterly defeated enemy is pursued further to the northeast on roads in a terrible conditions," 17. Armee reported on 17 September, and on the 18th Poltava was captured. The Soviet forces were in such disarray that they had not even demolished the 16-ton wooden bridge across River Vorskla, which runs through Poltava. Moreover, a considerable portion of the Soviet troops in the region became enveloped, with the result that the Germans took 4,000 prisoners and captured twelve tanks.[8]

The weather changed for the better, the roads dried up, and on 20 September the Germans already stood in Krasnograd, just 80 kilometers from Kharkov. The situation was absolutely disastrous for the Soviets. The first train with dismantled industrial equipment had left Kharkov only two days previously, but it would take at least four weeks to complete the evacuation. Ground troop reinforcements were on their way to the Kharkov area, but these had not yet reached the front. Furious over the loss of Poltava, Stalin immediately discharged the 38th Army's commander, General-Mayor Nikolay Feklenko – thus adding a command crisis to the general disaster. On top of everything

else, the Southwestern Front's commander, General-Polkovnik Mikhail Kirponos, was killed in Kiev on the same day, 20 September, and the commander of the Southwestern Front's Air Force, General-Leytenant Fyodor Astakhov, vanished in the Kiev encirclement.[*]

Also, there was no help to be expected from the 40th and 21st armies north of the 38th. At Romny, 100 kilometers north of Poltava, elements of Panzergruppe 2 had torn an 80-kilometer wide gap between these two armies. With the 40th mustering only 5,000 soldiers and ten tanks, the 21st had to dispatch all its available forces to prevent a major breakthrough in this sector – which otherwise might create a new dangerous threat against Kharkov from the north.[9]

South of the 38th Army stood the battered Southern Front. Its 6th Army, on the northern flank, had no more than 45,000 troops, and had been pushed towards the east by 17. Armee's southern army corps. Thus its northernmost division had its frontline strung out along 25 kilometers. Farther to the south, the 12th Army was no stronger. This had been reformed – after the first formation had been annihilated in Uman – on the basis of just an army corps with three divisions and two air regiments, and was

---

* Astakhov would make it back to Soviet lines in November.

This gunner of a Soviet Maxim machine gun was found dead as the German troops advanced. One of the latter took this photo. (Photo: Hans-Udo Schmitz-Wortmann.)

215

German pioneer troops during repair work on a bridge damaged by a Soviet fighter-bomber attack. (Photo: Via Daniel Johansson.)

This SS soldier on guard at the front line is assisted by his watchdog. (Photo: Via Daniel Johansson.)

mainly I-16s and I-153 biplanes, and with 4 RAG, a new phenomenon was introduced – the so-called "light night bombers" – old single-engine biplanes, the Polikarpov U-2 trainer, and discarded R-5 and R-Z reconnaissance planes.* But owing to the great distance from their airfields, there were hardly any German fighters to be seen, and the Soviet airmen were determined to accomplish what their weakened ground forces were unable to achieve – to slow down the German advance.

The result came instantly. On 21 September, 17. Armee reported: "Enemy air attacks throughout the day, particularly heavy raids in the Krasnograd and Poltava area, and against our advancing columns. Heavy losses, not least in horses." The roads along which 17. Armee advanced were marked with rows of horse carcasses, a reminder of Soviet strafing raids. The slow I-153 biplanes especially took a heavy toll on the horse-drawn columns.

The next day the army's report read, "Enemy air attacks throughout the day, mainly against Krasnograd and Poltava, and the roads along which we advance, caused significant own losses."[11] The most successful individual attack among these VVS missions on 22 September was carried out by Leytenant Grigoriy Kotseba from 44 IAD, who with his I-153 set fire to the construction equipment and pontoons intended for a German engineer bridge over the Orel River, south of Krasnograd. As a result of these air attacks, the rapid advance by 17. Armee, which had covered 150 kilometers in the first week of the offensive from Kremenchug – ground to an almost complete halt.

This allowed two new Soviet Rifle divisions and the 12th Tank Brigade to reach the area before Kharkov had fallen. Without a moments delay, these were hurled against 17. Armee at Krasnograd. The air above was filled with Soviet aircraft. A German fighter group that was sent forward to Poltava's airfield to deal with the Soviet air attacks, III./JG 3,was immediately hit by an air attack while its aircraft were on the ground, effectively neutralizing it. It was withdrawn after only a few hours.

On 21 September 1941, two of the best pilots of German fighter group III./JG 52, Leutnant Hermann Graf and Unteroffizier Leopold Steinbatz, were ordered to fly to the deserted Soviet airfield at Poltava in order to examine if it could be used by the Luftwaffe. This was badly needed, since the Soviet aviation had succeeded in halting the 17. Armee's advance towards Kharkov. The two German pilots beamed as they saw the base – nice, with concrete runways and solid houses, quite a contrast to the grassfields and tents that they had grown used to in recent times. They landed undramatically, and soldiers in field-gray battledress surrounded the two Bf 109s. Smiling ironically, the soldiers informed the two fliers that they had landed practically in the middle of the front line. In a forest only a few hundred yards away, straggling Soviet troops hid with mortars available.

fully occupied trying to hold the German Dnepr bridgehead at Dnepropetrovsk. A breakthrough here could cause the Southern Front's entire front to crumble.

The 38th Army was in a total shambles – its 199th Rifle Division could no longer be counted as a fighting unit, with only slightly more than two thousand largely demoralized troops and eight (8) cannon left remaining. It was in this situation that the Air Force of the Southwestern Front was ordered to concentrate on attacks against the German forces in this sector – thus abandoning the Kiev area. In mid-September, VVS Southwestern Front had only slightly over 200 aircraft, but the reserve aviation groups 1 RAG and 4 RAG now arrived from the Bryansk Front, thus increasing the strength to 470 aircraft.[10] Additionally, the Long-Range Aviation also deployed the two bomber corps 3 BAK and 4 BAK. This whole air armada was dispatched in a full-blown air offensive against the German advance, aimed at buying the GOSPLAN time. In fact, from 20 onwards the main battle stood between Soviet aircraft and German 17. Armee.

Among the new units were two Shturmovik groups, 241 and 503 ShAP. However, these were not in the best shape, with no more than a dozen Il-2s between them. The majority of the airmen also had nothing but rudimentary training. This was evident when 49 IAP was ordered to the front with 20 modern MiG-3 fighters; only twelve arrived at their destination – the remainder got lost and crashed during the transfer flight. Also, most of the aircraft in VVS Southwestern Front were outdated. The fighters were

---

* The frightening lack of combat aircraft as a result of huge losses in combination with an aircraft industry in disarray due to the German advance could be partly overcome through a quite ingenious measure in quite an ingenious way. There was no lack in the rear of old single-engine biplanes – the Polikarpov U-2 trainer, or the old discarded R-5 and R-Z reconnaissance planes. The Stavka decided to employ such aircraft in the role of light night bombers, and they formed LBAP regiments – light bombers – with the task of harassing the Germans at night time. With German night fighters in the East absent – all were needed to defend Germany itself against increasing RAF bombings at night – these biplanes proved fairly effective in the sense that they contributed to wear down already tired German troops.

A photo taken of Swedish Waffen-SS volunteer Markus Ledin. Born on 28 February 1921, Ledin became known as "The Terror of Midsommarkransen" ("Midsommarkransens Skräck") for his wild life in the Stockholm suburb of Midsommarkransen. He served as a volunteer in the Finnish Winter War and joined the Waffen-SS in 1941, fighting on the Eastern Front with SS Division "Wiking". Later he was transferred to 11. SS-Freiwilligen-Panzergrenadier-Division "Nordland," from which he deserted in September 1944 and made it back to Sweden via Finland. Ledin passed away on 10 December 1968.
(Photo: Via Martin Månsson.)

Graf looked at Steinbatz and saw that his face had grown pale. Getting shelled on the ground was the last thing the two fighter pilots wanted.

"Don't worry, blue boys," an artillery soldier chuckled: "We need you in the air. We'll get you airborne in the blink of an eye!"

Then disaster fell upon them in the shape of four of the most modern Soviet bombers, Petlyakov Pe-2s. Graf barely had squeezed himself into the cockpit of his Bf 109 as the sound of rattling machine guns and aircraft engines froze the blood in his veins. In a split second he had abandoned his aircraft and flung himself beneath one of the Messerschmitt wings – hardly a good place to hide from VVS airmen who were out to get German aircraft. But fear had gripped him, and both his brain and his body refused to work. Only when a small Soviet bomb came bouncing across the runway and landed just in front of him, did he come to his senses. He was up on his feet and ran, just ran to get away. A huge explosion flung him ten yards farther ahead.

Two destroyed Bf 109s were left behind. Graf and Steinbatz returned to base on board a Ju 52. Steinbatz's face was dressed with bandages, and the medic picked some small shrapnel from Graf's back.[12]

On 24 September Soviet aerial reconnaissance detected a concentration of large armored forces from Panzergruppe 1 at Dnepropetrovsk, 80 kilometers south of Krasnograd – indicating an upcoming attack. Soviet bombers had to be diverted against this sector, with 52 DBAD carrying out forty sorties with DB-3s against these troops on 24 September.[13] But the most effective air attacks were carried out by Fliegerkorps V, which from 24 September could be diverted from Kiev to support Panzergruppe 1. Attacks by He 111s and Ju 88s virtually paralyzed Soviet troops at Dnepropetrovsk, and the railway line from Stalino to Dnepropetrovsk was blocked. Other aerial bombardment against the rail lines leading north from Mariupol, Taganrog, and Rostov delayed the transfer of Soviet troops and materiel to the Kharkov sector.[14]

The next day, 25 September, Fliegerkorps V's bombers initiated a three-day offensive against VVS Southwestern Front's airfields around Kharkov and at Bogodukhov, claiming 43 aircraft destroyed on the ground. But on 26 September, VVS Southwestern Front and the DB-3s of the Long-Range Aviation were back in force over the battlefield southeast of Kharkov again. "Very heavy enemy air activity with bombing attacks and low-level machine gun attacks," complained 17. Armee.

That day, however, Generaloberst Ewald von Kleist's Panzergruppe 1 launched its attack from the Dnepropetrovsk Bridgehead and smashed 12th Army's weak positions. To 17. Armee, however, that brought no relief; Panzergruppe attacked towards the southeast. Next, 17. Armee was held up for several days owing mainly to fresh torrential rains and snow which once more made the roads impassable. When the skies cleared again on 2 October, Fliegerkorps V was dispatched in strength to help 17. Armee get moving through air attacks against Soviet troop and artillery positions. However, this was only a temporary show of strength, and could not be sustained for more than one day. Owing to the overall situation, the German bomber units were split between multiple tasks. Rail stations and railroads in the Soviet rear area were major targets in order to block the evacuation of the industries in the Donbass region. Nevertheless, the Soviets had built up a large repair organization, with reserve rails and repair stations placed at regular distances along the entire length of various routes.

During these days, the evacuation of the industries of Zaporozhye, 60 km south of Dnepropetrovsk, was completed. By 3 October, when the city fell into German hands, most of the industrial equipment was gone – including the gigantic steel and iron works Zaporizhtal; commencing production in 1931 this was the largest of its kind in the world. Its design capacity was 1,224 million tons of pig iron and 1.43 million tons of steel. Nearly ten thousand railway cars were used to relocate this plant alone – a good demonstration of the GOSPLAN's capacity.

Meanwhile, the evacuation of the industries in Kharkov continued at a high tempo. When the trains that were used to evacuate the industries returned to Kharkov to be loaded with new industrial equipment, they were filled with new troops to the Southwestern Front on their way west. Finally, this compelled Fliegerkorps V to divert a whole bomber wing, KG 55, exclusively for attacks against

The Soviet positions are observed by a German NCO, who is prepared for close combat. (Photo: Via Daniel Johansson.)

the Soviet railway network in the rear. Air attacks against the rolling stock, particularly railway engines, was considered to be most effective. KG 55's airmen were assigned to individual "free hunting" against rolling stock all across the huge area between Kursk in the north and Stalino in the south. They fitted their He 111s with a pair of extra nose-mounted 20mm automatic cannon for this purpose, and flying at low level were able to achieve some quite impressive initial success. Between 23 September and 12 October, the German bombers destroyed 95 trains and 12 locomotives.[15] But the Soviets countered this by shifting their railway movements in this area to night time, or to days with adverse weather.

Meanwhile however the Southern Front was plunged into disaster through Panzergruppe 1's breakthrough from Dnepropetrovsk. Von Kleist's forces were directed towards the southeast – heading for the northern shore of the Sea of Azov, with the aim of enveloping Southern Front's 9th and 18th armies south of the Dnepr Bend (in the southwest), and then turning east to break into the Caucasus and its oil fields through Rostov. The 12th Army, all the Southern Front had to meet the German attack with, was up against a terrific numerical superiority. Here, too, the Italian Army Corps that Mussolini had dispatched to the Eastern Front got its baptism of fire. Commanded by General Giovanni Messe, the CSIR (Corpo di Spedizione Italiano in Russia), put 60,000 troops at Panzergruppe 1's disposal.

A new Soviet army, the 56th, was hastily formed in the Caucasus and ordered to Rostov to block the German attack. But it would take at least three weeks for this army to form up and get in place. In the meantime, there was nothing but the 12th Army's 30,000 men and a handful of tanks between von Kleist's powerful Panzergruppe 1 and the oil fields in the Caucasus! Moreover, the 9th and 18th armies – with the bulk of Southern Front's strength – were tied up by Romanian 3rd Army south of the Dnepr Bend, 150 kilometers to the southwest. These suddenly faced the acute threat of being enveloped.

The 18th Army was disengaged from the front towards the west, made a 180-degree turn and slammed straight into von Kleist's eastern flank. Meanwhile, Polkovnik Vershinin, VVS Southern Front's commander, directed his whole aviation against Panzergruppe 1, and they received support from the Long-Range Aviation. Macchi MC.200 fighter planes of Italian 22 Gruppo had been assigned to provide Panzergruppe 1 with air cover, but these proved insufficient against this massive Soviet aerial onslaught. The 18th Army's attacks against von Kleist's eastern flank and the Soviet air attacks against the Panzergruppe's long supply lines and the bottlenecks at the river crossings, managed to temporarily halt von Kleist's advance at Orekhov, 100 kilometers north of the Sea of Azov. But that only bought Southern Front some time.

In an effort to bring about a change in the situation, the Germans temporarily diverted Fliegerkorps IV from operations in support of the attack against the Crimean Peninsula to support Panzergruppe 1. Early on 5 October, the Messerschmitt Bf 109 fighters of JG 77 swept VVS Southern Front from the skies. In one of the air combats on

that day, Feldwebel Eduard Isken and Oberfähnrich Friedrich-Wilhelm Grünewald of JG 77 shot down two MiG-3s which strafed German troops at Orekhov. The Soviet pilots, 55 IAP's Starshiy Leytenant Aleksandr Pokryshkin and Leytenant Stepan Komlev, were listed as missing.[16] The former nevertheless managed to make it back to Soviet lines, where he would eventually rise to become the second-ranking fighter ace of the VVS.

The relief from Soviet air attacks allowed Panzergruppe 1 to break through at Orekhov, and that evening its tanks stood in Semyonovka, just 70 kilometers from Berdyansk on the Sea of Azov. This caused a total panic on the Soviet side. One of the Soviet airmen who fought in this area, Leytenant Aleksandr Pavlichenko, described what happened at the airfield where his light bomber regiment 210 BBAP was stationed: "A staff aircraft landed at our airfield and a Polkovnik jumped out, crying: 'You who are sitting here. The Germans have broken through and are only six kilometers away! Hurry up and depart or destroy your planes!' Everybody was up on their feet and started running. All serviceable aircraft started taking off. Since our Su-2 was damaged from a combat mission on the previous day, I helped pilots from other regiments to try to set fire to unserviceable planes. But we didn't know how to do it. Then one soldier put two barrels of gasoline under

German troops cross a river on a truly makeshift bridge.
(Photo: Via Daniel Johansson.)

the wing of our plane. He opened the barrels and then we threw a torch at the fuel. The panic was awful. We made it to the maintenance base at Krasniy Luch. We found several aircraft parked there, mostly U-2 liaison planes. We were informed of the whereabouts of our 210 BBAP and reached our new base in a U-2. We received a warm welcome. Everyone had thought that we had been killed."[17] Southern Front's C.O., General-Leytenant Dmitriy Ryabyshev, was relieved on the same day. General-Polkovnik Yakov

A Soviet counter-attack with T-26 tanks supported by infantry.

Cherevichenko, who formerly had led the 9th Army, was appointed Front commander.

In a new attempt to get 17. Armee moving forward, a similar move was made on the German side. 17. Armee's commander, von Stülpnagel, was replaced with the man who was regarded as the most successful panzer general – Generaloberst Hermann Hoth, who hitherto had commanded Panzergruppe 3. On the day that this took place, 5 October, LV. Armeekorps of 17. Armee was subjected to forty-two Soviet air raids involving about 250 aircraft. The change in command resulted in no improvement for 17. Armee's situation.

But in the south, the whole Soviet defense collapsed. On 6 October SS-Brigade Leibstandarte Adolf Hitler of Panzergruppe 1 managed to capture most of the staff of the Soviet 9th Army. The army commander was able to escape in an aircraft at the last moment. Meanwhile, KG 27 and KG 51 started bombing Berdyansk, where German aerial reconnaissance had detected a Soviet sea evacuation underway. The following night, six KG 27 He 111s reported an "extremely successful" attack against trains on the railroad to Rostov.[18] This in fact was the trains carrying the bulk of Mariupol's industrial equipment – including the Ilyich Steel & Iron Works, a key manufacturer for the production of Il-2 assault planes. Much owing to this single Luftwaffe strike, Il-2 Shturmovik production actually temporarily ceased in October 1941.

On 7 October the Germans reached the coast of the Sea of Azov, sealing off Southern Front's 9th and 18th armies in the west. Again, the Soviets had to resort to their aviation

to save the situation as much as possible. Early on 8 October Vershinin sent his whole air force – over one hundred fighters, bombers, and Shturmoviks – into the sky to attack SS Leibstandarte as it stormed Mariupol.[19] This operation was launched just as the Messerschmitt 109s of Fliegerkorps IV had returned to operations over the Crimean Peninsula, more than 300 kilometers to the west. Thus, all attacks by VVS Southern Front on 8 October could be conducted without interference from German fighters.

One of the German fighter groups, II./JG 77 was hurriedly shifted back to provide Panzergruppe 1 with air cover on 9 October. Engaging 230 ShAD and Su-2-equipped 210 and 288 BBAP, its pilots claimed to have shot down five Il-2s and five Su-2s on 9 and 10 October. But with only around 15 Bf 109s available, the German fighter group would not suffice to halt the Soviet air offensive. On 10 October, SS Leibstandarte reported "heavy air attacks from groups of up to 20 aircraft."[20] Between 8 and 10 October, VVS Southern Front's round-the-clock offensive against Panzergruppe 1 resulted in the destruction of 62 German tanks and 680 other motor vehicles, according to Soviet estimations.[21] Even if these figures are exaggerated, Cherevichenko, Southern Front's new commander, asserted that it was owing to these operations by VVS Southern Front that the bulk of the 9th Army was able to slip out of the trap.[22] But the 18th Army could not be saved. It was totally annihilated, with 65,000 troops lost (while the Germans rounded up and sent over 100,000 Soviets into confinement).

The focus of the battle now shifted east, where Panzergruppe 1 headed for Rostov and the Caucasus. On 11 October SS Leibstandarte and SS-Division "Wiking" reached River Mius, just 55 kilometers west of Rostov. Thus, it also stood a mere 10 kilometers from Taganrog, another important industrial city. The evacuation of Taganrog's industries had begun in haste only on 4 October, when the first trains with the dismantled equipment of the Josef Stalin Instrumental Factory left for Novosibirsk. But most of the industry – including Aviation Factory No.31, the second largest producer of the modern LaGG-3 fighter – remained in place when the Germans began shelling the city.

With nothing but weak and dispersed Red Army units available to defend the road to Rostov, and the 9th Army in disarray following its swift escape from the trap, Cherevichenko had no choice but to continue to demand the utmost from his exhausted airmen. The Soviet air and ground units nevertheless had the advantage of being based close to large rail junctions such as Rostov and Stalino, and thus were well supplied.

On 11 October, VVS Southern Front made at least 300 sorties against SS Leibstandarte. II./JG 77 could bring only a handful of Bf 109s into the air to meet them, claiming three victories, while two of its best pilots were shot down. Oberfeldwebel Rudolf Schmidt was shot down and wounded shortly after achieving his 33rd kill, and Oberleutnant Anton Hackl was posted as missing after he had attained his 16th and 17th victories. Hackl nevertheless survived and returned to his unit the next day.[23]

VVS Southern Front's intensified activity compelled Fliegerkorps IV to resume its airbase raids, and in one

The resistance offered by the Red Army in September 1941 created time for the Soviets to evacuate many of their industries.

The heavy autumnal rains turned the ground into deep mud, forcing both sides to construct makeshift wooden "bridges" on roads. Seen in this photo are German pioneers. (Photo: Via Daniel Johansson.)

attack against an airfield near Stalino on 11 October, eight to ten Soviet aircraft were reportedly destroyed.[24] The attack was nevertheless far less successful than the Germans estimated, as VVS Southern Front lost only three aircraft to German air base attacks during the whole of October 1941.[25]

On 12 October, VVS Southern Front continued to pound 1. Panzerarmee's bridgehead across River Mius, and Mariupol was subject to seven bomb raids.[26] In response, II./JG 77 was able to mount only eighteen sorties, leading to a single MiG-3 getting shot down.[27]

Heavy rains suddenly changed the landscape into a blurry quagmire where supply vehicles got stuck. Danish volunteer SS-Sturmmann Ellef Henry Rasmussen of SS-Division "Wiking's" Scandinavian SS-Regiment "Nordland" recalled, "One sank down to the knees in the muddy paths, and the vehicles were buried to the axles. In general, we were only able to move forward in the tracks left from our tanks, and even then we had to pull our vehicles free over and over again. Owing to these miserable conditions, we were only able to move 10 to 15 km a day."[28] Over and over again, German vehicle columns that had got stuck in the mud repeatedly became helpless victims of Soviet planes which dropped out of the clouds to wreak havoc on the ground. This bought valuable time for the relocation of Taganrog's industry.

The Soviet pressure from the air was even stronger farther north, where 17. Armee on 9 October reported that air attacks had reached a point which simply made any further advance by the army impossible.[29] By this time, the autumnal rains were turning the roads in this sector too into deep mud, and many German supply columns, most of them horse-drawn, got stuck on the roads – making them vulnerable targets for Soviet planes. On 12 October alone, 17. Armee lost 200 soldiers and 238 horses in air raids.[30]

In fact, the entire Heeresgruppe Süd was about to ground to a halt exactly at a time when it was approaching its main goals – the Kharkov-Donets Basin industrial areas and, through the city of Rostov, the oil fields in the Caucasus. However, with 11. Armee tied down in attempts to seize the Crimea – another important goal for the army group – and the bulk of the German armor on the Eastern Front committed to Operation Typhoon, the offensive against Moscow, von Rundstedt had to make do with whatever resources were available to his army group. In order to relieve Panzergruppe 1 from the pressure from the air, a new fighter group, I.(J)/LG 2 was brought in on 14 October. Up until then, this unit had been based in Romania to protect the oil fields, and had seen relatively little combat. It thus had 30 operational Bf 109s when it was sent east.

On 15 October, the reinforced German fighter force had an immediate impact on the fighting on the ground and in the air. That day 18 Soviet planes were claimed shot down for no own losses over the Mius area, bringing considerable relief to the ground troops.[31] Testifying to the previous effect of the Soviet air attacks, Panzergruppe was able to break out of the bridgehead that it had previously established at River Mius, and penetrated Taganrog on 16 October. But by that time, between 70 and 75 per cent of the city's industrial equipment had been evacuated. Aviation Factory No.31, including 3,000 workers with their families and 50 finished LaGG-3s – arrived safely at Tbilisi in the Caucasus. The frustrated Germans had all Jews in Taganrog, around 2,500, executed.

General Giovanni Messe, the commander of the Italian Expeditionary Corps on the Eastern Front, offers his soldiers cigarettes during the advance towards Stalino.

Sharply deteriorated weather conditions limited the German air activity during the days that followed. The Soviets took advantage of this to dispatch their aviation in spite of the weather. On 19 October, 16 Il-2 Shturmoviks of 4 ShAP took off in a 25-meter cloud ceiling, fog and snowfall which limited visibility. They still managed to locate and attack a troop column of German 13. Panzer-Division, claiming nine vehicles destroyed. In reply to complaints from the ground troops about strong Soviet air attacks, several Bf 109s took off the next day to ward off these air attacks in the same weather conditions, but failed to shoot down more than a single Soviet plane. Meanwhile the ground troops fumed over "most heavy air attacks" with up to 42 bombers escorted by 18 fighters at the same time.[32] 4 ShAP alone was credited with the destruction of 20 vehicles on the ground.[33]

Nevertheless, it proved impossible to prevent the Germans from occupying the Donbass industrial area, on Panzergruppe 1's northern flank. Here, where 223 large industries and 54 small or medium factories were located, the evacuation did not work particularly well. Factories were blown up rather than evacuated. On 21 October, Stalino (today's Donetsk), the center of Donbass, was seized by the Germans. Only 17 of the 64 iron and steel plants in the Donbass were evacuated.

At this moment an additional new threat emerged against Kharkov, in the shape of General Walter von Reichenau's 6. Armee, which advanced from the west after completing the battle of Kiev, breaking through the lines of Soviet 21st Army to the north of the 38th at Kharkov. On 12 October, these troops stood at Bogodukhov, 65 kilometers northwest of Kharkov. Farther to the north, other elements of 6. Armee had seized Akhtyrka and Sumy, and continued eastward – threatening to outflank Soviet 38th Army. The evacuation of Kharkov's industries was still not completed. In desperation, the Soviets launched everything they had against this new danger. 150,000 workers and peasants were mobilized into a militia which made absolutely reckless attacks against the German troops. They were mown down in their thousands, but simultaneously intensified air attacks began to take their toll on 6. Armee's strength.

Flying from Poltava, the Messerschmitt pilots of III./ JG 52 – the only German fighter group in the region – did their utmost to relieve the ground troops. On 14 October they claimed to have shot down 17 Soviet aircraft for no own losses. But the Soviets struck back, dispatching a formation of Il-2s against the German fighter base. At night time, old biplanes of the types U-2 and R-5 made continuous harassment raids on the German troops, depriving them of their sleep, and the next day the fighters, Shturmoviks and twin-engine bombers were fully active again. "Numerous bombers and low-level assault planes in action against the marching columns of the attacking force," was noted in the German High Command's War Diary.[34] The construction of a bridge at Akhtyrka was held back by

SS troops in street fighting. The soldier in the front has a Mauser C96 semi-automatic pistol. The long barrel and high-velocity cartridge gave the C96 a better range and penetration than most other pistols. (Photo: Via Daniel Johansson.)

repeated bomber attacks. III./JG 52 was in action again, but this time failed to shoot down more than three Soviet planes. On 16 October alone, twenty-one air attacks were reported by 6. Armee.

Thus, the Germans were able to advance only step by step, at an agonizingly slow pace. Apart from the fighters of III./JG 52, von Reichenau could expect very little own air support; the whole of Luftflotte 2 was occupied supporting Operation Typhoon, and Luftflotte 4 found itself dispersed over a huge area, with heavy demands everywhere. And in Kharkov, GOSPLAN's agents struggled to complete their work before the enemy arrived.

A sudden weather change on 17 October, with heavy snowfall, rain and sleet, ruined all roads and further complicated matters for von Reichenau's troops.

18 October: The weather cleared again and the roads began to dry up. A pleasant surprise to 6. Armee's troops was the fact that hardly any Soviet aircraft turned up to attack them. The Germans forced their way through weakly held Red Army positions.

19 October: German advance columns penetrated the industrial area in western Kharkov. Report from the troops: "Industries are found to be systematically destroyed."[35] At the same time, in the center of the city, the very last of the planned trains left Kharkov's railway station. GOSPLAN had completed its work.

20 October: The German troops slowly fought their way through the industrial area in western Kharkov, but still were three kilometers from the city center.

21 October: Report from 6. Armee: "North and north-west of Kharkov the enemy offers a stiff resistance in small combat groups supported by tanks."

22 October: Report from 6. Armee: "Fierce fighting in the western outskirts of Kharkov. The city is burning in a large number of places."

23 October: Report from 6. Armee: "The enemy positions in the western outskirts of Kharkov were broken through."

23 October: Report from 6. Armee: "The right flank of the 6. Armee reached positions on both sides of Kharkov and forced the enemy to abandon the city."

As a result of this great battle, a total of no more than 1,720 POWs were recorded by the Germans. It was a genuine Pyrrhic victory. The true victor was the GOSPLAN, which had dismantled and relocated nearly all of Kharkov's industries. The machinery from Factory No.183 reached Nizhniy Tagil in the Ural region. Before even roofs had been built in the newly erected plant, and despite temperatures that fell to minus 40 degrees Celsius, production commenced in December 1941, when the first 25 T-34s were completed. Within a short period of time, it would be thousands. The Germans would take a terrible revenge on the citizens of Kharkov.

With most of the industrial park in Kharkov already dismantled and evacuated, the Stavka took the decision on 17 October to pull back Southwestern Front 120 kilometers east of the line Kharkov-Belgorod.

During the battle for eastern Ukraine, the Red Army offered a tenacious resistance in every town. These German soldiers are taking cover behind a ruined house. (Photo: Via Daniel Johansson.)

The Rasputitsa – the infamous autumnal mud in Russia and the Ukraine. This Panzer III, version G, of German 13. Panzer-Division has got stuck, and an attempt is made to pull it free with a Panzer II.

The GOSPLAN left a wasted industrial area to the Germans. Between July and November 1941, 1.5 million wagonloads carried industrial machinery, tools, material, and personnel eastward on the railway system. No fewer than 1,523 factories, installations, and research establishments, including 85 percent of Soviet airframe and aeroengine production facilities, were evacuated. From the Ukraine alone, 550 large factories were relocated, together with 3.5 million skilled workers. This laid the foundations for the resurrection of the Red Army following the disastrous losses in the summer and fall of 1941. The fact that the Soviet Union was able to dismantle and relocate the industry in the western parts of the country to the east, where the factories were set up again and production recommenced, in the midst of war and mobilization, is an astonishing accomplishment which is probably unparalleled in economic history.

Only in the Donbass could some industries be set to work for the Germans. However, Heeresgruppe Süd managed to occupy 63 per cent of all coal fields in the Soviet Union. Next, Generalfeldmarschall von Rundstedt aimed to crash through the gateway to the oil fields in the Caucasus – Rostov. However, confronted with a hardened resistance in the shape of the 56th Soviet Army – which from 17 October arrived to establish positions west of Rostov – and with roads turned into sticky morasses by heavy

downfalls, he decided to bide his time and wait for the roads to freeze so that he could get his armored force running at full speed.

Without any doubt, the Soviet air operations against Panzergruppe 1 were a key factor in von Rundstedt's decision. Without this air support, the weak remnants of Soviet 12th Army would never have been able to hold out for as long as they did. And although adverse road conditions put a severe brake on the German advance, it would probably have been possible to push forward to seize Rostov in just a couple of days after River Mius was reached on 11 October – had it not been for the intense air attacks against the supply lines. By that time, there was virtually nothing on the Soviet side to defend Rostov.

VVS Southern Front, which had 221 aircraft on 1 September, sustained 122 aircraft losses in that month.[36] By comparison, the losses sustained by its main opponent, Fliegerkorps IV, was only about half as large.

The Soviet aviation's contribution to propping up 17. Armee long enough to permit the dismantling and evacuation of the industries in Kharkov simply cannot be underestimated. This is a feat almost completely neglected in historiography. On the other side of the coin, in what was to come to characterize the air war on the Eastern Front, III./JG 52 achieved impressive numerical results during four weeks of service from Poltava Airdrome – 115 victories against only four losses – but still failed to accomplish its main task, namely to cover the German ground troops from Soviet air attacks. Confronted by an enemy with such a stamina, the qualitative superiority of the German fighters was simply not sufficient – if it was not coupled with considerable numerical advantage.[37] This also was demonstrated in the Crimean skies, where the latter factor came into decisive effect.

KHARKOV'S ORDEAL.

The city of Kharkov was dead-silent as the German troops marched in. The citizens remember this as an absolutely black day. Rain and snow fell over the blackened ruins. There were 460,000 people remaining in the city, but no one entered the streets.

The Germans immediately began to confiscate large quantities of food for their own troops, leaving very little for the population. Within a short period of time, around one-third of the people in Kharkov suffered from starvation. In scenes similar to those in Leningrad, thousands would die in the cold winter.

On 14 November, several buildings in the city were blown up by partisans. Generalleutnant Georg Braun, commander of 68. Infanterie-Division of 17. Armee, and fifteen other members of his staff were killed by a bomb planted at the headquarters at Dzhersinskiy Street 17. The German reaction was swift. Braun's division and the 57. Infanterie-Division of 6. Armee rounded up 1,200 citizens as hostages. Fifty were immediately hanged from balconies of large buildings, where they were left for several months. Posters were pinned all over the city, declaring that 200 hostages would be killed for each new bomb explosion. Shortly afterward, another 150 of the hostages were murdered.

To the day one month later, the City Commendant ordered the Jewish population to a hut settlement near Factory No. 183. When 20,000 people had assembled, Sonderkommando 4a, commanded by SS-Standartenführer Paul Blobel, of Einsatzgruppe C, moved in and began the killings. At first, this was done by shootings, but then a gas van was brought in to increase the tempo of the killings.

Meanwhile, other citizens died of starvation, and yet more were executed for the slightest reason. By the time Kharkov was liberated by the Red Army, 280,000 of its citizens had died. 160,000 had been deported as slave laborers to Germany. 195,000 had spent time under German arrest where they had been subject to torture and mistreatment. 23,000 people carried physical wounds. Hardly anyone came through the occupation without mental scars.

These civilians were hanged from balconies in Kharkov after the bomb strike against the headquarters of German 68. Infanterie-Division in the city on 14 November. The signs hung around their necks read, "Guilty of placing mines." (Photo: Edmund Rossmann.)

17: THE BATTLE OF THE CRIMEA.

"The enemy's air force was very active throughout the day. Successive attack waves of up to 27 aircraft bombed and machine-gunned living quarters, field positions, and resting troops, giving proof of a total air supremacy. Our troops sustain not insignificant losses, and this has a particularly negative impact on the mood among our troops."

– German LIV. Armeekorps, 3 October 1941.

Apart from the seizure of the Ukraine's industrial region, one main task assigned to Generalfeldmarschall von Rundstedt was to capture the Crimean Peninsula – the "natural aircraft carrier" from where Soviet air raids against the Romanian oil fields were carried out. This was to be made by two of Heeresgruppe Süd's southernmost armies, German 11. Armee and Romanian 3rd Army. Romanian 4th Army was unable to participate; it was tasked with seizing the important port city of Odessa, 100 kilometers west of the Dnepr's mouth. For over two months, all attempts to capture Odessa – first made in early August 1941 – had been frustrated by the Soviet Coastal Army, a force of

The troops of German 11. Armee became bogged down in trench warfare during its attempt to break through to the Crimea.

35,000 men that had been formed from the 9th Army's coastal group.

German 11. Armee had already crossed the mighty river at Berislav, 200 kilometers southwest of Dnepropetrovsk, by late August. This coincided with Southern Front's commander, General Ivan Tyulenev, getting badly wounded at Dnepropetrovsk on 29 August. 11. Armee consolidated the bridgehead and prepared to attack straight southwards, with the aim of capturing the Crimean Peninsula. Romanian 3rd Army was also brought into the bridgehead. The severely mauled Soviet 18th Army fought desperately to contain this foothold, but in vain. In one of the last orders issued as commander of the Southwestern Direction, Budyonnyy turned to what the Soviets so often resorted to as their last means – the aviation. On 8 September the Soviet Black Sea Fleet dispatched bomber brigade 63 BAB and fighter group 32 IAP on a Zveno raid against the Berislav Bridge. The Soviet aircraft were intercepted by Bf 109s of JG 77 and lost one I-16SPB fighter-bomber and one of the escorting Yak-1s while 131 IAP's Kapitan Andrey Milodan shot down one of JG 77's Bf 109s.[1] But the other I-16 fighter-bombers swept down over the bridge and managed to place their bombs right on the target. The bridge was not destroyed, but the damage sufficed to paralyze the traffic for two hours.

Possibly as a result of this, von Rundstedt ordered the 11. Armee to initiate the attack against the Perekop Isthmus – which connects the Crimea with the mainland – on 9 September. Generaloberst Eugen Ritter von Schobert, commanding 11. Armee, made an attempt to capture the eight-kilometer narrow Perekop Isthmus through a surprise attack with three reconnaissance battalions on 12 September. But the attack force was halted by well-directed Soviet artillery fire, and Generaloberst von Schobert was himself killed when his Fieseler Storch reconnaissance plane was shot down. The newly formed Soviet 51st Independent Army – under the very able command of General-Polkovnik Fedor Kuznetsov, who had previously led the Northwestern and the Central fronts – had managed to establish defensive positions on the Perekop Isthmus at the last minute. It also was provided with excellent air support. On 17 September, VVS Southern Front was reinforced with the Stavka's reserve air group 5 RAG – includ-

ing the refurbished 4 ShAP with 18 Il-2 Shturmoviks – to muster around 200 aircraft.[2] The Il-2s were immediately brought into action, with quite some success. The Black Sea Fleet had two aviation brigades, 62 IAB and 63 BAB, with approximately 200 aircraft based in the Crimea. On 18 September the Zveno fighter-bombers of 32 IAP/VVS ChF managed to destroy the Dnepr Bridge at Zaporozhye, thus severing the Wehrmacht supply lines to the front, which in turn delayed a German flanking attack from the north. On 21 September alone, one of the divisions of the 11. Armee was subject to twenty-two air attacks.[3]

But the Perekop Isthmus had to be forced. On 24 September, XIV. Armeekorps of 11. Armee attacked again. The importance of the Crimea to the German planners is evident from the fact that General Erich von Manstein, who commanded LVI. Panzerkorps in Heeresgruppe Nord, was sent to assume command of 11. Armee just when the Battle of Leningrad had reached a critical stage. A tremendous artillery barrage and bombings by Stukas tore up the Soviet defense positions before the German ground troops attacked. But the surviving Soviet troops fought back, greatly aided by the narrowness of the sector, filled with bunkers and trenches, and – not least – the aviation of the Black Sea Fleet and the Southern Front. TB-3s of 63 BAB even undertook some Zveno missions in this area. During an attack by I-16 fighter-bombers launched from two TB-3s, three German artillery batteries were destroyed. The fighting on the Isthmus on 24 September alone cost XIV. Armeekorps over one thousand casualties.

On 26 September, General-Leytenant Dmitriy Ryabyshev, who had succeeded in command of the Southern Front, attempted to counter-act by launching his 9th and 18th armies in an attack against Romanian 3rd Army, which covered 11. Armee's northern flank. The Romanians were pushed back, but the timing for the attack could have been better – on that very same day, German Panzergruppe 1 crashed out of its Dnepropetrovsk Bridgehead.

Ryabyshev directed most of VVS Southern Front to support the counter-attack, and these air units clashed violently with the bulk of Fliegerkorps IV's fighters, which were concentrated in this sector. In the air over the retreating Romanian army, JG 77 claimed 29 victories (five of them by Oberfeldwebel Heinrich Hackler of III./JG 77) against three own losses on 26 September, thus reaching its 600th victory in the East. The attempt to seal off or force 11. Armee to retreat beyond the Dnepr failed. The 18th Army and VVS Southern Front had to turn east to meet the threat from Panzergruppe 1.

Meanwhile, however, the Air Force of the Black Sea Fleet proved to be absolutely decisive in frustrating German 11. Armee's attempt to overrun the Crimea. On 28 September, this army's LIV. Armeekorps noted, "The enemy's numerically superiority in the air allowed him to inflict heavy losses on our troops and severe damage to our artillery, through 'rolling' air attacks, even at low altitude, with bombs and machine-guns."[4] General Von Manstein complained that "it reached a point where our AAA bat-

teries no longer dared to open fire, for fear of immediately getting eliminated by air attacks."[5]

Day and night 11. Armee was subject to this hailstorm of bombs. On the night of 1 October, 600-800 bombs were dropped on the positions of its 46. Infanterie-Division alone.[6] On 3 October, LIV. Armeekorps reported, "The enemy's air force was very active throughout the day. Successive attack waves of up to 27 aircraft bombed and machine-gunned living quarters, field positions, and resting troops, giving proof of a total air supremacy," which caused heavy losses and had "a particularly negative impact on the mood among our troops."[7]

In action over the Perekop Isthmus, III./JG 77 lost its leading ace, Oberleutnant Kurt Lasse – with 41 victories on his tally – in combat with two MiG-3s on 8 October. Lasse's compatriots paid this back the next day, when they attacked VVS ChF's 5/32 IAP over the forward clutch of Soviet airfields 40-50 kilometers south of the Perekop Isthmus. Three Yak-1s were shot down, two of them piloted by the aces Kapitan Ivan Lyubimov and Mladshiy Leytenant Allakhverdov. With the engine in his Yak-1 hit by bullets, Kapitan Lyubimov belly-landed. But the victorious Bf 109 pilot came back to strafe the downed Yak-1, and a machine-gun round tore off one-third of Lyubimov's chin. In his combat report from this day, Serzhant Nikolayev of 5./32 IAP (who also was shot down by a Bf 109), described how Mladshiy Leytenant Allakhverdov was lost: "Having belly-landed in the Munus-Tatarskiy region, I saw three Me 109s chasing my flight commander, Allakhverdov, at treetop level. In the air above Kir-Aktachi his aircraft burst into flames. He made a vertical climb, fell down over the wing, and tore into the ground. Both man and machine perished in the flames."[8] At the end of the day, III./JG 77 had claimed ten victories, including three MiG-3s during the same afternoon mission by Oberleutnant Kurt Ubben, who thus brought his total score to 44.

The increased pressure on both Odessa and the Crimea however compelled the Soviets to evacuate the former city and shift its defenders to the Crimea. This operation was carried out with quite some success between 14 and 17 October. In order to forestall the arrival of the Coastal Army's troops to the battlefield in northern Crimea, the Germans decided to once and for all deal with VVS ChF. For this purpose, Oberst Werner Mölders arrived to assume the role of Flieger-Nahkampfführer, directing the operations of German fighters over the Crimea. Mölders arrived straight from the Moscow front, and brought along Hauptmann Gordon Gollob's II./JG 3 to Chaplinka. Gollob by himself would play a significant role during the battle for air superiority over the Crimea. He started out on 17 October, when he escorted KG 27 He 111s against the Soviet Odessa evacuation fleet which entered Yevpatoria in the Crimea. VVS ChF dispatched MiG-3s to intercept the Germans, and two of them ended up on Gollob's victory tally, as Nos. 59 and 60. Next day 11. Armee made a fresh effort to break through. II./JG 3 and III./JG 77 were in continuous action, engaging large numbers of Soviet aircraft. Hauptmann Gollob took off on three successful missions – at 0647, bringing two victories; at 0945, with five; and at 1430 with two victories. He thus set a new record for a single day by shooting down nine aircraft.[9] But this still failed to ward off the Soviet air attacks. On 18 October, LIV. Armeekorps sustained over twelve hundred casualties in fruitless efforts to break through.[10]

Soviet counter-action to the increased presence of Luftwaffe fighters was also swift and effective. During the dark hours early on the morning of 19 October, VVS ChF's 40 BAP dispatched all available Pe-2s against Chaplinka. They flew at treetop level and caught the Germans off-guard when they attacked just before sunrise. The falling bombs were concentrated across the runway. No German aircraft were totally destroyed, but many were sufficiently damaged to be rendered unserviceable. "Only six Me 109s

General Ivan Yefimovich Petrov (right) in a forward observation post at Sevastopol. Petrov commanded the Coastal Army, which held out against the Romanians in Odessa for over two months between August and October 1941, and then prevented the Germans from seizing Sevastopol in 1941.

remain in operational condition," Gollob wrote in his diary.[11] For the next two days the Soviets were in almost total control of the air over Perekop. Meanwhile, the first elements of the Coastal Army began to arrive at the Perekop front. Between 19 and 22 October, LIV. Armeekorps sustained over two thousand casualties without being able to make any progress.[12]

VVS ChF's feat of holding the Wehrmacht at bay from the Crimea for a whole month was indeed remarkable. Between 1 and 20 October, the Soviet airmen claimed the destruction of 104 tanks, 700 trucks, fifty-four armored cars, eight infantry battalions, ten motorcycle columns, ten bridges, forty artillery pieces, and twenty-four anti-aircraft guns in this area. By now the Soviet positions were more favorable than before, with the Coastal Army taking up positions at the Perekop.

It was obvious to the Germans that the pressure from the air had to be taken away, but also – as Gollob remarked in his diary on 22 October – that the German fighters in the area were too few to handle this task. In consequence, III./JG 52, with 27 serviceable Bf 109s, flew down to Chaplinka from Poltava. On 23 October three fighter groups – II./JG 3, III./JG 52, and III./JG 77 – took off from Chaplinka to clear the Crimean skies once and for all. Oberst Mölders directed them via radio.

The Soviet airmen were shocked at the sudden onslaught by such large groups of aggressive enemy fighters. Dozens of Soviet aircraft fell prey to the merciless fighter attacks from above. Finally, the Soviet superiority in the air over Perekop was broken.

23 October brought a brutal end to the Soviet piggyback Zveno tactic. 63 BAB mounted two TB-3s escorted by eleven I-15bis and eight I-153s against artillery posi-

Air combat! Captured by the gun camera of a Messerschmitt Bf 109, this Soviet fighter plane has no chance of avoiding the German bullet tracers. (Photo: Hannes Trautloft.)

FLIEGERKORPS IV VERSUS SOVIET BLACK SEA FLEET.

Logistics was one of the main problems for the Axis forces on the Eastern Front. Heeresgruppe Süd's operations against the Crimea were severely hampered through shortage in supplies – a situation which was largely due to the fact that the Soviets were able to hold the major Black Sea port of Odessa for so long. When the first attack against the Crimea broke down in mid-September, the Soviet Coastal Army had resisted all attempts by Romanian 4th Army to seize Odessa for over one month. By that time, the Romanian casualties in the battle for Odessa had increased to around 60,000, and the Soviet defenders showed no signs of wavering. Meanwhile, Odessa's defenders received a steady flow of supplies from the Soviet Black Sea Fleet.

In an attempt to cut this sea lane, Fliegerkorps IV received instructions to concentrate the main firepower of its bombers on attacks against Soviet shipping in the Black Sea. The order was issued on 18 September, and that evening and throughout the following night, KG 27 dispatched sixty He 111s in "rolling attacks" against the town and port of Odessa, dropping 97 tons of bombs. The latter included forty 1,000-kg mine bombs.[1] With this, KG 27 initiated a series of nocturnal attacks against the port of Odessa, and operations in daylight against shipping between the Crimea and Odessa. On 19 September, 3./KG 27's commander, Oberleutnant Wolfgang Skorczewski, managed to sink the Soviet monitor *Udarnyy* east of Odessa. Eight days later Skorczewski was rewarded with the Knight's Cross.

Meanwhile, 6./StG 77 was shifted southward, abandoning its operations to support the advance toward Kiev. This squadron was commanded by Russian-born Oberleutnant Hermann Ruppert, who had distinguished himself with many daring dive-bomber attacks. Fortunately for the Axis, the Stukas arrived just in time to meet a Soviet counter-attack against the weakened Romanian forces.

In the evening of 21 September a group of Ju 87s led by Ruppert spotted the Soviet gunship *Krasnaya Armeniya* in the same fairwaters as Skorczewski had scored his success. Ruppert ordered his fliers to attack, and shortly afterward another two Soviet vessels appeared – the destroyer *Frunze* and the tugboat OP-8. Ruppert's Stukas hit and sunk all three vessels. Little did the Stuka fliers know that with *Frunze*, they had destroyed the ship that had Konteradmiral Lev Vladimirskiy onboard, and that he was assigned to lead a large-scale counter-strike operation. Vladimirskiy nevertheless survived.

Another group of German airmen, the crew of a KG 27 He 111, spotted the counter-strike's main task force at sea between the Crimea and Odessa in the evening of 21 September. Covered by a large group of naval vessels, including two cruisers and three destroyers, transport ships brought Soviet 3rd Marine Rifle Regiment to the shores of Grigorevka, southwest of Odessa, where the troops landed behind the Romanian lines during the following night. This was coordinated with an attack by two of the Coastal Army's divisions. Utilizing the moment of surprise, the Soviets succeeded in their task of pushing back the Romanian forces and thus neutralizing the threat against Odessa from the powerful Romanian coastal batteries which had been established in the area.

Frunze was an old Soviet destroyer, built for the Imperial Russian Navy in 1914.

230

Cont.

At the airdromes of Beltsy and Baden, 6./StG 77 was alerted and made ready to take off as soon as the morning dawned. But before the Ju 87s could take off, twenty I-16 Ishaks from 69 IAP strafed the Stuka bases, claiming twenty enemy aircraft put out of action on the ground for the loss of one Ishak. The captured pilot of a Romanian PZL P.11 shot down by 69 IAP's Batalyonnyy Komissar Nikolay Verkhovets had revealed the whereabouts of the Stukas on 21 September. Simultaneously, naval Starshiy Leytenant Konstantin Denisov led a group of I-15bis biplanes, Ishaks, Yak-1s and Il-2 Shturmoviks against Chaplinka Airdrome, father east – claiming eleven German aircraft destroyed.[2]

However, the Soviet claims proved to be over-optimistic. In fact, Oberleutnant Ruppert's 6./StG 77 was soon in full action against the Soviet fleet off Grigorevka. In a series of dive-bomber attacks on 22 September, Ruppert and his men managed to damage the two destroyers *Bezposhchadnyy* and *Bezuprechnyy* – with the latter receiving such severe damage that it had to be towed to Odessa. When KG 51 was sent out against the same target that day, one of its Ju 88s was rammed by a MiG-3 piloted by Starshiy Leytenant Semen Karasyov of 32 IAP/VVS ChF.[3]

Meantime, the fighters of 69 IAP and VVS ChF fought hard to secure the skies above the landing grounds, claiming twelve Axis aircraft shot down between 22 and 24 September. Oberleutnant Ruppert's Ju 87 was shot down over the sea on the 23rd, and the crew bailed out and spent many hours in a rubber dinghy before it was rescued. But the very next day, Ruppert was in action against the Soviet ships again. In total, his 6./StG 77 was credited with the destruction of five naval vessels and four transport ships, for only two losses during this battle.

The Soviet landing at Grigorevka succeeded in establishing a bridgehead which threatened the Romanian positions, but had it not been for 6./StG 77's achievements, it is possible that the landing operation could have developed into something even worse for the Romanians. Shortly afterward, 6./StG 77 was moved far beyond the Dnepr to support Panzergruppe 1 in its attack from the Dnepropetrovsk bridgehead.

1 IV. Fliegerkorps, Tagesabschlussmeldung 19 September 1941.
2 TsVMA, f. 149, d. 4750, l. 37.
3 TsVMA, f. 3, op. 2200, d. 8, l. 134.

---

tions near Perekop. As large numbers of Bf 109s suddenly appeared ahead of the target area, the I-16 fighter-bombers were jettisoned. Kapitan Arseniy Shubikov, the able commander of the 2nd squadron in 32 IAP/ VVS ChF, led the four I-16s against a tank concentration below. At the same time, a swarm of Bf 109s from III./JG 77 pursued them. Several Messerschmitts attacked the escort with terrifying effect, downing five of the eight I-15bis and I-153 biplanes of 8 IAP/VVS ChF. Leutnant Emil Omert and his wingman went after the diving I-16s. Closing in at high speed, Omert opened fire against one of them, sending Kapitan Shubikov plunging to his death.

The pilots of II./JG 3 and III./JG 52 meanwhile concentrated on the Soviet fighter escort, reportedly shooting down nineteen of these planes. The day's total was 33 victories. The only loss suffered by the participating Jagdgruppen was 9./JG 52's Feldwebel Ewald "Ede" Dühn. In the air over the Brom factory, III./JG 52 fell on six Pe-2s escorted by four Yak-Is of 5/32 lAP/VVS ChF. According to the Soviet loss list, all six Pe-2s and one Yak-1 were shot down. Shortly after sending his twenty-third victim, a Pe-2, to the ground, Ede Dühn was last seen pursuing another bomber at low level.

Following the 23 October massacre, the Soviet aviation regiments in the Crimea were in complete disarray. Several experienced airmen had failed to return from the missions this day, and others were hospitalized with bad injuries. Apart from the large numbers of aircraft destroyed, there were damaged aircraft in need of repair before they could be used again. But the greatest blow was dealt to the fighting spirit of the airmen. What discouraged them further were the replacement aircraft brought in from the mainland. Proud Yak-1, MiG-3, and Pe-2 pilots found that they had to fly obsolete aircraft models

Cruiser Molotov, launched in December 1939, was one of the most modern Soviet warships in 1941. By that time it was the only ship in the Soviet Navy with radar. Its main armament consisted of three 18 cm guns, and it had 13 anti-aircraft guns of between 45 and 12.7 mm.

again – I-16s, I-153s, and SBs. The bulk of the new modern aircraft emerging from the factories was earmarked for the defense of Moscow.

Another Luftwaffe success was achieved in the same area on 23 October, when He 111 torpedo planes from 6./KG 26 damaged the tanker *Sovetskaya neft* in the Black Sea. It barely managed to reach the port of Feodosiya.

On 24 October the Soviet presence in the air was weaker than ever in the Perekop skies. Faced with Bf 109 fighters, the Soviet bombers jettisoned their bombs and banked away.[13] Next, it was the turn of the Soviet ground troops to feel wrath from the air. StG 77's Stukas, and twin-engine bombers from KG 27 and KG 51 broke up the Soviet defensive positions. German pioneer troops did the final job with flamethrowers and hand grenades. Three days later, the entire Crimean front crumbled.

According to German sources, 140 Soviet planes were shot down during the final battle over the Perekop front, from 18 to 24 October: 124 by German fighters and 16 by ground fire. Suffering heavy losses during the following days and with no available replacements, the number of Soviet aircraft in the Crimea diminished rapidly. During the last seven days of October, 5 Eskadrilya/32 IAP/ VVS ChF lost fifteen of the seventeen Yak-1s it had on the evening of 23 October.

On 31 October a general Soviet retreat was ordered in the Crimea – with the Coastal Army falling back to Sevastopol and the 51st Army withdrawing to Kerch in the eastern part of the peninsula. With its aviation in shambles, the

Soviet Black Sea Fleet sent in its naval vessels to shell the advancing German army and support the withdrawal. Elements of the Coastal Army were evacuated by ships from Yevpatoria on the Crimea's western coast.

On 31 October the destroyer *Bodryy* subjected Taganrog and the German airfield to shelling. III./StG 77 was alerted, and although no bombs hit the ship, machine-gun fire from the Stukas injured fifty of *Bodryy*'s crewmembers, including the commander. On 2 November, three Ju 88s of KG 51 attacked the cruiser *Voroshilov* and scored two bomb hits, which put the ship out of action for several months.

One of the largest tragedies at sea in history occurred on 7 November, when 6./KG 26's torpedo planes hit and sank the passenger steamer *Armeniya*, which was evacuating soldiers and refugees from Sevastopol, in the Black Sea south of Yalta. Of an estimated five thousand people on board, all but eight perished in the sea. The cruiser *Molotov* fared better as it on 10 November managed to ward off attacks by 6./KG 26 after shelling German troops in the Feodosiya area in southeastern Crimea.

With the battle of the Crimea reaching what seemed to be a final conclusion, Fliegerkorps IV and the Black Sea Fleet clashed violently on 12 November. Led by Hauptmann Alfons Orthofer, II./StG 77's Stukas attacked the Soviet warships that supported the defenders of Sevastopol, the main port on the Crimean west coast. The cruiser *Chervona Ukraina* was sunk after receiving three bomb hits from Hauptmann Orthofer. Other Stuka pilots

Troops of 79th Naval Rifle Brigade boarding cruiser Krasnyy Kavkaz of Soviet Black Sea Fleet to be deployed to Sevastopol in December 1941. The Black Sea Fleet played a decisive role during the Soviet defense of Sevastopol.

managed to hit and damage the destroyers *Sovershennyy* and *Bezposhchadnyy*, all without any loss to the German airmen.

While the Coastal Army managed to establish defensive positions at Sevastopol, things looked grim for the battered 51st Army, which was pursued towards the southeast as it fell back to Kerch. Stalin decided to send one of his most loyal cronies, Marshal Georgiy Kulik, to assume superior command over the 51st Army. This proved to be a fatal mistake. As we have seen previously, Kulik was atrociously incompetent as a military commander. He also was terribly corrupt. After the fall of Kerch on the easternmost tip of the Peninsula on 17 November, Stalin's patience with Kulik was gone. Brought before court he was demoted and deprived of all his awards – a mild punishment in comparison to what other, far more able Soviet commanders faced. The verdict found him guilty of having increased the chaos and demoralization at Kerch, which was abandoned owing to Kulik's failure to organize the resistance. German accounts of the scene that met 11. Armee's troops as they approached Kerch seem to confirm the Soviet court's conclusion.

But the main port of Sevastopol, the greatest bait in the Crimea, remained in Soviet hands. Without doubt, this was largely due to the efforts of the Soviet airmen. As the balance sheet was drawn, it showed that they had held the Germans back for as long as it took to build up the defenses of Sevastopol – very similar to the performances by the VVS and DBA in the Ukraine by the same time.

While most of the Luftwaffe left the Crimea for other tasks – II./JG 3 to the Mediterranean theater, and III./JG 52 to Taganrog to support the offensive against Rostov – 11. Armee noted that the Soviets again took control of the air.[14] Indeed this captures the situation on the Eastern Front in a nutshell. In reality, this air superiority was upheld by a VVS ChF mustering only 59 aircraft, including 39 that were serviceable, in Sevastopol by 22 November.[15] But when a DB-3F of 63 BAB discovered a large concentration of German aircraft at Spat Airdrome, this force was sufficient to deal a devastating blow. Twenty-three Pe-2s, Il-2s, I-16s and MiG-3s attacked, and against the loss of a single aircraft they managed to knock out twelve of III./StG 77's Ju 87s – practically wiping out this Stukagruppe.[16]

Meanwhile, Einsatzgruppe D – subordinated to 11. Armee – carried out its gruesome task in the Crimea. Between 11 November and 11 December 1941, it reported the killings of 20,735 people, 95 % of them Jews. With that, Einsatzgruppe D had executed a total of 75,881 people since it began operations in the East. The largest single massacre took place at Simferopol between 9 and 13 December, when over 12,000 Jews and up to 1,000 Roma people were murdered. The commander of Einsatzgruppe D, SS-Standartenführer Otto Ohlendorf, was sentenced to death and executed by hanging in West Germany after the war.

233

THE END IN ODESSA.

On 29 September, the Soviets decided to evacuate Odessa and concentrate on the defense of the Crimea, which after all was of even greater strategic significance.

On 14 October, Vice-Admiral Oktyabrskiy dispatched his entire Black Sea Fleet to conduct a rapid evacuation of Odessa. While German air attacks against the ships were largely warded off by AAA and fighters – only the transport ship *Gruziya* received a bomb hit on 14 October – the embarkation onto the transport ships was prepared. In order to divert the enemy's attention, a final Soviet air raid against Constanta in Romania was flown on 15 October. Only on 16 October, when the last troops were being shipped away, did it dawn on the Axis what was taking place. All available German bombers were sent out to attack the fleet, but the powerful Soviet fighter cover, in combination with the anti-aircraft guns on the ships, provided the vessels with an effective shield. The War Diary of 2./KG 27 noted, "The sky above the convoys is filled with enemy fighters, and a fierce air battle is raging. We are able to count up to thirty fighters of all types, I-16s, I-17s, I-18s and Curtiss. In addition to that, we are beset by well-aimed AAA fire from the ships. We get involved in a whirling fight above the ships, which attempt to avoid the bombs by zig-zagging."[1]

The confused situation in the air over the convoy, to which the effect of smokescreens from the Soviet ships was added, caused the German bomber crews to misjudge the result of their attacks. They returned to base to submit claims for six freighters sunk, plus another eight transport ships and an MTB damaged.[2] In reality, the only success they managed to achieve against the evacuation fleet was the sinking of the ship *Bolshevik*, which went down with sixteen men after it had been hit by a torpedo from one of 1./KG 28's He 111 torpedo planes. A total of 350,000 soldiers and civilians, and 200,000 tons of materiel were ferried to Sevastopol.

The Romanian troops who marched into Odessa on 16 October were too exhausted and too humiliated to feel any triumph. The sixty-four-day-long siege of Odessa must be regarded as an important Soviet defensive success. Not only did the Coastal Army succeed in holding this strategically important port for so long – contributing decisively to delaying the Axis offensive against the Crimea and Rostov; it also ground down the Romanian Army and the whole Romanian Air Force to a point where the former was badly depleted and the latter had to be withdrawn from combat service on the Eastern Front for almost a whole year. While 16,578 of Odessa's Soviet defenders were reported killed or missing, and 24,690 were injured, the long siege of Odessa cost the Romanian Army around 100,000 casualties.

Among those evacuated from Odessa were tens of thousands of Jews, who were thus spared a fearsome fate. On 22 October, a delayed bomb exploded in the Romanian headquarters in the city, killing General Ioan Glogojeanu, the Romanian commander, and several other officers. Similar to what happened in Kiev at Babiy Yar, the Romanians blamed the Jews and took a terrible revenge. Romanian and German soldiers immediately began to seize and kill civilians, by shooting or hanging, most of them Jews. On the morning of 23 October, over 19,000 Jews were herded together in nine ammunition dumps. Many were shot and then the dumps were set on fire, with everyone inside being burned alive. Another 20,000 were forced into an anti-tank ditch where they were shot.

Colonel Radu Glogojeanu, who went to Odessa to retrieve his uncle's body, was terrified by what he saw. Afterward he said, "The scene in Odessa was horrific. I saw bodies hanging from telegraph poles. I saw groups of civilians rounded up by German soldiers."[3]

The remaining Jews were herded into the city's Jewish ghetto, where most of the buildings were destroyed. Left under open sky for ten days, many died of exposure.

Then 54,000 Jews were deported to the newly erected Romanian concentration camp at Bogdanovka. On 21 December, the annihilation of all inmates at Bogdanovka began. Five thousand sick and disabled prisoners were locked into two stables and burned to death. The rest of the prisoners were marched to the banks of a nearby river, where they were ordered to undress. Then the killings began. While thousands were shot in the back of their necks or butchered with hand grenades, others froze to death in the cold. Three days later, the killings stopped temporarily, but were resumed on 28 December. Only two hundred Jews were spared. For two months, these were forced to exhume the bodies. In the process, 150 of these last remaining prisoners succumbed to cold or hunger or were killed by their Ukrainian guards.[4]

The Romanian Army sustained very heavy personnel losses during the siege of Odessa. One of the most successful defenders was the Soviet female sniper Lyudmila Pavlichenko. Seen in the picture with her 7.62mm Tokarev SVT-40 semi-automatic rifle with 3.5X telescopic sight, she is regarded as the most successful female sniper in history. She was born in Biyala Tserkov in the Ukraine. When the war broke out she was a 24-year old history student at the University of Kiev. She was one among very many Soviet women and girls who volunteered to fight the invaders. Having trained in sharpshooting before the war, she became an Army sharpshooter and served with the 25th Rifle Division of the 9th Separate Army, which was later reorganized into the Coastal Army.

Pavlichenko scored 187 kills during the Battle of Odessa, and was afterwards evacuated to Sevastopol, where she increased her score to 309, including 36 enemy snipers, before she was injured by shrapnel in June 1942. Evacuated to the mainland just before Sevastopol fell, she was sent on a propaganda tour to the United States and the UK. Returning to the USSR in 1943, she was appointed a Hero of the Soviet Union and spent the remainder of the war training snipers. After the war she completed her studies to become a professional historian. Pavlichenko passed away on 10 October 1974, at the age of 58. She has been honoured with a song by American folk singer Woodie Guthrie, "Miss Pavlichenko," and the Russian-Ukrainian biographical film on her life, named "Battle for Sevastopol," was released in 2015.

1 Boelcke-Archiv, III.2./KG 27, Kriegstagebuch.
2 IV. Fliegerkorps, Tagesabschlussmeldung, 16 October 1941.
3 "The Odessa Massacre" in Radio Romania International, 2011-11-14.
4 Gilbert, *The Holocaust*, p. 217–218.

The Soviet counter-offensive.

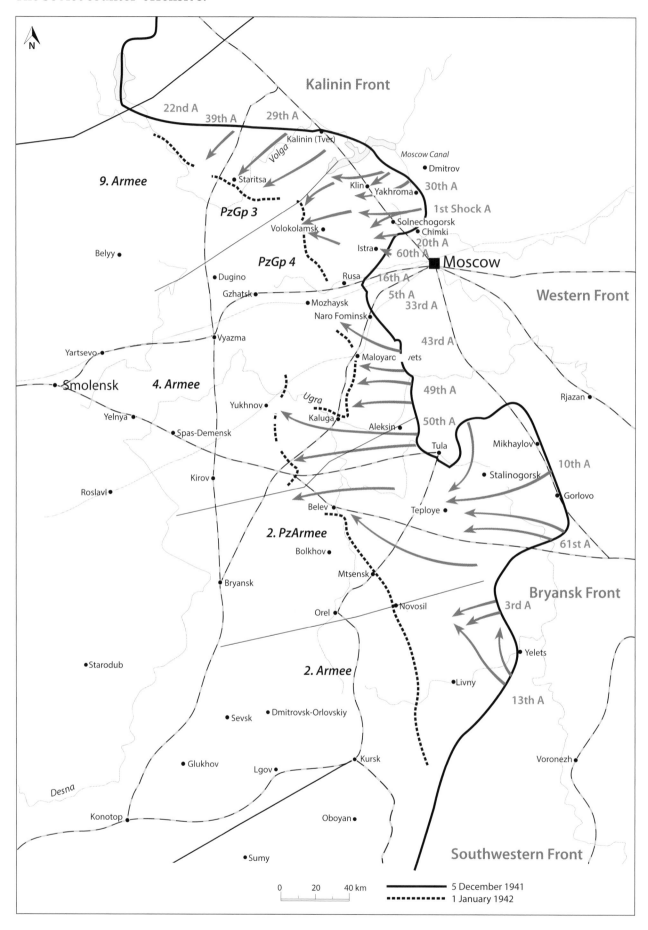

18: THE RED ARMY STRIKES BACK.

"Turn the gates of Moscow into a tomb for the German hordes!
Not a single step backwards – that is the demand of the Motherland!
We shall exterminate the Fascist plunderers, each one of them!
We shall not allow them to torment our country!"

– Polkovnik Leonid Sandalov, Chief of Staff of the 20th Army, 6 December 1941.

The Russian winter arrived in mid-November, making the soggy roads freeze and become passable again. On 15 November Heeresgruppe Mitte resumed Operation Typhoon, with Panzergruppe 3 attacking at Kalinin, north-west of Moscow. Simultaneously, the Kalinin Front's 30th Army attempted a counter-attack, which was completely smashed by German armor heavily supported by Stukas of Fliegerkorps VIII. The 30th Army's 58th Tank Division, which had just arrived from the Far East with 254 tanks – of which however only seven were KVs or T-34s – was completely routed. It was left with only one T-34 and 30 T-26 tankettes after just two days of fighting.[1] The divisional commander, General-Mayor Aleksandr Kotlyarov, committed suicide. Pushed back across the Moscow Channel at Yakhroma, the 30th Army was shifted to the Western Front's control. (Thus, the Kalinin Front was left with only three armies, the 22nd, 29th and 31st.)

In freezing temperatures on 16 November, Panzergruppe 4 attacked Soviet 16th Army with V. Armeekorps and XLVI. Panzerkorps – including the two rested 2. and 5. Panzer, which had arrived from Germany only

six weeks previously – to the south of Panzergruppe 3. "The time for waiting is over!" the commander, Hoepner, enthusiastically told his men: "We can attack again! The last Russian defense before Moscow is defeated. We must stop the beating of the heart of the Bolshevik movement in Europe!"

A fierce tank battle developed as the Soviets dispatched five tank brigades against the onslaught on Volokolamsk. Supported by 140 tanks – of which 46 were T-34s and KVs – the Soviets fought 400 German tanks for two whole days. Both sides were hampered by the deep snow, which made the men sink down to the waist, and the tanks able to maneuver only with the greatest difficulty. Supported by bombers and Stukas the Germans made repeated attempts to break through, without achieving any results for several days. In twilight in the forests and deep snow, individual Soviet *Frontovniki* could be quite effective against German tanks. Ivan Globin, a teenage Komsomol member from the village of Prochnookopskoy, hid behind a pine tree with a Molotov cocktail as a group of German tanks crept up. Their engines screamed in the cold. Their guns banged, their machine guns rattled. Tracer bullets whistled between the trees and into the snow. Globin calculated the distance to the closest tank. When no more than twenty-five steps lay between him and the tank, he prepared himself. The steel monster crawled past. Its machine gun peppered a pine tree next to the one behind which Globin was hiding. For a split second Globin thought he was going to faint, but then he pulled himself together, took a deep breath and jumped forward and threw the bottle. The breaking of glass was heard. Behind the turret of the tank a bright flame lit up. Then came smoke and in the next instant, a mighty flame shot up, setting a tree on fire. While the tank was fully ablaze, Globin hurled a bundle of grenades against a second tank. The German tanks stopped, allowing Mayor Skugaryov, the assistant regimental commander, to open fire at one of them, although he was wounded himself. Leytenant Zakharchenko's platoon of anti-tank guns managed to destroy two more tanks.

Although fiercely determined to fight the enemy, the recruits at Volokolamsk were terribly inexperienced, and this cost them bloody losses. Vsevolod Olimpev was one of them. He recalls how surprised he was to find the

German soldiers receive their first winter outfit in a village west of Moscow. The arrival of the winter, which caused the roads to freeze, was greeted with optimism by the Germans. (Photo: Arno Becker.)

near complete military ignorance not only among the soldiers, but also among the commanders who fought at Volokolamsk.

In the evening of 17 November, when the fighting had died down, the platoon to which Olimpev belonged sat down and took some vodka. Since the men had not eaten all day, they quickly became intoxicated by the alcohol, and suddenly a politruk stood up, cursing and toting a revolver, and yelled, "Forward! For your mother! Down with Fascism!" Immediately the whole group stood up and ran to attack the Germans. The drunken men were more of a crowd than an attack formation as they came dashing along a road in the darkness to charge a village occupied by the enemy. Several houses were still smoldering after the fighting during the day. Olimpev heard commands shouted in a foreign language, and suddenly they were covered with fire from the machine gun of a tank that stood parked not far away to the left. Almost simultaneously, two more machine guns opened up on their right hand side. The Soviet soldiers fell to the ground. Olimpev was lucky to fall into a ditch at the side of the road, and this saved his life. The shooting stopped, and the Germans seemed to have assumed that they had killed all the Soviets. Eventually the survivors managed to make it back to their own positions, but with half their number left behind.[2]

However, not all Soviet units were that inexperienced. The 1st Guards Tank Brigade – the renumbered 4th Tank

Brigade since 11 November – was quite successful in this battle, where it employed 39 tanks, of which 19 were T-34s. On 18 November, this unit's Starshiy Leytenant Dmitriy Lavrinenko repeated the feat he had achieved when he successfully ambushed 4. Panzer-Division at Mtsensk on 11 October. This time he made a lone attack with his T-34 against ten tanks of 2. Panzer-Division near Gusenevo, 15 kilometers east of Volokolamsk. Lavrinenko claimed to have knocked out seven enemy tanks before his own T-34 was badly hit, with two crew members getting killed. The war diary of 2. Panzer-Division confirms that five Panzer Is were knocked out.[3] Lavrinenko made it back to the own lines to continue the fight. Shortly afterward he was appointed a Hero of the Soviet Union, with a total of 37 tank kills on his account.

Cavalry Group Dovator (50th and 53rd Cavalry divisions) under General-Mayor Lev Dovator played an important role fighting the German infantry in this battle. Moving fast through the snow both day and night, the cavalrymen managed to inflict bloody losses in repeated raids against the German infantry. On 19 November, the 4th Squadron of the 37th Cavalry Regiment (50th Division) rode over a battalion of German Infanterie-Regiment 240, cutting down scores of German soldiers with their sabres. But then the horsemen came under fire from an artillery regiment of 106. Infanterie-Division. German war correspondent Paul Karl Schmidt witnessed the scene, vividly described in his post-war book about Operation Barbarossa:*

* Carell, *Unternehmen Barbarossa*, pp. 152–154, "Cavalry attack on Mussino," where Schmidt incorrectly described the Soviet unit as the "44th Mongolian Cavalry Division."

Cavalry Group Dovator (50th and 53rd Cavalry divisions) in December 1941. Led by General-Mayor Lev Dovator, this force achieved considerable success during the Soviet counter-offensive at Moscow, when deep snow hindered rapid movement by infantry in the terrain. But the unit also sustained bloody losses itself. General-Mayor Dovator himself was killed in action on 19 December 1941, and was posthumously appointed a Hero of the Soviet Union. (Photo: Krigsarkivet Stockholm.)

"The 3rd Battery of Artillery Regiment 107 of the 106th ID opens up from an open fire position. With great booms, the shells leave the pipes and explode in the midst of the attacking squadrons. The explosive shells from the Pak guns in the village, which had just been attacked by the T-34s, burst into the Russian lead group. Horses plunge, riders fly through the air. Flashes, smoke, fountains of dirt and fire. The regiment carries on. With an iron discipline, it even swings to the right and rides towards the village. But now the artillery fire comes crashing into the squadrons. The batteries launch ricocheting shells. The grenades explode at an altitude of eight meters. The fragment effect is terrible. The riders are torn apart in their saddles, the horses mown down."[4]

A Panzer III of 7. Panzer-Division, which managed to cross the partially frozen Moscow Channel at Yakhroma on 27 November 1941. The road signs have been scratched out by the German censor.

In this bloody battle, both sides exaggerated the enemy's losses. Indeed, the 50th Cavalry Division's combat report shows that 4th Squadron of the 37th Cavalry Regiment was completely annihilated in this action, but the losses were 36 killed and 44 wounded, not two thousand as Schmidt claims.[5] Neither was this, as Schmidt asserts, "one of the last great cavalry attacks of the war"; in fact, the Red Army used cavalry units with quite some success throughout the war, not least in their upcoming winter offensive. Lev Dovator himself was killed in action on 19 December 1941, and was posthumously appointed a Hero of the Soviet Union.

In a domino effect the German offensive extended southwards. On 18 November, 4. Armee – to which Panzergruppe 4 was subordinated – attacked all along the front from Volokolamsk in the north to Naro Fominsk in the south, while Guderian's 2. Panzerarmee joined in with a massive strike northwards in the Tula region. Fliegerkorps VIII supported the offensive by dispatching all available aircraft into attacks against Soviet field positions, troop concentrations, railways, and airfields. With Moscow nearly in sight, the German commanders expected the imminent seizure of the Soviet capital. It is indicative of the optimism on the German side at this stage that Guderian was assigned the task of advancing to Gorkiy – 400 kilometers east of Moscow![6]

On 19 November the War Diary of the German High Command noted, "Following heavy fighting, Panzergruppe 4 broke through the enemy lines along its entire front and gained much ground, particularly in V. Armeekorps' sector."[7] Soviet 16th Army had bled white in its attempts to halt the drive against Moscow from the west. By 21 November, cavalry and rifle regiments in the army were down at a strength of 150-200 men. Out of 140 tanks on 15 November, 54 had been lost. The 78th Rifle Division was hardest hit, having sustained 60 per cent losses in just one week.[8] Back in Berlin, Hitler was filled with new hope, stating that the success in Russia, which he described as "a prodigious achievement," was "of great political value."[9] On 23 November, Klin, half-way between Kalinin and Moscow, was seized by Panzergruppe 3.

Improved road conditions in the southern sector also enabled Generalfeldmarschall von Rundstedt's Heeresgruppe Süd to renew its attack against Rostov, the gateway to the oil fields in the Caucasus, on 17 November. By that time, Fliegerkorps V had been worn down to a mere 91 operational aircraft (figures for 15 November). Taken together, KG 54 and KG 55 could field no more than 16 serviceable bombers, while there were 17 serviceable Ju 87s in Stab and I./StG 77.[10] To counter VVS Southern Front's 120 serviceable aircraft (figures for 1 November) – 56 bombers, three Shturmoviks, and 61 fighters[11] – Fliegerkorps V possessed 41 serviceable fighters.

The Southern Front responded to von Rundstedt's attack by launching a powerful counter-attack from the northeast. The airmen of VVS Southern Front supported the offensive with nearly four hundred sorties on 19 November.[12] But this Soviet attack was defeated mainly through the vigorous action by StG 77 and the He 111s of KG 27 that were rushed in from Fliegerkorps IV. Despite a low cloud ceiling and snowfalls, the few remaining Ju 87s in StG 77 were in incessant action, blowing up any Soviet attempt to resist. On 20 November the German troops reached Rostov. The next day the city was in German hands.

With the capture of Rostov, Heeresgruppe Süd had exhausted its last strength. On the Soviet side, fresh rein-

A German Panzer III tank in fierce combat over possession of a village near Moscow.

239

German soldiers during the winter battle west of Moscow.
(Photo: Via Daniel Johansson.)

forcements were brought in to the north and east of Rostov. Farther to the north, the drive to the east by the German 6. and 17.armies was bogged down at Severniy Donets, southeast of the city of Kursk. A parallel situation developed along the entire Eastern Front. The physically and psychologically weakened German troops had lost the energy and the material requirements to withstand the upcoming wave of renewed local counter-attacks.

As a symbolic finale to the German victory march on the Eastern Front, the Luftwaffe's number-one ace, Oberst Werner Mölders, left Chaplinka Airdrome on the southern combat zone aboard an He 111 from KG 27 early in the morning of 22 November. Mölders had been ordered back to Germany to take part in the funeral of the late chief of supply and procurement of the Luftwaffe, Ernst Udet, who had committed suicide five days earlier. But Mölders never reached his destination. The aircraft crashed near Breslau and he was killed.

In late November 1941 the Wehrmacht on the Eastern Front was a mere shadow of what it had been five months previously. Losses had brought down the strength of army and Luftwaffe units to 30 or 40 percent, or even less, of their original strength. The veteran front-line *Landser* were badly effected by battle fatigue after five months of intense, incessant combat. Another major problem was the overextended supply lines, where columns traveling hundreds of miles on primitive roads ran the constant hazard of partisan ambushes. At this point the Germans also faced the stiffest Soviet resistance so far encountered.

On 27 November, Starshiy Leytenant Maksim Kulak of 120 IAP flew his I-153 directly into a large column of German troops west of the Moscow Channel, north of the Soviet capital.[13] German 7. Panzer-Division managed to cross the partially frozen Moscow Channel at Yakhroma, but on the 28th, six 150 SBAP SBs led by Mladshiy Leytenant Filipp Demchenkov managed to destroy the major bridge across the channel, thus disrupting the flow of German supplies. This allowed the new 1st Shock Army of the Kalinin Front to launch a successful counter-attack. For his feat, Demchenkov was posthumously appointed a Hero of the Soviet Union.

Three Soviet air divisions supported the counter-attack at Yakhroma. In spite of frightening losses – 627 IAP sacrificed all of its I-16s in only three days – these air units managed to carry out 150 to 180 sorties a day as long as the battle lasted. Inundated by falling bombs, the German tank division beat a hasty retreat back across the channel on 29 November.

South of Moscow, 2. Panzerarmee managed to occupy Mikhaylov, 90 km east of Tula, but then repeated air attacks managed to completely halt Guderian's advance – a fact which was recognized in a report to the German High Command.[14] Soviet 6 IAK carried out 370 close-support sorties, claiming the destruction of 77 tanks and 263 trucks during the last three days of November. Historian Robert Kershaw notes how German panzer soldier Leutnant Georg Richter repeatedly referred to Soviet air attacks in his diary during these days: "On 26 November he observed, 'there are heaps of Russian aircraft around – our own very seldom!' The following day, 'Russian aircraft totally dominate air space' over Panzergruppe 4, and as the advance got under way he declared, 'Russian flyers dominate the air and the ground'. Repeated references to Russian air superiority and strafing attacks are made on 29 November and 2 and 3 December. Every attack killed or wounded small numbers of artillerymen and began to significantly disable increasing numbers of artillery-towing vehicles. Russian air dominance had a cumulative and negative impact on morale. Attacks were more effective in winter than summer because men and vehicles were unable to quickly get off roads, hemmed in by piled up snow from clearance, and funnelled by the wooded terrain through which they advanced."[15]

These efforts by the Soviet air units gave the battered Soviet 50th Army time to regroup in the Tula sector, south of Moscow. This success further bolstered Soviet fighting spirits, as did news from the southern sector the following day. Here, Marshal Timoshenko, the commander in chief of the Red Army's Southwestern Direction, had brought forward strong Red Army reinforcements against the northern flank of the German 1. Panzerarmee in Rostov. These forces were launched in an energetic counter-offensive during the last days of November 1941. This time the German lines immediately crumbled. Von Rundstedt decided to pull back his weakened units to a defensive position along the Mius River. Although this saved 1. Panzerarmee from being surrounded, it cost von Rundstedt his command.

The liberation of Rostov on 30 November 1941 was the first major success in the war with Germany. Contrary to the situation on the Moscow front, the VVS in the South could play only a minor role during this campaign. With the cream of the modern production program allocated to the defense of the capital, the Soviet airmen in the South were largely left with obsolescent aircraft models, such as the SB bombers, I-16 fighters, and Polikarpov biplanes used in the ground-attack role. This inevitably resulted in considerable losses. During an upsurge in air fighting between

27 and 29 November, the three Luftwaffe fighter groups operating against VVS Southern Front claimed to have shot down 45 Soviet planes, of which III./JG 52 was responsible for more than half. VVS Southern Front recorded 90 aircraft lost in combat between 1 November and 1 December.[16] Nevertheless, the dogfights were not always one-sided. On November 28, 1941, Oberleutnant Günther Rall, the commander of 8./JG 52, was shot down and badly wounded by a Yak-1 to the west of Rostov. At the time, Rall had been credited with thirty-eight victories.

The weakness of the VVS in the southern combat zone is one of the main reasons why the Germans managed to hold out at the Mius line, fending off all Soviet attempts to break through.

Soviet infantry counter-attacks to retake Rostov in November 1941.

Meanwhile, Heeresgruppe Mitte was slowly closing in on Moscow from three directions. On 2 December, elements of 258. Infanterie-Division managed to penetrate Moscow's northwestern suburb of Khimki, only 15 kilometers from the Red Square. On 4. Armee's right flank, Naro Fominsk, 50 kilometers southwest of Moscow, was captured. 2 December was a day with clear skies and temperatures of minus 20 degrees Celsius.[17] Both sides sent their aviation into the air, and JG 51's War Diary described the day as "a big battle day," with claims for 17 Soviet aircraft shot down – four of them by Hauptmann Heinz Bär, who thus reached his 85th victory.[18] But Soviet fighter pilots also reported seventeen enemy aircraft shot down during forty aerial encounters in this area. Included among the victims on the German side was the Staffelkapitän of 5./StG 1, Hauptmann Joachim Rieger. Surprised by Soviet fighters, Rieger's wingman made a rash evasive maneuver and rammed his Staffelkapitän. Both Ju 87s went down. Rieger was one of the most experienced Stuka fliers in the Luftwaffe, having conducted 257 combat missions, for which he was posthumously awarded with the Knight's Cross.

Also on 2 December, the Il-2 Shturmoviks of 65 ShAP fell upon the German troops that were retreating from Yakhroma, northwest of Moscow, and reportedly destroyed nearly a hundred vehicles. With their supply columns in disarray through repeated air attacks, Hoepner's Panzergruppe 3 and Reinhardt's Panzergruppe 4 were forced to halt their offensives due to lack of fuel and ammunition. The Soviet aviation now shifted focus to attacks against the German troops and artillery positions in order to prepare the ground for the planned counter-offensive.

This was planned and organized by Zhukov during the transition from November-December 1941. It was to be initiated on 6 December with a strike against the flank of Guderian's 2. Panzerarmee at Yelets by a force of 60,000 troops from the Southwestern Front's northern flank. Next, the Kalinin and Western fronts would carry out a pincer movement, with the former attacking towards the south in the Kalinin sector, northwest of Moscow, and the Western Front striking in a westerly direction outside of Moscow.

New Soviet armies were being formed at a breathtaking pace. In October and November 1941, no less than eleven new armies were created. It is often said that back on 14 September 1941 the Soviet spy in Tokyo, Richard Sorge, had informed Stalin that Japan would not attack the Soviet Union until Moscow was captured by the Germans. It is commonly asserted that this information saved Moscow in the sense that it allowed the Red Army to release large numbers of troops – often depicted as well-equipped and highly trained – from the Far East to Moscow. But this must be dismissed as a myth, based purely on speculation. What Sorge actually found out was that Japan would not attack the Soviet Union *unless* "the USSR transfers troops on a large scale from the East."[19]

In fact, no more than three divisions were dispatched from the Far East to the Moscow sector during the whole period October–December 1941, the 32nd and 78th Rifle divisions and the 58th Tank Division. Two more divisions, the 93rd Rifle and 82nd Mechanized, arrived from the Trans Baykal Military District, and three – the 18th and 20th Mountain Cavalry divisions and the 238th Rifle Division – came from the Central Asian Military District. These were just nine out of a total of 219 divisions employed by the Red Army along the front on 1 December 1941.

But the eleven new armies and over two hundred divisions looked impressive only on the paper. In reality they were mere "skeletons," as one Red Army commander put it. The 18th Mountain Cavalry Divisions from the Central Asian Military District was down at one-third of its

Soviet Ilyushin Il-2 assault planes roam the skies over the Moscow front. (Photo via Drabkin.)

assigned troop strength. The armies were armies in name only. Western Front's new 20th Army, which was formed after the previous 20th Army had been destroyed in the Vyazma battle in October, comprised of just two Rifle divisions and three separate brigades. Many divisions were down at just slightly over two thousand men.

The new 10th Army (the previous one having been annihilated in the Biyalystok envelopment in June), formed on 8 November 1941, constituted of men who in most cases were between 30 and 40 years of age, and up to 65 % of these had no military training. After no more than 15 days of combat training it was sent to take on Guderian's 2. Panzerarmee during the upcoming counter-offensive.

A new kind of army, the so-called Shock Army, was introduced. Assigned with a high proportion of infantry, engineers and field artillery, its purpose was to create a breach in the German lines through its sheer weight. Next, mobile units such as tank and cavalry units would charge through the penetration and advance deep into the German rear area. The first among these, 1st Shock Army, was assigned to the Kalinin Front.

Archive in Podolsk (TsAMO), Moscow. These show that on 1 December 1941, Heeresgruppe Mitte was pitted against Soviet forces mustering a total of 576,500 troops, 5,000 artillery pieces and 574 tanks.

Red Army strength opposed to Heeresgruppe Mitte on 1 December 1941

Front	Troop strength	Artillery and mortars	Tanks
Western Front	441,920	4,495	537
Kalinin Front	74,601	117	7 [sic]
Right wing of South-western Front	60,000	388	30
Total	**576,500**	**5,000**	**574**

Sources: TsAMO, f. 208, op. 2511, d. 222; TsAMO, f. 213, op. 2002, d. 28; TsAMO, f. 202, op. 2231, d. 11.

Soviet soldiers with dogs, each with a 10 kg mine strapped to its back, to be used against German tanks on the Moscow front in December 1941. These dogs had been specially trained by giving them food under tanks. At the front line they were set loose against German tanks, with the idea that they would crawl under them and the mine would be set off as a lever that extended about 20 cm in height struck the bottom of the tank. In reality, these so-called "anti-tank dogs" proved relatively unsuccessful. They often were scared off by the sound of moving tanks and gunshots, and the Germans soon learned of their purpose and shot the dogs as they approached. Their employment was indicative of the desperate shortage of anti-tank weapons in the Soviet army in late 1941.

Figures on the strength of Soviet forces that would participate in Zhukov's offensive vary greatly between different sources, but mostly second-hand sources are referred to. It is quite remarkable that this state of affairs still prevails, since the actual figures are available in reports from each Front, army and division at the Russian State Military

Interestingly, the actual strength of Heeresgruppe Mitte is subject to some debate: According to German historian Klaus Reinhardt, citing an army group report, the troop strength was 1,929,409, but Niklas Zetterling and Anders Frankson dispute this, claiming the strength to have been slightly less than 1.2 million in November 1941.[20] Even if the latter figures are accepted, and although a substantial portion of these German troops were in the rear, Heeresgruppe Mitte enjoyed a substantial numerical superiority in troops when the Soviet offensive was opened.*

This also was the case with regard to armored forces. No exact figures for Heeresgruppe Mitte's tank strength in early December 1941 are available, but it may be assumed that its tank strength was on about the same level as when Operation Typhoon had commenced two months earlier, i.e. 1,800 tanks and assault guns. The total number of German tanks and assault guns on the Eastern Front on 30 September 1941 had been slightly over 2,000 (including 90 % in Heeresgruppe Mitte), and owing to replacements, this number *increased* to 2,177 on 30 November.[21] (Overall German tank strength increased from 4,874, including 4,002 operational, on 1 October 1941 to 5,004, including 4,084 operational, on 1 December 1941, while the number of operational assault guns increased from 508 to 598.[22]) Heeresgruppe probably enjoyed not only a three-fold numerical superiority in tanks, but of the Soviet tanks employed against it, only around 30 % were T-34s or KVs, with the remainder being obsolete tankettes.

Bearing in mind the disastrous Soviet losses during the double envelopment battles at Vyazma and Bryansk, it was quite logical that the Red Army forces opposed to Heeresgruppe Mitte were considerably weaker than they had been on the eve of Operation Typhoon in late September 1941.

---

* Soviet sources give the figure of (an additional) 240,862 troops in the rear area of the Red Army units involved in the Moscow offensive in December 1941. It should also be kept in mind that when the German front lines collapsed, a significant amount of the rear area troops were hurriedly rushed to the front line.

WHY WAS THE SOVIET FLOW OF REINFORCEMENTS NOT BLOCKED FROM THE AIR?

The steady flow of new troops and equipment to the Moscow area in November 1941 was indeed kept under close surveillance by the Luftwaffe's long-range air reconnaissance units. A question posed by many historians and other writers is why the Soviet flow of reinforcements was not blocked from the air.

Much has been said and written concerning the lack of a German strategic bomber fleet. Counterfactual allegations have been made of how the Germans would have been able to "win the war" if they had "thought of building a strategic bomber fleet." But this disregards the fact that the whole Blitzkrieg concept originated from Germany's economic situation – mainly its lack of strategic raw materials – which provided no alternative beyond a short and decisive war. Hence, to place the greatest emphasis on tactical missions for the bomber force was, after all, most rational from the perspective of Germany's prime strategic imperative.

Nevertheless, at precisely this stage, the German bombers in fact conducted more strategic missions than previously on the Eastern Front. On the night of 5–6 October, 1941, three He 111s of 9./KG 55 bombed the large tank factory at Kramatorskaya. The next night, an arms factory in Rostov was targeted. Two weeks later, the same squadron raided Aircraft Factory No. 18 Znamia Truda at Voronezh, where Il-2 assault planes were manufactured.

In October 1941, hardly a night passed without Luftwaffe bombers attacking Moscow, albeit at only a nuisance level. Nineteen raids were carried out against the Soviet capital that month, all but a few at night time. "Day by day the air bombings of Moscow were intensified," wrote Georgiy Zhukov. "Air raid sirens were heard almost every night."[1] The main target was the railways. The logbook of Oberleutnant Hansgeorg Bätcher of KGr 100, lists seven missions against Moscow in October 1941. During the daytime on the 14th, Bätcher reported 90 rail wagons destroyed in an attack against a rail station south of Moscow. On the 17th, again in daylight, Bätcher logged the dropping of eleven bombs over Moscow. That same afternoon he attacked trains south of Moscow. On 21 October there followed another daylight raid against Moscow.[2] On 5–6 November, German bombers attacked the large GAZ automobile plants in Gorkiy both day and night.

It was only owing to the fact that incessant pressure at the front compelled the German bomber force to be employed chiefly in tactical missions that the forces available for such strategic air operations never became sufficiently large to have any lasting impact. Normally less than ten bombers took part in each of these raids. The highly effective Soviet anti-aircraft artillery concentrations around these targets also played an important role. Hansgeorg Bätcher recalled that the intense AAA fire over Gorkiy prevented him from observing the result of the bombardment.[3]

All this led to the fact that the vast majority of the Soviet flow of reinforcements arrived without any interference from the Luftwaffe.

Hansgeorg Bätcher flew a higher number of combat missions than any other medium bomber pilot during the war, 658 in total. He was in combat service between 1939 and 1945 and survived the war. Bätcher passed away on 24 April 2003, at the age of 89. (Photo: Bätcher.)

1 Zjukov, *Minnen och reflexioner*, vol. II, p. 21.
2 Hansgeorg Bätcher, Flight Book.
3 Interview with Hansgeorg Bätcher.

Relations of strength Heeresgruppe Mitte and its opponent

1941	Troops, German:Soviet	Tanks, German:Soviet	Aircraft, German:Soviet
30 September	1:1	2:1	1:1
1 December	2:1	3:1	1:2

However, there was one field in which the Soviets had at least a numerical superiority, and that was in the air. As we have seen, Fliegerkorps II and many of the units of Luftflotte 2 were shifted to the Mediterranean area in November 1941. On 11 November, Generalfeldmarschall Kesselring's Luftflotte 2 and the headquarters of Fliegerkorps II left for the Mediterranean area, where they were tasked with organizing the Luftwaffe operations mainly against Malta. This left General von Richthofen's Fliegerkorps VIII in control of all Luftwaffe units remaining on the Moscow front. On 5 December the Soviets had amassed 1,376 aircraft against Heeresgruppe Mitte, against fewer than 600 in Fliegerkorps VIII.[23] While the Luftwaffe had only 487 fighters (200 serviceable) remaining on the *entire* Eastern Front on 6 December, there were 674 Soviet fighters (480 serviceable) in the Moscow area alone on 5 December.[24] An often overlooked fact is that Soviet air superiority was actually one of the most decisive factors in the Soviet success at the gates of Moscow.

The counter-offensive was actually opened earlier than initially planned, by the Kalinin Front in the north. At dawn on 5 December its 29th and 31st armies attacked German 9. Armee at Kalinin. 75 per cent of the whole Soviet aviation in the Moscow sector was concentrated in the Kalinin sector to bolster the attack, and the Red Army's onslaught received a massive – and, to the Germans quite shocking – air support. "Hundreds of assault aircraft and fighter-bombers attacked the freezing and hungry German soldiers with bombs and machine-guns, thousands of shells smashed into their shelters, and thousands upon thousands of voices yelled 'Hurrah!'", reads a German account.[25]

The VVS was active all along the Moscow sector. South of Moscow, the northern flank of Soviet Southwestern Front and its air force held the Germans down. In this sector, German 2. Armee reported on 5 December: "The advance by XXXXIV. and XXXV. Armeekorps is held up by sustained attacks by strong enemy aviation."[26] Generaloberst Guderian's 2. Panzerarmee had to hurriedly discontinue its offensive against Tula, and it began a strategic withdrawal behind the upper Don River.

On 6 December, the offensive spread westwards, with the 30th Army and the new 1st Assault Army joining in, so that the northern flank of the "Kalinin-Klin wedge" was under attack along a 140-km stretch, while the 20th Army assaulted the wedge from the west. The previous night, Polkovnik Leonid Sandalov, Chief of Staff of the 20th

A column of Soviet light tanks of the model T-40 plus infantry getting prepared to attack the Germans in a forest west of Moscow in December 1941. The T-40 was a quite modern tank, entering service just prior to the German attack in June 1941. This two-man amphibious vehicle was one of few tanks that was able to cross a river without a bridge, and was designed as a fast reconnaissance light tank. Weighing 5.5 tons it could make 44 km/h on paved road. However, owing to the immense Soviet tank losses in the summer and autumn of 1941, it had to be employed as an infantry tank during the Battle of Moscow. Armed with nothing but a 12.7mm and a 7.62mm machine gun and with only a 20mm armor, it was hardly suited for this role. Most of the 113 T-40s available to the Western Front on 28 October 1941 were lost during the counter-offensive in December 1941.

HOW DID THE TROOPS COPE WITH THE EXTREME COLD?

A popular concept of Operation Barbarossa is that the German front troops in general had not been assigned with winter clothes. But according to Generalfeldmarschall von Rundstedt, "it is not entirely true that preparations for a winter campaign were not made. The famous winter clothing was there, but it didn't arrive, owing to rail difficulties and road transport."[1] Nevertheless, the image of a whole army fighting in only in light summer uniforms is totally out of question. Such an image may make an enduring impression on people who have no real experience of such low temperatures, but medical research shows that a man clad in only an Army summer fatigue in minus 35 degrees Celsius will suffer death from hypothermia in between 50 minutes and two hours. Frost bite sets in after only about 20 minutes, and soon the person gets difficulty in moving the body, begins to hallucinate and falls into unconsciousness. As the war diary of the 18. Panzer-Division noted, in spite of the great cold, "the troops often had to spend day and night in the open."[2] In fact, the German troops who had not been supplied with sufficient winter clothing found others means to protect themselves against the cold; Guderian wrote that his troops "had got hold of Russian overcoats and fur caps and only the national emblem showed that they were German."[3] As soon as the temperatures dropped, the *Landser* began to systematically plunder the Soviet civilian population for any clothing that would offer some protection against the bitter cold. Since many of the Russian houses in the battle zone had been burned down to the ground, this in effect condemned many a Russian civilian to an agonizing death through freezing, and further increased the hatred against the German occupiers. The Soviet propaganda's *Smert fashistskim okupantam* – "Death to the Fascist occupiers" – was without doubt no empty slogan.

The common notion that the German tanks were unable to get their engines running in the low temperatures is also an exaggeration. "Fortunately we have so far been able to keep our fine tanks in running order," Guderian wrote on 8 December 1941.[4]

There is no doubt that the Landser at the Moscow front were badly supplied and suffered badly from the arctic cold, but so did the Soviets. Owing to the war, agricultural production in the Soviet Union fell by 40 per cent. "The food is bad, twice a day we get bread, sometimes 400 grams, sometimes 600, we never see more. The soup is like water," a soldier of the 33rd Army wrote in November 1941.[5] The rate at which the Red Army troops were supplied with winter equipment has also been exaggerated. Soviet soldiers also froze to death, and thousands suffered from frostbite. "Today it got cold. There are no warm clothes or boots," wrote a *Frontovnik* in November 1941.[6] A Soviet study established that 30 per cent of the censored letters from troops of the Kalinin Front in December 1941 were "negative," with complaints over inadequate food and the lack of warm clothes dominating.[7]

1 Messenger, *The Last Prussian*, p. 154.
2 Bundesarchiv-Militärarchiv, RH 27-18/84.
3 Guderian, *Panzer Leader*. Kindle edition. Location 3560.
4 Guderian, Location 3762.
5 Reese, *Why Stalin's Soldiers Fought*, p. 212.
6 Ibid., p. 214.
7 Ibid.

Army, had sent his troops an order of the day which would become famous: "Turn the gates of Moscow into a tomb for the German hordes! Not a single step backwards – that is the demand of the Motherland! We shall exterminate the Fascist plunderers, each one of them! We shall not allow them to torment our country!"[27]

On 7 December, the Western Front's 16th Army attacked the southeastern corner of the "Kalinin-Klin wedge." The aim was to envelop Panzergruppen 3 and 4 in conjunction with the attack from the north. It was a bold attempt, to say the least, considering the fact that the northern strike force was composed of only 30 tanks, while the 20th Army in the east had only 15, and the 16th Army began the attack with 124 tanks.[28] They were up against a foe with a superiority of probably more than five to one in tanks. Meanwhile, two Soviet armies and a cavalry corps attacked south of Moscow, intent on surrounding 2. Panzerarmee.

The Soviet offensive coincided with an unusual temperature drop, to below minus 35 degrees Celsius on 5 and 6 December.[29] Fighting in such an Arctic climate was fearsome in more than one way, as Soviet artillery soldier Pavel Osipov, who took part in the attack on 6 December, recalled, "The worse thing of all were the freshly killed bodies of soldiers left steaming. The air was filled with the peculiar stench of flesh and blood."

While much of Western historiography on Operation Barbarossa, based in the main on German sources, emphasizes the murderous freezing temperatures and explain that as a dominant reason for the German defeat, Soviet and subsequent Russian history writing in general dismisses the "weather factor" in the December battle at the gates of Moscow.

In fact, the Germans were able to ward off the Soviet attacks during these incredibly low temperature days. On 6 December, in a record minus 38 degrees below zero, German 9. Armee counter-attacked at Kalinin with heavy support from Panzergruppe 3 and pushed back Soviet 31st Army across River Volga again. In the process, Soviet 250th Rifle Division was completely routed and had to be withdrawn from combat. Between 5 and 7 December, the German High Command reported that the Soviet attacks in general were warded off.[30] "We failed during the first days," Zhukov blatantly admitted.

But on 8 December a low pressure ridge which brought thaw and heavy downfalls covered the Moscow region. The entries in the German High Command's Diary show that this weather would continue to hold the area in its grip for several days. On 8 December the German High Command's Diary noted, "Sudden weather change. Temperatures during day up to +4 degrees [Celsius], roads soft."[31] Interestingly, it was on that day that the Soviet troops achieved the first real breakthroughs. Red Army soldier Pavel Osipov recalls, "On the second or third day of the counter-offensive, on 7 or 8 December, it dawned on us that our attack was going successfully. Morale amongst all the soldiers, sergeants and officers soared. From then on we pushed forwards in order to overtake the Germans before they could set villages on fire. As a rule they torched everything before a withdrawal."[32]

In Zhukov's viewpoint, the main factor in the Soviet victory at Moscow was "the fantastic combat morale among the troops." He wrote, "Our forces were absolutely convinced that they were going to defeat the enemy at the gates of Moscow."[33]

In the evening of 8 December, Generalfeldmarschall von Bock desperately reported to the OKH that Heeresgruppe Mitte was in no position to withstand the concentrated Soviet attack.[34] On 9 December the temperature ranged between minus 5 and 0 degrees Celsius.[35] Now, the modern Soviet Pe-2 bomber appeared in larger numbers than ever before over the front lines. Pe-2-equipped 28 BAD flew ninety to a hundred sorties daily. On 9 December two Pe-2s of 23 SAD reportedly put ten German vehicles

The Red Army strikes back! A group of Soviet troops charge a German-occupied village west of Moscow. (Photo: Mikhail Savin.)

out of commission during three low-level attacks against a motorized column retreating from the Moscow Channel. Afterward, Zhukov wrote, "Our air units – those belonging to the [Western] Front, as well as those of the Air Defense and the Long-Range Air Force – made an important contribution to our counter-offensive at Moscow in December 1941. The airmen put up a skilful and courageous fight. For the first time since the outbreak of the war, our fliers deprived the enemy of his superiority in the air. Our air force maintained a systematic pressure against artillery positions, tank units, and command posts. And as the Nazi armies started retreating, our aircraft attacked and bombed the withdrawing troops without interruption. This resulted in all roads to the west becoming littered with equipment and vehicles abandoned by the Germans."[36]

On this same day, 9 December, von Bock sent an urgent request to the OKH: "Army Group needs more men!"[37] A deeply concerned Halder wrote in his diary: "Phone talk with Generalfeldmarschall von Bock: Guderian reports that the condition of his troops is so critical that he does not know how to fend off the enemy."[38]

That day, also, a discontented Zhukov reproached his army commanders for their erroneous tactic of attacking the enemy frontally instead of circumventing him. The object must be to occupy the roads in the opponent's rear, Zhukov emphasized. Thus changing their methods, tanks and cavalry of the 20th Army passed German positions

The Wehrmacht on the retreat west of Moscow.

to cut off the highway from Moscow to Leningrad north-west of Solnechogorsk, 65 km northwest of Moscow, on 10 December. Meanwhile, south of Moscow, General-Mayor Pavel Belov's 1st Guards Cavalry Corps broke through to Stalinogorsk (Novomoskovsk), 50 km WSW of Mikhay-lov – thus cutting off the withdrawal route for elements of Guderian's 2. Panzerarmee. Even further south, the Southwestern Front managed to tear a 25-km wide gap in 2. Armee's front lines, with 45. and 134. Infanterie divisions getting overrun. Halder wrote: "2. Armee is broken through near Livny. 45. and 134. Infanterie divisions are overrun! A big hole is gaping in our front!"[39]

The weather continued to be the same on 10 and 11 December, with only a light cold in the morning, and thaw in the afternoon. On the latter date, Belov's Cavalry Corps seized Stalinogorsk and captured a considerable war booty, including 50 tanks and 42 guns.[40] In rain and thaw on 12 December, German 2. Panzer-Division was ousted from Solnechogorsk – having been pushed back 40 km since the Soviet counter-offensive began.[41] That day, an increasingly desperate von Bock phoned the OKH again, reporting that the situation for Heeresgruppe Mitte had "reached an acutely critical stage."[42] The Southwestern Front's penetration in 2. Armee's front was further deepened through Livny in the direction of Orel. 45. Infanterie-Division was encircled and partially destroyed. "Very serious situation in Second Army," Halder noted in his diary.

Indeed, the turning point at Moscow is a most peculiar event. Some accounts point to the exhausted state of the German troops and the worn condition of much of their equipment; but these troops were well-trained and experienced, with highly qualified junior and senior commanders, and they faced enemy soldiers with often only rudimentary military training, suffering from shortages in equipment and ammunition.

In fact, the German troops, who had believed that their enemy was on the verge of collapsing, were psychologically totally unprepared for such a violent onslaught by highly

The dead crewmembers of a shot down Ju 88 are lined up and prepared for removal by Red Army troopers. The increased commitment of the Luftwaffe in late December 1941 brought great relief to the heavily pressed German ground troops.

motivated *Frontovniki*, to which was added the effect of the VVS air activity against their rear lines. They began to fall back, and soon the withdrawal turned into a flight. A mass psychosis had gripped the Wehrmacht soldiers. This fuelled combat spirits on the Soviet side even further. In many places, the battle developed into Red Army troops, drunk with success and eager for revenge, pursuing scattered Wehrmacht formations fleeing along the icy roads. It was a collapse in moral on the German side, nothing less. "Serious break of confidence in the field commands," was noted on the German side.[43]

When the skies temporarily cleared on 13 December, with temperatures dropping to minus 20 degrees Celsius,

Bodies of German soldiers and horses killed during the battle of Maloyaroslavets.

Red Army troops have captured a German supply train during their winter offensive. (Photo: Dmitriy Baltermants.)

the Soviet pressure from the air increased.[44] One of the Soviet aviation's most important tasks was to neutralize the German fighter force in the Kalinin sector – II./ JG 52 and the Spanish fighter squadron Escuadrilla Azul, based at Klin. A single attack by bombers of Moscow's Military District on the night of 13 December achieved this task. Thirteen Bf 109s were totally destroyed on the ground.[45]

During previous battles, the Germans had been greatly aided by their ever-present reconnaissance planes. But now these were prevented from carrying out their missions with the same effectiveness by "intense Russian fighter activity." [46]

Thus the Germans were taken completely by surprise when Soviet ground troops stormed Klin's airfield on 13 December. Panzergruppe 3, assigned to defend it, proved unable defend the base, and sustained heavy own materiel losses.[47] The large airbase was evacuated in what disintegrated into a headlong flight. All unserviceable aircraft were blown up. Unteroffizier Walter Tödt of JG 52 described the scene: "All of our aircraft, plus a Ju 88, and all fuel barrels were put together. An 8.8cm anti-aircraft gun fired into the heap. Then the AAA was also blown up [because] the engine of its towing vehicle refused to start. All German soldiers on the airfield entered the road to Rusa on foot."[48] Spanish Escuadrilla Azul came to an inglorious end. Only two of its aircraft escaped the destruction at Klin. Both Escuadrilla Azul and II./JG 52 were completely neutralized as flying units. In II./JG 52's case, a large part of the personnel were sent to Germany to rest and refit, and some of the personnel remained on the Eastern Front as an ad hoc ground fighting unit. In

Escuadrilla Azul's case, the personnel were simply repatriated to Spain.

The Battle of Klin was absolutely catastrophic for Panzergruppe 3; indeed, it sustained only about 2,500 casualties, but its headlong retreat cost General Reinhardt the loss of the majority of his artillery and vehicles.[49]

Actually, the entire Heeresgruppe Mitte was threatened with collapse. The tough panzer commander Guderian was clearly in a personal crisis. "I frequently cannot sleep at night," he wrote. My brain goes round and round while I try to think what more I can do to help my poor soldiers." [50] Generalleutnant Ferdinand Schaal – who had succeeded von Manstein as the commander of LVI. Panzerkorps of Panzergruppe 4 when he was appointed to command 11. Armee – described the situation in his once so successful panzer corps: "A growing number of soldiers started walking westward on their own initiative. ... Victims of the aerial attacks were no longer buried. ... All kinds of equipment were abandoned in the general confusion."

General-Leytenant Fyodor Lisitsyn of Soviet 1st Shock Army recalled the scenes that met the Soviet troops as they advanced along the road previously used by Schaal's retreating troops: "All the way from Yakhroma to Fyodorovka [a distance of 20 km], the road was completely blocked by abandoned German vehicles, tanks and guns. Never before had our soldiers seen such vast amounts of military equipment captured from the enemy. It boosted their moral and destroyed the myth of the invincible Hitlerite hordes."[51]

The repeated scenes that met the Soviet troops as they liberated more and villages and towns were appalling.

Two of Moscow's defenders. The soldier to the left is equipped with the PPSh-41 submachine gun. The other soldier has stuck an RPG-40 anti-tank hand grenade in his belt. The RPG-40, developed in 1940, was able to penetrate a 20-25 mm thick armor, and could be used to knock out German light tanks or armored personnel carriers. (Photo: Soviet Embassy, 1976.)

Whole villages were torched and plundered, streets littered with corpses - people who had frozen or starved to death when they had been deprived of their housing, warm clothes and food, the mentally and physically ill, rape victims, and there were scores of missing people, abducted for slave labor in Germany or in some cases disappeared without even a trace. "They have all perished," wrote a totally devastated *Frontovnik* when he entered his liberated hometown. "Our hut was burned down as a reprisal. Father and mother were shot. Little sister has been taken to Germany. Brother was hanged for cooperation with the partisans. My wife was beaten with a stick by order of the German commandant on account of allegedly lack of respect towards a policeman. Soon after that she died as a consequence of the beating. The children were taken by other people. I don't know where they are now. I must search in the neighbourhood." [52]

Hardly surprisingly, the Soviets often took a bloody revenge on many a captured German soldier. But in spite of everything, several *Frontovniki* still maintained a sense of humanity, as distilled in these lines in the diary of Soviet soldier V. Goncharyov: "When you watch the enemy, you feel pity for the people. How can anyone have left an army in such a condition! The horses don't pull the carriages any more. The roads are littered with dozens, hundreds of horses that have been shot, motor vehicles and tanks. Because of the bad condition of the roads and the fuel shortage everything is left behind. The automatic weapons fail,

the ammunition supply doesn't reach the front. Freezing temperatures, bad army fatigues, insufficient nourishment and our attacks torment the Germans. It will be interesting to see whether they will be able to dig trenches in order to offer any resistance to us." [53]

While inflicting severe losses on their enemy, the Soviet troops advanced 130 kilometers in ten days. On 15 December, a "very despondent" Commander-in-Chief of the German Army, Generalfeldmarschall Walther von Brauchitsch, said that he "could not see any way of extricating the Army from its present predicament." [54]

The difference between Zhukov's successful counter-offensive at Moscow and all previous Soviet offensives in 1941 was that it was more skillfully organized. The circumvention of the German positions, which developed into "infiltration" deep into Heeresgruppe Mitte's rear area by mobile forces such as Belov's cavalry group – which included both tanks and cavalry – was a late renaissance for the "deep operation" (*Glubokaya Operatsiya*) doctrine of the cursed and executed Marshal Tukhachevskiy. However, from all other aspects, the Soviet attack at Moscow in December 1941 was no different from the previous attacks against Heeresgruppe Mitte during the summer and autumn that failed so utterly, definitely not in numbers (where the opposite rather was the case), and not in terms of quality of the equipment or in the level of troop training or junior command either.

But the tactical reversal was not as complete as it could have been with a more daring leadership. The pre-war thinking still put its mark on operations, as a Soviet report on the 33rd Army in the Moscow counter-offensive reveals: "Tank brigades and separate tank battalions were often employed in small groups and uniformly distributed among rifle regiments and divisions. All 50 tanks supporting the 33rd Army on the Western Front were equally allocated to the five rifle divisions. The divisional commanders then redistributed these tanks to their front line regiments. As a result, tank density was only three per kilometre of front." [55]

Finally, Hitler made a quite decisive intervention. On 16 December, when the German troops were driven out of the city of Kalinin, he issued his famous "halt order," calling for a "fanatical resistance" without retreating another step. He discharged both the Commander-in-Chief of the German Army, Generalfeldmarschall Walther von Brauchitsch, and the commander of Heeresgruppe Mitte, Generalfeldmarschall Fedor von Bock, and took the former's place personally while filling the latter vacancy with Generalfeldmarschall Günther von Kluge. The Führer attempted to implement the same fear of reprisals among his army commanders as reigned on the Soviet side. Shortly afterwards he also had Generaloberst Heinz Guderian sacked.

Hitler initiated hectic activity. In spite of Heeresgruppe Mitte's numerical superiority, reinforcements had to be brought in from Heeresgruppe Süd.[56] He also turned to the Luftwaffe to save the situation. The air force was lucky to escape changes in the command structure. On the contrary, it received immediate reinforcements. II./KG 4 – with 29 He 111s – and II./KG 30 arrived straight from Germany. Also rushed in from afar were the Zerstörer of Stab and I./SKG 210 – now renumbered into Stab and I./ZG 1 – plus four air transport Gruppen with more than a hundred Ju 52s. One transport Gruppe was also transferred from Luftflotte 4. It was a last-minute effort, and it worked.

While the air transport fleet managed to improve the supply situation at the front, horizontal bombers, Stukas, and Zerstörer began to strike back at the advancing Soviet troops with a vengeance. In clear skies on 17 December, a large formation of Ju 87s surprised Zhukov's spearheads west of Tula and reportedly destroyed thirteen tanks and about two hundred motor vehicles. The VVS still had numerical superiority; on 18 December it claimed the destruction of 340 trucks, 11 artillery pieces, 100 ammunition carts, and 3 trains.

But where the Luftwaffe was not in place, the Soviets held the upper hand. On 18 December, the tank ace Starshiy Leytenant Lavrinenko of the 1st Guards Tank Brigade led the attack against the German positions in the village of Goryunov, wreaking havoc among German troops, tanks and other vehicles. In this combat, Lavrinenko was credited with his 52nd tank destruction. Unteroffizier Gustav Schrodek, tank commander in a Panzer III in 15. Panzer-Division, experienced Lavrinenko's attack. He described it in his diary:

"I received a call from the turret of my tank: 'Here they come!' I saw a T-34 rapidly approaching us. The worst part was that it started to go after me! I devoted my entire attention to the tank opponent in front of me. As a result, I did not notice that the other vehicle from my company was no longer operational and, indeed, had dead on board. I also did not immediately notice that panic had broken out among the riflemen. Something broke. The turret could no longer be traversed. 'Let's get out of here … give it some gas!' I yelled to the driver. The riflemen were in wild flight all along the line, hunted by the Russian tanks. The other tank from my company had been knocked out. By then, we were moving past another knocked-out tank. We no longer had any way on our tank to provide aimed fire. There was nothing more to be seen far and wide of the fourth tank. Eight riflemen were cowering on the front of my tank. Bunches of them were hanging off the sides. Despite that, more and more were attempting to climb up on the rear deck while we were moving. Many of them had already been wounded by all the shrapnel flying about. The road was open and we stepped on it. 'My' T-34 remained behind. We had escaped death one more time!"[57] The Luftwaffe kept attacking the Soviet troops daily during the remainder of December, claiming four tanks and fourteen motor vehicles on 18 December, seventy-five motor vehicles on 21 December, four tanks and sixty motor vehicles on 22 December, and two tanks and fifty motor vehicles on Christmas Eve. The challenge from the Soviet Air Force was met with pre-emptive airfield attacks. For example, Yelets Airdrome was bombed on 23 December, and Aleksin Airdrome was hit on the 23rd, 24th and 29th.

The Germans claimed that 119 Soviet planes were shot down from 15 to 30 December. Italian fighter pilots of Regia Aeronautica's 22 Gruppo contributed by claiming twelve Soviet planes shot down between 24 and 26 December for the loss of a single Mc.200 Saetta. During the same period, 52 German aircraft were destroyed and 46 severely damaged in action on the Eastern Front.[58]

Within two weeks, these blows from the air managed to take the wind out of the Soviet counter-offensive. On 28 December, with clear skies, and the temperature plummeting to minus 20 degrees Celsius, Heeresgruppe Mitte reported the front situation as weakly restored in most sectors.[59]

But the hurricane that was Operation Typhoon had also most definitely subsided. By New Year's Eve the prime objective of the Soviet counter-offensive – to push back the threat against Moscow – had been achieved. Operation Barbarossa was dead.

A Soviet boy sitting on a pile of German military equipment abandoned during the Wehrmacht's retreat west of Moscow in December 1941.

RESULTS AND CONCLUSIONS I:
THE MILITARY SCENE.

Thus ended the largest military campaign in history, in a total defeat. But before that, Operation Barbarossa had led to a row of unparalelled tactical victories for the attackers. In just five months, an area of around 1.4 million square kilometers – roughly the combined areas of all the U.S. states along the Atlantic coast, from Maine in the north to Georgia in the south plus Florida] – had been captured. Tremendous losses had been inflicted on the Soviet armed forces. According to the statistics provided by Russian researcher Grigoriy Krivosheev, 566,852 troops were listed as killed in action, 2,335,482 as missing in action (including POWs), and around around 500,000 Soviet reservists were captured while still mobilizing – making a total of approximately 3.4 million total losses. To that should be added 1,336,147 wounded or sick hospitalized by the Soviets (an additional undisclosed number of wounded ended up in German captivity).[1] David M. Glantz and Jonathan House present slightly different figures: 2,993,803 killed or missing and 1,314,291 wounded, making a total of 4,308,094 casualties. [2] The astronomical amount of 63,100 artillery pieces or mortars over 50mm caliber and 20,500 tanks were lost – 17,300 tankettes, 2,300 T-34s and 900 KVs.[3] (The Germans claimed to have destroyed or captured 21,391 tanks.) 10,600 aircraft were officially recorded as lost in combat between 22 June and 31 December 1941,

but considering the unaccounted for decrease of 5,420 aircraft during the five first chaotic weeks, the actual losses may be close to the 17,745 claimed by the Germans.[4] See Appendix 5, Table 1.

On 25 December 1941, the German Army High Command reported that 3,350,639 Soviet POWs had been taken since the beginning of the invasion.[5] A vast war booty including thousands of tanks and tens of thousands of artillery pieces was also registered. All of this was mainly the result of a series of huge battles of envelopment – at Biyalystok-Minsk in June, Smolensk in July, Uman and Gomel in August, Kiev in September, and north of the Sea of Azov and Vyazma-Bryansk in October. (See Appendix 5, Table 4.) Although the Germans also took civilians as prisoners of war, it may be assumed that the vast majority of the 2,335,482 military personnel recorded as missing in action in Krivosheev's figures were captured by the Germans and their allies. Added to the 500,000 reservists that were captured while still mobilizing, this gives a total sum of around 2.8 million. Thus it may be assumed that at least over half a million Soviet civilians, or every sixth prisoner, were rounded up by the Germans as prisoners of war.

These gigantic setbacks for the Red Army in 1941 were the result of the clash between two armed forces of diametrically opposed qualities. On one side was the Wehrmacht, without any doubt the world's most advanced military force. This state was based on a fortunate combination of on the one hand, the traditions of a most advanced military thinking of the 18th and 19th Century Prussian Army, deriving from the need to balance its numerical inferiority vis-à-vis its enemies, and on the other hand, the revolutionary new thinking which came as a result of the creation of a completely new Army and Air Force in the 1930s. On the other side were the Soviet armed forces, downtrodden, humiliated, decapitated and

The Red Army sustained immense losses during Operation Barbarossa, particularly in materiel such as artillery, tanks and aircraft. The photo shows two destroyed T-26 tankettes. The vehicle closest to the camera has been on fire, which is evident from the dead crew member, whose uniform has burned. The T-26, the most common tank in the Red Army in 1941, was very vulnerable to German anti-tank guns, and even to 20mm automatic cannons, and as a result sustained grievous losses.

terrorized by an autocratic and crude dictator with no military education whatsoever.

Probably the greatest cause of the disastrous Soviet losses in 1941 was a number of major flaws on the Soviet side, all of which were expressions of Stalin's autocratic rule:

1. Stalin's purges of the Red Army (including, most significantly, that of the military genius Mikhail Tukhachevskiy, Commander-in-Chief of the Red Army).
2. The subsequent incompetence of the new Soviet commanders.
3. The totally inadequate training of the troops of the Red Army.
4. Stalin's refusal to acknowledge the early warnings of an impending German attack and to put the troops in a state of alert.
5. A series of disastrous military decisions by an incompetent Soviet leadership, above all Joseph Stalin himself.

While Hitler's Wehrmacht was shaped for a war of conquest, Stalin fought an unofficial civil war against the Red Army itself, which he regarded as the main threat against his own power. In consequence, the Wehrmacht prioritised military competence and the Red Army loyalty towards Stalin.

Recent attempts by certain scholars to revise the image of the German commanders in the East as "grand operators" and bold "innovators of a revolutionary military concept" are, in fact, quite ill-founded. Considering all the circumstances, it is hard to see how any military commanders could have waged the war in the East in 1941 in a more skillful way. History is full of great mistakes by military commanders – the Allied neglect of the possibility of a German attack through the Ardennes in 1940 *and* 1944, Douglas McArthur's failure to secure the Philippines in 1941 after warnings from the high command that a Japanese attack was possible, and the Japanese decision not to carry out a follow-up attack against Pearl Harbor on 7 December 1941, just to mention a few. However, no such blunders were made by the German commanders on the Eastern Front in 1941. The conclusion must be that they made the best of the situation, in view of the circumstances.

The equivalent to Heinz Guderian on the German side was Grigoriy Kulik on the Soviet side. The former was the "Father of the German armored force," the developer of revolutionary maneuver warfare tactics and tank technology. The latter was a Stalin crony who bore a heavy responsibility for the erasing of Tukhachevskiy's modern warfare tactics and a man who branded submachine guns as a "bourgeois fascist affectation." While Guderian was known as a fiery leader who inspired his troops to great accomplishments through personal example, Kulik not only became famous for his personal motto, "Jail or Medal" (capturing his contrasting habits of either heaping awards on his subordinates or having them arrested), but also had a tendency to panic and sow demoralization among his subordinates.

On the German side, Generalfeldmarschall von Rundstedt's own judgement led him to turn his army to the

This dejected Red Army Polkovnik has just been captured by the Germans.

south in July 1941, instead of following Hitler's instructions and veering to the southwest – resulting in the great annihilation battle at Uman the following month. Meanwhile, his opponent, General-Polkovnik Mikhail Kirponos, followed Stalin's orders to the letter and sacrificed his entire armored force – the largest in the Red Army – in piecemeal counter-attacks that even Kirponos' Chief of Staff realized were doomed from the start. But there was no alternative to the blind adherence to orders from above which characterized the Soviet commanders. General Armii Pavlov, the C.O. of the Western Front, which faced the main German onslaught, had a saying unworthy of any true senior military commander: "Never mind – those at the top know better than we do."[6]

In fact, most of the senior Soviet commanders were not suited for their task. General-Polkovnik Kirponos was a talented divisional commander, but definitely not ready to be assigned with the command of the Southwestern Front with 864,600 troops, 5,956 tanks and 1,913 aircraft. On 10 July 1941, matters were made even worse when Budyonnyy – once described as "a man with a big moustache and a small brain" – took command as the superior commander of the Southwestern Direction. The direct result was the destruction of two Soviet armies in the encirclement battle at Uman four weeks later.

The constant reshuffling of Soviet commanders, which went on for the entire duration of the defensive fight

Among many Soviet soldiers that ended up as prisoners of war in 1941 was Joseph Stalin's son Yakov Dzhugashvili, seen here accompanied by a Luftwaffe officer. Yakov Dzhugashvili was serving as a Leytenant with the 7th Mechanized Corps when he was captured on 16 July 1941. He was killed by a guard in concentration camp Sachsenhausen on 14 April 1943. (Photo: Alfred Grislawski.)

Two Soviet officers study the map. (Photo: Soviet Embassy, 1976.)

in 1941, reflected both the inadequate quality of the commander and the desperation and organic mistrust among Stalin's leadership. For instance, the Northwestern Front changed commander three times in July and August 1941. The Western Front had its first commander, Pavlov – plus his Chief of Staff, the Artillery Commander, the Chief of the Communications Corps, and the Front's Air Force commander – arrested and shot. General-Leytenant Yeremenko was appointed Front commander on 30 June; he was replaced by Timoshenko on 2 July, was reinstalled on 19 July, and again replaced by Timoshenko on 30 July. On 12 September, General-Polkovnik Konev took command of the Western Front; less than a month later Stalin wanted

to have him shot, but he was saved by the intervention of Zhukov, who took over on 13 October. All of these changes in command led to a lack of stability in the command of the Red Army units.

The gap in quality between the German and Soviet commanders was immense, from the top down. This was quite obvious to both sides. To his despair, Leytenant Ivan Chernov, who fought in Soviet 5th Army, observed early in the first days of the war that "the Germans were considerably better led than our troops. That was particularly evident among their NCOs."[7] German soldiers frequently use words such as "predictable," "clumsy" and "senseless" to describe the Red Army's methods of combat through most of 1941. "When we neutralized their officer, the Russian soldiers would often be completely at a loss," is a frequent comment by German Eastern Front veterans – a result of the rigid command system on the Soviet side. Deprived of an officer to forward orders received from above, Red Army troops and airmen would often fight to the death, or – if surrounded – attempt a breakout, but tactically they would rarely carry out something which caught the Germans by surprise.

Completely different troop training left most Soviet troops and airmen tactically handicapped against their German counterpart, whose *Auftragstaktik* (Mission Command) encouraged self-initiative in combat.

Under the threat of dire consequences, the Soviet troop commanders were obliged to follow bureaucratic, textbook methods in any given situation. In the air war, their fighter pilots were rigidly bound to, for instance, patrols in a determined area and at a specific altitude: they were forbidden to

254

leave that restricted area, for example to pursue and finish off a damaged enemy aircraft, and often not even allowed to climb or descend to another altitude, whether offensively or defensively.* Meanwhile, the German fighter pilots were often dispatched on so-called "free hunting," which meant that they were free to go searching for opportunities to destroy enemy aircraft in the air; free to choose combat when they had an advantageous position and altitude, and also free to refrain from accepting combat under disadvantageous conditions.

While Soviet fighter pilots were under strict orders to operate in tight three-plane V-formations (which emanated from World War I, when the lack of radio equipment in the aircraft necessitated visual signals); these always tended to break up into each aircraft flying individually in fighter combat. The German fighter pilots, on the other hand, operated in the close team work of the *Rotte*: two aircraft fighting in a pair, the wingman (*Rottenflieger*) acting as the shield, covering the leader (*Rottenführer*), who was the sword, attacking the enemy – preferably in a dive from a higher altitude. Added to this was the superior performance of the German Messerschmitt Bf 109 fighter planes, the fact that radio receivers and transmitters were standard equipment in the German fighters (unlike Soviet fighters), the significantly better training standards of the Luftwaffe airmen, and their vastly greater experience. The result was a victory-to-loss ratio in the German fighter units on the Eastern Front in 1941 of 20 to 1. (See Appendix 5, Table 7.)

To the vast qualitative gap between the opposing forces should be added sheer luck on behalf of the Germans. Their opening air strike on 22 June 1941 – which would influence the entire campaign. not least the five first weeks – caught the Soviet Air Force precisely when its airfields in the West were completely littered with newly arrived modern aircraft that were to replace the older types, which also remained in place. Had all these modern aircraft arrived just a couple of weeks earlier – meaning all the phased out I-16 fighters, I-153 assault planes and SB bombers were secured as a reserve to be brought in against the invader – or the opening attack taken place only a couple of weeks later, it would have placed the Red Army in a far better position to stand up against the enemy.

Although the Luftwaffe remained considerably superior to the VVS, the air force proved to be the single most effective material asset on the Soviet side. During Heeresgruppe Süd's offensive against the Soviet industrial centers in the Ukraine and against the Crimea, operations by Soviet aviation was decisive in slowing down the Germans, and the VVS was also of probably decisive importance to the success of Zhukov's counter-attack in December 1941.

Equipped with Messerschmitt Bf 109s, the German fighter units enjoyed a total superiority in air fighting on the Eastern Front in 1941. Seen in this photo is one of the Luftwaffe aces, Günther Rall, in front of his Bf 109. Rall commanded 8./JG 52 in Luftflotte 4 and achieved 36 victories until he was shot down and wounded by a Yak-1 during the Battle of Rostov on 28 November 1941. Back in action again in 1942, he increased his score to 275. (Photo: Günther Rall.)

On the German side, the Luftwaffe and the armored forces – or rather their combined operations – were undoubtedly the most important material asset. The numerically very strong Soviet armored force proved to be extremely brittle – the result of the dominance of thinly armored and under-gunned obsolete tankettes. The only exception was very few skillfully led T-34 and KV units.**

The Soviet dictator Stalin made many grave misjudgements, but in one thing he was completely correct: "Any other state which had suffered such losses of territory as we did would not have stood the test and would have

---

* Quite indicative of the rigidity of the Soviet armed forces – indeed an expression of the leadership's mistrust in its subordinates – fighter pilot Aleksandr Pokryshkin was severely reprimanded for suggesting that the fighter pilots be authorized to carry out what in Soviet terminology was called "vertical combat" – i.e. to simply utilize the three dimensions in air combat.

** Ironically, some of the greatest "aces" during Operation Barbarossa were Soviet tank aces – such as Starshiy Leytenant Dmitriy Lavrinenko and Leytenant Zinoviy Kolobanov – and German fighter aces: Two fighter pilots, Oberst Werner Mölders of JG 51 and Major Günther Lützow of JG 3, each surpassed the 100-victory mark during Operation Barbarossa; both of these Jagdgeschwader could boast two other of the top aces at that time, Hauptmann Gordon Gollob of JG 3, with a total score of 85 kills at the end of 1941, and Oberleutnant Heinz Bär of JG 51, with 80 kills. Also, in JG 54, Oberleutnant Hans Philipp had a score of 73 as 1941 drew to a close.

collapsed," he said. This ability to survive rested on three pillars: The generation of new forces, the relocation of the industry to the east, and the incredible resilience of the Red Army's troops.

Thirteen new field armies were formed in July 1941, fourteen in August, one in September and four in October. Owing to this it was never necessary to bring in the bulk of the Far East armies (a myth which has been dispelled – see Chapter 18) – which otherwise might have provoked a Japanese attack.

Simultaneously, owing to the structure of a planned economy, it was possible to relocate 1,523 factories, installations, and research establishments to the east, thus saving them from German capture or destruction, and to restart production in record time.

Both of these factors were the result of the Soviet system itself, and so was the third cornerstone of the survival of the Soviet Union in 1941 – in fact the basic foundation of the two others: The stiff-necked determination among the Soviet population and troops to keep resisting the invaders. This was a completely unexpected factor for the Germans, who had initially believed that the Soviet Union would collapse under the weight of the first, massive military strikes – just as France had done in 1940.

It has been asserted that the Wehrmacht conducted the war in the East purely with an operational, impressionist thinking, at the expense of a strategic, overall view – indeed a harsh judgement of the German commanders.[8] However, the German strategy rested on the assumption of what Hitler had expressed before the attack – "all we have to do is to kick in the door and the whole rotten structure will come crashing down." This strategy was completely shattered by the Soviet refusal to bow down in spite of immense defeats, and thence the vast space of the Eastern war theatre did not allow the Germans to fight other than purely operationally, clinging to the only possible strategy, which proved to be an illusion. As we have seen, this led Hitler to openly admit regrets for having started the war with the Soviet Union even after less than two months. Only three weeks into the war, the Red Army had taught the Nazi dictator to reconsider his dismissal of the Russians as "subhumans" and instead describe the Russian as "a colossus and strong."

The Red Army inflicted losses on the Wehrmacht on a scale the Germans could not have imagined in view of their superior German commanders, methods, troop training, and equipment. The figures for the Ostheer's personnel losses between 22 June and 31 December 1941 vary between different sources – 656,691 according to the Wehrmacht monthly casual reports; 802,422 according to the Heeresarzt Heeresarzt 10-Day Casualty Reports, and 830,403 according to Generaloberst Halder's reports at the OKH general staff.[9] To these should be added the casualties of Germany's allies, around 150,000 Romanian, 75,000

Finnish soldiers on the march. By tying up at least two Soviet armies, the powerful Finnish army made an important contribution to Hitler's invasion of the Soviet Union. (Photo: SA Kuva.)

Finnish and around 10,000 Spanish, and Italian casualties – in total 235,000. See Appendix 5, Table 2.

Of a total of 4,192 German tanks in action on the Eastern Front (initial strength plus replacements and tanks of new units), 2,839 were destroyed, i.e. two-thirds.[10] The Luftwaffe recorded 1,730 aircraft totally destroyed in combat on the Eastern Front through 31 December 1941.[11] See Appendix 5, Table 3. The aircraft losses in the East between 22 June and 31 December 1941 were actually higher than during the same period one year previously during the Battle of Britain.

Over the years, the image of the differences in losses between the two warring sides during Operation Barbarossa as being something exceptional has prevailed. It is not uncommon to see totally unsupported claims of a difference between Soviet and German losses as 10 to 1 or even 20 to 1. A closer study, however, reveals this as just another myth, probably based on German accounts colored by racist prejudices. A comparison between the loss relations during Operation Barbarossa and the German Western Campaign in 1940 shows that the Germans actually inflicted higher losses on their Western enemies, in relation to their own losses, than they did to the Red Army. The relation between total casualties were 19 to 1 in favour of the Germans during the Western Campaign, and between 3.2 to 1 and 4.8 to 1 in favour of the Germans and their allies during Operation Barbarossa. Even if the prisoners of war of Germany's opponents are discounted, the ratios are still not better for the Germans on the Eastern Front: 2.3 to 1 in favour of the Germans during the Western Campaign, and between 1.9 to 1 and 2.4 to 1 in favor of the Germans and their allies during Operation Barbarossa. See Appendix 5, Table 6.

The popular image in the West of hundreds of thousands Soviet soldiers surrendering en masse without offering much resistance also proves to be a myth, possibly surviving due to German propaganda footage of huge assemblies of POWs. As David Stahel points out, the German image of the Soviet soldiers prior to Operation Barbarossa was influenced by the experience of the old Tsarist Russia's poor performance in World War I.[12] The Great War was also used as a point of reference in one of the earliest German reports on the soldiers of the young Soviet state: "What has become of the Russian of 1914-17, who ran away or approached us with his hands in the air when the firestorm reached its peak? Now he remains in his bunker and forces us to burn him out, he prefers to be scorched in his tank, and his airmen continue firing at us even when their own aircraft is set ablaze. What has become of the Russian? Ideology has changed him!"[13]

Indeed, Hitler was right when he described the war against the USSR as a clash between two diametrically opposed ideologies – Nazism and Communism. With similarities to a civil war rather than a regular military conflict, both sides fought on the grounds of ideological belief. The young German soldiers had been raised in the Hitler Jugend to believe that they were fighting a war that would alter history to the benefit of the German "race" for a thousand years to come.

The praiseworthy studies by Professor of history Omer Bartov at Brown University in the USA have contributed greatly in dispelling the myth of the "unpolitical Wehrmacht." A common misconception is that members of the Wehrmacht were not allowed to be a member of a political party. Under the impact of the growing Communist sympathies in society in 1918-19 and the Twenties, the Reichswehr – the German 100,000-man army intended mainly to secure internal political stability – banned its soldiers from joining any political party or even from voting in elections. However, in 1938, this was abolished by Hitler. In fact, the German officer corps appears to have had a 400 per cent over-representation among the Nazi Party members.* Around 30 per cent of the German officers in Bartov's study sample were members of the Nazi Party; the ratio was highest among upper middle class officers (61 per cent) and lowest among those from officer families (6 per cent).[14] The latter shows that the Wehrmacht was to a large extent a "new" army, the result of the Versailles Peace Treaty, which facilitated the Nazi Party's ambition to take control of the armed forces. It should also be kept in mind that the ideological influence of the Nazi Party was of course spread far beyond those who had actively become members of the Party. War-time letters and even recent interviews with *Landser* veterans display various levels of influence of Nazi ideas, although not all of them were in total agreement with the Party and its propaganda as such. After all, the Third Reich was a totalitarian state with an emphasis on what was called *Gleichschaltung* – ideological conformity; by the time Operation Barbarossa was launched, the state apparatus had been working twenty-four hours a day for eight years to permeate the of whole society with its ideas. That meant that a German soldier who was twenty when Operation

The campaign in the East cost the Germans and their allies much higher losses than anticipated. A group of German soldiers are collecting the bodies of their fallen comrades after a battle with Soviet troops.

* Around 7 % of the German adult population were members of the Nazi Party in 1940.

Women played a greater role in the Red Army than in any other armed forces during World War II. Seen in this photo are two young women keeping watch on a rooftop in Leningrad. (Photo: Soviet Embassy, 1976.)

own ideological point of view, such as Dutch SS volunteer Hendrik C. Verton, who wrote: "The Russian enemy fought like primitive, soulless robots, their patriotism and Bolshevik ideals not to be destroyed like bursting soap bubbles.... Their soldiers fought to their last breath, often committing suicide rather than being taken prisoner." [16]

The Soviet image of the German soldiers was also colored by their own ideology. At the outbreak of the war, they often made a class-based, clear distinction between ordinary German soldiers – who were regarded as "workers in uniform" – and officers of the upper class, who were blamed for all evils. However, after the first weeks of massive German atrocities – where obviously even the "workers in uniform" took part – this changed into an image of the German soldier as a beast, quite often a superhuman, and at the same time a de-humanized, murderous creature. Simultaneously, in contrast to this, Germany and the Germans were still regarded as a highly cultured nation.

Even Soviet men and women whose relatives had succumbed to Stalin's wave of political terror – and their number naturally was quite significant, bearing in mind that two million Soviet citizens were subject to political convictions between 1935 and 1940, of which around 700,000 were sentenced to death, in a country with 162 million inhabitants – would often fight with the same determination, for the same goals. One famous example is the female fighter ace Lidiya Litvyak, whose father was arrested in 1937 and later executed on trumped-up allegations of being a "traitor." The Soviet propaganda and, perhaps more importantly, their own experience of the October Revolution's positive social effects, convinced many among them to regard such tragic cases as "deviations" by individual, "corrupt" local leaders, and to believe that Stalin was not at fault. The personal cult created around Joseph Stalin fell on fertile soil in a country where Orthodox Christianity had for centuries taught the people icon devotion. The slogan *Za Stalina!* ("for Stalin") was painted on combat aircraft and tanks, and was shouted by assaulting *Frontovniki* with deep conviction. However, parallel to this, a scepticism towards the leadership was also widely present. Interviewed after the war, Red Army radio operator Boris Lyubovits recalled that in view of the great defeats early in the war, many were saying that they felt betrayed by those above." [17]

Barbarossa began, had been subjected to this massive propaganda since he was twelve.

His opponent, the young Soviet *Frontovnik*, often waged an even more determined struggle to defend what he or she apprehended as a development of a paradise resembling Communist society on Earth against its total opposite – darkness, Evil and absolute barbarity. The twenty-year-old Red Army trooper of 1941 had been subjected to a Communist propaganda no less intense throughout his whole life. Although attempts have been made in recent times – particularly after the fall of the Soviet Union in 1991 – to dismiss the influence of the Communist conviction as a source in the Soviet will to resist in the war, the Marxist outlook was very widespread among the *Frontovniki*. This is evident not only from all interviews the author has conducted with both Soviet and German war veterans, but also from German reports of the time. The Guidelines for the Behavior of the Troops towards Russians, submitted to the Ostheer in June 1941, emphasizes: "Do not speak, but act. You will never be able to 'persuade' or convince the Russian in a discussion, as he is better at discussing than you are; he is born with the dialectical method and you will lose any debate with him." [15]

From interviews with Soviet veterans and letters from others, a picture emerges where the bare Marxist ideas as such are perhaps not as important to the resilience of the Red Army as the enthusiasm that many felt about the considerable social gains (such as free and universal education and health care and increased living standards among major segments of the population) that visibly came as a result of the October Revolution.*

The stamina displayed by the *Frontovniki* was naturally interpreted by the Germans and their allies from their

It is often said that the incessant, albeit costly, Soviet counter-offensives throughout the summer and fall of 1941 wore down the Wehrmacht to the point where it was finally ripe for defeat at the gates of Moscow and Rostov in November-December 1941. However, closer scrutiny shows that this theory has no validity at all. It was indeed true that in late 1941 the *Ostheer* was exhausted and its equipment worn down. But at that stage, this was even more true of the Red Army.

Taken in isolation, these relentless counter-attacks produced some results that could be regarded as positive

---

* As a negative confirmation of this, people who had experienced the large-scale famine in the Ukraine in the Thirties, who belonged to oppressed nationalities, or who saw no positive change to their lives when their countries were swallowed up by the Soviet Union in 1939–40, often displayed Anti-Communist attitudes and fought without any enthusiasm when drafted into the Red Army. The majority of the deserters from the Red Army belonged to oppressed nationalities such as the Balts or West Ukrainians.

GEORGIY ZHUKOV – MOSCOW'S SAVIOR.

Georgiy Zhukov, born to a poor peasant family in 1896, was definitely one of the most talented military commanders in the Red Army and the whole Allied camp during World War II. Having served as an NCO in World War I, he joined the Bolshevik Party shortly after the October Revolution in 1917. Having fought as a cavalry commander in the Red Army during the Civil War, he received higher military education in the 1920s. Despite connections with supporters of Trotsky, he skilfully managed to survive political accusations during the Great Purge. In 1939 he took command of the Soviet-Mongolian forces that fought to ward off a Japanese attack at Khalkhin-Gol and turned defeat into victory, for which he was appointed a Hero of the Soviet Union.

Grigoriy Zhukov (right) earned fame for leading the troops in the Battle of Khalkhin-Gol, where this photo is taken, to victory in 1939. Here he is seen with the Mongolian leader Khorloogiyn Khoybalsan and (to the left) Grigoriy Shtern, the senior commander of the Red Army troops in the battle. Shtern was arrested on 7 June 1941, and under torture he "confessed" that he was a "Trotskyite" and a German spy. He was executed among several other imprisoned former senior Red Army commanders in connection with the suppression of the Moscow rebellion in October 1941.

Zhukov was one of the very few senior Soviet military commanders, who clearly saw the emerging threat from Germany, and acted accordingly. In February 1941 he started to work on a strategic plan for an upcoming war with Germany, which foresaw a Soviet mobilization and a pre-emptive strike. The plan was apparently never authorized by the Soviet High Command, but if it had been realized, it is possible that Operation Barbarossa would never have been launched and the Nazi rule could have been crushed much earlier.

Upon the master spy Sorge's report on 13 June 1941 about an imminent German invasion, Zhukov made fruitless efforts to convince Stalin of the need to mobilize the Red Army. In July 1941, he proposed – again without success – that Stalin authorize the

withdrawal of the Southwestern Front from its endangered position at Kiev. The consequence of Stalin's refusal to listen to Zhukov on this matter was the near total annihilation of the Southwestern Front and losses of 621,183 troops killed or missing, 28,419 artillery pieces and 411 tanks. With a timely withdrawal according to Zhukov's suggestion, a large share of this could have been deployed for the counter-offensive in December 1941 – with unforeseeable consequences.

The highlight in Zhukov's military career undoubtedly was the Moscow counter-offensive in December 1941 and the brilliant way in which it was conducted and led.

However, Zhukov's skills were also hampered by the constant circumvention of him by the bureaucratic and autocratic dictatorship. Stalin's purges led to him being over-promoted to the position of Chief of the General Staff in February 1941, a position that he himself admitted that he was not suited for. This took place when the former Chief of Staff, General Armii Kirill Meretskov, had been dismissed, eventually to be arrested and subjected to severe torture for an alleged "anti-Soviet military conspiracy."

Zhukov also made several major errors, such as his insistence on hopeless counter-attacks by the Southwestern Front in July 1941 and by the Western Front in August 1941. His greatest mistake was the failed counter-offensive west of Moscow in November-December 1942, which led to 760,000 casualties for virtually no gains at all.

Grigoriy Zhukov was no Manstein or von Rundstedt – he had neither their education, nor the professional military culture of the German General Staff – but he definitely compared well with the best American and British commanders. One of his greatest admirers was General Dwight D. Eisenhower, the Western Allied superior commander in Europe.

Fearing that Zhukov might become "another Tukhachevskiy," Stalin and Beriya attempted to topple Zhukov after the war. This time the Air Force commander Aleksandr Novikov – another of the most brilliant Soviet senior commanders during the war (he commanded the Air Force of the Northern Front in 1941) – was arrested and tortured until he agreed to testify against Zhukov. But again, Zhukov skillfully managed to evade the attacks.

In the mid-1950s, Zhukov was forced into an early retirement by Khrushchev for supporting the demand for the rehabilitation of Tukhachevskiy. He passed away in 1974.

for the Soviet side. However, from a wider perspective, they were a crude, unsophisticated way of wasting human and material resources. The German advance towards Moscow was halted in late summer and fall of 1941, and with the capture of the Yelnya Bulge, the Red Army achieved its first tactical victory of the war. But the cost of this was nearly 700,000 casualties from the Western, Reserve, and Central fronts between 10 July and 10 September.[18] As is evident from the experiences of the Soviet counter-offensives on the road to Moscow in July-September and in the Ukraine in July, and the defensive battles at Leningrad, Odessa, the Crimea, and Sevastopol, the Red Army was far more effective on the defense. A flexible defense in the region between Smolensk and Moscow in late summer and fall of 1941 would probably have produced better results at a lower cost, and would have laid the foundation for a more powerful counter-offensive in December 1941. But that would have required a more skillful Soviet High Command…

Not only does the whittling down of the Western and Reserve fronts through September 1941 neutralize the effect of the simultaneous wear and tear on Heeresgruppe Mitte; the German Army on the Eastern Front was actually in better shape in November 1941 – when it had received fresh units from Germany – than it had been two months earlier: On 30 September, the German tank strength in the East was 2,262, whereas on 30 November it numbered 2,480.[19] Contrary to this, the Soviet troop strength in front of Moscow dropped in both absolute figures and relative strength – from 1,250,000 troops, fairly on par with the Germans, on 30 September 1941, to 576,500 two months later, a numerical inferiority of two to one in comparison with the Germans.

The popular image in the West of relatively small German (and Finnish) forces standing against vast masses of Soviet troops – sometimes described as "hordes," straight from Goebbels' propaganda – belies the actual facts. One specific characteristic of the war on the Eastern Front in 1941 is that it was mainly fought with the Red Army in a position of numerical inferiority. This was not mainly caused, but was accentuated by the German method of focusing their troops to "points of concentration" (Schwerpunkt) – while the more static structure of the Soviet armed forces was completely at fault. As we have seen, the invasion began with 4.5 million troops attacking 2.3 million defenders.

And still, it ended in a German strategic defeat. The Soviets were not completely without brilliant commanders, and Grigoriy Zhukov was one of them. His counter-offensive at the gates of Moscow in December 1941 was definitely the Red Army's greatest feat during Operation Barbarossa, not least in view of the fact that the attacking Soviet forces were inferior to their German foe in all aspects but their fighting spirits and their air force – both of which were decisive factors in the outcome of the battle. The third factor which gave the Soviets the victory during this offensive was Zhukov's revolutionary method of focusing on infiltration of the German rear area with fast cavalry and armored forces. With this revival of elements of Tukhachevskiy's Deep Operations doctrine, Heeresgruppe Mitte – the most powerful military force in the world – was brought to the verge of collapse within a couple of days.

In one of the most dramatic turnarounds in military history, demoralization spread through the German ranks from top to bottom, and the commanders pleaded for a general retreat back to the Baltic states and Belarus. Many scholars agree that had such an order been issued, it is highly likely that it would have resulted in a general breakdown of moral in the Ostheer, and the retreat could easily have deteriorated into a wild flight, with unit cohesion melting away.

Most historians – as well as German veterans from the battle – agree that it was Hitler's resolute Halt Order that saved Heeresgruppe Mitte, and possibly the entire Ostheer, in that critical situation. The Führer's decision to relieve two of the psychologically exhausted and demoralized commanders in Heeresgruppe Mitte (von Bock and Guderian), as well as the equally demoralized Commander-in-Chief of the German Army, Generalfeldmarschall von Brauchitsch, was probably justified. This outweighs his simultaneous sacking of von Rundstedt (which he nevertheless soon admitted regrets over) for the unauthorized withdrawal from Rostov.

The two dictators actually played an equally important role in the survival of Heeresgruppe Mitte. While Zhukov saw the opportunity to shatter the German army group by concentrating all forces that could be spared from other sectors for a concentric blow in January 1942, Stalin overruled him and demanded a general offensive along the entire frontline from Leningrad to the Crimea. With its forces thus spread out, the Red Army's Winter Offensive ended in a strategic setback in the spring of 1942 – providing Hitler with the opportunity to seize the initiative again for a new Summer Offensive in 1942.

Ultimately, Operation Barbarossa, based on the huge misjudgements of racial prejudices, was Hitler's greatest military mistake, and led directly to Germany's defeat in the war. However, had it not been for Joseph Stalin's disastrously poor judgement and autocratic rule, the defeat of the Third Reich would have come much sooner. Thus, Hitler and Stalin share responsibility for the bulk of the tens of millions of Europeans who died in the tragedy that we know as World War II.

RESULTS AND CONCLUSIONS II:
THE WAR OF ANNIHILATION.

Germany's war on the Eastern Front was completely different from that against the Western Allies in that it was carried out as a full-scale War of Annihilation. Whereas the Germans committed war crimes at several places – such as Oradour-sur-Glane and Malmedy/Barugnez – in the West, the war against the Soviet Union can be described as a single, large "Oradour" or "Malmedy." The basis of this massive War of Annihilation – carried out both by the German forces and all of their allies on the Eastern Front – was anti-Communism and racist prejudices. According to historian Christian Streit, "the extreme anti-Bolshevism was the main factor that removed all concerns."[1]

More specifically, the Germans were led to this by a series of deadly instructions from their own leadership, as described by Professor Wendy Jo Gertjejanssen:

"Armed with the blessings of Hitler and the military leadership, the troops sent to the east were allowed 'all reprisals to be made against the inhabitants of Soviet cities and towns. In accordance with this order, military courts received instructions to ignore the complaints of the Ukrainian, Russian, and Belorussian population against the lawless acts committed by the soldiers and officers of the German army.' [. . .] The orders issued by the OKW and OKH were composed in four sets of instructions,

three of which allowed great freedoms for crimes against Soviet civilians:

1. Regulations concerning the activities of the Einsatzgruppen of the SS and SD, which enabled these murder squads to operate with relative freedom within the areas controlled by the army groups under the direct command of Reinhard Heydrich.
2. The curtailment of military jurisdiction (*Die Einschränkung der Kriegsgerichtsbarkeit*), which stipulated that guerrillas, and civilians suspected of assisting them, were to be shot by the army, and that in case no guilty party could be found, collective measures were to be taken against the civilian population in the area.
3. The Commissar Order, which called for the shooting of any Red Army political commissar captured by the troops.
4. The 'Guidelines for the Conduct of the Troops in Russia', which ordered ruthless measures against 'Bolshevik agitators, guerrillas, saboteurs and Jews' and called for the complete elimination of any active or passive resistance."[2]

While 8,300 out of 231,000 British and U.S. prisoners of war died in German captivity during World War II, estimates of the number of Soviet soldiers that died in German captivity range between 1.8 million and 4 million.[3] If those that died after the war of sickness and wounds inflicted during their captivity are included, estimates of the number of killed range as high as five million. The most commonly accepted figure is 3.3 million dead out of a total of 5.7 million Soviet POWs in German custody during the entire war (58 per cent) – including *2.8 million deaths out of a total of* 3.8 million Soviet POWs in German custody during the first eight months of the war, a harrowing death rate of 74 per cent.[4] The latter figure on Soviet POWs however is based on an erroneous Wehrmacht report on the number of prisoners of war; the number was corrected from 3.8 million to 3,350,639 in a report on 25 December

SS-Reichsführer Heinrich Himmler and Wehrmacht officers inspecting a Russenlager on the Eastern Front. (Photo: Via Martin Månsson.)

Remnants of Soviet prisoners of war in a German POW camp.

An anti-Communist cosack kills a Red Army prisoner of war with his sword as an amusement to a group of watching Hungarian soldiers.

1941.[5] That would give a death rate of 84 per cent. This extreme mortality is confirmed by statistics from German camps for Soviet POWs in occupied Poland, where 307,816 out of 361,612 – 85 per cent – perished through April 1942.[6] The actual figure is probably even higher. A large number of the POWs that were badly wounded – maimed, blinded or elsewhile handicapped – were released by the Germans and simply left on their own. (Others were shot.) It goes without saying that these were left to die. There are no other statistics on them other than the Wehrmacht statistics, according to which 484,000 Soviet POWs were released between June 1941 and January 1942.[7] Due to the Wehrmacht statistics, 3.4 million Soviet POWs were registered during the same time, and 363,331 remained in German custody on 1 February 1942. That amounts to 70 per cent of the total number and 88 per cent of the POWs not released. See Appendix 5, Table 5.

It should also be noted that owing to the extremely chaotic and brutal approach to Soviet prisoners of war, far from all Soviet POWs could be recorded by the Wehrmacht institutions; many were killed outright or perished in other ways before that. Moreover, the registration of prisoners in the POW camps began only when the mass death rate had reached its zenith.[8]

As we have seen, Soviet men and women in Finnish POW camps were also subject to brutal treatment, with 16,000 out of 47,000 POWs perishing in a ten-month period, i.e. a 34 per cent death rate.[9] The situation improved later on in the war, with the totals being 18,785 perished out of 64,188 Soviet POWs in Finnish confinement, a death rate of 29.3 per cent.[10] Although the death rate among Finnish POWs was above the average in Soviet POW camps, this nevertheless compares adversely with the death rate of Finnish POWs in Soviet captivity during the war: 17 per cent – 403 out of 2,377 – perished.[11]

Both the German and the Finnish treatment of Soviet POWs are worse even than the infamous Japanese treatment of Western Allied prisoners during the war.* The mortality rate of 58 per cent of Soviet POWs in German captivity compares most adversely with the mortality rate of 15 per cent of the German POWs in Soviet captivity.[12] The mortality among prisoners of the Axis states Romania, Hungary and Italy was 18 per cent.[13] Among volunteers in the German armed forces, 70 out of 452 Spaniards (15 per cent), 200 out of 4,730 Dutch (4.2 per cent), and 35 out of 456 Danes (7.6 per cent) died in Soviet captivity.[14]

This difference of course springs from the fact that whereas the Third Reich and its allies fought a war of aggression with the aim of annihilating the Soviet state and a large part of its population, the USSR was forced into a war where its only purpose was defending itself; in such a situation prisoners of war are valuable sources for the military intelligence. Moreover, their socialist ideology also led the Soviets to try to turn the POWs politically – with quite some success, as any German veteran from the Eastern Front can testify to – and thus use them for their own goals.**

It is often said – echoing wartime Nazi propaganda – that the Soviet Union did not sign the Geneva Convention relative to the Treatment of Prisoners of War of 1929, according to which POWs "shall at all times be humanely treated and protected, particularly against acts of violence, from insults and from public curiosity." This, however, is wrong. The Soviet Union did indeed sign the Geneva Convention relative to the Treatment of Prisoners of War on 27 July 1929. It is often said that the USSR did not ratify the

---

* According to the findings of the Tokyo Tribunal, the death rate of Western prisoners in Japanese custody was 27.1 per cent.
** According to Bodo Helms, a former Luftwaffe Leutnant and POW in the Soviet Union, later to advance to the rank of a colonel in the Bundesluftwaffe, around 45 per cent of the German officers and 75 per cent of the soldiers in Soviet captivity joined the pro-Soviet National Committee. (Helms, Von Anfang an dabei, p. 103.)

Convention, but the Soviet Regulations of Prisoners of War of 1931 prescribed "a regime for POWs in the USSR that was equivalent, if not better, than that guaranteed by the [Geneva] Convention."[15] (This was replaced by a new Regulation of the handling of POWs, passed on 1 July 1941, with basically the same content, mainly transferring the responsibility of the prisoners of war to the NKVD.) The Soviet Union had also ratified the Hague Convention of 1907, according to which POWs "must be humanely treated" and "treated as regards food, quarters, and clothing, on the same footing as the troops of the Government which has captured them." However, the Soviets failed to allow the International Red Cross to visit their POW camps.

Indeed, the situation for German POWs in Soviet captivity was very harsh, not least in the first period of the war, when malnutrition caused by the war affected the whole Soviet population.* The mortality rate of 15 per cent of the German and 17 per cent of the Finnish POWs in Soviet captivity is a clear indication that the regulations were not followed as they were supposed to be. This is supported by a vast amount of testimony from former POWs describing atrocities and inhumane regimes in Soviet captivity. Still, there is a huge difference between the treatment of Germans and Finns in Soviet captivity and that of Soviets in German or Finnish captivity.

It has been asserted that the extremely high mortality among Soviet POWs is due to the fact that the Germans and Finns were not prepared for such vast numbers of prisoners. First of all, this is a false statement: Not least owing to their contempt for the Russians the Germans and the Finns clearly expected such large numbers – if not even larger, considering that they had expected the Soviet Union to be defeated within six to ten weeks.

Secondly, there is clear evidence that this was a deliberate killing, through various means. In November 1941, General Karl Lennart Oesch, commander of the 4th Finnish Army Corps, issued the following written instructions for the treatment of captured Soviet soldiers: "Treatment of the prisoners has to be extremely strict. Any laxity is out of the question [...] Recalcitrant prisoners are to be executed on the spot to make an example for the others [...] One must bear in mind, that a Russki is always a Russki, and has to be treated and disciplined accordingly. Any mildness is out of the question, as the Russki is not accustomed to it and will consider it as a sign of weakness in his master [...] Recalcitrant prisoners and agitators (politruks) are to be done away without mercy. If executions are undertaken, such prisoners are to be marked in the documents as 'removed.'"[16] Quite revealing is the fact that the death rate among POWs in Finnish captivity was nearly eight times higher among prisoners of Russian origin than among those from the Baltic Soviet republics.[17]

The most obvious case of systematic POW killings is the German "Commissar order" which had led to the exe-

A Finnish Army officer and one of his soldiers among bodies of people shot near Petrozavodsk in Soviet Karelia. (Photo: SA Kuva.)

cution of approximately 42,000 Red Army political commissars by the time it was abandoned in May 1942.[18]

But indeed the whole German system for Soviet POWs was organized as a gigantic killing machine. Prior to Operation Barbarossa, the Germans constructed a large number of special POW camps, designed for the expected huge numbers of captured Soviet soldiers, so-called *Russenlager*, Russian camps. These differed substantially from POW camps assigned to Western prisoners. According to Organizational Order Number 37 of 30 April 1941, the *Russenlager* were to consist of mainly barbed-wire enclosures, watchtowers and housing for the guards. No hospitals or canteens were built.

These *Russenlager*, under German Army command, would claim the lives of hundreds of thousands of Soviets. Actually, when put into use, they were turned into de facto death camps. In a report to the German High Command (OKW), Alfred Rosenberg, the Reich minister of the Eastern Territories, noted that "in the majority of cases, the camp commanders have forbidden the civilian population

Former Red Army soldiers in the Mauthausen concentration camp.

---

* The worst case of German prisoners of war in World War II is that of the Stalingrad prisoners, of which only 6,000 survived. However, these surrendered after two months of envelopment, during which a totally inadequate amount of supplies were received. Out of 91,000 that surrendered in late January, 40,000 were injured, and the majority suffered from sickness such as typhus or diphtheria. Unfortunately, this extreme exception has occasionally been portrayed as the typical situation for German POWs in Soviet captivity. By the same logic, the forcible marching of German POWs through minefields in Denmark after the war could be portrayed as the average treatment of German POWs in Western captivity. ("*The Untold Horror of How Danes Forced German POWs to Clear Mines After WWII*" by Nir Levitan in Haaretz, 15 December 2015.) But German POWs were never subject to systematic mass killings similar to the politically motivated murders of 22,000 Polish officers in Soviet captivity in the spring of 1940.

THE SOVIET UNION AND THE GENEVA CONVENTION
RELATIVE TO THE TREATMENT OF PRISONERS OF WAR OF 1929.

It is asserted that the Geneva Convention was not ratified by the Soviet government. The following document, in the holdings of the State Archive of the Russian Federation, however sheds some new light on this.

Declaration
Hereby the People's Commissar of Foreign Affairs of the Union of Soviet Socialist Republics declares that the Union of Soviet Socialist Republics accepts the Convention relative to the Treatment of Prisoners of War, wounded, signed in Geneva on 27 July 1929. In order to verify it, the People's Commissar of Foreign Affairs of the Union of Soviet Socialist Republics, who has all the necessary mandates and powers, signs this declaration of acceptance. In accordance with a decision of the Central Executive Committee of the Union of Soviet Socialist Republics of 12 May 1930, this acceptance is final and does not need any further ratifications.
Moscow, 25 August 1930.
Signed Litvinov.

GARF, f. 9501, op. 5. d. 7 l. 22.
See also Slusser and Triska, *A Calendar of Soviet Treaties, 1917–1957*, p. 265.

from putting food at the disposal of prisoners and they have rather let them starve to death." The Commandant of Prison Camp Stalag 318, Oberst Falkenberg, noted in September 1941, "These damned *Untermenschen* [sub-humans] are eating grass, flowers and raw potatoes. If they can't find anything edible in the camp they turn to cannibalism." [19] Most of these camps did not even have any barracks. Oberst Falkenberg noted that in order to seek shelter against the cold, the desperate prisoners of war were "digging holes in the ground with their mess-kits and bare hands." The death figures for a selection of these camps are:

Stalag 372, Pskov: 50,000
Dulag 231, Vyazma: 17,000–25,000
Dulag 131, Bobruysk: 30,000–40,000
Stalag 131, Vitebsk: 76,000–120,000
Stalag 346, Kremenchug: 20,000
Dulag 160, Khorol: 57,000 [20]

Thus, in these six camps alone, the number of dead Soviet POWs approximately equals the total number of German POWs that perished in Soviet captivity between 1941 and 1956.

Before they even reached these camps, vast numbers of Soviet POWs succumbed to inhumane marches where they were subject to starvation, thirst and the brutality of the guards. "Whenever we halted," testified former Soviet prisoner of war Nikolay Obrynba, "thousands of those dying from hunger and cold remained or they collapsed as we marched along. Those still alive were finished off by soldiers wielding submachine guns. A guard would kick a fallen prisoner and, if he could not get up in time, fired his gun. I watched with horror as they reduced healthy people to a state of complete helplessness and death." [21] Of one column of 12,000 Soviet POWs that were marched from Vyazma to Dorogobuzh and Smolensk – a distance of 100 and 170 kilometers respectively – only 3,480 arrived at the destination. [22] In other cases, full-scale indiscriminate massacres of POWs were carried out, such as in the city of Smolensk on 19 October 1941, after which the streets of the city were covered with dead bodies. [23]

The situation hardly improved when Hitler in late 1941 ordered the surviving POWs to be transported to Germany, where many of them were to be used as slave laborers. They were transported by train, often in open freight cars in freezing conditions. According to a report by the Reichskommissariat Ostland on 5 December 1941, between 25 and 70 per cent of the prisoners perished during these transports. [24] A former Soviet prisoner described this: "The experience in the wagons can hardly be described in words. Wounds bled and turned everything black. Men died in each wagon. They died of blood loss, tetanus, blood poi-

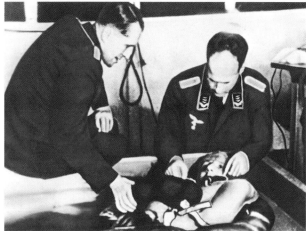

Victims of cruelty at the Bergen Belsen concentration camp. Out of 70,000 inmates that died at this place, around 30 per cent were Soviet prisoners of war. The camp commandant, SS-Hauptsturm-führer Josef Kramer, became known among the prisoners as "the Beast." He was captured when British soldiers liberated the camp in April 1945. Having been found guilty of selections for the gas chamber and other cruelties, he was sentenced to death and executed on 13 December 1945. (Photo: NARA.)

At Birkenau, Dachau and Auschwitz concentration camps, Soviet prisoners of war were subjected to human experiments by Luftwaffe doctor Sigmund Rascher. These included high-altitude/low-pressure experiments and freezing/hypothermia experiments, all of which led to a painful death. When SS-Reichsführer Himmler suggested that any prisoner who survived such a tortuous experiment should be released, Rascher replied that the victims were exclusively Poles and Russians, and although no one to date had survived, he was of the opinion that "they should be given no amnesty of any sort." The photo shows a prisoner in a vat filled with icy water during one of the freezing/hypothermia experiments.

During the doctors' trial at Nuremberg 1946–1947, former prisoner Walter Neff described one such experiment when two Soviet POWs managed to survive for several hours in the tank. After three hours, one of the Soviets said to the other: "Comrade, please ask the officer to shoot us," but received the reply that no mercy was to be expected from "the Fascist dog." The two Soviets shook hands and said "Farewell, comrade!" An attempt by a Polish interpreter to sedate the Soviets with chloroform was averted by Rascher, who pulled his pistol on the Pole. It took five hours before the last of the two prisoners of war had died from hypothermia.

The photo shows Dr Rascher (right) and his colleague, Professor Ernst Holzlöhner (left) during one of the freezing/hypothermia experiments. Holzlöhner was made rector at the University of Kiel in April 1945, but committed suicide two months later. Rascher was found guilty of kidnapping children, for which he was executed by the SS only days before the end of the war. (Photo: NARA.)

soning, or hunger, thirst and suffocation as well as other deprivation. This inhumane ordeal lasted for 10 days. The journey came to an end. At noon they unloaded the men. The dead were thrown out onto the platform."[25]

The fate that awaited the survivors in camps in Germany was in many cases even worse. The Army handed over tens of thousands of Soviets to the concentration camps, where the most grisly killings took place. In Gross-Rosen, over 65,000 Soviet POWS were killed within six months because they were given nothing but a thin soup of grass and water to eat.[26] In Flossenbürg, SS men burned Soviet prisoners alive.[27] Out of 2,000 Soviet POWs deported to Flossenbürg concentration camp in 1941, only 102 survived.

At Auschwitz on 3 September 1941, around 600 Red Army soldiers were murdered in the first Zyklon-B experiments.[28] Another 900 were murdered through the same means in December 1941, and when killings with gas began at Mauthausen-Gusen concentration camp shortly afterwards, Soviet prisoners of war were a major part of the first groups of victims. Large numbers of Soviet soldiers were also killed with Zyklon B at Neuengamme concentration camp.

In the concentration camp at Dachau, doctor Sigmund Rascher carried out human experiments for the Luftwaffe on Soviet POWs in ice cold water and in a low-pressure chamber to explore the endurance of the human body under extreme temperature and pressure conditions. (Generalfeldmarschall Erhard Milch, the Luftwaffe's Air Inspector General, expressed the gratitude of the Luftwaffe C-in-C, Reichsmarschall Göring, for Dr Rascher's "epoch-making human experiments.")

Large-scale atrocities against groups other than POWs were carried out on both sides during Operation Barbarossa. The most well-known among the Soviet atrocities are the massacres on political prisoners across the whole political spectra, from the left to the right. These

took place during the seemingly unstoppable advance of the Wehrmacht, when the Soviet authorities feared that they might be liberated. In June 1941, the NKVD was ordered to remove 140,000 prisoners from occupied eastern Poland/western Belarus, the Ukraine and the Baltic countries. Most of these were successfully evacuated, but according to NKVD reports in Russian archives, 8,789 political prisoners were killed by the NKVD in the prisons of the Ukrainian SSR.[29] Polish historian Albin Głowacki estimates that around 1,000 persons were killed in NKVD prisons in western Belarus.[30] Fewer were killed in the Baltic states because of the quick deportations of political prisoners in mid-June. In Vilnius and Kaunas, the NKVD murdered all the political prisoners – 260 in Kaunas alone – lest they were liberated by the LAF to reinforce its strength. Another 1,443 were reported shot during the evacuation, and 59 for attempting to escape. Twenty-three were killed in German air attacks, and 1,057 died from other causes. Thus, a total of around 13,000 political prisoners were murdered by the NKVD during the prison evacuations in June 1941.

These killings were exploited to the maximum by the German propaganda, designed to instigate the population

265

HOW MANY GERMAN PRISONERS OF WAR DIED IN SOVIET CAPTIVITY?

It is not uncommon to see figures on German soldiers perished in POW camps that even match the mortality rate of Soviets in German captivity, but these lack factual grounds. Immediately after the war, and not least as a defense during the Nuremberg Tribunals of war criminals in 1946, attempts were made by German officials and Nazi followers to relativize the German crimes on the Eastern Front by pointing out Allied war crimes.*

Mainly based on the list with the names of 1.1 million German soldiers still missing and presumed to be captives presented by West German Chancellor Adenauer in October 1951, claims of seven-digit numbers of perished German POWs have lingered on, much influenced by the Cold War. The West and the East both used Adenauer's figures to blame each other for these deaths, which – in spite of claims to the contrary – could not be tied to either the Eastern or the Western front.[1] In 1974, the West German so-called Maschke Commission, headed by former SA-member and Soviet POW, Erich Maschke, asserted that all of the 1.1 million German soldiers in Adenauer's list "more than likely died" died in Soviet captivity.[2]
Canadian writer James Bacque caused sensation in the West when he in 1989 claimed that the bulk of these – in total 900,000 to 1.2 million – died in Western custody.[3] Referring to official Western records, several historians have dismissed Bacque's figures.

Likewise, Adenauer's list has continued to be the point of departure for attempts to inflate the number of 363,000 German POWs[4] confirmed by the Deutsche Dienststelle (WASt) to have died in Soviet captivity.** This is not limited to politically tendentious publications (which commonly claim that "the chance of surviving captivity in the USSR was fifty-fifty); the perhaps most well-known writer to assert higher death rates is German military historian Rüdiger Overmanns. In *Deutsche militärische Verluste im Zweiten Weltkrieg,* he has picked up Maschke's method of adding missing Wehrmacht members on the Eastern Front to those registered as dying in Soviet captivity. Overmanns calculates that 700,000 of the missing died in captivity, and thus arrives at the conclusion that one million German POWs might have

*German prisoners of war, guarded by an NKVD officer.
(Photo: Krigsarkivet Stockholm.)*

died, including 90 per cent in Soviet captivity.[5] However, Overmann's and similar figures have also been questioned on grounds similar to those against Bacque.*** Just as Bacque's figures are refuted by U.S., British and French POW statistics, Maschke's and Overmann's figures are disproved by Soviet/Russian POW statistics. Since the Soviet archives were opened to the public in 1992, it has been possible to establish the exact number of POWs and their fate.

In a state such as Stalin's, where everything was kept under rigid control and anyone could be held accountable at any moment, records more detailed than anywhere else were kept. When the old Soviet archives were opened, it was established that there was an individual personal dossier kept for each prisoner, recording his unit, name, serial number, date of capture, and his personal history – including medical and legal history – while in captivity. The average length of these personal dossiers is 20 pages, occasionally covering 200 or more pages. The relatives of a POW had the full right to order a copy of the unexpurgated dossier.**** In such a system, there simply was no margin for hiding away disappeared prisoners of war.

These records show that a total of exactly 2,388,443 German servicemen were held as prisoners of war in the Soviet Union at any time during World War II. Of these, 356,700 died in captivity and 2,031,743 were repatriated to Germany.[6] This figure is just 6,000 lower than the German WASt figure – a discrepancy which might be explained through the fact that POWs sometimes died due to various causes before they were registered by the Soviet authorities.

---

* When American interrogators showed the Stuka ace and convinced Nazi Hans-Ulrich Rudel photos of atrocities in German Concentration camps in May 1945, Rudel replied that such photos could be seen in German cities that had been indiscriminately bombed by the Western Allies, and "if you gentlemen are interested in atrocities, you will find a sufficient amount of those at your Eastern ally." (Rudel, *Trotzdem*, p. 231.) That actually was a standard reply.

** The WaST contains detailed information on former members of the armed forces of the Third Reich.

*** Several of Overmann's figures are conspicuously high; thus his figure for Germans killed on the Eastern Front in 1941 is over 300,000. (Overmans, *Deutsche militärische Verluste im Zweiten Weltkrieg*, p. 266 and 277.) As showed in Appendix 5, Table 2, this differs considerably from the Wehrmacht monthly casual reports and the Heeresarzt 10-Day Casualty Reports, which give figures of 136,138 and 167,347 respectively. For a critical discussion on Overmann's methodology, see "Comments on 'Deutsche Militärische Verluste' by Rüdiger Overmans" at ww2stats. com/Overmans.pdf.

**** The author of these lines has had the opportunity to order the full dossier for the German POW Hermann Graf via his widow, and thus has been able to confirm this.

---

1 Bacque, *Other Losses: An Investigation into the Mass Deaths of German Prisoners of War at the Hands of the French and Americans After World War II*, p. xli.
2 Maschke, *Zur Geschichte der deutschen Kriegsgefangenen des Zweiten Weltkrieges. Band 15*, p. 185–230.
3 Ibid., p. lxii.
4 Overmans, *Deutsche militärische Verluste im Zweiten Weltkrieg*, p. 336.
5 Ibid., p. 292.
6 TsKhIDK, f. 1p, op. 32-6, d. 2, ll. 8–9. Today in the collections of the RGVA.

to carry out pogroms against the Jews, and unfortunately the echo of these deliberate exaggerations prevail to this day. One example suffices to illustrate this. In an internal report, the NKVD noted that of 696 convicts in the Dubno prison, 170 were released, 250 evacuated, and 230-260 selected for to be shot; 46 of the latter were not executed, bringing the total number of victims to between 184 and 214. The German army later gave figures of 400, 450, 500, or 550 victims of NKVD killings in that prison. The OUN inflated this to 800. Later, figures of thousands were widely propagated.[31] Today the latter figures are not infrequently reproduced in Western publications.

However, it must be kept in mind that these killings of political prisoners were carried out in the midst of a de facto civil war. Lithuanian and Latvian nationalist partisans were engaged in a bloody war against the Soviet authorities, and so was the OUN in the Ukraine. All of these cooperated closely with the Germans, and also had an anti-Semite agenda. The Polish guerilla movement ZWZ (the precursor of The Home Army, AK) had been active in Soviet-occupied eastern Poland since September 1939, liquidating Soviet agents, communist activists, etc.[32] By June 1941, the NKVD had arrested more than half the 25,000–30,000 guerillas of ZWZ.[33]

A funeral procession among Lithuanian deportees in the Verkhnyaya Ara-Kuorka settlement, Buryat ASSR, in the 1950s. Only days before the German invasion, the NKVD carried out a massive operation in the three Baltic states, whereby 9,146 Estonians, 15,000 Latvians and 17,000 Lithuanians suspected of political or armed opposition to the Soviet government were deported to settlements or prison camps in Siberia or elsewhere in the eastern parts of the Soviet Union. The majority of the Lithuanian deportees were employed by the logging and timber industry. The death rate was appalling during the initial years – reaching some fifty per cent among the Lithuanians – and the surviving deportees were only allowed to return home between 1947 and the late 1950s. (Photo: Genocide and Resistance Research Centre of Lithuania.)

Oberstleutnant Hasso von Manteuffel, a battalion commander in 7. Panzer-Division, threatened to arrest any SS, SD or Gestapo official who attempted to recruit his men for extra judiciary executions without his permission. Von Manteuffel went on to command Division Grossdeutschland, and during the Ardennes Offensive in 1944–1945 he led the 5. Panzerarmee with great success. After the war he joined the German Liberal Party and passed away on 24 September 1978, at the age of 81. (Photo: NARA.)

There was at least some military logic to the ruthless removal of these members of armed oppositions, contrary to the assassinations of "older" political prisoners in the Soviet interior later on. The two most well-known among these massacres in 1941 are the "Medvedev massacre" on, among others, several Old Bolsheviks in September, and the execution of 300 former military and political leaders, including three former Air Force commanders, in Kuybyshev in October. Other ruthless killings ordered by the Soviet authorities during Operation Barbarossa include the gunning down of hundreds of Muscovites during the rebellion in the Soviet capital in October 1941.

However, the renowned use of "blocking troops" ordered to shoot at their own retreating soldiers appears to be quite exaggerated in historiography. According to an NKVD report of 10 October 1941, a total of 657,364 soldiers had been arrested for unauthorized retreating or desertion. Among those, 632,486 were returned to the front line without any other repercussions, 10,201 were sentenced to death and executed, and only 3,321 were shot at the front line.

Soviet partisans – in reality a branch of the repressive authorities – carried out atrocities against the civilian population on a large scale. A German report covering the period 11 December 1941–23 January 1942 established that three out of four victims of partisan killings were Soviet civilians.[34] The fact that several among those executed were collaborators and killers of hostages and Jews, and the presence of "false partisans" does not alter the fact that the partisans upheld Stalin's rule of terror over the population.

However, not even the atrocities of Joseph Stalin's henchmen in 1941 are remotely comparable to the vast war crimes committed by Hitler's forces. The atrocities of the partisans paled in comparison with the reprisals carried out by the occupation forces. Nazi leaders also exploited the partisan activity, as the head of the Nazi Party Chancellery, Martin Bormann, wrote on 16 July 1941, "The partisan warfare provides us with a great advantage: it gives us the opportunity to extinguish anything that stands against us."[35] Nevertheless, such an excuse was not needed, nor were the German atrocities merely a reply to Soviet actions; the war against the Soviet Union was planned beforehand to be one of annihilation.

The greatest suffering was inflicted on the Jewish population of the USSR. According to Holocaust scholar Yitzhak Arad at Yad Vashem, between 2,509,000 and 2,624,500 Jews in the Soviet territories occupied by Germany and its allies

Lithuanian nationalists during a pogrom against Jewish Lithuanians in Kaunas on 27 June 1941.

perished during the war, i.e. a death rate of between 86 and 95 per cent.[36]

Hundreds of thousands were executed by the five Einsatzgruppen, each consisting of between 500 and 990 men. The so-called Jäger Report, recording the executions of Einsatzkommando 3 of Einsatzgruppen A between 22 June and 1 December 1941, is quite indicative of the murderous activities of these death squadrons. Compiled by the commander, Karl Jäger, it lists the executions of nearly 140,000 civilian people in the region entrusted to Heeresgruppe Nord: 136,421 Jews (46,403 men, 55,556 women and 34,464 children), 1,064 Communists, 653 mentally disabled, and 134 others.

However, it is also a fact that possibly even larger number of Soviet civilians fell prey to the executions of Germany's regular police force, the Ordnungspolizei (Order Police), which was deployed in the occupied territories. "Police battalions and other units of the Order Police commenced slaughtering Jews en masse with the beginning of the simultaneous onslaught against the Soviet Union and its Jews, and continued as long as Germans continued to kill Jews systematically. It cannot be said precisely in how many deaths police battalions were complicit. The number is certainly over one million, and could be three times as high."[37]

Members of the Waffen-SS also committed atrocities against civilians in the occupied parts of the USSR, and so did members of the Wehrmacht; particularly by providing the means for the murders – trucks, ammunition, etc – but many soldiers even took active part in the killings. How-

ever, most of the latter belonged to so-called "security divisions" (*Sicherungsdivision*), composed of older men with only little military training. The most notorious among these was the 707. Infanterie-Division, which is supposed to have killed more than 10,000 Jews in the rear area of Heeresgruppe Mitte in the fall of 1941.[38]

The Wehrmacht had a profound complicity in crimes against the Soviet POWs, but the extent to which it participated in the mass killings of Jews has been exaggerated – e.g. by the 1995 Wehrmacht Exhibition ("Verbrechen der Wehrmacht"), which was proved to contain many factual errors.

Whereas many Wehrmacht commanders and soldiers appear to have been in agreement with – or at least almost completely insensitive to – the ruthless treatment of Soviet POWs and partisans, they showed decidedly different attitudes to the mass killings of obviously innocent civilians. In a report on 9 December 1941, Rudolf Christoph von Gersdorff, the intelligence officer in Heeresgruppe Mitte, established the fact that the mass killings of the Jews were not only fully known about by the officers at the front, but also "generally rejected" by them.[39] Historian Dieter Pohl adds that "also in letters written by common soldiers, a strong criticism against this genocide was evident."[40]

Incidents when Wehrmacht officers and soldiers protested against, and occasionally even stopped, such massacres are quite common. The mass killings of Jews in Heeresgruppe Mitte's rear area in October 1941 (see Chapter 15) evoked strong protests from the headquarters of the army group.[41]

Oberstleutnant Hasso von Manteuffel, a battalion commander in 7. Panzer-Division, openly declared that he "would arrest any SS, SD or Gestapo official who attempted to recruit his men for any duties without his express permission." Von Manteuffel also refused to allow his troops become involved in SD actions. This, however, led to no repercussions for von Manteuffel.[42] Similarly, when Major Günther Lützow, the commander of JG 3, was visited by representatives of an Einsatzgruppe who asked if he could detach some of his men for a liquidation of Communists and Jews, he assembled his whole unit. Then, in the presence of the SD officials, he addressed his men, telling them that anyone who would like to participate in such "criminal actions" (as he put it), thereby violating his "honor as a soldier" should step forward, although that would cause the immensely popular Lützow to immediately apply for a transfer to another unit. Of course, no one volunteered for the shootings.[43] Lützow also did not face any repercussions; he continued to command JG 3 until August 1942, when he was promoted to become Inspector of the Day Fighters in the West.

In Heeresgruppe Nord, Oberstleutnant Arno Kriegsheim, Chief of Staff of the Berück, did not get off as lightly. His statement that the shootings of Jews were "ignoble" (unwürdig) cost him not only his position, but he was also dismissed from the ranks of the Wehrmacht.[44]

On 3 July, Oberstleutnant Helmuth Groscurth, operations officer in 295. Infanterie-Division, and Oberst Otto

Korfes, one of the division's regimental commanders, intervened with force against a massacre on Jews carried out by Waffen-SS soldiers, men of Einsatzgruppe C and Ukrainian nationalists. In his description of this event, Korfes wrote:

In a 5-meter deep and 20-meter wide ditch, stood or lay a group of 60 to 80 persons, mainly Jews – men, women and children. Moaning and screaming could be heard. Hand grenades detonated between the people. … 10 to 12 men in civilian dress, some of whom had hand grenades stuck into their belts, and some with spades in their hands, stood on top of the ditch. As far as I could see, they were led by a couple of SS-men. Just as I arrived in company with Oberleutnant [Ernst] Huar [Korfe's adjutant], one of the civilians stepped forward, holding a hand grenade which he was about to hurl into the ditch. I wrested the hand grenade from him and yelled at the men to stop killing. Then I told the soldiers who stood around to leave the citadel and took command of the officers, medical officers and NCOs. Most of the soldiers passed through the exits. Two officers, two medical officers and around 15 NCOs, most of them belonging to the Luftwaffe, reported to me. I let the NCOs block all entrances, and sent my adjutant to Oberstleutnant [Eitel-Friedrich] Patzwahl [a battalion commander in Korfe's regiment] in order to bring in a company and a physician and medics with first aid kit. Then I asked the people to climb out of the ditch…"

One of the Jews that thus was saved turned out to be a German emigrant who had served as a soldier in World War I, where he had been awarded the Iron Cross.[45]

In August, Oberstleutnant Groscurth also attempted, unsuccessfully, to prevent the killings of Jewish children by Sonderkommando 4a/ Einsatzgruppe C in Biyala Tserkov (see Chapter 11). When Generalfeldmarschall von Rundstedt became aware of such atrocities, he explicitly prohibited the soldiers of Heeresgruppe Süd from taking part in them.[46]

Contrary to German first-line troops, a fairly large number of Romanian soldiers committed atrocities against civilians – mainly Jews and Roma people – not only in the occupied territories, but also against those ethnical groups in Romania proper. German soldiers were shocked to see Romanian soldiers herding thousands of Jews and Roma people into the occupied Transnistria. Karl Holland, a Luftwaffe mechanic, wrote: "The Romanians herded Gypsies or Jews past our airfield. I followed them for a while and then I heard machine gun fire."[47] In July, the commander of 170. Infanterie-Division, Generalmajor Walter Wittke, intervened and stopped Romanian troops from continuing the pogrom against Jews that they had commenced on 8 July.[48] In Bukovina and Bessarabia, Romanian soldiers carried out pogroms in at least fifty towns or villages, which caused outrage among many German soldiers, and several also intervened to stop the atrocities.[49]

However, Hitler's other main ally, Finland, distinguished itself in one regard in that it did not deliberately single out Jews for killings. To the contrary, Jews served with the Finnish Army.

The German executioners routinely forced their victims to undress before they killed them. After the war the victims in this photo were identified as Mia Malka (sitting) and her brother Max Epstein, two Latvian Jews from Liepāja (Libau). The photo was taken at the dunes outside the town of Šķēde, north of Liepāja between 15 and 17 December 1941, when German SD and police forces and the 21st Latvian Police Battalion shot 2,731 Jews and 23 communists at this place. Pēteris Galiņš, in charge of the Latvian forces during this massacre, was killed in 1943. Dr. Fritz Dietrich, the commander of the German Order Police in Libau, was sentenced to death by a U.S. war crimes court and executed at the Landsberg Prison 22 October 1948.

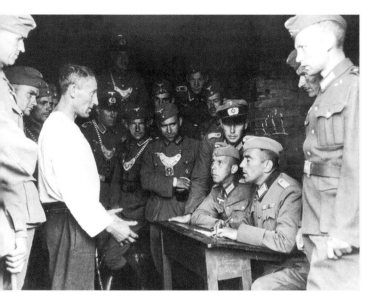

A Soviet civilian is interrogated by German field police. One can almost read his fate in the eyes of some of the Germans.

But this was the exception; elsewhere large-scale pogroms were carried out by local anti-Semites in the western parts of the Soviet Union – the territories that had been annexed by the USSR in 1939 and 1940. Some of the worst pogroms took place in Lithuania and Latvia, where they were initiated by nationalist partisans even before the arrival of German troops. In western Ukraine, at least fifty-eight local pogroms took place, with estimations of the number of victims ranging between 13,000 and 35,000.[50] The Polish population living under Soviet rule was no exception. A report from the Polish armed resistance movement ZWZ on the period 1-15 July 1941, stated: "In a number of cities (Brest, Lomza, Biyalystok, Grodno) pogroms have taken place and even the massacre of Jews by local Poles, unfortunately, acting together with German soldiers."[51] Historian Andrzej Zbikowski has found that between 22 June and 4 July 1941 alone, local Polish anti-Semites initiated pogroms against their Jewish neighbors in fifty-one localities in formerly eastern Poland.[52]

However, within the pre-1939 Soviet borders, the population was significantly less prone to anti-Semitism. A German report of 11 August 1941 on the attitudes of the population in these territories noted, "Attempts to instigate pogroms have failed. The reason is that in the eyes of the average Russian, the Jew leads a proletarian life and thus cannot be subject to attacks."[53]

The notion of an official Soviet anti-Semitism during the war years completely belies actual facts. Altogether, 270 generals and admirals that served with the Red Army and the Red Fleet during the war were of Jewish origin. Included among those were four army commanders, twenty-three corps commanders, seventy-two divisional commanders, and 103 brigade commanders.[54] Yitzhak Arad establishes that "in no army of the Allies, not even in the U.S., did Jews occupy such high positions, as in the Soviet Army."[55] Hundreds of thousands of Soviet soldiers, airmen and sailors also were of Jewish origin, and between 120,000 and 180,000 of them were killed in action.[56]

Gentile civilians did not have an easy time of it either; for them also life in occupied Soviet Union was a collective trauma. "The Germans tortured and murdered civilians at the slightest pretext," wrote historian Nina Tumarkin.[57] The same could probably be said for the troops of any of Germany's allies. "People had a sense that their lives and the occupiers were out of control," concluded professor Wendy Jo Gertjejanssen after conducting extensive interviews with people who lived through the German occupation. "I don't know how I survived," said Mikhail Potapov, a young boy in Gomel during the war. "We were constantly afraid, always hungry, always terrorized by the German soldiers who appeared as non-human monsters to me as a child. They could do anything they wished to you, and they did. I got used to see beatings, hangings, dead people in the streets. My mother and two sisters were tortured and killed. The same happened to many of our neighbors. My grandmother and I barely survived. I wept until I had no more tears. Not once did I see a German behave decently. Then I began to feel a glowing hatred against anything German. If I had the chance, I would have killed each one of them. But I was just a boy of between six and eight years of age. I still have nightmares."[58]

Aleksandr Tolstik, a construction engineer in Minsk, describes the situation during the first days of the German occupation: "On 1 July, a notice was posted everywhere: all men between 16 and 50 years of age should come to a certain place. Anyone who fails to turn up will be shot. When I arrived, there were already 140,000 men. The camp was set up by the Wehrmacht and was enclosed by barbed wire. 15 rolls over each other. We were all searched through. They took the money from us, the identity cards and all our work stuff. Everything we had. We stood very tight on the court. 140,000 men. Five or six men on one square meter. At night we had to lie down on the ground. Whoever stood up, was shot. At first they shot over our heads, then lower. It was hot. 35 degrees. In July. There was no food, no water, no toilets, no medical care. Nothing. I was there for seven days. During that time, 3,000 men died."[59]

A correspondent from the by then still neutral United States, Alvin J. Steinkopf, described the scenes that met him as he was allowed to visit German-occupied Smolensk in August 1941: He saw "ragged" children in the streets of a city in ruins with 20,000 "frightened and resourceless" people remaining. He wrote: "I found the German commander of Smolensk eating a thick soup from a dish on a dirty tablecloth spread in what was once the director's room of a savings bank. Civilian organizations under the leadership of an appointed Russian lawyer 'who secretly had been an anti-Communist' as burgomaster [mayor]…"[60]

Owing to the orders that the German Army was to live off the conquered land, widespread plunder was the rule. Based on archive material, historian Omer Bartov gives the example of one German unit: "The troops of the 18. Panzer-Division plundered and looted the population wherever they could lay their hands on their possessions. Boots and furs were particularly high on the soldiers' lists of priorities, as were potatoes, flour and cattle. The men broke into houses and indeed stripped whole villages of their food reserves, shooting down any person who tried to resist them."[61]

The occupation of large areas of the western Soviet Union was an economic disaster to the country in several aspects. By November 1941 those areas that had fallen under occupation had previously provided the country with the following percentage of production:

Minerals:[62]
Iron 68 %
Coal 63 %
Aluminum 60 %
Steel 58 %

Foodstuff:[63]
Sugar 84 %
Pigs 60 %
Grain 38 %
Cattle 38 %

Agricultural production fell by 40 per cent. Added to the decline in the work force and other war-related negative effects on food production and distribution, this resulted in a nourishment problem throughout the whole Soviet Union. A single letter by a Soviet soldier of the 33rd Army in November 1941 is quite indicative of the situation: "The food is bad, twice a day we get bread, sometimes 400 grams, sometimes 600, we never see more. The soup is like water."[64] But counteracting against rising malnourishment, which reduced people's immune protection, the Soviet authorities rapidly organized sanitation stations all over the free areas of the country, often on trains, for obligatory health controls of the entire population, and launched a widespread immunization program. In spite of the war needs, the national budget for healthcare was considerably increased. Owing to these great efforts, there were no large-scale epidemics in the free parts of the country during the war.[65]

The situation was immensely worse in the occupied parts, where the Germans and their allies actively killed millions of people through a deliberate starvation policy according to the pre-war Hunger Plan. The minutes from a conference with amongst others the former "white" émigre Alfred Rosenberg, Reich Minister for the Occupied Eastern Territories, Generalmajor Rudolf Gercke, the commander of the German Field Transport Service and Reichsmarschall Hermann Göring, the Luftwaffe commander and the Minister of Economics in the Reichsluftfahrtministerium on 13 November 1941, reads – on the latter's statements: "The fate of the large cities, especially Leningrad, is of no importance to him. This war will witness the greatest death toll since the Thirty-Years' War. If the grain cannot be transported from the Ukraine, it must be used for pig-breeding."[66]

It is impossible to establish how many Soviet people succumbed to hunger and hunger-related disease owing to the policy of Germany and its allies, but their number is in the millions. During the first two years of occupation, the quantity of foodstuffs that the Germans exported from the occupied parts of the Soviet Union amounted to 4,372,339 tons of grain, 1,895,775 tons of potatoes, 495,643 tons of meat, and 723,450 tons of cooking oil and other fats.[67] German economic historian Götz Aly has showed that this converts into 106,268,262 so-called cereal units. According to UN standards, a human being needs about 2.5 cereal units per year to survive. This proves that in theory, 21.3 million people were deprived their means of survival during those two years in the occupied parts of the Soviet Union – the besieged city of Leningrad not included. To this should be added all that was stolen from the population by the millions of occupation troops.

Owing to the chaotic wartime situation, it is impossible to estimate with any accuracy the total number of deaths in the Soviet Union during the war. A study by the Russian Academy of Sciences in 1994 estimated total Soviet war-related population losses between 1941 and 1945 at 26-27 million, including nearly 20 million civilians.[68] Ukrainian historian Viktor Korol however disputes this, and instead has calculated the Soviet loss of life due to the war as over 40 million.[69] On one of the displays at the Russian memorial complex at Poklonnaya Gora, Moscow, the figure of 37.2 million Soviet people killed during the war is given.

Russian military historian Grigoriy Krivosheev estimates that 4.1 million Soviet civilians perished due to starvation and malnutrition-related disease during the war. According to Russian researcher A.A. Shevyakov, 14.3 million Soviet civilians were shot, gassed, tortured to death or otherwise killed by Germany and its allies during the war, with another 6.4 million civilian victims of starvation during the war.[70] Recent German research has arrived at an even higher number of victims of man-made starvation in German-occupied Soviet Union: 7 million.[71] For instance, according to Soviet figures, nearly one-third of the whole Russian civilian population in occupied Eastern Karelia alone (14,000 out of 50,200) succumbed to the Finnish occupation policy.[72] As we have seen, 280,000 of the 460,000 Kharkov citizens that remained in the city when it was occupied, died – 60 per cent.

Almost all of the people living in the Soviet Union during the occupation that were interviewed by professor Gertjejanssen told her that the Germans took all their food. "Many still cried about this, and it was very apparent that they had suffered tremendously because of this lack of sustenance."[73]

The victims of starvation of course were not merely statistical figures. Elena Kozhina, then a young girl, described in her memoirs how she and her family suffered from the man-made starvation under the German occupation: "I heard a scream. It was such a scream... even I perked up, and weakly screamed something in reply. I tried to get up but could not. Mama ran out into the yard with Tanya in her arms. My little sister's head was lolling on Mama's shoulder, her eyes already closed. Only her tiny mouth was still moving, trying to open, gasping for air. 'My little bird! My little bird, don't fly away!' And with her last remaining strength, Mama was raising Tanya's tiny body up, up to the blackened sky, full of smoke and thunder, as if there she might breathe easier. 'My little bird!' But my little sister was already dead."[74]

A report by German 12. Infanterie-Division noted that "the land has been exploited to the utmost," causing

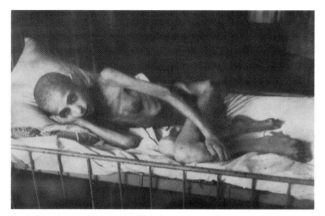

A victim of starvation caused by the Wehrmacht: A young Soviet woman sick with dystrophy, a degeneration of tissue due to malnutrition. This photo was taken in the besieged Leningrad, where she could at least receive medical treatment. The situation was even worse in the occupied parts of the USSR, where millions of people starved to death.

The sight of people dying from starvation in the streets was common during the German occupation of the Soviet Union. This photo shows a street in Kiev during the occupation.

"a situation of a general lack of food supplies for the civilian population," which in some cases even "caused starving Russian civilians to turn to German units and ask for relief or beg to be shot."[75] Ironically, often German soldiers that had managed to resist becoming permeated with the inhuman Nazi ideology meant the difference between life and death to starving Soviet civilians. The practice of housing Germans in Soviet houses both enabled and encouraged German troops to help their Soviet household members to survive. It has not been uncommon for the author to meet German veterans who have described absolutely trustworthy stories of how they helped the people with whom they shared housing – Alfred Grislawski, Hansgeorg Bätcher and Friedrich Lang to mention just a few. There also are several Soviet accounts that confirm this.* Frieda Frome described in her memoirs how a non-commissioned German officer came to stay with her family. She wrote how they all "trembled with dread" at first, and that she and her sister hid "most of the time," but

that the German turned out to be a "godsend," because he brought them a little extra food.[76]

Tatyana Vasilyeva, in 1941 a 13-year-old girl in the town of Siverskaya south of Leningrad, supplies us with another example in her memoirs: She and her family were so weak from hunger that they were confined to bed when a group of Germans took over two rooms in their house. One of the Germans felt pity for the Russians when he saw their poor condition, saying that he was fully aware that it was the German occupation policies that caused her family to starve. He promised to help them and gave them a loaf of bread almost every day, but told them not to reveal it to the other Germans. The bread from this German enabled Tatyana and her mother to get up after a couple of weeks. Her father nevertheless remained ill, and her toddler sister, Olya, still could not walk because her legs had become useless from the starvation. And ironically Tatyana's recovery caused her to be captured and deported to Germany for slave labor; she would spend three years working 12-hour days in factories, all the while enduring violence, hunger and other privations.[77]

The worst suffering was however wrought upon the Jews in German-occupied Soviet Union, who received a daily ration of no more than 420 kilocalories and were also forbidden by the occupation authorities to purchase meat, milk, eggs, butter and vegetables.[78] There was hardly any way even the most good-natured Germans could possibly help them, as they were isolated in the ghettos.

Throughout the occupation, there was a permanent curfew, and this was used in a particularly sinister way by many German soldiers to find victims to rape, as one of many similar testimonies describes: "During the night we would hide in the village. We'd get together in just one house. And here they would knock in the windows and take the young ones. Then there was a knock. 'Open, Mother!' We would open. Then he would look and see which one was young. 'Komm!' We would yell. The mothers were running after us. They were also yelling. They killed my aunt. [The Germans] were pulling her daughter and she was screaming and he shot into her and killed my aunt."[79]

Sexual violence, including mass rape, was an integrated phenomenon of the War of Annihilation against the Soviet Union, although this has escaped the attention of most Western scholars on the subject of the Eastern Front. To the contrary, Western writers have been quite successful in establishing the terrible wave of rapes committed by Soviet soldiers in Germany and Poland towards the end of the war as a general public knowledge. For instance, in his epic book on the Battle of Berlin, historian Antony Beevor deals with the rape of German or Polish women by Soviet soldiers on twenty-eight different pages.[80] When dealing with rape, the victim's perspective must of course dominate, and thus it is absolutely justified and a moral obligation to deal with these atrocities. What makes the whole matter even more tragic is that German rapes of Polish and Soviet women, probably on an even larger scale and definitely preceding these Soviet rapes, are ignored by nearly all Western historians. This cannot be explained entirely

---

* Hansgeorg Bätcher even visited the families that he thus saved in the Crimea in the 1990s, and received a warm welcome.

through a lack of available documents, since an abundance of such records are to be found among the documents presented at the Nuremberg War Crimes Trial.

Indeed, the wording in some accounts on rape on the Eastern Front during World War II reveals more about the scholar than about what really happened, as Professor Gertjejanssen put it: "The assumption that men from the east, especially from the Far East, rape more than men from the west, for example."[81] Gertjejanssen's comment is just as harsh as it is striking: "The propaganda Germany employed against the 'barbaric Soviet people' certainly has been pervasive."[82]

However, this applies only to a minority of writers, conscious of their own ideological perspective to a greater of lesser degree. In most cases regarding the majority of myths and misconceptions concerning the Eastern Front during World War II, the explanation is the circumstances and the specific historiographical tradition in which the scholar works – what is called *den fjättrade Clio* in Swedish historiographic theory.* First of all, surviving victims in the West are far more attainable for Western scholars than their fellow sufferers in the East. Secondly, while rapes committed by Soviets/Russians in Germany were exploited for propaganda reasons during and after the Cold War, a "silence of shame" stopped victims of rape by Western soldiers from stepping forward.** Secondly, a lack of criticism of the sources has caused many a writer to pay too much attention to statements by veterans. But while the same Western writers critically take note of the fact that many Soviet veterans are quite unwilling to admit that mass rapes took place, they swallow whole German veterans' assertions that there were never any German rapes – thus completely ignoring even the simple fact that it can still be dangerous for citizens of a country which lost the war to admit such a crime.

There also is a widespread myth that Jews were not sexually assaulted by Germans. Evidence from all over Europe, including the occupied territories and the Concentration Camps, prove that this is not true. The Nazi laws against having sex with a Jewish woman only pertained in cases of consensual sex. As Professor Myrna Goldenberg, who has closely studied the subject, states, "In Nazi Germany, rape and other forms of sexual abuse against Jewish women were not defined as crimes."[83]

Even in spite of their official military and racial laws and rules, Germans of the Wehrmacht, the SS, the Police, the civilian administration, and their allies, were engaged in mass rape, including gang rape on an enormous and routine scale, in the occupied territories of the Soviet Union and Poland. The victims were Jews as well as gentiles; women and girls as well as men and boys; and victims were from the youngest of ages. There are examples of a 90-year old female rape victims as well as nine- or eight-

year-old girls.[84] A testimony recorded in United States Holocaust Memorial Museum reads: "They [Germans and Lithuanian partisans] tied a twelve-year-old [Jewish] girl to a bench, and six Germans and six Lithuanians finished the sexual act twice each, and the poor girl wasn't let go. And the mother was forced to stay during this and watch so that the child wouldn't scream. After that the mothers were forced to completely undress, were put against a wall with hands tied upwards toward the head, and they pulled out all the hair on naked places. They were ordered to stick out their tongues, and they stuck needles into them. Then they all came over and urinated and smeared their faeces over their eyes. The men were told to take out their sexual organs, on which they put red hot pokers and held it until the poker became black. During that time they said it's enough to live, you Jews, we will murder all of you."[85] Mikhail Temchin, a Soviet doctor, recalls how "one girl of twelve was so badly mauled during such an 'act of collective love' that she required about five or six stitches to restore her into halfway human shape."[86]

Historian Alana Fangrad has arrived at the conclusion that "on the whole, Nazi authorities accepted these forms of sexual violence."[87] As Antony Beevor establishes,

This pregnant Soviet woman was raped and killed by German troops.

Rape by German soldiers was widespread on the Eastern Front.

---

* "The Shackled Clio," an expression coined by Swedish historian Hugo Valentin (1888–1963), pertaining to Clio, the muse of lyre playing, also referred to as "the Proclaimer, glorifier and celebrator of history, great deeds and accomplishments," who nevertheless remains shackled to the immediate present – meaning that history is always interpreted from the interpretors own perspective and values.

** It is only with German historian Miriam Gebhardt's Als die Soldaten kamen, which was published in 2015 (Deutsche Verlags-Anstalt, Munich), based on the most profound research material on rapes committed against German civilians during World War II to date, that a balance has been achieved; Gebhardt's results actually shows that rape was a more common phenomenon among American soldiers than among Soviet soldiers, when compared to the number of servicemen in Germany.

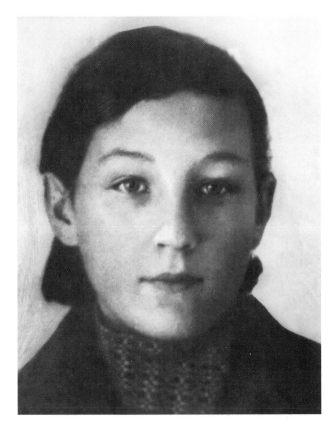

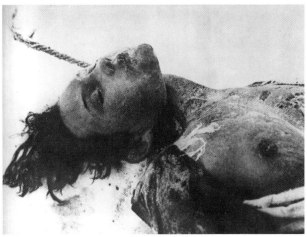

← ↑ *Zoya Kosmodemyanskaya, a 17-year-old Soviet girl, was arrested by the Germans when she attempted to burn down a German Army stable in the village of Petrishchevo on the evening of 27 November. For two days she withstood severe torture by soldiers of German 197. Infanterie-Division, but refused to reveal anything but her cover name, "Tanya." On 29 November she was publicly hanged in the center of the village. Before she was hanged, she is reported to have cried: "You cannot hang us all!" After the execution, the Germans took the photo to the right of her tortured body.*

a "Jurisdiction Order" signed by Generalfeldmarschall Keitel on 13 May 1941 "deprived Russian civilians of any right to appeal, and effectively exonerated soldiers from crimes committed against them, whether murder, rape or looting."[88] In her study on Sexual Violence on the Eastern Front during World War II, Professor Wendy Jo Gertjejanssen found that "a few men were punished," but the available evidence indicates that these were in fact exceptions.[89] In the relatively few cases where Germans were sentenced for rape on the Eastern Front, *visibility* during the act seems to have been the dominating issue.[90] Gertjejanssen concludes that not only did the German military command fail to do much to prevent this mass rape, but "rape was deployed as a means of terror," and "there was a tacit understanding that the armed men had a right or even permission to rape women and girls."[91] The common notion that this reflected the "sexual need" of front soldiers is refuted by the simple fact that Slavs and Jews were subject to mass rape by the Germans and their allies, while Estonian's and Latvians seemed to have suffered far less from this fate.[92]

Males and young boys also suffered rape and sexual abuse.[93] Although probably millions of Soviet citizens, primarily women and girls, became rape victims the topic has been grossly understudied. One exception however is Professor Gertjejanssen who in her doctoral studies conducted a large number of interviews in the former Soviet republics. She found that "most people" in the places she visited said that rape actually was "a common phenomenon" in their villages during the Germans occupation.[94]

It seems as though much of the Goebbels exaggerations on Soviet crimes against German civilians have been borrowed from actual German atrocities committed against Soviet civilians. One such example is the notorious crucifixion of raped women on barn doors in Nemmersdorf.* There are several more trustworthy examples of such brutal practices committed by German and their allied troops against Soviet women. Wendy Jo Gertjejanssen relates to one example which came up during one of her interviews:

"One Soviet officer told us about a brutal gang rape, murder and mutilation, the remains of which he was shown as they entered a village in eastern Europe. His troops arrived in this village about the same time the main army took the Cherkassy Pocket. The Germans had retreated in a hurry. This was evident because they left behind two railroad cars full of sugar. One of the officer's men came running to him and told him he had to show him something. We went, not too far away was a house. In the house you could see that the Germans had been there. The icons were on the floor, broken. On the table there was food and alcohol. So that's what remained on the table. Where the icon was supposed to be there stood an undressed young girl, about fifteen to sixteen years old, and in that place [vagina] there was a bottle stuffed. The breast was cut into four pieces and the blood was running down her legs and onto the floor. And she was raspiata [arms like Jesus Christ]. When I saw it I was so fearful, so I came out and started to collect the people so that they would see, so that they wouldn't say that our soldiers did it. She was cold already. So when I brought the people and they looked, oh my god, it was awful, it was scary. Such a girl, just like a flower and so beautiful, such a nice figure. So they killed her, and just like Jesus Christ on

---

* For instance, a recent study by German Ph.D. Bernhard Fisch has found that the crucifixion barn doors in the German propaganda photographs were not even in Nemmersdorf. (See "Nemmersdorf 1944: nach wie vor ungeklärt" by Bernhard Fisch in Gerd R. Ueberschär, *Orte des Grauens. Verbrechen im Zweiten Weltkrieg.* Gebundene Ausgabe – 2003.)

Public hangings of people accused of cooperation with the partisans was commonplace all over the occupied parts of the Soviet Union. (Photo: Via Martin Månsson.)

a cross they put the nails, and where the icons were hanging they tied her head to some kind of stick, and to kill her where the very important icon was. And the legs were hanging. Oh it was so scary.

Assistant: Did you find out who did it?

Veteran: Germans, Germans. There was a Stab [headquarters] there, they were drinking there, they were having fun there.

Assistant: And about this girl, do you remember, what was said? Who was she? How did she behave? What made it so that they did such a thing to her?

Veteran: She was the owner of that house.

Assistant: Oh, owner of that house?

Veteran: Yea, owner of that house.

Assistant: Yea, yea, a girl?

Veteran: And that means that they were drinking there and shooting there and shooting through the icons, and they left those icons on the table. ... Yea, they did it before they had to retreat, that's when they did it.

Assistant: Yea, yea, it was said and everybody says that when they were leaving...

Veteran: I can swear on the bible that this is true. I never do any propaganda."

Gertjejanssen concludes: "The man who told the story was well-educated, and he told of rape by Soviet soldiers as well. He was well aware of the propaganda used by the Soviet state to incite him and his soldiers to fight to the end. In other words, this man was believable because he had a critical stance in the retelling of many events." [95]

Lilya Samoilovna Gleizer, a Jewess in the Minsk ghetto, recalled how "drunken Germans and policemen raped young Jewish girls without a trace of shame. They took their knives and cut out sexual organs ... cut off noses, breasts, and ears." [96] Nukhim Polinovsky, who was ordered to dig up and cremate the bodies of a massacre against Jews at Bialystok, testified that in a pit with 700 women, "the bodies were absolutely naked, the breasts of many of the victims had been cut off." [97]

Such horrible stories can only be grasped when we consider that just as in the case with the victims of famine, the voluntary acts of other German soldiers would often be the only protection against rape on the Eastern Front. Several of the women interviewed by Gertjejanssen said that they felt safer when they had an officer staying in or nearby their house, because they would often protect the women. One of the women said: "[This German officer]

276

A PARTISAN AND HER EXECUTIONER.

Three Soviet citizens, accused of being partisans, are led to their hanging by Lithuanian auxiliary policemen in Minsk on 26 October 1941: To the left, World War I veteran Kiril Trus, and to the right, 16-year-old Volodya Shcherbatsiyevich. The girl with the defiant look in the center is 17-year-old Mariya Borisovna Bruskina. The sign hung around her neck reads: "We are partisans and have shot at German soldiers." That was not true, since Bruskina's only "crime" was to have helped wounded Soviet soldiers to escape by smuggling civilian clothing and false identity papers into the hospital.

The execution was filmed by the Lithuanians. A Russo-German sympathizer with the partisans who worked at a photo shop in Minsk was entrusted to develop the film. He secretly made copies of stills and hid them until the liberation of Minsk by the Red Army in 1944.

The execution of Mariya Borisovna Bruskina was carried out by the 2nd Lithuanian Police Battalion. Commanded by Antanas Impulevičius-Impulėnas, this infamous unit killed about 46,000 people, including about 9,000 Soviet prisoners of war, in the fall of 1941. The members of the unit acted with such sadism that the German commander in Slutsk, south of Minsk, wrote a note of complaint to his superior, and asked, "in future, I ask you to keep this battalion away from me." Impulevičius-Impulėnas, a former Lithuanian army major, had been arrested by the NKVD in 1940, but was freed by partisans in June 1941.

Impulevičius-Impulėnas, seen in the photo, fled to Germany in 1944 and emigrated to the United States after the war. In 1962 a Soviet Lithuanian court sentenced him to death in absentia, but the US authorities refused to extradite him. He passed away in Philadelphia, Pennsylvania on 4 December 1970 at the age of 63.

was taking only one room, a bedroom, so my mother would make some soup in the evening, and he would eat it. So he wouldn't even let anybody in the house."[98]

A form of systematic gang rape that the Germans did not intervene against however was sexual slavery. This phenomenon in World War II is also almost totally unknown, apart from the Japanese so-called "Comfort Women". "The Japanese army was not unique in its practice of sexual slavery during World War II. So too did the Germany army. Women and girls in the east were forced into such fates because of the lack of food due to the German invasion, subsequent occupation, and deliberate policy of starvation. Other women and girls were forced into this kind of work at gunpoint. Still others were given the so-called choice of living (and dying) in a concentration camp or working in a brothel."[99]

Again, the explanation why this remains relatively unknown has sociologic and psychological reasons and does not relate at all to the amount of documentation available; in fact the sexual slavery practised by the Germans on the Eastern Front is supported by a "vast amount of German documentation and a large number of Soviet interrogations of civilians both during and after the war exist. Some of these documents have only recently become available in archives in countries such as Latvia, Estonia, Ukraine, and Russia. Many of these are available at the United States Holocaust Memorial Museum in Washington, D.C. Finally, a multitude of novels and memoirs exist."[100] The current German state, which has set an example of self-criticism and acknowledgement of guilt when it comes to many war crimes, however has not acknowledged the victims of sexual violence, nor has it admitted its complicity in these kinds of sexual crimes. Thus it is hardly surprising that this dark chapter has escaped the attention of military historians.

The extensive network of German military brothels is a typical example of the double standards of the otherwise puritan Nazi ideology. One of the basic foundations of this ideology was homophobia. As in all male armies, military service provided good opportunities for homosexual relations – although severely punished when detected. This was not unkown to the political and military leaders. SS Leader Himmler was one of them; already in a speech about homosexuality to the SS Gruppenführer in 1937, he had said: "We will be exceedingly generous in this matter because one cannot, on the one hand, want to prevent all the youth from drifting toward homosexuality and, on the other hand, block for them every [sexual] outlet." He also was of the opinion that sexual intercourse in a brothel with a woman of "an alien race" did no harm to the German.[101] Hundreds of Wehrmacht and SS brothels were formed before Operation Barbarossa, usually with the Feldkommandant in any given area in charge, but often also privately controlled by individual businessmen.[102]

The women and girls who were forced into this state-controlled sexual slavery often did not survive long owing to illness caused by mistreatment, suicide or murder.[103] A German medical officer reported that one girl in a brothel received thirty-two "visits" between four and nine o'clock in the evening; because of the high demand, the men were limited to ten minutes before the duty sergeant yelled "Next!"[104]

The Germans were constantly in search for new women and girls to replace the "losses" in the field brothels. In the occupied villages and cities of the Soviet Union, the Germans routinely and repeatedly searched for "suitable" women and girls to become sexual slaves. One account serves as an example: In the village of Kabana near Kiev, a local teacher named Vera K. testified that "the Germans gathered women and girls in a brothel and exposed them to massive rapes there."[105] This practise was carried out parallel to the continual hunt for slave laborers. Besides this, women deported to Germany as slave workers also were subject to mass sexual harrassment.[106] No less than 8.7 million Soviet citizens were deported as slave laborers.[107]

Victims of a German massacre at Bagerovo, Crimea.

The stereotype in the Third Reich of the "Russian," the product of a society filled with racial prejudice and Nazi propaganda, cannot be separated from the Nazi image of "the cruel, inhumane Jew," neither can it be detached from crude anti-Communism. The Nazi linking of "Judeo-Bolshevism" as an inseparable whole formed the actual basis of National Socialism. This caused many Germans to close their eyes to their own – even personal! – atrocities and create an image of the war as being "a mission to protect Western civilization from Stalin's barbarism."[108] The fact that the German image of the Eastern Front was completely distorted – with a common notion being that of "decent" German invaders fighting a "primitive" and "cruel" enemy – is a good example of how propaganda and selective perception can influence a person's judgement. (That this image has been adapted by many a Western scholar on the war in the East, however, perhaps is less understandable.) When Dutch SS volunteer Hendrik

The eyes of this young Soviet combat engineer on the Moscow front in the winter of 1941/1942 have probably seen too much of human cruelty. Little could he know that three and a half years of relentless fighting remained before the war would be over.

C. Verton described the character of the war in the East, he wrote: "The war with the Soviet Union, and the form which they directed it, escalated and surpassed all cruelty and hardship experienced in any former combat since 1939." Reading further, it becomes evident that Verton means the Soviet side when he speaks of cruelties: "Hitler described it as the biggest crusade in world history, resembling the German crusaders, who had to fight the hordes of Genghis Khan in Silesia. That we could fight such an unrelenting enemy with the motto 'it's you or me!' was thanks to the truncheon-hard training that we had received."[109]

It is as the British say, that the proof of the pudding is in eating. It should be kept in mind what Omer Bartov so pertinently points out – but what several Western scholars often seem to forget: "The German army in Russia ... fol-

lowed a clear policy of subjugation and extermination. Had Germany won the war, Russia would have disappeared as a political entity, and millions more Russians would have been murdered, with the rest being enslaved by their German colonizers. .... [On the other hand,] the Red Army in Germany had no policy of decimating the German population and turning Germany into a wasteland fit for Russian colonization. Had this been the case, we would not have seen the recent reunification of Germany, for there would have been nothing to unite with. ... If the Soviet Union installed brutal dictatorships in the East European countries it conquered, these were nevertheless not genocidal regimes."[110]

The same phenomenon applies to Germany's allies. It was a common notion among the Finnish soldiers – and indeed among Finnish historians of today – that they represented a civilized outpost against a ruthless, barbaric enemy, striving to enslave and massacre them. However, in reality, it was the Finns who sent thousands of inhabitants of the occupied territories to concentration camps, and it was the Finns who were responsible for a death rate of POWs that exceeded the death rate of Allied soldiers in Japanese POW camps. The Finnish policy when it attacked in 1941 rested on the hope of the total annihilation of the Soviet Union, whereas after both wars with the Soviet Union (1939–1940 and 1941–1944), Finland survived as an independent state.

Much of the self-image of the attackers can be described on a psychological level as a case of simple blame shifting, such as the following lines in a letter from a German soldier on the Eastern Front in August 1941: "Thank God that [the Russians] have been thwarted from plundering and pillaging our homeland."[111] Regrettably, some modern scholars have been unable to free themselves from the impact of this distorted self-image of the attackers.

But many a German and Finnish soldier managed to see through the propaganda. "May God preserve us from losing the war, because if revenge is taken, things will be bad for us," wrote a German soldier under the impression of massacres against Jews in Lithuania.[112]

On the other side of the hill, Soviet soldier Pavel Gurevich expressed the feelings among the *Frontovniki*: "I thought that we shall stop those reptiles at any cost. We were all boys, 18 and 19 years of age, and it was only when I heard the screams and howls from the wounded that I understand how terrible war is. But in spite of all horrors, you would not let go of your rifle, you would not run. Instead, you are overwhelmed by a great rage and only have one thing in mind: To shoot those Fascists, to shoot them all! German tanks and infantry opened fire at us with all might. We had already been under a fierce bombardment for a long time, but I remember quite distinctly that what surprised me most was that I and my comrades would not leave the battlefield. Such was our rage – we had only one desire: to seek revenge for our comrades, to destroy those reptiles!"[113]

Twelve months after the launching of Operation Barbarossa, Hitler led his troops towards Stalingrad and a revengeful Red Army...

279

APPENDIX 1: **ORDER OF BATTLE ON 22 JUNE 1941.**

GERMANY AND ITS ALLIES.

LUFTFLOTTE 5. *(German)*
Generaloberst Hans-Jürgen Stumpff
in the Nordic countries

The Luftwaffe forces in the Nordic countries were grouped into Generaloberst Hans-Jürgen Stumpff's Luftflotte 5, which on 21 June 1941 could muster a total of 240 aircraft. The main units were KG 30, I./KG 26, parts of JG 77, and IV.(St)/ LG 1. But only a part of this force was brought up against the Soviet Union. These were organized in Fliegerführer Kirkenes under Oberst Andreas Nielsen. On 21 June 1941, the following units stood at Oberst Nielsen's disposal:

5./KG 30 at Banak (northern Norway) with ten Ju 88s
IV.(St)/LG 1 at Kirkenes (northern Norway), with thirty-six Ju 87s
1./JG 77 at Kirkenes with ten Bf 109 E and Bf 109 T
Stab/ZG 76 at Kirkenes with six Bf 110s
1.(F)/124 at Kirkenes with three Ju 88s
1.(H)/ 32 at Kemijärvi and Rovaniemi (northern Finland) with seven Hs 126s and three Do 17 P
l./KüFlGr 406 at Banak with He 115s and Do 18s.

Also, two He 111s and two Ju 88s of a weather reconnaissance Schwarm and eleven Ju 52s of a Transportstaffel were attached to Luftwaffekommando Kirkenes.

ARMEE NORWEGEN. *(German)*
Generaloberst Nikolaus von Falkenhorst

Gebirgskorps Norwegen – General Eduard Dietl
2. Gebirgs-Division – Generalmajor Ernst Schlemmer
3. Gebirgs-Division – Generalmajor Hans Kreysing
Höheres Kommando zbV XXXVI – General Hans Feige
169. Infanterie-Division – Generalmajor Kurt Dittmar
SS-Kampfgruppe "Nord" – SS-Brigadefuhrer Karl-Maria Demelhuber
6. divisioona (Finnish 6. Division) – Eversti (Colonel) Verner Viikla

SUOMEN ILMAVOIMAT.
(Finnish Air Force)
Kenraalimajuri (Major General) Jarl Lundqvist
Lentorykmentti 1 (Flying Regiment 1)
Lentolaivue 12 (Flying Squadron 1) – reconnaissance
Lentolaivue 32 – fighters
Lentorykmentti 2 (Flying Regiment 2)
Everstiluutnantti (Lieutenant Colonel) Richard Lorentz
Lentolaivue 16 – reconnaissance
Lentolaivue 28 – fighters
Lentorykmentti 3 (Flying Regiment 3)
Everstiluutnantti (Lieutenant Colonel) Einar Nuotio

Lentolaivue 24 – fighters
Lentolaivue 26 – fighters
Lentolaivue 34 – fighters
Lentorykmentti 4 (Flying Regiment 4)
Everstiluutnantti (Lieutenant Colonel) Toivi Somerto
Lentolaivue 42 – bombers
Lentolaivue 44 – bombers
Lentolaivue 46 – bombers
Lentolaivue 48 – bombers
Lentorykmentti 5 (Flying Regiment 5)
Lentolaivue 14 – reconnaissance
Lentolaivue 6 – bombers
Lentolaivue 30 – fighters
Separate squadrons
Lentolaivue 10
Lentolaivue 15
Merivoimien Esikunta (Meriv.E)
(Naval Forces Staff)
Lentolaivue 6

SUOMEN MAAVOIMAT. *(Finnish Army)*
Suomen marsalkka (Marshal of Finland) Gustaf Mannerheim
14. divisioona (14th Finnish Division) – Eversti (Colonel) Erkki Raappana

Karjalan armeija (Finnish Karelian Army).
Kenraaliluutnantti (Lieutenant General Erik Heinrichs)
1. divisioona (1st Finnish Division) – Eversti (Colonel) Paavo Paalu
17. divisioona (17th Finnish Division) – Eversti (Colonel) Aarne Snellman
163. Infanterie-Division (German) – Generalleutnant Erwin Engelbrecht
Ryhmä Oinonen (Finnish Group Oinonen) – Kenraalimajuri (Major General) Woldemar Oinonen

Suomen VI armeijakunta. *(Finnish VI Army Corps)*
Kenraalimajuri (Major General) Paavo Talvela
5. divisioona (5th Finnish Division) – Eversti (Colonel) Eino Koskimies
11. divisioona (11th Finnish Division) – Eversti (Colonel) Kaarlo Heiskanen
Jääkäriprikaati (Jäger Brigade) – Eversti (Colonel) Ruben Lagus

Suomen VII armeijakunta. *(Finnish VII Army Corps)*
Kenraalimajuri (Major General) Woldemar Hägglund
7. divisioona (7th Finnish Division) – Eversti (Colonel) Antero Svensson
19. divisioona (19th Finnish Division) – Eversti (Colonel) Hannu Hannuksela

Suomen VII armeijakunta. *(Finnish VII Army Corps)*
Kenraalimajuri (Major General) Taavetti Laatikainen
2. divisioona (2nd Finnish Division) – Eversti (Colonel) Aarne Blick
15. divisioona (15th Finnish Division) – Eversti (Colonel) Niilo Hersalo

18. divisioona (18th Finnish Division) – Eversti (Colonel) Aaro Pajari
Reserve:
10. divisioona (10th Finnish Division) – Eversti (Colonel) Jussi Sihvo

---

LUFTFLOTTE 1. *(German)*
Generaloberst Alfred Keller
in East Prussia

KGrzbV 106 – Ju 52.
2.(F)/ObdL – Do 215. At Norkitten.
Westa 1 – miscellaneous. At Jürgenfelde.

Fliegerkorps I.
General Helmuth Förster
4., 5./JG 53 Pik As – Bf 109 F. At Neusiedel.
Stab, I., II., III./JG 54 Grünherz – Bf 109 F. HQ: Lindental.
Stab, II., III./KG 1 Hindenburg – Ju 88 A. HQ: Powunden.
Stab, I., II., III./KG 76 – Ju 88 A. HQ: Gerdauen.
Stab, I., II., III./KG 77 – Ju 88 A. HQ: Heiligenbeil.
5.(F)/122. At Jürgenfelde.

Fliegerführer Ostsee.
Oberstleutnant Wolfgang von Wild
KGr 806 – Ju 88 A. At Prowehren.
1.(F)/125 – He 59. At Fischhausen.
2., 3. (F)/125 – He 114 and Ar 95.

Luftgaukommando I.
Generalleutnant Richard Putzier (reserve)

Erg.Gr./JG 52 – Bf 109 E. At Neuhausen.
Erg.Gr./JG 54 – Bf 109 E. At Neuhausen.

HEERESGRUPPE NORD. *(German)*
Generalfeldmarschall Wilhelm von Leeb

Heeresaufklärer
Koluft Heeresgruppe Nord
- 1.(F)/22
- 3.(F)/Nacht

18. Armee (German).
Generaloberst Georg von Küchler
(Chief of Staff – Maj.Gen. Kurt Waeger)
XXVI. Armeekorps – General Albert Wodrig
61. Infanterie-Division – Generalleutnant Siegfried Haenicke
217. Infanterie-Division – Generalleutnant Richard Baltzer
291. Infanterie-Division – Generalleutnant Kurt Herzog
XXXVIII. Armeekorps – General Friedrich-Wilhelm von Chappuis
58. Infanterie-Division – Generalleutnant Karl von Graffen
254. Infanterie-Division – Generalleutnant Walter Behschnitt
I. Armeekorps – General Kuno-Hans von Both
1. Infanterie-Division – Generalleutnant Philipp Kleffel
11. Infanterie-Division – Generalleutnant Herbert von Böckmann
21. Infanterie-Division – Generalleutnant Otto Sponheimer

Heeresaufklärer
Koluft 18. Armee
- 3.(F)/10
I. AK - 7.(H)/21
XXVI. AK - 4.(H) 21
XXXVIII. AK - 2.(H)/21

Panzergruppe 4. *(German)*
Generaloberst Erich Hoepner
XLI. Armeekorps (mot.)/Panzerkorps[1] – General of Panzer Georg Hans Reinhardt
1. Panzer-Division – Generalleutnant Friedrich Kirchner
6. Panzer-Division – Generalleutnant Wilhelm Ritter von Thoma
269. Infanterie-Division – Generalleutnant Ernst von Leyser
36. Infanterie-Division (mot.) – Generalleutnant Otto-Ernst Ottenbacher
LVI. Armeekorps (mot.)/Panzerkorps[2] – General Erich von Manstein
8. Panzer-Division – Generalleutnant Erich Brandenberger
3. Infanterie-Division (mot.) – Generalleutnant Curt Jahn
290. Infanterie-Division – Generalleutnant Theodor Freiherr von Wrede
SS- Division "Totenkopf" – SS-Obergruppenführer Theodor Eicke

Heeresaufklärer
Koluft Panzergruppe 4
- 4.(F)/33
XLI. PzK - 4.(H)/31
.1 PzD - 2.(H)/23
6. PzD - 3.Pz(H)/23
LVI. PzK - 8.(H)/32
8. PzD - 3.(H)/41

16. Armee. *(German)*
Generaloberst Ernst Busch
II. Armeekorps – General Walter von Brockdorff-Ahlefeldt
12. Infanterie-Division – Generalleutnant Walther von Seydlitz-Kurzbach
32. Infanterie-Division – Generalleutnant Wilhelm Bohnstedt
121. Infanterie-Division – Generalleutnant Otto Lancelle
X. Armeekorps – General Christian Hansen
30. Infanterie-Division – Generalleutnant Kurt von Tippelskirch
126. Infanterie-Division – Generalleutnant Paul Laux
XXVIII. Armeekorps – General Mauritz von Wiktorin
122. Infanterie-Division – Generalleutnant Siegfried Macholz
123. Infanterie-Division – Generalleutnant Walter Lichel

Heeresaufklärer
Koluft 16. Armee
- 3.(F)/22
II. AK - 2.(H)/13
X. AK - 4.(H)/23
XXVIII. AK - 1.(H)/12

Berück Heeresgruppe Nord.
207. Sicherungs-Division
281. Sicherungs-Division
285. Sicherungs-Division

Army Group reserves.
XXIII. Armeekorps
251. Infanterie-Division
206. Infanterie-Division

OKH reserve behind Heeresgruppe Nord.
L. Armeekorps
86. Infanterie-Division
SS Polizei-Division

LUFTFLOTTE 2. *(German)*
Generalfeldmarschall Albert Kesselring
in Poland
Stab, I., III./JG 53 Pik As – Bf 109 F. HQ: Krzewica.
IV./KGzbV 1 – Ju 52.
Stab, 2.(F)/ 122 – Ju 88 A, Bf 110, Bf 109 E. At Warsaw.
Westa 26 – Bf 110, Do 17 Z, He 111 H. At Warsaw-Bielany.

Fliegerkorps VIII.
General Wolfram Freiherr von Richthofen
Stab, II., III./JG 27 – Bf 109 E. HQ: Subolevo.
II./JG 52 – Bf 109 E, Bf 109 F. At Subolevo.
Stab, I., II./ZG 26 Horst Wessel – Bf 110. At Suwalki.
II.(S)/LG 2 – Bf 109 E. At Praschnitz.
10.(S)/LG 2 – Hs 123 A. At Praschnitz.
Stab, I.,8., 9./KG 2 Holzhammer – Do 17 Z. HQ: Arys-Rostken.
III./KG 3 Blitz – Do 17 Z. At Suwalki.
Stab, II., III./St.G. 1 – Ju 87 B. At Radczki.
Stab, I., III./St.G. 2 Immelmann – Ju 87 B, Ju 87 R, Bf 110.
At Praschnitz.
2.(F)/11 – Do 17 P. At Suwalki.

Fliegerkorps II.
General Bruno Loerzer
Stab, I., II., III., IV./JG 51 – Bf 109 F. HQ: Siedlce.
Stab, I., II./SKG 210 – Bf 110. HQ: Radzyn.
Stab, I., II./KG 3 Blitz – Do 17 Z, Ju 88 A. At Deblin.
Stab, I., II., III./KG 53 Legion Condor – He 111 H, He 111 P.
HQ: Radom.
Stab, I., II., III./St.G. 77 – Ju 87 B, Bf 110. HQ: Biala Podlaska.
1.(F)/122 – Ju 88 A, Bf 110. At Warsaw.

Luftgaukommando II.
General Hellmuth Bieneck (reserve)
Erg.Gr./ZG 26 – Bf 110. Poznan area.
Erg.Gr./JG 51 – Bf 109 E. Poznan area.

HEERESGRUPPE MITTE. *(German)*
Generalfeldmarschall Fedor von Bock

Heeresaufklärer
Koluft Heergesgruppe Mitte
- 4.(F)/14
- 2.(F)/Nacht

9. Armee. (German).
Generaloberst Adolf Strauss
V. Armeekorps – General Richard Ruoff
5. Infanterie-Division – Generalleutnant Karl Allmendinger
35. Infanterie-Division – Generalleutnant Walther Fischer
von Weikersthal
VI. Armeekorps – General Otto-Wilhelm Förster
6. Infanterie-Division – Generalleutnant Helge Auleb
26. Infanterie-Division – Generalleutnant Walter Weiss
VIII. Armeekorps – General Walter Heitz
8. Infanterie-Division – Generalleutnant Gustav Höhne
28. Infanterie-Division – Generalleutnant Johann Sinnhuber
161. Infanterie-Division – Generalleutnant Hermann Wilck
XX. Armeekorps – General Friedrich Materna
162. Infanterie-Division – Generalleutnant Hermann Franke
256. Infanterie-Division – Generalleutnant Gerhard Kauffmann

Heeresaufklärer
Koluft 9. Armee
- 1.(F)/33
V. AK - 4.(H)/10

XVII. AK - 2.(H)/10
XX. AK - 5.(H)/41
VIII. AK - 1(H)/31

Panzergruppe 3. *(German)*
Generaloberst Hermann Hoth
XXXIX. Armeekorps (mot.)/Panzerkorps [3] – General Rudolf
Schmidt
7. Panzer-Division – Generalleutnant Hans Freiherr von Funck
20. Panzer-Division - Generalleutnant Horst Stumpff
14. Infanterie-Division (mot.) – Generalleutnant Friedrich Fürst
20. Infanterie-Division (mot.) – Generalleutnant Hans Zorn
LVII. Armeekorps (mot.)/Panzerkorps [4] - General Adolf-Friedrich
Kuntzen
12. Panzer-Division – Generalmajor Josef Harpe
19. Panzer-Division – Generalleutnant Otto von Knobelsdorff
18. Infanterie-Division (mot.) – Generalleutnant Friedrich
Herrlein

Heeresaufklärer
Koluft Panzergruppe 3
- 2(F)/33
LVII. PzK - 7.(H)/13
12. PzD - 3.(H)/12
19. PzD - 2.(H)/32
XXXIX. PzK - 4.(H)/12
7. PzD - 1.(H)/11
20. PzD - 1.Pz(H)/13
IV. AK- 2.(H)/12

4. Armee. *(German)*
Generaloberst Günther von Kluge
VII. Armeekorps – General Wilhelm Fahrmbacher
7. Infanterie-Division – Generalleutnant Eccard Freiherr von
Gablenz
23. Infanterie-Division – Generalleutnant Heinz Hellmich
258. Infanterie-Division – Generalleutnant Waldemar Henrici
268. Infanterie-Division – Generalleutnant Erich Straube
IX. Armeekorps – General Hermann Geyer
137. Infanterie-Division – Generalleutnant Friedrich Bergmann
263. Infanterie-Division – Generalleutnant Ernst Haeckel
292. Infanterie-Division – Generalleutnant Martin Dehmel
XIII. Armeekorps – General Hans Felber
17. Infanterie-Division – Generalleutnant Herbert Loch
78. Infanterie-Division – Generalleutnant Curt Gallenkamp
XXXXIII. Armeekorps – General Gotthard Heinrici
131. Infanterie-Division – Generalleutnant Heinrich
Meyer-Buerdorf
134. Infanterie-Division – Generalleutnant Conrad
von Cochenhausen
252. Infanterie-Division – Generalleutnant Diether
von Boehm-Bezing

Heeresaufklärer
Koluft 4. Armee
- 4.(F)/11
XLIII. AK - 7.(H)/12
IX. AK - 2.(H)/41
VII. AK - 1.(H)/10
XIII. AK - 5.(H)/12

Panzergruppe 2. *(German)*
Generaloberst Heinz Guderian
XII. Armeekorps – General Walther Schroth
31. Infanterie-Division – Generalleutnant Kurt Kalmukoff
34. Infanterie-Division – Generalleutnant Hans Behlendorff

45. Infanterie-Division – Generalleutnant Fritz Schlieper
XXIV. Armeekorps (mot.)/Panzerkorps[5] – General Leo Geyr von Schweppenburg
3. Panzer-Division – Generalleutnant Walter Model
4. Panzer-Division – Generalleutnant Willibald Freiherr von Langermann und Erlencamp
10. Infanterie-Division (mot.) – Generalleutnant Friedrich-Wilhelm von Loeper
1. Kavallerie-Division – Generalleutnant Kurt Feldt
255. Infanterie-Division – Generalleutnant Wilhelm Wetzel
267. Infanterie-Division – Generalleutnant Robert Martinek
XXXXVI. Armeekorps (mot.)/Panzerkorps[6] – General Heinrich von Vietinghoff
10. Panzer-Division – Generalleutnant Ferdinand Schaal
SS-Division "Das Reich" – SS-Obergruppenführer Paul Hausser
Infanterie-Regiment "Grossdeutschland" – Generalmajor Wilhelm-Hunert von Stockhausen
XXXXVII. Armeekorps (mot.)/Panzerkorps[7] – General Joachim Lemelsen
17. Panzer-Division – Generalleutnant Hans-Jürgen von Arnim
18. Panzer-Division – Generalleutnant Walther Nehring
29. Infanterie-Division (mot.) – Generalleutnant Walter von Boltenstern
167. Infanterie-Division – Generalleutnant Hans Schönhärl

Heeresaufklärer
Koluft Panzergruppe 2
- 3.(F)/31
XXIV. PzK - 7.(H)/32
3. PzD - 9.(H)/LG 2
4. PzD - 6.Pz(H)/41
XII. AK - 1.(H)/21
XLVII. PzK - 5.(H)/23
17. PzD - 6.(H)/32
18. PzD - 6.Pz(H)/13
XLVI. PzK - 6.(H)/31
10 .PzD - 3.(H)/14

Berück Heeresgruppe Mitte.
102. Sicherungs-Division – Generalleutnant Johann Pflugbeil
286. Sicherungs-Division – Generalleutnant Kurt Müller
403. Sicherungs-Division – Generalleutnant Wolfgang Ditfurth

Army Group reserve.
293. Infanterie-Division – Generalleutnant Justin von Obernitz

OKH reserve behind Heeresgruppe.
Höheres Kommando zbV XXXV
15. Infanterie-Division – Generalleutnant Ernst-Eberhard Hell
52. Infanterie-Division – Generalleutnant Dr. Lothar Rendulic
106. Infanterie-Division – Generalmajor Ernst Dehner
110. Infanterie-Division – Generalleutnant Ernst Seifert
112. Infanterie-Division – Generalleutnant Friedrich Mieth
197. Infanterie-Division – Generalleutnant Hermann Meyer-Rabingen
Lehr-Brigade (mot.) 900 – Oberst Walther Krause

LUFTFLOTTE 4. *(German)*
Generaloberst Alexander Löhr
in southern Poland and Romania
KGrzbV 50 – Ju 52.
KGrzbV 104 – Ju 52.
4.(F)/122 – Ju 88, Bf 110. At Reichshof.
Westa 76 – He 111 H, Ju 88 A, Bf 110. At Reichshof.

Fliegerkorps V.
General Robert Ritter von Greim
in southern Poland
Stab, I., II., III./JG 3 – Bf 109 F. HQ: Hostynne.
Stab, I., II., III./KG 51 Edelweiss – Ju 88 A. HQ: Krosno.
Stab, I., II./KG 54 Totenkopf – Ju 88 A. At Lublin-Swidnik.
Stab, I., II., III./KG 55 Greif – He 111 H, Bf 110. HQ: Labunie.
4.(F)/121 – Ju 88 A. At Zamosc.

Fliegerkorps IV.
Generalleutnant Kurt Pflugbeil
in Romania
Stab, II., III./JG 77 Herzas – Bf 109 E, Bf 109 F. HQ: Bacau.
I.(J)/LG 2 – Bf 109 E. At Janca.
Stab, I., II., III./KG 27 Boelcke – He 111 H. HQ: Focsani-South.
II./KG 4 General Wever – He 111 H. At Zilistea.
3.(F)/121 – Ju 88 A, Bf 110. At Ramnicul-Sarat.

Deutsche Luftwaffenmission Rumänien.
Generalleutnant Hans Speidel
in Romania
Stab/JG 52 – Bf 109 F. At Bucharest and Mizil.
III./JG 52 – Bf 109 E, Bf 109 F. At Mizil and Pipera.

Luftgaukommando VIII.
Generalleutnant Bernhard Waber (reserve)
Erg.Gr./JG 3 – Bf 109 E. Breslau area.
Erg.Gr./JG 27 – Bf 109 E. Breslau area.

Luftgaukommando XVII.
General Friedrich Hirschauer (reserve)
Erg.Gr./JG 77 – Bf 109 E. Vienna area.

AERONAUTICA REGALĂ ROMÂNĂ (ARR).
(Royal Romanian Air Force)
Gruparea Aeriană de Luptă (GAL) (Romanian)
(Combat Air Grouping)
Grupul 4 vânătoare (4th Fighter Group) – fighters
Grupul 5 vânătoare – fighters
Grupul 6 vânătoare – fighters
Grupul 7 vânătoare – fighters
Grupul 8 vânătoare – fighters
Grupul 1 bombardament (1st Bomber Group) – bombers
Grupul 2 bombardament – bombers
Grupul 4 bombardament – bombers
Grupul 5 bombardament – bombers
Grupul 6 bombardament – bombers
Flotila 1 informatie – reconnaissance
Flotila 2 informatie – reconnaissance
Flotila 3 informatie – reconnaissance

HEERESGRUPPE SÜD.
Generalfeldmarschall Gerd von Rundstedt
Heeresaufklärer
Koluft Heeresgruppe Sud
- 2.(F)/11
- 1.(F)/Nacht

6. Armee. *(German)*
Generaloberst Walther von Reichenau
XVII. Armeekorps – General Werner Kienitz
56. Infanterie-Division – Generalleutnant Karl von Oven
62. Infanterie-Division – Generalleutnant Walter Keiner
XXIX. Armeekorps – General Hans von Obstfelder

284

44. Infanterie-Division – Generalleutnant Friedrich Siebert
111. Infanterie-Division – Generalleutnant Otto Stapf
299. Infanterie-Division – Generalleutnant Willi Moser
XXXXIV. Armeekorps – General Friedrich Koch
9. Infanterie-Division – Generalleutnant Siegmund Freiherr von Schleinitz
297. Infanterie-Division – Generalleutnant Max Pfeffer

Heeresaufklärer
Koluft 6. Armee
- 3.(F)/11
XLIV. AK - 4.(H)/41
XVII. AK - 6.(H)/21

Panzergruppe 1. *(German)*
Generaloberst Paul Ludwig Ewald von Kleist
III. Armeekorps (mot.)/Panzerkorps [8] – General Eberhard von Mackensen
13. Panzer-Division – Generalleutnant Friedrich-Wilhelm von Rothkirch und Panthen
14. Panzer-Division – Generalleutnant Friedrich Kühn
25. Infanterie-Division (mot.) – Generalleutnant Erich-Heinrich Clößner
XIV. Armeekorps (mot.)/Panzerkorps [9] – General Gustav Anton von Wietersheim
9. Panzer-Division – Generalleutnant Alfred Ritter von Hubicki
SS-Division (mot.) "Leibstandarte SS Adolf Hitler" – SS-Obergruppenführer Sepp Dietrich
SS- Division "Wiking" – SS-Brigadeführer Felix Steiner
XXXXVIII. Armeekorps (mot.)/Panzerkorps [10] – General Werner Kempf
11. Panzer-Division – Generalleutnant Ludwig Crüwell
16. Panzer-Division – Generalleutnant Hans-Valentin Hube
16. Infanterie-Division (mot.) – Generalleutnant Sigfrid Henrici

Heeresaufklärer
Koluft Panzergruppe 1
- 7.(F)/LG 2
XXXXVIII. PzK - 5.(H)/32
11.PzD - 5.Pz(H)/11
III. PzK - 4.(H)/22
14. PzD - 4.(H)/13
9. PzD - 1.(H)/23
13. PzD - 3.(H)/21
16. PzD - 5.Pz(H)/14

17. Armee. *(German)*
Generaloberst Carl-Heinrich von Stülpnagel
IV. Armeekorps – General Viktor von Schwedler
24. Infanterie-Division – Generalleutnant Hans von Tettau
71. Infanterie-Division – Generalleutnant Alexander von Hartmann
262. Infanterie-Division – Generalleutnant Edgar Theißen
295. Infanterie-Division – Generalleutnant Herbert Geitner
296. Infanterie-Division – Generalleutnant Wilhelm Stemmermann
XXXXIX. Gebirgskorps – General Ludwig Kübler
68. Infanterie-Division – Generalleutnant Georg Braun
257. Infanterie-Division – Generalleutnant Karl Sachs
1. Gebirgs-Division – Generalleutnant Hubert Lanz
LII. Armeekorps – General Kurt von Briesen
101. leichte Infanterie-Division – Generalleutnant Erich Marcks
97. leichte Infanterie-Division – Generalmajor Maximilian Fretter-Pico
100. leichte Infanterie-Division – Generalmajor Werner Sanne

Heeresaufklärer
Koluft 17. Armee
- 3.(F)/33
LII. AK - 4.(H)/32
IV. AK - 1.(H)/41

Armata a 3-a Română. *(3rd Romanian Army)*
General Petre Dumitrescu
Brigada 1 Vânători de munte (Mountain Brigade)
Brigada 2 Vânători de munte (Mountain Brigade)
Brigada 4 Vânători de munte (Mountain Brigade)
Brigada 5 Cavalerie (Cavalry Brigade)
Brigada 6 Cavalerie (Cavalry Brigade)
Brigada 8 Cavalerie (Cavalry Brigade)
Corpul 3 Armată (3rd Army Corps)
Divizia 6 Infanterie (7th Infantry Division)
Divizia 7 Infanterie (7th Infantry Division)

11. Armee. *(German)*
Generaloberst Eugen Ritter von Schobert
XI. Armeekorps – General Joachim von Kortzfleisch
76. Infanterie-Division – Generalleutnant Maximilian de Angelis
239. Infanterie-Division– Generalleutnant Ferdinand Neuling
Divizia 1 Blindată (1st Romanian Armored Division) – Brigadier General Ioan Sion
Brigada 6 Cavalerie (6th Romanian Cavalry Brigade) – Major General Aurel Racoviţă
XXX. Armeekorps – General Hans von Salmuth
198. Infanterie-Division – Generalleutnant Otto Röttig
Divizia 8 Infanterie (8th Romanian Infantry Division) – Brigadier General Alexandru Orasanu
Divizia 13 Infanterie (13th Romanian Infantry Division) –Brigadier General Gheorghe Rozin
Divizia 14 Infanterie (14th Romanian Infantry Division) – Brigadier General Gheorghe Stavrescu
LIV. Armeekorps – General Erick-Oskar Hansen
50. Infanterie-Division – Generalleutnant Karl-Adolf Hollidt
170. Infanterie-Division – Generalleutnant Walter Wittke
Divizia 5 Infanterie (5th Romanian Infantry Division) – Brigadier General Petre Vlasescu

Heeresaufklärer
Koluft 11. Armee
- 2.(F)/22
LIV. AK - 3.(H)/13
XXX. AK - 5.(H)/13
XI. AK - 6.(H)/12

Armata a 4-a Română. *(4th Romanian Army)*
- Lieutenant General Nicolae Ciupercă
Corpul 3 Armată (3rd Army Corps) – Major General Vasile Atanasiu
Divizia de Garda (Guards Division) – Major General Nicolae Sova
Divizia 15 Infanterie (15th Infantry Division) – Major General Cosma Marin Popescu
Divizia 35 Infanterie (35th Infantry Division) – Brigadier General Emil Procopiescu
Corpul 5 Armată (5th Army Corps) – Lieutenant General Gheorghe Leventi
Diviziei 1 grăniceri (1st Border Division) – Brigadier General Gheorghe Potopeanu
Divizia 21 Infanterie (21st Infantry Division) – Major General Cristache Popescu
Corpul 11 Armată (11th Army Corps) – Major General I. Aurelian

Two fortress brigades
Corpul 2 Armată (2nd Army Corps) – Major General Nicolae Macici
Divizia 9 Infanterie (9th Infantry Division) – Brigadier General Hugo Schwab
Divizia 10 Infanterie (10th Infantry Division) – Brigadier General Ion Glogojanu
Divizia 11 Infanterie (11th Infantry Division) – Brigadier General David Popescu
Brigada 7 Cavalerie (7th Cavalry Brigade) – Colonel Gheorghe Savoiu

SOVIET UNION.

SEVERNYY FLOT (SF).
(Northern Fleet)
Kontr-admiral (Counter-Admiral) Arseniy Golovko
3 old destroyers (*Kuybyshev, Uritski, Karl Libknekht*) 5 modern destroyers (*Grozny, Gromki, Stremitelny, Sokrushitelny, Gremyashchi*), 7 patrol boats, 3 large, 6 medium and 6 small submarines, 2 minesweepers, 15 small patrol boats, and 2 torpedo boats and auxiliary ships.

VVS SF.
(Air Force of the Northern Fleet)
General-Mayor Aleksandr Kuznetsov
72 SAP , 118 RAP, 49 ORAE, 24 Aviazveno Svyazi.
A total of 116 aircraft.

VVS LENINGRADSKIY VOYENNYY OKRUG/VVS SEVERNYY FRONT.
(Air Force of the Leningrad Military District/VVS Northern Front)
General-Mayor Aleksandr Novikov
1 SAD, subordinate to the 14th Army, between Murmansk and Kandalaksha.
10 BAP, 137 BAP, 145 IAP, 147 IAP
55 SAD, subordinate to the 7th Separate Army in the Petrozavodsk area.
72 SBAP.
5 SAD, subordinate to the 23rd Army on the Karelian Isthmus.
7 IAP, 159 IAP, 158 IAP.
41 BAD, subordinate to the 23rd Army in the Siverskaya area.
201 SBAP, 202 SBAP, 205 SBAP.
3 IAD, assigned to the air defense of Leningrad.
19 IAP, 44 IAP.
54 IAD, assigned to the air defense of Leningrad.
26 IAP, 157 IAP, 311 RAP.
2 SAD to the south of Leningrad.
2 SBAP, 44 SBAP, 58 SBAP, 65 ShAD.
39 IAD to the south of Leningrad.
154 IAP, 155 IAP, 156 IAP.
In total 1,270 aircraft.

LENINGRADSKIY VOYENNYY OKRUG/SEVERNYY FRONT.
(Leningrad Military District/Northern Front)
General-Polkovnik Markian Popov
177-ya strelkovaya diviziya (117th Rifle Division) – Polkovnik A.F. Mashoshin
191-ya strelkovaya diviziya (191th Rifle Division) – Polkovnik D.K. Lukyanov
1-ya mekhannizirovannyy korpus (1st Mechanized Corps) – General-Mayor M. L. Cherniavsky
3-ya tankovaya diviziya (3rd Tank Division) – Polkovnik K.Yu. Andreev
163-ya motostrelkovaya diviziya (163rd Motor Rifle Division) – General-Mayor N.M. Kuznetsov

14-ya armiya. *(14th Army)*
General-Leytenant Valerian Frolov
14-ya strelkovaya diviziya (14th Rifle Division) – Polkovnik A.A. Zhurba
52-ya strelkovaya diviziya (52nd Rifle Division) – General-Mayor N.N. Nikishin
1-ya tankovaya diviziya (1st Tank Division) – General-Mayor V.I. Baranov
42-y strelkovyy korpus (42nd Rifle Corps) – General-Mayor Roman Ivanovich Panin
104-ya strelkovaya diviziya (104th Rifle Division) – General-Mayor S.I. Morozov
122-ya strelkovaya diviziya (122nd Rifle Division) – General-Mayor P.S. Shevchenko
1st Mixed Aviation Division

7-ya otdelnaya armiya. *(7th Separate Army)*
General-Leytenant Filipp Danilovich Gorelenko
54-ya strelkovaya diviziya (54th Rifle Division) – Mayor Gen. I.V. Panin
71-ya strelkovaya diviziya (71st Rifle Division) – Polkovnik V.N. Fedorov
168-ya strelkovaya diviziya (168th Rifle Division) – Polkovnik A.L. Bondarev
237-ya strelkovaya diviziya (237th Rifle Division) – Mayor Gen. D.F. Popov

23-ya armiya. *(23rd Army)*
General-Leytenant Pyotr Pshennikov
19-y strelkovyy korpus (19th Rifle Corps) – General-Mayor Mikhail Gerasimov
142-ya strelkovaya diviziya (142nd Rifle Division) – General-Mayor S.P. Mikulskiy
115-ya strelkovaya diviziya (115th Rifle Division) – General-Mayor V.F. Kon'kov
50-y strelkovyy korpus (50th Rifle Corps) – General-Mayor Vladimir Shcherbakov
43-ya strelkovaya diviziya (43rd Rifle Division) – General-Mayor V.V. Kirpichnikov
123-ya strelkovaya diviziya (123rd Rifle Division) – Polkovnik Ye.Ye. Tsukanov
10-ya mekhannizirovannyy korpus (10th Mechanized Corps) – General-Mayor Ivan Lazarev
21-ya tankovaya diviziya (21st Tank Division) – Polkovnik L.V. Bunin
24-ya tankovaya diviziya (24th Tank Division) – Polkovnik M.I. Chesnokov
198-ya motostrelkovaya diviziya (198th Motor Rifle Division) – General-Mayor V.V. Kryukov

286

KRASNOZNAMENNIY BALTIYSKIY FLOT (KBF).
(Red Banner Baltic Fleet)
Vitse-Admiral Vladimir Tributs
2 battleships (*Marat, Oktyabrskaya Revolutsiya*), 2 heavy cruisers (*Kirov, Maksim Gorki*), 2 flotilla leaders (*Leningrad, Minsk*), 7 old destroyers (*Yakov Sverdlov, Kalinin, Karl Marks, Lenin, Artyom, Engels, Volodarskiy*), 12 modern destroyers (*Gnevniy, Gordiy, Grozyashchi, Smetlivy, Steregushchiy, Storozhevoi, Serdity, Stoiki, Silny, Surovy, Slavny, Smely*), 7 patrol boats, 11 large, 36 medium and 23 small submarines, 6 mineships, 33 minesweepers, 1 gunship, 48 torpedo boats.

VVS KBF.
(Air Force of the Red Banner Baltic Fleet).
General-Mayor Vasiliy Yermachenkov
8 BABr
10 SABr
61 IABr
15 OMRAP.
Plus seven independent aviation Eskadrilyas.
A total of 707 aircraft.

VVS PRIBALTIYSKIY VOYENNYY OKRUG (VVS PBVO)/VVS SEVERO-ZAPADNYY FRONT.
(Air Force of the Baltic Special Military District/ VVS Northwestern Front)
General-Mayor Aleksey Ionov
312 RAP
8 SAD at Kaunas and Alytus.
15 IAP, 31 IAP, 61 ShAP.
57 IAD between Vilnius and Daugavpils.
42 IAP, 54 SBAP, 49 IAP.
7 SAD in northern Lithuania.
10 IAP, 9 SBAP, 46 BAP, 241 SBAP.
6 SAD between Riga and Liepaya.
21 IAP, 31 SBAP, 40 BAP , 148 IAP.
4 SAD in Estonia.
38 IAP, 35 SBAP, 50 SBAP, 53 SBAP.
In total 1,211 aircraft.

PRIBALTIYSKIY VOYENNYY OKRUG (PBVO)/SEVERO-ZAPADNYY FRONT.
(Baltic Special Military District/Northwestern Front)
General-Polkovnik Fyodor Kuznetsov
5-y vozdushno-desantnyy korpus (5th Airborne Corps) – General-Mayor Ivan Bezugly
9-y vozdushno-desantnoy brigadyy (9th Airborne Brigade)
10-y vozdushno-desantnoy brigadyy (10th Airborne Brigade)
201-y vozdushno-desantnoy brigadyy (201st Airborne Brigade)

8-ya armiya (8th Army)
General-Leytenant Pyotr Sobennikov
10-y strelkovyy korpus (10th Rifle Corps) – General-Mayor Ivan Nikolayev
10-ya strelkovaya diviziya (10th Rifle Division) – Polkovnik I.I. Fadeyev
48-ya strelkovaya diviziya (48th Rifle Division) – General-Mayor P.V. Bogdanov

90-ya strelkovaya diviziya (90th Rifle Division) – Polkovnik V.P. Yevdokimov
11-y strelkovyy korpus (11th Rifle Corps) – General-Mayor Mikhail Shumilov
11-ya strelkovaya diviziya (11th Rifle Division) – Polkovnik N.A. Sokolov
125-ya strelkovaya diviziya (125th Rifle Division) – General-Mayor P.P. Bogaychuk
12-ya mekhannizirovannyy korpus (12th Mechanized Corps) – General-Mayor Nikolay Shestopalov
23-ya tankovaya diviziya (23rd Tank Division) – Polkovnik T.S. Orlenko
202-ya motostrelkovaya diviziya (202nd Motor Rifle Division) – Polkovnik V.K. Gorbachyov

11-ya armiya. *(11th Army)*
General-Leytenant Vasiliy Morozov
23-ya strelkovaya diviziya (23rd Rifle Division) – General-Mayor V.F. Pavlov
126-ya strelkovaya diviziya (126th Rifle Division) – General-Mayor M.A. Kuznetsov
128-ya strelkovaya diviziya (128th Rifle Division) – General-Mayor A.S. Zotov
16-y strelkovyy korpus (16th Rifle Corps) – General-Mayor Fyodor Ivanov
5-ya strelkovaya diviziya (5th Rifle Division) – Polkovnik F.P. Ozerov
33-ya strelkovaya diviziya (33rd Rifle Division) – General-Mayor K.A.Zheleznikov
188-ya strelkovaya diviziya (188th Rifle Division) – Polkovnik P.I. Ivanov
29-y strelkovyy korpus (29th Rifle Corps) – General-Mayor Aleksandr Samokhin
179-ya strelkovaya diviziya (179th Rifle Division) – Polkovnik A.I. Ustinov
184-ya strelkovaya diviziya (184th Rifle Division) – Polkovnik M.V. Vinogradov
3-ya mekhannizirovannyy korpus (3rd Mechanized Corps) – General-Mayor Aleksey Kurkin
2-ya tankovaya diviziya (2nd Tank Division) – General-Mayor E.N. Solyankin
5-ya tankovaya diviziya (5th Tank Division) – Polkovnik F.F. Fyodorov
84-ya motostrelkovaya diviziya (84th Motor Rifle Division) – General-Mayor P.I. Fomenko

27-ya armiya. *(27th Army)*
General-Leytenant Nikolay Berzarin
16-ya strelkovaya diviziya (16th Rifle Division) – General-Mayor I.M. Lyubovtsev
67-ya strelkovaya diviziya (67th Rifle Division) – General-Mayor N.A. Dedayev
3-ya strelkovaya brigada (3rd Rifle Brigade)
22-y strelkovyy korpus (22nd Rifle Corps) – General-Mayor Mikhail Dukhanov
180-ya strelkovaya diviziya (180th Rifle Division) – Polkovnik I.I. Missan
182-ya strelkovaya diviziya (182nd Rifle Division) – Polkovnik I.I. Kuryshev
24-y strelkovyy korpus (24th Rifle Corps) – General-Mayor Kuzma Kachalov
181-ya strelkovaya diviziya (181st Rifle Division) – Polkovnik P.V. Borisov
183-ya strelkovaya diviziya (183rd Rifle Division) – Polkovnik P.N. Tupikov

287

VVS ZAPADNOGO OSOBOGO VOYENNOGO OKRUGA (VVS ZOVO)/VVS ZAPADNYY FRONT.
(Air Force of the Western Special Military District/VVS Western Front)
General Andrey Tayurskiy
313 RAP, 314 RAP.
9 SAD, subordinate to the 10th Army in the Bialystok border area.
13 SBAP , 41 IAP, 124 IAP, 126 IAP, 129 IAP.
10 SAD, subordinate to the 4th Army in the Brest-Litovsk border area.
33 IAP, 74 ShAP, 123 IAP, 39 SBAP.
11 SAD, subordinate to the 3rd Army in the Grodno–Lida area.
16 SBAP , 122 IAP, 127 IAP.
12 BAD in the Vitebsk area.
6 SBAP , 43 SBAP, 128 SBAP, 209 SBAP, 215 SBAP.
43 IAD between Minsk and Smolensk.
160 IAP, 161 IAP, 162 IAP, 163 IAP.
13 BAD in the Bobruysk area.
24 SBAP, 97 SBAP, 121 SBAP, 125 SBAP, 130 SBAP.
In total 1,789 aircraft (including 252 of "modern" fighter types).

ZAPADNOGO OSOBOGO VOYENNOGO OKRUGA (ZOVO)/ZAPADNYY FRONT.
(Western Special Military District/Western Front)
General-Polkovnik Dmitriy Pavlov
2-y strelkovyy korpus (2nd Rifle Corps) – General-Mayor Arkadiy Yermakov
100-ya strelkovaya diviziya (100th Rifle Division) – General-Mayor I.N. Russiyanov
161-ya strelkovaya diviziya (161st Rifle Division) – Polkovnik A.I. Mikhailov
21-y strelkovyy korpus (21st Rifle Corps) – General-Mayor Vladimir Borisov
17-ya strelkovaya diviziya (17th Rifle Division) – Polkovnik T.K. Batsanov
24-ya strelkovaya diviziya (24th Rifle Division) – General-Mayor K.N. Galitskiy
37-ya strelkovaya diviziya (37th Rifle Division) – Polkovnik A.E. Chekharin
44-y strelkovyy korpus (44th Rifle Corps) – General-Mayor Vasiliy Yushkevich
64-ya strelkovaya diviziya (64th Rifle Division) – Polkovnik S.I. Iovlev
108-ya strelkovaya diviziya (108th Rifle Division)
47-y strelkovyy korpus (47th Rifle Corps) – General-Mayor Stepan Povetkin
50-ya strelkovaya diviziya (50th Rifle Division) – Polkovnik V.P. Yevdokimov
55-ya strelkovaya diviziya (55th Rifle Division) – Polkovnik D.I. Ivanyuk
121-ya strelkovaya diviziya (121st Rifle Division) – General-Mayor P.M. Zykov
143-ya strelkovaya diviziya (143rd Rifle Division) – General-Mayor D.P. Safonov
4-y vozdushno-desantnyy korpus (4th Airborne Corps) – General-Mayor Aleksey Zhadov
7-y vozdushno-desantnoy brigadyy (7th Airborne Brigade)
8-y vozdushno-desantnoy brigadyy (8th Airborne Brigade)
214-y vozdushno-desantnoy brigadyy (214th Airborne Brigade)
17-ya mekhannizirovannyy korpus (17th Mechanized Corps) – General-Mayor Mikhail Petrov
27-ya tankovaya diviziya (27th Tank Division) – Polkovnik A.O. Akhmanov

36-ya tankovaya diviziya (36th Tank Division) – Polkovnik S.Z. Miroshnikov
209-ya motostrelkovaya diviziya (209th Motor Rifle Division) – Polkovnik A.I. Muravyev
20-ya mekhannizirovannyy korpus (20th Mechanized Corps) – General-Mayor Andrey Nikitin
26-ya tankovaya diviziya (26th Tank Division) – General-Mayor V.T. Obukhov
38-ya tankovaya diviziya (38th Tank Division) – Polkovnik S.I. Kapustin
210-ya motostrelkovaya diviziya (210th Motor Rifle Division) – General-Mayor F.A. Parkhomenko

3-ya armiya. *(3rd Army)*
General-Leytenant Vasily Kuznetsov
4-y strelkovyy korpus (4th Rifle Corps) – General-Mayor Yevgeniy Yegorov
27-ya strelkovaya diviziya (27th Rifle Division) – General-Mayor A.M. Stepanov
56-ya strelkovaya diviziya (56th Rifle Division) – General-Mayor S.P. Sakhnov
85-ya strelkovaya diviziya (85th Rifle Division) – General-Mayor A.V. Bondovskii
11-ya mekhannizirovannyy korpus (11th Mechanized Corps) – General-Mayor Dmitriy Mostevenko
29-ya tankovaya diviziya (29th Tank Division) – Polkovnik N.P. Studnev
33-ya tankovaya diviziya (33rd Tank Division) – Polkovnik Mikhail Panov
204-ya motostrelkovaya diviziya (204th Motor Rifle Division) – Polkovnik A.M. Pirogov

4-ya armiya. *(4th Army)*
General-Leytenant Aleksandr Korobkov
49-ya strelkovaya diviziya (49th Rifle Division) – Polkovnik C.F. Vasilyev
75-ya strelkovaya diviziya (75th Rifle Division) – Polkovnik Nedvigin
28-y strelkovyy korpus (28th Rifle Corps) – General-Mayor Vasiliy Popov
6-ya strelkovaya diviziya (6th Rifle Division) – Polkovnik M.A. Popsiu-Shapko
42-ya strelkovaya diviziya (42nd Rifle Division) – General-Mayor I.S. Lazarenko
14-ya mekhannizirovannyy korpus (14th Mechanized Corps) – General-Mayor Stepan Oborin
22-ya tankovaya diviziya (22nd Tank Division) – General-Mayor V.P. Puganov
30-ya tankovaya diviziya (30th Tank Division) – Polkovnik Semen Bogdanov
205-ya motostrelkovaya diviziya (205th Motor Rifle Division) – Polkovnik F.F. Kudyurov

10-ya armiya. *(10th Army)*
General-Leytenant Konstantin Golubev
1-y strelkovyy korpus (1st Rifle Corps) – General-Mayor Fyodor Rubtsov
-ya strelkovaya diviziya (2nd Rifle Division) – Polkovnik M.D. Grishin
8-ya strelkovaya diviziya (8th Rifle Division) – Polkovnik N.I. Fomin
5-y strelkovyy korpus (5th Rifle Corps) – General-Mayor Aleksandr Garnov
13-ya strelkovaya diviziya (13th Rifle Division) – Polkovnik A.Z. Naumov

86-ya strelkovaya diviziya (86th Rifle Division) – Polkovnik M.A. Zashibalov

113-ya strelkovaya diviziya (113th Rifle Division) – General-Mayor Kh.N. Alaverdov

6-y kavaleriyskiy korpus (6th Cavalry Corps) – General-Mayor Ivan Nikitin

6-ya kavaleriyskaya diviziya (6th Cavalry Division) – General-Mayor M.P. Konstantinov

36-ya kavaleriyskaya diviziya (36th Cavalry Division) – General-Mayor E.S. Zybin

6-ya mekhannizirovannyy korpus (6th Mechanized Corps) – General-Mayor Mikhail Khatskilevich

4-ya tankovaya diviziya (4th Tank Division) – General-Mayor A.G. Potaturchev

7-ya tankovaya diviziya (7th Tank Division) – General-Mayor S.V. Borzilov

29-ya motostrelkovaya diviziya (29th Motor Rifle Division) – General-Mayor I.P. Bikdyanov

13-ya mekhannizirovannyy korpus (13th Mechanized Corps) – General-Mayor Pyotr Akhliustin

25-ya tankovaya diviziya (25th Tank Division) – Polkovnik N.M. Nikiforov

31-ya tankovaya diviziya (31st Tank Division) – Polkovnik S.A. Kalikhovich

208-ya motostrelkovaya diviziya (208th Motor Rifle Division) – Polkovnik V.I. Nichiporovich

---

VVS KIEVSKOGO OSOBOGO VOYENNOGO OKRUGA (VVS KOVO)/VVS YUGO-ZAPADNIY FRONT.
(Air Force of the Kiev Special Military District/VVS Southwestern Front)
General-Leytenant Yevgeniy Ptukhin

315 RAP, 316 RAP.

14 SAD, subordinate to the 5th Army in the Lutsk area.

17 IAP, 46 IAP, 89 IAP.

62 BAD, subordinate to the 5th Army in the Kiev area.

52 SBAP, 94 SBAP, 243 SBAP, 245 SBAP.

15 SAD, subordinate to the 6th Army in the Lvov area.

23 IAP, 28 IAP, 66 ShAP, 164 IAP.

16 SAD, subordinate to the 6th Army in the Ternopol area.

86 SBAP, 87 IAP, 92 IAP, 226 SBAP, 227 SBAP.

63 SAD, subordinate to the 26th Army in the Stryy area.

20 IAP, 62 ShAP, 91 IAP, 165 IAP.

64 SAD, subordinate to the 12th Army in the Stanislav area.

12 IAP, 149 IAP, 166 IAP, 246 IAP, 247 IAP.

17 BAD in the Proskurov area.

48 SBAP, 224 SBAP, 225 SBAP, 242 SBAP, 244 SBAP.

36 IAD in the Kiev area.

2 IAP, 43 IAP, 254 IAP, 255 IAP.

19 BAD in the Biyala Tserkov area.

33 SBAP, 136 BAP, 138 SBAP.

44 IAD in the Vinnitsa area.

88 IAP, 248 IAP, 249 IAP, 252 IAP.

In total 1,913 aircraft.

Note: Shortly after the outbreak of the war, 18 DBAD was subordinated to the staff of VVS Southwestern Front in the Kiev area.

KIEVSKOGO OSOBOGO VOYENNOGO OKRUGA (KOVO)/YUGO-ZAPADNIY FRONT.
(Kiev Special Military District/Southwestern Front)
General-Polkovnik Mikhail Kirponos

31-y strelkovyy korpus (31st Rifle Corps) - General-Mayor Anton Lopatin

193-ya strelkovaya diviziya (193rd Rifle Division) – Polkovnik A.K. Berestov

195-ya strelkovaya diviziya (195th Rifle Division) – General-Mayor V.N. Nesmelov

200-ya strelkovaya diviziya (200th Rifle Division) – Polkovnik I.I. Lyudnikov

36-y strelkovyy korpus (36th Rifle Corps) – General-Mayor Pavel Sisoev

140-ya strelkovaya diviziya (140th Rifle Division) – Polkovnik L.G. Bazanets

146-ya strelkovaya diviziya (146th Rifle Division) – General-Mayor I.M. Gerasimov

228-ya strelkovaya diviziya (228th Rifle Division) – Polkovnik A.M. Ilin

49-y strelkovyy korpus (49th Rifle Corps) – General-Mayor Ivan Kornilov

190-ya strelkovaya diviziya (190th Rifle Division) – Polkovnik G.A. Zverev

197-ya strelkovaya diviziya (197th Rifle Division) – Polkovnik S.D. Gubin

199-ya strelkovaya diviziya (199th Rifle Division) – Polkovnik A.N. Alekseyev

55-y strelkovyy korpus (55th Rifle Corps) - General-Mayor Konstantin Koroteyev

130-ya strelkovaya diviziya (130th Rifle Division) – General-Mayor V.A. Vizzhili

169-ya strelkovaya diviziya (169th Rifle Division) – General-Mayor I.E. Turunov

189-ya strelkovaya diviziya (189th Rifle Division)– Combrig A.S. Chichkanov

1-y vozdushno-desantnyy korpus (1st Airborne Corps) – General-Mayor Matvey Usenko

1-y vozdushno-desantnoy brigadyy (1st Airborne Brigade)

204-y vozdushno-desantnoy brigadyy (204th Airborne Brigade)

211-y vozdushno-desantnoy brigadyy (211th Airborne Brigade)

213-ya motostrelkovaya diviziya (213rd Motor Rifle Division) – Polkovnik V.M. Osminskiy

24-ya mekhannizirovannyy korpus (24th Mechanized Corps) – General-Mayor Vladimir Chistyakov

45-ya tankovaya diviziya (45th Tank Division) – Polkovnik M.D. Solomatin

49-ya tankovaya diviziya (49th Tank Division) – Polkovnik K.F. Shvetsov

216-ya motostrelkovaya diviziya (216th Motor Rifle Division) – Polkovnik A. Sarkisyan

5-ya armiya. *(5th Army)*
General-Leytenant M.I. Potapov

15-y strelkovyy korpus (15th Rifle Corps) – General-Mayor Ivan Fedyuninsky

45-ya strelkovaya diviziya (45th Rifle Division) – General-Mayor G.I. Sherstyuk

62-ya strelkovaya diviziya (62nd Rifle Division) – Polkovnik M.P. Timoshenko

27-y strelkovyy korpus (27th Rifle Corps) – General-Mayor Pavel Artememko

87-ya strelkovaya diviziya (87th Rifle Division) – General-Mayor F.F. Alyabushev

124-ya strelkovaya diviziya (124th Rifle Division) – General-Mayor F.G. Sushiy

135-ya strelkovaya diviziya (135th Rifle Division) – General-Mayor F.N. Smekhotvorov

22-ya mekhannizirovannyy korpus (22nd Mechanized Corps) – General-Mayor Semyon Kondrusev

19-ya tankovaya diviziya (19th Tank Division) – General-Mayor K.A. Semenchenko

41-ya motostrelkovaya diviziya (41st Tank Division) – Polkovnik P.P. Pavlov

215-ya motostrelkovaya diviziya (215th Motor Rifle Division) – Polkovnik P.A. Barabanov

9-ya mekhannizirovannyy korpus (9th Mechanized Corps) – General-Mayor Konstantin Rokossovskiy

20-ya tankovaya diviziya (20th Tank Division) – Polkovnik M.E. Katukov

35-ya tankovaya diviziya (35th Tank Division) – General-Mayor N.A. Novikov

131-ya motostrelkovaya diviziya (131st Motor Rifle Division) – Polkovnik N.V. Kalinin

19-ya mekhannizirovannyy korpus (19th Mechanized Corps) – General-Mayor Nikolay Feklenko

40-ya tankovaya diviziya (40th Tank Division) – Polkovnik M.V. Shirobokov

43-ya tankovaya diviziya (43rd Tank Division) – Polkovnik I.G. Tsibin

6-ya armiya. *(6th Army)*

Leytenant-General Ivan N. Muzychenko

6-y strelkovyy korpus (6th Rifle Corps) – General-Mayor Ivan Alekseyev

41-ya strelkovaya diviziya (41st Rifle Division) – General-Mayor G.N. Mikushev

97-ya strelkovaya diviziya (97th Rifle Division) – Polkovnik N.M. Zakharov

159-ya strelkovaya diviziya (159th Rifle Division) – Polkovnik I.A. Mashchenko

37-y strelkovyy korpus (37th Rifle Corps) – General-Mayor Semyon Zybin

80-ya strelkovaya diviziya (80th Rifle Division) – General-Mayor V.I. Prokhorov

139-ya strelkovaya diviziya (139th Rifle Division) – Polkovnik N.L. Loginov

141-ya strelkovaya diviziya (141st Rifle Division) – General-Mayor Ya.I. Tonkonogov

5-y kavaleriyskiy korpus (5th Cavalry Corps) – General-Mayor Fyodor Kamkov

3-ya kavaleriyskaya diviziya (3rd Cavalry Division) – General-Mayor M.F. Maleyev

14-ya kavaleriyskaya diviziya (14th Cavalry Division) – V.D. Kryuchenkin

4-ya mekhannizirovannyy korpus (4th Mechanized Corps) – General-Mayor Andrey Vlasov

8-ya tankovaya diviziya (8th Tank Division) – Polkovnik P.S. Fotchenkov

32-ya tankovaya diviziya (32nd Tank Division) – Polkovnik E.G. Pushkin

81-ya motostrelkovaya diviziya (81st Motor Rifle Division) – Polkovnik P.M. Varipayev

8-ya mekhannizirovannyy korpus (8th Mechanized Corps) – General-Mayor Dmitry Ryabyshev

12-ya tankovaya diviziya (12th Tank Division) – General-Mayor T.A. Mishanin

34-ya tankovaya diviziya (34th Tank Division) – Polkovnik I.V. Vasilyev

7-ya motostrelkovaya diviziya (7th Motor Rifle Division) – Polkovnik A.G. Gerasimov

15-ya mekhannizirovannyy korpus (15th Mechanized Corps) – General-Mayor Ignatiy Karpezo

10-ya tankovaya diviziya (10th Tank Division) – General-Mayor S.Ya. Ogurtsov

37-ya tankovaya diviziya (37th Tank Division) – Polkovnik F.G. Anikushkin

212-ya motostrelkovaya diviziya (212th Motor Rifle Division) – General-Mayor S.V. Baranov

26-ya armiya. *(26th Army)*

General-Leytenant Fyodor Kostenko

8-y strelkovyy korpus (8th Rifle Corps) – General-Mayor Mikhail Snegov

72-ya gornostrelkovaya diviziya (72nd Mountain Division) – General-Mayor P.I. Abramidze

99-ya strelkovaya diviziya (99th Rifle Division) – Polkovnik N.I. Dementyev

173-ya strelkovaya diviziya (173rd Rifle Division) – General-Mayor S.V. Verzin

12-ya armiya. *(12th Army)*

General-Leytenant Pavel Ponedelin

13-y strelkovyy korpus (13th Rifle Corps) – General-Mayor Nikolay Kirillov

44-ya gornostrelkovaya diviziya (44th Mountain Division) – General-Mayor S.A. Tkachenko

58-ya gornostrelkovaya diviziya (58th Mountain Division) – General-Mayor N.I. Proshkin

192-ya gornostrelkovaya diviziya (192nd Mountain Division) – Polkovnik S.D. Gubin

17-y strelkovyy korpus (17th Rifle Corps) – General-Mayor Ivan Galanin

60-ya gornostrelkovaya diviziya (60th Mountain Division) – General-Mayor M.B. Salikhov

96-ya gornostrelkovaya diviziya (96th Mountain Division) – General-Mayor I.M. Shepetov

164-ya strelkovaya diviziya (164th Rifle Division) – Polkovnik A.N. Chervinskiy

16-ya mekhannizirovannyy korpus (16th Mechanized Corps) – General-Mayor Aleksandr Sokolov

15-ya tankovaya diviziya (15th Tank Division) – Polkovnik V.I. Polozkov

39-ya tankovaya diviziya (39th Tank Division) – Polkovnik N.V. Starkov

240-ya motostrelkovaya diviziya (240th Motor Rifle Division) – Polkovnik I.V. Gorbenko

CHERNOMORSKIY FLOT (ChF).
(Black Sea Fleet)

Vitse-Admiral Filipp Oktyabrskiy

1 battleship (*Parishskaya Kommuna*), 2 modern cruisers (*Voroshilov, Molotov*), 3 old cruisers and 1 school cruiser (*Krasnyy Kavkaz, Krasnyy Krym, Chervona Ukraina* and *Komintern*), 3 flotilla leaders (*Moskva, Kharkov* and *Tashkent*), 5 old destroyers (*Frunze, Dzerzhinski, Nezamozhnik, Shaumyan, Zheleznyakov*) and 8 modern destroyers (*Bodry, Bystry, Boiki, Besposhchadnyy, Bezuprechnyy, Bditelny, Smyshlennyy, Soobrazitelny*), 2 patrol boats, 47 submarines, 84 torpedo boats, and 15 mine sweepers.

VVS ChF.
(Air Force of the Black Sea Fleet)

General-Mayor Vladimir Rusakov

62 IABr

63 BABr

119 OMRAP

Plus eleven independent aviation Eskadrilyas.

A total of 624 aircraft.

VVS ODESSKIY VOYENNYY OKRUG (VVS OVO)/VVS YUZHNYY FRONT.

(Air Force of the Odessa Military District/VVS Southern Front)
General Fyodor Michugin
146 RAP, 317 RAP.
20 SAD between Beltsy and Tiraspol.
4 IAP , 45 SBAP , 55 IAP, 211 SBAP.
21 SAD to the north of the Black Sea coast from Bolgrad in the west to Vorms in the east.
5 BAP , 69 IAP, 67 IAP, 168 IAP , 299 ShAP.
45 SAD from Razdelnaya in the west to Fedorovka in the east.
131 IAP, 132 SBAP, 232 SBAP, 210 SBAP.
In total 950 aircraft (including over 100 modern MiG-3 fighters).

ODESSKIY VOYENNYY OKRUG (OVO)/YUZHNYY FRONT.

(Odessa Military District/Southern Front)
General-Polkovnik Ivan Tyulenev
7-y strelkovyy korpus 7th Rifle Corps) – General-Mayor Konstantin Dobroserdov
116-ya strelkovaya diviziya (116th Rifle Division) – Polkovnik Ya.F. Yeremenko
196-ya strelkovaya diviziya (196th Rifle Division) – Mayor Gen. K.E. Kulikov
206-ya strelkovaya diviziya (206th Rifle Division) – Polkovnik S.I. Gorshkov
9-y strelkovyy korpus 9th Rifle Corps) – General-Mayor Pavel Batov
106-ya strelkovaya diviziya (106th Rifle Division) – Kombrig M.S. Tkachev
156-ya strelkovaya diviziya (156th Rifle Division) – General-Mayor P.V. Chernyaev
32-ya kavaleriyskaya diviziya (32nd Cavalry Division) – Polkovnik A.I. Batskalevich
3-y vozdushno-desantnyy korpus (3rd Airborne Corps) – General-Mayor Vasiliy Glazunov
5-y vozdushno-desantnoy brigadyy (5th Airborne Brigade) – Polkovnik Alexander Rodimtsev
6-y vozdushno-desantnoy brigadyy (6th Airborne Brigade) – Polkovnik Viktor Zholudev
212-y vozdushno-desantnoy brigadyy (212th Airborne Brigade) – Polkovnik Ivan Zatevakhin
47-ya strelkovaya diviziya (47th Rifle Division)

9-ya otdelnaya armiya. *(9th Separate Army)*
General-Leytenant Yakov Cherevichenko
14-y strelkovyy korpus 14th Rifle Corps) – General-Mayor Daniil Yegorov
25-ya strelkovaya diviziya (25th Rifle Division) – Polkovnik A.S. Zakharchenko
51-ya strelkovaya diviziya (51st Rifle Division) – General-Mayor P.G. Tsirulnikov
35-y strelkovyy korpus 35th Rifle Corps) – General-Mayor Ivan Dashichev
95-ya strelkovaya diviziya (95th Rifle Division) – General-Mayor A.I. Pastrevich
176-ya strelkovaya diviziya (176th Rifle Division) – General-Mayor V.M. Martsinkevich
48-y strelkovyy korpus 48th Rifle Corps) – General-Mayor Rodion Malinovsky
30-ya gornostrelkovaya diviziya (30th Mountain Division) – General-Mayor S.G. Galaktionov
74-ya strelkovaya diviziya (74th Rifle Division) – Polkovnik F.Ye. Sheverdin

150-ya strelkovaya diviziya (150th Rifle Division) – General-Mayor I.I. Khorun
2-y kavaleriyskiy korpus (2nd Cavalry Corps) – General-Mayor Pavel Belov
5-ya kavaleriyskaya diviziya (5th Cavalry Division) – Polkovnik V.K. Baranov
9-ya kavaleriyskaya diviziya (9th Cavalry Division) – Polkovnik A.F. Bychkovskiy
2-ya mekhannizirovannyy korpus (2nd Mechanized Corps) – General-Mayor Yuriy Novoselskiy
11-ya tankovaya diviziya (11th Tank Division) – Polkovnik G.I. Kuzmin
16-ya tankovaya diviziya (16th Tank Division) – Polkovnik M.I. Mindro
15-ya motostrelkovaya diviziya (15th Motor Rifle Division) – Polkovnik N.N. Belov
18-ya mekhannizirovannyy korpus (18th Mechanized Corps) – General-Mayor Pyotr Volokh
44-ya tankovaya diviziya (44th Tank Division) – Polkovnik V.P. Krimov
47-ya tankovaya diviziya (47th Tank Division) – Polkovnik G.S. Rodin
218-ya motostrelkovaya diviziya (218th Motor Rifle Division) – General-Mayor F.N. Shilov

DALNE-BOMBARDIROVOCHNAYA AVIATSIYA (DBA).

(Long-Range Bomber Aviation)
In the western parts of the USSR
1 BAK in the Novgorod area
40 DBAD at Soltsy and Krechvitsy.
53 DBAP, 200 DBAP, 7 TBDAP.
51 DBAD at Yedrovo.
7 DBAP, 203 DBAP, 204 DBAP.
2 BAK in the Kursk area
35 DBAD at Bryansk, Orel and Karachev.
100 DBAP, 219 DBAP, 223 DBAP.
48 DBAD at Kursk, Shchigry and Oboyan'.
51 DBAP, 220 DBAP, 221 DBAP, 222 DBAP.
3 BAK in the Smolensk area
52 DBAD at Shatalovo, Seshcha and Smolensk.
3 TBDAP, 98 DBAP, 212 DBAP
42 DBAD at Borovskoye and Shaykovka.
1 TBDAP, 96 DBAP, 207 DBAP.
4 BAK in the Zaporozhye area
22 DBAD at Zaporozhye and Saki/Crimea.
8 DBAP, 11 DBAP, 21 DBAP.
50 DBAD at Rostov-on-the-Don and Novocherkassk/Caucasus.
81 DBA , 299 DBAP, 231 DBAP, 228 DBAP.
18 DBAD (an independent Diviziya) at Skomorokhy and Borispol'.
14 TDBAP, 90 DBAP, 93 DBAP.
In total 1,332 aircraft, including 1,122 DB-3Fs and DB-3s, 201 TB-3s and nine TB-7s.

APPENDIX 2: GERMAN AND SOVIET UNIT STRUCTURES IN JUNE 1941.

German infantry division.

Assigned wartime strength 1941: 16,900 men
Headquarters
Supply troops
One artillery regiment (2,500 men) and an artillery battalion
Three infantry regiments (each 3,250 men), each consisting of three battalions (each 861 men plus support troops), each consisting of three infantry companies (each 191 men), each consisting of three infantry platoons (each 52 men).

Support troops consisted of supply, reconnaissance, signals, engineer, service troops, etc.

In 1941 a German first-line infantry division included around 16,900 men with 516 trucks, 237 lighter transports, 753 motor cycles and 1,189 horse teams. Armament included 72 anti-tank guns, 138 mortars and 74 artillery pieces.

The divisions and infantry regiments were individually numbered, while the battalions of each regiment were numbered with Roman characters from I to III. Thus, 4. Infanterie-Division consisted of:
Infanterie-Regiment 10 (I. – III- Bataillon)
Infanterie-Regiment 52 (I. – III- Bataillon)
Infanterie-Regiment 103 (I. – III- Bataillon)
Artillerie-Regiment 4 (I.-III. Abteilung)
Artillerie-Regiment 40 (I. Abteilung)
Aufklärungs-Abteilung 4
Panzerjäger-Abteilung 4
Pionier-Bataillon 13
Nachrichten-Abteilung 4

Note:
Abteilung was the German designation of a battalion in artillery, armor or cavalry.

Soviet infantry division.

Assigned wartime Strength 5 April 1941: 14,439 men
Headquarters (130 men)
One artillery cannon regiment (1,038 men)
One artillery howitzer regiment (1,277 men)
Three infantry regiments (each 3,182 men), each consisting of support troops and
three infantry battalions (each 778 men plus support troops), each consisting of
three infantry companies (each 178 men plus support troops), each consisting of
three infantry platoons (each 51 men)

Support troops consisted of supply, reconnaissance, signals, engineer, service troops, etc.

The assigned strength of a Soviet rifle division just prior to Operation Barbarossa was 14,439 men with 585 trucks, 22 light transports and 1100 horse teams. Armament included 54 anti-tank guns, 150 mortars and 78 artillery pieces.

However, the assigned strength is misleading in the Soviet case. In June 1941, no Soviet infantry division had its assigned strength. The average Soviet rifle division had between 8,000 and 12,000 men.

In July 1941 the assigned strength of the rifle division decreased to 10,859 men, 203 motor vehicles and 54 artillery pieces. By that time, however, the average strength was 6,000 men and between 50 % and 64 % of the assigned numbers of motor vehicles and artillery pieces. In mid-September the rifle division was further reduced by detaching one of its two artillery regiments.

The Structure of the Luftwaffe.

Luftflotte, normally comprised of one or two Fliegerkorps
Fliegerkorps, comprised of several Geschwader
Geschwader, comprised of a Stabstaffel (12 aircraft) and three Gruppe* (each a Stabsschwarm of 4 aircraft) and three Staffel (each 12 aircraft), each comprised of three Schwarm (each 4 aircraft) in fighter units or four Kette (each 3 aircraft)

Note:
The Schwarm was divided into two Rotte, each of two aircraft.

The Geschwader were individually numbered, while each Gruppe of the Geschwader were numbered with Roman characters from I to III:
III./JG 52 = third Gruppe of Jagdgeschwader 52.

The Staffel of each Geschwader were assigned with an Arabic number from 1. to (in the case of a three Gruppe-Geschwader) 9. The Staffel in each Gruppe was numbered with Arabic numerals:
9./JG 52 = ninth Staffel of Jagdgeschwader 52.
The Schwarm and the Rotte were not numbered.

* There were units with only two Gruppe, and others with up to five Gruppe, but these were exceptions.

The exception was the Reconnaissance Group (Aufklärungsgruppe), which was simply abbreviated according to its strategical (Fernaufklärungsgruppe) or tactical (Heeresaufklärungsgruppe) role. Such as: 4.(F)/122 = 4th Staffel of Fernaufklärungsgruppe 121, or 1.(H)/32 = 1st Staffel of Heeresaufklärungsgruppe 32. A particular Reconnaissance Group was Aufklärungsgruppe Oberbefehlshaber der Luftwaffe (AufklObdL), which was directly subordinate to the commander of the German Air Force, Reichsmarschall Hermann Göring.

The Structure of the Soviet Air Forces.

From 1935 onwards, the Soviet military air force, VVS, was divided between the army (VVS KA) and the navy (VVS VMF).

At the outbreak of the war, the VVS KA had been split into four separate organizations, mainly due to conclusions drawn from the Winter War against Finland.

A considerable lack of coordination between the ground forces and the aviation had been noted during the early stages of the Winter War. In order to create a better coordination between close-support aviation and the ground troops the air units of the Soviet Northwestern Front were subordinated to the commanders of the (ground) armies. This system was soon implemented in the entire VVS KA.

All Shturmovik units and a large part of the VVS fighter units lost their independence and were put under direct command of individual (ground) armies.

At the outbreak of the war in 1941, the forces of the VVS of the Red Army were divided as follows:

The aviation subordinate to the ground forces
Sixty-one Aviatsionnaya Divizii (eighteen fighter, nine bomber and thirty-four 'composite', Smeshannaya, i.e. 'mixed', Divizii) and five Aviation Brigades. These units were divided between:

- The Front Air Forces, divided into separate Military Districts (later Fronts', and the Home Defense, PVO. Comprised 40.5 per cent of the total number of combat aircraft in the entire VVS of the Red Army.

- The Army Air Forces, divided between separate (ground) armies. Comprised 43.7 per cent of the total number of the combat aircraft in the entire VVS of the Red Army.

- The Liaison Squadrons of the (ground army) Corps (KAE) – individual aviation squadrons assigned to the different army corps. The KAEs comprised 2.3 per cent of the total number of combat aircraft in the VVS of the Red Army at the outbreak of the war in 1941.

The aviation directly subordinate to the High Command
Thirteen bomber and five fighter Aviatsionnaya Divizii (the latter were in their initial stages of forming and were never completed), all grouped into:

- The Long-Range (bomber) Aviation, DBA, controlled directly by the High Command. Comprised 13.5 per cent of the total number of combat aircraft.

Experience gained in the Spanish Civil War and the war in China resulted in the restructuring of the VVS units in the late 1930s.

The Aviatsionnaya Eskadrilya (or, shortly, Eskadrilya) was reduced from 32–43 aircraft to 12–15 and replaced as the main tactical aviation unit by the Aviatsionnyy Polk (or, shortly, Polk), or Regiment.

At the outbreak of the war with Germany in 1941, each Aviatsionnaya Eskadrilya comprised of four or five basic tactical formations, the so-called Zveno, three or four aircraft.

In June 1941, the structure of the Soviet Air Forces was the following:

Zveno – Three aircraft.
Eskadrilya – Four or five Zveno.
Polk – *Fighter and ground-attack:* Four Eskadril'i of each 15 aircraft plus a Staff Flight, a total of 62 aircraft. *Bomber:* Five Eskadriliy of each 12 aircraft plus a Staff Flight, a total of 62 aircraft. *Heavy bomber:* 40 aircraft.

Note:
On 10 August 1941, the VVS High Command issued an order, changing the designated strength of ground-attack regiments (Shturmovoy Aviatsionnyy Polk) to two Il-2 equipped Eskadril'i of each 10 aircraft, plus one fighter Eskadrilya of 10 aircraft and one Su-2 equipped Zveno, totaling 33 aircraft. At the same time, new short-range bomber Polki were formed, each consisting of a designated strength of two bomber Eskadril'i of each 10 aircraft plus one fighter Eskadrilya with 10 aircraft, and two staff aircraft, totaling 32 aircraft.

On 20 August 1941, an order was issued from the Stavka, according to which all Polki equipped with 'modern' combat aircraft types were to be made up of two Eskadril'i with 9 aircraft each, plus 2 staff aircraft, i.e. a total of only 20 aircraft.

Between four and six Polki formed an Aviatsionnaya Diviziya (Aviadivizi).

There were purely fighter, purely bomber (and high-speed and heavy bomber) and purely ground-attack Divizii and Polki and composite Divizii and Polki. In 1941, the largest tactical unit of the VVS was the Aviatsionnyy Korpus (AK, Aviation Corps). Apart from this, there were some independent Eskadrili, OAE.

APPENDIX 3: TANKS
IN OPERATION BARBAROSSA.

Light tanks.

Vehicle	Main armament	Frontal armor	Dimensions	Engine power /ton	Max speed on road	Crew
GERMAN TANKS.						
Panzerkampf-wagen I Ausf. B	2 x 7.92 mm	13 mm / 27–63°	L = 4.42 m W = 2.06 m H = 1.72 m W = 6.00 ton	16.7 hp/ton	40 km/h	2
Panzerkampf-wagen II Ausf. A, B, C	1 x 20 mm L/55	30 mm	L = 4.81 m W = 2.22 m H = 1.99 m W = 8.90 ton	14.7 hp/ton	40 km/h	3
Panzerkampf-wagen 35(t)	1 x 37.2 mm L/40	25 mm / 30°	L = 4.90 m W = 2.16 m H = 2.21 m W = 10.67 ton	11.2 hp/ton	35 km/h	4
Panzerkampf-wagen 38(t) Ausf. E/F	1 x 37.2 mm L/47.8	50 mm	L = 4.61 m B = 2.14 m H = 2.25 m W = 9.85 ton	12.6 hp/ton	42 km/h	4
SOVIET TANKS.						
T-26	1 x 45 mm L/46	16 mm	L = 4.60 m W = 2.45 m H = 2.65 m W = 9.60 ton	9.5 hp/ton	27 km/h	3
T-40	1 x 20 mm or 1 x 12.7 mm	15 mm / 80°	L = 4.11 m W = 2.33 m H = 1.91 m W = 5.50 ton	15.5 hp/ton	44 km/h	2
BT-2	1 x 37 mm L/45	13 mm	L = 5.35 m W = 2.23 m H = 2.20 m W = 11.30 ton	35.4 hp/ton	52 km/h (72 km/h on wheels)	2–3
BT-5	1 x 45 mm L/46	13 mm	L = 5.35 m W = 2.23 m H = 2.25 m W = 11.50 ton	34.8 hp/ton	52 km/h (72 km/h on wheels)	3
BT-7	1 x 45 mm L/46	20 mm / 18°	L = 5.66 m W = 2.23 m H = 2.70 m W = 13.80 ton	28.8 hp/ton	52 km/h (72 km/h on wheels)	3

Note: Ausf. = Ausführung, model (German)

Medium tanks.

Vehicle	Main armament	Frontal armor	Dimensions	Engine power /ton	Max speed	Crew
GERMAN TANKS.						
Panzerkampf-wagen III Ausf. G	1 x 50 mm L/42	30 mm / 70–80°	L = 5.41 m W = 2.92 m H = 2.44 m W = 20.3 ton	14.8 hp/ton	40 km/h	5
Panzerkampf-wagen IV Ausf. D, E	1 x 75 mm L/24	30 mm / 80°	L = 5.92 m W = 2.84 m H = 2.68 m W = 20.0 ton	15 hp/ton	40 km/h	5
SOVIET TANKS.						
T-28E	1 x 76.2 mm L-10	30 mm / 90°	L = 7.37 m W = 2.87 m H = 2.63 m W = 25.4 ton	19.7 hp/ton	42 km/h	6
T-34/76A (model 1940)	1 x 76.2 mm L-11	45 mm / 60°	L = 5.92 m W = 3.00 m H = 2.41 m W = 25.6 ton	19.5 hp/ton	55 km/h	4
T-34/76B (model 1941)	1 x 76.2 mm F-34	45 mm / 60°	L = 5.92 m W = 3.00 m H = 2.41 m W = 25.6 ton	19.5 hp/ton	54 km/h	4

Heavy tanks.

Vehicle	Main armament	Frontal armor	Dimensions	Engine power /ton	Max speed	Crew
SOVIET TANKS.						
T-35	1 x 76.2 mm LS-3 plus 2 x 45 mm M32	50 mm / 90°	L = 9.72 m W = 3.20 m H = 3.43 m W = 50.0 ton	10.0 hp/ton	29 km/h	11
KV-1	1 x 76.2 mm L-11 or F-32 or F-34	60 mm / 70°	L = 6.68 m W = 3.32 m H = 2.71 m W = 45.0 ton	12.0 hp/ton	34 km/h	5
KV-2	1 x 152 mm L/24	75 mm / 70°	L = 6.95 m W = 3.32 m H = 3.25 m W = 57.0 ton	10.5 hp/ton	25 km/h	6

Assualt gun.

Vehicle	Main armament	Frontal armor	Dimensions	Engine power /ton	Max speed	Crew
GERMAN.						
Sturmgeschütz III Ausf. B	1 x 75 mm L/24	50 mm / 21°	L = 5.40 m W = 2.93. m H = 1.98 m W = 20.2 ton	15.8 hp/ton	40 km/h	4

Note: Ausf. = Ausführung, model (German)

APPENDIX 4: **AIRCRAFT IN OPERATION BARBAROSSA.**

Fighters.

Aircraft	Max speed at 3000 m	Propulsion	Dimensions		Armament	Crew
GERMAN.						
Messerschmitt Bf 109 F-2	531 km/h	1 x 1175 hp	Wingspan Length	9.97 m 8.94 m	1 x 15 mm + 2 x 7.92 mm	1
Messerschmitt Bf 109 F-4	558 km/h	1 x 1350 hp	Wingspan Length	9.97 m 8.94 m	1 x 20 mm + 2 x 7.92 mm	1
SOVIET.						
Polikarpov I-16 Mark 17	425 km/h	1 x 750 hp	Wingspan Length	9.00 m 5.86 m	2 x 20 mm + 2 x 7.62 mm	1
Polikarpov I-16 Mark 24	490 km/h	1 x 1100 hp	Wingspan Length	9.00 m 6.13 m	4 x 7.62 mm + 8 x 82 mm rocket projectiles	1
Mikoyan-Gurevich MiG-3	555 km/h	1 x 1200 hp	Wingspan Length	10.2 m 8.25 m	1 x 12.7 mm + 2 x 7.62 mm + 8 x 82 mm rocket projectiles	1
Lavochkin, Gorbunov & Gudkov LaGG-3	532 km/h	1 x 1050 hp	Wingspan Length	9.80 m 8.81 m	3 x 12.7 mm + 2 x 7.62 mm + 8 x 82 mm rocket projectiles **or** 1 x 20 mm + 1 x 12.7 mm	1
Yakovlev Yak-1	540 km/h	1 x 1050 hp	Wingspan Length	10.0 m 8.48 m	1 x 20 mm + 1 x 7.62 mm	1

Assualt planes and dive-bombers.

Aircraft	Max speed	Propulsion	Dimensions		Armament	Crew
GERMAN.						
Henschel Hs 123A-1	340 km/h @ 1200 m	1 x 880 hp	Wingspan upper under Length	10.50 m 8.00 m 8.33 m	2 x 7.92 mm + 450 kg bombs	1
Messerschmitt Bf 110 E-1	562 km/h	2 x 1175	Wingspan Length	16.25 m 12.07 m	Frontal 2 x 20 mm + 4 x 7.92 mm, rear 1 x 7.92 mm + 1000 kg bombs	2
Junkers Ju 87 B-2	390 km/h	1 x 1200 hp	Wingspan Length	13.80 m 11.00 m	Frontal 2 x 7.92 mm, rear 1 x 7.92 mm + 1 000 kg bombs	2
SOVIET.						
Polikarpov I-153*	427 km/h	1 x 1100 hp	Wingspan Length	10.00 m 6.12 m	4 x 7.62 mm + 8 x 82 mm rocket projectiles	1
Ilyushin Il-2		1 x 1660 hp	Wingspan Length	14.60 m 11.65 m	2 x 20 mm + 2 x 7.62 mm + 8 x 82 mm rocket projectiles + 600 kg bombs	1

* Also served as a fighter plane.

Bombers.

Aircraft	Max speed	Propulsion	Dimensions		Armament	Crew
GERMAN.						
Heinkel He 111 H-4	435 km/h	2 x 1350 hp	Wingspan Length	22.60 m 16.40 m	1 x 20mm + 1 x 13mm + 7 x 7.92mm + 3600 kg bombs	5
Junkers Ju 88 A-4	510 km/h @ 5300 m	2 x 1400 hp	Wingspan Length	20.80 m 14.36 m	6 x 7.92 mm + 1400 kg bombs	4
Dornier Do 17 Z-2	410 km/h @ 4000 m	2 x 1000 hp	Wingspan Length	18.00 m 15.80 m	6 x 7.92 mm + 1000 kg bombs	4
SOVIET.						
Tupolev TB-3, 1936 model	300 km/h	4 x 830 hp	Wingspan Length	41.80 m 25.10 m	6 x 7.62 mm + 2000 kg bombs	6
Tupolev SB	458 km/h	2 x 1050 hp	Wingspan Length	18.00 m 12.78m	4 x 7.62 mm + 1500 kg bombs	3
Ilyushin DB-3	439 km/h	2 x 950 hp	Wingspan Length	21.40 m 14.22 m	3 x 7.62 mm + 2500 kg bombs	3
Ilyushin DB-3F	435 km/h	2 x 1100 hp	Wingspan Length	21.44 m 14.79 m	3 x 7.62 mm + 2500 kg bombs	3
Petlyakov Pe-2	540 km/h @ 5000 m	2 x 1050 hp	Wingspan Length	17.15 m 12.78 m	4 x 7.62 mm + 1000 kg bombs	3
Sukhoy Su-2	460 km/h	1 x 1100 hp	Wingspan Length	14.30 m 10.25 m	6 x 7.62 mm (4 in wings, 1 in upper turret, 1 in floor hatch) + 400 kg bombs or 10 × 82 mm rocket projectiles	2

APPENDIX 5: **LOSS TABLES.**

Soviet losses in 1941 in relation to the strength in the western parts of the country on 22 june 1941.

TABLE 1.			
	Strength 22 June 1941	Combat losses	Losses as percentage of strength
Troops	2.3 million	3.4 million killed or missing in action	148 %
Tanks	12,800	20,500	160 %
Artillery pieces & mortars over 50mm caliber	46,630	63,100	135 %
Aircraft	8,642 *	16,000 **	185 %

* Aircraft of the Military districts in the West, the DBA, and the fleets in the North, the Baltic Sea and the Black Sea.
** Estimation.

Personnel losses of the Ostheer in 1941 according to different sources.

TABLE 2.					
Source	Killed in action	Missing in action	Wounded	Totals	Totals including casualties of Germany's allies
Wehrmacht monthly casual reports	136,138	24,824	495,579	656,691	892,000
Heeresarzt 10-Day Casualty Reports	167,347	34,527	600,584	802,422	1.04 million
Generaloberst Halder, OKH, diary reports	173,722	35,873	621,308	830,403	1.07 million

German losses in troops, tanks and aircraft on the Eastern Front.

TABLE 3.

1941	June	July	August	September	October	November	December	Total
Troop casualties*	41,064	164,988	189,913	131,584	113,765	84,051	77,093	802,422
Tank losses	118	732	638	257	337	382	375	2,839**
Aircraft combat losses	273	487	251	230	241	139	109	1,730

* Killed in action, missing in action and wounded.

** The author is grateful for the following comment by historian Christopher Lawrence: "The Germans tended not to actually record a tank as destroyed, even though it could be in the repair depot for months. Comparing German tanks destroyed to Soviet tanks destroyed creates a very lop-sided ratio. For my book *Kursk: The Battle of Prokhorovka* (2015) I used destroyed and damaged compared to destroyed and damaged as I think it gave a more meaningful comparison of performance differences (and even then, it was not favorable to the Soviet Union). For the Germans there were probably about 10 tanks damaged for every one destroyed, while for the Soviets it was more like 2 damaged for each destroyed (ref. figures in Appendix IIII in *Kursk: The Battle of Prokhorovka*). The problem is that comparing destroyed to destroyed is as much a comparison of their repair and refurbishment capabilities as it is of their combat capabilities."

Sources: *Troop casualties:* Bundesarchiv-Militärarchiv, RW 19/1387-1392, Heeresarzt Heeresarzt 10-Day Casualty Reports per Theater of War. *Tank losses:* "Das Scheitern der wirtschaftlichen 'Blitzkriegstrategie'" by Rolf-Dieter Müller in Boog, Horst, Jürgen Förster, et al. Das Deutsche Reich und der Zweite Weltkrieg. Band 4: Der Angriff auf die Sowjetunion, p. 977. *Aircraft losses:* Bundesarchiv/Militärarchiv RL 2 III/754-756. Loss returns to the Generalquartiermeister der Luftwaffe.

Prisoners of war and war booty reported by the Germans during large battles of envelopment.

TABLE 4.

Envelopment battle	Prisoners of war	Captured tanks	Captured artillery pieces
Biyalystok-Minsk, June	323,898	3,332	1,809
Smolensk, July	310,000	3,205	3,120
Uman, August	103,054	317	858
Gomel, August	78,000	144	700
Kiev, September	665,212	824	3,018
North of Sea of Azov, October	64,325	126	519
Vyazma-Bryansk, October	657,948	1,241	5,496
Totals	**2.2 million**	**9,189**	**15,520**

Wehrmacht figures on losses among Soviet prisoners of war in German custody June 1941–January 1942.

TABLE 5.	
Soviet POWs registered June 1941–January 1942	3,411,388
Released	484,000
POWs not released	3,048,077
Soviet POWs remaining in German custody 1 February 1942	363,331
Decrease*	2,400,000
Decrease in percentage of total number	70 %
Decrease in percentage of POWs not released	88 %

* It should be noted that during this period, no substantial numbers of POWs are recorded as having escaped.
Sources: BundesarchivMilitärarchiv RW 6/543-548 and RW 19/415.

Comparison of casualties during the Western Campaign in May–June 1940 and Operation Barbarossa in 1941.

TABLE 6.		
A) INCLUDING POWS		
Casualties	**Western Campaign May–June 1940**	**Operation Barbarossa June–December 1941**
Allied/Soviet	3.010 million	3.4 million to 4.3 million
German	157,621	892,000 to 1.07 million**
Loss relations Allied/Soviet to German	19:1	3.2:1 to 4.8:1

A) EXCLUDING POWS		
Casualties	**Western Campaign May–June 1940 excluding Allied POWs**	**Operation Barbarossa June–December 1941 excluding Soviet POWs**
Allied/Soviet	360,000	2 million*
German	157,621	850,000 to 1.03 million**
Loss relations Allied/Soviet to German	2.3:1	1.9:1 to 2.4:1

* Estimation.
** Germany and its allies.

300

Records for Luftwaffe fighter units on the Eastern Front 22 June 1941–5 December 1941.

TABLE 7.				
Unit	Victories*	Losses in the air **	Losses on the ground **	Total losses **
JG 3	1,298	58	10	68
JG 27	289	27	11	38
JG 51	1,881	84	1	85
JG 52	881	56	5	61
JG 53	762	35	2	37
JG 54	1,078	46	1	47
JG 77 plus I.(J)/LG 2	1,166	52	2	54
Totals	7,255	358	32	390

All losses are damaged between 60 %–100 % (i.e. aircraft totally destroyed) due to hostile activity.

* **Source:** Prien, Rodeike, and Bock, *Die Jagdfliegerverbände der Deutschen Luftwaffe 1934 bis 1945. Teil 6/I: Unternehmen „Barbarossa" Einsatz im Osten 22.6. bis 5.12. 1941*, p. 32.

** **Source:** Bundesarchiv/Militärarchiv RL 2 III/754-756.

SOURCES.

Archives.

4 GIAP/VVS VMF Museum and Archive.
108 Rava-Russkiy GvShAP Archive.
146 GvIAP/PVO Private Museum.
Central Military Archive, TsAMO, Podolsk.
Central Naval Archive TsVMA, Gatchina.
Luftfahrtmuseum Hannover-Laatzen.
Monino Air Force Museum, Moscow.
Genocide and Resistance Research Centre of Lithuania, Vilnius
National Archives, Kew.
National Archives and Records Administration, Washington, D.C.
Rosvoyentsentr, Moscow.
Russian State Archive of Social-Political History in Moscow, RGASPI.
Russian State Military Archive, RGVA, Moscow.
State Archive of the Russian Federation, GARF, Moscow.
Suchgruppe 45, Salzwedel.
United States Holocaust Memorial Museum.
WASt Deutsche Dienststelle, Berlin.

Literature.

Abramov, A.S. *Dvyenadtsat' taranov*. Sredne-Ural'skoe knizhnoe izdatel'stvo, Sverdlovsk, 1970.

Abramovich, Aron. *V reshayoshchey voyne: Uchastne I rol yevdeyev SSR v voyne protiv natsizma*. n.p., Tel Aviv 1981.

Achkasov, V., and B. Vayner. *Krasnoznanyenniy Baltiyskiy flot v Velikoy Otyechyestvyennoy voyne. Voyenizdat*, Moscow 1957.

Ailsby, Christopher. *Images of Barbarossa*. Ian Allan Publishing, Shepperton 2001.

Anttonen, Ossi, and Hannu Valtonen. *Luftwaffe Suomessa – In Finland 1941–1944*, Helsinki 1976, 1980.

Arad, Itskhak. *Kholokaust: Katastrofa evropeyskogo evreysta (1933–1945)*. Yad Vashem, Jerusalem 1990.

Armstrong, John Alexander (ed.). *Soviet Partisans in World War II*. University of Wisconsin Press, Madison 1964.

Arnstad, Henrik. *Skyldig till skuld: En europeisk resa i Nazitysklands skugga*. Norstedts, Stockholm 2009.

Artemyev, A.M. *Morkaya Aviatsiya Rossii*. Voyenizdat, Moscow 1996.

Askey, Nigel. *Operation Barbarossa: The Complete Organisational and Statistical Analysis, and Military Simulation, Volume I*. Lulu Publishing, 2013.

-----. *Operation Barbarossa: The Complete Organisational and Statistical Analysis, and Military Simulation, Volume IIa*. Lulu Publishing, 2013.

-----. *Operation Barbarossa: The Complete Organisational and Statistical Analysis, and Military Simulation, Volume IIb*. Lulu Publishing, 2014.

Baade, Fritz, Richard F. Behrendt, and Peter Blachstein (ed.). *"Unsere Ehre heisst Treue", Kriegstagebuch des Kommandostabes RFSS, Tätigkeitsberichte der 1. und 2. SS-Kav.-Brigade und von Sonderkommandos der SS*. Europa Verlag, Wien 1965.

Bacque, James. *Other Losses: An Investigation into the Mass Deaths of German Prisoners of War at the Hands of the French and Americans After World War II*. Talonbooks, Vancouver 2011.

Bagramjan, I. Ch. *So begann der Krieg*. Militärverlag der Deutschen Demokratischen Republik, Berlin 1972.

Baird, J. W. *The Mythical World of Nazi War Propaganda, 1939–1945*. University of Minnesota Press, Minneapolis 1974.

Balke, Ulf, *Kampfgeschwader 100 "Wiking"*. Motorbuch Verlag, Stuttgart 1981.

-----. *Der Luftkrieg in Europa 1939–1941*. Bechtermünz Verlag, Augsburg 1997.

Barabanshchikov, M., and A. Nekrylov, *Sbornik lyotchiki*. Molodaya Gvardiya, Moscow 1978.

Barbas, Bernd, *Die Geschichte der II. Gruppe des Jagdgeschwaders 52*. Traditionsgemeinschaft JG 52, Überlingen 2005.

Barkan, Elazar, Elizabeth A. Cole, and Kai Struve (eds.). *Shared History, Divided Memory: Jews and Others in Soviet-occupied Poland, 1939–1941. Leipziger Beiträge zur Jüdischen Geschichte und Kultur. Band V*. Leipziger Universitätsverlag, Leipzig 2007.

Bartov, Omer. *Hitler's Army: Soldiers, Nazis, and War in the Third Reich*. Oxford University Press, Oxford 1992.

-----. *The Eastern Front*. Palgrave, New York 2001.

-----. *Germany's War and the Holocaust: Disputed Histories*. Cornell University Press, Ithaca and London 2003.

Bekker, Cajus. *The Luftwaffe War Diaries*. Ballantine Books, New York 1969.

Beevor, Antony. *Berlin: The Downfall 1945*. Penguin Books, London 2007.

Bentzien, Hans. *Division Brandenburg: Die Rangers von Admiral Canaris*. Edition Ost, Berlin 2004.

Bergström, Christer and Andrey Mikhailov. *Black Cross/Red Star: The Air War Over the Eastern Front. Vol. 1, Operation Barbarossa*. Pacifica Military History, Pacifica 2000.

Bergström, Christer and Andrey Mikhailov, in cooperation with Alfred Griskawski. *Graf & Grislawski: A Pair of Aces*. Eagle Editions, Hamilton 2003.

Bergström, Christer, Eric Mombeek, and Martin Pegg. *Jagdwaffe: Barbarossa, the Invasion of Russia June–December 1941*. Ian Allan Publishing Ltd. 2003.

Bernád, Denes. *Rumanian Air Force: The Prime Decade, 1938–1947*. Squadron/Signal Publications, Carrollton 1999.

-----. *Rumanian Aces of World War 2*. Osprey Publishing, Wellingborough 2003.

Bitva za Moskvu. Moskovskiy rabochiy, Moscow 1966.

Boldin, Ivan Vasilyevich. *Stranitsyy zhizni*. Voyenizdat, Moscow 1961.

Bonn, Keith E. (ed.) *Slaughterhouse: The Handbook of the Eastern Front*. The Aberjona Press, Bedford, PA, 2005.

Boog, Horst, Jürgen Förster, et al. *Das Deutsche Reich und der Zweite Weltkrieg. Band 4: Der Angriff auf die Sowjetunion*. Deutsche Verlags-Anstalt, Stuttgart 1983.

Boyarskiy, Vyacheslav Ivanovich. *Partizany i armiya: Istoriya uteryannyykh vozmozhnostey*. AST, Moscow 2001.

Boyevoy put' Sovyetskogo Voyenno-Morskogo Flota. Voyenizdat, Moscow 1988.

Braatz, Kurt. *Gott oder ein Flugzeug: Leben und Sterben des Jagdfliegers Günther Lützow*. NeunundzwanzigSechs Verlag, Moosburg 2005.

Braithwaite, Rodric. *Moskva 1941*. Historiska Media, Lund 2007.

Brandon, Ray, and Wendy Lower. *The Shoah in Ukraine: History, Testimony, Memorialization*. Indiana University Press and the United States Holocaust Memorial Museum, Bloomington and Indianapolis 2010.

Browning, Christopher. *Helt vanliga män: Reservpolisbataljon 101 och den slutliga lösningen i Polen*. Norstedts, Stockholm 2006.

Brütting, G. *Das waren die deutschen Kampffliegerasse 1939–1945*. Motorbuch Verlag, Stuttgart 1975.

Bunte, Rune and Lennart Jöberg. *Historia i siffror*. Gleerups, Lund 1968.

Burkhart, Generalmajor, in cooperation with Generaloberst Franz Halder and Generalleutnant Emil Leeb. *German Tank Strength and Loss Statistics*. Study MS P-059. Historical Division U.S. Army, European Command, New York 1950.

Buxa, Werner. *Weg und Schicksal der 11. Infanterie-Division*. Dörfler Verlag, Eggolsheim-Bammersdorf 2004.

Caldwell, Erskine. *Moscow Under Fire: A Wartime Diary*. Hutchinson & Co., London 1942.

Carell, Paul. *Unternehmen Barbarossa; der Marsch nach Russland*. Verlag Ullstein, Frankfurt-am-Main 1963.

Chavchavadze, Paul Avinov and Marie Avinov. *Marie Avinov: Pilgrimage Through Hell*. University of California, Prentice-Hall 1968.

Cholawski, Shalom. *Soldiers from the Ghetto: The First Uprising Against the Nazis*. A.S. Barnes & Co., San Diego and New York 1980.

Clark, Alan. *Barbarossa: The Russo-German Conflict 1941–45*. Quill, New York 1985.

Cohen, Laurie R. *Smolensk under the Nazis: Everyday Life in Occupied Russia*. University of Rochester Press, Rochester, NY 2013.

Cooper, Matthew. *The Phantom war: The German Struggle against Soviet Partisans, 1941–1944*. Macdonald and Janes, London 1979.

Cottam, Kazimiera J. (ed.). *Defending Leningrad: Women Behind Enemy Lines*. New Military Publishing, Nepean, ON 1998.

de Zayas, Alfred-Maurice, with Walter Rabus. *The Wehrmacht War Crimes Bureau, 1939–1945*. University of Nebraska Press, Lincoln 1989.

Dickfeld, Adolf. *Footsteps of the Hunter*. J.J. Fedorowicz Publishing, Winnipeg 1993.

Dierich, Wolfgang. *Kampfgeschwader 51 Edelweiss,* Motorbuch Verlag, Stuttgart 1975.

-----. *Kampfgeschwader 55 Greif.* Motorbuch Verlag, Stuttgart 1975.

Drabkin, Artem and Oleg Sheremet. *T-34 in Action*. Pen & Sword, Barnsley 2006.

Drabkin, Artem. *Stalins slägga: Ryska artillerister i strid med Wehrmacht*. SMB, Höganäs 2010.

Drabkin, Artem, Alexei Isaev and Christopher Summerville. *Barbarossa Through Soviet Eyes: The First twenty-four Hours*. Pen & Sword, Barnsley 2012.

Durasova, T. B. *Budet zhit rodina – budem zhit I myy*. Kareliya, Petrozavodsk, 1985.

Ehrenburg, Ilya, and Vasily Grossman, edited by David Patterson. *The Complete Black Book of Russian Jewry*. Transaction Publishers, New Brunswick 2009.

Elleinstein, Jean. *Stalinfenomenets historia*. Arbetarkultur, Lund 1977.

Epstein, Barbara. *The Minsk Ghetto 1941-1943: Jewish Resistance and Soviet Internationalism*. University of California Press, Berkeley 2008.

Erickson, John. *The Road to Stalingrad*. Cassel, London 2003.

Ericson, Edward E. *Feeding the German Eagle: Soviet Economic Aid to Nazi Germany, 1933–1941*. Greenwood Publishing Group, 1999.

Fangrad, Alana. *Wartime Rape And Sexual Violence: an examination of the perpetrators, motivations, and functions of sexual violence against Jewish women during the Holocaust*. Author House, Bloomington, IN, 2013.

Fast, Niko. *Das Jagdgeschwader 52*. Bensberger Buch-Verlag, Bergisch Gladbach, 1988-1992.

Fiala, Josef. *"Österreicher" in den SS-Einsatzgruppen und SS-Brigaden: die Tötungsaktionen in der Sowjetunion 1941–1942*. Diplomica Verlag, Hamburg 2010.

Forczyk. *Tank Warfare on the Eastern Front 1941-1942: Schwerpunkt*. Pen and Sword, Pen & Sword, Barnsley 2014.

Frankson, Anders, and Niklas Zetterling. *Slaget om Kursk*. Norstedts förlag, Stockholm 2002.

Frisch, Franz A.P. and Wilbur D. Jones, Jr. *Condemned to Live: A Panzer Artilleryman's Five-Front War*. Burd Street Print, 2003.

Frome, Frieda. *Some Dare to Dream: Frieda Frome's Escape from Lithuania*. Iowa State Pr., 1988.

Gertjejanssen, Wendy Jo. *Victims, Heroes, Survivors: Sexual Violence on the Eastern Front during World War II*. PhD diss. University of Minnesota 2004.

Gilbert, Martin. *The Holocaust*. Fontana Press, London 1986.

Glantz, David M. and Jonathan House. *When Titans Clashed: How the Red Army Stopped Hitler*. University Press of Kansas, 1995.

Glantz, David M. *The Initial Period of War on the Eastern Front, 22 June–August 1941*. Routledge, London and New York 2001.

-----. *Barbarossa Derailed The Battle for Smolensk 10 July–10 September 1941. Volume I: The German Advance, the Encirclement Battle, and the First and Second Soviet Counteroffensives, 10 July–24 August 1941*. Helion & Co., Solihull 2010.

Goldenberg, Myrna and Amy H. Shapiro (ed.). *Different Horrors/Same Hell: Gender and the Holocaust*. University of Washington Press, Seattle 2013.

Goldhagen, Daniel. *Hitler's Willing Executioners: Ordinary Germans and the Holocaust*. Abacus Books, London 1997.

Golubev, V. F. *Vtoroye dykhani*. Lenizdat, Leningrad 1988.

Gordon, Yefim and Dmitri Khazanov. *Soviet Combat Aircraft of the Second World War. Volume One: Single-Engined Fighters*. Midland Publishing Ltd., Earl Shilton 1998.

-----. *Soviet Combat Aircraft of the Second World War. Volume Two: Twin-Engined Fighters, Attack Aircraft and Bombers*. Midland Publishing Ltd., Earl Shilton 1999.

Grenkevich, Leonid D. and David M. Glantz (ed.). *The Soviet Partisan Movement, 1941–1944: A Critical Historiographical Analysis*. Frank Cass, London 1999.

Groehler, O. *Geschichte des Luftkriegs*. Militärverlag, Berlin (GDR) 1981.

Guderian, Heinz. *Panzer Leader*. E.P. Dutton, New York 1952.

Guderian, Heinz. *Panzer Leader*. Da Capo Press, Boston 2001.

Gundelach, Karl. *Kamfgeschwader General Wever 4*. Motorbuch Verlag, Stuttgart 1978.

Gyllenhaal, Lars, and James F. Gebhardt. *Slaget om Nordkalotten*. Historiska Media, Stockholm 2001.

Habeck, Mary R. *Storm of Steel: The Development of Armor Doctrine in Germany and the Soviet Union, 1919–1939*. Cornell University Press, London 2003.

Hackler, Erwin. *Vom Hoffen und Irren: eine deutsche Jugend in der Weimarer Republik und dem Deutschen Reich*. PS:KonText, Mainz-Bretzenheim 1995.

Halder, Generaloberst Franz. *The Private War Journal of Generaloberst Franz Halder*. Combined Arms Research Library: Digital Library. http://cgsc.contentdm.oclc.org.

Hanski, Raija. *Behandlingen av krigsfångar under vinter- och fortsättningskriget: en folkrättslig studie*. Institutet för mänskliga rättigheter, Åbo akademi, Åbo 1990.

Hart, Stephen and R. Hart. *German Tanks of World War II*. Spellmount Publishers Ltd, 1998.

Haupt, Werner. *Die 8. Panzer-Division im 2. Weltkrieg*. Podzun-Pallas Verlag, Eggolsheim, 1987.

-----. *Army Group Center: The Wehrmacht in Russia 1941–1945*. Schiffer, Atglen 1997.

-----. *Army Group North: The Wehrmacht in Russia 1941–1945*. Schiffer, Atglen 1997.

-----. *Army Group South: The Wehrmacht in Russia 1941–1945*. Schiffer, Atglen 1998.

Heaton, Colin D. *German Anti-Partisan Warfare in Europe: 1939–1945*. Schiffer Military History, Atglen 2001.

Heim, Heinrich, and Werner Jochmann. *Adolf Hitler Monologe im Führerhauptquartier 1941–1944*. Albrecht Kraus, Hamburg 1980.

Helms, Bodo. *Von Anfang an dabei: Mein abenteuerliches Fliegerleben 1939–1980*. Vowinckel Verlag, Berg am Starnberger See, n.d.

Hoppe, Bert (ed.). *Die Verfolgung und Ermordung der europäischen Juden durch das nationalsozialistische Deutschland 1933-1945. Band 7. Sowjetunion mit annektierten Gebieten I: Besetzte sowjetische Gebiete unter deutscher Militärverwaltung, Baltikum und Transnistrien*. Oldenbourg Verlag, Munich, 2011.

Hoth, Hermann. *Panzer Operations: Germany's Panzer Group 3 during the Invasion of Russia, 1941*. Casemate, Philadelphia & Oxford 2015.

Ilin, N. G. *Gvardeutsyy v vozdukhe*. DOSAAF, Moscow 1973.

Inozemtsev, I.G. *Pod krylom – Leningrad*. Voyenizdat, Moscow 1978.

Inozemtsev, Nikolay. *Frontoy dnevnik*. Nauka, Moscow 2005.

Irving, David. *Goebbels: Mastermind of the Third Reich*. Parforce, London 1996.

-----. *Hitler's War and The War Path*. Focal Point, n.d.

Isayev, Aleksandr Valeryevich. *Kotlyy 41-go: Istoriya VOV, kotoruyu myy ne znali*. Yauza, Moscow 2005.

Isayev, Aleksey V. *Ot Dubno do Rostova*. AST, Tranzitkniga, Moscow 2004.

Jacobsen, Hans-Arnold and Jürgen Rohwer. *Entscheidungsschlachten des zweiten Weltkrieges*. Bernard & Graefe Verlag, Munich 1960.

Jatkosota-Kronikka. Gummerus Kustannus Oy, Jyväskylä 1991.

Jentz, Thomas L. *Panzertruppen 1: The Complete Guide to the Creation & Combat Employment of Germany's Tank Force, 1933–1942*. Schiffer Military History, Atglen, PA, 1996.

Josephson, Paul, Nicolai Dronin, et al. *An Environmental History of Russia*. Cambridge University Press, New York 2013.

Kamenir, Victor J. *The Bloody Triangle: The Defeat of Soviet Armor in the Ukraine, June 1941*. Zenith Press, Minneapolis 2008.

Katukov, Mikhail Yefimovich. *Na ostriye glavnogo udara*. Voyenizdat, Moscow 1974.

Kempowski, Walter. *Das Echolot: Barbarossa '41, ein kollektives Tagebuch*. btb Verlag, Munich 2004.

Kershaw, Ian and Moshe Lewin (ed.). *Stalinism and Nazism: Dictatorships in Comparison*. Cambridge University Press, Cambridge 1997.

Kershaw, Robert J. *War without Garlands: Operation Barbarossa 1941/42*. Da Capo Press, Boston 2000.

Kinnunen, Tiina, and Ville Kivimäki (ed.). *Finland in World War II*. Brill, Boston 2012.

Kirchubel, Robert, and Steven J. Zaloga. *Barbarossa: Armégrupp Nord*. SMB, Höganäs 2010.

-----. *Barbarossa: Armégrupp Syd*. SMB, Höganäs 2010.

Kirchubel, Robert, Peter Abboy, and Nigel Thomas. *Barbarossa: Armégrupp Mitt*. SMB, Höganäs 2010.

Klee, Ernst, Willi Dressen, and Volker Riess. *"The Good Old Days": The Holocaust as Seen by its Perpetrators and Bystanders*. Konecky & Konecky 1991.

Kornyukhin G. F. *Sovetskie Istrebitel v Velikoy Otechestvennoy Voyne*. Smolensk 2000.

Kozhina, Elena. *Through the Burning Steppe: A Wartime Memoir*. Riverhead Books, New York 2000.

Krivosheev, G. (ed.). *Grif sekretnosti snyat. Poteri vooruzhyonnykh sil SSSR v voynakh, boyevykh deystviyakh i voyennykh konfliktakh*. Voyenizdat, Moscow 1993.

-----. *Soviet Casualties and Combat Losses in the Twentieth Century*. Greenhill Books, London 1997.

-----. *Rossiya i SSSR v voynakh XX veka: Poteri vooruzhennykh sil*. OLMA-Press, Moscow 2001.

Kulikov, Viktor. *Operatsiya Barbarossa*. OOO Strategiya KM, Moscow 2000.

Lawrence, Christopher A. *Kursk: The Battle of Prokhorovka*. Aberdeen Books, Sheridan, Colorado 2015.

Lefevre, Eric. *Brandenburg Division: Commandos of the Reich*. Histoire & Collections, Paris 2000.

Lehwess-Litzmann, Walter. *Absturz ins Leben*. Dingsda-Verlag, Querfurt 1994.

Lopukhovsky, Lev. *The Viaz'ma Catastrophe, 1941: The Red Army's Disastrous Stand Against Operation Typhoon*. Helion, Solihull 2013.

Luknitskiy, Pavel Nikolayevich. *Leningrad deystvuyet*. Sovyetskiy Pisatel, Moscow 1971.

Mahlke, Helmut. *Stuka: Angriff: Sturzflug*. Verlag E. S. Mittler & Sohn, Berlin 1993.

Mangulis, Visvaldis. *Latvia in the Wars of the 20th Century*. Cognition Books, Princeton Junction 1983.

von Manstein, Erich. *Verlorene Siege*. Athenäum, Bonn 1955.

Marrus, Michael. *The "Final Solution": The Implementation of Mass Murder, Volume 1. The Nazi Holocaust*. Marrus, Westpoint, CT 1989.

Martin, Bernd (ed.). *Tagebuch eines sowjetischen Offiziers vom 1. Januar 1942-8. Februar 1942*. Wehrwissenschaftliche Rundschau 17, 1967.

Maschke, Erich. *Zur Geschichte der deutschen Kriegsgefangenen des Zweiten Weltkrieges. Band 15*. E. und W. Gieseking, Bielefeld 1974.

Maslennikov, Yu. I. *Taktika v boyevykh primerakh*. Voyenizdat, Moscow 1985.

Medvedev, Roy A. *Stalin och stalinismen*. Prisma, Stockholm 1981.

Messenger. Charles. *The Last Prussian: A Biography of Field Marshal Gerd Von Rundstedt, 1875–1953*. Brassey's: Putnam Aeronautical, 1991.

Mitcham, S. W. *The Panzer Legions*. Stackpole Books, Mechanicsburg, PA, 2007.

Møller Hansen, Peter. *Troskab: Dansk SS-frivillig E.H. Rasmussens erindringer 1940-45*. Lindhardt og Ringhof, Copenhagen, 2015.

Moore, Bob, and Barbara Hately-Broad (ed.). *Prisoners of War, Prisoners of Peace: Captivity, Homecoming and Memory in World War II*. Berg, Oxford & New York 2005.

Moroko, V. M. *Dviproges: Chyornyy serpen 1941 roku*. Historical Faculty, Zaporizhia University 2010.

Morozov, K. A. *Kareliya v godyy Velikoy Otechestvennoynyy (1941 – 1945)*. Petrozavodsk 1983.

Müller, Rolf-Dieter, and Gerd R. Ueberschär. *Hitler's War in the East, 1941–1945: A Critical Assessment*. Berghahn Books, New York 2002.

Murphy, David E. *What Stalin Knew: The Enigma of Barbarossa*. Yale University Press, New Haven & London 2005.

Nagorski, Andrew. *The Greatest Battle: Stalin, Hitler, and the Desperate Struggle for Moscow That Changed the Course of World War II.* Simon & Schuster, New York 2007.

Nauroth, Helmut. *Stukageschwader 2 Immelmann.* Verlag K.W. Schütz, Preussisch Oldendorf 1988.

Nikžentaitis, Alvydas, Stefan Schreiner and Darius Staliūnas. *The Vanished World of Lithuanian Jews.* Rodopi, Amsterdam, 2004.

Noggle, Anne. *A Dance with Death: Soviet Airwomen in World War II.* Texas A&M University Press,College Station 1994.

Nolte, Hans-Heinrich. *Kleine Geschichte Russlands.* Stuttgart 1998.

Novikov, Aleksandr A. *V Nebe Leningrada.* Voyenizdat, Moscow 1970.

Õispuu, Leo. *Estonians in Russian Armed Forces in 1940–1945, Part 3. (Selmet-Üüde).* The State Archives of Estonia, Memento Tallinn Association, Tallinn University of Technology 2011.

Osipov, G. A. *V nebe bombardirovshchiki.* Biblioteka zhurnala Shchelkovo, Shchelkovo 2003.

Ostermann, Max-Hellmuth. *Vom Häschen zum As.* Potsdam: Ludwig Voggenreiter Verlag, 1944.

Overmans, Rüdiger. *Deutsche militärische Verluste im Zweiten Weltkrieg.* Oldenbourg Verlag, München 2000.

Pietrow-Ennker, Bianca. (ed.) *Präventivkrieg: Der deutsche Angriff auf die Sowjetunion.* Fischer Taschenbuch Verlag, Frankfurt a.M. 2001.

Pleshakov, Constantine. *Stalin's Folly: The Tragic First Ten Days of World War II on the Eastern Front.* First Mariner Books, 2006.

Plocher, H. *The German Air Force Versus Russia, 1941.* USAF Historical Division, Arno Press, New York 1968.

Pobratimy Nikolaya Gastello. MOF "Pobyeda-1945 GOD", Moscow 1995.

Pohl, Dieter. *Die Herrschaft der Wehrmacht: Deutsche Militärbesatzung und einheimische Bevölkerung in der Sowjetunion 1941–1944.* Fischer Taschenbuch Verlag, Frankfurt am Main 2011.

Pokryschkin, Alexander I. *Himmel des Krieges.* Deutscher Militärverlag, Berlin (GDR) 1970.

Prien, Jochen. *Geschichte des Jagdgeschwaders 77.* Struve-Druck, Eutin 1992-1994.

Prien, Jochen, Gerhard Stemmer, Peter Rodeike, and Winfried Bock. *Die Jagdfliegerverbände der deutschen Luftwaffe 1934 bis 1945, Teil 6/II.* Struve Druck, Eutin 2004.

-----. *Die Jagdfliegerverbände der deutschen Luftwaffe 1934 bis 1945, Teil 6/II.* Struve Druck, Eutin 2004.

Pshenyanik, G. A. *Sovyetskie Voyenno-vozdushnye sily v bor'bye s Nemetsko-fashistskoy aviatsiyey v lyetnyeosyennyey kampanii 1941 g.* Voyenizdat, Moscow, 1961.

Raus, Erhard. *Panzer Operations: The Eastern Front Memoir of General Raus, 1941–1945.* Da Capo Press, Boston 2003.

Reese, Roger R. *Why Stalin's Soldiers Fought The Red Army's Military Effectiveness in World War II.* University Press of Kansas, Kansas 2011.

Rhodes, Richard. *Masters of Death: The SS-Einsatzgruppen and the Invention of the Holocaust.* Vintage Books, New York 2002.

Riebenstahl, Horst. *The 1st Panzer Division 1935–1945.* Schiffer Publishing, Atglen, PA 2004.

Ring, Hans, and Werner Girbig. *Jagdgeschwader 27: Die Dokumentation über den Einsatz an allen Fronten 1939–1945.* Motorbuch Verlag, Stuttgart 1972.

Rokossovskiy, Konstantin K. *Soldatskiy Dolg.* Voyenizdat, Moscow, 1988.

Rossolinski, Grzegorz. *Stepan Bandera: the Life and Afterlife of a Ukrainian Nationalist: Fascism, Genocide and Cult.* ibidem-Verlag, Stuttgart 2014.

Ryabyshev, Dmitriy Ivanovich. *Pervyy god voynyy.* Voyenizdat, Moscow 1990.

Salisbury, Harrison E. *The 900 Days: The Siege of Leningrad.* Da Capo Press, Boston 2003.

Sana, Elina. *Luovutetut; Suomen ihmisluovutukset Gestapolle.* W. Söderström, Helsingfors 2003.

Sandström, Allan. *Fortsättningskriget 1941–1944.* Libris, Örebro 1991.

Satjukow, Silke and Rainer Gries. *"Bankerte!" Besatzungskinder in Deutschland nach 1945.* Campus Verlag, Frankfurt 2015.

Schäufler, Hans. *Panzer Warfare on the Eastern Front.* Stackpole Books, Mechanicsburg 2012.

------. *Knight's Cross Panzers.* Stackpole Books, Mechanicsburg 2010.

Scheja, Oskar and Dan Chiariello. *The Man in the Black Fur Coat: A Soldier's Adventures on the Eastern Front.* CreateSpace Independent Publishing Platform 2014.

Schick, Albert. *Combat History of the 10. Panzer Division.* Fedorowicz Publishing, Winnipeg 2013.

Schramm, Percy E. (ed.). *Kriegstagebuch des Oberkommandos der Wehrmacht 1939–1945.* Bernard & Graefe Verlag, Munich 1982.

Schrodek, Gustav. *Ihr Glaube galt dem Vaterland: Geschichte des Panzer-Regiments 15.* Podzun-Pallas Verlag, Wolfersheim 1976.

-----. *Die 11. Panzer-Division.* Dörfler Verlag, Eggolsheim-Bammersdorf 2004.

Shaposhnikov, Boris Mikhaylovich. *Bitva za Moskvu: Moskovskaya operaysiya Zapadnogo fronta 16 noyabrya g.–31 yanvarya 1942 g.* Voyennoye izdatelstvo NKO Soyuza SSR, Moscow 1943.

Shirer, William. *Det tredje rikets uppgång och fall.* Forum, Stockholm 1989.

Shukman, Harold (ed.). *Stalin's Generals.* Grove Press, New York 1993.

Skripko, N. S. *Po tselyam blizhnim I dalyim.* Voyennoye Izdatelstvo Ministerstva oboronyy SSSR, Moscow 1980.

Slepyan, Kennet. *Stalin's Guerillas Soviet Partisans in World War II.* University Press of Kansas, Kansas 2006.

Slusser, Robert M., and Jan F. Triska. *A Calendar of Soviet Treaties, 1917–1957.* Stanford University Press, Stanford 1959.

Smilovitsky, Leonid. *Holocaust in Belorussia, 1941–1944.* Biblioteka Motveya Chernogo, Tel Aviv 2000.

Snyder, Timothy. *Bloodlands: Europe between Hitler and Stalin.* Basic Books, New York 2010.

Snyder, Timothy, and Ray Brandon (ed.). *Stalin and Europe: Imitation and Domination, 1928–1953.* Oxford University Press, New York 2014.

Stahel, David. *Operation Barbarossa and Germany's Defeat in the East.* Cambridge University Press, Cambridge 2015.

Stoll, Walter. *Nomaden in Uniform: meine Erinnerungen an die Kriegsjahre 1939–1945. Geschichte des Infanterie-Regiments 107.* Eigenverlag/Kameradschaft Rgt. 107, 1978.

Strauss, Franz Josef. *Die Geschichte der 2. (Wiener) Panzer-Division.* Dörfler, Eggolsheim, n.d.

Temchin, Michael. *The Witch Doctor: Memoirs of a Partisan.* Holocaust Library, New York 1983.

von Tettau, Hans. *Die Geschichte der 24. Infanterie-Division.* Dörfler Verlag, Eggolsheim-Bammersdorf 2005.

The German Army and the Genocide: Crimes Against War Prisoners, Jews, and Other Civilians, 1939–1944. The New Press, New York 1999.

Thurston, Robert W. and Bernd Bonwetsch (ed.). *The People's War: Responses to World War II in the Soviet Union.* University of Illinois Press, Chicago 2000.

Tieke, Wilhelm. *Kampf um die Krim.* Private edition, Erbland, n.d.

Tolstoy, Nikolay. *Stalin's Secret War.* Pan Books, London 1982.

Tooze, Adam. *The Wages of Destruction: The Making and Breaking of the Nazi Economy.* Penguin Books, London 2008.

Tumarkin, Nina. *The Living And The Dead: The Rise And Fall Of The Cult Of World War II In Russia.* Basic Books, New York 1995.

Ueberschär, Gerd R. and Wolfram Wette (ed). *Der deutsche Überfall auf die Sowjetunion.* Fischer Taschenbuch Verlag, Frankfurt a.M. 1999.

Vershinin, K. A. *Chetvertaya vozdushnaya.* Voyenizdat, Moscow 1975.

Verton, Hendrik C. *In the Fire of the Eastern Front: The Experiences of a Dutch Waffen-SS Volunteer, 1941–45.* Stackpole Books, Mechanicsburg 2005.

Voznesensky, N. A. *Soviet Economy during the Second World War.* International Publishers, New York, n.d.

Waiss, Walter. *Boelcke-Archiv, Band III: Chronik Kampfgeschwader Nr. 27 Boelcke: Teil 2: 01.01.1941–31.12.1941.* Private edition, Neuss, n.d.

Wassiljewa, Tatjana. *Hostage To War: A True Story.* Scholastic Inc., New York 1, 1999.

Die Wehrmachtsberichte 1939–1945. Band 1 – 1. September 1939 bis 31. Dezember 1941. Gesellschaft für Literatur und Bildung, Köln 1989.

Wegner-Korfes, Sigrid. *Weimar, Stalingrad, Berlin: Das Leben des deutschen Generals Otto Korfes.* Verlag der Nation, 1994.

Weiss, Jakob. *The Lemberg Mosaic: The Memoirs of Two Who Survived the Destruction of Jewish Galicia.* Alderbook Press, New York 2011.

Westerlund, Lars (ed.). *Prisoners of War and Internees: A Book of Articles by the National Archives / Sotavangit ja internoidut: Kansallisarkiston artikkelikirja.* National Archives of Finland, Helsinki 2008.

Whymant, Robert. *Stalin's Spy: Richard Sorge and the Tokyo Espionage Ring.* Palgrave MacMillan, New York 1996.

Winter, Franz F. *Die deutschen Jagdflieger: Eine Dokumentation.* Universitas Verlag, Munich 1993.

Zetterling, Niklas, and Anders Frankson. *The Drive on Moscow: Operation Taifun and Germany's First Great Crisis in World War II.* Casemate, Philadelphia & Oxford 2012.

Ziemke, Earl. *The German Northern Theater of Operations, 1940–1945. Pamphlet No. 20-271.* Department of the Army, Washington 1959.

Zimmerman, Joshua D. *The Polish Underground and the Jews, 1939–1945.* Cambridge University Press, New York 2015.

Zjukov, Georgij. *Minnen och reflexioner.* Progress, Moscow 1988.

Zubkov, R. A. *Tallinskiy Krasnoznamyonnogo flota.* Kuchkovo pole, Moscow 2012.

Zvyagintsev, Vyacheslav Yegorovich. *Tribunal dlya "Stalinskikh sokol".* Terra, Moscow 2008.

Periodicals.

Aviamaster.
Aviatsiya i Kosmonavtika.
Baltic Defence Review.
Espacio, tiempo y forma. Serie V, Historia contemporánea.
Europe-Asia Studies.
Haaretz.
Journal of Military and Strategic Studies.
Journal of Slavic Military Studies.
Journal of the Army War College Carlisle.
Krasnaya Zvezda.
Lithuanian Quarterly Journal of Arts and Sciences.
Mir Aviatsii.
Sotsiologicheskie issiedovaniya.
Sunday Times.
US Army Reserve, Journal of the Army War College Carlisle.
Vierteljahrsheften für Zeitgeschichte.
Voyenno-Istoricheskiy Zhurnal.
World War II Magazine.
Yad Vashem Studies.

CHAPTER NOTES.

Notes to Chapter 1.

1   Medvedev, Roy A. *Stalin och stalinismen*, Stockholm: Prisma, 1981, p. 116.
2   Elleinstein, Jean. *Stalinfenomenets historia*, Lund: Arbetarkultur, 1977, p. 133.
3   "The Terror of Bureaucratic Self-Preservation", 6 September 1935. In Trotsky, Leon, *Writings of Leon Trotsky, 1935–36*. New York: Pathfinder Press, 1977. p. 120.
4   "The Beginning of the End", 12 June 1937. In Trotsky, Leon, *Writings of Leon Trotsky, 1936–37*. New York: Pathfinder Press, 1978. p. 325.

Notes to Chapter 2.

1   "Hitlers Entschluss zum 'Lebensraum'–Krieg im Osten." In *Der deutsche Überfall auf die Sowjetunion*, ed. Gerd R. Ueberschär and Wolfram Wette. Frankfurt am Main: Fischer Taschenbuch, 1999. p. 19.
2   Ericson, *Feeding the German Eagle: Soviet Economic Aid to Nazi Germany, 1933–1941*, pp. 195–199.
3   Halder, Diary, Vol. V, p.50.
4   International Military Tribunal, Nürnberg, 14 November 1945 to.October 1946, Volume 31, p. 84, Doc.. 2718-PS.
5   Hillgruber, Andreas, "War in the East and the Extermination of the Jews", in Marrus, Michael. Part 3, *The "Final Solution": The Implementation of Mass Murder*, Volume 1. The Nazi Holocaust. Westpoint, CT, 1989: Meckler. pp. 85–114.
6   Oberkommando der Wehrmacht, WFST/Abt. L. (IV/Qu) Nr. 44822/41 g.K.Chefs.

Notes to Chapter 3.

1   "The Fall and Rise of Marshal Tukhachevsky" by Major William J. Mc Granahan, US Army Reserve, Journal of the Army War College Carlisle, PA, 1978.
2   Ibid.
3   Habeck, *Storm of Steel: The Development of Armor Doctrine in Germany and the Soviet Union, 1919–1939*, p. 277.
4   Glantz and House, *When Titans Clashed*, p. 24.
5   Forczyk, *Tank Warfare on the Eastern Front 1941–1942*, p. 15.
6   Habeck, *Storm of Steel: The Development of Armor Doctrine in Germany and the Soviet Union, 1919–1939*, p. 276.
7   Halder, Diary, 19 July 1941.
8   Askey, *Operation Barbarossa: the Complete Organisational and Statistical Analysis*, Vol. IIa, p. 93.
9   "Das Scheitern der wirtschaftlichen 'Blitzkriegstrategie" by Rolf-Dieter Müller in Boog, Horst, Jürgen Förster, et al. *Das Deutsche Reich und der Zweite Weltkrieg. Band 4: Der Angriff auf die Sowjetunion*, p. 977.
10 Generalmajor Burkhart, in cooperation with Generaloberst Franz Halder and Generalleutnant Emil Leeb. Study MS P-059. *German Tank Strength and Loss Statistics*, p. 26.

Notes to Chapter 4.

1   Halder, Diary 30 March 1941.
2   Ziemke, *The German Northern Theater of Operations, 1940–1945*. Kindle ed., Location 2528.
3   yale.edu/lawweb/avalon/imt/proc/02-08-46.htm.

4   Murphy, *What Stalin Knew*, p. 91.
5   Ibid., p. 85.
6   Ibid., p. 65.
7   Ibid., p. 65.
8   Ibid., p. 69.
9   Ibid., p. 165.
10 Tolstoy, *Stalin's Secret War*, pp. 219–220.
11 Murphy, p. 69.
12 Ibid., p. 69.
13 Ibid., p. 101.
14 "Offense, Defence or the Worst of Both Worlds? Soviet Strategy in May–June 1941" by Alexander Hill in Journal of Military and Strategic Studies. Vol. 13, Issue 1, Fall 2010.
15 Murphy, p. 101.
16 TsAMO, f. 11th Army.
17 "Razvedka Bila Trevogu" by Pyotr I. Ivashutin in Krasnaya Zvezda, 2 February 1991. Quoted in Murphy, p. 149.
18 Pleshakov, *Stalin's Folly: The Tragic First Ten Days of World War II on the Eastern Front*, p. 99.
19 Boldin, *Stranitsyy zhizni*, p. 83.

Notes to Chapter 5.

1   Ostermann, *Vom Häschen zum As*, p. 121.
2   TsAMO, f. 122 IAP.
3   TsAMO, f. 70 GShAP.
4   Bundesarchiv-Militärarchiv. RL 2 II/246.
5   Kempowski, *Das Echolot*, p. 22.
6   Interview with Roman Yevseyevich by Artem Drabkin.
7   G. Habedanck, "Bei Brest-Litovsk über die Grenze" in *Die Wehrmacht*, 1941.
8   Scheja and Chiariello, *The Man in the Black Fur Coat: A Soldier's Adventures on the Eastern Front*, p. 12.
9   Kempowski, p. 36.
10 Ibid., p. 54.
11 Tolstoy, p. 226.
12 Boldin, p. 84.
13 Pleshakov, p. 106.
14 Erickson, *The Road to* Stalingrad, p. 119.
15 Boldin, p. 85.
16 Erickson, p. 120.
17 Halder, Diary 22 June 1941.
18 Balke, *Der Luftkrieg in Europa 1939–1945*, p. 427.
19 Bundesarchiv-Militärarchiv, RL 2 II/246.
20 Quoted in Balke, p. 308.
21 TsAMO, f. 35, op. 11285, d. 233, l. 1, 16; TsAMO, f. 208, op. 2526, l. 214–215; Skripko, *Po tselyam blizhnim I dalyim*, p. 68.
22 Kamenir, *The Bloody Triangle: The Defeat of Soviet Armor in the Ukraine, June 1941*, p. 77.
23 Bagramjan, *So begann der Krieg*, pp. 96–97.
24 Kamenir, p. 81.
25 Kulikov, *Operatsiya Barbarossa*, p. 42.
26 Ibid., p. 23.
27 Halder, Diary, 22 June 1941.
28 Bundesarchiv/Militärarchiv, RL 10/287.
29 Hannes Trautloft, Diary, 22 June, 1941.
30 Bekker, *The Luftwaffe War Diaries*, p. 317.
31 Halder, Diary, 22 June 1941.
32 Kriegstagebuch Panzergruppe 3.

33 Hoth, *Panzer Operations: Germany's Panzer Group 3 During the Invasion of Russia, 1941*. Kindle version, Location 755.

34 Kriegstagebuch 7. Panzer-Division

35 TsAMO, f. 5th Tank Division.

Notes to Chapter 6.

1 Clark, *Barbarossa*, p. 51.
2 TsAMO, f. 38, op. 11360, d. 1, l. 65.
3 Boldin, p. 89.
4 Ibid.
5 Ibid., p. 90.
6 Ibid., p. 95.
7 TsAMO, f. 38, op. 11360, d. 2, l. 290, 291.
8 Interview with Hermann Neuhoff.
9 Boldin, p. 99.
10 TsAMO, f. 9. Op. 39. D. 98. L. 330–340.
11 Boldin, p. 100.
12 Guderian, *Panzer Leader*, p. 154.
13 Glantz and House, *When Titans Clashed*, p. 52.
14 Kempowski, p. 191.
15 Fiala, *"Österreicher" in den SS-Einsatzgruppen und SS-Brigaden: die Tötungsaktionen in der Sowjetunion 1941–1942*, p. 63.
16 Bundesarchiv/Militärarchiv, RH 27-18/24.
17 Bundesarchiv/Militärarchiv, RH 27-18/175.
18 Ibid.
19 Fiala, p. 64.
20 Interview with Malkus Boris Lyubovits by Artem Drabkin.
21 Bagramjan, p. 97.
22 Halder, Diary 23 June 1941.
23 TsAMO, f. 212 AP DD.
24 Kulikov, p. 46.
25 Mahlke, *Stuka, Angriff: Sturzflug*, p. 141.
26 TsAMO, f. 43 IAD; Bundesarchiv/Militärarchiv RL 2 III/755.
27 Bundesarchiv/Militärarchiv RL 2 III/755.
28 Kohl, *Ich wundere mich, dass ich noch lebe*, p. 68.
29 Mahlke, p. 141.
30 Rhodes, *Masters of Death*, p. 38.
31 Kempowski, p. 79.
32 Gertjejanssen, *Victims, Heroes, Survivors: Sexual Violence on the Eastern Front during World War II*, p. 267.
33 Interview with Friedrich Falevich. Centropa. Preserving Jewish memory–Bringing history to life. centropa.org/biography/friedrich-falevich.
34 Bundesarchiv-Militärarchiv RH 26-5/7, Kriegstagebuch (Ia) der 5. Infanteriedivision, 28 June 1941, p. 55.
35 Bundesarchiv-Militärarchiv. RL 2 II/246.
36 Bundesarchiv/Militärarchiv RL 2 III/755.
37 Bundesarchiv/Militärarchiv RL 2 III/755.
38 Tagesmedlungen der Operations-Abteilung des GenStdH, 28 June 1941. Schramm (ed.), *Kriegstagebuch des Oberkommandos der Wehrmavht. Teilband II*–hereafter KTB KOW, Vol. II, p. 499.
39 Bundesarchiv-Militärarchiv RH 19/II/128. Tagesmeldungen der Heeresgruppe Mitte.
40 NARA, T-315, Roll 876, Frame 307. Kriegstagebuch der 34. Infanterie-Division, Kriegstagebuch Nr. 4: Tätigkeitsbericht vom 27. August 1941 für die Zeit vom 1. Juli – 31. Juli 1941.
41 Kriegschronik Band XIV, from Winter, Die deutschen Jagdflieger, p. 98.
42 Plocher, *The German Air Force Versus Russia 1941*, p. 88.
43 Zjukov, *Minnen och reflektioner*, p. 275.
44 Bundesarchiv/Militärarchiv RL 2 III/755
45 Schäufler, *Panzer Warfare on the Eastern Front*, p. 13.

46 Bundesarchiv-Militärarchiv. RL 2 II/247.
47 Erickson, p. 158.
48 Tagesmedlungen der Operations-Abteilung des GenStdH, 30 June 1941. KTB OKW, Vol. II, p. 502.
49 Krivosheev, *Rossiya i SSSR v voynakh XX veka: Poteri vooruzhennykh sil*, p. 267.
50 NARA, T-315, Roll 876, Frame 1082. Korpsbefehl (XII. A.K.) vom 4. Juli 1941 für die Fortsetzung des Vormarsches am 5. Juli 1941, AZ: Ia op. Nr. 13 (Anlagenband Nr. 1 zum Kriegstagebuch Nr. 4).
51 Reese, *Why Stalin's Soldiers Fought*, p. 90.
52 Cohen, *Smolensk under the Nazis: Everyday Life in Occupied Russia*, p. 49.
53 Plocher, 1941, p. 91.
54 Pshenyahik, *Sovetskie Voenno-vozdushnye sily v bor'be s nemetsko-fashistskoy aviatsiey v letne-osenney kampanii 1941 g.*, p. 94.
55 Ibid.
56 Bundesarchiv/Militärarchiv RL 2 III/754–756.

Notes to Chapter 7.

1 Bundesarchiv-Militärarchiv, RH 27-8/9: Kriegstagebuch 8. Panzer-Division.
2 KTB OKW, Vol. II, p. 491.
3 TsAMO, f. 5th Tank Division.
4 Glantz, *The Initial Period of War on the Eastern Front, 22 June–August 1941*, p. 93.
5 Interview with Hans-Ekkehard Bob.
6 Glantz, *The Initial Period of War on the Eastern Front, 22 June–August 1941*, p. 90.
7 Bundesarchiv/Militärarchiv RL 2 III/754.
8 Nikžentaitis, Schreiner, and Staliūnas, *The Vanished World of Lithuanian Jews*, p. 195.
9 Rhodes, p. 45.
10 NARA, NA film T311, roll 53, Heeresgruppe Nord War Diary.
11 "The Lithuanian Revolt Against the Soviets in 1941" by Zenonas Ivinskis, University of Bonn, in Lituanus: Lithuanian Quarterly Journal of Arts and Sciences, Volume 12, No.2–Summer 1966.
12 Raus, *Panzer Operations*, p. 22.
13 Ibid., p. 22.
14 Ibid., p. 36.
15 Bundesarchiv/Militärarchiv, RL 10/529.
16 Interview with Gerhard Baeker.
17 TsAMO f. 290, op. 3284, d. 19.
18 Hannes Trautloft, Diary 30 June 1941.
19 Bundesarchiv/Militärarchiv, RL 10/440.
20 Bundesarchiv/Militärarchiv, RL 10/529.
21 Bundesarchiv/Militärarchiv RL 2 III/754–756.
22 TsAMO, f. 41 SAD.
23 *Pobratimyy Nikolaya Gastello*, p. 278.
24 Bundesarchiv-Militärarchiv, RL II/267. Geheim-Akten über Lagebericht (Lw) vom 1.7. 1941 bis 12.7. 1941.
25 Carell, *Unternehmen Barbarossa*, p. 198.
26 Novikov, *V Nebe Leningrada*, p. 85.
27 KTB OKW, vol. II, p. 518.
28 Hannes Trautloft, Personal Diary. 27 July, 1941.
29 TsAMO, f.217, op.1221, d.4, ll.21–22.
30 Haupt, *Heeresgruppe Nord*, p. 56.
31 *Pobratimyy Nikolaya Gastello*, p. 304.
32 Hannes Trautloft, Diary 16 July 1941.
33 Ibid.
34 Halder, Diary, 13 July 1941.
35 Bundesarchiv-Militärarchiv, RH 21-3/46; Halder, Diary, 13 July 1941.
36 Halder, Diary, 16 July 1941.

37 Ibid.
38 Raus, p. 54.
39 Ibid.
40 Hannes Trautloft, Diary 16 July 1941.
41 *Pobratimyy Nikolaya Gastello*, p. 309.
42 Askey, *Operation Barbarossa: The Complete Organisational and Statistical Analysis, and Military Simulation, Volume IIa*, p. 383.
43 Forczyk, *Tank Warfare on the Eastern Front 1941–1942: Schwerpunkt*, p. 71.
44 Halder, Diary, 29 July 1941.

Notes to Chapter 8.

1 Kamenir, pp. 7 and 34.
2 Interview with Vasiliy Kurayev.
3 Bundesarchiv-Militärarchiv. RL 2 II/246.
4 Interview with Vasiliy Kurayev.
5 Bundesarchiv-Militärarchiv, RL II/267. Geheim-Akten über Lagebericht (Lw) vom 16.6. 1941 bis 30.6. 1941. Lagebericht Nr. 699.Lagebericht Nr. 654.
6 Bundesarchiv-Militärarchiv. RL 2 II/246.
7 Bundesarchiv-Militärarchiv RL 2 III/754–756.
8 TsAMO, f. VVS Southwestern Front, 1f, op. 181, d. 47, ll. 40-77.
9 Bundesarchiv-Militärarchiv, RL II/267. Geheim-Akten über Lagebericht (Lw) vom 16.6. 1941 bis 30.6. 1941. Lagebericht Nr. 699.Lagebericht Nr. 654.
10 Interview with Ariya Simeon Lvovich by Artem Drabkin.
11 Kamenir, p. 129.
12 Schrodek, *Ihr Glaube galt dem Vaterland: Geschichte des Panzer-Regiments 15*, pp. 127–128.
13 Ryabyshev, *Pervyy god voynyy*, p. 24.
14 TsAMO, f. 8th Mechanized Corps.
15 Ryabyshev, p. 24.
16 Rokossovskiy, *Soldatskiy Dolg*, pp. 16–17.
17 Interview with Sergey Andreyevich Otrochenkov by Artem Drabkin.
18 Bundesarchiv-Militärarchiv, RL II/267. Geheim-Akten über Lagebericht (Lw) vom 16.6. 1941 bis 30.6. 1941. Lagebericht Nr. 655.
19 Zjukov, p. 262.
20 Bundesarchiv/Militärarchiv RL 7/471.
21 Schrodek, p. 131.
22 Kamenir, p. 183.
23 TsAMO, f. 86 BAP.
24 Bagramjan, p. 150.
25 Kamenir, pp. 42 and 242.
26 Krivosheev, *Rossiya i SSSR v voynakh XX veka: Poteri vooruzhennykh sil*, p. 268.
27 Dierich, *Kampfgeschwader 51 "Edelweiss"*, p. 159.
28 Kempowski, p. 163.
29 Kempowski, p. 208.
30 Rhodes, p. 64.
31 Rossolinski, *Stepan Bandera: the Life and Afterlife of a Ukrainian Nationalist: Fascism, Genocide and Cult*, p. 193.
32 Reese, p. 182.
33 de Zayas, *The Wehrmacht War Crimes Bureau, 1939–1945*, p. 164.
34 Brandon and Lower, *The Shoah in Ukraine*, p. 27.
35 Bundesarchiv-Militärarchiv, RL II/267. Geheim-Akten über Lagebericht (Lw) vom 1.7. 1941 bis 12.7. 1941.
36 Bundesarchiv/Militärarchiv RL 2 III/754–756.
37 Bagramjan, p. 180.
38 Ibid., p. 182.
39 Ibid., p. 189.
40 Mir Aviatsii, 2/97.
41 Halder, Diary, 11 July.
42 TsAMO, f. 74 ShAP.

Notes to Chapter 9.

1 Hoth, *Panzer Operations: Germany's Panzer Group 3 During the Invasion of Russia, 1941*. Kindle version, Location 1301.
2 Glantz, *Barbarossa Derailed*, p. 59.
3 Watch at youtube.com/watch?v=ZORVvgTrUlg.
4 Glantz, *Barbarossa Derailed*, Vol. 1, p. 57.
5 Kempowski, p. 225.
6 Gertjejanssen, p. 300.
7 Interview with Ion Lazarevich Degen by Artem Drabkin.
8 Bundesarchiv-Militärarchiv. RL 2 II/248.
9 *Pobratimy Nikolaya Gastello*, p. 241.
10 Bundesarchiv-Militärarchiv, RL II/267. Geheim-Akten über Lagebericht (Lw) vom 1.7. 1941 bis 12.7. 1941.
11 Glantz, *Barbarossa Derailed*, p. 68.
12 NARA, T-313 Roll 86. 2nd Panzer Army War Diary (Kriegstagebuch), Russia Jul–Oct 41.
13 Bundesarchiv/Militärarchiv RL 8/49.
14 Bartov, *The Eastern Front, 1941–1945*, p. 19.
15 TsAMO, f. 3431, op. 1, d. 1, l. 39.
16 Mitcham, *The Panzer Legions*, p. 137.
17 Halder, Diary, 8 July 1941.
18 Guderian, *Panzer Leader*, Kindle Version, Location 2686.
19 Luftwaffe loss list via Matti Salonen.
20 iremember.ru/memoirs/minometchiki/ostapchuk-grigor-iy-danilovich.
21 Cohen, *Smolensk under the Nazis: Everyday Life in Occupied Russia*, p. 59.
22 Stahel, *Operation Barbarossa and Germany's Defeat in the East*, p.273.

Notes to Chapter 10.

1 Glantz and House, *Clash of Titans*, p. 68.
2 Bundesarchiv/Militärarchiv RL 21-2/927.
3 Bundesarchiv/Militärarchiv RH 27-4/10.
4 Bundesarchiv/Militärarchiv RH 24-47/2.
5 Bundesarchiv/Militärarchiv RL 10/287.
6 Interview with Nina Erdman by Artem Drabkin.
7 "Oruzhie Peshki" by V. Markovskiy and A. Medved, in *Aviamaster* 2/97.
8 TsAMO, f. 3 BAK.
9 Bundesarchiv-Militärarchiv RH 26-14/10. Kriegstagebuch Ia 14. Infanterie-Division (mot) vom 25.5.41–1.10.41.
10 TsAMO, f. 208, op. 2589, d. 3, l. 28.
11 NARA, Record Group No. 242/1028. Frontverluste der Fliegertruppe der SU, Ic/Ost. OKL/863.
12 Luftwaffe loss list via Matti Salonen.
13 Jentz, *Panzertruppen 1 : The Complete Guide to the Creation & Combat Employment of Germany's Tank Force, 1933–1942*, p. 212.
14 Halder, Diary, 4 and 17 August 1941.
15 Bartov, *The Eastern Front, 1941–1945*, pp. 19–20.
16 Halder, Diary, 26 July 1941.
17 Stahel, p. 309.
18 Ibid., p. 304.
19 NARA, T-313 Roll 86. 2nd Panzer Army War Diary (Kriegstagebuch), Russia Jul–Oct 41.
20 Barabanshchikov and Nekrylov, *Sbornik lyotchiki*, p. 35.
21 Plocher, p. 97.
22 KTB OKW, vol. II, p. 1040.
23 Stahel, p. 328.
24 Guderian, *Panzer Leader*, Kindle Version, Location 2791.
25 NARA, T-313 Roll 86. 2nd Panzer Army War Diary (Kriegstagebuch), Russia Jul–Oct 41.
26 Guderian, *Panzer Leader*, Kindle Version, Location 2791.
27 Halder, Diary 28 July 1941.
28 Erickson, p. 198.
29 Glantz, *Operation Barbarossa*, p. 76.

30 Heinrich Hoffmann, logbook.
31 Osipov, *V nebe bombardirovshchiki*, p. 147.
32 Bundesarchiv-Militärarchiv. Feindlagebericht Horchkompanie 611/AOK 2. 15 August 1941.
33 TsAMO, f. 69 GIAP.
34 Bundesarchiv-Militärarchiv. Feindlagebericht Horchkompanie 611/AOK 2. 17 August 1941.
35 TsAMO, f. 3 BAK.
36 KTB OKW, Vol. II, p. 565.
37 Plocher, 1941, pp. 103–104.
38 Bundesarchiv-Militärarchiv RL 10/287.
39 Interview with Hermann Neuhoff.
40 Ilin, *Gvardeutsyy v vozdukhe*, pp. 32–36.
41 Halder, Diary 22 August 1941.
42 Tagesmedlungen der Operations-Abteilung des GenStdH, 22 August 1941. KTB OKW, Vol. II, p. 584.
43 Bundesarchiv-Militärarchiv. RL 2 II/255.
44 Bundesarchiv-Militärarchiv. Feindlagebericht. Horchkompanie 611/AOK 2. 25 August 1941.
45 Frisch and Jones, *Condemned to Live: A Panzer Artilleryman's Five-Front War*, pp. 74–78.
46 Krivosheev, *Rossiya i SSSR v voynakh XX veka: Poteri vooruzhennykh sil*, p. 348.
47 NARA, T. 314, Roll 347, Frame 000628.
48 Stahel, p. 402.
49 Guderian, *Panzer Leader*, Kindle Version, Location 2897.

Notes to Chapter 11.

1 Kulikov, p. 50.
2 Bundesarchiv/Militärarchiv RL 7/471.
3 Inozemtsev, *Frontoy dnevnik*, Nauka, p. 28.
4 Halder, Diary, 8 August 1941.
5 Bundesarchiv/Militärarchiv RL 7/467.
6 Krivosheev, *Grif sekretnosti snyat: poteri vooruzhyonnykh sil SSSR v voynakh, boevykh deystviyakh i voennyh konfliktakh*, pp, 166–167.
7 KTB OKW, Vol. II, p. 560. 8 August 1941.
8 iremember.ru/memoirs/minometchiki/adamskiy-izo-davidovich.
9 Brandon and Lower, p. 28.
10 Baade, Behrendt and Blachstein, *"Unsere Ehre heißt Treue", Kriegstagebuch des Kommandostabes RFSS, Tätigkeitsberichte der 1. und 2. SS-Kav.-Brigade und von Sonderkommandos der SS. Europa Verlag*, pp. 105–106.
11 Klee, Dressen and Riess, *"The Good Old Days": The Holocaust as Seen by its Perpetrators and Bystanders*, p. 150.
12 Brandon and Lower, p. 30.
13 See yadvashem.org/untoldstories/database/germanReports.asp?cid=278&site_id=288.
14 TsAMO, f. 9. Op. 39. d. 98. ll. 315–317.
15 TsAMO, f. 88 IAP.
16 Bundesarchiv/Militärarchiv RL 2 III/754–756.
17 TsAMO, f. 88 IAP.
18 *Pobratimyy Nikolaya Gastello*, p. 265.
19 KTB OKW, vol. II, p.588.
20 Plocher, p. 72.
21 TsAMO, f. 228, op. 724, d. 32.
22 KTB OKW, vol. II, p. 594.
23 NARA, T-314 Roll 1097.XLVII Corps War Diary (Kriegstagebuch), Russia May–Sep 41.
24 Halder, Diary, 31 August 1941.
25 Tagesmedlungen der Operations-Abteilung des GenStdH, 1 September 1941. KTB OKW, Vol. II, p. 605.
26 Halder, Diary, 4 September 1941.
27 Guderian, *Panzer Leader*, Kindle Version, Location 3120.
28 National Archives, Kew. PRO Air 3/6.
29 Ibid.

30 Halder, Diary 9 September 1941.
31 Bagramjan, p. 325.
32 TsAMO, f. 346, op. 6755, d. 121.
33 NARA, T-313 Roll 86. 2nd Panzer Army War Diary (Kriegstagebuch), Russia Jul–Oct 41.
34 KTB OKW, vol. II, p. 632. September 13, 1941.
35 Plocher, pp. 127–128.
36 Bundesarchiv/Militärarchiv RL 7/471.
37 Plocher, p. 130.
38 KTB OKW, vol. II, p. 661.
39 Krivosheev, *Grif sekretnosti snyat: poteri vooruzhyonnykh sil SSSR v voynakh, boevykh deystviyakh i voennyh konfliktakh*, pp. 166–167.
40 Ibid.

Notes to Chapter 12.

1 Artemyev, *Morkaya Aviatsiya Rossii*, pp. 153–154; Boyevoy put'Sovetskogo Voyenno-Morskogo Flota, 4th ed., p. 242.
2 KTB OKW, Vol. II, p. 522. 13 July 1941.
3 TsAMO, f. 217, op. 1260, d. 947, l. 2; Bundesarchiv-Militärarchiv, RL 2 III/754–756.
4 Halder, Diary, 26 July 1941.
5 Bundesarchiv/Militärarchiv, RL 10/529.
6 Bundesarchiv/Militärarchiv, RL 10/526.
7 Baltic Defence Review No. 9 Volume 1/2003, p. 180.
8 OKL, Führungsstab Ic, geheime Kommandosachen, Lagebericht Nr. 702. 11 August 1941.
9 TsAMO, f. 217, op. 1260, d. 283.
10 KTB OKW, vol. II, p. 564.
11 Inozemtsev, *Pod Krylom Leningrad*, p. 61; Bundesarchiv/Militärarchiv RL 2 III/754–756.
12 OKL, Führungsstab Ic, geheime Kommandosachen, Lagebericht Nr. 702. 11 August 1941.
13 Inozemtsev, *Pod Krylom Leningrad*, p. 61.
14 TsVMA, f. 3, op. 2421, d. 8, l. 86.
15 Raus, p. 75.
16 Salisbury, *The 900 Days*, p. 197.
17 Archiv JG 54. Staffel-Chronik der III. Jagdgeschwader 54, 7. Staffel. 18 August 1941.
18 Haupt, *Die 8. Panzer-Division im 2. Weltkrieg*. Podzun-Pallas Verlag, Eggolsheim, 1987, p. 168.
19 TsAMO, f. 11-y otdel, nagradnaya kartochka Z.G. Kolobanova.
20 Forczyk, *Tank Warfare on the Eastern Front 1941–1942*. Kindle version, location 1835.

Notes to Chapter 13.

1 Ziemke, *The German Northern Theater of Operations, 1940–1945*. Kindle edition, Location 2528.
2 Ibid., p. 43.
3 Ziemke, Location 2793.
4 Ibid., Location 2825.
5 Sandström, p. 48.
6 Carell, p. 370.
7 Via Carl-Fredrik Geust.
8 Anttonen and Valtonen, *Luftwaffe Suomessa – in Finland 1941–1944*, p. 15.
9 Ziemke, Location 2825.
10 Halder, Diary, 25 June 1941.
11 Interview with Nikolay Gapeyonok.
12 "V boyah uchilis' pobezhdat" by V. Babkin in *Aviatsiya i Kosmonavtika*, 8/1991.
13 Halder, Diary, 9 July 1941.
14 Quoted in "Baptism in the Northwoods: SS-Kampfgruppe Nord at Salla, 1941" by Jason Long, Sturmvogel, members.tripod.com/~Sturmvogel/nord-salla.html.
15 TsAMO, f. 3000, op. 1, d. 1, l. 42.

16 Bundesarchiv-Militärarchiv, RL II/219. ObdH, FSt Ic. Lagebericht Nr. 667 and 668.

17 TsAMO, f. 3000, op. 1, d. 1, l. 42.

18 Durasova, *Budet zhit rodina–budem zhit I myy*, p. 8.

19 Halder, Diary, 6 July 1941.

20 TsAMO, f. 214, op. 1566, d. 1.

21 TsAMO, f. 217. op. 1260, d. 93, l. 440, 450.

22 Luftwaffe loss list via Matti Salonen.

23 Kursenkow, *Jagdflieger*, p. 25.

24 Luftwaffe loss list. Via Matti Salonen.

25 Ailsby, *Images of Barbarossa*, p. 130; Ziemke, p. 184.

26 Rune Rautio in Anttonen and Valtonen, p. 157.

27 Bundesarchiv/Militärarchiv RL 2 III/754–756.

28 Via Raimo Malkamäki.

Notes to Chapter 14.

1 TsAMO, f. 217, op. 1260, d. 93, ll. 4, 17.

2 Gundelach, *Kampfgeschwader General Wever 4*, p. 151.

3 TsVMA, f. 3 GIAP.

4 TsAMO, f. 217, op. 1260, d. 71, ll. 73–76.

5 KTB OKW, vol. II, p. 631.

6 Hannes Trautloft, Diary, 15 September 1941.

7 Luknitskiy, *Leningrad deystvuyet*, p. 188.

8 Bundesarchiv/Militärarchiv RL 2 III/754–756.

9 Ring and Girbig, *Jagdgeschwader 27*, p. 70.

10 Golubev, *Vtoroye dykhani*, pp. 62–63.

11 Haupt, *Heeresgruppe Nord*, p. 97.

12 Ibid., p. 97.

Notes to Chapter 15.

1 NARA, Record Group No. 242/1028. Frontverluste der Fliegertruppe der SU, Ic/Ost. OKL/863.

2 Zetterling and Frankson, *The Drive on Moscow*, p. 253.

3 Lopukhovsky, *The Viaz'ma Catastrophe, 1941: The Red Army's Disastrous Stand Against Operation Typhoon*, p. 79.

4 TsAMO, f. 208, Op. 2513, d. 83, l. 176.

5 Krivosheyev, *Grif sekretnosti snyat. Poteri vooruzhyonnykh sil SSSR v voynakh, boyevykh deystviyakh i voyennykh konfliktakh*, p. 171; Groehler, *Geschichte des Luftkriegs*, p. 331.

6 Hansgeorg Bätcher, logbook.

7 Bundesarchiv-Militärarchiv, RL II/269. ObdH, FSt Ic. Lagebericht Nr. 755.

8 Bundesarchiv-Militärarchiv, RL 2 III/754–756 and RL 2 II/262.

9 KTB OKW, Vol. II, p. 675.

10 Bundesarchiv-Militärarchiv, RL II/269. ObdH, FSt Ic. Lagebericht Nr. 756.

11 Schäufler, *Panzer Warfare on the Eastern Front*, p. 37.

12 Heinrich Hoffmann, logbook.

13 TsAMO, f. 6 IAK.

14 Ibid.

15 NARA, T-314 Roll 1310. LIII Corps Diary (Kriegstagebuch), Russia Feb–Dec 41.

16 Bundesarchiv-Militärarchiv, RL II/269. ObdH, FSt Ic. Lagebericht Nr. 757.

17 Katukov, *Na ostriye glavnogo udara*, pp. 35–36.

18 Lopukhovsky, p. 135.

19 Zetterling and Frankson, p. 76.

20 Erickson, p. 217.

21 Bundesarchiv-Militärarchiv, RL 2 II/263.

22 *Pobratimy Nikolaya Gastello*, p. 281.

23 Schäufler, *Knights Cross Panzers*, p. 132.

24 Katukov, p. 44.

25 Bundesarchiv-Militärarchiv, RL II/269. ObdH, FSt Ic. Lagebericht Nr. 758.

26 Fast, *Das Jagdgeschwader 52*, vol. I, p. 137.

27 Plocher, p. 231.

28 Erickson, p. 221.

29 Viktor Anfilov, "Georgiy Konstantinovich Zhukov," in Shukman, Harold (ed.). *Stalin's Generals*, p. 350.

30 Bundesarchiv-Militärarchiv, RL II/269. ObdH, FSt Ic. Lagebericht Nr. 781.

31 Balke, p. 377.

32 Kriegstagebuch 4. Panzer-Division.

33 TsAMO, f. 4 SAD.

34 Fast, Vol. II, p. 64.

35 National Archives, Kew. PRO Air 40/1968.

36 Bundesarchiv/Militärarchiv RL 2 III/754–756.

37 Erickson, p. 219

38 Plocher, p. 231.

39 Hackler, *Vom Hoffen und Irren: eine deutsche Jugend in der Weimarer Republik und dem Deutschen Reich*, p. 205.

40 Nagorski, *The Greatest Battle*, p. 174.

41 Braithwaite, *Moskva 1941*, p. 307.

42 Ibid., p. 304.

43 Ibid., p. 312.

44 Shaposhnikov, *Bitva za Moskvu*, p. 56.

45 Interview with Gabass Zhurmatovich Zhurmatov by Artem Drabkin.

46 Kershaw, *War without Garlands*, p. 103.

47 Bundesarchiv/Militärarchiv, RL 8/49.

48 Stoll, *Nomaden in Uniform: meine Erinnerungen an die Kriegsjahre 1939–1945. Geschichte des Infanterie-Regiments 107*, p. 64.

49 Carell, p. 135.

50 Stoll, p. 64.

51 NARA, T-315, Roll 876, Frame 0518. Kriegstagebuch der 34. Infanterie-Division, Kriegstagebuch Nr. 4, Teil II. 30 October 1941.

52 Strauss, *Die Geschichte der 2. (Wiener) Panzer-Division*, p. 96.

53 Rokossovskiy, *Soldatskiy dolg*, p. 68.

54 Fast, *Das Jagdgeschwader 52*, vol. II, pp. 71–75.

55 Nauroth, *Stukageschwader 2 Immelmann*, p. 171.

56 Carell, p. 137.

57 Heim and Jochmann, *Adolf Hitler Monologe im Führerhauptquartier 1941–1944*, p. 22.

58 Irving, *Goebbels: Mastermind of the Third Reich*, p. 674.

59 Irving, *Hitler's War and The War Path*, p. 452.

60 Gilbert, *The Holocaust*, p. 184.

61 Smilovitsky, *Holocaust in Belorussia, 1941–1944*, p. 207.

62 Ibid., p. 58.

63 Interview with Fredrich Lang.

Notes to Chapter 16.

1 "Das Unternehmen Barbarossa als wirtschaftlicher Raubkrieg" by Rolf-Dieter Müller in Ueberschär and Wette, *Das deutsche Überfall auf die Sowjetunion*, p. 141.

2 Bunte and Jöberg. *Historia i siffror*, p. 33.

3 Ibid., p. 33.

4 Voznesensky, *Soviet Economy during the Second World War*, p. 39.

5 Ibid., p. 37.

6 "Das Unternehmen Barbarossa als wirtschaftlicher Raubkrieg" by Rolf-Dieter Müller in Ueberschär and Wette, *Das deutsche Überfall auf die Sowjetunion*, p. 145.

7 Bagramjan, p. 311.

8 KTB OKW, Vol. II, p. 657.

9 Bagramjan, p. 325.

10 Skripko, *Po tselyam blizhnim I dalyim*, p. 143.

11 KTB OKW, vol. II, p. 653.

12 Bergström, *Graf & Grislawski*, p. 43.

13 TsAMO, f. 24 AD.

14 Bundesarchiv/Militärarchiv, RL 7/471.

15 Plocher, p. 207.
16 TsAMO, f. 16 GIAP.
17 Interview with Aleksandr Pavlichenko.
18 IV. Fliegerkorps, Tagesabschlussmeldung October 7, 1941.
19 Vershinin, *Chetvertaya vozdushnaya*, p. 95.
20 KTB OKW, vol. II, p. 690.
21 TsAMO, f. 4 VA.
22 Vershinin, p. 95.
23 National Archives, Kew. PRO Air 334/11.
24 IV. Fliegerkorps, Tagesabschlussmeldung October 11, 1941.
25 TsAMO, f. 228, op. 724, d. 32.
26 KTB OKW, vol. II, p. 699.
27 National Archives, Kew. PRO Air 334/11.
28 Møller Hansen, *Troskab: Dansk SS-frivillig E.H. Rasmussens erindringer 1940–45*, p. 44.
29 KTB OKW, vol. II, p. 688.
30 Ibid., p. 699.
31 Ibid., p. 704.
32 Ibid., p. 712.
33 TsAMO, f. 7 GShAP.
34 KTB OKW, vol. II, p. 701.
35 Ibid., p. 710.
36 TsAMO, f. 228, op. 724, d. 32.
37 Bundesarchiv-Militärarchiv. RL 2 II/262–267.

Notes to Chapter 17.

1 TsAMO, f.131 IAP.
2 TsAMO f. 228, op. 724, d. 32.
3 KTB OKW, vol. II, p. 650.
4 Bundesarchiv-Militärarchiv, LIV. AK: Kriegstagebücher mit Anlagen für die Zeit vom 1.9. 1941–15.7.1942. Quoted in Tieke, Kampf um die Krim 1941–1944, p. 21.
5 Manstein, *Verlorene Siege*, p. 225.
6 KTB OKW, vol. II, p. 673.
7 Bundesarchiv-Militärarchiv, LIV. AK: Kriegstagebücher mit Anlagen für die Zeit vom 1.9. 1941–15.7.1942.
8 TsVMA, f. 11 GIAP.
9 Gordon Gollob, logbook.
10 Tieke, *Kampf um die Krim*, p. 29.
11 Gordon Gollob, Diary, 19 October 1941.
12 Tieke, pp. 31–35.
13 Bundesarchiv/Militärarchiv, RL 7/471.
14 Tieke, p. 68.
15 TsAMO, f. 288, op. 9900, d, 15, l. 7.
16 Luftwaffe loss list via Matti Salonen.

Notes to Chapter 18.

1 TsAMO, f. 208, op. 2511, d. 222.
2 Interview with Vsevolod Olimpev by Artem Drabkin.
3 Kriegstagebuch 2. Panzer-Division.
4 Carell, pp. 152–153.
5 TsAMO, f. 3rd Guards Cavalry Division.
6 Guderian, *Panzer Leader*, Kindle Version, Location 3524.
7 KTB OKW, Vol. II, p. 766.
8 Shaposhnikov, *Bitva za Moskvu*, pp. 34 and 36.
9 Halder, Diary, 19 November 1941.
10 National Archives, Kew. PRO Air 40/1989.
11 TsAMO, f. 228, op. 724, d. 32.
12 Bagramjan, p. 449.
13 *Pobratimyy Nikolaya Gastello*, p. 271.
14 KTB OKW, vol. II, p. 781.
15 Kershaw, *War without Garlands*, p. 117.
16 TsAMO, f. 228, op. 724, d. 32.
17 KTB OKW, vol. II, p. 789.
18 Kriegstagebuch JG 51. Quoted in Prien et al, *Die Jagdfliegerverbände der Deutschen Luftwaffe 1934 bis 1945, Teil 6/I*, p. 328.

19 Whymant, *Stalin's Spy: Richard Sorge and the Tokyo Espionage Ring*, p. 244.
20 Zetterling and Frankson, p. 253.
21 "Das Scheitern der wirtschaftlichen 'Blitzkriegstrategie" by Rolf-Dieter Müller in Boog, Horst, Jürgen Förster, et al. *Das Deutsche Reich und der Zweite Weltkrieg. Band 4: Der Angriff auf die Sowjetunion*, p. 977.
22 Hildebrand, Study MS P-059. *German Tank Strength and Loss Statistics*, p. 26.
23 TsAMO, f. 208, op. 2511, d. 222; TsAMO, f. 213, op. 2002, d. 28; TsAMO, f. 202, op. 2231, d. 11; Bundesarchiv/Militärarchiv RL 2 III/754–756.
24 Prien et al, *Die Jagdfliegerverbände der Deutschen Luftwaffe 1934 bis 1945, Teil 6/I*, p. 28; TsAMO, f. 208, op. 2511, d. 222; TsAMO, f. 213, op. 2002, d. 28; TsAMO, f. 202, op. 2231, d. 11.
25 Haupt, *Heeresgruppe Mitte*, p. 103.
26 KTB OKW, Vol. II, p. 794.
27 *Bitva za Moskvu*, p. 250.
28 TsAMO, f. 208, op. 2511, d. 222; TsAMO, f. 213, op. 2002, d. 28; TsAMO, f. 202.
29 KTB OKW, Vol. II, pp. 795 and 797.
30 Ibid., pp. 794–798.
31 Ibid., p. 801.
32 Kershaw, *War without Garlands*, p. 131.
33 Zjukov, p. 37.
34 Halder, Diary, 8 December 1941.
35 KTB OKW, vol. II, p. 806.
36 Zjukov, p. 45.
37 Halder, Diary, 9 December 1941.
38 Ibid.
39 Ibid., 10 December 1941.
40 TsAMO, f. 1st Guards Cavalry Corps.
41 KTB OKW, vol. II, p. 816.
42 Halder, Diary, 12 December 1941.
43 Halder, Diary, 9 December 1941.
44 KTB OKW, Vol. II, p. 820.
45 Bundesarchiv/Militärarchiv RL 2 III/754–756.
46 Guderian, Location 3709.
47 Halder, Diary, 14 December 1941.
48 Fast, *Das Jagdgeschwader 52*, vol. I, p. 140.
49 Forczyk, *Tank Warfare on the Eastern Front 1941-1942*. Kindle version, location 3844.
50 Guderian, Location 3815.
51 *Bitva za Moskvu*, p. 300.
52 Boris Olsyhanskiy, unpublished manuscript, quoted in Reese, *Why Stalin's Soldier's Fought*, p. 180.
53 V. Goncharyov in Martin, *Tagebuch eines sowjetischen Offiziers vom 1. Januar 1942–8. Februar 1942*, p. 354.
54 Halder, Diary, 15 December 1941.
55 Begishev, *Primenenie tankov*, quoted in "The Economics of War in the Soviet Union during World War II" by Jacques Sapir in Kershaw and Lewin (ed.), *Stalinism and Nazism: Dictatorships in Comparison*, p. 218.56 Halder, Diary 10 December 1941.
57 Schrodek, *Ihr Glaube galt dem Vaterland: Geschichte des Panzer-Regiments 15*.
58 Bundesarchiv/Militärarchiv RL 2 III/754–756.
59 KTB OKW, Vol. II, p. 865.

Notes to Results and Conclusions I.

1 Krivosheev, *Soviet Casualties and Combat Losses in the Twentieth Century*, pp. 95–98.
2 Glantz and House, *When Titans Clashed*, p. 292.
3 Krivosheev, pp. 95–98.
4 Ibid; TSAMO, f. 35, op. 11333, d. 23, l. 353; Bergström, Black Cross Red Star, Vol. I, p. 252.

5   KTB OKW, vol. II, p. 1106.

6   Pleshakov, *Stalin's Folly: The Tragic First Ten Days of World War II on the Eastern Front*, p. 99.

7   Kempowski, *Das Echolot*, p. 56.

8   See, e.g. Stahel, *Operation Barbarossa and Germany's Defeat in the West*, p. 446.

9   Bundesarchiv-Militärarchiv, RW 6/543, 19/1387–1392, KTB OKW, vol. II, pp. 1120–1121, Halder, Diary, 5 January 1942.

10 "Das Scheitern der wirtschaftlichen 'Blitzkriegstrategie" by Rolf-Dieter Müller in Boog, Horst, Jürgen Förster, et al. *Das Deutsche Reich und der Zweite Weltkrieg. Band 4: Der Angriff auf die Sowjetunion*, p. 977.

11 Bundesarchiv/Militärarchiv RL 2 III/754–756. Loss returns to the Generalquartiermeister der Luftwaffe.

12 Stahel, *Operation Barbarossa and Germany's Defeat in the West*, p. 445.

13 Kriegschronik Band XIV, from Winter, *Die deutschen Jagdflieger*, p. 98.

14 Bartov, *The Eastern Front 1941–45*, pp. 49–51.

15 Ueberschär, *Der deutsche Überfall auf die Sowjetunion*, p. 327.

16 Verton, *In the Fire of the Eastern Front*, p. 92.

17 Interview with Malkus Boris Lyubovits by Artem Drabkin.

18 Krivosheev, *Grif Sekretnosti*, pp. 168–171.

19 "Das Scheitern der wirtschaftlichen 'Blitzkriegstrategie" by Rolf-Dieter Müller in Boog, Horst, Jürgen Förster, et al. *Das Deutsche Reich und der Zweite Weltkrieg. Band 4: Der Angriff auf die Sowjetunion*, p. 977.

Notes to Results and Conclusions II.

1   Ueberschär and Wette, *Der deutsche Überfall auf die Sowjetunion*, p. 180.

2   Gertjejanssen, *Victims, Heroes, Survivors: Sexual Violence on the Eastern Front during World War II*, pp. 285–286.

3   Müller and Ueberschär, *Hitler's War in the East, 1941–1945: A Critical Assessment*, p. 215.

4   Goldhagen, *Hitler's Willing Executioners: Ordinary Germans and the Holocaust*, p. 290.

5   KTB OKW, vol. II, p. 1106.

6   "Die Behandlung der sowjetischen Kriegsgefangenen und völkerrechtliche Probleme" by Christian Streit in Ueberschär and Wette, p. 381.

7   Bundesarchiv-Militärarchiv, RW 19/415.

8   "Die Behandlung der sowjetischen Kriegsgefangenen und völkerrechtliche Probleme" by Christian Streit in Ueberschär and Wette, p. 160.

9   Westerlund, *Prisoners of War and Internees: A Book of Articles by the National Archives / Sotavangit ja internoidut: Kansallisarkiston artikkelikirja*, p. 9.

10 Hanski, *Behandlingen av krigsfångar under vinter- och fortsättningskriget: en folkrättslig studie*, p. 72.

11 TsKhIDK, f. 1p, op. 32-6, d. 2, ll. 8-9. Today in the collections of the RGVA.

12 Ibid.

13 Ibid.

14 Ibid.

15 Moore and Hately-Broad, *Prisoners of War, Prisoners of Peace: Captivity, Homecoming and Memory in World War II*, p. 124.

16 Limits of Intentionality by Oula Silvennoinen in Kinnunen and Kivimäki, *Finland in World War II*, p. 379.

17 Westerlund, p. 9.

18 Pohl, *Die Herrschaft der Wehrmacht: Deutsche Militärbesatzung und einheimische Bevölkerung in der Sowjetunion 1941–1944*, p. 231.

19 "Soviet Prisoners of War: Forgotten Nazi Victims of World War II" by Jonathan North in *World War II Magazine*, Jan./Feb. 2006.

20 Pohl, pp. 221–226.

21 "Soviet Prisoners of War: Forgotten Nazi Victims of World War II" by Jonathan North in *World War II Magazine*, Jan./Feb. 2006.

22 Pohl, p. 209.

23 Ibid.

24 "Die Behandlung der sowjetischen Kriegsgefangenen und völkerrechtliche Probleme" by Christian Streit in Ueberschär and Wette, p. 172.

25 "Soviet Prisoners of War: Forgotten Nazi Victims of World War II" by Jonathan North, in World War II Magazine, January/February 2006.

26 United States Holocaust Memorial Museum, "The Treatment of Soviet POWs: Starvation, Disease, and Shootings, June 1941–January 1942." ushmm.org/wlc/en/article.php?ModuleId=10007183.

27 Ibid.

28 Ibid.

29 Rossolinski, *Stepan Bandera: the Life and Afterlife of a Ukrainian Nationalist: Fascism, Genocide and Cult*, p. 193.

30 Snyder and Brandon, *Stalin and Europe: Imitation and Domination, 1928-1953*, p. 109.

31 Barkan, Elazar, et al, *Shared History, Divided Memory: Jews and Others in Soviet-occupied Poland, 1939–1941*, p. 292.

32 Ibid., p. 156.

33 Snyder and Brandon, p. 109.

34 Slepyan, *Stalin's Guerillas*, p. 80.

35 Ueberschär and Wette, p. 276.

36 "The Holocaust of Soviet Jewry in the Occupied Territories of the Soviet Union" by Yitzhak Arad in *Yad Vashem Studies* No. 21, 1991, p. 47.

37 Goldhagen, p. 202.

38 "Täter aus Überzeugung? Oberst Carl von Andrian und die Judenmorde der 707. Infanteriedivision 1941/42" by Peter Lieb in *Vierteljahrsheften für Zeitgeschichte*, Heft 4/2002. ifz-muenchen.de/heftarchiv/2002_4_1_lieb.pdf.

39 Pohl, p. 279, referring to Bundesarchiv-Militärarchiv, RH 19 II/127.

40 Ibid., p. 280.

41 Ibid., p. 270.

42 Heaton, *German Anti-Partisan Warfare in Europe: 1939–1945*, p. 207.

43 Braatz, *Gott oder Flugzeug*, p. 266.

44 Pohl, p. 269.

45 Korfes, *Weimar, Stalingrad, Berlin: Das Leben des deutschen Generals Otto Korfes*, pp. 90–91.

46 Barkan, Elazar, et al, p. 307.

47 Prien, *Geschichte des Jagdgeschwaders 77*, p. 692.

48 Pohl, p. 247.

49 Ibid., p. 245.

50 "Anti-Jewish Pogroms in Western Ukraine–A Research Agenda" by Dieter Pohl in Barkan, et al, *Shared History, Divided Memory: Jews and Others in Soviet-occupied Poland, 1939–1941*, p. 306.

51 Zimmerman, *The Polish Underground and the Jews, 1939–1945*, p. 96.

52 "Pogroms in Northeastern Poland – Spontaneous Reactions and German Instigations" by Andrzej Zbikowski in Barkan, Elazar, et al, *Shared History, Divided Memory: Jews and Others in Soviet-occupied Poland, 1939–1941*, p. 316.

53 Pohl, p. 245, referring to Bundesarchiv-Militärarchiv RW 4/v. 252.

54 Abramovich, *V reshayoshchey voyne: Uchastne I rol yevdeyev SSR v voyne protiv natsizma*, vol. 2, p. 536.

55 Arad, *Kholokaust: Katasrrofa evropeyskogo evreysta (1933–1945)*, p. 93.

56 Arad, *The Holocaust of Soviet Jewry in the Occupied Territories of the Soviet Union*, p. 47.

57 Tumarkin, *The Living And The Dead: The Rise And Fall Of The Cult Of World War II In Russia*, p. 68.

58 Interview with Mikhail Potapov.

59 Kohl, *Ich wundere mich, dass ich noch lebe*, p. 78.

60 "Holding a Heap of Ashes and Rubble" by Alvin J. Steinkopf, in New York Times, 12 August 1941, quoted in Cohen, *Smolensk under the Nazis: Everyday Life in Occupied Russia*, p. 59.

61 Bartov, *The Eastern Front 1941–45*, referring to Bundesarchiv-Militärarchiv, 27-18/181.

62 Josephson, Dronin, et al, *An Environmental History of Russia*, p. 116.

63 Ibid., p. 116.

64 Reese, p. 212.

65 Gertjejanssen, p. 74.

66 Ueberschär and Wette, p. 332.

67 Bundesarchiv, R 2/30675. RFM: Bedeutung der besetzten Ostgebiete nach der dt. Ein- und Ausfuhrstatistik (Ostbilanz), 30. Juli 1943.

68 "Soviet Deaths in the Great Patriotic War: A Note" by Michael Ellman and S. Maksudov in *Europe-Asia Studies*, Vol. 46, No. 4, 1994, p. 677.

69 "The Price of Victory: Myths and reality" by V. E. Korol in *Journal of Slavic Military Studies*, No. 9, June 1996, pp. 417–423.

70 "Zhertvy sredy mirnogo nasseleniya v gody otechestvennoy voyny" by A.A. Shevyako in *Sotsiologicheskie issiedovaniya*, No. 11, 1992.

71 Nolte, *Kleine Geschichte Russlands*, pp. 259f.

72 Morozov, *Kareliya v godyy Velikoy Otechestvennoynyy (1941–1945)*, p. 10.

73 Gertjejanssen, p. 72.

74 Kozhina, *Through the Burning Steppe: A Wartime Memoir*, pp. 43–44.

75 Bundesarchiv-Militärarchiv, RH 26-12/140. Kriegstagebuch 12. Infanterie-Division, 16.12 1941–31.8. 1942.

76 Frome, *Some Dare to Dream: Frieda Frome's Escape from Lithuania*, p. 37.

77 Wassiljewa, *Hostage To War: A True Story*, pp. 14–15.

78 Tooze, *The Wages of Destruction*, p. 483.

79 Interview by Professor Wendy Jo Gertjejanssen, Gertjejanssen, pp. 269–270.

80 Beevor, *Berlin: the Downfall 1945*.

81 Gertjejanssen, p. 319.

82 Ibid., p. 320.

83 "Sex-Based Violence and the Politics and Ethics of Survival" by Myrna Goldenberg, Ph.D. in Goldenberg, Myrna and Shapiro, *Different Horrors/Same Hell: Gender and the Holocaust*, p. 101.

84 Gertjejanssen, pp. 293–294, 298, 311; United States Holocaust Memorial Museum, RG-06.025: RIGA N-18313, tom 18, doc. 117.

85 Gertjejanssen, pp. 293–294, 298, 311; United States Holocaust Memorial Museum, RG-06.025: RIGA N-18313, tom 18, doc. 117.

86 Temchin, *The Witch Doctor: Memoirs of a Partisan*, p. 36.

87 Fangrad, *Wartime Rape And Sexual Violence: an examination of the perpetrators, motivations, and functions of sexual violence against Jewish women during the Holocaust*, p. 40.

88 Beevor, *Stalingrad*, p. 14.

89 Gertjejanssen, p. 254.

90 Ibid., p. 290.

91 Ibid., p. 254.

92 Ibid., p. 258.

93 Ibid., p. iii.

94 Ibid., p. 261.

95 Ibid., pp. 296–297.

96 Fangrad, p. 84.

97 Goldenberg and Shapiro, *Different Horrors/Same Hell: Gender and the Holocaust*, p. 109.

98 Gertjejanssen, p. 271.

99 Ibid., p. 154.

100 Ibid., p. 155.

101 Bundesarchiv-Militärchiv H 20/840. Bericht des Leitenden Sanitätsoffiziers beim Militärbefehlshaber im Generalgouvernement vom 2.10.1940.

102 Gertjejanssen, p. 172.

103 Ibid., p. 177.

104 "The Brothel Brigade" by W. Frischauer in *Sunday Times, Color Supplement*, 30 April 1972.

105 TsDAVOV (Kiev) f.1, op. 22, d.123, ll .13-15, cited in Gertjejanssen, p. 172.

106 Gertjejanssen, pp. 284ff.

107 Josephson, Dronin, et al. *An Environmental History of Russia*, p. 117.

108 Rees, *Their Darkest Hour*, p. 68.

109 Verton, p. 93.

110 Bartov, *Germany's War and the Holocaust*, p. 13.

111 Bartov, *Hitler's Army*, p. 156.

112 Ibid., p. 126.

113 Interview with Pavel Gurevich by Artem Drabkin.

Notes to Appendix I.

1 Reorganized into a Panzerkorps in July 1942, but since it operated as a Panzer corps in 1941, it is designated as a Panzerkorps in the narrative.

2 Reorganized into a Panzerkorps in March 1942, but since it operated as a Panzer corps in 1941, it is designated as a Panzerkorps in the narrative.

3 Reorganized into a Panzerkorps in July 1942, but since it operated as a Panzer corps in 1941, it is designated as a Panzerkorps in the narrative.

4 Reorganized into a Panzerkorps in June 1942, but since it operated as a Panzer corps in 1941, it is designated as a Panzerkorps in the narrative.

5 Reorganized into a Panzerkorps in June 1942, but since it operated as a Panzer corps in 1941, it is designated as a Panzerkorps in the narrative.

6 Reorganized into a Panzerkorps in June 1942, but since it operated as a Panzer corps in 1941, it is designated as a Panzerkorps in the narrative.

7 Reorganized into a Panzerkorps in June 1942, but since it operated as a Panzer corps in 1941, it is designated as a Panzerkorps in the narrative.

8 Reorganized into a Panzerkorps in June 1942, but since it operated as a Panzer corps in 1941, it is designated as a Panzerkorps in the narrative.

9 Reorganized into a Panzerkorps in June 1942, but since it operated as a Panzer corps in 1941, it is designated as a Panzerkorps in the narrative.

10 Reorganized into a Panzerkorps in June 1942, but since it operated as a Panzer corps in 1941, it is designated as a Panzerkorps in the narrative.

INDEX.

A.

Adamskiy, Izo 150, 151
Alex, Ernst 113
Allakhverdov, Mladshiy Leytenant 228
Alperenko, V. I. 124
Amarilis, ship 120
Antonescu, Ion 45, 47, 151
Arājs, Viktors 104
Arkhipenko, Fyodor 55, 69
Armeniya, passenger ship 230, 232
Astakhov, Fyodor 118, 159, 215
Avdeyev, Aleksandr 188
Avdeyevskiy, Feodosiy 114

B.

Baeker, Gerhard 53, 54, 57, 96
Bagramyan, Ivan 118
Bandera, Stepan 114, 115
Bär, Heinz 125, 135, 141, 156, 241, 255
Bätcher, Hansgeorg 51, 129, 130, 133, 143, 243
Belov, Pavel 247, 250
Belskiy brothers 146
Bereznikova, V. N. 124
Berggren, Hans 177
Beriya, Lavrentiy 114, 191, 199, 201, 202, 259
Beyer, Franz 118
Bezposhchadnyy, destroyer 231, 233
Bezuprechnyy, destroyer 231
Bix, Hermann 194
Blazytko, Franz 189
Blobel, Paul 153, 226
Blumentritt, Günther 205
Blunt, Anthony 49
Blyukher, Vasiliy 37
Bob, Hans-Ekkehard 100, 109, 211
von Bock, Fedor 28, 86, 128, 134, 138, 139, 144, 156, 157, 246, 247, 250, 260
Bodryy, destroyer 232
Bogdanov, Ivan 134
Boldin, Ivan 60, 71
Bolshevik, transport ship 234
Bolygin, Nikolay 224
Boos, Hans 141
Borisenko, Yevgeniy 75
Bormann, Martin 268
Borok, Robert 66
Boy-Zelenski, Tadeusz 115
Brandt, Wim 124, 126
von Brauchitsch, Walther 134, 139
Braun, Georg 226, 285
Bretnütz, Heinz 62
Brinko, Pyotr 185

British units
  81 Squadron, RAF 182
  134 Squadron, RAF 182
  151 Wing, RAF 182
  801 Squadron, Fleet Air Arm 176
  809 Squadron, Fleet Air Arm 176
  812 Squadron, Fleet Air Arm 176
  817 Squadron, Fleet Air Arm 176
  827 Squadron, Fleet Air Arm 176
  828 Squadron, Fleet Air Arm 176–177

Broich, Paul 229
Bruskina, Mariya Borisovna 129
Budyonnyy, Semyon 277
Buchholz, Max 79
Bagurskiy, Politruk 195, 196
Bukatschek, Otto 84
Bulganin, Nikolay 199
Bulvičius, Vytautas 92
Burda, A. 195
Buschenhagen, Erich 46

C.

Cairncross, John 49
Canaris, Wilhelm 48
Carius, Otto 64
Carol, Romanian king 45
Chebotaryov, Ivan 104
Chelpan, Konstantin 38
Cherevichenko, Yakov 221
Chernov, Ivan 59, 254
Chernykh, Sergey 54, 63
Chervona Ukraina, cruiser 232
Chulkov, Ivan 129
Churchill, Winston 144, 158, 176
Cohrs, Alexander 74
von Cossart, Manfred 54
von Cossel, Hans-Detloff 123, 126, 197

D.

Danilov, Andrey 61
Degen, Ion 124
Deicke, Joachim 152
Dekanozov, Vladimir 50
Demchenkov, Filipp 240
Demelhuber, Karl 272
Demyonok, Vasiliy 153
Denikin, Anton 37
Denisov, Konstantin 231
Dietl, Eduard 170, 173
Dietrich, Fritz 270
Dietrich, Josef "Sepp" 149
Dinort, Oskar 128

Previous books by Christer Bergström

Luftstrid över Kanalen, 1983

Mot avgrunden: Spelet som ledde till andra världskriget, 1991

Luftwaffe Fighter Aircraft in Profile, 1997

Deutsche Jagdflugzeuge, 1999

Black Cross/Red Star: The Air War over the Eastern Front, Vol. 1, 2000

Black Cross/Red Star: The Air War over the Eastern Front, Vol. 2, 2001

More Luftwaffe Fighter Aircraft in Profile, 2002

Graf & Grislawski: A Pair of Aces, 2003

Jagdwaffe: Barbarossa – the Invasion of Russia, 2003

Jagdwaffe: The War in Russia January–October 1942, 2003

Jagdwaffe: The War in Russia November 1942-December 1943, 2004

Jagdwaffe: War in the East 1944-1945, 2005

Black Cross/Red Star: The Air War over the Eastern Front, Vol. 3, 2006

Luftstrid över Kanalen, 2006

Barbarossa: The Air Battle, 2007

Stalingrad: The Air Battle, 2007

Kursk: The Air Battle, 2008

Hans-Ekkehard Bob, 2008

Max-Hellmuth Ostermann, 2008

Bagration to Berlin, 2008

Andra världskriget så alla förstår – nya rön om andra världskriget, 2009

Hitlers underhuggare, 2010

The Ardennes 1944–1945: Hitler's Winter Offensive, 2014

The Battle of Britain, 2015

Berömda flygaress, 2015